COMPOUND WORDS IN SPANISH

CURRENT ISSUES IN LINGUISTIC THEORY

AMSTERDAM STUDIES IN THE THEORY AND HISTORY OF LINGUISTIC SCIENCE – Series IV

General Editor

E.F.K. KOERNER

Zentrum für Allgemeine Sprachwissenschaft, Typologie
und Universalienforschung, Berlin
efk.koerner@rz.hu-berlin.de

Current Issues in Linguistic Theory (CILT) is a theory-oriented series which welcomes contributions from scholars who have significant proposals to make towards the advancement of our understanding of language, its structure, functioning and development. CILT has been established in order to provide a forum for the presentation and discussion of linguistic opinions of scholars who do not necessarily accept the prevailing mode of thought in linguistic science. It offers an outlet for meaningful contributions to the current linguistic debate, and furnishes the diversity of opinion which a healthy discipline must have.

A complete list of titles in this series can be found on *http://benjamins.com/catalog/cilt*

Volume 316

María Irene Moyna

Compound Words in Spanish. Theory and history

COMPOUND WORDS
IN SPANISH

THEORY AND HISTORY

MARÍA IRENE MOYNA

Texas A&M University

JOHN BENJAMINS PUBLISHING COMPANY
AMSTERDAM/PHILADELPHIA

^{TM} The paper used in this publication meets the minimum requirements of American National Standard for Information Sciences – Permanence of Paper for Printed Library Materials, ANSI z39.48-1984.

Library of Congress Cataloging-in-Publication Data

Moyna, María Irene.
  Compound words in Spanish : theory and history / María Irene Moyna.
      p.   cm. (Amsterdam studies in the theory and history of linguistic science. Series IV,
         Current Issues in Linguistic Theory, ISSN 0304-0763 ; v. 316)
  Includes bibliographical references and index.
  1. Spanish language--Compound words. 2. Spanish language--Word formation. I. Title.
  PC4175.M69   2011
  465'.9--dc22   2011000203
  ISBN 978 90 272 4834 3   (Hb ; alk. paper)
  ISBN 978 90 272 8713 7   (Eb)

John Benjamins Publishing Co. · P.O. Box 36224 · 1020 ME Amsterdam · The Netherlands
John Benjamins North America · P.O. Box 27519 · Philadelphia PA 19118-0519 · USA

Table of contents

List of figures

List of tables

List of abbreviations used

1	first person	GEN	genitive
2	second person	GendP	gender phrase
3	third person	Gr.	Greek
Ø	empty head	Hisp. Arab.	Hispano-Arabic
ACC	accusative	IMPERF	imperfective
ad	by the year	IND OBJ	indirect object
A, ADJ	adjective	It.	Italian
ADV	adverb	L	lexical [feature]
AdvP	adverbial phrase	Lat.	Latin
AgrP	agreement phrase	L.Lat.	Late Latin
AGT	agentive	lit.	literally
AN FUT	analytical future	MASC	masculine
AP	adjectival phrase	NEG	negation
Arab.	Arabic	N	noun
AspP	aspect phrase	NP	noun phrase
AuxP	auxiliary phrase	NumP	number phrase
c.	circa	Occ.	Occitan
Cast.	Castilian	PART	partitive
Cat.	Catalan	PartP	partitive phrase
CL	classifier	PERF	perfective
CONJ	conjunction	PERS-A	personal 'a' (direct object animacy marker)
DegP	degree phrase	PL	plural
DIM	diminutive	Port.	Portuguese
DIR OBJ	direct object	PP	prepositional phrase
DP	determiner phrase	PREP	preposition
Eng.	English	PRES	present
F	functional [feature]	PRET	preterite
FEM	feminine	QP	quantifier phrase
Fr.	French	Rom.	Romanian
Gal	Galician	SC	small clause

SG	singular	V	verb
Sp.	Spanish	VP	verb phrase
SUFF	suffix	WCM	word class marker
SYN FUT	synthetic future	WCMP	word class marker phrase
ThP	theme phrase	X	variable for lexical category
UNACC	unaccusative verb		

Abbreviated primary sources

Dictionaries and databases (for complete citations, cf. References)

A	Diccionario medieval español [Alonso Pedraz]
AD	Archivo Digital de Manuscritos y Textos Españoles [ADMYTE]
Au	Diccionario de Autoridades
C	Tesoro de la lengua castellana o española [Covarrubias]
CORDE	Corpus Diacrónico del Español
CREA	Corpus de Referencia del Español Actual
CS	Suplemento al Tesoro de la lengua castellana o española [Covarrubias]
G	Google
K&N	Diccionario de la Prosa Castellana de Alfonso X [Kasten & Nitti]
M	Diccionario de uso del español [Moliner]
N	Vocabulario romance en latín [Nebrija]
ON	Dictionary of the Spanish Contained in the Works of Antonio de Nebrija [O'Neill]
LHP	Léxico hispánico primitivo [Menéndez Pidal et al.]
DRAE	Diccionario de la lengua castellana por la Real Academia Española (1884)
S	Diccionario del español actual [Seco et al.]
T	Tentative Dictionary of Medieval Spanish [Kasten & Cody]
TL	Tesoro Lexicográfico de la Real Academia Española [Real Academia Española]

Texts

AC	Arte Cisoria
TC	Tratado de Cetrería
LAC	Libro de los Animales de Caza
LCA	Libro de la Caza de las Aves
LH	Libro de los Halcones
LM	Libro de la Montería
MDM	Menor Daño de Medicina
CR	Cirugía Rimada

Preface & acknowledgments

To say that compounding has been of interest to linguists from the earliest times may sound trite, but it is true. This is evident, for example, in the nomenclature used to identify compound patterns, which is still based on choices made by Pāṇini some 2,500 years ago. Words like *dvandva*, *tatpuruṣa*, and *dvigu* may be mystifying and slightly frustrating to the non-initiate and complicated to typeset even with modern computer keyboards, but they have stood the test of time as a visible manifestation of the collective expertise on compounding accumulated for over two millennia.

Yet, it was not really until the second half of the 20th century that the descriptive accounts typical of earlier periods gave way to theoretical debates. Compounds became a hot topic, because they were possibly the clearest example of the kinds of problems faced by generative grammarians as they tried to tease apart the territories of morphology and syntax. Are compounds rule-generated or stored lexical objects? The more we consider the question with data from language acquisition and processing, the more the answer seems to be 'Yes'.

When I started working on compounding at the tail end of the 20th century, that debate was raging and in many ways, it still is. However, more recent studies have begun to look at compounds for what they are, rather than for what they have to say about the relationship between different modules of grammar. The past decade has seen the publication of a handbook devoted entirely to compounds, as well as works focused on specific compound patterns and their cross-linguistic similarities and differences. Moreover, there are new edited collections that consider compounding from interdisciplinary perspectives including typology, acquisition, and psycholinguistic processing.

For all that, the field still lacks a modern treatise on the historical development of compounding patterns in any given language. To be sure, there is an entire volume of the *Transactions of the Philological Society* devoted to compounding in historical languages (Volume 100, 2002), but the articles are not diachronic in the sense that they do not systematically document the evolution of compounding over time. The chapter in the *Oxford Handbook of Compounding* devoted to diachrony (Kastovsky 2009) presents a taxonomy of the compounding types in the Indo-European family, but it does not trace each pattern chronologically. This book comes to fill a descriptive and theoretical vacuum by taking a first stab at the topic with data from Spanish.

The title of the book is dual, because I expect it to have two main audiences. The first group of readers will probably be theoretical linguists who may come looking for fresh data to prove one or another hypothesis. The second group will be made up of historical linguists who may seek in this book a description of the changes in the compounding patterns of Spanish. Because I cannot predict how much theoretical background historical linguists will have on the issue of compounding or how much theoretical linguists will agree with my point of departure, I have included a couple of chapters that lay down the theoretical basis for the rest of the book. Readers more interested in description may prefer to skip these chapters or simply scan them for specific information. My hope is that, whatever they opt to do, they will find the book useful and the story of compounding as fascinating and as puzzling as I still do, after all these years of working with them.

This book owes much to the help, inspiration, and encouragement of many people. My initial interest in compounds developed at the University of Florida, where I carried out my doctoral dissertation under the supervision of Gary Miller. I did extensive additional data collection and all of the writing while working at the Department of Hispanic Studies at Texas A&M University. I am grateful to our two department heads during that period, Víctor Arizpe and Larry Mitchell, for allowing me the time I needed to complete the project. I also gratefully acknowledge a stipend and time release granted by the TAMU Office of the Vice President for Research, through the Program to Enhance Scholarly and Creative Activities, and another grant from the Glasscock Center, which helped defray part of the cost of indexing this book.

If the first draft was a long-drawn and lonely effort, its many subsequent rewrites have been more collective and infinitely more enjoyable. First, I wish to thank my writing group at TAMU, organized by Prudence Merton. The members of the group provided the best non-expert feedback one could hope for, a generous supply of dark chocolate, and much needed comic relief and companionship over long months of work. I also wish to thank the linguists who have commented on portions of this work, in particular John Lipski, Esther Torrego, and Robert Smead. Israel Sanz carefully went over my Latin translations, and Steven Dworkin, Larry Mitchell, David Pharies, Juan Uriagereka, and Roger Wright read the entire manuscript and provided valuable feedback that improved its content and readability many times over. David Pharies must be thanked for believing that I would complete this project, at times when my own certainty flagged. For my first single-author book, I was very fortunate to have the guidance and gentle prodding of my editor, E.F.K. Koerner, the unfailing good will and assistance of Anke de Looper, who was in charge of the entire production process, and the collaboration of Do Mi Stauber, who drew up the index. I appreciate their useful suggestions and experience almost as much as their patience. I owe my largest debt of gratitude to my parents, Patrick Moyna and María Cristina Borthagaray, and to my daughter, Matilde Castro, who supported me in too many ways to count.

María Irene Moyna   College Station, November 2010

I guess being an unsuccessful poet
isn't as attractive as it used to be.
But where's the risky spirit,
the headlong leap into the vast
unknown of love, where anything
and everything might happen? Where's
the wish to be surrounded by poems,
the great sustaining luxuries and dangers
of poems, or to make one's life itself
a poem, unpredictable, meaning
many things, a door into the other world
through which even a child might walk?
Words have such power, I wanted to tell her.
You never know what may come of them.
Or who will be the beneficiary.

From "On Love and Life Insurance: An argument" by John Brehm (reproduced by kind permission from the author).

Introduction

1. Overview

This work traces the origins and development of the major compounding patterns of Spanish by documenting them from their earliest lexicographical attestations to the present. It thus fills a gap in scholarship, since the history of Spanish compound words has not received due attention. Next to the extensive bibliography on the history of Spanish suffixation (for a thorough alphabetical compendium and bibliography, cf. Pharies 2002), works on compounding history are few in the Romance family (Bierbach 1982; Bork 1990; de Dardel 1999; Klingebiel 1988, 1989) and even fewer in Spanish (Lloyd 1968). With few exceptions, these studies have concentrated on a small number of compounding patterns instead of providing a panoramic view of the evolution of the process. For their part, the classic early treatises (Darmesteter 1967 [1884]; Diez 1973 [1874]; Meyer-Lübke 1923 [1985]) provide general overviews of compounding but do not distinguish synchrony from diachrony or provide quantitative data.

The resulting lack of information in primary literature is reflected in the *gramáticas históricas*, i.e., the general histories of the Spanish language (Alvar & Pottier 1987; Lapesa 1980; Lloyd 1987; Penny 1991), which devote extensive sections to the origins of suffixation and prefixation, but are very terse about the concurrent history of compounding (cf. also Sánchez Méndez 2009). Works with a synchronic focus (Alemany Bolufer 1920; Bustos Gisbert 1986; Lang 1990; Rainer 1993) justifiably deal with historical examples only insofar as they still belong in the lexicon of Spanish. Until now, the need to study the history of compounding may have been overshadowed by the higher relative frequency of derivation in Spanish and other Romance languages. However, the growing use of compounding as a source of neologisms in the twentieth century and beyond calls for a careful reexamination of its historical antecedents.

A compound is characterized pre-theoretically as a word created by combining two words. This brings up at least two matters that are ill-defined and debatable. The first is the slippery category of 'word', both as it applies to the constituents of a compound and to the resulting complex form. The second is the minimum fixity required of the combination. What for some authors is a compound on the grounds of its semantic and formal stability, is not so for other authors, because its constituents are not structurally atomic. As we shall see in Chapter 1, if we use the semantic criterion alone, then *tomar el pelo* 'pull someone's leg', lit. 'pull the hair' should be considered a compound. However, the fact that the verb and its object are not inseparable (*me han tomado mucho el pelo* 'they have pulled my leg a lot', lit. 'me-IND OBJ have-3PL taken a

lot the hair') weakens this claim (Val Álvaro 1999: 4830–34). The pre-theoretical notion of compound is thus neither clear nor uniform across the literature. Different
theoretical approaches have led to different proposals concerning the boundary between compounding and other related phenomena such as derivation, syntactic phrase
formation, and idiomatic expressions (ten Hacken 1994; Val Álvaro 1999). In the specific case of Romance compounding, an especially complicated issue is distinguishing
compounds from syntactic phrases with idiomatic meaning. This matter is discussed
in depth in Chapter 1.

Because all the definitions available have their problems, this work starts by defining and describing compounding and justifying the criteria applied to distinguish this
process from other types of complex word formation. Providing a definition has two
positive consequences: first, it brings the theoretical assumptions to the surface, and
second, it makes it possible to focus only on properties that are relevant to Spanish.
Moreover, because the definition provided is internally consistent and explicit, readers
whose starting point is different from the one laid out in this work should be able to
translate the model presented into theirs.

Throughout the book, native compounding is to be understood as including patterns that were inherited or developed in Spanish on the basis of native stems and
combining principles. Broadly speaking, compound constituents have to exist independently at the time the compound is first attested in order for the complex form to
be considered a compound. The native speaker's awareness that a word is made up of
pre-existing words seems the most direct evidence available of structural transparency.
For earlier historical periods, the only evidence we have of this awareness is provided
by the presence of the constituents as independent entries in dictionaries. As a consequence, the study excludes compounds borrowed from other languages, such as composite foreign words (e.g., *living room, mass media*); this is because, even if these loan-
words are recorded in Spanish dictionaries (Seco et al. 1999), the absence of independent
entries for their constituents suggests that the whole is not analyzable for the average
monolingual speaker. More importantly, the study also excludes learned compounds
formed by combining Latin or Greek stems, in spite of their popularity as a mechanism of word formation in certain registers. The simultaneous presentation of native
and learned patterns would have been unwieldy and would have blurred the boundary
between core and periphery word formation processes. Given the very special characteristics of learned patterns, an independent treatment seems more appropriate.

2. Structure of the book

The book is organized in three parts. The first part, which includes Chapters 1 through
3 and fits under the theoretical portion alluded to in the title, lays out the assumptions
about what a compound is and explains how those assumptions were used for data
collection. The main purpose of Chapter 1 is to define the types of objects that are

included under the term 'compound' in this work. It discusses and justifies the properties that define the category, and uses these properties to distinguish between compounds and other similar constructions excluded from consideration. Chapter 2 provides the criteria of classification used to establish the main compound types, which are based on the internal structure and the semantics of each compound type. Finally, Chapter 3 contains a description of the data sources, including the reasons for each choice and the ways in which the data from each source were handled. It also includes the tests employed to identify compounds in historical digital corpora and the criteria used to classify them.

The second part of the book (Chapters 4 through 8), is a diachronic presentation of the major Spanish compounding patterns, and thus constitutes the history of compounding proper. To be characterized as 'major' a compounding pattern has to be represented by over 1% of the data across historical periods. For example, compounds with the structure numeral quantifier + noun, such as *milhombres* 'small, noisy man', lit. 'thousand-men' are included because they meet the minimum frequency requirement. By contrast, the pattern preposition + noun (e.g., *sinsabor* 'misfortune', lit. 'without-taste') does not reach this threshold and is therefore not included in the description. The 1% cut-off point was selected for several reasons. Patterns below that threshold tend to be semantically and syntactically idiosyncratic, following no obvious compounding principles. Including them would therefore only confound the main objective of this book, which is a general description of compounding in Spanish. Moreover, minor patterns pose methodological complications, since they are only sporadically represented, and the resulting gaps make it difficult to trace their evolution.

The major compounding patterns of Spanish were classified into four main groups, according to the position and nature of their constituents (especially the core constituent, or 'head', cf. Chapter 1). Chapters 4 and 5 are devoted to compounds whose head is the second constituent. Chapter 4 deals specifically with those whose non-head constituent is an adverb (e.g., *maldormir* 'to sleep badly', lit. 'badly-sleep'), and divides them into subcategories according to the lexical category of the head. Chapter 5 deals with those whose non-head constituent is a noun (e.g., *maniatar* 'to tie by the hands', lit. 'hand-tie'), and again divides them according to the lexical category of the head. Chapter 6 includes compounds whose head constituent is a nominal and whose non-head is another nominal or an adjective modifier (e.g., *malahierba* 'weed', lit. 'bad-herb', *hierbabuena* 'mint', lit. 'herb-good'). Chapter 7 considers structurally exocentric compounds, i.e., those whose internal head fails to pass on its syntactico-semantic features to the whole (e.g., *sacacorchos* 'corkscrew', lit. 'remove-corks', not a type of *saca* 'remove' or a type of *corchos* 'corks'). Finally, Chapter 8 deals with concatenative compounds, i.e., those whose constituents are of the same hierarchical level (e.g., *falda-pantalón* 'skort', lit. 'skirt-pants').

The way compounds are classified is a departure from previous studies, which have tended to group them according to the grammatical category of the compound itself. That classification system is avoided in this book because it has two main drawbacks.

First, because nominal patterns tend to be overwhelmingly preferred in Spanish, classifying compounds by lexical category would have resulted in chapters of very uneven length. Second, and more importantly, using a system based solely on the category of the compound obscures historically relevant connections among patterns that cut across grammatical category. For example, compounding patterns with their head on the right and an adverbial non-head on the left (e.g., [Adv + A]$_A$ in *maleducado* 'ill-bred', lit. 'badly-educated', [Adv + V]$_V$ in *malvender* 'sell for too little', lit. 'badly-sell', [Adv + N]$_N$ in *malcriadeza* 'bad education', lit. 'badly-raising') share the fact that they are much more abundant in the earlier periods. They are also concentrated in some areas of the lexicon and exhibit certain constituent elements recurrently. Those common properties give clues about how these compound structures have changed and influenced each other over time. This fact would be obscured by considering the grammatical category of the compound alone, since the latter is a property they do not share.

As stated earlier, within each chapter, compound types are subdivided according to the grammatical category of the compound and its constituents. For instance, among the exocentric compounds in Chapter 7, [V + N]$_N$ (e.g., *sacacorchos* 'corkscrew', lit. 'remove-corks') and [V + Adv]$_N$ (e.g., *catalejo* 'small telescope', lit. 'see-far') are distinguished from [Q + N]$_N$ (e.g., *sietemachos* 'bully', lit. 'seven-males'). Each pattern is introduced with a general discussion of its internal structure and meaning. The constituents are analyzed from the point of view of their position with respect to each other and their morphological properties, such as the internal structure of their constituents (e.g., *gallocresta* 'wild sage', lit. 'rooster-comb' vs. *gallicresta* 'id.'). Constituents are also described in terms of their lexical or semantic restrictions, including preferences for certain specific constituents in the head or the non-head position (e.g., the prevalence of the adverbs *mal* 'badly' and *bien* 'well' in [Adv + V]$_V$ and [Adv + A]$_A$ compounds). This is followed by a discussion of compound headedness, i.e., the structural and semantic relationship that holds between constituents. The meaning of compound constituents is then contrasted with their meaning in isolation to determine what kind of systematic semantic specialization occurs in each compounding pattern.

The synchronic presentation is followed by a diachronic analysis, starting with a discussion of historical antecedents in Latin and other historical languages. This historical background is followed by comparative data for each pattern in the Romance languages, and by some examples of the earliest attestations of the pattern in the Spanish data used in the study. These qualitative data are accompanied by quantification and tabulation of the pattern's frequency and productivity over time. The frequency of a given pattern is measured as a function of the number of all compounds documented with a pattern in a given period, relative to the total number of all compounds for the same period. In other words, high frequency can result from the accumulated effect of the use of a pattern in previous periods. By contrast, productivity is measured as the ratio between new compounds created in a century and those already existing (for details, cf. Chapter 3, Section 3.4). After the presentation of the quantitative data, the discussion moves on to the degree of inseparability of the constituents over time, through the analysis of their orthographical variants and other structural properties (cf. Chapter 3, Section 3.2.2). The description concludes with a discussion of changes in compound lexical category, which may result in exocentric compounds even if a pattern is generally endocentric (e.g., *bienestar* 'wellbeing', lit. 'well-be'). Because some patterns are related to others, cross-comparisons between compounds in several sections and in different chapters are sometimes necessary. For example, head-initial [N + N]$_N$ compounds in Chapter 6, Section 6.1, are cross-referenced with their head-final counterparts in Section 6.2 (e.g., *gas ciudad* 'city gas', lit. 'gas city', vs. *gasoducto* 'gas pipe').

The third and last section, Chapter 9, brings together theory and history, by considering the overall trends only noticeable if all patterns are considered together and drawing general theoretical conclusions from those tendencies. In that regard, the most notable tendency is a shift from head-final to head-initial compounding. This shift came about as a result of two main processes: first, the increased use of head-initial patterns, and second, the internal rearrangement of head-final compounds so they would fit the new preferred word order. The chapter discusses the increase in frequency of the head-initial patterns that led to the shift in word order, and also exceptions to this trend, represented by the appearance of pockets of head-final compounding, most notably during the 15th and the 20th centuries. Chapter 9 shows that these novel head-final compounds tend to be associated to specific semantic fields, and are often due to calquing or partial borrowing from classical languages or English. Moreover, the new head-final compounds exhibit special morphological features because the leftmost non-head appears in stem form. The chapter ends by considering what the history of Spanish compounding has to tell us about morphological change in general. In particular, it proposes that, all other things being equal, patterns that offer advantages in the process of language acquisition by children will tend to prevail.

At the end of the book, the Appendix lists all the compounds found in the study, classified by compound type and listed chronologically and then alphabetically. Each compound appears in its spelling most compatible with compound status, even if that spelling is not the most frequently attested. Thus, whenever there is a one-word variant, that one is chosen as the headword. This is followed by the exact transcription of the first attestation, included to facilitate the search for those looking to confirm the earliest occurrence. For example, the headword for the [Adv + A]$_A$ compound *biensonante* 'harmonious', lit. 'well-sounding', appears in its unitary form, followed by *bien sonantes* [1255], its actual earliest attested form. Lack of space prevents the inclusion of all attested spelling variants for each form, but the reader can locate these exhaustively in CORDE/CREA by using asterisks in place of the letters more prone to spelling variation in the history of Spanish orthography. Since it would be impossible to include all meanings, each compound is accompanied by a listing of the lexicographical sources where it was found. Readers who are interested in the meanings of each compound may search them in those sources, which are quite easily accessible in print or online.[1] Finally, the list includes the earliest and latest attestation of each compound in the databases where it was found.

This book is designed so that each chapter and the appendix can be consulted independently by those searching for specific answers. I strived to make each section self-contained and self-explanatory, with cross-references to relevant material in other parts of the book. However, this is not a dictionary, and most readers will find it easier and more fruitful to read the text in the order in which it is presented.

3.   Methodological considerations

To provide evidence for the expansion or retraction of compound patterns, this work considers a historical database culled from a variety of lexicographical sources. The use of dictionaries was deemed the most efficient way to search for compounds, since these types of lexemes are not frequent in Spanish discourse. One should bear in mind, though, that lexicographical sources also have limitations. For example, databases capture compounds effectively attested in the language, as opposed to potential compounds that would be understood and accepted by native speakers in a given period. The problem is that judgments about potential words can only be provided by living informants, which would restrict the scope of the study to the past century. Since a century is too narrow a window to document the slow changes typical of compounding, dictionaries are the only feasible alternative.

An additional advantage of using dictionaries is that although they do not record all the effectively attested compounds created with a given pattern, they do give a good idea of frequencies. Allow me to illustrate the extent of the gap between the compounds found in texts and those found in dictionaries, and to show that this gap is of little theoretical consequence. A wildcard search in digital databases (CORDE/CREA) for compounds with the internal structure $[N + A]_A$ whose first constituent is *boqui-* (e.g., *boquiduro* '[of a horse] hard-mouthed', lit. 'mouth-hard') found 36 such compounds. Of those, only 21, or a little under 60%, were also found in the ten dictionaries consulted. The missing compounds included perfectly transparent examples, such as *boquilimpio* 'clean-mouthed', lit. 'mouth-clean' and *boquibermejo* 'red-mouthed', lit. 'mouth-red'. At first glance, these gaps in coverage appear to call into question the thoroughness and reliability of dictionaries. However, a more careful examination shows that compounds unattested in dictionaries are also highly infrequent: most of them have only one token in CORDE/CREA. By contrast, those that are recorded in dictionaries have much higher token frequency. To summarize, dictionaries do not

---

1.   It is important to note that the work of collating data was carried out by a single person, working alone. Every compound was checked at least twice in the sources, but it would be surprising, given the size of the database, if there were no mistakes. The author assumes responsibility for any errors, but welcomes comments that will help improve the database in future.

record every compound that appears in textual sources, but compounds that appear with any observable frequency are never missing. Given that most compound patterns are abstract templates, quantitative comparisons such as that carried out for *boqui-* compounds are impractical on a larger scale, and the extent of the gap between both types of sources cannot be fully addressed. However, the data from the dictionaries, checked against the digital databases for first and last attestation, can be considered a good approximation to the frequent compounds of Spanish.

The specific types and quantity of dictionaries used in the study are discussed in greater detail in Chapter 3. However, general comments are warranted here concerning the thoroughness of the compilation. The choice of dictionaries out of the vast array of possible options was prompted by the need to balance coverage with practical constraints. Some of these were quite straightforward, like the need to complete data collection by a specific date. This meant that dictionaries such as Nieto Jiménez and Alvar Ezquerra's very valuable *Nuevo Tesoro lexicográfico del español (s. XIV-1726)* (Nieto Jiménez & Alvar Ezquerra 2007), were only consulted *a posteriori* to corroborate data but not as first-hand sources.

Moreover, one should note that there is a point of diminishing returns in the search for data, because the same compounds appear in more than one dictionary. The more dictionaries one adds, the greater the chances that a given compound will have been recorded before in another, especially given the tendency of some dictionaries to copy content from others. Indeed, about half of the compounds found are recorded in at least two dictionaries, and some of them in as many as nine. Since the total number of compounds is a little under 3,600, it is probable that the addition of more dictionaries would increase the number of repetitions without greatly affecting the conclusions of this work. It must be remembered that the ultimate objective of this project is not to produce an exhaustive list of all the compound *words* ever recorded, but of all the major compound *patterns* represented by those individual compound words. Drawing from my experience, I believe that the addition of newer data would not greatly influence the final results or the general tendencies discussed in Chapter 9. This hypothesis can be confirmed or corrected, of course, with the later addition of new data sources.

4. Morphological change and compounds

The study of the history of compounding sheds light on morphological change in several ways. In part, compounding resembles derivation, since both are processes of word formation whose outputs are stored in the mental lexicon. In the case of derivational suffixes and prefixes, the main historical issues are how certain affixes are incorporated into the language, how they acquire, expand, or contract their meaning, and how their applicability is reduced, lost, or increased at the expense of other competing processes. Similarly, new patterns of compounding are created over time as old ones disappear. Yet, because compounding patterns are abstract, they need to be traced independently of the surface segments involved.

It is possible for the compounding pattern and the individual compounds created with that pattern to undergo similar or different fates. One possibility is that both compounding patterns and individual compounds decrease or increase in tandem. Thus, the constituents of compounds created with obsolete patterns may lose independent status, turning what was once a compound into a combination of word and affix or even a monomorphemic word. For example, the [N + V]$_V$ pattern is no longer productive; similarly, words created with that pattern such as *mantener* 'maintain', lit. 'hand-hold' are no longer analyzable by speakers. Sometimes, though, the fate of individual compounds does not reflect that of the pattern itself. For example, compounds created with obsolete patterns may continue to be analyzable by native speakers and to spawn occasional new compounds. Such is the case of *misacantano* 'priest who can say mass', lit. 'mass-singer' [c. 1215], which continues to be analyzable, although its compounding pattern is obsolete. Its analyzability is evidenced by a more recent compound in bullfighting, *toricantano* 'novice bullfighter' [1597–1645], created analogically by comparing the rookie bullfighter with a new priest, and where *cantano* 'singer' makes no specific semantic contribution to the meaning of the entire compound. In a few isolated cases, it is also possible for a compound created with a very productive pattern to eventually become eroded and no longer recognizable as such. Thus, although [V + N]$_N$ compounding is highly vital in modern Spanish, most native speakers fail to recognize *matambre* 'rolled flank steak', lit. 'kill-hunger' [1840] as a token of the pattern, although the older spelling *matahambre* is structurally transparent. These situations of mismatch between pattern productivity and lexeme transparency are infrequent in affixation, where the process of affixation and the segment affixed are normally closely intertwined.

Compounds can undergo other changes over time, which distance them even more from derivation and highlight their parallels with syntax. For example, compound constituents may modify their internal morphological structure or change position with respect to each other. Both of those processes can be illustrated with one example. The early compound *gallocresta* 'wild sage', lit. 'rooster-comb' [c. 1300], whose head constituent appears on the right, undergoes several different structural modifications over time that make it fit the preferred syntactic order of Spanish, where the head is on the left. In one such modification, *gallicresta* [1494], the word class marker of the non-head element, *gallo*, is replaced by a linking vowel (for more on word class markers, cf. Chapter 1, Section 1.2.4.3). In another change, it is restructured as the phrase *cresta de gallo* [ad 1500], which later loses its internal preposition and results in *crestagallo* [Google, 2009]. In all cases, the changes clarify the hierarchical relationship between the two constituents in ways that are explored further in Chapter 6.

The above summary shows that an inquiry into the process of compounding over time has a number of theoretical consequences. For example, the findings of this inquiry have to be brought to bear in discussions of the morphology-syntax interface.

An ongoing debate in theoretical linguistics is the degree of overlap between morphology and syntax. For some authors, these two components of grammar are ruled by discrete sets of principles, an idea stated in Chomsky (1970), and further developed in Selkirk (1982), and di Sciullo and Williams (1987), among many others. Others have proposed various degrees of overlap, usually subordinating morphology to syntax (Hale & Keyser 1992; 1993; 1997; Halle & Marantz 1993; Harley 2009). The analysis of compounds is particularly sensitive to this tug-of-war. On the one hand, even the most fervent proponents of the separation of morphology and syntax acknowledge that compounds are created by processes parallel to those that create phrases in syntax (Anderson 1992: 294). On the other hand, the output of compounding, like that of derivation, is a new item stored in the lexicon and as such, it often undergoes semantic specialization. The analysis of changes in the structure and meaning of compounds over time provides a new point of comparison to assess their relative position with respect to syntactic phrases and complex morphological objects.

I hope that the general conclusion that will be drawn from this work is that much remains to be done in the study of Spanish compounding history, and that this work is worth doing. For example, the study can be expanded by considering data from different linguistic varieties found in dialectal dictionaries and glossaries. This will complement the sources used here, which tend to document the common core lexicon of Spanish, and will provide a clearer idea of which patterns are the most successful cross-dialectally. It is also of interest to analyze compounding in specialized jargons and argots, in order to identify possible deviations from the core patterns presented here, and to see to what extent those deviations anticipate future changes in general Spanish.

I also hope that by the end of the book, readers will have concluded that the interest in Spanish compounding goes beyond the descriptive. In fact, the historical study of compounds in Spanish provides support to the view that language change can be fueled by children as they acquire their native language (Kiparsky 1982a, Lightfoot 1993). Specifically, the shift in preference from head-final to head-initial patterns in compounding is a morphological consequence of the shift from head-final to head-initial syntactic constructions, and can be accounted for by a change in parameter setting. More direct evidence of the importance of child acquisition to language change is probably the increased productivity of the Spanish $[V + N]_N$ compounding pattern over time. As we shall see in Chapter 9, this pattern occurs spontaneously in the process of acquisition of many languages, even some for which it is not conventional in adult language. In languages where $[V + N]_N$ compounds are not possible in adult language, children later unlearn this pattern. In Spanish, where no such barriers to $[V + N]_N$ exist, the innate child pattern has been allowed to spread beyond its original confines. This type of evidence of the effect of natural language acquisition on language change has the potential to illuminate areas outside of compounding and languages other than Spanish, providing historical linguists with new tools to explain old problems.

CHAPTER 1

Definitions

1.1 Introduction: The problem with compounds

Compounding is a deceptively simple notion. Every educated Spanish speaker knows that a compound is a word made up of other words, and can cite some typical examples such as *hombre lobo* 'werewolf', lit. 'man-wolf' or *sacapuntas* 'pencil sharpener', lit. 'sharpen-points'. Beyond these, disagreements start. For example, at different points in time compounding has been interpreted to include words such as *hágalo* 'do it!', *correveidile* 'gossipmonger', lit. 'run-go-and-tell-him/her', *evidentemente* 'evidently', and *vosotros* 'you-PL', lit. 'you-others'. The first two are transparently made up of several words each, and a smart high school student with a knack for etymology will spot Latin MENS, MENTIS in the adverb *evidentemente,* and *vos* 'you' and *otros* 'others' in *vosotros*. However, most linguists today would agree that none of those words are compounds, and this chapter summarizes their reasons. In turn, even linguists have had their disagreements about the status of some complex lexemes. For example, *patata frita* 'French fry', lit. 'potato fried' and *dulce de leche* 'caramel paste', lit. 'sweet of milk', have unitary meaning but exhibit structural properties typical of phrases. Their status will depend on the semantic and structural criteria used to define compounds.

This section discusses in detail the problem of defining compounding. This is followed by a presentation of some preliminary notions to be used throughout the study and a description of the structural properties of compounds. Finally, the chapter goes over various complex structures that are excluded from consideration, either because they do not fit the definition of compounding or exhibit special characteristics.

In the Romance tradition, compounding has been defined as the creation of a new word through the combination of pre-existing words (Diez 1973 [1874]; Real Academia Española's *Esbozo* of 1986: 169) or of words and stems (Alemany Bolufer 1920: 155; Bello 1928: 24; Benczes 2005; Meyer-Lübke 1923 [1895]: 625). In practice, however, all these studies tacitly assume the second definition, since they include compounds made up of bare stems and of full-fledged words (e.g., _patitieso_ 'flabbergasted', lit. 'leg-stiff' and _pata dura_ 'clumsy person', lit. 'leg-stiff'). Yet, even the second definition, which is adapted to the internal structure of Spanish words, is not by itself adequate to distinguish compounds from other similar constructions. For that, we must have recourse to a theory that clearly defines words and how they may combine to generate new ones. To illustrate the problem, consider the examples in (1).

(1) a. *ojo* 'eye'
     b. *ojal* 'buttonhole'
     c. *abrojo* 'star thistle'
     d. *ojialegre* 'happy-eyed', lit. 'eye-happy'
     e. *ojo de buey* 'porthole', lit. 'eye of ox'
     f. *ojo de la cerradura* 'keyhole', lit. 'eye of the lock'
     g. *No lo mira con buenos ojos.* '[s/he] does not like it', lit. 'NEG it look-3 SG with good eyes'.
     h. *No veo nada de este ojo.* 'I cannot see anything with this eye', lit. 'NEG see-1 SG nothing of this eye'.

Which of those are compounds? Clearly, *ojo* 'eye' cannot be decomposed into constituent parts and is therefore a simple word – though, as will be shown in Section 2.2.2, even this notion is not as straightforward as it looks. Speakers would also agree that while *ojal* 'buttonhole' contains a stem *oj-* as one of its components, *-al* is not an independent word of Spanish, so *ojal* is not a compound either. If they recognize *-al* in words such as *puñal* 'dagger' (< *puño* 'fist' + *-al*) and *dedal* 'thimble', (< *dedo* 'finger' + *-al*), they will classify *ojal* as derived by the same pattern. They will probably fail to find *ojo* 'eye' in *abrojo* 'star thistle' unless they chance upon the word's etymology – from Lat. APĔRI ŎCŬLOS 'open the eyes!' (Corominas & Pascual 1980–91: v.1, 22) or, alternatively, from Lat. APĔRI OCŬLUM 'open the eye!' (Real Academia Española 1992) – at which point they may recognize its complex origin. Yet this is unlikely to change their views about the word's internal structure, since phonetic erosion masks the presence of *abre* 'open', and the semantic contribution of the word *ojo* to *abrojo* is tenuous today. Thus, by any definition, the words *ojo, ojal,* and *abrojo* are not compounds. It is also quite clear that the sentence *No veo nada de este ojo* (1h) does not qualify as a compound because it is not "fixed" in any way. It is a completely non-idiomatic sentence, culled by combining words to express a novel meaning. The meaning of the whole is compositional in the sense of Frege (1993 [1892]), i.e., it can be calculated on the basis of the meaning of the parts and the way they are combined.

What about the remaining examples, (1d–g)? Of those, *ojialegre* is obviously a compound: it is related to *ojo* and *alegre*, both in form and meaning. Additionally, *ojo* appears in a shape that forces its attachment to *alegre* through specific combinatorial principles (cf. *alegreoji 'happy-eye'). The three remaining structures are more problematic. Neither the constituents nor their order can be changed, and the combinations have non-compositional meanings. For example, speakers may deduce the meaning of *ojo de buey* lit. 'eye of ox' compositionally, interpreting the expression literally. Importantly, however, the expression can also denote an opening on the side of a ship. This is not a compositional meaning, and would therefore be an argument for considering *ojo de buey* 'porthole' a compound. Yet, constructions like these can be interrupted by various functional elements: *ojos de buey* 'portholes', lit. 'eyes of ox', *ojito de la cerradura* 'little keyhole', lit. 'eye-DIM of the lock', *no lo miraría con muy buenos ojos* 's/he would not like it very much', lit. 's/he would not look at it with very good eyes'. If preeminence is given to non-compositionality of meaning, then all three have some claim to wordhood, and so, to compoundhood, but if structural inseparability is used as a criterion, then they do not. So how can we distinguish compounds from non-compounds? The answer will depend on the underlying theory of compounding. For example, though most authors have been reluctant to call structures such as (1h) compounds, some have used their idiomatic nature as an argument to include them as a verbal subtype (Val Álvaro 1999: 4830 et passim). And while most have remarked that the structures in (1e, f) differ in important ways from (1d), they have found reasons to include both as different kinds of compounds (but cf. Rainer & Varela 1992: 120, where this solution is rejected). The decision cannot be made without recourse to an implicit or explicit theory of compounding, an issue that will be tackled in Section 3, after presenting some definitions that will simplify later exposition.

1.2 Some preliminary definitions

1.2.1 Words and lexemes

The pre-theoretical definition of a compound as a word made up of other words leads to the problems described in Section 1 because the notion of 'word' is polysemous. As pointed out in di Sciullo & Williams (1987: 1), a word can be understood as a *morphological object*, i.e., an entity created by combining smaller indivisible units, or morphemes. Thus, *ojialegre* 'happy-eyed', lit. 'eye-happy' can be analyzed as containing at least two distinct units, *oj-* 'eye' and *alegre* 'happy'. However, these two constituents within the word are invisible to the operations of syntax, so the whole behaves as an indivisible building block in sentence formation, a *syntactic atom*: *Estaban muy ojialegres* 'They were very happy-eyed', lit. 'eye-happy-P' vs. **estaban muy ojisalegres*, 'they were very happy-eyed', lit. 'eye-PL-happy-PL'; ** estaban oji muy alegres* 'they were eye very happy-PL'. In this second sense, *ojialegre* 'happy-eyed', lit. 'eye-happy' is distinguishable from *ojo de buey* 'porthole', lit. 'eye of ox' in that the latter is not atomic: *ojos de buey* 'portholes', lit. 'eyes of ox'. A word can also be taken to be a unit of idiosyncratic meaning, a *listeme*, regardless of internal structure or syntactic indivisibility. Listemes may range from individual items (e.g., *bird, hand, bush*), to full sentences whose meaning is not derivable from the meaning of their parts (e.g., *A bird in the hand is worth two in the bush*). If listemes are understood at all, it is because the speaker has previously paired each one with an arbitrary meaning and stored these pairings in a mental repository, the *lexicon*. In that sense, *ojo de buey* 'porthole' and *mirar con buenos ojos* 'consider positively' are as much 'words' as *ojialegre* and *ojo*. One last possibility, not discussed by di Sciullo and Williams, is to consider a *prosodic unit* a phonological word (Anderson 1992: 306). In that sense, *tráelo* 'bring it!' is a word because it has single stress, although it is clearly made up of two syntactic units.

This level of confusion makes the term 'word' a less than ideal starting point for a theory of compounding, so it will be avoided in this book, as will the expression *word formation*. Instead, I will use *lexeme formation* to mean the process of creation of *lexemes*, as I will call the members of the major lexical categories (in principle, noun, verb, and adjective/adverb). These are distinguishable from functional categories (including plural, gender, and case marking, tense, aspect, agreement, and so on) (cf. grammatical formatives in Aronoff 1994: 13–14). Intuitively, the former are the conceptual bricks of a sentence, while the latter are the mortar that holds those content-bearing bricks together and make the sentence grammatical. Thus, for example, whereas both *Doggie run* (as said by a two-year-old) and *The doggie is running* (as said by his mother) have the same content words, only the second one has the added layer of functional elements required by English. This distinction seems straightforward, but exactly what is lexical and what functional is less easy to delimit. I come back to this issue in Section 1.2.4 because it is crucial to my definition of compounding.

1.2.2   Internal structure of lexemes

When considering lexemes internally, it is apparent that some are simpler than others. Some contain just one unit of sound/meaning, while others can be broken down into smaller ones. For example, in English, *hand* or *bush* are simple, whereas *hand-y* and *bush-y* are divisible into two parts, each contributing some meaning to the whole. But whereas *hand* and *bush* can appear as *free forms*, -*y* is an *affix* and can only appear attached to others. I will reserve the term *stem* for a simple free form that participates in a process of affixation or compounding (e.g., *hand* in *hands, handy,* or *handfeed*), and *base* as a more general term, to refer to any stem, simple or complex, thus manipulated (e.g., *handy* in *handily* or *handyman*). Note from the examples that the base can be coextensive with a stem, if only one affixation or compounding process has applied. To avoid proliferation of synonyms, I will generally avoid the term *root*, except to refer to an abstract, non-categorical bundle of semantic features (cf. Distributed Morphology, Halle & Marantz 1993), which becomes a stem when inserted into a categorical terminal node (e.g., Spanish $\sqrt{\text{CONT}}$, present in $[[cuent]o]_N$ 'story' or $[[cont]ar]_V$ 'to tell').[1] In general, however, I will assume the starting point of compounding to be lexical bases, so that roots will seldom be invoked in this work.

---

1.   Because the root is abstract, it may be realized in different guises depending on a number of factors. The alternation in the example is motivated by stress properties; unstressed mid-vowels alternate with stressed diphthongs. Other alternations may be lexical, such as cases of suppletive stems *ir, fue, voy* 'to go, he went, I go'.

1.2.3 Inflection and derivation

Affixation processes can be *inflectional*, when they instantiate syntactic categories above the level of the individual lexeme, or *derivational*, when they affect features internal to the lexeme with no phrasal consequences (Anderson 1982: 83; Aronoff 1994: 15; Stump 1998: 14 et passim). Thus, for example, the plural marker on a noun is a manifestation of agreement, a syntactic relation between it and other sentential constituents: *los buenos muchachos vinieron* 'the-MASC PL good- MASC PL boys came-PL' vs. **el buen muchachos vino* 'the-MASC SG good- MASC SG boys came-SG'. By contrast, the presence of a given derivational affix does not have this kind of consequence elsewhere in the sentence. For example, nouns created by addition of different agentive suffixes, say, *-ero* or *-dor*, do not trigger distinct agreement or concord: *el buen panadero/vendedor vino* 'the- MASC SG good- MASC SG baker/seller came-SG'. Other oft-cited differences between inflection and derivation are the higher productivity, semantic regularity and transparency, and non-recursiveness of inflection, which contrast with the fact that derivation may apply recursively and result in new lexeme formation by changing the meaning or grammatical category of the base. Additionally, inflection follows derivation: $[vende]_V dor]_N es]_{Npl}$ vs. $*[vende]_V s]_{pl} dor]_{Npl}$, $[felic]_A idad]_N es]_{Npl}$ vs. $*[felic]_A es]_{pl} idad]_{Npl}$. The distinction between inflection and derivation is supported by evidence from acquisition and aphasia studies (Badecker & Caramazza 1998: 400 et passim; Clark 1998: 388).

Ultimately, as pointed out by Aronoff (1994: 126) and Stump (1998: 19), derivation and inflection are not two kinds of affixation but two uses of affixation, and the same affix could be inflectional in certain uses and derivational in others. A case in point is presented in Spanish by affective suffixation, which is often classified as inflectional because it does not change the grammatical category or semantic matrix of the base (e.g., *muchacho* 'young man' > *muchachito* 'little young man', *loco* 'crazy' > *loquito* 'crazy-DIM'). However, on occasion it can be found in derivational uses, when a diminutive form has lexicalized (e.g., *bolso* 'bag' > *bolsillo* 'pocket', lit. 'bag-DIM', *central* 'central office' > *centralita* 'telephone exchange', lit. 'central office-DIM'). This has to be kept in mind when analyzing compound words that contain inflectional affixes, an apparent counterexample to the sequencing of lexeme formation before inflection.

1.2.4 Functional and lexical categories

As stated earlier, lexemes belong in a given lexical class, which in principle includes nouns, verbs, adjectives, and adverbs (Baker 2003). The categories of adjective and adverb have been considered to be one and the same (for arguments, cf. Baker 2003: 231 et passim). However, in this work I retain the classic distinction between adverbs, which act as adjuncts to verbs or to adjectives, and adjectives, which adjoin to nominals. These classes share the fact that they are 'contentful', i.e., they denote lexico-conceptual notions: *cat, sleep, black*. By contrast, in order to be used intentionally, i.e., to build propositions that can refer to the extralinguistic world, they must be accompanied by individuative functional elements: *The black cat is sleeping on the mat*. Lexical and functional categories are distinguished even in traditional grammar: the former constitute large, constantly expanding open classes; the latter are closed classes with few members. Lexical categories are normally made up of free forms, whereas functional categories may be expressed through free forms and affixes.

(2)   Lexical phrase   Functional phrase
       NP   DP
       black bird   the black bird
       red eyes   my red eye

       VP   AuxP
       eat   have eaten
                               is eating

       AP   DegP
       nice   much nicer
       well fed   so much better fed

       AdvP   DegP
       well   extremely well

It seems uncontroversial that verbs like *eat*, nouns like *bird* or *eyes*, and adjectives and adverbs like *black*, *nice*, and *well*, are lexical, while determiners (*the*, *my*), auxiliaries (*have*, *be*), and degree phrases (*so*, *much*) are functional. However, the lexical/functional split encounters difficulties when attempting to classify all syntactic heads. For one thing, there are categories whose members seem to spread over both camps. I will illustrate this problem with two classes relevant to compounding, viz., prepositions (1.2.4.1) and quantifiers (1.2.4.2). An additional problem with consequences for compounding is that some formants seem to exhibit features of both lexical and functional elements simultaneously. I will illustrate this issue with the Spanish word class marker (1.2.4.3). Finally, two items may be both of the same type and yet exhibit radically different characteristics. I will illustrate this point by contrasting person/number agreement marking with tense/aspect marking on verbs (1.2.4.4). Although this last issue is not directly relevant to compounding, it is worth bringing up because it further highlights the insufficiencies of the lexical/functional distinction and the need for a more nuanced analysis.

1.2.4.1 *Prepositions and the lexical/functional distinction*
The status of prepositions as lexical or functional has been the subject of much debate. One position, held in Chomsky (1970) and Jackendoff (1977), proposes that they are a fourth lexical category, besides nouns, verbs, and adjectives. In this view, the four categories are defined through two binary features, [N], and [V]. Verbs are [+ V, –N], nouns are [–V, +N], adjectives are [+V, +N], and prepositions are [–V, –N]. However,

Baker (2003: 303 et passim) claims that adpositions (i.e., pre- and postpositions), are functional, not lexical. He argues that, like other functional categories, they are few in number, constitute a non-productive closed class, have vague meaning, and do not participate in derivation. Baker also deploys evidence from a variety of incorporating languages to demonstrate that prepositional heads act as barriers to lexical incorporation, and inversely, allow functional incorporation, which he takes to be evidence of their functional nature.

It seems that both positions are too extreme and fail to recognize the distinct behavior of different types of prepositions. The facts of Spanish and other languages support a distinction between two types of prepositions. On the one hand, *functional prepositions* do indeed have vague meaning and are present mostly to mark core case relations (3). They do not come in pairs of opposites, and do not accept degree phrases (4) (Miller 1993). By contrast, *lexical prepositions* introduce adverbial expressions they often come in pairs of opposites and accept degree phrases (5). In Spanish dialects that allow it, additional evidence for the difference in behavior between lexical and functional prepositions can be obtained from stranding: *¿De qué edificio, está cerca t, la facultad?* 'What building is the university close to?' lit. 'Of what building is close the university?' (Campos 1991).

(3) a. *Le di el libro a Juan.* (dative)
    IND OBJ gave-1SG the book to Juan.
    'I gave the book to Juan'.

   b. *Vi a mi hermano con su novia.* (animate accusative).
    Saw-1SG PERS-a my brother with his girlfriend.
    'I saw my brother with his girlfriend'.

   c. *la casa de mi hermano* (genitive)
    the house of my brother
    'my brother's house'

(4) a. *Ese libro es (*exactamente) de matemáticas.*
    'This book is (*exactly) of mathematics'.

   b. *Dale el libro (*exactamente) a José.*
    'Give the book (*exactly) a José'.

(5) a. *El libro está (exactamente) sobre la mesa.*
    'This book is (exactly) on the table'.

   b. *El libro está (exactamente) bajo la mesa.*
    'The book is (exactly) under the table'.

   c. *El conejo está (completamente) adentro de la galera.*
    'The rabbit is (completely) inside [of] the hat'.

   d. *El conejo está (completamente) afuera de la galera.*
    'The rabbit is (completely) out of the hat'.

Evidence for the distinction between lexical and functional prepositions is also provided by complex lexeme formation, and in particular by compounding. In this regard, Baker's claim that prepositions are not lexical because they do not participate in word formation through derivation is weakened, because lexical propositions do participate in compounding (cf. 6a and c, for Spanish and English examples), while functional prepositions do not (6b and d) (Dressler 2005: 29 and references therein). Because this is a matter that concerns compound formation directly, we will come back to it in Section 3.1.

(6)   a.   Eng. outgrow, inbreed, overthrow, inhouse, online

     b.   Eng. *of-grow, *for-breed, *to-throw

     c.

compound	literal gloss	meaning
sinvergüenza	without shame	cheeky person
sinsabor	without taste	hardship
fueraborda	outboard	outboard [motor]
delantealtar	before-altar	altar ornament

     d.

compound	literal gloss
*devergüenza	of-shame
*desdeescuela	from-school
*atrabajo	to-work

1.2.4.2 *Quantifiers and the lexical/functional distinction*

Let us now turn to the issue of quantifiers, elements that specify the quantity of individuals in the domain of discourse to whom a given predicate applies (Larson & Segal 1995: 226) (7).

(7)   a.   *Todos los estudiantes aprobaron el examen.*
       'All the students passed the exam'.

     b.   *Algunos estudiantes aprobaron el examen.*
       'Some students passed the exam'.

     c.   *Tres estudiantes aprobaron el examen.*
       'Three students passed the exam'.

     d.   *Ningún estudiante aprobó el examen.*
       'No student passed the exam'.

Quantifiers are typically considered a functional category, like determiners. The two share distributional properties: *los amigos* 'the friends', vs. *algunos amigos* 'some friends', *tres amigos* 'three friends'. Moreover, quantifiers, like determiners, bind a noun phrase so that it can refer to some class of individuals in the extralinguistic world: *gato* 'cat' vs. *el gato de mi hermana* 'my sister's cat'.

However, it is recognized that the class of quantifiers is heterogeneous. Binary (or strong) quantifiers (such as *all, every, most*) have two arguments (restriction and scope), while others, known as unary (or weak) quantifiers (e.g., the numerals) have only one argument. This leads to contrasts in contexts other than (7). For example, binary quantifiers are non-reversible, whereas unary quantifiers are reversible. This difference can be seen in the contrast between the pairs of sentences in (8) and (9). In a case such as (8), the truth of (8b) does not follow from the truth of (8a), because *la mayoría* 'most' is a binary quantifier. By contrast, if (9a) is true, it follows that (9b) is also true, evidence that *algunos* 'some' is a unary quantifier.

(8)   a.   *La mayoría de los vascos son españoles.*
           'Most Basques are Spaniards'.

      b.   *La mayoría de los españoles son vascos.*
           'Most Spaniards are Basques'.

(9)   a.   *Algunos/tres millones de vascos son españoles.*
           'Some/three million Basques are Spaniards'.

      b.   *Algunos/tres millones de españoles son vascos.*
           'Some/three million Spaniards are Basques'.

There are other differences between binary quantifiers and a specific type of unary quantifiers, the numerals. Whereas binary quantifiers pattern distributionally with determiners and cannot be regular lexical predicates (10), numerals do not have the restrictions of determiners, but rather, pattern with regular lexical predicates (11). Note also that, while binary quantifiers constitute a closed class with few members, the category of numerals is, by definition, infinite.

(10) a.   **los todos apóstoles*
           the all   apostles

      b.   **Los apóstoles son todos.*
           The apostles   are   all.

(11) a.   *los doce   apóstoles*
           The twelve apostles

      b.   *Los apóstoles son doce.*
           The apostles   are   twelve.
           'There are twelve apostles'.

The distinction between binary quantifiers and numerals is manifested in compounding. While binary quantifiers are barred from appearing in compounds, numerals are possible.

(12) a.   Eng. two-step, three-pile, four-way
      b.   Eng. *most-step, *all-pile, *every-way

c.	compound	literal gloss	meaning
	milpiés	thousand-feet	millipede
	sietemachos	seven-males	brave man

d.	compound	literal gloss
	*todospiés	all feet
	*cadamacho	every-male

In sum, when attempting to apply the notions of lexical/functional to an entire word class, this may mask differences between the behavior of its members. Such is the case of prepositions and quantifiers: some are contentful, and therefore fulfill some functions typical of lexical elements, whereas others are not, and therefore cannot fulfill these functions.

1.2.4.3 *Word class markers and the lexical/functional distinction*

Nominals are prominently represented in Spanish compounding, which reflects a universal tendency (Dressler 2005: 32). However, Spanish nominals are morphologically complex, because they have a terminal element not present in other languages, as in *tí-o* 'uncle', *tí-a* 'aunt', *president-e* 'president-MASC', *president-a* 'president-FEM', *puert-a* 'door' *puert-o* 'port'. Those terminal elements are not necessarily marks of biological sex, since they appear on nouns that do not denote sexed entities (cf. *puerta* 'door' and *puerto* 'port'). They do not hold a one-to-one relationship to grammatical gender, either. In spite of some general tendencies, the concord requirements imposed on the rest of the noun phrase are independent of the shape of the terminal element: *el mapa bonito* 'the-MASC map-MASC beautiful-MASC', *la prima bonita* 'the-FEM cousin-FEM beautiful-FEM'; *el corte nuevo* 'the-MASC cut-MASC new-MASC' *la corte nueva* 'the-FEM court-FEM new-FEM'; *el bikini chiquito* 'the-MASC bikini-MASC small-MASC', *la mini chiquita* 'the-FEM miniskirt-FEM small-FEM', *el primo perdido* 'the-MASC cousin-MASC lost-MASC', *la moto perdida* 'the-FEM motorcycle-FEM lost-FEM'; *el espíritu primitivo* 'the-MASC spirit-MASC primitive-MASC', *la tribu primitiva* 'the-FEM tribe-FEM primitive-FEM' *el papel caro* 'the-MASC paper-MASC expensive-MASC', *la pared cara* 'the-FEM wall-FEM expensive- FEM'.[2]

In his extensive analysis, Harris (1991) concludes that *-a, -e, -i, -o, -u,* and *-Ø* are **word class markers**, i.e., 'markers of pure form', unrelated to gender or sex; they delimit word classes whose only commonality is their ending. They appear at the outer periphery of a lexeme, after all derivation has taken place (*muchacho* 'boy' → *muchachada*

---

2.   For a complete listing of word class markers and their possible pairings, cf. Harris 1991: 30–31). Harris observes several mismatches between word endings and the marking of biological gender. For instance, in some pairings there is no difference between male and female (*el/la estudiante* 'the MASC-FEM student MASC-FEM') and there are cases where the noun itself is incapable of indicating the sex of the denotatum (*cocodrilo ~ *cocodrila* 'crocodile-MASC-FEM', **balleno ~ ballena* 'whale-MASC/FEM'; cf. *cocodrilo hembra*, 'female crocodile', *ballena macho* 'male whale').

'group of boys', *muchachoada* 'id'.; *casa* 'house' → *casero* 'housekeeper', **casaero* 'id'.), but before number inflection (*muchacho* 'boy' → *muchachos, *muchachso*).

According to Harris, word class markers are not limited to the class of nouns, but are also present in verbs, adjectives, and adverbs. Additionally, they have 'no meaning or function; they obey no higher semantic or syntactic authority'(1991: 59). I will take issue with this assertion, and argue that in the case of nouns, these class markers may have no lexical semantic content, but they do in fact contribute to sentence semantics by making the nouns 'referable', i.e., capable of bearing referential properties akin to classifier systems in several Asian languages (cf. Muromatsu 1995; 1998).[3] Until it is provided with a word class marker, a nominal stem cannot participate in syntax: **El gat- se escapó otra vez por la ventana.* 'The cat escaped through the window again'; **En Chincha comen gat-* 'In Chincha they eat cat'. Without it, a nominal stem denotes a pure abstract quality, i.e., it is pure predicate: *gat-* 'catness'. From this, it follows naturally that the class marker should be absent until all derivational suffixation has been added, because derivation involves semantic operations on the lexico-conceptual structure of the stem that precede its use in a referable expression. The adjective *gatuno* for example, can only mean 'pertaining to cats in general', not 'pertaining to such-and-such an individual cat'. The verb *gatear* is 'to crawl', i.e., 'to walk in a cat-like manner', and cannot mean 'to walk like my cat Gigi'.

---

3.   In spite of their similarities, the classifier systems of many East Asian languages and the word class marker of Spanish are not identical. The most obvious difference regards their positional freedom. Classifiers are preposed clitics, appearing with the nominal only in certain syntactic environments, where they are required by the presence of numerals. On the other hand, the word class marker is always a bound terminal element of the nominal, required for morphological wellformedness even in its citation form (cf. i a–c for Japanese, d–e for Spanish). In that sense, the alternation is reminiscent of the marking of verbal agreement, which is a bound morpheme in some languages and a clitic in others.

(i)   a.   *enpitu*   *kuruma*   *Japanese* (Muromatsu 1995: 151)
            pencil   car
            'pencil/pencils'   'car/cars'

      b.   **ni   no   enpitu   *san   no   kuruma*

            two   GEN pencil   three   GEN car

            'two pencils'   'three cars'

      c.   *ni   hon   no   enpitu   san   dai   no   kuruma*

            two   CL   GEN pencil   three   CL   GEN car

            'two pencils'   'three cars'

      d.   *casa,*   **casø*   *carro,*   **carrø*   *Spanish*
            house   car

      e.   *una casa,*   *dos casas*   *un carro,*   *dos carros*
            one house,   two houses   one car,   two cars

(13)   N_L

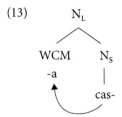

WCM   N_S
-a |
              cas-

The word class marker is a problem for the lexical/functional split hypothesis. Suppose we assume the structure in (13) for Spanish nominals (where WCM stands of word class marker, N_S represents the nominal stem prior to word class marker adjunction, and N_L the nominal lexeme resulting from this adjunction), and all terminal nodes must be classifiable as one or the other. In that case, where does the word class marker fall? On the one hand, it is inside a lexical constituent, and should thus be lexical. On the other, the difference between the stem and the lexeme is not one of content, but of its ability to refer, a syntactic property, so the WCM has functional properties. The lexical/functional split cannot categorize this item satisfactorily.

1.2.4.4 *Verb/aspect vs. person/number as functional heads*

There is another way in which the lexical/functional split is unsatisfactory, viz., it fails to tease apart meaningful from meaningless functional elements. Consider the case of verbal inflection. There would be little argument that both verb/aspect and person/number are functional heads, represented in languages such as English and Spanish as suffixes, free forms, or a combination of both (cf. 14).

(14) a. She go<u>es</u> there often.
   b. She <u>will</u> go there next week.
   c. *Nosotros* <u>*seguiremos*</u>   *adelante.*
       'We   continue-1 PL SYN FUT forward'.
   d. *Nosotros* <u>*vamos a seguir*</u>   *adelante.*
       'We   continue-1 PL AN FUT forward'.

However, the semantic import of tense and aspect is clear, whereas that of person/number is not so obvious. If tense and aspect features change, the truth value of a proposition changes with them (15a, c); if person/number specifications on the verb change, the sentence becomes ungrammatical, but it does not become a different proposition with a different truth value (15 d-f). The traditional lexical/functional split has simply nothing to say about this.

(15) a. *Las chicas fueron*   *al cine.*
       'The girls go-3 PL PRET to the movies'.
   b. *Las chicas van*   *al cine.*
       'The girls go-3 PL PRES to the movies'.

    c. *Las chicas siguen*   *yendo al cine.*
        'The girls continue-3 PL PRES going to the movies'.

    d. **Las chicas fue*   *al cine.*
        'The girls go-3 SG PRET to the movies'.

    e. **Las chicas va*   *al cine.*
        'The girls go-3 SG PRET to the movies'.

    f. **Las chicas sigo*   *yendo al cine.*
        'The girls continue-1 SG PRES going to the movies'.

In the following section, the lexical/functional split is redefined in terms of features internal to the system, instead of as a general classification used to sort items in the lexicon. This may seem like a small distinction, but it is not: it allows for a clearer delineation of the types of constituents possible inside compounds.

1.2.5 The lexical/functional feature hypothesis

Up until now, the lexical/functional split has been presented as a metalinguistic description of types of word classes. In contrast, the present proposal incorporates the split into the level of the terminal node itself. This move presupposes that if the lexical/functional split works, it is because items do indeed differ in some internal dimension, represented featurally, on a par with others such as telicity and animacy. I thus propose two binary features [L] and [F], present in all heads and defining four possible types, defined through all their logical combinations.[4] The traditional lexical classes of noun, verb, and adjective/adverb stems will be defined as [+L, –F] heads. For their part, standard interpretable functional heads with sentence-semantic value, such as determiner, strong quantifier, complementizer, degree word, tense, aspect, and verbal mood will be defined as [–L, +F]. But there are now two additional combinations of features, namely [+L, +F] and [–L, –F], which, due to their apolar combinatorial nature, are not contemplated in the previous lexical/functional split. I propose that the first combination of features ([+L, +F]) represents heads such as numerals and contentful prepositions of the kind defined here as 'lexical'. It also includes heads that have until now been poorly understood and accounted for in the morphological literature of Spanish, such as the word class marker of nouns and the thematic vowels required by verbs prior to inflection. Finally, the category [–L, –F] corresponds to uninterpretable functional elements, i.e., items that have no semantic content and no structural function (concord, case, and agreement markers, expletive subjects such as *It seems that ...* and *There are men...*). These are assumed to be erased at the point of semantic interpretation (Chomsky 1995).

---

4.   This move is inspired by Muysken's (1982) solution to the question of how many bar levels are possible in X-bar. I am grateful to Juan Uriagereka for extensive discussion of this point.

Table 1.1 Classification of head types according to the [L, F] feature hypothesis

	+L	−L
+F	Word class marker, verbal theme, contentful prepositions, numerals and other weak quantifiers, modal verbs	Determiners, strong quantifiers, tense/mood/aspect markers, auxiliary verbs, degree words
−F	Noun, verb, adjective, adverb stems	Expletives, case inflection, person/number verbal inflection

Items that are [+L] are lexical in one of two ways: they are either conceptually meaningful themselves [+L, −F], or are required by meaningful items to be used referen-
tially [+L, +F]. Items that are [−L] fulfill exclusively sentence syntactic functions. Those
that are [−L, +F] derive their meaning from their syntactic function as operators.
Those that are [−L, −F] do not, and are assumed to be subject to deletion in the semantic component.[5]

1.3   Definitional properties of compounds

To define compounding and distinguish it from other processes, it is necessary to delimit (a) its possible constituents; (b) its possible outputs; and (c) its possible internal
operations. Different authors have drawn the line in different places, which is to be
expected since the notion itself is not clear-cut or uniform across languages and gray
areas abound (Dressler 2005: 24).

1.3.1   Lexical input

The impressionistic view that compounds have a 'stripped down syntax', or a microsyn-
tax (Benveniste 1966: 145), can be accounted for in terms of a structural property that
defines compounds in general, and Spanish compounds in particular, i.e., that their constituents must bear the feature [+L]. Thus, within a compound we find [+L, −F] constituents (N, V, A, Adv) and [+L, +F] constituents (word class marker, verbal theme, numeral
and other weak quantifiers, modal verbs), but no [−L] (determiners, pronouns, tense and

---

5.   Some categories, such as the marks of adjectival concord, are less obviously classifiable. On
the one hand, one might want to include them with case and agreement, as meaningless uninterpretable features that merely mark the relation of dependency between the adjective and the
noun whose gender it adopts. However, the marks themselves are not simply copied: *hombre
alto* 'the tall man', lit. 'the man tall', *hombre grande* 'the big man', lit. 'the man big', *perro alto* 'the
tall dog', lit. 'the dog tall', *perro grande* 'the big dog', lit. 'the dog big' (cf. **hombre alte*, **perro
grando*). Some recent theoretical accounts also support the view of a distinction between case
and agreement, on the one hand, and concord, on the other (Uriagereka 2008).

agreement markers, auxiliaries, expletives, case) (cf. Leffel 1988; Miller 1993: 89 for earlier formulations). This seems to be a general feature of core compounding types across languages (with few counterexamples, cf. Fabb 1998: 77–78; Toman 1998: 316).

The lexical/functional feature hypothesis accounts well for the types of constituents that are possible and impossible within English and Spanish compounds. Compounds may include lexical and modal verbs but exclude auxiliary, tense, and agreement projections (cf. the contrast in grammaticality in 16d, e, for English and 17c for Spanish). The same pattern obtains with adjectival phrases versus degree phrases (cf. 16a and 17b), and noun phrases versus determiner phrases (16b, c and 17a, c).

(16)   Data in a–d from Miller (1993: 91)
    a.   blackbird   *veryblackbird
    b.   Bronx-hater   *the-Bronx-hater
    c.   book-reading   *what-reading, *it-reading
    d.   book-reading   *book-having-read
    e.   must-see   *must-have-seen
    f.   three-piece   *most-piece
    g.   outsource   *ofsource

(17)

	compound	literal gloss	meaning
a.	*hombrelobo*	man-wolf	werewolf
	*hombreellobo	man-the-wolf	
	*hombrequien	man-who	
b.	*pelirrojo*	hair-red	redhead
	*pelimuyrrojo	hair-very-red	
	*peliextremadamenterrojo	hair-extremely-red	
c.	*sacacorchos*	remove-corks	corkscrew
	*sacaqué	remove-what	
	*sacaeste	remove-this one	
	*sacancorchos	remove-2 PL PRES-corks	
	*sacabascorchos	remove-2 SG IMPERF-corks	
	*hasacadocorchos	remove-2 SG PERF-corks	
d.	*cuatro-ojos*	four-eyes	four-eyes
	*todos-ojos	all-eyes	
	*ningún-ojo	no-eye	

The reader may have noted two specific gaps in the Spanish data, when compared to English compounds. The first is the absence in Spanish of modal verbs as a category with different syntactic behavior from lexical verbs. This accounts for the absence in Spanish of compounds of the type *puede-hacer* 'can-do' or *debe-leer* 'must-read'. The second gap has to do with the scarcity of compounding with prepositions (but recall examples such as *sinvergüenza* in 6c). This seems to be related to the fact that most lexical prepositions seem to have special allomorphs when they are used in complex lexemes, i.e., prefixes. Thus, *poner antes* 'place before' alternates with *anteponer* 'antepose', *poner después* 'place afterward' with *posponer* 'postpose'. At this point, I simply point out this fact, without exploring any further the possible relationship between compounding and prefixation (for a discussion, cf. Varela & Martín García 1999: 4995).

Defining compounds as created exclusively through the combination of [+L] constituents narrows down the possible patterns in a principled way. For instance, it allows for a simple distinction between quantifiers that can and cannot participate in compounding. Weak quantifiers, such as numerals, are expected as compounding constituents, whereas strong quantifiers are not (17d). The distinction also provides a rationale to exclude phrasal constructions containing functional prepositions, i.e., those that instantiate agreement relations between sentence constituents (in Spanish, typically, *de* 'of, from' and *a* 'to') (Barlow & Ferguson 1988). This eliminates from consideration constructions of the type *dulce de leche* 'caramel paste', lit. 'sweet of milk' and *cuerno de la abundancia* 'cornucopia', lit. 'horn of the abundance', which include functional categories in their internal structure ($[N + prep + N]_N$ and $[N + prepDP]_N$ respectively). Since this is a complex issue and one not universally agreed upon, I leave detailed discussion of it for Section 1.5.4.

The case of lexical prepositions is less clear, because, as pointed out earlier, it is often not obvious whether a given complex lexeme involves prefixation or compounding with prepositions. For example, it is very possible that *sobre-* 'over' in *sobrevolar* 'fly over', lit. 'over-fly' and *sobrehueso* 'bony outgrowth', lit. 'overbone' could have the internal structure $[P + V]_V$ and $[P + N]_N$ respectively, given the semantic interpretation of *sobre* as a locative and the possibility of analyzing it as a case of incorporation (Baker 1988): *sobrevolar el mar* ~ *volar sobre el mar* 'over-fly the sea, fly over the sea'. However, it is unlikely that we can give the same analysis to *sobrealimentar* 'overfeed' or *sobrenombre* 'nickname', lit. 'over-name' since the locative meaning is not present and thus an incorporation analysis is precluded: *sobrealimentar al niño* 'overfeed the child' ~ **alimentar sobre el niño* 'feed over the child'.

A case-by-case consideration is impractical for the purposes of the present work, so the alternatives would be to either include all prepositions/prefixes in the analysis or, on the contrary, to exclude them all. The position followed here has been to exclude from consideration all prepositions except those that cannot be taken to be prefixes (cf. also the argument of 'system adequacy' in Rainer & Varela 1992: 118, which is based on Wurzel 1984). For a particle to be counted as a preposition it must have a form that makes it impossible to be interpreted as a prefix and it must exhibit distinct distributional properties, i.e., it must precede a noun with which it constitutes a prepositional phrase. This would exclude for example, lexemes such as *sobreventa* 'oversale', and *sobrevolar* 'fly over', lit. 'overfly', *anteponer* 'antepose', lit. 'fore-put' and *antesala* 'hall', lit. 'fore-room', which are considered instances of prefixation. By contrast, forms such as *sinrazón* 'nonsense', lit. 'without reason' are considered compounds, since Spanish has no prefix *sin-* with the relevant meaning.

Table 1.2 Lexemes and stems in Spanish compounding

	Stem	Lexeme
nominal	*ajiaceite* 'type of sauce', lit. 'garlic-oil'	*ajoarriero* 'type of stew', lit. 'garlic-muleteer'
verbal	*aliquebrar* 'break the wings [of a bird]', lit. 'wing-break'	*quiebrahacha* 'type of hard wood', lit. 'break-ax'
adjectival	*blanquiverde* 'white and green', lit. 'white-green'	*manjar blanco* 'blancmange', lit. 'delicacy white'
numeral	*cuatrimotor* 'four-engine plane', lit. 'four-engine'	*cuatro ojos* 'person who wears glasses', lit. 'four-eyes'

1.3.1.1 *Lexemes and stems in compounding*

The lexical/functional feature hypothesis also accounts for differences among compounds in terms of their internal make-up. Thus, for example, it predicts that compounds may either exhibit [+L, –F] constituents only, or both [+L, –F] and [+L, +F] constituents (cf. Table 1.2).[6] This fact can be used to draw distinctions between languages, since not all of them present this duality. Whereas Spanish exhibits constituents of both kinds, English has no lexeme/stem distinction in nouns and verbs, because the [+L, +F] category of word class marker and verbal theme is absent. As a result, stems are homophonous with lexemes and alternations like the ones in Table 2 are not found.

1.3.2 Lexical output

Several early authors consider as a compound any kind of word made up of pre-existing free forms (Alemany Bolufer 1920: 153; Darmesteter 1967 [1884]: 72–88; Real Academia Española 1986: 169), but others (Diez 1973 [1874]; Meyer-Lübke 1923 [1895]) restrict their object of study to lexeme creation exclusively. It is this second position that has prevailed and that will be adhered to throughout this work. Simply put, a new compound is a lexeme, i.e., it belongs to one of the major lexical categories

---

6.   It is interesting to note the absence of a distinction between stems and lexemes in adverbial constituents. Thus, for example, the adverbs *mal* 'badly' and *bien* 'well' always appears in the same guise when they participate in compounding and when they appear as free forms: *malvivir* 'survive', lit. 'badly-live', *biencasado* 'happily married', lit. 'well-married'. Since very few adverbs participate in compounding (they are limited to *mal* 'badly' and *bien* 'well', with others such as *siempre* 'always' appearing infrequently) it is hard to tell whether the lack of alternation is an accidental gap, due to the fact that those particular adverbs lack an overt word class marker. It can be proven that other adverbs do in fact show alternations between stems and lexemes: *lejos* 'far' → *lejitos* 'somewhat far', lit, 'far-DIM, *lejanía* 'distance' lit., 'far-N SUFF'

of noun, verb, adjective, adverb, or numeral (18).[7] Functional words such as pronouns or discourse markers are not considered compounds, even if they are internally complex (19).

(18) a. Eng. boathouse (N), windsurf (V), waist-deep (A)

	b.	compound	literal gloss	meaning
		casacuna (N)	house-crib	orphanage
		maniatar (V)	hand-tie	tie by the hands
		carilargo (A)	face-long	long-faced

(19) a. Eng. nevertheless, moreover, y'all

	b.	Spanish	literal gloss	meaning
		sin embargo	without hindrance	however
		asimismo	thus-same	likewise
		nosotros	we-others	we
		vosotros	you-others	you-PL

1.3.3   Syntactic internal relations

A first description of Spanish compounds shows that relations between constituents can be characterized with syntactic labels such as coordination, apposition, complementation, and modification (cf. 20a for sentence-level syntax and 20b, for lexeme-internal syntax). Those syntactic relations are of two basic types and define two basic types of compounds, which will be called *hierarchical compounds* (also known as sub-compounds) i.e., those with a head and a dependent constituent, and *concatenative compounds* (also known as co-compounds) those that are non-hierarchical (cf. Toman 1998: 311–12 for a similar distinction).

	a.	syntax		meaning
		coordination:	*Juan y Pedro*	'Juan and Pedro'
		apposition:	*Juan, mi hermano*	'Juan, my brother'
		modification:	*su cara muy larga*	'his very long face'
		complementation:	*abre la lata*	'[S/he] opens the can'.

	b.	compound	literal gloss	meaning
		coordination:		
		coliflor	cabbage-and-flower	cauliflower
		rojiverde	red-green	red-green
		materno-infantil	mother-child-ADJ	[of] mother and child

---

7.   Adverbial compounds are absent in Spanish, an accidental gap which does not affect the main argument (for an alternative account, which considers *-mente* adverbs compounds with the structure [A + N], cf. Zagona 1990, Baker 2003: 234).

apposition:

| *escritor-director* | writer-director | writer-director |

modification:

| *cara larga* | face-long | long-faced |

complementation:

| *abrelatas* | open-cans | can opener |

In spite of the similarities between (20a) and (20b), there are differences between these operations at the sentence and lexeme level. On the one hand, sentence syntax often requires the presence of overt functional elements for certain relations to be licensed (21).

(21) a. *Robert Redford es actor director.*
Robert Redford is actor director.

  b. *Robert Redford es actor y director.*
Robert Redford is actor and director.
'Robert Redford is an actor and a director'.

In contrast, syntactic constituents may be separated (22a, e) or moved from their base-generated positions (22c), whereas this is impossible lexeme-internally (22b, d, f).

(22) a. *Robert Redford es actor y además director.*
Robert Redford is actor and also director.
'Robert Redford is an actor and also a director'.

  b. **Robert Redford es un actor-además-director.*
Robert Redford is an actor-also-director.
'Robert Redford is an actor and also a director'.

  c. *¿Qué$_i$ sacaste t$_i$?* *El corcho.*
What remove-2SG PRET? The cork.
'What did you remove? The cork.

  d. **¿Qué$_i$ compraste un saca t$_i$?* *Corcho.*
What buy-2SG PRET a remove? Cork.
'What did you buy a remover of? Cork'.

  e. *Abrió rápidamente las latas.*
Opened-2SG PRET quickly the cans.
'He opened the cans quickly'.

  f. **el abre-rápidamente-latas.*
The open-quickly-cans
'the fast can-opener'

There is also a notable absence from the compound-internal syntactic relationships, namely, subject-predicate. For example, verbal compounds of the structure $[V + X]_N$ can exhibit complements (e.g., themes, locatives, manner complements): *vendepatria* 'traitor', lit. 'sell-country', *correcaminos* 'roadrunner', lit. 'run-roads', *mandamás* 'boss', lit. 'order-most'; by contrast, the subject of a verb is impossible: *lava-mujer* 'wash-woman', *corre-hombre* 'run-man'. That, together with the restriction on long-distance movement in compounds mentioned earlier (cf. 22d), suggests that the syntactic operations available to compound constituents are limited to those involving a head and an internal argument, but not specifiers. Therefore, in later discussion I will avail myself of complementation and modification as the two main processes that relate constituents in hierarchical compounds. The structure and semantic properties of each one of these general types will be considered in depth in Chapter 2.

1.4 Properties of compounds

Compounds exhibit formal features typical of lexemes, such as fixity, syntactic atomicity, and semantic idiomaticity. They also exhibit evidence of the syntactic nature of the process in the productivity of some patterns and their possibility of recursion. I discuss these five properties in turn.

1.4.1 Fixity

One of the facts that makes compounds different from syntactic phrases is that, once they are created, their elements become fixed in an invariable order that cannot be altered. Additionally, the replacement of constituents results in a different compound (23).

(23) | compound | literal gloss | meaning |
| --- | --- | --- |
| *casacuna* | house-crib | orphanage |
| *cunacasa* | crib-house | |
| *residencia-cuna* | residence-crib | |
| *casa-cama* | house-bed | |

A number of prosodic and phonetic features follow from the formal fixity of compounds (Bloomfield 1933: 228). Of these, one common across languages is word stress, which involves the de-stressing of one of the two constituents (Fabb 1998: 79). In Spanish, single main stress is a feature of certain patterns of compounding, such as [V + N]$_N$ (*sacacórchos* 'corkscrew', lit. 'remove-corks', *pisapapéles* 'paperweight', lit. 'step-papers'), but it is not categorical. Concatenatives can have more than one stressed syllable: *directór-actór, matérno-infantíl* '(related to) mother and child'. In other cases, there is variation between different tokens of the same pattern: *agua fuérte* 'etching', lit. 'water strong', but *água régia* 'hydrochloric and nitric acid solution', lit. 'water regal'. Normally, the more lexicalized the compound, the more likely it is to have single lexeme stress, but variation among speakers or dialects is possible, as evinced by Eng. *íce cream, ice cream* (Bloomfield 1933: 180). Other phonetic changes present in Spanish include the elimination of hiatic vowels, especially if they are identical: *para + aguas > paraaguas > paraguas* 'umbrella', lit. 'stop-waters'.

Prosody and phonetics are useful diagnostic tools to ascertain compound status in contemporary studies, but they are of limited usefulness in work with a historical focus. Access to prosody and sounds in general is mediated by orthography and thus, by the criteria of the scribe and/or the lexicographer. This issue is taken up in Chapter 2, Section 2.3 when discussing tests for compoundhood.

1.4.2 Atomicity

The lexemes that make up a compound cannot be targeted for individual syntactic operations, a feature they share with the output of morphological derivation. For example, no material may be inserted between the constituents, either through modification or parentheticals (24) (for the earliest formulation, cf. Bloomfield 1933: 180).

(24)		compound	literal gloss	meaning
	a.	*buque escuela*	ship school	training ship
		*buque pequeño escuela	ship small school	small training ship
	b.	*hombre rana*	man frog	frogman
		*hombre viejo rana	man old frog	old frogman
	c.	*pollera pantalón*	skirt trousers	skort
		*pollera larga pantalón	skirt long trousers	long skort
	d.	*magia negra*	magic black	black magic
		*magia muy negra	magic very black	very black magic

Another manifestation of this feature is the fact that no anaphoric reference can be made to the non-head element, just as it cannot in suffixation, in contrast with syntactic phrases (25).

(25) a. phrases:
   La madre   del niño$_i$ lo$_i$ vio en   el jardín.
   The mother of the child$_i$ DIR OBJ M SG$_i$ saw him$_i$ in the garden.

   b. compounds:
   *Esta telaraña$_i$ la   hizo la$_i$ gorda.
   This cloth-spider$_i$ DIR OBJ F SG$_i$ made the$_i$ fat$_i$.
   'This spider web was made by the fat spider'.

   c. suffixation:
   *Fui   a la panader$_i$ía. No lo$_i$ vi.
   Go-1 SG PRET to the baker$_i$y. NEG DIR OBJ M SG$_i$ see-1SG PRET.
   'I went to the bakery. I did not see the baker'.

All these examples show that the compound behaves as a block immune to syntactic operations in a manner no different from single lexemes. This behavior is crucial to distinguish certain types of compounds from syntactic structures that resemble them on the surface, as shall be seen in Section 1.5.

1.4.3 Idiomaticity

Because they are lexemes, all compounds may undergo meaning displacements that result from lexicalization (Penny 1991: Ch. 5). This is especially true of the kinds of compounds this study is about, i.e., those recorded in dictionaries. The most common semantic displacement involves a restriction of the possible denotations to a specific subtype (cf. *black bird* vs. *blackbird*, in Bloomfield 1933: 180). For example, *lavaplatos* 'dishwasher', lit. 'wash-dishes', and *lavavajilla* 'dishwasher', lit. 'wash-crockery' could theoretically both be applied to anything or anyone that washes dishes (i.e., worker or machine). The fact that the first term is used with both meanings but the second is reserved for the household item is an arbitrary restriction resulting from usage.

Meaning changes involving metaphor/metonymy are even harder to predict (Lakoff 1990; Lakoff & Johnson 1980). To illustrate the problem, let us consider the $[V + N]_N$ compounds in (26), which show how the same pattern can result in compounds with different degrees of semantic transparency/opacity.

(26)	compound	literal gloss	meaning
a.	*matambre*	kill-hunger	rolled flank stake
b.	*matasuegras*	kill-mothers-in-law	party whistle
c.	*matamoros*	kill-moors	brave man, bully
d.	*matarratas*	kill-rats	rat poison

At one end we have *matambre*, which is etymologically a compound but is no longer analyzable by native speakers as made up of constituents. It is semantically opaque in that computing its meaning does not involve any operation with its parts, because strictly speaking there are no parts. Other compounds with the same internal structure are compositional: the meanings of the parts and the rules of combination (in this case, verb-complement) account for the semantics of the whole. That is the case with *matarratas*, which is indeed something that kills rats. Note, however, the semantic specialization mentioned above: the noun tends to be reserved for a poisonous powder, rather than for a baseball bat, slingshot, or other instrument that could be employed for the task of getting rid of rodents. The trickier cases are those in (26b, c), whose combination of constituents was metaphoric to begin with, or, if it ever was literal, this information is now unavailable to all but the most erudite of native speakers. In this case, the meaning of the compound is also non-compositional. For example, a *matasuegras* 'party whistle' is not something that kills mothers-in-law. Yet, it is still possible for native speakers to analyze the constituents and note this discrepancy.[8] This reveals that even if compounds are stored in the lexicon as unanalyzed wholes, their constituents may be accessed independently (Libben 2005).

In sum, compound meaning may be atomic, when it is impossible to decompose the whole into independent units. It may also be compositional, when knowing the meanings of the constituents and the structure of the combination is enough to deduce a range of possible meanings for the whole. The most salient or frequent of these semantic relations tend to lexicalize, so that the compound denotes a subcase within the range of possibilities. Compounds can also exhibit more complex interpretation due to metonymic/metaphoric uses. However, if the constituents retain their form, stored figurative meanings do not preclude access to compositional meaning.

1.4.4 Productivity

Compounding involves certain combinatorial processes whose renewed use may yield neologisms. For example, the pattern $[V + N]_N$ keeps producing new terminology in dialects and semi-technical fields (e.g., *sacaleche* 'breast pump', lit. 'get-milk'), as well as nonce neologisms readily interpreted by native speakers. However, not all compounding patterns are equally productive at any given point in time. In contrast with $[V + N]_N$, other patterns are found in a handful of items, mostly archaic (e.g., $[N + V]_V$, *maniatar* 'tie by the hand', lit. 'hand-tie'). Still others have numerous dictionary entries, but seem to have decreased their relative productivity in modern Spanish (e.g., $[Adv + V]_V$, *malcasarse* 'marry the wrong person', lit. 'badly-marry'). The issue of defining and measuring productivity in morphology is by no means simple, however, and the number of tokens in itself is not sufficient to determine it. This issue is taken up again in Chapter 3, Section 3.4, where several methods for calculating productivity in diachrony are discussed.

1.4.5 Recursion

The last property to be discussed is recursion, i.e., the possibility of applying the process of compounding to previous outputs of compounding. The name 'recursion' is reserved for those cases in which merge operations are involved, i.e., where a new

---

8. To wit, the following authentic quote from Google: *Día mundial del matasuegras: Ese día puedes matar a cualquier suegra del mundo porque nadie se va a enterar porque como ya te dan el arma dentro del cotillón pues tú llegas a la fiesta, localizas a tu suegra, te vas para ella y le das con el matasuegras así como el que no quiere la cosa. Claro después es muy difícil encontrar el arma homicida entre tanto matasuegras.* 'International day of the party whistle (*matasuegras*, mother-in-law killer): That day you can kill any mother-in-law because nobody will find out. They give you your weapon when you go to the party store, so you arrive at the party, find your mother-in-law, approach her, blow the party whistle (*matasuegras*, mother-in-law killer) in her face when nobody's looking. Of course after that it is very hard to find the killer weapon among all the party whistle'.

nested binary complex is created (27a–d, e-f). It has parallels in syntax: *el hombre de pantalón negro* 'the man in black trousers', *el perro del hombre de pantalón negro* 'the dog of the man in black trousers', *la pulga del perro del hombre de pantalón negro* 'the flea of the dog of the man in black trousers'. Concatenative compounds are created by a process that adds constituents without adding structural layers, so there is no authentic recursion, but rather, iteration: *poeta-pintor-escultor-pensador* 'poet-painter-sculptor-thinker' (unattested).

(27) a. *parabrisas* 'windshield', lit. 'stop-breezes' (attested)
      b. *limpiaparabrisas* 'windshieldwiper', lit. 'clean-stop-breezes' (attested)
      c. *arreglalimpiaparabrisas* 'windshieldwiperfixer', lit. 'fix-clean-stop-breezes' (unattested)
      d. *guardaarreglalimpiaparabrisas* 'windshieldwiper-fixer-keeper', lit. 'keep-fix-clean-stop-breezes' (unattested)
      e. *anuncio tatuaje* 'tattoo advertisement', lit. 'advertisement tattoo' (attested)
      f. *hombre anuncio tatuaje* 'tattoo advertisement man', lit. 'man advertisement tattoo' (unattested)

Recursive compounds such as those in (27) are possible, though not frequently attested in Romance. An additional observation is that recursion in Spanish exhibits a structural restriction: patterns such as $[V + [V + [V + [V + N]_N]_N]_N]_N$ and $[N + [N + N]_N]_N$ are exclusively left-branching (i.e., they exhibit tail recursion). This limitation is language-specific, since it clearly does not apply to compounding in Germanic languages (cf. the hypothetical but transparent examples in 28).

(28) a. $[[[[pipe]_N clog]_N remover]_N unit]_N$
      b. $[[nursing home]_N [bingo club]_N [talent show]_N]_N$

Although at this point the matter will not be exhausted, it bears mentioning that the restrictions on recursion mentioned above correlate with language-specific characteristics. Notably, full (left and right) recursion is impossible in Spanish, a language that also happens to have complex lexeme structure (stem + WCM), whereas it is possible in English, whose lexemes do not exhibit this morphological complication. It is worth exploring whether the internal structure of constituents is correlated with the different behavior of recursion across languages, a matter I leave open for further investigation.[9]

1.5 Some exclusions by definition

This section goes over some structures that have been included at some point or another in the literature on compounding, but are excluded from consideration here. It

---

9.   It may be related to derivational 'timing' restrictions of the kind mentioned in Lasnik (1999) for verbal ellipsis.

is shown that they are not *bona fide* cases of compounding because they fail to exhibit one or more of the defining characteristics laid down earlier.

1.5.1 Etymological compounds

The lexemes in (29) were formed through the compounding of two free forms, as noted. However, the passage of time has caused loss of compositionality through phonetic erosion, semantic change, or both. Most early philologists, who did not clearly distinguish synchrony and diachrony, equated the complex status of a lexeme at the time of its creation with its status later on (Alemany Bolufer 1920; Diez 1973 [1874]; Meyer-Lübke 1923 [1895]). However, a synchronic approach has prevailed in later works, such as the Real Academia Española's *Esbozo* (1986), Bustos Gisbert (1986), Lang (1990), Rainer & Varela (1992), Rainer (1993), and Val Álvaro (1999: 4831).

(29) a. *hilván* 'basting' < *hilo* 'thread' + *vano* 'vain'
      b. *carcomer* 'gnaw' < *carne* 'flesh' + *comer* 'eat'
      c. *zaherir* 'insult' < *fazferir* 'face-hurt' < Lat. FACIEM FERIRE 'id'.

The latter position is also taken throughout this work. In other words, the focus is diachronic but not etymological: historical comparisons are established over time, but for each period only analyzable forms are considered. In the absence of native speaker intuitions, lexicographical and textual databases were consulted to ascertain whether or not a form was made up of two independent stems. Note that this does not mean the problem is completely solved, because analyzability of a form may be a matter of degree, depending on the linguistic awareness of individual speakers, their knowledge of other languages, and so on. It may also depend on the existence of more or less transparent parallel constructions that may be simple orthographic variants of each other and thus aid native speakers in finding internal structure (e.g., more or less opaque *benedito, benedicto, bendito* vs. transparent *biendicho* 'blessed', lit. 'well-said'). These methodological challenges are addressed in Chapter 3, Section 3.2.

1.5.2 Syntactic freezes

Spanish has composite nominal lexemes (N^0) that contain sentences complete with subject (*cristofué*), inflectional marks on the verb (*met-o, entiend-o*), and referential pronouns (*correveidile, bienmesabe, no te entiendo*) (30). These constructions have been included as miscellaneous and unclassifiable types of compounding in several accounts (Bustos Gisbert 1986: 318; Rainer 1993: 298; Val Álvaro 1999: 4837).

(30)	**Complex form**	**literal gloss**	**meaning**
a.	*correveidile*	run-go-and-tell-him/her	gossipmonger
b.	*bienmesabe*	well-me-tastes	meringue dessert
		[it tastes good to me]	

c.	*cristofué*	Christ was [after its call]	tyrant flycatcher
d.	*metomentodo*	meddle-myself-in-all [I meddle in everything]	meddler
e.	*no te entiendo*	not-you-understand [I don't understand you]	person of mixed race
f.	*siguemepollo*	follow me chicken	ribbon on back

Similar constructions are reported for the Germanic languages, where they are adjectival, rather than nominal (31).

(31)   Data from Lieber (1992: 11–23)
  a.   an [[I ate too much] headache]   *English*
  b.   [[God is dood] theologie] '[God is dead] theology'   *Afrikaans*
  c.   [[lach of ik shiet] humor] '[laugh or I shoot] humor'   *Dutch*
  d.   Die [[Wer war das] Frage] 'the [who was that] question'   *German*

Although superficially these constructions look like compounds in that they are syntactic atoms created through the combination of free forms, here it is argued that they are not actual compounds. All of the examples in (30) and (31) are complete declarative, interrogative, or imperative sentences used as quotes (Bresnan & Mchombo 1995). Thus a *[God is dead] theology* is a theology that can be summarized in the motto "God is dead". Eating the sweet called *bienmesabe* presumably leads the taster to utter that sentence, and so on. Because these constructions are quotations out of their context of utterance, they are not referential, so that although they have sentential structure, they are syntactically inert.

One argument against considering these lexemes as compounds is the fact that they are not created through regular patterns, so that their form is completely idiosyncratic and their meaning is equally unpredictable. In spite of the existence of *correveidile*, for example, speakers do not create names of professions or occupations by stringing together imperatives to describe their associated activities. Thus, although *examinaauscultapinchayrecétale* 'examine, listen, inject, and prescribe to him/her' would be a brief summary of what a doctor does, coinages of this kind cannot be understood. This is in stark contrast with nonce formations such as *curalocos* 'cure-crazies', to mean a psychiatrist, or *pinchaniños* 'inject-children', to denote a pediatrician, which any native speaker would understand as tokens of the general type $[V + N]_N$.

Structural idiosyncrasy and semantic opaqueness are related to measurable differences in frequency. For example, the database of verbal compounds in Bustos Gisbert (1986) includes 32 constructions with the irregular type of pattern described above. They are greatly outnumbered by the 871 perfectly regular $[V + N/Adv]_N$ compounds in the same database (almost 97% of the data). Structures of the *correveidile* kind have been called **syntactic freezes** to capture their full-fledged but inert syntactic structure (Miller 1993: 93), and they are not considered compounds in this work.

1.5.3 Idiomatic expressions

In recent works, idiomatic expressions of the sort in (32) have been considered cases of Spanish compounding (cf. *locuciones verbales* in Val Álvaro 1999: 4830). Like compounds, these idiomatic phrases have non-compositional meaning and fixed constituent order.

(32)   Data from Val Álvaro (1999: 4831)

  a. *tomar el pelo* 'to tease', lit. 'to take the hair'
      vs. **tomar el cabello, *coger el pelo*

  b. *hacer de tripas corazón* 'to sacrifice', lit. 'to make of guts heart'
      vs. **hacer de corazón tripas, *hacer de intestinos corazón*

  c. *estirar la pata* 'to die', lit. 'to stretch the leg'
      vs. **alargar la pata, *estirar la pierna*

However, there is a difference in their level of insertion in the syntactic structure (di Sciullo & Williams 1987: 5). A compound is inserted in an X^0 position and is therefore opaque to the operations of syntax, as seen in Section 4.2. By contrast, an idiom is a maximal projection (XP). This is reflected in the fact that phrases inflect for tense and agreement, their internal pronouns are subject to the principles of agreement, and other phrases may be inserted between their constituents (33). These verbal locutions are good examples of listemes (i.e., objects stored in the lexicon) that are not lexemes.

(33)   a. *Habías estado <u>tomándome el pelo</u> desde el principio*   (8.12.07, Google)[10]
          'You had been teasing me from the start'. (lit. 'pulling me the hair')

  b. *[...] creo que ha llegado el momento de que <u>hagas de tus tripas corazón</u> y veas "La Comunidad".*   (8.12.07, Google)
      'I think it's time you suck it up and watch "La Comunidad"' ('lit. 'you make of your guts heart')

  c. *¿Qué haces aquí? ¿Te han enterrao así, sentao, o no <u>has estirao aún la pata</u>?*
                                    (1930, Ramón Sender, CORDE)
      'What are you doing here? Have they buried you like that, sitting, or haven't you kicked the bucket yet?' (lit. 'you have not stretched yet the leg')

---

10. In this and all later data obtained from Google, the citations are presented exactly in the spelling and punctuation of the original, regardless of whether they agree with the orthographic conventions of Spanish. This is done to facilitate the work of anyone attempting to google the same data in future, although it must be borne in mind that it may be impossible to locate old webpages, given the transience of Google.

1.5.4 Phrasal constructions

We finally come to one of the most problematic issues of Spanish, indeed of Romance, compounding. The term 'phrasal compound' has been used to refer to constructions such as *hierbabuena* 'mint', lit. 'herb good', *malasombra* 'evil person', lit. 'bad shadow', *dulce de leche*, 'caramel', lit. 'sweet of milk', or *árbol de la cera* 'wax myrtle', lit. 'tree of the wax', which have an internal structure undistinguishable from regularly constructed syntactic phrases (e.g., nominal phrases such as $[N + prep + N]_N$ and $[N + A]_N$ or $[A + N]_N$). However, they have become lexicalized, which entails formal fixity and semantic specialization.

In the past, authors have tended to include these constructions in their compounding taxonomies, while at the same time acknowledging their syntactic pedigree. Thus, Darmesteter (1967 [1884]), Diez (1973 [1874]), and Meyer-Lübke (1923 [1895]) and the Real Academia (1986) identify them as compounds by 'juxtaposition', as opposed to compounds by 'apposition'. The former (also known as phrasal or improper compounds) include combinations that follow regular syntactic patterns and draw their meaning from them (e.g., Fr. *chef-d'oeuvre* 'masterpiece', lit. 'chief-of-work'). The latter (also known as proper compounds) involve combinations that have no overt syntactic relation and whose sense is derived precisely from their position with respect to each other (e.g., Fr. *chou-fleur* 'cauliflower', lit. 'cabbage-flower').

More recently, these complex lexemes have been excluded from some analyses on account of their phrasal structure (Rainer & Varela 1992). However, the more general approach has been to include both phrasal and non-phrasal compounds, while recognizing their formal differences (Bustos Gisbert 1986; Lang 1990; Rainer 1993: Ch. 3; Val Álvaro 1999). Here it will be argued that both of these approaches are too extreme in treating all these constructions identically and that it is sounder to distinguish among them, including some and excluding others.

Consider the examples in (34), all of which have patterns that have at one point or another been called compounds (cf. Bustos Gisbert 1986: 69; Rainer 1993; Val Álvaro 1999: 4824–30).

(34)	compound	literal gloss	meaning
a.	$[A + N]_N$		
	vanagloria	vain-glory	vainglory
	gentilhombre	gentle-man	gentleman
	ricadueña	rich-lady	noblewoman
	medianoche	half-night	midnight
b.	$[N + A]_N$		
	paso doble	step double	pasodoble [music]
	olla podrida	pot rotten	stew
	nochebuena	Christmas Eve	night good
	hielo seco	ice dry	dry ice

c. [N + prep + N]$_N$

dulce de leche	sweet of milk	caramel paste
traje de baño	suit of bath	swimsuit
diente de león	tooth of lion	dandelion
hombre de paja	man of straw	strawman

d. [N + prep + DP]$_N$

pipa de la paz	pipe of the peace	peace pipe
manzana de la discordia	apple of the discord	apple of discord
culo del mundo	ass of the world	hole of a place
abogado del diablo	lawyer of the devil	devil's advocate

The [N + DP]$_N$ structures in (34d) are the easiest to exclude from compounding. A large database (Google) provides examples in which the constituents in these complex forms appear separated, evidence that they are not syntactically atomic (35).

(35) a. *ETA enciende la pipa de su paz.*   (6.14.07, Google)
'ETA lights the pipe of its peace'.

b. *El pensar diferente que impera entre nosotros en el aspecto político partidista no debe ser la manzana de nuestra discordia.*   (6.14.07, Google)
'Our different ideas about party politics should not be the apple of our discord'.

c. *el que sangra y se retuerce/Es el gran culo de este mundo* (6.14.07, Google)
'What bleeds and squirms/is the great ass of this world'.

d. *En fin, haces de abogado de un diablo que hace años escribió un artículo muy curioso sobre por qué ETA no debería de atentar en Cataluña.*
(6.14.07, Google)
'In sum, you are playing advocate of a devil who some years ago wrote a very funny article about why ETA should not carry out attacks on Catalonia'.

The rest of the examples have a great deal more structural fixity. Thus, for example, *dulce de leche* 'sweet of milk' in the relevant sense has no alternatives of the type **dulce de la leche*, **de esta leche*, **de nuestra leche* 'sweet of the milk, of this milk, of our milk', and *hielo seco* 'dry ice', lit. 'ice dry' cannot be qualified as **hielo muy seco*, ** hielo tremendamente seco* 'very dry ice, terribly dry ice', both of which would be possible in syntactic constructions (cf. *dulce de higos* 'fig preserve' vs. *dulce de los higos del árbol* 'sweet of the figs of the tree', *dulce de mis higos* 'sweet of my figs'; *carne seca* 'dry meat' vs. *carne muy seca* 'very dry meat', *carne tremendamente seca* 'terribly dry meat'). Yet, these two constructions differ in terms of their structural complexity. The simpler ones in (34a, b) involve a relationship between two lexical constituents, with an adjective acting as a preposed (34a) or postposed (34b) modifier to a noun. The relation is internal to the noun phrase and marked by gender concord: *nochebuena*, 'Christmas Eve', lit. 'night-FEM good-FEM', vs. **nochebueno* 'night-FEM good-MASC'. The examples in (34c) involve additional syntactic machinery: the first nominal requires a functional preposition to case-mark the lower nominal with the genitive, in violation of the definition of compounding as involving exclusively [+L] constituents (cf. also Dressler 2005).

Additional evidence can be provided to support a distinction between $[N + A]_N$ and $[A + N]_N$, on the one hand, and $[N + prep + N]_N$, on the other. Part of the evidence is linguistic, based on the behavior of these complexes in derivational processes, and part of it is neurolinguistic, and comes from studies of aphasic patients.

When a $[N + A]_N/[A + N]_N$ complex undergoes morphological derivation, it retains its internal gender concord (36a, b). However, when a $[N + prep + N]_N$ complex undergoes derivation, functional elements are lost in an overwhelming majority of cases (cf. 36c–e, data from Google, 6.14.07). There are thus valid linguistic grounds for distinguishing $[N + A]_N$ from $[N + prep + N]_N$.

(36)   **base**   **derived form**

a.   *medio campo*   >   *mediocampista*
      middle-MASC field-MASC   middle-MASC field- AGT SUFF
      'midfield'   'midfielder'

b.   *vanagloria*   >   *vanagloriarse*
      vain-FEM glory-FEM   vain-FEM glory-SUFF V
      'vainglory'   'to boast, to brag'

c.   *luna de miel*   >   *lunamielero*
      moon of honey   moon-honey-AGT SUFF
      'honeymoon'   'honeymooner'

d.   *hijo de puta*   >   *hijoputesco*
      son of prostitute   son-prostitute-ADJ-SUFF
      'bastard'   'bastardly'

e.   *caja de ahorros*   >   *cajaahorrista*
      box of savings   box-savings-AGT SUFF
      'savings account'   'owner of a savings account'

In studies with aphasic patients, $[N + A]_N$ and $[A + N]_N$ compounds also behave differently from $[N + prep + N]_N$, in ways that parallel the facts presented above. For example, Italian-speaking aphasics with grammatical impairments exhibit considerably fewer concord errors inside $[N + A]/[A + N]_N$ lexemes (e.g., *croce rossa* 'red cross', lit. 'cross-FEM red-FEM') than they do in phrases with the same internal structure (e.g., **croce giallo* 'yellow cross', lit. 'cross-FEM yellow-MASC') (Mondini et al. 2002). By contrast, in tests with $[N + prep + N]_N$ lexemes, they make mistakes in preposition selection at rates comparable to errors with non-lexicalized phrases (e.g., *canna da pesca* for *canna di pesca* 'fishing rod', lit. 'rod of fishing', *sacco in pelo* for *sacco a pelo* 'sleeping bag', lit. 'bag of hair', *mulino vento* for *mulino a vento* 'windmill', lit. 'mill of wind') (Mondini et al. 2005). This suggests that $[N + A]/[A + N]_N$ lexemes are more often retrieved as unanalyzed wholes, and therefore not affected by the aphasic's impairment in the manipulation of functional items, whereas [N + prep + N]$_N$ listemes are truly syntactic.

The above notwithstanding, no one would argue against the historical connection between [N + prep + N]$_N$ and [N + N]$_N$ merge compounds. It is often the case that phrasal constructions with intervening prepositions are compound precursors. For example, the evolution of *telaraña* 'spider web', lit. 'cloth spider' proceeded by elimination of functional elements over time in the overall sequence [N + prep + DP]$_N$ > [N + prep + N]$_N$ > [N + N]$_N$: *tela de la araña* [c. 1250], *tela del aranna* [c. 1275], *tela de arañas* [1378–1406], *tela de araña* [c. 1400], *telarañas* [1379–1425], *tela arannjas* [c. 1471]. The [N + prep + DP]$_N$ form disappears early, but the others have coexisted all the way to the present. Yet, only *telaraña/tela araña* is a compound by the definition presented here.

By the time the preposition is lost, there is little doubt that the nouns have been compounded. So why not accept these antecedent forms as compounds, too? Because not all [N + prep + N]$_N$ reach the point where their functional elements are lost (cf. the pairs in 37). This is not simply a function of the passage of time: *cepillo de dientes* 'toothbrush', lit. 'brush of teeth', which has been around since the 19th century [1884, CORDE], retains its prepositional element much more robustly than *ducha de teléfono* 'moveable shower head', lit. 'shower of telephone', a newer bathroom fixture. The matter is taken up in Chapter 6, Section 6.1.2.3, when discussing the origins of head-initial [N + N]$_N$ compounds.

(37)	complex form	literal gloss	meaning
a.	*casa (de) cuna*	house (of) cradle	orphanage
b.	*ducha (de) teléfono*	shower (of) telephone	hand shower
c.	*casa *(de) citas*	house *(of) trysts	hotel
d.	*cepillo *(de) dientes*	brush *(of) teeth	toothbrush

In brief, the definition of compounding presented calls for the exclusion of lexemes that have lost compositionality through phonetic erosion and have become monomorphemic. It also distinguishes compounds from other multi-morphemic structures that may have non-compositional meaning (e.g., locutions, [N + prep + DP]$_N$) and even a high degree of inseparability (e.g., [N + prep + N]$_N$), but are not made up exclusively of lexical constituents.

1.6 Some exclusions by justified stipulation

The previous section discussed constructions that can be excluded from the study of compounding on linguistic grounds, because they simply do not fit the definition. This section adds two exclusions that are not motivated on linguistic grounds but are simply a function of the nature of this study, i.e., its aims, its design, and its scope.

1.6.1   Learned compounds

Spanish shares with many other languages of Western Europe a tendency to borrow compounding stems from the classical languages to create lexemes in certain semantic fields. Unlike native stems, these learned stems do not have the possibility of appearing as free allomorphs (e.g., *No sé qué *logía voy a estudiar* 'I don't know what science I'm going to study'). To create new forms, they appear in combination with other learned stems (38a) and also with native stems or lexemes to create rightheaded compounds (38b).

(38)		**lexeme**	**literal gloss**	**meaning**
	a.	*psico-logía*	mind-science	psychology
		agri-cultura	field-culture	agriculture
	b.	*hidro-terapia*	water-therapy	hydrotherapy
		tomati-cultura	tomato-culture	tomato growth
		ciclo-vía	cycle-way	bike lane

Although their compound status is not put into question, the types in (38) will not be considered here. In that respect, this study differs from Kastovsky's, which proposes to consider neoclassical compounds together with their native counterparts, based on their increasing frequency in European languages and on their semantic parallels with native compounds (2009: 326). There are several reasons to exclude learned compounding. A practical reason is the need to constrain the study to a homogeneous set of lexemes with common combination patterns. Learned compounds tend to be quite different from native Spanish compounds in features such as their constituent order. Another reason is theoretical and has to do with learnability. The meaning of learned stems and the rules of their combination are not available to native speakers during early acquisition, but require explicit instruction. This happens at school, well after native compounding has been acquired.[11] Additionally, coinages of this type are not spontaneous but restricted to specialized domains (science, medicine, technology). Thus, although neoclassical compounds are undeniably productive, they are so in a very selective way. It should be noted, however, that the distinction between native and learned compounding has started to blur with the existence of forms such as *fango-terapia* 'mud-therapy' (possibly modelled after *hidroterapia* and the like), whose constituents are *bona fide* native Spanish stems but whose order is that of a learned compound. Compounds of this kind are included in the study, because identifiable native roots make the combination transparent to Spanish speakers, even if their order is calqued. This matter will be taken up at length at the appropriate points in this work

---

11.   I lack bibliographical references to back up this claim, but it is my own experience as a native speaker that learned compounds associated with various scientific disciplines are routinely explicated whenever they are first encountered in school textbooks. This would be unnecessary if these compounds were part of the regular inherited lexicon.

(cf. especially the discussion of [N + N]$_N$ right-headed compounding in Chapter 6, Section 6.2).

1.6.2   Proper names

Several accounts define compounds as common, generic words that entail a permanent and fixed semantic relationship between their constituents (di Sciullo & Williams 1987: 50; Gleitman & Gleitman 1970: 96). The survival and storage of compounds in the lexicon reveal social agreement about categories deserving of a separate designation. Proper names (e.g., *Hotel California, Kennedy Center*), are supposed to be different in that they are arbitrarily chosen or invented to denote without ascribing properties (Levi 1978: 7). However, it has been shown that this distinction between compounds and complex proper names is not so clear, since compounding can be activated not just to denote classes but also to create non-generic deictic devices (Downing 1977: 823). Additionally, even if they are used for naming individuals, proper names must be created following the principles of word combination made available by the grammar. Thus, the name *Kennedy Center* may be an arbitrary designation for a center for the arts in Washington D.C., but its rightheaded structure is not. To wit, the Spanish version of the name is *Centro Kennedy*, not *Kennedy Centro*, in accordance with the language's principles of headedness.

Complex proper names, therefore, involve combinations of constituents that follow grammatical principles and can provide clues to word formation in general. In fact, several diachronic studies include patronyms and toponyms as evidence of the productivity of compounding patterns. For example, the surname *Villagodos* lit. 'town Goths' appears, among many others, as an example of [N + N]$_N$ in de Dardel (1999: 189), and *Tallaferro* lit. 'cut-iron' or *Miraualles* lit. 'look-valleys' are presented in Lloyd (1968: 12–19) as examples of [V + N]$_N$. More modern examples include the name of cities, e.g., *Buenos Aires* 'lit. good-PL air-PL' ([A + N]$_N$), topographical landmarks, e.g., *Punta Gorda* 'lit. Point Fat', ([N + A]$_N$), and buildings, e.g., *Casa Pueblo* 'lit. House Village' (name of a restaurant/hotel) ([N + N]$_N$). Yet, this study excludes proper names. One reason is practical: most of the data come from lexicographical databases that only record common names. The other is methodological. Since proper names sometimes involve constituents with no dictionary entry (e.g., *Inclán* in *Valle Inclán*), it is difficult to assign them a grammatical category, gender, and other features necessary for satisfactory classification.

A related problem is presented by compound lexemes made up of one or two proper names as constituents (39a). These types of compounds pose methodological problems because it is sometimes difficult to assign grammatical categories to constituents and decide on the syntactic relation between them. For example, it is doubtful whether in *pedrojiménez* 'variety of grape' the head is the first name *Pedro* or the surname *Jiménez*. These complications make it preferable to eliminate such compounds from consideration in a study of this sort. Since they are infrequent, the decision is of little consequence to the overall outcome. A different situation is presented by the words in (39b), where a proper name does not refer to any given individual but is used as a generic term to denote a class (e.g., *María* standing for 'woman'). Those forms are considered legitimate compounds and are included in the data.

(39)	lexeme	literal gloss	meaning
a.	*reinaluisa*	queen Louise	lemon verbena
	martín pescador	Martin fisherman[12]	kingfisher
	pedrojiménez	Pedro Jiménez	grape variety
b.	*marisabidilla*	Mary know-it-all	know-it-all
	marimacho	Mary male	tomboy
	marimandona	Mary bossy	bossy woman
	marimorena	Mary dark	quarrel

1.7 Summary of chapter

This chapter has presented a definition of compounding as a process involving the creation of lexemes on the basis of other lexemes. However, what at first blush seemed like a simple and intuitive proposition, turned out to be more complex and nuanced than expected. It led to a theoretically-based formulation of the types of possible constituents in terms of two binary features, [L]exical and [F]unctional. Only [+L] constituents are possible in compounds. In Spanish this includes nouns, verbs, adjectives, adverbs, and numerals, and some associated lexical/functional categories such as the word class marker and the verbal theme.

Compound constituents combine by following syntactic principles; at the same time, the resulting complexes behave like syntactic atoms in being inseparable and opaque to operations that single out individual constituents. In their meaning, compounds also straddle the categories of phrase and lexeme: although their structure determines their semantic interpretation compositionally, most compounds listed in lexicographical sources have specialized their meaning unpredictably. The ambiguous nature of compounding has led to several approaches regarding what structures should be included and excluded, and has resulted in differences from one study to another. However, the definition in terms of [+L] heads presented here provides a clear-cut distinction based on a simple set of featural combinations. Rather than representing an abandonment of tradition, this approach crystallizes a collection of apparently haphazard observations into a coherent theoretical apparatus. Chapter 2 considers in greater detail the internal structure of Spanish compounds, including the types of possible relationships between the constituents and how to determine which of them is the head.

---

12.   Incidentally, the Eng. bird name *martin* is also a proper name turned common name, since supposedly it originated in Saint Martin, due to the fact that the bird's migration occurred around Martinmas, on November 11.

CHAPTER 2

The internal structure of compounds

Chapter 1 covered some general definitions of what is and is not considered a compound in this study. The present chapter completes the presentation of the notion of compounding by considering the internal structure and semantic properties of various compound types. It shows that compounds exhibit two basic general structures, viz., hierarchical and non-hierarchical. In the former, one of the constituents is the head and the other one is subordinate to it in some way (e.g., *hombre lobo* 'werewolf', lit. 'man wolf'). In non-hierarchical compounds, there are no dependent constituents, so both (or all, in the case of compounds with more than two constituents) are heads (e.g., *sofá cama* 'sofa bed'). Both hierarchical and non-hierarchical compounds exhibit a variety of syntactic relationships between their constituents, as we shall see. Independently of these internal relationships, one must also consider the relationship between the constituents and the higher node, which stands for the entire compounded structure. When constituents pass on their syntactico-semantic properties to the whole, then the compound is said to be endocentric (e.g., a *pájaro campana* 'bell bird', lit. 'bird bell' is a type of bird). If they do not, the resulting compound is exocentric (e.g., a *sacacorchos* 'corkscrew', lit. 'remove-corks' is neither a type of *saca* 'remove' nor of *corchos* 'corks'). This chapter explores these different structural configurations and their semantic consequences.

2.1 Preliminaries

When compounding is defined as proposed in Chapter 1, as a process of lexeme formation on the basis of lexical heads exclusively, this limits not just the types of constituents available, but the possible relationships between them. This is because, as shown in Fukui and Speas (1986: 285), lexical and functional heads project different types of structures. In particular, only functional heads are capable of projecting specifiers. This means that if the process of compounding involves the combination of lexical heads exclusively, then it follows that compound structures cannot have specifiers. This provides a principled way to limit possible compound structures to two general hierarchical patterns: head-complement and head-adjunct. In non-hierarchical configurations, only head-head is possible, since the presence of complements and adjuncts is a manifestation of a dependency relationship (*complement-complement, *adjunct-adjunct). As we shall see in the following sections, the entirety of Spanish compounding patterns is limited to those patterns of relationship. In the sections that follow, I consider hierarchical compounds of the type head-complement, of the type head-adjunct, and finally, those that involve only heads.

2.2 Hierarchical compounds

In hierarchical compounds (or sub-compounds, Kiparsky 2009) two lexical constituents are combined through some form of association operation under a single node, with one of them being structurally preeminent. In technical terms, one constituent is the head, i.e., its morphosyntactic and semantic features are copied onto the higher node (on morphological heads, cf. Zwicky 1985). The non-head is responsible for some kind of syntactico-semantic operation on the head, either complementation (1a) or modification (1b).

(1)	compound	literal gloss	meaning
a.	*aliquebrar*	wing-break	break the wings [of a bird]
	maniatar	hand-tie	tie by the hands
	sacacorchos	remove-corks	corkscrew
b.	*malcasar*	badly marry	make a bad marriage
	bienvenido	well-come	welcome
	hierbabuena	herb-good	mint

To understand the hierarchical relationship between the two constituents, consider, for example, *aliquebrar* in (1a). In this compound there are two constituents, one of which is the verb *quebrar* 'break', which is responsible for the verbal properties of the whole. The other is the nominal stem *al-* 'wing', which acts as the complement of *quebrar* and absorbs its theme role. Similarly, in *malcasar* (1b), the compound is a verb and so is the constituent *casar* 'to marry', while *mal* 'badly' modifies the manner of the event denoted by the verb, and is thus a modifier. In both cases, there is a constituent that combines two nodes (sisters, in standard syntactic terms), under a single node V^0 that contains them.

(2)

As it is presented in (2), the internal structure of the two compounds seems identical (and indeed, this is what has been claimed in the past in Harley 2009; Moyna 2004; Roeper et al. 2003). However, if that were the case, there would be no principled way to distinguish between compounds whose non-head acts as a complement and is assigned a thematic role by the head (e.g., *aliquebrar* 'break the wings [of a bird]', lit.

'wing-break'), those in which it is a modifying predicate (e.g., *hierbabuena* 'mint', lit. 'herb-good'), and those in which it is an adjunct (e.g., *malcasar* 'marry the wrong person', lit. 'badly-marry'). In what follows I propose ways to distinguish these relationships formally and thus explain the different semantics that hold between the constituents in each case.

2.2.1 Merge compounds

In merge compounds, the lexeme-internal operation that combines the head and the non-head parallels syntactic Merge, an operation that creates syntactic phrases (Chomsky 1995: 172). In a merge operation, one of the two constituents combined, the head, projects to the immediately higher node, i.e., it is responsible for the category label and other syntactic-semantic properties of the whole (3b). The other constituent is the first sister to the head; between the two, they constitute the first possible bracketing of constituents: [[[[wash] cars] for the school drive] on Friday]. The first sister, or complement, is a maximal projection, i.e., it fails to project its features any further. For example, in the merge between *wash* and *cars*, it is *wash* that projects its features to the whole *wash cars* (*wash* is a verb, and *wash cars* is a V[erb] P[hrase]).

The difference between syntactic and morphological merge lies in the fact that in morphological merge only lexemes may occupy both positions and the result of the merge is still a lexeme, i.e., a syntactic atom (X^0) that occupies a single node in a syntactic tree. For its part, Merge in syntax creates a phrase (XP) with the same category as the head element but more structural complexity (i.e., it takes up several terminal nodes) (3).

(3) a. Morphological merge   b. Syntactic merge

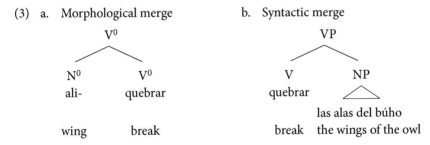

As a corollary, a phrase created through syntactic Merge, such as *quebrar las alas* 'break the wings' can be expanded, while a compound created through morphological merge, such as *aliquebrar* 'break the wings', lit. 'wing-break' is inert to syntax and its constituents cannot be separated. Compare: *quebrar las largas alas* 'break the long wings' vs. *largasaliquebrar* 'long wing-break'.

2.2.2 Predicative compounds

Many asymmetrical compounds have an internal structure involving a predication, i.e., an argument and a predicate. The simplest kind is modification, in which one head is adjoined to another head. Some examples of compounds that involve nominal modification are presented in (4a) and represented formally in (4b). When the combination involves verbs with adverbial expressions, of the type presented in *malgastar* 'waste', lit. 'badly-spend', it is often referred to as adjunction (4c). It can be considered different from modification in the sense that here the adverb is a subsidiary predication on the event denoted by the verb, itself a predicate on the external argument represented by the subject. This is different from the primary predication configuration represented by the adjective-noun relationship, which involves only an argument and a predicate. However, it is also possible to see verbs as arguments themselves, since a verb is 'an event of x-ing' (*eat* = *an event of eating*). This will be the approach followed here because it simplifies exposition by allowing us to consider modification of nominals and adjunction of verbals (and deverbal adjectives) as one and the same operation (4d).

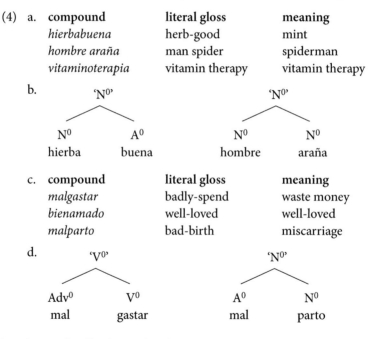

(4) a. **compound**   **literal gloss**   **meaning**
         hierbabuena   herb-good   mint
         hombre araña   man spider   spiderman
         vitaminoterapia   vitamin therapy   vitamin therapy

     b.   'N⁰'   'N⁰'

          N⁰   A⁰   N⁰   N⁰
          hierba   buena   hombre   araña

     c. **compound**   **literal gloss**   **meaning**
         malgastar   badly-spend   waste money
         bienamado   well-loved   well-loved
         malparto   bad-birth   miscarriage

     d.   'V⁰'   'N⁰'

          Adv⁰   V⁰   A⁰   N⁰
          mal   gastar   mal   parto

Although superficially identical to the Merge operation presented in 2.2.1, in predication the association between the two constituents is weaker, something captured notationally by the quotes around the higher node. The complement of a verb 'completes' the phrase, affecting its internal event properties. For example, *eating bananas* is quite a different operation from *eating oysters*, and both are vastly different from *eating crow* or *eating one's heart out*. The relationship between a head and its modifier is not intimate. Adjectival or adverbial predication does not change the semantics of the verb or noun involved in such drastic ways (cf. *eating quickly* vs. *eating slowly*; *ripe bananas* vs. *green bananas*). The meaning of the modifier must be intersected with the meaning of the head to establish the actual coverage of the expression. For instance, *green bananas* are all the items that are both in the set of *bananas* and in the set of *green* things. By contrast, if the head *eat* appears with the complement *crow*, it no longer belongs in the set of 'events of eating' in any meaningful way.

2.3 Concatenative compounds

In concatenative compounds (or co-compounds, Wälchli 2005) the constituents are combined in a flat (i.e., non-hierarchical) structure (5). In a sense, the compound has as many heads as it has constituents (it is thus n-ary) and these must belong to the same lexical class. In principle, there is no limit to the number of constituents that can be strung together: e.g., *[situación] económico-social-personal-laboral...*'.economic-social-personal-employment... [situation]'; *Leonardo da Vinci era poeta-pintor-escultor-científico....* 'Leonardo da Vinci was a poet-painter-sculptor-scientist...'. However, forms with more than two constituents are unusual and normally not listed in the dictionary.

(5)

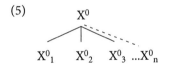

(6)

	compound	literal gloss	meaning
a.	*económico-social*	economic-social	economic-social
	rojiverde	red-green	red and green
	verdiazul	green-blue	green and blue
b.	*amigo-enemigo*	friend-enemy	friend-enemy
	compraventa	sale	sale-purchase
	ajoaceite	garlic-oil	type of sauce

These compounds have traditionally been called *dvandva* or coordinative compounds, which assumes the same internal structure for all of them. However, it has been shown that the class includes several different configurations and warrants a more fine-grained analysis (Bauer 2008). In Spanish, the first subtype of concatenative compounds is made up of two constituents that are coextensional, such as *actor-bailarín* 'actor-dancer', the denotation of which is an individual who is both an actor and a dancer. These compounds can be identified because they pass the test 'an x that is a y, a y that is an x'. They have been called appositional compounds (Spencer 1991: 311), but since the notion of syntactic apposition is complex and controversial, here I will prefer the more neutral term 'identificational compounds'. In the second subtype, the constituents have non-overlapping denotations. In some languages, such as Sanskrit, the denotation can be plural or dual (*hastyaçvās* 'elephants and horses', *chattropānaham* 'an umbrella and a shoe' (Olsen 2001: 285; Whitney 1941 [1879]: 485–486). However, in Spanish, English, and many other languages, these compounds are only possible as predicates of a higher nominal, which requires a plural complement, in a manner to be discussed shortly. For example, in *[relaciones] madre-niño*, 'mother-child [relations]', the denotation of the expression covers two different notions, somehow linked by an external head. I will call them additive compounds, which seems more transparent than other nomenclatures used in the past (e.g., translative compounds in Bauer 2001a: 700). Finally, there are other $[N + N]_N$ compounds that "blend" or combine semantic features of the relevant portions of the constituent denotation into a novel singular predicate. For example, *centro-derecha* 'center-right' describes an ideology somewhere between the center and the right. These I will call *hybrid dvandvas*.

The semantic differences between appositional compounds, on the one hand, and additive and hybrid compounds, on the other, can be shown with contrasts such as those in (7). Whereas identificational compounds can be replaced by either of their constituents to yield the same denotation (7a, b), this cannot be done with the other types, which define mutually exclusive sets (7c, d).

(7)   a.   *El salón comedor es un salón. El salón comedor es un comedor.*
'The living room-dining room is a living room. The living room-dining room is a dining room'.

b.   *La madre-esposa es una madre. La madre-esposa es una esposa.*
'The mother-wife is a mother. The mother-wife is a wife'.

c.   #*Una relación madre-niño es una relación madre. Una relación madre-niño es una relación niño.*[1]
'A mother-child relationship is a mother relationship. A mother-child relationship is a child relationship'.

d.   #*El sureste es el sur. El sureste es el este.*
'The southeast is the south./The southeast is the east.'

In additive *dvandvas* the constituents act as if they were joined by an implicit coordination: *coordenadas (de) espacio y tiempo* 'space and time [coordinates]', *rivalidad (entre) campo y ciudad* 'country <u>and</u> city rivalry'. In some languages, the resulting compound has a plural denotation, equal to the addition of the two constituents, such as Sanskrit *satyānŗté* 'truth and falsehood',(Whitney 1941 [1879]: 481). However, in Spanish and other languages the coordinated constituents are always in a head-complement relationship with the external noun through a null preposition:

---

1.   Whereas the asterisk (*) is reserved for ungrammatical sentences, the hash sign (#) is used to mark a sentence as nonsensical, even if structurally grammatical.

[rivalidad[ø[ciudad-campo]$_{NP}$]$_{PP}$]$_{NP}$ (cf. Toman 1985 for German). Most often, they apply to converse relationships (Lyons 1977: 279) or relational predicates, such as kinship terms and reciprocal social roles (Olsen 2001): *(relación) marido-mujer* 'husband-wife (relationship)', lit. '(relationship) husband-wife'; *(diálogo) norte-sur* 'north-south (dialogue)', lit. '(dialogue) north-south'. I propose that the compound structure merely provides a basic coordination, while the exact semantic nuances are given by the context, including the (external) head nominal. Thus, for example, an opposition interpretation may result if the head nominal demands a relational predicate (e.g. *rivalidad* 'rivalry'), but an additive interpretation may obtain when no relational predicate is present (e.g. *coordenadas* 'coordinates').

The evidence above suggests that the internal structure of additive *dvandvas* is coordination, with a null conjunct. This leads to the need to decide among competing accounts of coordination, an issue that exceeds the confines of this work. The reader may want to consult Goodall (1983) for a tridimensional account, van Oirsouw (1987) for a deletion account, Kayne (1994) for one based on asymmetry, Camacho (1999) for hierarchical dominance without asymmetry, and, more recently, de Vries' (2005) proposal of a three-dimensional model based on the notion of 'behindance'. Suffice it to say that whatever the correct structure may be for coordination, a structure along those lines ought to account for these compounds. For the purposes of this work, I will adopt the structure of deletion proposed by van Oirsouw (1987), for two reasons. The first is that, unlike the type of asymmetric structure presented by Kayne (1994: 57 et passim), an account through ellipsis does not require positing a specifier position in coordination, which would run counter to assumptions made earlier about the lexical nature of compound constituents (cf. Section 2.1). The second reason is that an ellipsis account can be helpful in yielding the semantic properties of additive compounds, as we will see presently.

Let us begin by illustrating the concern in sentential syntax. Consider sentence (8), whose unmarked interpretation is that a portion of the argument denotation is covered by one of the two coordinated predicates (i.e., some Uruguayans are white), while the other denotation portion is covered by the other (some Uruguayans are black). (For the time being we ignore the second less salient – but possible – reading, according to which both predicates apply to the entire argument, i.e., 'all Uruguayans are both black and white'.) This suggests that context variables have to be incorporated into the structure as in (8b), to somehow establish an apportioning of the argument into relevant subsets, each one with its own independent predicate (black and white). The interpretation in question can be accounted for through conjunctive reduction, i.e., the ellipsis of one of the two coordinated arguments even when they are not coextensional. After ellipsis, the two predications continue to be disjoint in the appropriate sense and to apply to distinct parts of the argument. Although many more details could be discussed in relation to these very interesting sorts of examples, this brief sketch will suffice for our word-internal purposes, to which I turn next.

(8) a. *Los uruguayos son blancos y negros.*
         Uruguayans are white and black.

     b. *Los uruguayos [pertinentes] son blancos y los uruguayos [pertinentes] son*
         negros.
         [The relevant] Uruguayans are white and [the relevant] Uruguayans are
         black.

     c. *Los uruguayos ~~[pertinentes] son~~ blancos y los uruguayos [pertinentes] son*
         negros.
         [The relevant] Uruguayans are white and black.

Similar reasoning can be applied to cases such as the predication established by the
conjunct *espacio-tiempo* 'space-time' in *coordenadas espacio-tiempo* 'space-time coordinates', whose two predicates are not applied to the argument as a whole, but really to
different constituents, as in (8b): *coordenadas [pertinentes] de espacio y coordenadas*
[pertinentes] de tiempo '[relevant] coordinates of space and [relevant] coordinates of
space > *coordenadas espacio-tiempo* 'space-time coordinates'. In other words, whatever
accounts for conjunctive reduction in syntax – and this matter is by no means settled
– must be at play at the word level, too (9).[2]

(9)

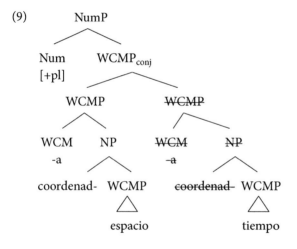

Finally, let us consider the third group of concatenative $[N + N]_N$ compounds, hybrid
dvandvas. In this unusual case, there is a partial blend of the features of two constituents

---

2.   It could be argued that this very syntactic approach to word formation requires transformations, and as such, would require compounds to have the full machinery of syntax, including
specifier positions, to do so. However, since Emonds (1976), transformations have been divided
into two categories: local transformations, in charge of local operations such as affix hopping
and the like, and structure preservation transformations responsible for long-distance movement. I argue only local transformations are involved in word formation, and specifier positions
are thus not required.

to create a new individual denotation, distinct from both of its parts: *gallipavo* 'American turkey', lit. 'rooster-turkey'. This is not an identificational compound, however, as it is impossible for the two constituents to have any extensional overlap in these cases (e.g., no rooster is a turkey, and no turkey is a rooster). Moreover, the compound does not simply add the denotations of the two constituents (as in *pelea gallo-pavo* 'rooster-turkey fight'). In *gallipavo* 'American turkey', lit. 'rooster-turkey' some of the features of *gallo* 'rooster' and *pavo* 'turkey' have been somehow combined to denote a third species, with features of each one of the constituent denotations. In other words, the entity is in some relevant sense rooster-like, and in another turkey-like.

In order to achieve this strange interpretation, we can again, perhaps, invoke conjunctive reduction (intuitively, the animal is like a rooster in some relevant sense, and a turkey in another relevant sense). However, in this instance the reduction must involve the predicates themselves, before they acquire any referential properties.[3] In other words, the conjunctive reduction must involve the noun stems before attachment of the WCM, as represented in (10).

(10)

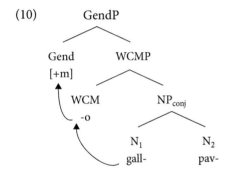

The exact extent of the semantic combination cannot be formulated a priori and is not determined syntactically. At one end of the continuum, the addition of semantic features contributed by both conjuncts is just one part of the meaning of the whole, i.e. a *pars pro toto* metonymy: *ajoaceite* 'type of sauce with garlic, oil, and other ingredients', lit. 'garlic-oil' (cf. co-hyponomic compounds in other languages in Bauer 2001a: 700; 2008: 9). At the other end, there are cases in which each constituent provides exactly half of the features: *sureste* 'southeast' is the cardinal point exactly halfway between the south and the east (compromise compounds, Bauer 2008: 10). In between, we have cases in which all the compatible features combine in the compound, in some

---

3.   This is not the standard view in semantics, according to which the meaning of predicates rests on their referential properties. For example, the meaning of a predicate such as "This leaf is green" is normally assumed to come from a previously defined set of green objects to which the leaf, as a referential expression, is said to belong. Examples such as the ones presented here, where a stem has meanings that can be manipulated and operated on before the attachment of morphological formants that endow them with referentiality (cf. Muromatsu 1998), favor a different definition of meaning.

undetermined percentage. Thus, *marxismo-leninismo* 'marxism-leninism' can be understood as a political philosophy that combines principles of Marxism compatible with those of Leninism, a characterization that might vary from one speaker to the next.

There is much more to say about the class of concatenative compounds, both in terms of their structural and semantic properties. The reader is directed to Chapter 8 for further discussion of the structure, meaning, and evolution of these compounds.

2.4 Endocentricity and exocentricity

Section 2 considered *endocentric* compounds, i.e., those in which the internal head constituent is also the head of the entire compound. However, many languages, including Spanish, have compounds in which no constituent percolates its syntactic-semantic features to the whole. For example, the combination of two adjectives *alto* 'tall' and *bajo* 'short' somehow results in a noun, *altibajo* 'vicissitude', lit. 'high-low' (cf. Eng. ups and downs). In *lavaplatos* 'dishwasher', lit. 'wash-dishes', neither of the two constituents is responsible for the category of the compound, since it is neither a verb nor a plural masculine noun (11). The syntactic-semantic features of the compound must therefore come from somewhere else, from 'outside' the compound, hence the term *exocentric*. Note that the internal structure of exocentric compounds may involve a merge operation, if one of the constituents does indeed govern the other one (*lavaplatos*), or concatenation, if both (or all) constituents do (*altibajo*). What they have in common is that, in either case, the structural head of the entire compound is an empty category external to either of its constituents.

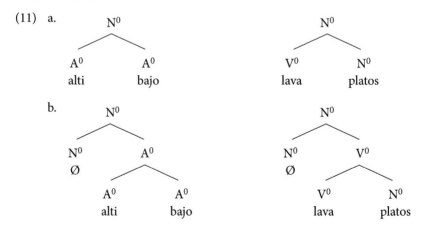

(11) a.

Spanish has several regular and productive patterns of exocentric compounding (12). They include the Pan-Romance $[V + N]_N$ pattern (12a), and the pattern termed *bahuvrihi* by Pāṇini, in which the relationship between the compound and its denotation is possessive or part-whole: *cararrota* 'cheeky person', lit. 'face broken', is someone whose face has the properties described by the compound (12b). Additionally, a variety of concatenative structures may be used exocentrically (12c). As the examples below show, all regular patterns of exocentric compounding in Spanish are nominal, a fact to which I will come back later.

(12)		compound	literal gloss	meaning
	a.	*abrelatas*	open-cans	can-opener
		sacacorchos	pull-corks	corkscrew
		pelapapas	peel-potatoes	potato-peeler
	b.	*cararrota*	face broken	cheeky person
		casco azul	helmet blue	blue helmet [UN soldier]
		dedos verdes	fingers green	someone with a green thumb
	c.	*altibajo*	high-low	vicissitude
		claroscuro	light-dark	chiaroscuro
		subibaja	go up-come down	seesaw
		duermevela	sleep-wake	light sleep

Apart from those regular exocentric patterns, any compound of any structure can be nominalized or used exocentrically, including, for example, $[Adv + V]_V$, $[N + A]_A$, and numerals (13).[4]

(13)		compound	literal gloss	meaning
	a.	*bienestar*	well-be	well-being
		malestar	badly-be	malaise
		malanda	badly-walk	wild hog
	b.	*boquirrubio*	mouth-blond	conceited youth
		colirrojo	tail-red	redstart [bird]
		manigordo	hand-fat	ocelot
	c.	*ochomil*	eight thousand	summit over 8,000 meters
		siete octavos	seven eighths	short overcoat

2.4.1 Headedness of hierarchical compounds

When presented with a hierarchical compound, native speakers generally have intuitions about which of the two constituents is the head and is therefore responsible for the features of the whole. If a theory is to reflect the knowledge that native speakers have about their language, then one of our goals should be to assign headship in

---

4.   In some cases, the corresponding verbal compound does not exist: *bienestuve en tu casa* 'I well-was at your house', *malandaba por la calle* 's/he badly went down the street'.

hierarchical compounds unambiguously and in a principled way. In English this tends to be a straightforward matter, since the head coincides with the last constituent, as summarized in the Righthand Head Rule (Williams 1981). Thus, in (14) an *apron string* is a subtype of *string*, of the kind found in *aprons*, and *honey-sweet* is a specific property, *sweet*, of the type found in *honey*.[5]

(14)   Data from Selkirk (1982: 14–15)
      a.   N: apron <u>string</u> $[N + N]_N$, small<u>pox</u>, $[N + A]_N$, over<u>dose</u> $[P + N]_N$, rattle-<u>snake</u> $[V + N]_N$
      b.   A: honey-<u>sweet</u> $[N + A]_A$, white-<u>hot</u> $[A + A]_A$, under<u>ripe</u> $[P + A]_A$
      c.   V: out<u>live</u> $[P + V]_V$

In Spanish, however, the distribution of the head is not fixed for all types of compounds (15). Adjectival and verbal compounds are right-headed: *drogadicto* is an adjective like *adicto*, and *maltratar* is a verb, like *tratar*. Nominal compounds can be both left- and right-headed, regardless of the lexical category of the non-head. Thus, an *hombre-masa* is a special kind of *hombre*, and a *mesa redonda*, a kind of *mesa*, but *organoterapia* is not a kind of *órgano* but a kind of *terapia*, based on organ transplants, and *malaventura* is a type of *ventura*, of the *mala* type.

(15)   Data from Rainer (1993: Ch. 3)

	literal gloss	meaning
a. **Nominal compounds**		
$[N + N]_N$		
hombre-masa	man-mass	mass man
organoterapia	organ-therapy	organ-therapy
$[N + A]_N$		
mesa redonda	table round	round table
$[A + N]_N$		
malaventura	bad fortune	misfortune
b. **Adjectival compounds**		
$[N + A]_A$		
drogadicto	drug-addict	drug-addict
pelirrojo	hair-red	redhead
c. **Verbal compounds**		
$[Adv + V]_V$		
maltratar	badly-treat	mistreat
$[N + V]_V$		
maniatar	hand-tie	tie by the hand

---

5.   There are exceptions, however, such as head-initial compounds (*pickpocket, gadabout*, etc.).

2.4.1.1 *Some preliminary notions*

To account for headship assignment in Spanish hierarchical compounds, it helps to have recourse to so-called thematic information. This is a property related to the argument structure of verbs, i.e., their capacity to assign roles to the various nominal participants in the sentence; a useful simile would be the roles played by actors in a performance. It is assumed to be a part of the verb's lexical entry (also called its thematic grid) how many and precisely which arguments (or theta roles) it has to assign. Thus, for example, in (16), the verb *put* has three specific roles, and must assign them all, each to a different NP argument (i.e., each role is played by a different actor). Any alternative will result in ungrammaticality either because the verb has not discharged (i.e., used up) all its roles (16c–e), or because there are arguments in the sentence with no thematic role (16f).

(16) a.   put ⟨agent, theme, locative⟩
       b.   She put her three children in childcare.
       c.   *Put her three children in childcare.
       d.   *She put her three children.
       e.   *She put in childcare.
       f.   *She put her three children in childcare the bus.

Higginbotham (1985) calls this kind of thematic information 'theta marking'. It is generally associated with verbal dependencies, but may extend to some nominals, as shown below. There are two other modes of thematic dependency that interest us here and which are canonically associated with nouns and adjectives. Higginbotham shows that any nominal has at least one theta role, which allows for its predicative use. Aside from being arguments of verbs (participating in whatever event these verbs denote), nominals can also function as predicates in their own right. This contrast can be seen in the different use of *socios* 'partners' in the examples in (17a, b). Whereas in (17a) the nominal is the argument of the verb, in (17b) the quality of being partners is assigned as a property, i.e., it is a predicate of *ustedes*. When the noun appears accompanied by a determiner, as it does in (17a), the property stays within the determiner phrase, according to Higginbotham, 'bound' by the quantifier. In the process of theta binding a predicative nominal becomes an argument, incapable of assigning a role, but capable of receiving one. This explains the ungrammaticality of *Yo los considero a ustedes unos socios* 'I consider you some partners'.

(17) a.   *Acabo*   *de conocer a <u>unos socios</u>.*
            Finish-1SG PRES of meeting PERS-a some partners.
            'I have just met some partners'.

      b.   *Yo los   considero a   ustedes   <u>socios</u>.*
            I   2 PL DIR OBJ consider   PERS-a 2 PL DIR OBJ partners.
            'I consider you partners'.

Finally, thematic information can also be used to account for the notion of modification. In the general cases relevant here, modification can be viewed as a relationship of coordination between the denotation of a nominal (itself a predicate) and the secondary predicate that the adjective introduces. For instance, if something is a long road, it is taken to have the properties of being a road and long. The thematic relationship between the argument and its modifier is defined by Higginbotham as theta identification: the position in the adjective that corresponds to its referential variable is identified with the corresponding position within the nominal (18). In turn, the nominal theta role is bound by a quantifier or verb, so that the adjective piggybacks onto whatever role the nominal performs, be it argumental or predicative (19).

(18)

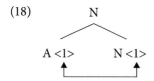

(19) a. *Yo los   considero a   ustedes   socios vitalicios.*
          I   2 PL DIR OBJ consider PERS-a 2 PL DIR OBJ partners life-ADJ.
          'I consider you partners for life'.

      b. *Acabo   de conocer a   unos socios vitalicios.*
          Finish-1 SG PRES of knowing PERS-a some partners life-ADJ.
          'I have just met some partners for life'.

Now, as alluded above, although a great many 'simple' nominals (*man, dog, rose*) have only one theta position, others are in fact more like verbs, in that they open up several argument positions that must be filled. That is the case of deverbal nominals, which often inherit the argumental structure of the verb they are derived from (20).

(20) a. The Romans destroyed the city.
          destroy: ⟨agent, theme⟩

      b. the destruction of the city by the Romans.
          destruction: ⟨agent, theme⟩

This is also true for nouns whose very meanings imply the existence of a whole of which they are a part, i.e., possession (e.g., *hand, mouth, nose, eye, leg,* all of which imply a body). For these nominals, the argument structure must reflect this multiple dependency. On the one hand, their referential role is bound by a determiner; on the other, their relational role is expressed as something possessed by the nominal of which they are a part. Kinship terms also fall in this category (Pustejovsky 1995). Their relational role is assigned to the corresponding kinship counterpart, so that, for instance, the relational role of 'father' is implicitly assigned to 'son/daughter', and so on.

2.4.1.2 *Headship assignment in hierarchical compounds*

Head assignment in Spanish hierarchical compounds depends on theta assignment operations between constituents. In this section three specific patterns, one endocentric and two exocentric, are used to illustrate the phenomenon by considering the formal mechanisms needed to account for each one. The first example is that of endocentric hierarchical compounds of the structure $[N + A]_N$, in which the semantic relationship between head and non-head is one of modification, i.e., theta identification (21).

(21)

	compound	literal gloss	meaning
a.	$[A + N]_N$		
	malasangre	bad-blood	worry
	medianoche	middle-night	midnight
	buenaventura	good-venture	good fortune
b.	$[N + A]_N$		
	avefría	bird-cold	lapwing [bird]
	camposanto	field holy	cemetery
	cajafuerte	box-strong	strongbox

In the examples in (21), the nominal head carries the main denotation, i.e., it retains a theta role that can be bound by an external determiner. The non-head lacks a denotative function: it is theta-identified with the head and acts as its predicate. The order of this predication is what one would expect from Spanish syntax generally (cf. the compounds in 21a, b and the phrases in 22a, b). Presumably, the same set of syntactic principles governs both word orders.

(22)

	phrase	literal gloss	meaning
a.	*mala película*	bad movie	bad movie
	media banana	half banana	half a banana
	buena amiga	good friend	good friend
b.	*sopa fría*	soup cold	cold soup
	niño santo	child saintly	saintly child
	silla fuerte	chair strong	strong chair

Let us turn to the second illustrative pattern, exocentric compounds of the internal merged structure $[V + N]_N$ (23). In this case, the account involves two different types of theta discharge, viz., theta-marking of the kind that obtains between verb and arguments, and theta-binding, of the kind that discharges the theta role of a nominal in a determiner phrase or of the predicate when it is bound by the subject (Higginbotham 1985: 561). First, theta-marking takes place between the verb and the nominal that takes on one of its thematic roles, the two most frequent being theme and locative.

(23) a. *cuidacoches*   *cuidar*   *coches*
       'car keeper', lit. 'keep-cars'   ⟨agent, theme⟩   ⟨1⟩

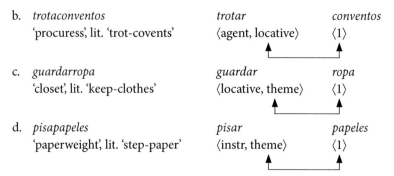

b. *trotaconventos*
   'procuress', lit. 'trot-covents'

c. *guardarropa*
   'closet', lit. 'keep-clothes'

d. *pisapapeles*
   'paperweight', lit. 'step-paper'

The verb + noun complex functions as a predicate, with at least one unassigned thematic role. But since these compounds are nominal, not verbal, there must be more structure than appears from the surface constituents. I propose that they involve a second merge between an empty nominal head and the [V + N] complex (24).[6]

(24)

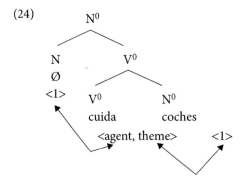

The empty nominal head has a syntactic and a semantic role. Syntactically, it guarantees that this type of noun, like all nominals in Spanish, has the appropriate morphological structure required for referability (cf. Section 2.2.2). In other words, it is governed by a word class marker, which in this case is null (as in *papel* 'paper', and *pared* 'wall'). Semantically, it binds the unassigned thematic role of the verbal predicate. Depending on the roles to be assigned, the nominal may be a human agent (as in *cuidacoches* 'car guard', lit. 'protect-cars'), an instrument (as in *pelapapas* 'potato-peeler', lit. 'peel-potatoes'), or a locative (*posavasos* 'coaster', lit. 'put-glasses'), and so on.

Finally, let us consider one more type of merge compounds involving more than one theta discharge operating simultaneously, namely *bahuvrihi* or possessives (cf. Section 3.4.3). In this case theta discharge proceeds through theta binding and theta identification. The analysis presented here rests on the fact that the nominals involved are parts that can be used to refer to a whole, i.e., the possessor (Booij 1992; Lieber 2004). Thus, they have not just one but two theta roles, one referential, and one

---

6.   This empty category parallels proposals for noun-to-verb conversion, i.e., denominal verbal derivation with no overt suffixation (Hale and Keyser 1992, 1993, 1997).

relational. For example, the noun *mano* 'hand' has a role that is assigned to the denotatum itself, but indirectly, it presupposes the existence of a whole of which it is a part.
In a compound such as *mano larga* 'person who likes to touch others', lit. 'hand long',
the adjective is theta-identified with the referential role of the noun. This referential
role of N, in turn, participates in external theta-binding (25). The relational role of the
nominal is matched word-internally, when it is bound with a word class marker (null,
like in [V + N]$_N$). The existence of this second nominal head allows for the possibility
of using a part to denote the whole. It also accounts for any gender mismatches between the nominal in the compound and the compound itself, since the gender of the
null nominal head is independent of that of the nominal constituent: *un mano larga* 'a
man who likes to touch others', lit. 'a-MASC hand-FEM long-FEM'.

(25)

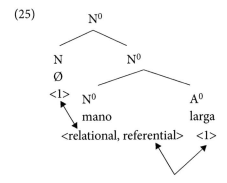

As these illustrative cases show, the notions of thematic information can be used to
account for headship assignment in compounds even in the absence of clear word order rules like those of English. A more exhaustive and nuanced description of how this
works for every compounding pattern will be presented in the relevant descriptive
chapters.

2.4.1.3 *Headedness and hyperonymy*

In several works on compounding, the head is defined as the constituent that can function as the hyperonym of the entire compound (Rainer 1993: 61). For example, in *coche cama* 'sleeper car', lit. 'car bed', the head is *coche* because *coche cama* is a kind of
coche and not a kind of *cama*. This criterion is also found in Brousseau (1989: 287), and
implicitly in Lang (1990). There are problems, however, with the notion of hyperony-
my/hyponymy that militate against it. It can be highly subjective whether a compound
is a hyponym of the constituent that can be shown to be the head based on independent syntactic evidence. An oft-cited example in English is *greenhouse*, which some
speakers may not think of as 'a kind of house' and yet must be responsible for the
nominal lexical class of the whole (Aronoff & Fuderman 2005: 108). Similar examples
could be invoked for Spanish. Thus, for example, the noun *aguardiente* 'brandy', lit.
'water burning' denotes a type of drink, but whether this is considered enough to make
it a hyperonym of water or not will depend very much on the speaker. For some, the

fact that both are liquid and drinkable may be enough semantic justification to consider *aguardiente* a subset of *agua*. Others may balk at including in the semantic category of water a liquid whose most remarkable feature is its high alcoholic content. The
criteria outlined above, which resort to the semantics of theta role assignment, rather
than to lexical semantic notions such as set/subset relations, are much more accurate.
In the case in question, it can be shown that *agua* and not *ardiente* is the head because
after the process of composition, the adjective's theta role has been theta-identified
(through modification), but the nominal theta role is still open for binding. The nominal is thus the head, regardless of the vagaries of lexical meaning.

2.5 Compounding and inflection

One last structural issue to be addressed before moving on to the meaning of compounds is the interaction between inflectional suffixation and compounding. According to accounts that assume the precedence of lexeme formation over inflection, inflectional affixation should normally be attached after compounding (Kiparsky 1982b).
The fact is, however, that plural inflection does appear inside compounds; inflectional
suffixes may even be inserted between constituents, in apparent violation of compound
atomicity.

In Spanish, plural inflection always appears to the right of the word class marker
(cf. Section 2.2.2), so it is attached to compound constituents that are lexemes, not
stems: *atar las manos* 'to tie the hands' > *maniatar* vs. **manisatar, *manosatar*, and *gallipavos* vs. **gallispavos, *gallospavos*. The inflection that pluralizes the entire compound
lexeme can appear on any constituent – the head (26a), the non-head (26b), or both
(26c). It may also appear in all the constituents of concatenative compounds, which all
have head status (26d).

(26)		compound	literal gloss	meaning
	a.	*hombres anuncio*	men poster	poster men
		premios consuelo	prizes consolation	consolation prizes
		fotonovelas	photo-novels	photographic comic strips
		gentilhombres	gentle-men	gentlemen
	b.	*los buscapiés*	the-PL search-feet	the firecrackers
		los lavaplatos	the-PL wash-dishes	the dishwashers
		los sacacorchos	the-PL remove-corks	the corkscrews
	c.	*malas lenguas*	bad- PL tongues	gossipmongers
		ricas dueñas	rich- PL women	noblewomen
		dedos verdes	fingers green- PL	green fingers
		caras rotas	faces broken- PL	cheeky people

d.	*diccionarios-enciclopedias*	dictionaries encyclopedias	dictionaries-encyclopedias
	marxismos-leninismos	Marxism-PL-Leninism-PL	Marxisms-Leninisms
	[relación] alumnos-profesores	[relationship] students teachers	student-teacher [relationship]

The plural marks on the head constituent are sentence-syntactic, in that they have reflexes at the phrasal level: *el hombre anuncio estaba en la esquina* 'the-SG man-SG advertisement-SG was in the corner', *los hombres anuncio estaban en la esquina* 'the-PL man-PL advertisement were in the corner'. The same can be said of the pluralization of both head constituents in a concatenative compound. The situation with the compounds in (26b) is a bit more complex. The plural marks on non-head constituents may be simply due to compound-internal requirements, e.g., a *lavaplatos* 'dishwasher', lit. 'wash-dishes' washes more than one dish (for further discussion, cf. Chapter 7, Section 7.1.1.1). In that case, they have no syntactic repercussions outside of the compound (*el lavaplatos nuevo* 'the-MASC SG dishwasher-MASC SG new-MASC SG' vs. **el lavaplatos nuevos* 'the-MASC SG dishwasher-MASC SG new-MASC PL'). However, in the cases presented in (26b), the denotation is plural; just as other nouns that end in *-s* in the singular, these compounds have no additional overt marking of the plural (cf. *la crisis – las crisis* 'the crisis, the crises', *el lunes – los lunes* 'the Monday, the Mondays').[7]

In lexeme-lexeme compounds, the plural inflection of the compound appears on the head, regardless of its position, in agreement with the principle that it is the locus of inflection (cf. Zwicky 1985) (*hombres anuncio, fotonovelas*). A leftmost non-head can also appear with inflection if it fulfills internal concord requirements between head and non-head, breaking up the compound's integrity (*malas lenguas*). In lexicalized compounds plural inflection may appear only at the end of the entire structure (27a, b), while if the non-head appears to the right and is invariably plural (27c), the plural marker may be reanalyzed as corresponding to the entire compound, and eliminated from the singular form.

(27) a. *malas venturas* > *malaventuras*
          bad-PL fortunes   bad-fortunes
          'misfortunes'
          medias noches   > *medianoches*
          half-PL nights   half-nights
          'midnights'

---

7.   This is distinct from the proposal in Booij (1996), for whom plural inflection is inherent (as is comparative/superlative degree, tense and aspect on verbs), whereas contextual (sentence syntactic) inflection includes categories such as person/number on verbs, required for agreement with subjects and objects, concord markers for adjectives, and structural case for nouns. Note that Booij's distinction can be described in terms of lexical/functional features as [−L, +F] (inherent inflection) and [−L, −F] (contextual inflection).

b. *hombres lobo(s)>*   *hombrelobos*
    man-PL wolf-(PL)   man-wolves
    'werewolves'
    aguas malas   >   *aguamalas*
    waters bad-PL   water-bad-PL
    'jelly fishes'

c. *abrelatas*   >   *abrelata*
    open-cans   open-can
    'can-opener'
    posabrazos   >   *posabrazo*
    rest-arms   rest-arm
    'armrest'

2.6 Meaning of compounds

Some of the semantic properties of compounds have been discussed earlier because
they are naturally related to their structure. To summarize those observations, endocentric hierarchical compounds denote a subcase of the denotation of the head.
Thus, for example, a *ducha teléfono* 'hand shower', lit. 'shower telephone' is a kind of
ducha; *hierbabuena* 'mint', lit. 'herb good' a kind of *hierba*; and the adjective *maleducado* 'ill-bred', lit. 'badly educated' is predicated of someone who is *educado* in a
certain way, *mal*. In neologisms such as those in (28), each of the compounds denotes a subcase of the noun *mujer* 'woman', to which the second nominal acts as a
predicate.

(28) *Hay   mujeres veneno, mujeres imán,/hay   mujeres consuelo,*
      There are women-poison, women-magnet, there are women consolation,
      mujeres puñal   (J. Sabina, 1994)
      women-dagger.
      'There are poison women, magnet women, consolation women, dagger women.'

It is hard to establish exactly the possible relationships between the constituents in
hierarchical compounds, i.e., precisely how the non-head carves out the subset denotation. It may do so by specifying location (e.g., *maestrescuela* 'schoolteacher', lit,
'teacher school'), material (*cañamiel* 'sugarcane', lit. 'cane honey'), or location (e.g., *coche cama* 'sleeper car', lit. 'car bed'), among several possibilities. Attempts have been
made to limit these possible relations (Levi 1978), and some regular gaps have been
found, such as the absence of a goal interpretation (Fabb 1998: 74). For example, a
hypothetical compound *tren ciudad* 'city train', lit. 'train city', could not mean 'train to
the city', but 'train of the city' or 'within the city'. Beyond those restrictions, however,
the actual semantic relationship between constituents is ultimately arbitrary in

lexicalized compounds. Yet, it has been noted that at the point of neologistic creation, the most salient features of the denotatum are normally the ones highlighted by the compound (Dressler 2005).

Endocentric concatenative compounds involve an addition or a disjunction of the meanings of the constituents. Although there may be no formal indication of the actual relationship in the compound, the syntactic context disambiguates possible meanings quite readily (29).

(29)   a.   *Las relaciones actor-director fueron muy turbulentas durante*
            The relations   actor-director were   very turbulent   during
            la filmación.
            the filming.
            'The relationship between the actor and the director was very turbulent during the filming.'

       b.   *El   actor-director   teme al fracaso.*
            The actor-director fears   failure.

The meaning of exocentric patterns can be quite regular, but their interpretation always involves more than the mere compositionality of the overt constituents. For example, in *bahuvrihi* (posessive) patterns the compound constituents and the denotation have a part-whole relationship: *mano larga* 'thief', lit. 'hand long', *cuatro ojos* 'person that wears glasses', lit. 'four eyes' (Section 2.4.1.2). In the case of $[V + N]_N$, the compound satisfies an argument of the verb, normally the agent/instrument.

2.7 Summary of chapter

To recap Chapter 2, the distinction between hierarchical and concatenative compounds is based on whether or not the relation between constituents exhibits internal dependencies. Within hierarchical compounds, one of the constituents is the head, and one is. the non-head, of which there can be two main types, i.e., complements or adjuncts (modifiers). Moreover, the head can precede or follow the non-head, creating another possible distinction among hierarchical compounds. Any compound, regardless of its internal structure, can be used exocentrically. In that case, its category features come not from the internal head(s) but from a higher nominal node. Table 2.1 summarizes and exemplifies the various compounding types present in Spanish.

Table 2.1 Classification and exemplification of Spanish compound types

| | Hierarchical | | Concatenative |
	Head-initial	Head-final	
Endocentric	$[N + N]_N$ ducha teléfono 'hand shower' $[N + A]_N$ hierbabuena 'mint'	$[N + N]_N$ casamuro 'rampart' $[A + N]_N$ gentilhombre 'gentleman' $[N + A]_A$ ojialegre 'happy-eyed' $[Adv + A]_A$ maleducado 'ill-bred' $[N + V]_V$ aliquebrar 'break the wings' $[Adv + V]_V$ maltratar 'ill-treat'	$[N + N]_N$ casatienda 'house-store' $[A + A]_A$ rojiverde 'red-green'
Exocentric	$[V + N]_N$ matarratas 'rat poison' $[N + N]_N$ puntapié 'kick'	$[Adv + V]_V$ bienestar 'wellbeing' $[A + N]_N$ mala lengua 'gossipmonger'	$[A + A]_N$ altibajo 'vicissitude' $[V + V]_N$ vaivén 'oscillation'

The meaning of the compound depends on the meaning of its constituents, on its structure, and on whether it is transparent or lexicalized. For example, hierarchical endocentric compounds denote a class of individuals that are a subset of those denoted by the head constituent. In concatenative endocentric compounds, the meanings of all the constituents contribute equally to the meaning of the whole, in different ways depending on whether or not their referential variables are identified. With time, like any lexeme, a compound can acquire idiosyncratic meanings not attributable to the constituents or their relationship.

CHAPTER 3

Finding compounds

Data sources, collection, and classification

Chapters 1 and 2 outlined the definition of compounding that underpins this entire work, informing data selection and classification for all historical periods. This third chapter presents the historical periods considered, together with a description of the data sources selected for each one. Subsequently, the procedures used to find compounds and ascertain their status are discussed, together with the dating of first attestations and the measurements of relative pattern frequency and productivity. The chapter closes with an explanation of the criteria used to classify compounds.

3.1 Data sources and their limitations

The compilation includes data from the earliest lexicographical sources of Spanish up to the present, providing coverage at regular intervals. It must be noted that although diachronic exhaustiveness is one of the aims of this work, it has not been achieved at the expense of methodological reliability. As will become apparent in the remainder of the chapter, large corpora are needed to ascertain the compound status of certain lexical complexes. At the present state of Spanish lexicography, no information is available for any period prior to 700, and very little before 1100. One can gather an idea of the passage from Latin to Romance compounding through consultation of earlier manuscripts, but for the time being this lacks the rigor sought in this work. It is hoped that with increasing efforts in lexicography and digitalization, those earlier periods will also soon become open to scientific exploration of the type designed here.

For the centuries between 700 and 1399, the study relies on modern historical dictionaries whose corpus is a selection of period texts. After 1400, it includes works by lexicographers from each period separated by no more than 150 years.[1] Because earlier centuries are less well documented, additional data have been obtained through direct consultation of texts. However, no primary sources have been used to supplement the later periods, because the density of compounds in Spanish texts is rather low and an examination of lexicographical sources is more profitable. In what follows, the

---

1.   There are 119 years between Nebrija and Covarrubias, 128 between Covarrubias and Autoridades, 145 between Autoridades and DRAE 12th edition, 114 between DRAE 12th edition and Moliner 2nd edition, and 115 between DRAE 12th edition and Seco et al.

sources are described in some detail, including an assessment of their strengths and weaknesses, and the measures taken to guarantee their reliability.

For the earliest centuries (700–1099), one lexicographical source is available, the *Léxico hispánico primitivo (siglos VIII al XII)*, compiled by the Real Academia Española on the basis of work carried out over fifty years mainly by Menéndez Pidal and Lapesa (henceforth, LHP).[2] Its data must be taken with some caution, since the editors openly admit to its preliminary nature and its limitations (Menéndez Pidal et al. 2003: XVIII et passim). The wordlist is still incomplete because the project started before the discovery and transcription of numerous period documents. Additionally, the publication has not undergone a complete final revision, nor can the data from this source be corroborated in large databases of the kind used for other periods. Still, it is the only available lexicographical source that can link what is known about Latin compounding to later developments in Hispano-Romance.

For the centuries between 1100 and 1399, three dictionaries and five texts have been used. The dictionaries include the *Diccionario medieval español: desde las Glosas emilianenses y silenses (s. X) hasta el siglo XV* (Alonso Pedraz 1986, henceforth A), the second edition of the *Tentative Dictionary of Medieval Spanish* (Kasten & Cody 2001, T), and the *Diccionario de la prosa castellana de Alfonso X el sabio* (Kasten & Nitti 2002, K&N). Five texts were selected from ADMYTE (Micronet 1992, AD) from the fields of science and technology: *Libro de la Caza de las Aves* (LCA), *Libro de la Montería* (LM), *Tratado de Cetrería* (TC), *Libro de los Halcones* (LH), and *Libro de los Animales de Caza* (LAC) (Table 3.1). This choice was motivated by the fact that science and technology fields tend to be lexically innovative. The expectation was that these texts were more likely to have compounds not previously recorded in dictionaries than other fields, such as religion and the law. As can be seen from consulting the Appendix, this expectation was not borne out in the data: barely any of the compounds were found exclusively in the ADMYTE corpus, although several of the ones found in lexicographical sources could be confirmed.

The three dictionaries complement each other. Two of them, A and T, include literary and non-literary sources and cover the entire medieval period. A's stated coverage ranges between the 10th and the 15th centuries, while T includes texts between 1140 and 1489. Of the two, A is less reliable, due to inconsistent spelling, unsophisticated analysis, and choice of editions, as noted in Dworkin (1994). Words found in it have been checked against other sources (Corominas & Pascual 1980-91; Davies

---

2.   In general, when the dictionary or database already have an accepted abbreviation, this one was preferred (CORDE, DRAE, etc.). Otherwise, a short version of the title was created, with several objectives in mind. The first was to keep each abbreviation as short as possible, so that it would fit in the small space available in the Appendix. It was also important to keep each short form as distinct as possible from the others. For example, in the case of the *Léxico hispánico primitivo* the initials LHP were considered ideal. Yet, if abbreviations of the name were too similar to others, the initials of the author were preferred, as in the case of M for Moliner's dictionary.

2002–; Herrera 1996; Müller 1987–; Real Academia Española [2006–2010]). Any un-corroborated entries have been excluded. T is a more updated source, based on the 1946 original edition but expanded in its wordlist by 50%. It still has the possible disadvantage of being based on later editions of medieval texts, transcribed following a number of different criteria. The third medieval dictionary, K&N, is the most exhaustive but also the narrowest in historical and textual scope. It only includes documents from the Alfonsine scriptorium, produced between 1254 and 1284 (K&N, Presentation). K&N was meticulously prepared on the basis of original manuscripts. Additionally, it employs a vast selection of texts (approximately 5 million words) covering all fields of medieval knowledge, making it a good source to document lexical creativity. Finally, the dictionary lists attested spellings, a useful feature because this allows for more accurate digital searches.

For the centuries between 1400 and 1699, four dictionaries have been employed, together with three texts. The lexicographical works include Nebrija's *Vocabulario romance en latín* (Nebrija 1973 [1495?], N), supplemented by O'Neill (1997), which contains a dictionary with definitions in modern Spanish of all Castilian lexemes in Nebrija's entire production.[3] Additionally, the *Tesoro de la lengua castellana o española* (Covarrubias Orozco 2006 [1611], C) and its *Suplemento* edited by Dopico and Lezra (Covarrubias 2001 [1613], CS) have been employed. These were accompanied by three scientific texts from ADMYTE: *Menor Daño de Medicina* (MDM), *Cirugía Rimada* (CR), and *Arte Cisoria* (AC) (cf. Table 3.1). Again, scientific texts were chosen because they seemed more likely to contain neologisms unattested in dictionaries, but this was not borne out after all.

The selection of items for inclusion in the wordlists is based on each lexicographer's often implicit criteria. In the case of Covarrubias at least, the descriptive nature of the dictionary is demonstrated by the inclusion of words marked by the author as 'rustic' or typical of the urban popular classes (Gordon Peral 2003), evidence of a certain degree of social and stylistic variation. Nebrija's work poses an additional challenge, since the Spanish-to-Latin version was heavily influenced by the Latin-to-Spanish glossary that preceded it. It is well attested that one of the most important sources of Spanish headwords in the Spanish-to-Latin *Vocabulario* were the Spanish renderings of Nebrija's earlier Latin-to-Spanish *Diccionario* (Guerrero Ramos 1995: 147). Although this process was in no way mechanical or unreflective, it certainly presents some problems when trying to ascertain the lexical status of complex Spanish headwords in the *Vocabulario*. The crucial issue is whether a given complex Spanish headword is an authentic compound lexeme or simply a descriptive syntactic phrase

---

3. The full list of the works covered in O'Neill (1997) includes: *Introductiones latinae* (1481), *Introductiones latinae contrapuesto el latín al romance* (1488?), *Dictionarium latino-hispanicum* (1492), *Gramática de la lengua castellana* (1492), *Dictionarium hispano-latinum* (1495?), *Repetitio quinta* (1508), *Tabla de la diversidad de los días y horas* (1516–1517), and *Reglas de la orthographia en la lengua castellana* (1517).

included in the Latin dictionary to define a Latin term in the absence of an exact lexical rendering. Any doubtful cases have been corroborated in additional databases, and the have been discarded if not confirmed.

For the centuries between 1700 and 1899, two Academic dictionaries have been included, viz., the *Diccionario de autoridades* (Real Academia Española 1979 [1726–1739], Au) and the 12th edition of the *Diccionario de la lengua castellana por la Real Academia Española* (Real Academia Española 1884, DRAE). Given the stated prescriptive goal of the Academy, a possible drawback is the exclusion of popular, nonstandard language in favor of the language of authoritative sources. However, together with their didactic and prescriptive objective, Academic dictionaries also have a historical and testimonial purpose (Hernando Cuadrado 1997; Ruhstaller 2004: 123). As a consequence, some of their 'authorities' are not literary sources but a variety of nonliterary texts, and they thus provide at least a good approximation to the general lexicon of Spanish (Real Academia Española 1979 [1726–1739]: v et passim).

Finally, the 20th century is represented by the second edition of the *Diccionario de uso del español* (Moliner 1998, M) and the *Diccionario del español actual* (Seco et al. 1999, S), which, as their titles suggest, attempt to describe actual usage. Seco et al'.s work

Table 3.1 Authentic texts used in the study

Title	Author	Approximate date	Subject	Linguistic characteristics
Libro de la Caza de las Aves	Pedro López de Ayala	1385 a quo 1388 ad quem	Falconry	Prose, written in Castilian
Libro de la Montería	Alfonso XI	1342 a quo 1355 ad quem	Hunting	Prose, written in Castilian
Tratado de Cetrería	Gerardus Falconarius	1220–1300	Falconry	Prose, translated from Latin to Castilian
Libro de los Halcones	Guillermus Falconarius	1200–1300	Falconry	Prose, translated from Latin to Castilian
Libro de los Animales de Caza	Muhammed ibn'abd Allah ibn 'Umar al-Bayzar	Copied 1390–1410	Falconry	Prose, translated from Arabic to Castilian
Menor Daño de Medicina	Alfonso Chirino	1419 ad quem	Medicine, medicinal plants, recipes	Prose, written in Castilian
Cirugía Rimada	Diego de Cobos	1419, copied 1493	Medicine	Verse, written in Castilian
Arte Cisoria	Enrique de Aragón (Villena) † 1434	Copied 1400–1500	Food carving and serving	Prose, written in Castilian

achieves this to a greater extent by being based on a corpus from the second half of the 20th century, rather than on previously published dictionaries (Haensch 2004; Seco et al. 1999: xi). Moliner's dictionary is less useful, since it is partly based on previous editions of Academic dictionaries, and thus, even in this second edition, still incorporates a fair number of archaisms (Gutiérrez 2000: 35).

In spite of their heterogeneity and limitations, the dictionaries selected provide a wealth of data on Spanish compounding over the period covered (cf. Table 3.2). The uniform treatment of the data, especially as regards verification and dating of first attestations, to be explained shortly, minimizes some of their drawbacks.

One final note on the reasons for excluding other sources is in order. Historical dialectal glossaries and dictionaries (such as Mackenzie 1984) have been discarded, because they may document some trends that ultimately did not prevail in standard Castilian. For similar reasons, specialized technical dictionaries and glossaries (e.g., Herrera 1996) do not constitute main sources, although they are useful ancillary materials. Other general historical lexicographical works are of limited use because they have been discontinued (Müller 1987–; Real Academia Española 1960–).

The dictionaries chosen reflect Peninsular Spanish more than American varieties, which should not be interpreted as any perceived preeminence of the former over the latter. The geographical restriction of the corpus helps preserve continuity and some degree of homogeneity. Attempting to include a larger sample of Latin American varieties would add the complicating effect of contact with indigenous and other European languages, matters beyond the scope of the present volume. There are also practical considerations, since many varieties of Spanish of the Americas lack the extensive lexicographical documentation needed to investigate compounding exhaustively.

Table 3.2 Number of compounds obtained from each lexicographical source

Source	Number of compounds
Léxico hispánico primitivo [LHP]	26
Diccionario medieval español [A]	207
ADMYTE [AD]	61
Diccionario de la prosa castellana de Alfonso X [K&N]	171
Tentative Dictionary of Medieval Spanish [T]	98
Vocabulario romance en latín [N]	153
O'Neill [ON]	40
Tesoro de la lengua castellana o española [C] and Suplemento [CS]	280
Diccionario de Autoridades [Au]	779
Diccionario de la lengua castellana por la Real Academia Española [DRAE]	1112
Diccionario de uso del español [M]	2236
Diccionario del español actual [S]	2020
Total (excluding repetitions)	3,558

A feasible and highly desirable future project would be the expansion of this study to the varieties that are better represented, for example by consulting Harris and Nitti's (2003) edition of Boyd-Bowman's *Léxico hispanoamericano*, Lara (1996) for Mexican Spanish, and Chuchuy (2000) and the Academia Argentina de Letras (2003) for Argentine Spanish.

3.2 Identification of compounds

To establish that a complex form is a compound in a given period, the first step is to ascertain that its constituents were indeed lexical stems at the time of attestation, according to the theoretically motivated decisions of Chapter 1. Further, it must be established that the combination of constituents is a unit, not simply a frequent but separable collocation. The following sections explain the criteria adopted to guarantee this throughout the study.

3.2.1 Independent status of constituents

To confirm the independent existence of all the lexemes that appear complex, the constituents have been searched in the same lexicographical sources and/or in digital databases (Corpus del Español, CORDE, and CREA), and Corominas & Pascual (1980–91). Only those complex formations that can be confirmed as formed by at least two native stems are included. Given the complex relationship between Romance and Classical sources, especially Latin, borrowings from those sources pose several challenges that require some discussion.

Latin complex lexemes with both learned/semi-learned and native counterparts are included only as variants of the latter, e.g., the native form *biendicho* appears listed as the main entry for variants *bendicho, bendito, bendicto, benedito,* and *benedicto* < Lat. BENEDICTUS 'blessed'. One of the forms is transparent, and the others are assumed to be simple spelling variants in a period of vacillating writing conventions (Blake 1991).

Latin complex forms that have lost internal compositionality are included if they have been reanalyzed through folk etymology, e.g.: *gordolobo* 'mullein [Verbascum L.]' < *godalobo* 'id'. < L.Lat. CŌDA LUPĪ 'id', lit. 'tail of wolf' (Real Academia Española 1992), reanalyzed as *gordo* + *lobo* 'fat wolf'. Even though they are not perfect compounds, in the sense that the semantic relationship between constituents has been obscured, the reanalysis carried out by native speakers confirms the reality of the $[A + N]_N$ compounding pattern.

By contrast, compounded forms are excluded if they have lost internal compositionality through phonetic erosion or because their constituents are not independently attested. This happens frequently with foreign borrowings. For example, *membrillo* 'quince' and its variants *membriello, miembrollo, bembrillo, bembriello* are not considered a compound form, although they are etymologically related via Lat. MELIMĒLUM 'sweet apple' to the Greek compound μελίμηλον 'melimelon' 'id'. contaminated by Lat. MELOMĔLI 'quince paste', both from μέλι 'meli' 'honey' and μῆλον 'melon' 'apple' (Corominas & Pascual 1980–91: vol. 4, 32–33). Another example is *zabalmedina* 'type of magistrate', lit. 'chief of the city', a borrowing from Arabic whose internal structure is a sequence of two nominals normally known as a 'construct state', *çahib almedina* 'chief-the-city', and thus a multimorphemic lexeme. However, neither *çahib* 'chief' nor *medina* 'city' were borrowed independently into Spanish, so that the complex form is opaque. The case of *çauacequia* 'chief of the irrigation ditch' (< Arab. *çahib al saqiya* 'chief-the-irrigation ditch'), presents an intermediate situation, since *acequia* 'irrigation ditch' was indeed borrowed independently. However, the word is not included, since there is no evidence that the first constituent was ever analyzable as a free form in Spanish.

Inherited forms are also discarded if phonetic erosion or lexical loss turned at least one of the constituents opaque, since in that case only part of the complex is discernible. Consider, for example, *benévolo* 'kind', lit. 'well-wanting' < Lat. BENEVŎLUS 'id', a compound of BENE 'well' and VELLE 'to want' (Corominas & Pascual 1980–1991: vol. 1, 563), where *ben* 'well' is transparent, but the verbal stem VELLE was not inherited independently in Spanish. Items are also discarded if they contain Latin stems that have become affixes in Spanish. For example, although Latin verbal stems such as *-ific-* and *-ifer-* are diachronically related to the independent Latin verbs FACERE 'to make, to do' and FERRE 'to carry', Latin compounds containing these stems are excluded because the relationship between forms has been lost in Spanish. For instance, *mundificativo* 'medicine that cleans or purges' derives from *mundificar* from Lat. MUNDIFICĀRE < Lat. MUNDUS 'clean' and FACERE 'make' (cf. *mondo*, Corominas & Pascual 1980–91: vol. 4, 125–26), but most native speakers of Spanish would not have been aware of the fact.

Complex forms are excluded if their constituents have no independent existence in Spanish in the period in question, even if they continue to be actively involved in the coinage of specialized terminology. Normally these words have special phonological and semantic characteristics that flag them as learned, such as complex consonant clusters and/or specialized meanings (*caputpurgio* 'procedure to purge the head' < Lat. CAPUT 'head' + PURGARE 'to purge', Du Cange 1937 [1883–1887]).

Finally, some forms are excluded due to etymological uncertainty about their constituents. For example, *cartapacio* 'writing notebook' is variously claimed to be related to L.Lat. CHARTAPĀCIUM 'letter of peace' (Corominas & Pascual 1980–91: vol. 1, 900, 901; Real Academia Española 1992), to Lat. CHARTOPHYLACIUM from Gr. Χαρτοφυλάκιον 'chartophylákion' 'file' (Corominas & Pascual 1980–91, citing el Brocense), to an augmentative of *cartapel* (Corominas & Pascual 1980–91), and finally, to CARTA with an uncertain derivational or compositional element (Alonso Pedraz 1986: vol. 1, 639). None of these hypotheses is strongly supported, so the term is not included.

3.2.2 Compoundhood

The final wordlist (cf. Appendix) has been checked in order to ascertain the compound status of all its forms. This section presents the morphological, distributional, semantic, syntactic, and orthographic evidence employed in doing so.

3.2.2.1 *Morphological evidence*
Some compounds can be unequivocally identified on morphological grounds, if, for example, one of their two constituents appears as a bound stem. Thus, it is unproblematic to class *avutarda* 'bustard', lit. 'bird-slow', *maniatar* 'tie by the hand', lit. 'hand-tie' and *patitieso* 'flabbergasted', lit. 'foot-stiff' as compounds, since the forms *avu-*, *mani-*, and *pati-*, with final linking vowels, are only possible as combining stems (cf. *av-e*, *man-o*, *pat-a*). The bound status of one constituent can also result from phonetic erosion of its word class marker: e.g., *piedrasufre* 'sulphur', lit. 'stone-sulphur' (cf. *piedra azufre*). As the example in (1) shows, when morphological evidence is robust, variable spelling does not interfere with correct identification of compounds.

(1) *La músico terapia es una técnica terapéutica que utiliza la música en todas sus formas con participación activa o receptiva por parte del paciente. (Congreso Mundial de Musicoterapia, París, 1974).*   (8.21.07, Google)
'Music therapy is a therapeutic technique that uses music in all its forms with the active or receptive participation of the patient. World Conference on Music Therapy'.

3.2.2.2 *Distributional evidence*
Distributional properties can also help to classify some forms as compounds. For example, the presence of [V + N]$_N$ and [P + N]$_N$ constructions in nominal slots is only grammatical if they are interpreted as compounds (2a, b). As with morphological evidence, distributional evidence does not require orthographic consistency to corroborate it (cf. the variants in 3).

(2) a. *Se rellena una buena aceituna con alcaparras y anchoas picadas, y después de haberla echado en adobo de aceite, se introduce en un picafigo o cualquiera otro pajarito.*   (1913, Emilia Pardo Bazán, CORDE)
'You fill a good olive with capers and chopped anchovies, and after marinating it in oil, you place it inside a figpicker or any other little bird'. (lit. 'pick-fig')

    b. *pocos monarcas han tenido más sinsabores en su vida que este gran soberano.*   (1877, Valentín Gómez, CORDE)
'Few monarchs have had more misfortunes in their life than this great sovereign'. (lit. 'more without-tastes').

(3) a. [...] *cuando te atienden no te tratan como un cliente sino como un <u>rompe</u>*
        <u>huevos</u>   (8.21.07, Google)
        '[....] when they serve you they treat you not like a client but like a pain in
        the ass (lit. 'like a break-eggs')

     b. *Somos unos <u>rompehuevos</u>.*   (8.21.07, Google)
        'We are a pain in the ass', lit. 'break-eggs'.

     c. *por la <u>telaraña</u> o araña Arachneus* (Antonio de Nebrija, 1492, Corpus del
        español)
        'for the spiderweb or spider Arachneus' (lit. 'clothspider')

     d. *[...] despues del humor cristalino en la parte de dentro es una <u>tela araña</u> [...]*
                                          (1494, Fray Vicente de Burgos, CORDE).
        'after the chrystaline humor in the inside there is a spider web [...]' (lit.
        'cloth spider')

The possible distribution of phrasal constituents sometimes changes over time. For
example, in Modern Spanish a manner adverb may not appear preposed to a verb in a
VP, so there is no doubt that a [Adv + V]$_V$ complex is a compound. Yet, in earlier
stages of the language the adverb could indeed appear preposed in a verb-final VP, so
that the same combination cannot automatically be taken to be a compound. Consider
the examples in (4).

(4) a. *[...] por que quien <u>mal vivió</u>, muera peor.* (1589, Juan de Pineda, CORDE)
        'so that he who led a bad life, should die a worse death', lit. 'he who badly
        lived, dies worse'.

     b. *[...] el visorey les dijo que parecía <u>mal vivir</u> en casas de los vecinos y comer
        a costa dellos [...]*   (1551, Pedro Cieza de León, Corpus del Español).
        '[...] the viceroy told them that he seemed to barely survive in his neigh-
        bors' houses and eat what they gave him [...]'

     c. *Desde hace cuatro años nuestro invitado <u>malvive</u> con su mujer y sus seis
        hijos en una mísera chabola [...]*
                                (20th Century, Oral Corpus, Corpus del Español)
        'For the last four years our guest has been living miserably with his wife
        and six children in a squalid hut [...]'

     d. *La música, entre nosotros, no vive: <u>malvive</u>.*
                                (20th Century, José Luis Rubio, Corpus del Español)
        'Among us, music does not live: it barely survives'.

In (4a), *mal vivió* 'led a bad life', lit. 'badly lived' is a verb-final phrase with a preposed
adverb, as the parallelism between *mal* 'badly' and the comparative *peor* 'worse' of the
following clause shows. By contrast, in (4c, d) *malvive* 'barely survives', lit. 'badly-lives'
is a compound, since modern Spanish does not allow this word order. This can be
proven syntactically, since in (4c, d) *mal* 'badly' cannot be modified by a degree phrase,

a possibility that would have been open to (4a): cf. *quien muy mal vivió* 'he who led a very dissolute life', lit. 'very badly lived', vs. *la música entre nosotros no vive: *muy malvive* 'among us music does not live; it barely survives', lit. 'very badly-lives'. There is also semantic evidence that *malvivir* has become a single lexical unit. It is now specialized in meaning, since the material but not the moral interpretation of *mal* is possible. Example (4b) also seems to be a compound, although this is harder to prove: in the absence of native speakers from the period, a full array of syntactic tests cannot be performed, and databases are not always forthcoming with the kind of evidence needed. The context suggests a meaning in line with its compound interpretation, i.e., the person referred to barely scrapes a living and has to ask others for free food and lodging, and that will have to suffice as evidence. In so far as possible, the same procedure has been followed in other ambiguous cases, though it must be acknowledged that the evidence to make this decisions is not always forthcoming.

3.2.2.3 *Semantic evidence*

Semantic criteria are based on the fact that the compound normally acquires a stable meaning in the course of its history. First, it is used to name a subset of the more general category denoted by its head, and later, it becomes idiomatically restricted to an even narrower subset of its possible denotata. Consider, for example, the case of *malvivir* above, which denotes a type of the more general verb *vivir*, characterized by 'badness', and is later restricted to living affected by one particular cause for badness, i.e., indigence. Semantic narrowing has been adduced by most traditional Spanish literature as a definitional property of compounding (cf. Alemany Bolufer 1920; Bustos Gisbert 1986: 112–14; Lang 1990) and is indirectly endorsed in this work by the use of lexicographical sources. However, this type of sources can lead us both to under- and overstatement of the number of compounds.

Using lexicographical data can underestimate the number of compounds by favoring lexicalized forms over novel coinages, since only the former are generally recorded. To put this in quantitative perspective, Bauer (2001b: 36) found that only 55% of the compounds in an English text were recorded in the *Oxford English Dictionary*. Even taking into consideration the lower productivity of Spanish compounding, disparities such as these are also likely to be found in this language. However, the conservative approach implicit in the use of dictionaries is not in itself a fatal flaw, since, by using the same type of data collection for all stages of the language, a certain degree of uniformity is achieved.

A more serious problem of considering meaning as the sole criterion is that it may lead to overestimate the number of compounds. The fact that a complex form with specialized meaning has a dictionary entry does not guarantee that it also behaves like a syntactic atom. For example, both *caña azucarera* 'sugar cane', lit. 'cane sugar-ADJ. SUFF'. and *cañahueca* 'reed [Arundo donax L.]', lit. 'cane hollow', with the internal structure [N + A]$_N$, have lexical entries in Seco et al. (1999). However, only the latter is a compound, as the contrasts in (5) show.

(5)   a.   *Para implementar el reemplazo progresivo de los cultivos de <u>caña y remola-</u>*
         <u>cha azucarera</u> *se creará el Fondo Nacional de Reconversión.*
                                                (8.21.07, Google)
         'To implement the progressive replacement of sugar cane and sugar beet
         a National Reconversion Fund will be created'. (lit. 'cane and beet sugar-
         ADJ SUFF')

     b.   *Nombre común o vulgar: Caña común, Guajara, Caña de Castilla, Caña de*
         güín, Caña gigante, Caña guana, Caña guin, Cañabrava de Castilla, <u>Caña-</u>
         <u>*hueca*</u>*, Cañavera (*cañahueca o vera, *caña hueca o común)*
                                                (8.21.07, Google)
         'Common name: [list of names for Arundo donax L.]'

The possibility of coordinating two independent heads *caña* 'cane' and *remolacha* 'beetroot' and of modifying both with the adjective *azucarera* 'sugar-ADJ SUFF' shows that *caña* and *azucarera* are separable and thus, not compounded. By contrast, *caña* 'cane' and *hueca* 'hollow' in *cañahueca* 'reed [Arundo donax L.]', lit. 'cane hollow' cannot be separated or coordinated independently of one another. This is good evidence that the two constituents are compounded. The dictionary provides both complexes with an entry, since each one has a meaning, but this should not blind us to their structural differences.

Given the drawbacks of the semantic criterion, the presence of unitary meaning has been corroborated with syntactic evidence of compoundhood before adding any complex nominal to the final wordlist. However, it is recognized that even if the constituents in a complex appear separated some of the time, this does not necessarily mean that the complex is never a compound. An alternative interpretation is that a single surface structure corresponds to a compound and to a homonymous syntactic phrase. Stringent verification methods were applied, which probably led to a somewhat conservative final wordlist (cf. Section 3.2.24). This has been considered preferable to having a larger database with dubious items.

3.2.2.4 *Syntactic evidence*
The type of problem posed by examples like *caña azucarera* and *cañahueca* in (5) arises in Spanish in a subset of compounds with the same surface structure as regular syntactic phrases. This includes compounds with the structure $[N + A]_N$ and $[A + N]_N$, $[Adv + A]_A$ (e.g., *hierbabuena* 'mint', lit. 'herb good', *gentilhombre* 'gentleman', and *malcriado* 'spoilt', lit. 'badly-raised', respectively), and, in earlier periods of Spanish, also $[Adv + V]_V$ (e.g., *malcriar* 'spoil', lit. 'badly-raise'). In order to tease apart phrases from genuine compounds with the same structure, two criteria were used: structural tests and frequency tests. Each one is considered in turn.

3.2.2.4.1 *Structural tests.* To establish the compoundhood of a complex, three tests were devised, based on the fact that constituents are fixed and inseparable. The first checks for the possibility of inserting material between constituents (6). The second

examines the possibility of constituent deletion under coordination (noun phrase ellipsis), something that can be done with phrases but is impossible with compounds (7). The last test confirms the stability of the complex, by ascertaining the possibility of moving constituents relative to each other (8).[4]

(6)   Inseparability
   a.   **phrase:**
      planta buena   *planta muy buena*
      lit. plant good   plant very good
      'good plant'   'very good plant'

   b.   **compound:**
      hierbabuena   **hierba muy buena*
      lit. herb good   *herb very good
      'mint'

(7)   Deletion under coordination
   a.   **phrase:**
      el hombre alto y el hombre bajo → el hombre alto y el ... bajo
      lit. the man tall and the man short → the man tall and the short
      'the tall man and the short man' → 'the tall man and the short one'

   b.   **compound:**
      el hombre rana y el hombre lobo → *el hombre rana y el ... lobo
      lit. the man frog and the man wolf → the man frog and the wolf
      'the frogman and the werewolf'

(8)   Fixity of constituent order
   a.   **phrase:**
      la caña delgada   *la delgada caña*
      lit. the can thin   the thin cane
      'the thin cane'
      el hombre santo   *el santo hombre*
      lit. the man saintly   the saintly man
      'the saintly man'

   b.   **compound:**
      la cañahueca   **la huecacaña*
      lit. the cane hollow   the hollow cane
      'the reed [Arundo donax L.]'
      el camposanto   **el santocampo*
      lit. the field holy   the holy field
      'the cemetery'

---

4.   There would be no shortage of additional possible tests (cf. Gross 1990a, 1990b; ten Hacken 1994), but the ones selected are quite robust and easy to run on a large number of possible compounds, a valuable feature for a work of this breath.

The tests have been performed with CORDE/CREA, where wildcards make it possible to check abstract syntactic configurations simultaneously. For instance, by simply entering the two constituents separated by an asterisk (e.g., *hierba * buena* 'mint', lit. 'herb good') it is possible to search the entire database for any evidence of separability for the complex (e.g., hypothetical *hierba muy/tan/nada buena* 'lit. herb very/so/not good'). In contemporary data, native speaker intuitions were deemed sufficient as evidence of compoundhood. When these intuitions were not robust, they were checked against contemporary databases, such as Corpus del Español, CREA, and even Google. Although the latter was not designed to be used as a lexicographical database and it cannot provide evidence of certain phenomena, its vastness, spontaneity, and currency are unsurpassed and make it an invaluable ancillary database. For example, throughout the work, it has provided much more vivid illustrations of lexeme usage than anything that could have been imagined by this author. Google's main limitation is historical: it can only be used for (very recent) contemporary data. Other drawbacks are the fleetingness of the material posted and the difficulty in ascertaining its origin.

Forms that fail any of those tests have not been included in the database. For example, *pescado salado* 'salted fish', lit. 'fish salted', is not included because it appears with insertions: *pescado chico salado* 'small salted fish', lit. 'fish small salted'. The form *cal viva* 'quicklime', lit. 'live lime', is discarded because of the possibility of head deletion in *cal viva y amatada* 'quicklime and slaked lime', lit. 'lime live and deadened'. Finally, cases such as *aves mayores* 'large birds', lit. 'birds large' are discarded because they can appear as *mayores aves* 'large birds'.

3.2.2.4.2 *Frequency tests.* Since the study is designed to identify established compounds, evidence of structural integrity cannot come from one example alone. Inseparable multi-word items with phrasal structure are only included if they pass certain minimum frequency thresholds, measured relative to the total number of words contained in the digital corpora.[5] Table 3.3 presents the frequency that a compound has to meet in order to be counted. These frequency requirements have been adjusted to reflect the fact that the CORDE/CREA database is larger for the later periods than for the earlier ones. If a form is recorded in more than one period, its frequency requirement is that of its latest period of attestation.

---

5.   Although it has been recognized that *hapaxes*, i.e., words that appear only once, can be used to measure productivity (Baayen & Lieber 1991), in the particular case of compounds the risk of corrupting the database with the inclusion of non-compounds is too great. *Hapaxes* with phrasal structure have not been included, even if their semantics and orthography suggest compoundhood, because there is no possibility of carrying out the syntactic verification tests.

Table 3.3 Minimum frequency requirements relative to size of historical corpora

Years	CORDE/CREA[6]	Minimum frequency
700–1099	NA	3
1100–1199	16 mi.	5
1200–1299	16 mi.	5
1300–1399	16 mi.	5
1400–1499	16 mi.	5
1500–1599	40 mi.	10
1600–1699	40 mi.	10
1700–1799	60 mi.	15
1800–1899	60 mi.	15
1900+	190 mi.	40

Evidence against compound status is taken as a gradient measure, given that a complex form may show repeated evidence of inseparability and fixity and yet exhibit a few instances incompatible with compound status. This is the case, for example, of *agua rosada* 'rose water', lit. 'water rose-ADJ SUFF', which has almost 600 inseparable tokens vs. 37 examples of non-compounded use in CORDE. In those cases, the decision is based on the percentage of occurrences incompatible with compound status with respect to the total number. If this figure exceeds 10%, the form is discarded. This does not mean that we are certain it is not a compound, but that we cannot be certain it is.

3.2.3   Prosody and orthography

A useful criterion to distinguish compounds from syntactic phrases, particularly in synchronic studies, is stress. For example, in English, whose stress patterns have been studied in great detail, compounds have been shown to share prosodic properties with words: they exhibit only one main stress and lower the degree of stress in other syllables: *bláckbìrd* vs. *bláck bírd* (Bloomfield 1933: 89–90; Chomsky & Halle 1968). Yet, this phenomenon, which has come to be known as the compound stress rule, has been shown to have exceptions. For instance, compounds whose internal structure is non-hierarchical fail to exhibit de-stressing: *wríter-diréctor*. Additionally, even in compounds with a head and a non-head constituent, the stress rule does not always apply,

---

6.   Data from www.rae.es (CORDE/CREA) figures are approximate because the Real Academia does not break them down by century. The total number of words for CORDE is estimated at 300 million, broken down into three periods: 21% for the Middle Ages (1100–1492), 28% for the Golden Age (1493–1713), and 51% for the Contemporary period (1714–1974). CREA has 150 million words and includes exclusively the last twenty-five years, which at the time of writing covered the period between 1975 and 2000, later expanded to 2004. Figures are calculated assuming the percentage of words within a given period is spread equally among all centuries.

to the point that some authors today question the very existence of a compound stress rule (Plag et al. 2008, Giegerich 2009). In spite of these problems, in cases where a sequence of lexemes could be interpreted as a phrase or a compound, stress still offers a useful first approximation to distinguish between them in English. The question now is whether stress processes have any usefulness for the study of Spanish compounding history. The first issue to consider is to what extent compounds in Spanish behave like those of English in terms of word prosody. The second issue is how the prosodic criteria can be applied to historical written data (for a discussion of these problems in English, cf. Nevalainen 1999: 407–08). Let us consider each one of these issues in turn.

There are very few studies of Spanish compound stress, and those available are not based on experimental data. However, the limited information we have suggests that at least some Spanish compounding patterns do present distinctive stress properties. In some respects, these stress properties resemble those of their English counterparts. One similarity is that many Spanish compounds undergo de-stressing: *cámpo* 'field' + *sánto* 'holy' > *camposánto* 'cemetery'. Another similarity is that this de-stressing is not categorical for all compounds. For example, some never undergo destressing (e.g., *hómbre lóbo* 'werewolf', lit. 'manwolf'), while others may exhibit variable stress properties (e.g., *guárdia civíl* vs. *guardia civíl* 'policeman', lit. 'guard civilian') (Hualde 2006/2007: 70).

There are also differences between Spanish and English compounds in terms of their stress properties. One difference is that in Spanish de-stressing is manifested as stress loss rather than the mere lowering of stress prominence. As a result, the stress pattern of a compound such as *lavaplátos* 'dishwasher', lit. 'wash-dishes', is much the same as that of a derived word such as *lavadóra* 'washer' (Hualde 2006/2007: 67). Another important difference is that in Spanish it is the first constituent that undergoes de-stressing, not the last: *cára* 'face' *dúra* 'hard' > *caradúra* 'cheeky person'; *hiérba* 'herb' + *buéna* 'good' > *hierbabuéna* 'mint' (cf. Eng. *réd* + *heád* > *rédheàd*).

Once we have established the stress properties of Spanish compounds, and in particular their stress loss, the second issue to consider is how these properties can be retrieved reliably from written data. An obvious manifestation of loss of stress in one of the compound constituents is unitary spelling, a criterion alluded to, directly or indirectly, by many accounts of compounding. However, it must be remembered that the orthographic criterion is far from infallible and cannot be relied on exclusively.

The first problem with the orthographic criterion is that not all compounds are spelled as one word. As we have repeatedly seen in previous sections, compound status is not reflected consistently through orthography, even in cases in which there is sufficient independent linguistic evidence to ascertain it. This may reflect the lack of uniformity of single stress that was noted above, or it may show writers' reluctance to innovate in writing, long after changes have already consolidated in speech. For whatever reason, alternations and inconsistencies are frequent. Consider, for example, forms such as *gallocresta* and *gallo cresta* 'wild clary', lit. 'rooster comb', which are found 22 and ten times in CORDE, respectively. In some restricted historical periods, hyphenated spelling has been another way to represent the tension between the perceived status of compounds, halfway between words and phrases (e.g., *calienta-platos* 'plate warmer', lit. 'heat-plates').

The second problem with spelling is that not everything that is spelled as one word is a compound. As a consequence, if the orthographic criterion is applied unreflexively to poorly documented periods, compound status can be mistakenly attributed to non-compounds. Consider the case of *botalyma* 'blunt file', which is included as a headword in Alonso Pedraz (1986), and which, by the orthographic criterion, should be added to the list of compounds. Careful examination shows that this [A + N] complex appears only once in Corpus del Español, whereas CORDE has the variant *bota lima*, in a different edition of the same text.[7] These are simply spelling variants, attributable to orthographic vacillation on the part of the scribe or the transcriber; there is no reason to consider *botalyma* anything but an alternate spelling for the syntactic noun phrase *bota lima*.

With the provisos mentioned above, spelling can be an important clue to the univerbation of a two-constituent complex. It is an especially helpful secondary criterion to decide on the status of complex forms whose internal structure is compatible both with compound and phrasal structure. For example, if a clear progression from two-word to one-word spelling is documented, this adds weight to claims that the complex form has become compounded. For example, the adjective *mal acostumbrado* 'spoilt', lit. 'badly-accustomed' can be found in constructions compatible with a phrasal or a lexical analysis (e.g., *lo han acostumbrado mal* 'they have spoiled him', vs. *lo han mal acostumbrado* 'id.', *está peor acostumbrado* 'he is more spoiled', vs. *está más mal acostumbrado* 'id.'). In spite of this ambiguity, the increased use of the spelling *malacostumbrado* over time helps categorize the form as a compound. By contrast, the absence of unitary spellings can certainly weaken claims that a given combination of words is a compound. Spelling is therefore one of the criteria considered in the discussion of each compound pattern.

3.3 Historical periodization

3.3.1 Periods

Rather than follow artificial divisions based on cultural or historical milestones with little linguistic significance, the data are classified in periods drawn at regular intervals of a century (from 1000 to 1099, and so on) (cf. Wright 1999). Yet, given that compounding is not as frequent as other morphological phenomena such as inflectional or

---

7.   Both variants appear in versions of the *Cancionero de Baena*; *botalyma* is from the Electronic Texts and Concordances of the Madison Corpus of Early Spanish Manuscripts and Printings (O'Neill 1999) and *bota lima* comes from the Dutton and González Cuenca (1993) edition.

derivational affixation, sometimes centuries must be grouped together for analysis, since scarcity of data makes it difficult to distinguish stages without shrinking the pool to the point of distortion. This is especially true of the earliest periods, prior to 1200, which are normally treated together.

3.3.2   Dating of compounds

Compounds have been assigned a historical range starting with their earliest first attestation and ending with their latest attestation. Three different sources have been consulted for this: (a) the dictionaries and texts used in data collection; (2) the CORDE/CREA digital databases; (3) the digital *Tesoro Lexicográfico de la Lengua Española* (Real Academia Española 2001-). These sources exhibit different degrees of inter-reliability, depending on the specific compound being dated, which underscores the importance of using several. Some sources are known to be problematic, such as Alonso Pedraz's (1986) dictionary, so data that only appear documented there have been discarded outright.

As a general rule and as one would expect, the CORDE/CREA corpus has the advantage of being both the most reliable and normally the earliest to attest forms, since it reflects actual written usage rather than lexicographical record. For example, *altisonancia* 'high-sound', lit. 'high-sounding', appears much earlier in CORDE [1737–1789] than in dictionaries [1925]. By contrast, *altiplanicie* 'high plain', lit. 'high-plain' appears both in CORDE and in the Academic dictionaries within a few years ([1880–1882] vs. [1914]). In a minority of cases, CORDE lags behind the dictionaries, as in the case of *altarreina* 'yarrow [Achillea ageratum L.]', lit. 'high-queen' ([1962] vs. [1884]).

While the first attestation is the earliest one found in any reliable source, the latest attestation is selected exclusively from those in authentic corpora (CORDE/CREA or Seco et al. 1999). Attestations in Academic dictionaries or in Moliner (1998), unsupported by other sources, have not been considered, unless they are the only ones available, given the tendency of those dictionaries to retain lexemes that have become obsolete. Data found exclusively in Academic dictionaries have been deemed to be less trustworthy than those attested in multiple independent sources, so if their relative weight is high for a given compound pattern, this has been noted in the sections on that particular pattern's productivity. In general, the dates of attestation for doubtful cases have been adjusted with Corominas & Pascual (1980–91) if possible.[8]

The continued use of a compound over time has been checked by consulting dictionaries and CORDE/CREA. Compounds that appear in two non-consecutive periods have been taken to exist in all intervening periods, even if not actually documented. It has been assumed that the form exists continuously and fails to leave traces in writing, rather than being coined independently on two separate occasions. Forms

---

8.   Checking in CORDE is only possible for compounds recorded on or after 1100. In other words, compounds collected from the *Léxico hispánico primitivo* cannot be confirmed against any other source and their dating has to be taken at face value.

marked as antiquated or obsolete in a given source are only included if they are corroborated in earlier sources, either lexicographical or digital. Compounds not recorded after a certain point are assumed to have fallen out of use.

Let us illustrate how the historical range of a compound was established with one
concrete example. The first record of *benefacere* 'protect', lit. 'well-do' (vars. *benefacer,
bien fer, bienfacer, bienhacer*) as an inseparable form appears in a document dated between 1085 and 1109 in the *Léxico hispánico primitivo* (9c). In earlier attestations presented in the same source, the constituents are not compounded, since they are still
separable or can be targeted for syntactic operations independently (cf. comparative
modification in (9a) and separation of constituents in (9b)). The form is therefore included as a compound starting in the 1000–1099 century. At the other end of the time
range, the latest attestations (now in the variant *bienhacer*) are no longer verbs but
have been recategorized as nominals, i.e., they are exocentric. The latest of them appears in 1932, so that the total time span for the compound in both endocentric and
exocentric uses starts in the 1000s and ends in the 1900s.

(9)   a.   *[...] et post mortem meam vadas inter filios et neptos de fratribus meis domno Monnio et domno Gutetier [...] vel qui tibi melior fecerit.*   (1062, LHP)
'[...] and that after my death you should go with the children and grand-
children of my brothers to master Monnio and master Gutetier [...] who-
ever offers you the best protection'.

b.   *Et si isti bene tibi non fecerint, vadas sub sancto Facundo.*   (1077, LHP)
'and if these do not support you, seek the protection of San Facundo [pos-
sibly, the monastery of Sahagún]'

c.   *et teneat illo Petro Michaelleç meo filio et sedeat cum illo homine de Sancta
Iuliana a bien fer cum honore et prestamo et caballo.*   (1085–1109, LHP)
'and I order that my son Petro Michaelleç should have it and should remain in good terms with the man of Santa Juliana with honor, and land,
and horse'.

d.   *El "qué" va, así, íntimamente vinculado y orientado al bienhacer [...]*
(1932–1944, Xavier Zubiri, CORDE)
'The "what" is, therefore intimately linked and oriented towards good-
ness'

The issue of whether the written record of compounding patterns can be taken to be a
reliable reflection of their use in speech is complex. First written attestations should of
course not be taken to be contemporary with first oral attestations, so that century-by-
century measures of frequency only make sense if one takes into consideration this
oral-to-written time lag. In a sense, this is nothing but a manifestation of the pitfalls of
historical research in general. In the case of compounds the issue is aggravated because
these lexemes are not frequent in the language to begin with, so gaps can make the
overall picture grainier than for other structures. Perhaps more importantly, stylistic

restrictions may have affected different compound patterns unevenly, favoring those that appear in the more formal registers typical of the types of historical texts available. More informal compounds closer to the vernacular are less likely to be well documented, which can potentially skew the whole picture of compounding for earlier periods. Not much can be done about these issues, other than to be mindful of them and to comment on them at the appropriate places.

3.4 Productivity

3.4.1 Measuring productivity

Modern treatises often comment on the productivity (or lack thereof) of compounding in Romance vis-à-vis other language families. They also assess the relative productivity of one compound pattern of Spanish with respect to others (Rainer 1993: 245; Sánchez Méndez 2009). However, there has been no systematic study of compound productivity in Spanish, so that even if these impressionistic assessments seem essentially correct, the methods used to arrive at them are not explicit, let alone measurable. In most cases, references to productivity are based on the frequency with which certain patterns recur in the data. Yet, frequency of use is not the same as productivity (for extensive discussion, cf. Bauer 2001b: 48 et passim).

To my knowledge, this is the first study to actually measure the productivity of Spanish compounding patterns through the application of an explicit quantitative methodology. It does so by measuring the absolute and relative increase in the use of a given pattern over time as well as the ratio of new compounds to old compounds for every period. I explain each measurement in turn.

Compound patterns can be quantified by considering the absolute number of compounds that are formed with a given pattern in each period, i.e., *overall frequency*. Thus, in a general sense, a compounding pattern can be said to increase in frequency if in Period 2 it is represented by more new compounds than in an earlier Period 1. By the same token, it is less frequent if these numbers decrease over time. For example, if a given pattern has ten compounds in Period 1 and 15 in Period 2, it has undergone a 50% increase (+50%). By contrast, if it has eight compounds in Period 2, then it has undergone a loss of 20% (–20%). This measure is very approximate, however, since gains and losses can be due simply to the fact that the later period is better or less well documented. This problem can be corrected by taking into consideration the size of the lexicographical sources for each period, but such a correction is difficult to establish: it is often hard to find out the exact number of headwords for a dictionary, a figure that has been described as the best kept secret in lexicography (Gutiérrez 2000: 32). Additionally, the low overall density of compounding in Spanish makes measures of frequency relative to the total number of words insignificantly low for all patterns, so that comparisons become unintuitive.

The second measure attempts to provide a corrective for the insufficiencies mentioned above. Instead of presenting the number of compounds as an absolute figure or as a ratio over total number of words, it measures the *relative frequency* of a pattern, i.e., its frequency in a given period against the total number of compounds for the period. Thus, a comparison between a pattern in Period 1 and 2 can be established as the difference in its frequency relative to all compounds in each of the two periods. This keeps the comparison 'fair' by adjusting totals to the number of compounds in each period as a common baseline. Thus, for example, if in Period 1 there are 100 recorded compounds and 30 of them are created with a certain pattern, then it constitutes 30% of the total for Period 1. If in Period 2 there are 200 compounds and 50 of them use the same pattern, this represents 25% of the total, a drop of 5%. Note that this is in spite of the fact that there were 20 more compounds with the pattern in Period 2 than in Period 1.

Studies that compare relative frequencies of synonymous suffixes (e.g., *-ity* and *-ment*) are often based on the assumption that these are gaining or losing ground with respect to each other (Anshen & Aronoff 1999). This does not hold for comparisons among compound types, since the various patterns belong to different grammatical categories and no competition between them is possible. Moreover, when it occurs, competition for lexical space is not limited to other compounding patterns but also with affixation, phrasal locutions, and a variety of other word formation mechanisms. In the calculations presented here, the total number of compounds should be taken simply as a substitute for the total number of words in general.

The last measure is meant to assess the *productivity* or neologistic activity of a given pattern. Rather than simply comparing frequencies or percentages in two periods, it establishes a difference between old and new compounds for a single pattern. To do this, compounds of a given pattern in Period 2 are contrasted against those of the same pattern in Period 1. Those that appear in both periods are 'old compounds' in Period 2, i.e., they are carried over. This figure is then compared against the number of compounds not attested in Period 1, which are considered 'new compounds' in Period 2. The ratio between new and old compounds gives a measure of the vitality of the pattern, i.e., its capacity to be activated to coin novel forms. By contrast, there may be compounds that are not carried over, i.e., that are present in Period 1 but not in Period 2. The ratio between lost and old compounds establishes a measure of the pattern's obsolescence, i.e., its loss of vitality. It is expected that loss of tokens of a given pattern eventually results in lack of models for further compounding, as it erodes the input necessary to extend it.

Pattern productivity can be established as a net gain or loss, i.e., the difference between the rates at which new compounds are created and old compounds are lost. Suppose, for example, that a given pattern has 100 compounds in Period 1, out of which 90 are carried over to Period 2. Suppose also that the pattern is found in 20 new forms in Period 2, absent from Period 1. Thus, its overall productivity index is calculated as 20/100 (net gain of 0.2) minus 10/100 (net loss of 0.1), for a positive value of

0.1 (10%). If a pattern exhibits no gains or losses, its 'maintenance' value is 0, i.e., it is surviving mostly on the strength of its past productivity. If a pattern exhibits a value of −0.5 (-50%), this indicates that whatever new forms have been created are not enough to make up for the loss of old compounds, so that the vitality of the pattern is weakening overall. A value of 0 may also mean that the pattern has lost and gained tokens at comparable rates, i.e., that its productivity is negatively affected by the transience of its coinages. However, since the measure is a composite that distinguishes gains from losses, these subtleties can also be reflected and discussed whenever appropriate.

3.4.2   Limitations to productivity

It has been pointed out in works on derivational productivity that the set of possible bases to which an affix can attach may act as a bottleneck for its expansion: e.g., *step-*, which can only apply to family relations such as *stepmother*, *stepbrother*, and so on (Bauer 2001b: 48). Therefore, it is not 'fair' to compare a suffix that is limited by its meaning or form to a certain subset of bases with another one with no such limitations.

In the case of compounds, in principle this should not be an issue because compounding does not seem to impose any kind of requirement on constituents other than membership in a certain grammatical category. Thus, for example, although it is true that $[N + N]_N$ compounds are more productive with certain first constituents than with others, this seems more an accident of history than a linguistically driven limitation (cf. for example, the compounds in (10), where the * indicates that they were unattested in Google on 28.8.07).

(10)		compound	literal translation	meaning
	a.	*hombre anuncio*	man poster	sandwich man
		hombre araña	man spider	spiderman
		hombre lobo	man wolf	werewolf
		hombre masa	man mass	massified man
	b.	*mujer anuncio*	woman poster	sandwich woman
		mujer araña	woman spider	spider woman
		mujer lobo	woman wolf	wolfwoman
		mujer masa	woman mass	massified woman
	c.	**computadora anuncio*	computer poster	poster computer
		*computadora araña	computer spider	spider computer
		*computadora lobo	computer wolf	wolf computer
		*computadora masa	computer mass	mass computer

However, there are some restrictions that are part and parcel of certain compound patterns. Thus, for example, $[V + N]_N$ compounds disallow stative and unergative verbs. This fact is not just an accidental or cultural gap, but a restriction of the pattern itself:

to be able to fit the pattern, the verb must be capable of discharging an agent/instrument and a theme/location, minimally (11) (cf. Chapter 7, Section 7.1.1).

(11)		compound	literal gloss	meaning
	a.	*portaaviones*	carry-airplanes	airplane carrier
		cazafantasmas	hunt-ghosts	ghostbuster
		chupacirios	suck-candles	pious person
		matarratas	kill-rats	rat poison
	b.	*tienehambre	have-hunger	hungry person
		*poseegafas	possess-glasses	wearer of glasses
		*parecemuerto	seem-dead	seemingly dead person
		*muerepronto	die-fast	fast dying person

Other cases seem to be somewhere between intrinsic linguistic and extrinsic cultural limitations. That is the case of [N + A]$_A$ compounds (12). These compounds should in principle be possible with any plausible noun-adjective combination, but are in fact restricted to nouns of inalienable possession, which limits them to parts of the body of animates (12a). Even then, some quite salient parts of the body are inexplicably absent (12b), pointing to formal (phonological?) as well as semantic restrictions. It would be conceivable to expand this pattern to other fields, such as internal organs of humans or animates, and even to plant or object description, but this has only happened occasionally (García Lozano 1993; Zacarías Ponce de León 2009) (12c).

(12)		compound	literal gloss	meaning
	a.	*astifino*	horn-thin	of thin horns [cattle]
		pechihundido	chest-sunken	with a sunken chest
		cejijunto	eyebrow-together	with knitted eyebrows
		boquiflojo	mouth-soft	of soft-mouth [horse]
	b.	*naricifino	nose-thin	of thin nose
		*corazoniduro	heart-hard	of hard heart
		*codidelicado	elbow-delicate	of delicate elbows
		*tripiflojo	gut-soft	of soft guts
	c.	*techihundido	roof-sunken	of sunken roof [house]
		*callilimpio	street-clean	of clean streets [city]
		*verduribarato	vegetable-cheap	of cheap vegetables [market]
		*quesisalado	cheese-salty	of salty cheese [dish]

All of the above points to a complex constellation of factors affecting productivity, even in cases in which no specific set of bases is predetermined. Any such relevant factors will be discussed at the appropriate points in the descriptive chapters.

3.4.3 Productivity vs. institutionalization

Since it is based on lexicographically recorded compounds, this study favors institutionalized compounds over more creative word formation 'on the fly'. Compounds become institutionalized not necessarily because they are created by application of frequent word formation processes, but because of the cultural relevance of the item they name. On occasion, highly infrequent patterns may become institutionalized because they refer to a novelty that lacks a term to denote it. To illustrate, consider the case of the Spanish noun *colaless* 'thin thong', lit. 'butt-naked', formed by analogy with the English *topless*, reinterpreted as being a nominal with the meaning 'naked breast' and the internal structure 'breast-naked'.[9] Although the word has popularized in some dialects (it is the most generalized term for 'thong' in Río de la Plata Spanish), derivation by attaching *less* with the meaning of 'naked' is not productive in any variety.

If estimations of productivity are based on lexicographically attested forms, instead of hapaxes that do not make it to the dictionaries, the results may favor patterns that are not necessarily the most productive. That criticism can be countered by arguing that terminological creativity is likely to be randomly distributed among all lexeme formation patterns, rather than concentrated on infrequent ones. This is not to deny that a higher concentration of certain types of compounds is more likely in certain semantic fields and/or registers than in others. Any such specializations are dealt with in the relevant sections of Chapters 4 through 8.

3.4.4 The representativeness of dictionary data

In the remainder of this work, comparisons between the productivity of a compound pattern in different periods and between different patterns in the same period are measured as a function of the frequency with which these patterns are attested in dictionaries. But how valid are *attested* compounds to draw conclusions about a process that is unbounded by definition (Chapter 1, Section 1.4.5)? At issue is the notion of creativity from a formal perspective, technically called 'recursiveness'. Once this notion is

---

9.   It is understandable that the lexical category of *colaless* (and *topless*) in Spanish should be a matter of some puzzlement, since the English model for these words is an adjective. However, consider the following authentic examples that serve to clarify the matter.

a.   *En algunos países de Sudamérica la prenda se denomina* **colaless** *y en inglés se denomina* thong *(cuando la parte de atrás va de uno a dos centímetros) o* g-string *(si es una simple cuerda).*
'In some countries of South America the garment is called colaless and in English it is called a thong (when the backside is no wider than an inch) or g-sting (if it is merely a string)'.   (10.13.09, Google, Wikipedia)

b.   *Video: Christian y Ahahi opinan sobre* **el topless** *de Belinda.*
Video: Christian and Ahahi give their opinion about Belinda's topless.
(10.13.09, Google)

invoked, it must be assumed 'all the way', making it unclear how to compare the various outputs of a recursive system.

The issue is thus whether establishing compound frequencies through dictionary data is a valid option. As was shown in the introduction, more compounds could indeed be culled by consulting texts directly, providing a closer picture of 'real' frequencies. Unfortunately, the low density of compound attestations in Spanish corpora makes these more exhaustive searches unrealistic. Moreover, with all their limitations, dictionaries never fail to record compounds that appear frequently in the corpora. In any case, finding more compounds in a written corpus, no matter how big, still would not be an accurate reflection of the staggering size of the oral production they are meant to reflect, let alone the mental capacities that underlie this production. For the purposes of this work, then, we will content ourselves with the fact that all compound types have been collected following a uniform methodology. No compound pattern is more or less likely to be represented lexicographically, so that any gaps between dictionaries and other possible types of data sources will be assumed to have little or no effect on cross-pattern and cross-period comparisons.

3.4.5   Academic folk etymologies

The use of old dictionaries affords us an unexpected bonus to study compound patterns, namely, the etymologies provided by lexicographers as they attempt to account for items that appear to be polymorphemic but are no longer transparent. When lexicographers invoke patterns as the basis for these lexemes, they provide evidence of the patterns available in their grammar and, indirectly, in that of their contemporaries. This is true even when their justifications are completely or partially erroneous.

For example, several etymologists, including Covarrubias, have suggested that *calabozo* 'dungeon', comes from a putative Arabic noun *cala* (or *qál⁽ᵉ⁾a*) 'fort, castle' and *pozo* 'well', "as if one said *fuerte pozo* 'fort well'" (Covarrubias 1611: 396–97). Other authors have tried to explain the same lexeme by applying other compounding patterns. For example, João Ribeiro (cited in Corominas & Pascual 1980: vol. 1, 396–97) proposes it is a Portuguese compound of *calar* 'to shut up' and *boço* var. of *boca* 'mouth', because "the dungeon is the punishment for people who talk too much". Both of these suggestions are discarded by Corominas and Pascual, who themselves propose a third hypothesis, also based on the idea that *calabozo* is etymologically related to a compound. This time, it is traced back to a reconstructed vulgar Latin form CALAFŎDIUM, a compound of pre-Romance *cala* 'haven, cove', and Latin FŎDĔRE 'dig'. In spite of the tentative nature of these explanations, they have in common that their proponents motivate the lexeme in some compounding pattern of Spanish or early Romance. Thus, Covarrubias' proposal is evidence for the reality of head-final $[N + N]_N$ compounds. Ribeiro's proposal is based loosely on the $[V + N]_N$ pattern, while Corominas and Pascual's assumes a $[N + N]_N$ pattern, with a deverbal nominal head as second constituent.

A similar situation arises with a second opaque example, *mariposa* 'butterfly', for which Covarrubias and Corominas and Pascual propose a compounded etymon. In this case, their two proposals are closer, in that both assume that the second constituent is a form of the verb *posar* 'to perch'. However, they differ in what they take the first constituent to be. Covarrubias proposes that the first constituent is the adverb *mal* 'badly', since *mariposa* is "almost *maliposa*" (lit. 'badly-perch'), justifying it semantically because the insect *se asienta mal en la luz de la candela donde se quema* "makes the mistake of coming to sit on the flame of a candle" (Covarrubias 1611: 1247). For their part, Corominas and Pascual propose that the first constituent is the name *María* 'Mary' (Corominas & Pascual 1980–91: vol. 3, 894). In other words, in both cases the polysyllabic lexeme is attributed the structure of a head-final verb phrase, in one case with an adverbial non-head $[[\text{Adv} + \text{V}]_V]_N$, and in the other with a nominal non-head $[[\text{N} + \text{V}]_V]_N$.

Finally, the etymological explanations proposed may be based on patterns that include constituents of the same lexical categories, but differ in the type of relationship suggested between these constituents. For example, to explain the relationship between the form and meaning of *mojigato* 'prudish, prim', several etymologists suggest an $[\text{N} + \text{N}]_N$ pattern, but differ in the nouns they propose and in the type of relationship that holds between them. Covarrubias suggests (and *Autoridades* echoes) that the origin of the lexeme must be a compound of the structure $[\text{N} + \text{N}]_N$, with two nominal bases, *mus* 'mouse' and *gato* 'cat', presumably linked through the vowel -*i*-, because "it was said by allusion to the cat, when it lies in wait for the mouse". This etymology is discarded by Corominas and Pascual, who replace it by another based on a different type of $[\text{N} + \text{N}]_N$ compounding pattern. They propose that the two constituents are in fact synonymous and hierarchically identical: a hypothesized *mojo* 'kitty' and *gato* 'cat'; the first constituent is a hypochoristic with parallels attested in other Romance languages such as Mallorcan *moix* 'kitty' (cf. discussion in Corominas & Pascual 980–91: vol. 4, 117). In this last case, then, Covarrubias' mistaken etymology is based partly on one of the constituents possibly present in the original compound. His interpretive contribution, though erroneous, corroborates that one of the active compound formation patterns in his grammar is a head-final $[\text{N} + \text{N}]_N$ pattern, while Corominas and Pascual's suggestion is based on a concatenative $[\text{N} + \text{N}]_N$ compound pattern.

Examples like these are frequent. Given that these folk etymologies can add evidence of the reality of a certain pattern of compounding they are sometimes included in the descriptions of individual compounding patterns.

3.5 Classification of compounds

3.5.1 Lexical category

To carry out the analysis, compounds have been classified according to their own lexical category as well as the lexical categories of their constituents. As stated in Chapter 1,

Table 3.4 Examples of compounds by lexical category of compound and constituents

	Example patterns	Example compounds
Nominal	$[N + N]_N$	*aguapié* 'bad wine', lit. 'water foot'
	$[N + A]_N$	*aguaviva* 'jelly fish', lit. 'water alive'
	$[Q + N]_N$	*milhojas* 'millefeuille', lit. 'thousand-leaves'
	$[V + N]_N$	*majahierro* 'ironsmith', lit. 'hit-iron'
Verbal	$[N + V]_V$	*manentrar* 'to attack', lit. 'hand-enter'
	$[Adv + V]_V$	*maltraer* 'mortify', lit. 'badly-bring'
		menospreciar 'scorn', lit. 'less-value'
Adjectival	$[N + A]_A$	*bocarroto* 'loose-mouthed', lit. [horse] 'mouth-broken'
		boquimuelle 'loose-mouthed', lit. [horse] 'mouth-soft'
	$[Adv + A]_A$	*malferido* 'seriously injured', lit. 'badly-hurt'
	$[Q + A]_A$	*cuatropartido* 'divided in four' lit. 'four-split'
Adverbial	Miscellaneous	*bien gent* 'gently', lit. 'well gentle'
		salva fe 'with certainty', lit. 'safe faith'
Numeral	$[Q + Q]_Q$	*ocho mil* 'eight thousand'
		cuarenta y ocho 'forty-eight', lit. 'forty and eight'

compounds can belong to the lexical categories N[oun], V[erb], A[djective], Adv[erb], and [Numeral] Q[uantifier] and can be formed through different constituent combinations (e.g., [N + N], [Adv + A], etc.) (cf. Table 3.4 for examples). On the table and in subsequent chapters, patterns are identified by their internal structure between square brackets and the grammatical category of the resulting complex, which appears as a subscript.

Very few adverbs have ever been created through compounding, although there are examples of compounds as part of adverbial expressions (*a mansalva* 'completely', lit. 'to hand-safe', *a matacaballo* 'very fast', lit. 'to kill-horse'). By contrast, numerals are possible both as compounds and as compound constituents. To obtain data on compound numerals, the digital databases (Corpus del español, CORDE, CREA) have been preferred to the dictionaries, since the latter are not always exhaustive in the inclusion of numerals. By contrast, it is relatively straightforward to carry out exhaustive searches of numerals in digital databases because their constituents are limited to a small set of lexemes. Compounds combining numerals with constituents of a different category are classified according to their internal structure: e.g., $[Q + N]_N$ *ciempiés* 'centipede', lit. 'hundred-feet', $[Q + A]_A$ *cuatralbo* '[horse] whose four legs are white', lit. 'four-white'.

In Spanish, the lexical category of some constituents is ambiguous, especially when it comes to distinguishing nouns from adjectives. For example, the second constituents in *maldecidor* 'swearer', lit. 'badly-sayer' and *malandante* 'unfortunate', lit. 'badly-walking' can both be interpreted as deverbal nouns or adjectives. In general, however, constituents fall more squarely into one category than the other. Consider the examples in (13).

(13) a. *Era el capitán Martín de Robles (no le conocí) hombre que se picaba de*
          gracioso y <u>decidor</u> [...]. (1569, Reginaldo Lizárraga, Corpus del Español)
          'Captain Martín de Robles (whom I never met) was said to be a funny and
          <u>talkative</u> man'.

      b. *[...] cumple a un veedor fiel cerrar los ojos, ni a un <u>decidor</u> leal decir menos*
          de las maravillas que está viendo. (1874, José Martí, Corpus del Español)
          'A faithful seer must close his eyes, and a loyal <u>sayer</u> must not understate
          the marvels he is seeing'.

      c. *[...] que si es escudero él de un gigante pagano, yo lo soy de un caballero*
          <u>andante</u> cristiano y manchego [...] (1605, Miguel de Cervantes Saavedra,
          Corpus del Español)
          '[...] for if he is the shield bearer of a pagan giant, I am the shield bearer of
          a knight <u>errant</u>, a Christian, and a man from La Mancha [...]'

      d. *el <u>andante</u> sobre alas de viento [...]* (1086–1141, Jehuda ha-Levi, Corpus
          del Español)
          'the <u>walker</u> on the wings of wind'

Although *decidor* 'sayer' can appear both in adjectival and nominal uses (13a and b, respectively), the latter are more frequent. The reverse is true for *andante* 'walker, walking'
(13c, d). Higher frequency of use is the criterion employed to decide in these cases, unless
the structure or meaning of the compound clearly favors the less frequent interpretation.

One final observation concerns compounds that can be classified in more than
one grammatical category. A contemporary example is *pechiazul* lit. 'throat-blue',
which can be used as an adjective to refer to any creature that is blue-throated, but
more often denotes a specific bird with that feature, i.e., the bluethroat [Luscinia sveci-
ca L.]. That is, the compound can be endocentric $[N + A]_A$ or an exocentric $[[N + A]_A]$
$_N$. There are also historical examples: the combination *bien gent* 'decent', lit. 'well-gen-
tle', could be used in Medieval Spanish as an adjective or as an adverb, i.e., 'decent/de-
cently'. In these cases, the compound is classified using the exocentric interpretation,
which tends to come as a later development.

3.5.2 Headedness properties

A second criterion used to classify compounds is their headedness, i.e., whether they
are endocentric or exocentric. Recall form Chapter 2 that the first category includes
compounds in which at least one of the constituents is responsible for the syntactico-
semantic properties of the whole. Let us consider some examples.

(14) | compound | literal gloss | meaning |
        |---|---|---|
        | a. $[N + N]_N$ | | |
        | *hombre orquesta* | man orchestra | one-man band |
        | $[N + A]_A$ | | |
        | *camposanto* | field holy | graveyard |

b. [V + N]$_N$
   comecocos   eat coconuts [brains]   puzzle
   [Q + N]$_N$
   milhojas   thousand leaves   millefeuille

c. [N + N]$_N$
   puntapié   tip foot   kick
   [N + A]$_N$
   cabeza loca   head crazy   crazy person

In (14a), both compounds are interpretable as a semantic subset of the first constituent. For example, they are masculine singular nouns, a trait they inherit from their heads (e.g., *el hombre orquesta* 'the-MASC SG man- MASC SG orchestra-FEM SG', *el hombre* 'the-MASC SG man-MASC SG', vs. *la orquesta* 'the-FEM SG orchestra-FEM SG'). Semantically, *hombre orquesta* is a type of man, and *camposanto* is a type of field. By contrast, in exocentric compounds the head is an empty category, associated with a null nominal WCM. For example, in the patterns in (14b), although the verb *comer* clearly governs the nominal complement *cocos*, the nominal features of the compound cannot be inherited from either of the constituents present; they must come from a head with no phonetic realization. The same can be argued for *milhojas*, which does not inherit its syntactico-semantic properties from either the numeral or the nominal constituent. The patterns in (14b) are always exocentric, whereas those in (14c) have exocentric or endocentric uses. In the latter case, exocentric interpretations of the pattern tend to be derivative and are discussed separately in subsequent chapters.

3.5.3 Relationship between constituents

Compounds are also classified according to the internal relationship between constituents. In hierarchical compounds, one of the constituents (the non-head) is subordinate to the other (the head) in a relationship of complementation or adjunction. These compounds are subdivided into head-initial and head-final, depending on whether their head element is on the left or on the right (15a, b).

(15)	compound	literal gloss	meaning
a.	Head initial		
	[N + N]$_N$		
	casa cuna	house crib	orphanage
	[V + N]$_N$		
	rompecabezas	break-heads	puzzle
b.	Head-final		
	[A + N]$_N$		
	gentilhombre	gentle-man	gentleman
	[Adv + V]$_N$		
	maltrabaja	badly-work	lazy person

These two configurations are possible both in endocentric and exocentric compounds. For example, both the endocentric *casa cuna* and the exocentric *rompecabezas* are head-initial, because the second constituent is subordinated to the first. In contrast, both the endocentric *gentilhombre* and the exocentric *maltrabaja* are head-final, because the first constituent is subordinated to the second. The difference between the endocentric and the exocentric examples is that in the former the head also percolates its features to the entire compound, whereas in the latter there is no such process. In concatenative compounds (Chapter 2, Section 2.3), constituents are hierarchically equal, joined through a relation of identity or addition (16).

(16)	**Concatenative compound**	**literal gloss**	**meaning**
	$[A + A]_A$		
	cóncavo-convexo	concave-covex	concave-convex
	$[N + N]_N$		
	mesa camilla	table stretcher	table stretcher
	$[V + V]_N$		
	duermevela	sleep-wake	light sleep

3.5.4 Internal structure of constituents

Finally, because the distinction between stems and lexemes is important in Spanish compounds (cf. Chapter 1, Section 1.2.2), the internal structure of constituents is also considered in the classification. In most cases, it is the first element that is of interest, as it is the one that may exhibit variability. By contrast, the second constituent appears overwhelmingly in full form and is of little classificatory value. Compounds are therefore divided according to whether this first constituent appears in bare stem form (without its terminal element) or in lexeme form (stem + WCM) (17).

(17)		**compound**	**literal gloss**	**meaning**
	a.	Stem compounds		
		dulciamargo	sweet-sour	sweet-and-sour
		dormivela	sleep-wake	light sleep
		gallicresta	rooster-comb	wild sage
		cristianodemocracia	Christian democracy	Christian democracy
	b.	Lexeme compounds		
		dulceamargo	sweet-sour	sweet-and-sour
		duermevela	sleep-wake	light sleep
		gallocresta	rooster comb	wild sage
		disco-pub	disco-bar	disco-bar

The missing terminal element is often replaced by -*i*- or -*o*-, creating forms that are different from lexemes in their phonological properties (*galli* ~ *gallo, dormi* ~ *duerme*) or in their inertness to concord: *cristiano̲democracia* 'Christian democracy' vs. *democracia cristiana̲*, **democracia cristiano̲* 'id'. However, there are ambiguous cases, whose first constituent could be considered either a lexeme or a stem. Thus, in *fangoterapia* 'mud therapy' or *radiotransmitir* 'broadcast by radio', lit. 'radio-broadcast' it is impossible to tell whether the first constituent is a lexeme (*fango, radio*) or the stem accompanied by a linking vowel (*fang-o, radi-o*). In those cases, the lexeme interpretation is generally preferred, based on the premise that the simplest hypothesis for learners would be to assume that if a string looks like a full fledged lexeme on the surface, then it is. Yet, this premise has occasionally been revised, in light of the fact that the interpretation of the internal structure of a given compound is probably influenced by the existence of others with parallel structure whose constituents are unambiguously stems (e.g., for *fangoterapia*, consider *vitamin-o-terapia* 'vitamin therapy', *music-o-terapia* 'music therapy', and the like).

3.6 Summary of chapter

The sources and the criteria used to select data are worthy of the detailed attention they have received in the previous sections, because they are foundational to the remainder of the study. They underpin the descriptive portions of the book, including those devoted to specific patterns (Chapters 4 to 8), as well as to cross-pattern generalizations (Chapter 9). Indirectly, they are also at the root of the more theoretical conclusions of the entire work. As I hope to have demonstrated, there is nothing mechanical about finding compounds in dictionaries and digital databases. Whereas in diachronic studies of derivation it is possible to carry out searches for specific surface strings of characters, with orthographic variation constituting the main methodological complication, in the case of compounding there is no uniform surface form. Compounding patterns are abstract and often indistinguishable from homophonous phrases, so that ascertaining their syntactic behavior is as important as considering their constituent structure.

In order to achieve a high degree of certainty about the compound status of the items, stringent criteria have been preferred. It may be argued that this has probably led to the elimination of at least some likely compounds, as is undoubtedly the case. At the same time, the study has one advantage over those based primarily on semantic and/or orthographic criteria: the compound status of the data is quite unassailable.

As with all studies, this one is as solid as its weakest link, both in terms of the data obtained and the certainty of their dating. For example, given the size of the database, it was impossible to check the dates of first attestation for all compounds in sources other than CORDE/CREA, so any weaknesses in those databases will have repercussions for this work. Although the resources and methods used are the best available within the constraints of the project, no doubt better ones will eventually become available. For example, the Real Academia's stated commitment to complete the

Diccionario Histórico del Español within our lifetime (Abraham Madroñal p.c.) will provide ample opportunities for correction. In the meantime, I hope this study will help shed light on a facet of Spanish word formation that has remained in the shadows for too long.

The next two chapters describe two sets of compound patterns whose head is on the right. Chapter 4 tackles patterns that have adverbial non-heads, such as [Adv + V]$_V$ (e.g., *maldormir* 'to sleep badly', lit. 'badly sleep'). Chapter 5 focuses on head-final patterns with nominal non-heads, such as [N + V]$_V$ (e.g., *maniatar* 'to tie by the hands', lit. 'hand-tie'). Two other head-final compounding patterns have been deferred until Chapter 6, specifically, those with the constituent structure [N + N]$_N$ (*vitaminoterapia* 'vitamin therapy') and [A + N]$_N$ (*ricadueña* 'noble woman'). There they are dealt with together with their mirror patterns, head-initial [N + N]$_N$ (*hombre lobo* 'werewolf', lit. 'man-wolf') and [N + A]$_N$ (*hierbabuena* 'mint', lit. 'herb-good'), with which they exhibit many similarities.

CHAPTER 4

Endocentric compounds with adverbial non-heads

Bienquerer, bienquisto, bienquerencia

This chapter starts the description of the history of Spanish compounding patterns whose head constituent appears on the right, by tackling specifically those that have adverbial non-heads. There are three main such patterns: [Adv + V]$_V$, [Adv + A]$_A$, and [Adv + N]$_N$. As the examples in Table 4.1 show, the three compound patterns form a natural cluster with related structure and meaning, and, very often, with derivational relationships. They also share a very early appearance and higher levels of productivity in the earliest periods, with waning vitality over time. After each of the three patterns is described individually, these connections are explored at some length (Section 4.4).

4.1 The [Adv + V]$_V$ pattern: *Bienquerer*

The [Adv + V]$_V$ pattern has a non-head adverbial as its first constituent, followed by the verbal head. When used endocentrically, the resulting compound is a verb, with the adverb acting as a predicate of the event denoted (*maldormir* 'to sleep badly', lit. 'badly-sleep' denotes a subset of the events denoted by *dormir*). However, as we shall see later in this section, the pattern is quite frequently used exocentrically, i.e., merged with an empty nominal head, which results in a nominal compound (*bienestar* 'wellbeing', lit. 'well-be').

Table 4.1 Endocentric head-final compounds with adverbial non-heads

Pattern	Example	Found in →
[Adv + V]$_V$	*bienquerer* 'to love', lit. 'well love'	Chapter 4, Section 4.1
[Adv + A]$_A$	*bienquisto* 'well-loved'	Chapter 4, Section 4.2
[Adv + N]$_N$	*bienquerencia* 'love', lit. 'well-love-N SUFF'	Chapter 4, Section 4.3

4.1.1   Structure

4.1.1.1   *Constituents*

Only a handful of adverbs can appear as the non-head constituent in [Adv + V]$_V$ compounding. The overwhelming majority of these compounds are formed with one of two adverbs of manner: *mal* 'badly' (43 attested cases, e.g., *malvender* 'sell for a low price', lit. 'badly-sell', *malquerer* 'dislike', lit. 'badly-love') and *bien* 'well' (eight cases, e.g., *bienvivir* 'live well', lit. 'well-live'). A distant third is an adverb of quantity, *menos* 'less' (three cases, e.g., *menospreciar* 'despise', lit. 'less-value'). In the older compounds, the adverb may appear in an undiphthongized alternative form, such as *ben-*, as in *bendecir* 'to bless', lit. 'to well-say', or reduced through consonantal loss, such as *ma-* in *maherir* 'injure', lit. 'badly-injure'. Of the two adverbs, *mal* has been more productive, especially since the 1500s.[1]

The verbal constituents cover the semantic range of possible Aktionsart (Vendler 1967), including states (*creer* 'believe', *querer* 'want'), activities (*mirar* 'look', *vivir* 'live'), achievements (*meter* 'put', *perder* 'lose'), and accomplishments (*parir* 'bear [a child]', *interpretar* 'interpret'). As far as the formal features of the verb, the process of compounding in general does not affect its subcategorization frame. This is expected, since the addition of an optional adverb should not affect the basic verbal thematic grid.

Thus, for example, in (1a) *malperder* 'spoil', lit. 'badly-lose' discharges a theme role on its direct object, just as *perder* 'lose' would. There are a few exceptions to this rule, especially in older lexicalized compounds. For example, whereas *decir* 'to say' requires a nominal or clausal direct object complement (*dijo la verdad* 'she told the truth', *dijo que vendría* 's/he said that she'd come'), *bendecir* 'to bless' and *maldecir* 'to curse' can also be used intransitively (1b) or with an indirect object beneficiary (1c).

(1)   a.   *dejaba* <u>*malperder*</u> *sus frutos codiciados en todos los mercados*
(cf. <u>*perder* *sus frutos codiciados*</u>)   (5.17.08, Google)
'he allowed for his sought-after fruit to go to waste (lit. 'to be badly-lost')
in all the markets' (cf. '[he] allowed for his sought-after fruit to be lost')

   b.   *En el tiempo de los patriarcas, la cabeza de cada tribu y familia* <u>*bendecía*</u>.
(cf. ******la cabeza de cada tribu y familia* <u>*decía*</u>)   (5.17.08, Google)
'In the time of the patriarchs, the head of each tribe and family blessed
(lit. 'well-spoke')' (cf. *'the head of each tribe and family said')

---

1.   Because prepositions have been excluded from this study of compounding (cf. Chapter 1, Section 1.3.1), possible contrasts such as *subestimar* 'underestimate' and *sobreestimar* 'overestimate' are not considered. It is interesting, though, that the adverb *menos* 'less' is not matched by *más* 'more' in compounds, although made-up examples such as *maspreciar* 'more-value' and *masvalorar* 'more-value' would be transparent.

    c. *El obispo <u>bendijo</u> a los atletas mexicanos que fueron a Pekín.* (cf. **el obispo* <u>*dijo* a los atletas mexicanos</u>)   (9.2.08, Google)
        'The bishop blessed (lit. 'well-said') the Mexican athletes who went to Beijing' (cf. *'the bishop said the Mexican athletes')

Even more recent examples can also undergo similar changes that relax the requirement of an obligatory complement. Note that in (2a) the verb *malacostumbrar* 'spoil', lit. 'badly-accustom' discharges theta roles on an animate direct object and also a prepositional complement, just as *acostumbrar* 'accustom' would. Yet, (2b) shows that the prepositional complement is no longer obligatory.

(2) a. *No hay que <u>malacostumbrar</u> a Giancarlo <u>a tanto protagonismo</u>*
       (cf. <u>*acostumbrar* a Giancarlo a tanto protagonismo</u>)   (5.17.08, Google)
       'We shouldn't spoil (lit. 'badly-accustom') Giancarlo with so much protagonism' (cf. 'accustom Giancarlo to so much protagonism')

     b. *pero se corre el riesgo de <u>malacostumbrar</u> a las nuevas generaciones.*
       (**<u>*acostumbrar* a las nuevas generaciones</u>')   (Google, 5.17.08)
       'but we run the risk of spoiling (lit. 'badly accustoming') the new generations' (cf. *'accustoming the new generations')

Several of the most frequent verbs used in this type of compound appear both with *mal* and with *bien* (seven pairs in the database, including *bienestar* 'wellbeing', lit. 'well-be' vs. *malestar* 'discomfort', lit. 'badly-be'; *bendecir* 'bless', lit. 'well-say' vs. *maldecir* 'curse', lit. 'badly say'; *bienquerer* 'love', lit. 'well-love' vs. *malquerer* 'dislike', lit. 'badly-love').

4.1.1.2 *Compound structure*

The [Adv + V]$_V$ compound results from an operation that associates the adverbial non-head and the verbal head through adjunction, since the adverb does not absorb any of the theta roles the verb has to discharge (3). Headedness is determined through cyclic interpretation: the non-head is sent to interpretation early, whereas the head stays in the derivation and is responsible for the syntactic-semantic properties of the whole (Uriagereka 1999).

(3)   'V'

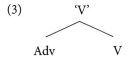

     Adv   V

Head assignment is the result of a process of modification, akin to that already illustrated for nominal phrases in Chapter 2 (Section 2.4.1). The modification here involves theta identification between the eventive predicate denoted by the verb and the secondary predicate introduced by the adverb (<1> in (4)), similar to the theta identification between a noun and an adjective. The verb retains the same number of theta roles to discharge, independently of the adverbial modification.

(4)

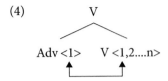

An additional structural observation, whose import will be clarified shortly, concerns the relative position of the constituents: in this particular type of compound the non-head appears invariably to the left of the head, unlike what happens with other compounds whose non-head is a predicate. For example, in the mirror pair $[N + A]_N$ and $[A + N]_N$ the head can be on either side of the non-head (*hierbabuena* 'mint', lit. 'good-herb', vs. *buenaventura* 'good luck').

4.1.1.3 *Compound meaning*
$[Adv + V]_V$ compounds are typically equivalent in meaning to the phrasal combination of verb and adverb: *malvender* 'to sell for a low price', lit. 'to badly-sell'. However, the compound always has a more restricted meaning than the phrase. If we compare *vender mal* and *malvender*, for example, the former has a much wider range of possible meanings than the latter, including the possiblity of selling an item at the wrong time, using the wrong procedure, illegally, and so on. For example, a statement such as *esa vendedora vende mal* 'that seller sells badly' could be interpreted in a number of ways, including that she does not sell very much because she is not persuasive, that she is an effective seller but is rude when doing it, etc. By contrast, *malvender* 'badly-sell' is restricted to the meaning of selling for too little in return. The contrast is shown clearly in the authentic example in (5), where *vivir bien/vivir mal* 'live well/live badly' are polysemous, whereas *bien vivir/mal vivir*, lit. 'well-live/badly-live' are restricted to the economic sense of 'live confortably/live poorly'.

(5)   *[...] No se vive bien en España, pero aunque así fuera, no debemos olvidar nunca la distancia que media entre "bien vivir" y "vivir bien". Muchos de vosotros habéis salido de nuestro país por dos razones: porque no queríais vivir mal, ni malvivir.*   (1966–1974, Enrique Tierno Galván, CORDE)
'People don't live well in Spain, but even if they did, we should never forget the distance between "living comfortably" (lit. 'well-living') and "living well". Many of you have left our country for two reasons: because you did not want to live badly, or eke out a living (lit. 'badly-live').'

The adverbs *mal* 'badly' and *bien* 'well' create pairs of negative-intensive compounds when they attach to the same verb. This same effect has been noted for syntax in structures such as *she does go* vs. *she doesn't go*, the intensive and negative counterparts of the neutral *she goes* (Laka 1994; Lasnik 1972; Pollock 1989). The possibility of creating the same pairings in compounding proves that the phenomenon is true both above and below sentence syntax. When verb and adverb share positive or negative semantic features, their combination simply intensifies the verbal meaning: *malherir* 'to injure seriously', lit. 'badly-hurt', *bienquerer* 'to love dearly', lit. 'well-love'. The parallel phrases do not convey intensity: *herir mal* 'to injure wrongly', *querer bien* 'to love correctly'. When the verb and the adverb do not share semantic features, the addition of *mal* can be equivalent to negation: *malquerer* 'to hate', lit. 'badly-love', *malograr* 'to spoil', lit. 'badly-achieve', *malentender* 'misunderstand', lit. 'badly-understand'. These highly lexicalized compounds cannot be paraphrased:?*querer mal* 'love wrong', *lograr mal* 'achieve wrongly' (but cf. *entender mal* 'misunderstand').

4.1.2 Diachrony

This section discusses the evolution of the [Adv + V]$_V$ pattern, from its inherited origins to the present. The frequency of the pattern is measured both in absolute terms, as a raw count of distinct compounds identified in each century, and in relative terms, as a percentage of the total number of different compounds over time. However, the timeline presented is approximate, and possibly somewhat delayed (cf. discussion in Chapter 3, Section 3.3.2). I will assume that written documentation is reliable to date the age of compounds with respect to each other, so that general trends are accurate, even if not exactly reflective of real time.

This historical section also presents syntactic evidence of the tightness of the relationship between the constituents, including any changes over time. Spelling is discussed as an ancillary means to ascertain the prosodic status of compounds. The section ends with a brief discussion of the recategorization of [Adv + V] compounds from verbs to nouns, and with a discussion of some exceptional cases.

4.1.2.1 *Historical antecedents and comparative data*

According to Kastovsky (2009: 338), compounds that combine a particle or adverb with a verb are probably the result of univerbation of an originally loose sequence. The Latin antecedents of the [Adv + V]$_V$ pattern are well documented (Bader 1962; 301; Fruyt 1990: 198; Oniga 1992: 102). One study in particular documents the stages in the univerbation process of Lat. BENE FACERE, from its initial state as a phrase, with componential meaning and separable constituents, until it becomes a fixed structure with idiomatic meaning (Brunet 2005). However, the Romance reflexes of the [Adv + V]$_V$ pattern are only mentioned explicitly in some general descriptions of compounding such as Gràcia & Fullana (1999: 247) and Mascaró (1986) for Catalan, Zwanenburg (1992) for French, and Mallinson (1986) for Romanian. Yet, comparative evidence can be mustered from lexicographical sources for most Romance varieties: Port. *bem-querer* 'to love well', lit. 'well-love', Cat. *malviure* 'to eke out a living', lit. 'badly live', Fr. (rare) *bienvenir* 'to welcome', It. *malguidicare* 'make an unfair decision', lit. 'badly-judge', Rom. *maltrata* 'mistreat', lit. 'badly-treat'. The presence of [Adv + V]$_V$ compounds across the Romance family is evidence of the pattern's early origin and inherited status. There are also many early examples in Spanish, including some attested prior to 1000 and during the early centuries of the medieval period (6).

(6)   Early attestations of Spanish [Adv + V]$_V$ compounds

    a.   *[....] ipsa hereditate qui tibi <u>benefecerit</u> in terra Legionense*

                                                (951–957, Sahagún, LHP)

        'that land that benefits you in León'

    b.   *Et si dos omnes travaren, maguer qu'el maiorino ó 'l saion davant esté, non a i nada, si uno d'elos non il da sua voz, si ferro esmoludo non í sacar'á <u>mal fazer</u>.*   (1155, *Fuero de Avilés*, CORDE).

    c.   *Por <u>maldezir</u> mios enemigos te clamé, e tu <u>bendezistlos</u> .iij. vezes*

                                            (c. 1200, Almerich, CORDE)

        'I asked you to curse my enemies, and you blessed them thirty times'.

    d.   *Fasta en Alménar, a moros <u>malfaçaron</u>, muchos fueron los presos, muchos los que mataron*   (c. 1250, *Poema de Fernán Gómez*, CORDE)

        'All the way to Almenar, they persecuted the moors, they took many prisoners, and they killed many'.

4.1.2.2 *Frequency and productivity*

Overall, the pattern [Adv + V]$_V$ is represented by a total of 55 different compounds in the entire database (1.6%) (Table 4.2). It must be clarified that the frequency of each of the compounds (i.e., the number of times the same compound appears in the databases) is irrelevant to the total count. In other words, the totals presented are for distinct compounds attested in each period (e.g., *alicortar, aliquebrar, cabizbajar, maniatar....*), rather than for the times each one of those compounds appeared repeatedly in the texts or dictionaries. The total numbers increase quickly between 1000 and 1500, and much more slowly after that. However, when considered in terms of relative pattern frequency, these compounds decrease over time with respect to all new compound forms attested in each century from their peak in the 1300s until they become negligible.

The decrease in the productivity of [Adv + V]$_V$ is illustrated in Table 4.3. The first column (*Carried over*) indicates the compounds carried over from the previous period. The second column (*Lost*) contains the number of old compounds no longer attested in or after that century, whereas the third (*New*) shows the number of compounds that appear for the first time. The totals column is calculated by adding gains and subtracting losses to the initial figure. Finally, the productivity ratio in the last column is calculated by dividing the net gain (new compounds minus lost compounds) by the total number in a given period. For example, a ratio of 0.33 in a century indicates

Table 4.2 [Adv + V]$_V$ compounds attested by century, as totals and as a percentage of all compounds

	[Adv + V]$_V$	All compounds	[Adv + V]$_V$ as % of all compounds
1000s–1200s	18	349	5.2
1300s	26	434	6.0
1400s	37	709	5.2
1500s	44	1073	4.1
1600s	43	1237	3.5
1700s	44	1360	3.2
1800s	45	1842	2.4
1900s–2000s	50	3005	1.7
Total	55	3451	1.6

Table 4.3 Productivity of [Adv + V]$_V$ compounds by century

	Carried over	Lost	New	Total	Productivity Ratio
1200s	2	(0)	16	18	NA
1300s	18	(1)	9	26	0.31
1400s	26	(0)	11	37	0.30
1500s	37	(2)	9	44	0.16
1600s	44	(2)	1	43	−0.02
1700s	43	(0)	1	44	0.02
1800s	44	(0)	1	45	0.02
1900s–2000s	45	(0)	5	50	0.10

that, adjusting for losses, 33% of the compounds in that period were new. This table demonstrates that for [Adv + V]$_V$ compounds, th totals in the later periods are due mostly to the preservation of compounds from earlier centuries, with little neologistic activity after the 1500s.[2] The [Adv + V]$_V$ pattern is inactive but stable, as the majority of these compounds continue to be employed over the centuries with few losses.

4.1.2.3 *Inseparability of constituents*
The issue of the syntactic inseparability of constituents affects the very question of whether a complex form is in fact a compound or just a frequent syntactic phrase. Recall from Chapter 1 (Sections 1.4.1–1.4.2) that one of the criteria for compoundhood

---

2. Possible reasons for this decrease can be speculated to be related to the loss of V2 effects in Spanish. This would have made the syntactic order adverb-verb less likely, and less frequent in the input children received from adult speakers, thus eliminating a possible source of the Adv + V compound patterns. More discussion will be presented in Chapter 9.

is the evidence that constituents appear in a fixed order and cannot be separated. These properties are not always verifiable with the early compounds, given that the numbers of examples are low and native speakers are unavailable to confirm them. Additionally, it is possible to find examples that violate the principle of inseparability and fixed order (7), but they may very well have been parallel phrases and not the compounds in question.

(7)   a.   *[...] son syn cuenta los moujmientos del coraçon a cobdiçiar/o a <u>mal querer</u>*
                  (1293, *Castigos*, CORDE)
  'the heart has countless urges to cupidity or hate'

  b.   *E no deuen <u>querer mal</u> a los omnes; por los yerros que fazen.*
              (1256–1263, Alfonso X, CORDE)
  'and they shouldn't hate men because of the mistakes they make'

  c.   *¡Oh cuán bien decía el divino Platón, es a saber: "que no debrían fatigarse los hombres por mucho vivir, sino por <u>muy bien vivir</u>"!*
          (1521–1543, Fray Antonio de Guevara, CORDE)
  'Oh, how rightly did the divine Plato say: "that men shouldn't strive to live long, but to live very well"!'

Over time, the Adv + V complex undergoes a series of changes, including orthographic univerbation or narrowing of meaning (8a), as discussed in Section 4.1.1.3. Note, however, that if univerbation entails semantic specialization, the latter does not require the former, underscoring once more the unreliability of orthography alone as a diagnostic for compound status. It takes more than a formal surface difference to distinguish the compound from an [Adv + V] phrase that retains the less specialized meaning (8b).

(8)   a.   *Ya le seguiremos en su interesante regreso al escondrijo donde <u>mal vive</u>.*
           (1897, Benito Pérez Galdós, CORDE)
  'We will follow him on his interesting journey back to the hideout where he barely survives'.

  b.   *quien <u>mal vive</u> peor muere*   (1703, Francisco Garau, CORDE)
  'He who lives badly, dies worse'.

It is tricky to date when the Adv + V construction ceases to be a possible phrasal structure and can therefore be assumed to be a compound. No specific information is available in Keniston (1937), Lapesa (1980), Penny (1991), or Company Company (2006) concerning the issue of adverb placement over time. However, a preliminary search in CORDE shows that preposed adjunction of *mal/bien* is possible until the 1600s (9a), after which the structure with preposed adverbs survives only in a handful of proverbs and idiomatic expressions, known to retain archaic word order (9b, c).

(9) a. *Qui mal piensa con ojos espantosos, mordiendo sus labros mal faze e acába-*
lo.   (ad 1280, Alfonso X, CORDE)
'He who thinks mistakenly with horrified eyes, biting his lips, does badly
and ends it'.

    b. *Kien mal piensa, mal dispensa, i mal le da Dios.*
(1627, Gonzalo Correas, CORDE)
'He who thinks badly [of others], fails to forgive, and God treats him badly'.

    c. *No es esto Rethórica, ni Lógica, ni Arte Combinatorio, como mal piensa el*
padre maestro Feyjoo   (1745, Benito Jerónimo Feijoo, CORDE)
'This isn't rhetoric, or logic, or combinatory art, as master Feijoo mistakenly believes'.

The evidence above suggests that until the 1600s, a sequence of Adv + V can legiti-
mately be considered phrasal. To favor a compound interpretation over a phrasal interpretation more robust evidence is required, such as clear specialized meaning and
unitary spelling. It is reasonable to assume, then, that in the earliest compounds created with the $[\text{Adv} + \text{V}]_V$ pattern, the precedence of the adverb is simply a reflection of
an acceptable phrasal order that becomes fixed as the phrase lexicalizes. Later compounds of this type are unlikely to have been created through simple univerbation of a
phrase, given that by then syntax no longer allowed placing adverbs before verbs. In
these later compounds it must be surmised that the pattern alone provides a template
for further coinages. The decreased productivity of $[\text{Adv} + \text{V}]_V$ may thus be linked to
the two factors: on the one hand, the loss of the verb-final order that would allow for
the creation of these compounds syntactically, and on the other, the scarcity of examples of this compound pattern in speech, which reduces the possibility of modeling
new compounds based on it.

4.1.2.4 *Orthographic representation*

$[\text{Adv} + \text{V}]_V$ compounds may appear written as an orthographic unit or not. Unitary
spelling suggests word stress and lexicalized meaning, but the small number of examples for some compounds does not always provide evidence of a clear progression
from two-word to one-word spelling. As one would expect in the case of compounds
that are created by gradual agglutination of juxtaposed phrases, it is possible for a
compound to be spelled as two words before it is spelled as one (10a, b). There are also
examples that present both orthographies simultaneously (10c, d).

(10) a. *Apenas alcanzo para mal comer, y por eso me ayudo de este modo.*
(1818, José Joaquín Fernández de Lizardi, CORDE)
'I can barely feed myself (lit. 'badly-eat'), so I help myself this way'.

b. *no es lo mismo lo de su niña, la Paquita, que después de todo vive decente-
mente, aunque sin los papeles en orden, que lo de ésta, que anda por ahí
rodando como una peonza y sacándole los cuartos a cualquiera para mal-
comer.*   (1951–1969, Camilo José Cela, CORDE)
'What your daughter Paquita does is not the same thing, because after all
she lives decently, even without the marriage licence. This one, however,
goes round and round like a top, getting money from anyone to feed her-
self (lit. 'badly-eat')'.

c. *et no ayan poder de mal meter ende nada, si no por debda propria que deba
el huerphano*   (c. 1242, *Fuero de Brihuela*, CORDE)
'and they are not entitled to spoil anything there, unless the orphan him-
self owes something'

d. *La rrayz non sea nunca detrançar, nin de malmeter*
                                  (1218 – c. 1250, *Fuero de Zorita de los Canes*, CORDE)
'The property should never be destroyed or spoilt'

The reasonable assumption is that unitary spelling confirms the compound status of
an [Adv + V]$_V$ complex, while the orthographic separation of the constituents does
not, by itself, disprove it.

4.1.2.5 *Endocentric and exocentric uses*

[Adv + V] compounds are typically endocentric, so that the resulting compound is a
verb. However, there are several examples of nominalization with no overt suffixation,
i.e., V → N conversion (11a–c). In a few of these cases, only a nominal interpretation is
attested for a compound (e.g., *malpensar* in (11a)). In other cases, both verbal and
nominal interpretations are found (e.g., *mal vestir* in (11b, c)).

(11) a. *por non dar lugar al su mal pensar, mandolo prender e ençerraren una
torre, jurando que y lo farie fazer penitençia de su maldat.*
                        (1284, translation of the *Cantigas de Santa María*, CORDE)
'and in order not to permit his bad thoughts, he had him captured and put
prisoner in a tower, swearing that he would make him do penance for his
wrongdoing'.

b. *Aparejarnos devemos antes del menester contra lo que puede hazer la ventura, provando algunas vezes aspera vianda e mal vestir*
                                            (c. 1430, *Floresta de philósophos*, CORDE)
'We should ready ourselves against what fate may have in store for us, by
occasionally trying bad food and bad clothing'

c. *Acomodábase a todo, a bien vestir y mal vestir*
                                     (1611, Sebastián de Covarrubias, CORDE)
'He could become accustomed to everything, both good clothes and bad
clothes (or: to dressing well and dressing poorly)'.

    d. *ques departién de las otras yentes en la ley e aun en* el vestir *mismo, como*
      firmes a su Dios en todo. (c. 1275, Alfonso X, CORDE)
      '[....] that they were different from other peoples in their laws and in their
      very clothing, because they were attached to their God in everything'.

In some of the examples that can be interpreted as verbal or nominal, in fact there is
evidence that V → N conversion occurred earlier than the process of compounding. In
other words, although at the surface level the compound structure can be analyzed as
$[[Adv + V]_V]_N$, the historical facts favor an analysis of the nominal compounds as having the internal structure of a nominal phrase whose noun is the product of verb-to-
noun conversion, modified by an adjective: $[A + [V]_N]_N$. For example, the verbal example in (11c) is preceded by almost two centuries by the nominal in (11b), which in
turn is preceded by numerous early examples of nominalized *vestir* 'clothing' (11d).
This suggests that *malvestir* 'poor clothing', lit. 'bad-clothing' is more appropriately
analyzed as an $[A + N]_N$ compound. However, because the adjective and the noun are
homophonous with an adverb and a verb, respectively, this pattern offers a possible
'reverse' etymological source for other $[Adv + V]_V$ compounds.

4.1.3 Special cases

As seen in the last section, the interplay between compounding and nominalization of
the head constituent may result in some degree of structural ambiguity. It is also possible for the [Adv + V] surface structure to be only apparent, since the putative verbal
constituents are not attested. That is the case with *malhumorar* 'to anger', *menoscabar*
'to diminish', and *malquistarse/bienquistarse* 'to be on good terms/to be on bad terms'.
Since the verbs **humorar*, **cabar*, and **quistar* were not found in the database or in any
lexicographic source, these cases are better interpreted as verbal conversions from
nominal and adjectival bases (*malhumorar* ← *malhumor* 'bad mood', lit. 'bad humor',
menoscabar ← *menoscabo* 'damage', lit. 'less-end', *bien/malquistar* ← *bien/malquisto*
'well loved/unloved', lit. 'well-/badly-loved').

4.2 The $[Adv + A]_A$ pattern: *Bienquisto*

Of the three patterns with adverbial non-heads, $[Adv + A]_A$ has the largest number of
compounds. Although at first blush it seems to be derived from $[Adv + V]_V$ through
participial suffixation, several compounds in this class do not have deverbal heads.
Even when they do, the $[Adv + A]_A$ compounds themselves are not always preceded by
a previously attested verbal counterpart, a matter that will be discussed at greater
length in Section 4.4.

4.2.1 Structure

4.2.1.1 *Constituents*

Like their verbal counterparts, [Adv + A]$_A$ compounds exhibit almost exclusively the adverbs *bien/ben* 'well' and *mal/male-* 'badly' in non-head position. However, they also exhibit a slightly wider array of possible adverbs, since *menos* 'less' is sporadically joined by *siempre* 'always' and other adverbial roots such as *pleni-* 'fully' (a shortened allomorph of the complex form *plenamente* 'fully' (e.g. *plenisonante* 'resounding', lit. 'fully-sounding').

An overwhelming majority of the adjective heads in this class are deverbal, with past participles, both regular and irregular, figuring prominently (almost 70% of the total): *malparida* '[woman] who's had a miscarriage', lit. 'badly-delivered', *bien nacido* 'high born', lit. 'well born'. Other less frequent deverbal adjectives are present participles (16%): *maldoliente* 'suffering', lit. 'badly-suffering', *bienoliente* 'aromatic', lit. 'well-smelling'. There are also several agentives derived through suffixation of *-(d)or* (*bienhechor* 'beneficial', lit. 'well-doing', *malgastador* 'extravagant', lit. 'badly-spender'), and less frequent endings such as *-ero* (*bienjusticiero* 'fair', lit. 'well-avenger'), *-ible* (*maldecible* 'despicable', lit. 'badly-sayer'), *-ivo* (*menospreciativo* 'scornful', lit. 'less-value-SUFF'), *-izo* (*malcontentadizo* 'unhappy', lit. 'badly-content-SUFF'), and *-oso* (*bienquerencioso* 'loving', lit. 'well-loving'). Most of these suffixes are deverbal (cf. *comer* 'eat' → *com<u>ible</u>* 'edible', *decorar* 'decorate' → *decor<u>ativo</u>* 'decorative', *escurrir* 'slip' → *escurri<u>dizo</u>* 'slippery'), but a few are denominal (*cana* 'white hair' → *can<u>oso</u>* 'white-haired'). This indicates that nominal compounds of the type [Adv + N]$_N$ are also a potential source of adjectival compounds: *bienquerencia* 'good will' → *bienquerencioso* 'with good will'.

Finally, there are a number of compounds whose adjectival head is unlikely to be deverbal. This may be because the verb is unattested, such as the case of *siempretieso* 'tumbler [toy]', lit. 'always-stiff', since there is no verb **tiesar* 'stiffen'. Alternatively, it may be because there is no formal or historical evidence to assert its precedence over the adjective. That is the case of *malcontento* 'unhappy', lit. 'badly-happy', where the verb *contentar* 'to make content' cannot be said to be the basis for the adjective *contento* 'content', nor does it precede it historically (cf. also *maldigno* 'shameful', lit. 'badly-dignified', and *malsano* 'unhealthy', lit. 'badly-healthy').

4.2.1.2 *Compound structure*

Like the verbal compounds described in Section 4.1, [Adv + A]$_A$ compounds result from an operation that associates the adverbial non-head and the adjectival head, resulting in a modification (12). The head of the compound is the head of the predicate, i.e., the adjective. Like before, the quotation marks around the higher node are meant to represent the fact that the association between constituents is not one of head-complement.

(12)   'A'

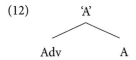

Adv   A

Modification involves theta identification between the predicate introduced by the adjective and the secondary predicate of the adverb (<1> in 13). In turn, the variable of the adjective is theta-identified with whatever nominal head it modifies. The adjective may have theta roles to discharge, but these are not altered by the presence of the adverbial, since the latter does not absorb any of these theta roles: *amado por todos* 'loved by everyone' → *bienamado por todos* 'well-loved by everyone'. Like in the [Adv + V]$_V$ compounds, the non-head appears invariably to the left.

(13)   A

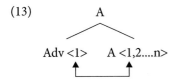

Adv <1>   A <1,2....n>

4.2.1.3 *Compound meaning*

Many [Adv + A]$_A$ compounds are equivalent to the phrasal combination of the adverb and the adjective: *malaconsejado ~ aconsejado mal* 'ill advised', lit. 'badly advised', *bientratado ~ tratado bien* 'well treated'. However, a certain degree of semantic narrowing is concomitant with compounding. Thus, *malcriado* 'brattish', lit. 'badly-raised' no longer conveys the full array of possible phrasal meanings of *criado mal*. If a child is described as *un niño criado mal* 'a child raised badly', this may refer to the process followed in his education as well as the resulting behavior; only the second meaning is conveyed by the compound. Thus, it is not contradictory to say: *Pepito es un niño or criado mal, pero por suerte no es malcriado* 'Pepito is a badly raised child, but fortunately he is not a brat'.

Like in their verbal counterparts, the meaning of the adjective and the adverb may involve the intensification of positive or negative meaning: *maldoliente* 'suffering', lit. 'badly-suffering', *bienamado* 'well loved'. The use of *mal* 'badly' with positive adjectives has the semantic effect of negation: *malagradecido* 'ungrateful', lit. 'badly-grateful', *malcontento* 'unhappy', lit. 'badly-happy'.

Finally, some adjectives are unattested except in the compound. For example, *malhablado* 'dirty-mouthed', lit. 'badly-spoken', is based on a putative adjective *hablado* 'spoken' that is not attested independently as an agentive (cf. Eng. *John is soft-spoken* vs. **John is spoken*). Likewise, *bienoliente* 'fragrant', lit. 'well-smelling' is unlikely to have been modeled on the marginal adjective *oliente* 'smelling'.

4.2.2 Diachrony

4.2.2.1 *Historical antecedents and comparative data*

Compounds with an adverbial non-head and an adjectival head are attested for several Indo-European languages (Olsen 2002: 239 for Armenian; Whitney 1941[1879]: 498, 500 for Sanskrit). More directly relevant to our purposes is the presence of these compounds in Latin: MULTICUPIDUS 'desiring much', MALE SĀNUS 'unhealthy', lit. 'badly-healthy' (Bader 1962: 301; Oniga 1992: 102). The pattern has also been described by several authors in Romance languages such as Portuguese (Villalba 1992: 207), Catalan (Gràcia & Fullana 1999: 247; Mascaró 1986: 69), French (Zwanenburg 1992: 224–28), and Romanian (Mallinson 1986: 33). The restriction to the pair of manner adverbs *bien/mal* 'well/badly' holds true for all Romance languages attested, with very few exceptions: Port. *bem-visto* 'well reputed', lit. 'well-seen', *malpropício* 'improper', lit. 'badly-propitious', Cat. *benvingut* 'welcome', *malcontent* 'unhappy', lit. 'badly-happy', Fr. *bienheureux* 'happy', lit. 'well-happy', *maladroit* 'clumsy', lit. 'badly-able', It. *benavventurato* 'fortunate', lit. 'well-adventured', *malformato* 'malformed', lit. 'badly formed', Rom. *binecrescut* 'well-bred' (but note also *nou-născut* 'newborn').

In Spanish the [Adv + A]$_A$ pattern is first attested as early as [Adv + V]$_V$ compounds, in the 1100s, reinforcing the notion that both types are inherited simultaneously and adjectives are not historically derived from verbs. Among these early attestations there are deverbal participial adjectives (14a) but also others derived by suffixation (14b), and even examples wit a non-deverbal adjective (14c). These early compounds are used both endocentrically (14a–c) and exocentrically (14d). In other words, various possible mechanisms of formation and interpretation are available for [Adv + A]$_A$ compounds from the earliest dates. Therefore, it cannot be adduced that any of them has preceded or spawned the rest, at least during the historical period under analysis.[3]

(14) Early attestations of Spanish [Adv + A]$_A$ compounds

    a. *antes perderé el cuerpo e dexaré el alma, pues que tales malcalçados me vencieron de batalla*   (*Poema de Mio Cid*, CORDE)
        'I would rather lose my body and my soul, because those worthless men (lit. 'poorly shod') defeated me in battle'

    b. *Pasava un gran recuero por cabo de un aldea, e entró en ella un gran ladrón e muy malfechor*   (c. 1253, *Sendebar*, CORDE).
        'while a great mule driver was going through a village, a very evil (lit. 'badly-doing') thief entered the town'

    c. *la cosa muerta o ferida ola menoscabada, ssea del demandado.*
                (c. 1196, *Fuero de Soria*, CORDE)
        'the dead or injured or damaged (lit. 'less-end-ADJ SUFF') thing shall belong to the defendant'

---

3. This is not to say that there could not be historical precedence of some patterns over others. It is simply a statement about the impossibility of proving it with the available evidence.

d. *pueda demandar lo que auje el malfechor ala sazon que fizo la malfecha &*
   non mas   (c. 1196, *Fuero de Soria*, CORDE)
   'he can claim whatever the damager had at the time he committed the
   damage (lit. 'badly-done') and no more'

4.2.2.2 *Frequency and productivity*

The overall total of [Adv + A]$_A$ compounds in the database is 144 (4.2%). If we consider the absolute total numbers per century, the totals peak in the 1500s, after which
they plateau and start to decrease. The decline in relative terms starts much earlier,
since the percentage of [Adv + A]$_A$ compounds vis-à-vis the total per century starts at
around 20% in the earliest period but decreases gradually and steadily to less than 4%
(Table 4.4).

The vitality of the [Adv + A]$_A$ compound pattern is highest during the earliest
periods. The early totals are very high, while new compounds are added at a modest
but steady pace to this inherited base until the 1500s. Over half of [Adv + A]$_A$ compounds are attested before 1300, and over three fourths by 1400 (Table 4.5). Expansion
of the pattern tapers off by the 1500s and it is often outweighed by losses, with the result that the ratio of new to old compounds in all periods after that is under 5%, and
occasionally dips into the negatives as the absolute number of [Adv + A]$_A$ compounds
declines.

4.2.2.3 *Inseparability of constituents*

We must decide whether the [Adv + A] combinations are inseparable, and thus, compounds, or merely phrases with a high degree of semantic cohesiveness. It has already
been shown how in the verbal compounds, early examples were formed through agglutination, i.e., the univerbation of syntactic combinations of a verb and an adverbial
clitic (Fruyt 1990). Later compounds could not be thus formed because preposing

Table 4.4 [Adv + A]$_A$ compounds attested by century, as totals and as a percentage of all
compounds

	[Adv + A]$_A$	All compounds	[Adv + A]$_A$ as % of all compounds
1000s–1200s	70	349	20.1
1300s	83	434	19.1
1400s	108	709	15.2
1500s	113	1073	10.5
1600s	113	1237	9.1
1700s	112	1360	8.2
1800s	116	1842	6.3
1900s–2000s	118	3005	3.9
Total	144	3451	4.2

Table 4.5 Productivity of [Adv + A]$_A$ compounds attested by century

	Carried over	Lost	New	Total	Productivity Ratio
1200s	5	(0)	65	70	NA
1300s	70	(8)	21	83	0.16
1400s	83	(2)	27	108	0.23
1500s	108	(5)	10	113	0.04
1600s	113	(2)	2	113	0.00
1700s	113	(5)	4	112	−0.01
1800s	112	(0)	4	116	0.03
1900s–2000s	116	(4)	6	118	0.02

adverbs to verbs became illicit in sentence syntax. With [Adv + A]$_A$ compounds matters are a little murkier, because the possibility of preposing the adverb to the adjective it modifies persists to the present. Therefore, position of the constituents with respect to each other is not enough by itself to ascertain compound status.

The compoundhood of [Adv + A] forms must therefore be established in some other way, based on the syntactic properties of compounds vis-à-vis phrases. Table 4.6 provides one such measure by quantifying a random selection of [Adv + A] constructions with respect to the frequency with which the non-head may appear modified independently. Recall from Chapter 3, Section 3.2.2.4, that independent syntactic operations on the non-head are impossible with genuine compounds. Syntactic atomicity was checked by comparing the frequency of constructions of the type *más bienvenido* or *más bien venido* [[más [[bien]$_{Adv}$ venido]$_{Adj}$]$_{DegP}$ vs. *mejor venido* [[mejor]$_{Adv}$]$_{DegP}$] venido]$_{Adj}$ in Google. Only the first possibility should be available to forms that have been compounded. Table 4.6 shows results for a sample of ten [Adv + A] combinations. It shows the first attestation of each compound, together with the totals and percentages of word sequences compatible and incompatible with compound status (Google, 6.24.08). For the purpose of clarity, compounds with the adverb *bien* 'well' are separated from those with *mal* 'badly'.

Table 4.6 shows that [Adv + A] combinations run the gamut from those that are used exclusively as lexicalized forms (semantically non-compositional, syntactically atomic), to others for which compounded interpretations coexist with looser combinations. Thus, for example, *bienvenido* 'welcome' and *malcriado* 'ill raised', lit. 'badly-raised', are used virtually always as compounds, but *malpensado* 'ill thinking', lit. 'badly thinking' is quite balanced between compounded and non-compounded uses. By contrast, *bienamado* 'well-loved', and *malcomido* 'ill fed', lit. 'badly fed', are more common in their non-compounded use. Although it would make sense for the loss of independence of the constituents to be related to the historical depth of the compounds, this is not always borne out in the data. Some very early combinations (*bienamado* [1240–1251], *malcalzado* 'poorly shod', lit 'badly-shod', [1140]) are used more often as phrases in the contemporary data, whereas later ones, such as *maleducado* 'lit bred', lit. 'badly-educated' [1781], are much more likely to be used as compounds.

Table 4.6 Frequency of compounded vs. non-compounded uses of ten [Adv + A] combinations in contemporary Spanish

[Adv + A]$_A$	First attest.	Más + [Adv + A]	%	Mejor/peor + [A]	%
bien + venido	c. 1236	32,200	99.5	173	0.5
bien + visto	1323	65,000	94.2	4,000	5.8
bien + parido	c. 1541–1545	578	77.2	171	22.8
bien + intencionado	1535–1602	1,510	37.8	2,490	62.3
bien + amado	1240–1251	68	16.2	352	83.1
mal + criado	1275	1,989	95.5	94	4.5
mal + educado	1781	5,030	90.8	507	9.2
mal + pensado	1378–1406	1,200	59.4	820	40.6
mal + calzado	1140	2	1.8	111	98.2
mal + comido	1471–1476	7	1.0	691	99.0

It should be noted, however, that a low percentage of compounded uses does not, in and of itself, constitute evidence against interpreting an [Adv + A] complex as a compound. The sheer volume of data in Google makes it impossible to check each token to establish identity of meaning among putatively parallel examples. In fact, any example of *más/menos* + *mal/bien* + A is positive evidence that in some meaning and for some speaker, the complex is indeed a compound. For example, (15a) and (15b) illustrate the compounded and phrasal uses of *mal pensado*, respectively.

(15) a. *por aquí fijo que hay alguien más mal pensado/a que yo* (6.24.08, Google)
'Around here for sure there is someone more evil-minded (lit. 'more badly thought') than me'

  b. *Es el edificio peor pensado que he visto en mi vida.*   (6.24.08, Google)
'This is the most ill-conceived (lit. 'worst thought') building I have ever seen in my life'.

4.2.2.4 *Orthographic representation*
Like [Adv + V]$_V$ compounds, the adjectival pattern has the possibility of appearing spelled as one word or two. It also holds true in this case that unitary spelling gives evidence of the prosodic and semantic unification that comes from wordhood, but separation of the two constituents in spelling is not necessarily counterevidence for compound status. For a majority of the [Adv + A]$_A$ compounds with documented alternative spellings, there is a progression from two-word to one-word spelling over time. The tendency is much clearer than for the [Adv + V]$_V$ compounds described in Section 4.1.2.4, because [Adv + A]$_A$ compounds are more frequent, making the progression easier to document. For example, out of the random sample presented in Table 4.7, over two thirds are attested in two-word spelling before they are spelled as one word, while two more appear in both spellings simultaneously.

Table 4.7 Earliest attested forms of a selection of [Adv + A]$_A$ compounds

	First attestation two-word spelling	First attestation one-word spelling
bien + apreso	c. 1236	1330–1343
bien + casado	c. 1240	1956
bien + criado	c. 1275	1576–1577
bien + faciente	1330–1343	1440–1455
bien + mandado	1240–1250	c. 1580
bien + oliente	1246–1252	ad 1540
bien + queriente	c. 1236	c. 1236
bien + sonante	c. 1255	1593
mal + acostumbrado	1250–1300	ad 1435
mal + agradecido	c. 1514–1542	c. 1430
mal + avenido	1270–1284	1443–1454
mal + mandado	c. 1250	c. 1378–1406
mal + parado	c. 1240–1250	1264
mal + sonante	c. 1527–1561	1545–1565
mal + sufrido	1481–1496	c. 1550–1606
mal + traedor	1337–1348	c. 1270

4.2.2.5 Endocentric and exocentric uses

Most [Adv + A]$_A$ compounds are used endocentrically, that is, the grammatical category of the compound is inherited from that of the adjectival head: *contento* 'happy' → *malcontento* 'unhappy', lit. ' badly happy'; *criado* 'raised' → *biencriado* 'well educated', lit. 'well-raised'. There is, however, a small number that have converted to the nominal category permanently. Some are used exclusively as nouns: e.g., *malentendido* 'misunderstanding', lit. 'badly-understood'; others are attested both in endo- and exocentric uses: *bienfecho* 'well done' or 'benefit', lit. 'well-done'.

4.3 The [Adv + N]$_N$ pattern: *Bienquerencia*

Unlike the adjectival compounds in the previous section, the nominal pattern [Adv + N]$_N$ is derivative of the [Adv + V]$_V$ pattern. This can be corroborated by the fact that the nominal heads in this class of compounds are always deverbal. In fact, all of them have compounded verbal counterparts, and even allowing for gaps in the historical database, it is normally possible to establish the chronological precedence of the latter, a matter that will be dealt with in Section 4.4.

4.3.1 Structure

4.3.1.1 *Constituents*

As in their verbal counterparts, these nominal compounds exhibit exclusively three adverbs in non-head position, *bien/ben* 'well', *mal* 'badly', and *menos* 'less'. It is the presence of *bien* 'well', an incontrovertible adverb, which allows us to categorize the remainder of the first constituents as adverbs, since *mal* and *menos* are ambiguous as adjective/adverb and quantifier/adverb, respectively. Unlike in the case of verbal compounds, in the nominals no adverb emerges as much more frequent (13 with *bien/ben*, 14 with *mal*, six with *menos*), and none is preferred in modern compounding.

The nominal constituent is always deverbal and normally derived through suffixation: *bendecir* 'to bless', lit. 'well-say', → *bendición* 'blessing', lit. 'well-saying', *bienestar* 'wellbeing', lit. 'well-be' → *bienestancia* 'wellbeing', *malandar* 'to go badly', lit. 'badly-go' → *malandanza* 'misadventure', lit. 'badly-going', *maldecir* 'to curse', lit. 'badly-say' → *maldecimiento* 'curse', lit. 'badly-saying', *maltraer* 'to mortify', lit. 'badly-bring' → *maltraedor* 'persecutor', lit. 'badly-bringer', *malfacer* 'to do ill', lit. 'badly-do' → *malfechura* 'bad construction', lit. 'badly-doing'. As a consequence, the nominal compounds fall quite neatly into two categories: agentive nominals (*menoscabador* 'one who harms', *maldecidor* 'one who curses') and nomina actionis (*bendición* 'blessing', *bienaventuranza* 'beatitude'). Like the verbs they are related to, several of these nominal compounds come in pairs of opposites: *bendecidor* 'one who blesses' vs. *maldecidor* 'one who curses', *bienquerencia* 'love' vs. *malquerencia* 'dislike', *bienandanza* 'good fortune' vs. *malandanza* 'misfortune'.

4.3.1.2 *Compound structure*

[Adv + N]$_N$ compounds do not result from a process of compounding *per se*. Rather, they are the result of later suffixation on a compounded base, a merge of the verbal head with a nominal head that is overtly expressed by the suffix (16).

(16)
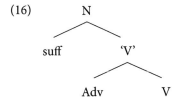

This structure does not affect the internal modification that holds between the verb and its adverbial predicate, nor does it alter the order of the constituents whose compounded structure it nominalizes. Additional evidence for a structure in which nominalization is higher than the compounded constituents is the fact that adverbs do not ever modify nouns in syntax, not even those with eventive meaning: *desplazarse rápidamente* 'to move quickly' → *desplazamiento rápido* 'quick movement', **desplazamiento rápidamente* 'quickly movement'; *ordenar bien* 'organize well' → *buena ordenanza* 'good ordinance', *bien ordenanza 'well ordinance', presentar mal 'to present badly' → mala presentación 'bad presentation', *mal presentación 'badly presentation'.[4]

However, the fact that the adverb and the derived nominal are still both discernible in the [Adv + N]$_N$ structure makes these compounds different from cases such as ropavejero 'seller of old clothes', lit. 'clothes-old-AGT SUFF'. The latter is truly parasynthetic, i.e., it involves simultaneous compounding and suffixation, since ropa vieja 'old clothes', lit. 'clothes old' is not a compound in the sense specified, nor is vejero 'old-AGT SUFF' an attested agentive. In the [Adv + N]$_N$ pattern the nominals exist independently of the compound, which can thus be analyzed as made up by its two constituent parts.

4.3.1.3 Compound meaning

[Adv + N]$_N$ compounds inherit the semantic specialization of their bases. Thus, malquerencia 'ill-will', lit. 'badly-loving' is really a nominalization of the base malquerer 'to wish ill', lit. 'badly-love'. Occasionally, nominalization itself will add more layers of semantic narrowing. Thus, bienaventuranza 'blessing', lit. 'well-adventure' is restricted in use to the religious meaning of the beatitudes of Jesus' Sermon on the Mount.

4.3.2 Diachrony

4.3.2.1 Historical antecedents and comparative data

Deverbative nominal compounds based on the [Adv + V]$_V$ pattern through suffixation are attested in several Indo-European languages such as Sanskrit (Whitney 1941 [1879]: 494–95) and the Baltic languages (Larsson 2002: 211). Again, it is their existence in Latin that is more meaningful for our purposes: BENEFACTUM 'benefit, good deed' (Bader 1962: 301). There are also examples for a variety of Romance languages, although this is not normally discussed in compounding compendia. Consider, for example, Port. bem-aventurança 'happiness', lit. 'good-fortune', malquerença 'ill will', lit. 'badly-loving', Cat. malastrugança 'misfortune', benaventurança 'beatitude', lit. 'well-adventure', Fr. bienveillance 'good will', lit. 'well-willing', malfaisance 'ill will', lit. 'badly-doing', It. benemerenza 'quality of being deserving', lit. 'well-deserving', maldicenza 'slander', lit. 'badly-speaking', Rom. binefăcător 'well-doer'.

Additional evidence for the historical depth of this pattern is that several of the examples in Spanish are only analyzable in the earliest period, later becoming

---

4.   The occasional use of bien 'well' to modify nouns, such as chica bien 'upper class girl', lit. 'girl well' is not a counterargument to this claim. This use of adverbials as nominal modifiers is highly restricted. For one thing, only bien is possible: *un chico mal 'a lower class boy', lit. 'boy badly'. In most dialects bien is impossible in predicative positions: *Es una persona muy bien 'S/he is a very distinguished person', lit. 'S/he is a person very well'. In the most permissive dialects, which do allow it in postverbal position (such as my own), the adjective use of bien 'well' has semantic restrictions, as it can only modify human nominals: una persona bien, *un libro bien,??un perro bien 'a noble person, *a noble book,?? a noble dog', lit. 'a person well, a book well, a dog well'. Finally, it is restricted to postnominal position: *una bien chica 'a well girl'.

semantically opaque and/or structurally fused due to phonetic erosion, loss of the deverbal stem from the lexicon, or both. Consider, for example, *behetría* 'population entitled to choose its own lord', lit. 'well-being', which exists until the present but whose
constituents have lost structural independence, and compare it with its more transparent earlier variants *benefectria, benefactoria, benefactura,* and so on. Note that some of
the early compounds in this pattern drop out of the language altogether (e.g., *bienes-
tança* 'wellbeing', unattested after the 15th century, (17)).

(17)   a.   *mas en cabo finco Antonjo uençudo. ca lo desampararon sus compannas
            assi cuemo omnes que no cataron debdo de derecho nj bien estança. & fue-
            ronse pora Octauiano.*   (c. 1270, Alfonso X, CORDE)
            'But in the end Anthony was vanquished, because he was abandoned by
            his companies and by the men who didn't realize that they owed him a
            debt by law and by wellbeing and they went over to Octavian'.

4.3.2.2 *Frequency and productivity*

The total number of $[Adv + N]_N$ compounds is even smaller than that of its verbal
counterpart (only 46 examples, or 1.3% of the total data). Since this is a secondary pattern, its productivity is limited by its very restricted domain of application. The total
number of $[Adv + N]_N$ compounds remains stable over the years, whereas their relative frequency drops from a high of 7.4% in the earliest period attested to a virtually
negligible 1.1% in contemporary Spanish.

As Table 4.9 shows, the neologistic activity of $[Adv + N]_N$ has been very low over
all the historical periods studied. Starting from a set of inherited forms attested between the 1000s and the 1200s, very few new forms are added over time. At no point
is the percentage of new compounds higher than 11%, and it is often negative, as losses cancel out gains.

Table 4.8 $[Adv + N]_N$ compounds attested by century, as totals and as a percentage of all
compounds

	$[Adv + N]_N$	All compounds	$[Adv + N]_N$ as % of all compounds
1000s–1200s	26	349	7.4
1300s	25	434	5.8
1400s	27	709	3.8
1500s	28	1073	2.6
1600s	25	1237	2.0
1700s	28	1360	2.1
1800s	31	1842	1.7
1900s–2000s	34	3005	1.1
Total	46	3451	1.3

Table 4.9 Productivity of [Adv + N]$_N$ compounds attested by century

	Carried over	Lost	New	Total	Productivity Ratio
1200s	8	(0)	18	26	NA
1300s	26	(3)	2	25	−0.04
1400s	25	(2)	4	27	0.07
1500s	27	(3)	4	28	0.04
1600s	28	(4)	1	25	−0.12
1700s	25	(0)	3	28	0.11
1800s	28	(0)	3	31	0.10
1900s–2000s	31	(0)	3	34	0.09

4.3.2.3 *Inseparability of constituents*

Unlike [Adv + V]$_V$ compounds, these derived compounds never exhibit any evidence of phrasal status. This is because adverbial modification of nominals is impossible, and therefore, the only source for these compounds is the nominalization of their verbal counterpart, with no alternative syntactic route available.

4.3.2.4 *Orthographic representation*

Like their verbal counterparts, the idiosyncratic meaning of these compounds can be conveyed through one-word or two-word spellings virtually through their entire history (as in 18a–c). In other cases, unitary spelling precedes spelling as two words, possibly due to gaps in the data in such a scarcely represented class (18d, e). However, unlike in the case of [Adv + V]$_V$ and [Adv + A]$_A$ compounds, unitary spelling is not needed to ascertain compoundhood, given that adverb-noun are not a licit syntactic combination.

(18)   Orthographic representation of [Adv + N]$_N$ compounds

    a.   *Si alguno [....] fiziere homicidio en eilla, lo que fazer non se puede sin me-*
        nospretio de la fe   (c. 1250, *Vidal Mayor*, CORDE)
        'If anyone commits a homicide in it, which cannot be done without disregard for the faith'

    b.   *Aquesto es establido en menos precio de los usureros*
                                            (1247, *Fueros de Aragón, BNM 458*, CORDE)
        'That is established in spite of usurers'

    c.   *con menos precio de los dogmas de la economía política, la libertad de in-*
        dustria y la competencia que de ella nace son calificadas de cosa detestable
                                          (1843–1844, Antonio Alcalá Galiano, CORDE)
        'in spite of the dogmas of political economy, freedom of industry and the competition that derives from it are held to be detestable'

   d. *Este sant Esidro fue [...] Perseguidor & maltraedor de las heregias. & de los*
       hereges   (c. 1270, Alfonso X, CORDE)
       'This San Isidro was a persecutor and an enemy of heresies and of heretics'

   e. *Et esto quiere dezir que el mal traedor de la sçiençia que es testigo de la*
       neçedat   (1337–1348, Juan Manuel, CORDE)

       'And this means that the enemy of science is a witness for stupidity'

4.3.2.5 *Endocentric and exocentric uses*

All of the compounds in this class are endocentric: once the nominalization process takes place, there is no conversion of the outcome to other word classes. It is true that agentives derived from [Adv + V]$_V$ through the suffixation of -*(d)or* are ambiguous between nominal and adjectival uses (19a, b), but this is not a property linked to the compounding process itself but more generally attributable to the ambiguity of the suffix.

(19) a. *Polyphemo fue un cruelísimo tirano de Sicilia, soberbio y muy menosprecia-*
          dor de los dioses.   (21.05.08, Google)
          'Polyphemus was a very cruel tyrant of Sicily, arrogant and very contemptuous towards the gods'.

      b. *Esa crítica ha sido muy bienhechora, porque representó un sacudimiento.*
                                                                    (21.05.08, Google)
          'That criticism has been very positive, because it meant a shake-up'.

4.4 Relationship between [Adv + V]$_V$, [Adv + A]$_A$, and [Adv + N]$_N$ compounds

Comparison of the patterns [Adv + V]$_V$, [Adv + A]$_A$, and [Adv + N]$_N$ shows that they constitute a family. This is apparent in their parallel forms and morphological relatedness, their meanings and semantic fields, and their history. For instance, all of these compounds show the same preference for the adverbs *bien/mal* as the non-head. Their heads are often derivable from each other, which creates small subsets of compounds with common stems. Their early attestations point to a specialized, semi-learned use in legal and religious texts, although they have generalized quite freely to everyday vocabulary. Although this specialization could simply be an artifice of the types of texts more likely to be preserved from early historical periods, [Adv + X]$_X$ compounds are not as frequent in poetry or fictional prose, genres quite well documented in early texts.

   Total frequencies show the preeminence of adjectivals, which constitute more than half of all the compounds with adverbial non-heads (Table 4.10). Although all classes prefer *mal/bien* 'well/badly' over other adverbs, this preference is clearer in verbal compounds, with adjectival and nominal patterns exhibiting a little more variety (for a similar observation for Latin, cf. Bader 1962: 301). Of the *mal/bien* pair, verbal compounds favor *mal* more markedly, whereas the preference is less categorical in adjectivals and nominals.

Table 4.10 Percentages and totals of adverbial non-heads in [Adv + X]$_X$ compounds

Adverb	[Adv + V]$_V$ (n)	[Adv + A]$_A$ (n)	[Adv + N]$_N$ (n)	Total (n)
mal-	80 (44)	57.6 (83)	58.7 (27)	62.9 (154)
bien-	14.5 (8)	35.1 (52)	26.1 (12)	29.4 (72)
Other	5.5 (3)	6.3 (9)	15.2 (7)	7.7 (19)
Total	100 (55)	100 (144)	100 (46)	100 (245)

In diachronic terms, these compounds are Latin inheritances or early Romance creations. They share a pattern of high early frequency that tapers off over the centuries. Considered as a group, all compounds with adverbial non-heads constitute a sizeable portion of the total compounds up until the 1300s (30%), but by the 20th century they are less than 10% of the total (Table 4.11). Their productivity also exhibits a strikingly similar pattern, with modest early productivity followed, in almost all cases, by ratios of under 10% of new compounds in each century. It should be noted that even the adjectival pattern, the most frequent of the three, is of very marginal productivity in contemporary Spanish.

Table 4.11 Relative frequency of [Adv + X]$_X$ compounds attested by century

	[Adv + V]$_V$	[Adv + A]$_A$	[Adv + N]$_N$	Total freq.
1200s	5.2	20.1	7.4	32.7
1300s	6.0	19.1	5.8	30.9
1400s	5.2	15.2	3.8	24.2
1500s	4.1	10.5	2.6	17.2
1600s	3.5	9.1	2.0	14.6
1700s	3.2	8.2	2.1	13.5
1800s	2.4	6.3	1.7	10.4
1900s–2000s	1.7	3.9	1.1	6.7
Totals	1.6	4.2	1.3	7.1

Table 4.12 Productivity of [Adv + X]$_X$ compounds attested by century

	[Adv + V]$_V$	[Adv + A]$_A$	[Adv + N]$_N$
1200s	NA	NA	NA
1300s	0.31	0.16	−0.04
1400s	0.30	0.23	0.07
1500s	0.16	0.04	0.04
1600s	−0.02	0.00	−0.12
1700s	0.02	−0.01	0.11
1800s	0.02	0.03	0.10
1900s–2000s	0.10	0.11	0.09

The family resemblance among [Adv + V]$_V$, [Adv + A]$_A$, and [Adv + N]$_N$ is underscored by the morphological relationship between their head constituents. Verbal compounds are often the derivational base for the others: *malquerer* 'to wish ill', lit. 'to badly-love' → *malquisto* 'unloved', lit. 'badly-loved' (*quisto*, irregular participle of *querer*); *malquerer* → *malquerencia* 'ill will', lit. 'badly-loving'; *maldecir* 'to curse', lit. 'badly-say' → *maldecidor* 'someone who curses', lit. 'badly-sayer'. As stated earlier, the derivative status of most [Adv + N]$_N$ is clear, since all of those with the adverbs *bien/ mal* 'well/badly' have deverbal nominal heads and meanings directly linked to a [Adv + V]$_V$ compound: *bienquerer* 'to love well, lit. 'well-love' → *bienquerencia* 'loving well', lit. 'well-loving'.

However, [Adv + V]$_V$ compounds cannot always be found in the lexicographical sources for all the [Adv + A]$_A$ compounds. As the examples in (20a, b) show, some of these gaps may be due to the fact that the database lacks compounded verbal bases that did indeed exist in the language, and that can be filled by direct consultation of digital databases such as CORDE. Thus, the verbs *bien oler* 'to smell well', lit. 'well-smell' and *bien aparentar* 'to have a good appearance', lit. 'to well appear' are attested in texts, although they are not listed in the same dictionaries that include *bienoliente* 'perfumed', lit. 'well-smelling' and *bienaparente* 'good-looking', lit. 'well-appearing'.

(20) a. *esta piedra si la meten en el vino fazelo <u>bien oler</u> maravillosamente*
       (ad 1467, *Traducción del Mapa mundi de San Isidro*, CORDE)
       'this stone, if placed in the wine makes it smell well (lit. 'well-smell') beautifully'

   b. *el rey mandó llamar al punto a su físico, que era un hombre atezado y de sombrío semblante, el cual, con venir vestido a la cristiana, <u>bien aparentaba</u> haber nacido en las márgenes del Muluya*
       (1852, Antonio Cánovas del Castillo, CORDE)
       'the king sent immediately for his physician, who was a swarthy and somber-looking man, and who although dressed in Christian clothes, really seemed (lit. 'well-seemed') to have been born on the shores of the Muluya [river in Morocco]'

For other [Adv + A]$_A$ compounds no verbal bases can be found in either lexicographical or textual sources. Thus, *bien tallado* 'well shaped' and *mal agestado* 'with an unpleasant look', lit. 'badly-looking' are not matched anywhere by the compounded verbs *bien tallar* or *mal agestar*.

Additional evidence that the verb is not always the derivational base is the fact that several adjectival compounds are denominal rather than deverbal: *bienfortunado* 'fortunate', lit. 'well-fortunate' (← *fortuna* 'fortune'), *malfamado* 'ill-reputed', lit. 'badly-famed' (← *fama* 'fame'), *malgeniado, malgenioso* 'bad-tempered' (← *genio* 'temper'). Finally, dates of first attestations suggest that verbal compounds do not always precede the others, as one would expect if they were their etymological source. This fact is impossible to establish when the entire set of related forms is present from the earliest period (e.g., *benefacere* 'well-doing', *benefectria* 'protection, well-doing'), but even in the cases in which there are differences in the first attestations, the earliest of the related compounds may be adjectival and nominal as well as verbal: *malcasado* 'unhappily married', lit. 'badly-married' [c. 1240] > *malcasar* 'marry the wrong person', lit. 'badly-marry' [1330–1343]; *menoscabo* 'damage', lit. 'less-end' [c. 1150] > *menoscabado* 'damaged' [c. 1196] > *menoscabar* 'to damage' [c. 1236].

4.5 Summary of chapter

To summarize this chapter, compounds with the structure $[Adv + X]_X$ have an internal structure of adjunction when the head is a verb or an adjective. The much rarer nominal pattern is derived from the others through suffixation. In all cases, the non-head is a manner adverb, predominantly *bien* 'well' or *mal* 'badly'. At least in the earliest periods, the verbal and adjectival patterns are the result of univerbation of juxtaposed phrasal constituents. Around the 1500s, the parallelism between compounds and phrases ceases in the case of $[Adv + V]_V$ compounds, since adverbs can no longer be preposed to the verbs they modify in sentence syntax. For adjectives, this continues to be possible, and the compounded status of $[Adv + A]_A$ can only be ascertained through tests of constituent separability and independence (such as the replacement of *mal/bien* by the comparatives *mejor/peor*).

Historically, all three patterns are inherited from Latin, and exhibit their highest productivity in the earliest part of the period considered. Over time, they became inactive, with a net loss of exponents as older lexemes with this pattern dropped out of the language, or as their constituents became unrecognizable as independent lexemes.

CHAPTER 5

Endocentric compounds
with nominal non-heads

Maniatar, manirroto, maniobra

This chapter continues with the treatment of head-final compounding by focusing on three patterns whose non-head is a nominal (Table 5.1). Among them, the most productive are adjectival $[N + A]_A$ patterns. There is also a truly archaic verbal $[N + V]_V$ pattern, with very few examples and virtually no present productivity. Although some of its exponents are related to the $[N + A]_A$ pattern, it has not shared its productivity or evolution. The last head-final pattern is $[N + N]_N$, whose nominal head on the right is related to the verbal or adjectival classes mentioned above. For $[N + N]_N$ head-final patterns whose head is not deverbal, readers are directed to Chapter 6, where those patterns are explored together with their head-initial counterparts.

5.1 The pattern $[N + V]_V$: *Maniatar*

In this endocentric pattern the verbal constituent to the right is the head of the structure, whereas the non-head noun is placed to its left. In its endocentric uses, the resulting compound is a verb, with the nominal acting as an incorporated complement. This pattern has two historical layers. The first one is older; it exhibits nominal incorporation and was inherited from Latin through early Romance. The second layer is modern and owes some of its productivity to the verbalization of $[N + A]_A$ compound bases. In much of the discussion, these two classes must be kept apart because they differ in structure and meaning as well as in stylistic restrictions.

Table 5.1 Endocentric head-final compounds with nominal non-heads

Pattern	Example	Found in →
$[N + V]_V$	*maniatar* 'tie by the hand', lit. 'hand-tie'	Chapter 5, Section 5.1
Integral $[N + A]_A$	*manirroto* 'generous', lit. 'hand-broken'	Chapter 5, Section 5.2.1
Deverbal $[N + A]_A$	*insulinodependiente* 'insulin-dependent'	Chapter 5, Section 5.2.3
Deverbal $[N + N]_N$	*maniobra* 'maneuver', lit. 'hand-work'	Chapter 5, Section 5.3

5.1.1   Structure

5.1.1.1   *Constituents*

In the earliest compounds (before 1500) the nominal is normally a part of the body, usually *mano* 'hand' or some alternative combination form (*mamparar, manparar* 'to protect', lit. 'hand stop', *manutener, mantener* 'to support, to sustain', lit. 'hand-hold'), but also *cabo* 'head' (in *caboprender* 'include, comprehend', lit. 'head-grasp', *cabtener, captener* 'conserve, protect', lit. 'head-keep'). It should be noted that in modern Spanish *cabo* has been replaced by *cabeza* in the anatomical sense, whereas is continues to be used with other meanings (e.g., the end of something, the tip of a rope, etc.). As Klingebiel (1989) notes, *mano* and *cabo* refer to the two most human parts of the body, and are often used figuratively to refer to the entire person. *Mano* can stand for power (*mamparar* 'to protect'), work (*maniobra* 'maneuver'), and ritual gestures (*mancuadra* 'oath', lit. 'hand-square'); *cabo* can mean end, chapter, paragraph, or legal head of the household. All through history *mano* continues to be predominant in this compound subset (12 out of the 37 compounds). Sometimes it is a constituent in its own right, making a clear semantic contribution to the whole (*manuscribir* 'to handwrite'), whereas at other times the verb is derived from a previously compounded base and the contribution of the nominal to the overall meaning is blurred: *maniobrar* 'to maneuver', lit. 'hand-work' (< *maniobra* 'maneuver', lit. 'hand-labor'), *mancomunar* 'to put together resources', lit. 'hand-common' (< *mancomún* 'agreement', lit. 'hand-common').

In compounds created after 1500, new parts of the body are added: *aliquebrar*, 'to break the wings [of a bird]' lit. 'to wing-break' [1654], *cabizbajar* 'to lower one's head', lit. 'head-lower' [1605], *perniquebrar* 'to break the legs', lit. 'leg-break' [1536–1538]. These admittedly infrequent examples are related to earlier or simultaneous [N + A]$_A$ compounds, i.e., *aliquebrado* 'with broken wings', lit. 'wing-broken' [1654], *cabizbajo*, 'depressed', lit. 'head-lowered' [1514–42], *perniquebrado* 'with a broken leg', lit. 'leg-broken' [1554]. In the more modern compounds there are a few non-anatomical expansions: *radiodifundir* 'to broadcast by radio', lit. 'radio-broadcast', *fotocopiar* 'to xerox', lit. 'photo-copy'.

The first constituent may appear in two morphological guises, i.e. as a full-fledged noun complete with base and word class marker (*man-o*), or as a combining stem, which may be bare (*man-*), accompanied by combining vowels (*mani-, manu-*), or entirely unique to these forms (*cabiz-*, cf. *cabez-a* 'head'). The most frequent and only truly productive pattern combines stems, normally with a linking vowel: *maniatar* 'to tie by the hands', lit. 'hand-tie', [1527–1550], *pintiparar* 'compare', lit. 'spot-lift', [1597–1645], *rabiatar* 'to tie by the tail', lit. 'tail-tie' [1803]. Compounds created by combining full-fledged nouns are archaic and infrequent: *caboprender* 'include', lit. 'head-hold' [1252–1270]. In a small subset, the nominal and the combining form are indistinguishable, which means that the first constituent can be interpreted as either a full noun or a stem (*radio-difundir* or *radi-o-difundir*; consider the alternations *radio-cita* ~ *radi-ecita, radio-actividad* ~ *radi-actividad*, which show the ambiguous status of the final -*o* in *radio*).

A variety of different verbal bases can participate in this type of compounding, by undergoing common structural processes that will be discussed in the next section.

5.1.1.2 *Compound structure*

The head in these compounds is the verb, since it is responsible for the grammatical category of the whole, while the non-head nominal can be an incorporated direct object or an instrument. In the first situation, the verb itself must have one or two internal arguments to begin with. The incorporation of the noun absorbs the canonical case that the verb would otherwise assign, so that transitives become intransitives, and in ditransitives the indirect object is promoted to accusative status. Thus, for example: *el gato echó el pelo* 'the cat lost its hair' → *el gato pelechó* 'the cat molted', lit. 'hair-lost'; and, more infrequently, *el niño le quebró las alas a un loro* 'the child broke the wings of a parrot' → *el niño aliquebró un loro* 'the child wing-broke a parrot'.[1] If the incorporated nominal is a direct object, it has a part-whole relationship with the newly promoted indirect object (*aliquebrar al loro* 'to wing-break the parrot', *'ala del loro* 'wing of the parrot'). Notice that incorporation is only possible when the nominal is incapable of bearing the case assigned by the verb, as would be the case when it appears in stem form (1b), whereas if it appears in full form, it receives case *in situ* (1a).

(1) a.

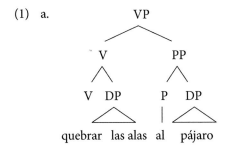

b.

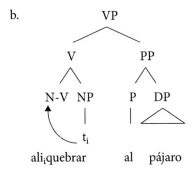

---

1. Note that if the direct object were definite, it would require the personal *a*: *El niño aliquebró al loro*, lit. 'The child wing-broke PERS a-the parrot'. This is part of a complex relationship between accusatives and datives in Spanish which manifests itself independently of compounding. Consider, for example the licit alternation between *El niño vio el/al perro* 'The child saw the dog', and the impossibility of doing the same with *El niño vio a Juan/*El niño vio Juan*.

When the incorporated nominal is an instrumental, no theta roles are absorbed in the process: *escribió el documento a mano* → *manuscribió el documento* 'he wrote the document by hand', lit. 'he hand-wrote the document', *difundieron la noticia por radio* → *radiodifundieron la noticia* 'they broadcast the news on the radio', lit. 'they radio-broadcast the news'. Unlike in the cases of object incorporation, in instrumental incorporation no part-whole relationship holds (*radiodifundir la noticia* 'to radio-broadcast the news', **radio de la noticia* 'radio of the news'). This suggests that in cases of object incorporation, the lower nominal governed by the PP is in fact one of the members of an integral small clause (Hornstein et al. 1994). This small clause contains the whole (*el loro*) and its parts (*las alas*), out of which the latter constituent is raised into the first argument position, while the whole remains downstairs. Instrumental incorporation lacks this small clause structure under the PP, which accounts for the differences between the two types of structures, a matter that deserves further exploration.

The diagrams in (2a-c) contrast the syntactic phrasal structure *difundir la noticia por radio* 'to broadcast the news over the radio' and the incorporated structure *radiodifundir la noticia* 'radio-broadcast the news'. They differ only in the presence of an overt preposition as the head of PP. If the preposition is present, the lower nominal must appear in its full form, with a word class marker head, allowing it to absorb case and preventing further movement. By contrast, if there is no overt preposition the lower nominal must appear in its bare form, which cannot be assigned case (2b). Devoid of case, the nominal will incorporate, first into the head of P, and later, into the head of the verb, through head-to-head adjunction (2c). This process is in line with Baker's (1988) proposal that if a nominal complement is not assigned case, as an alternative to satisfy its visibility conditions it must incorporate as a modifier into the head to which it acts as a complement.

(2)   a.

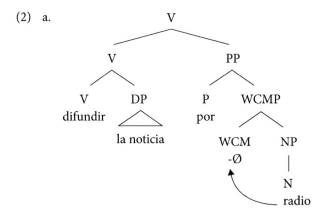

b.

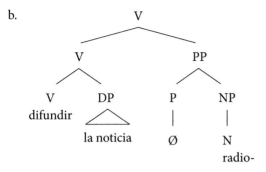

c.

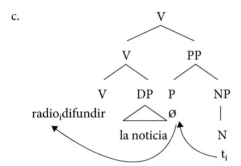

5.1.1.3   Compound meaning

Because they represent different historical depths, [N + V]$_V$ compounds have undergone different degrees of semantic drift. Most compounds created before the 1500s are
highly lexicalized and semantically opaque. Thus, for example, *mantener* 'to support' is
not synonymous with *tener con la mano* 'hold with the hand', and *zaherir* < *fazferir* 'to
insult' is not synonymous with *ferir la faz* 'injure the face'. Strictly speaking, these compounds are so only from a historical, not synchronic, perspective. By contrast, compounds formed after the 1500s tend to be formally and semantically transparent, i.e.,
they have two distinct constituents, each of which makes a distinct semantic contribution: *pelechar* 'molt', lit. 'hair-lose', *fotocopiar* 'xerox', lit. 'photo-copy'. Note that both
direct objects and instrumental adjuncts can be incorporated with or without infix-
ation of a linking vowel: *pel-echar, man-i̯-atar* (object + V), *man-tener, man-i̯-obrar*
(adjunct + V).

5.1.2   Diachrony

5.1.2.1   *Historical antecedents and comparative data*

According to Kastovsky, compounds combining nominal modifiers and verbal
heads did not occur in Indo-European, and were rare in the daughter languages
(2009: 338). There are certainly some examples of the compounding pattern
[N + V]$_V$ in Latin, such as ANIMADVERTERE 'blame', lit. 'spirit-pay attention' and

TERGIVERSARI 'hesitate', lit. 'back-turn' (Fruyt 1990: 177 et passim; Oniga 1992: 102). The pattern appears in Spanish in a number of learned compounds, such as *pacificare* (*pacifikare*, LHP) 'pacify', lit. 'peace-make', whose constituents were no longer free-standing lexemes. Only *manutenere*, by virtue of its non-learned transmission, offered a viable model for further developments in Romance (Klingebiel 1989). Its reflexes in Catalan, Provençal, and Occitan have been extensively studied by Klingebiel (1986; 1988; 1989), with the result that this is one of the best historically and synchronically described compounding patterns in Western Romance. It is also mentioned in synchronic panoramic accounts of Catalan compounding (Hualde 1992: 364; Mascaró 1986: 68), and more extensively in Gràcia & Fullana (1999) and Adelman (2002).

Beyond the languages documented by Klingebiel, the pattern $[N + V]_V$ is very restricted in Romance. Judging from the information on panoramic studies of compounding in Portuguese and Romanian, it is not present in those languages. It also receives only a passing reference for French in Zwanenburg (1992: 224), and it is specifically labeled as unproductive in Italian by Scalise (1992: 177), who provides examples such as *manomettere* 'emancipate [a slave]', lit. 'hand-put' and *crocefiggere* 'crucify', lit. 'cross-fix'. In Spanish, first attestations of the use of $[N + V]_V$ come very early in time (3).

(3)   Early attestations of $[N + V]_V$ compounds in Spanish

    a.   *Et si mester non ouiere & aquel a quien deuiere la debda lo quisiere tener, <u>mantengalo</u>, & siruasse del quanto meior pudiere.*

                                (c. 1196, *Fuero de Soria*, CORDE)

        'and if he [the debtor] should have no need, and the creditor to whom he owes the debt wants to have him, he should support (lit. 'hand-have') him and use him any way he wants'.

    b.   *non podiendo en ssí sser cabopreso nin ençerrado por ninguna manera, quiso <u>caboprender</u> e ençerrar al ssu ffijo Ihesu Cristo, queriendo que rreçibiese nuestra carne*   (c. 1270, Alfonso X, *Setenario*, CORDE)

        'Not being in himself limited or closed in in any way, he [God] wished to limit and enclose his son Jesus Christ, giving him our flesh'

5.1.2.2 *Frequency and productivity*

$[N + V]_V$ compounds constitute a rarity in Spanish compounding all through history, totaling 37 examples in the data (1.1%). Unlike the head-final patterns seen in Chapter 4, they never exhibit very high frequencies, their percentages hovering around 2% (Table 5.2). This is true whether frequency is measured in absolute terms or relative to the total number of compounds.

The pattern's productivity, measured as the ratio of new compounds to the totals for each period, remains modest for the entirety of the timespan examined (Table 5.3). For all centuries, most compounds are inherited from the preceding stages. By

Table 5.2 $[N + V]_V$ compounds attested by century, as totals and as a percentage of all compounds

	$[N + V]_V$	All compounds	$[N + V]_V$ as % of all compounds
1000s–1200s	10	349	2.9
1300s	9	434	2.1
1400s	9	709	1.3
1500s	13	1073	1.2
1600s	15	1237	1.2
1700s	16	1360	1.2
1800s	21	1842	1.1
1900s–2000s	29	3005	1.0
Total	37	3451	1.1

Table 5.3 Productivity of $[N + V]_V$ compounds attested by century

	Carried over	Lost	New	Total	Productivity Ratio
1200s	3	(0)	7	10	NA
1300s	10	(1)	0	9	−0.11
1400s	9	(1)	1	9	0.00
1500s	9	(1)	5	13	0.31
1600s	13	(2)	4	15	0.13
1700s	15	(2)	3	16	0.06
1800s	16	(0)	5	21	0.24
1900s–2000s	21	(1)	9	29	0.28

contrast, few of these compounds are lost over the centuries, evidence of the pattern's stability.

5.1.2.3 Inseparability of constituents

In the majority of $[N + V]_V$ compounds, the first constituent appears in bound form. It follows that it cannot ever be moved or separated from the second by the insertion of extraneous materials: *aliquebrar* 'wing-break' vs. **quebrar ali*; *aliquebró muchos pájaros* 'he broke the wings of many birds', lit. 'he wing-broke many birds' vs. **ali muchos pájaros quebró*. No counterexamples were found in the database.

5.1.2.4 Orthographic representation

$[N + V]_V$ compounds are spelled as a unit, given that the first term normally appears as a bare nominal stem, a form that cannot be used in isolation. There are very few exceptions to this, mostly in the earlier periods (4a, b).

(4)   a.   *Et todas estas cartas ssobredichas en esta ley an nonbre generales por que <u>cabo</u>
            <u>prenden</u> en ssi muchas cosas.*   (ad 1260, *Espéculo de Alfonso X*, CORDE)
            'And all these charters mentioned earlier in this law are called general
            because they include (lit. 'head-hold') many things within'.

       b.   *Su espada y sus consejos fueron bien útiles [....] al licenciado Espinosa en las
            guerras peligrosas y obstinadas que los Españoles tuvieron que <u>man tener</u>
            con las tribus belicosas situadas al oriente de Panamá*
                                            (1832, José Manuel Quintana, CORDE).
            'His sword and advice were very useful [...] to the esquire Espinosa in the
            dangerous and stubborn wars that the Spaniards had to maintain
            (lit. 'hand hold') with the bellicose tribes on the east of Panama'

5.1.2.5   *Endocentric and exocentric uses*

All [N + V]$_V$ compounds in this class are verbal, and thus, endocentric.

5.1.3   Special cases

Several compounds in the [N + V]$_V$ class are not created through straightforward
nominal incorporation to a verbal head. Alternative formation routes include concatenation of two nominal or adjectival bases that are then verbalized: *salpimentar* 'to
add salt and pepper', lit. 'salt-pepper-v SUFF' (< *sal* 'salt' + *pimienta* 'pepper'); *calosfriarse*
'to have chills, to feel hot and cold', lit. 'hot-cold-v SUFF' (< *calor* 'heat' + *frío* 'cold'). In
spite of their concatenative base, these compounds are still amenable to an alternative
analysis as [N + V]: *salpimentar* ← *sal* 'salt' + *pimentar* 'to pepper'. Another possible
mechanism for the formation of [N + V]$_V$ compounds is through the addition of two
concatenated verbal bases, only the latter of which appears with its verbal ending:
salar 'to salt' + *prensar* 'to press' > *salpresar* 'to salt and press', lit. 'salt-press'. Finally,
some compounds in this class are the result of verbal suffixation to compounds from
other categories: *mancomunar* 'to put together resources', lit. 'hand-common'
(< *mancomún* 'association', lit. 'hand-common'), *alzaprimar* 'to lever up -v SUFF', lit
'lift-press-v-SUFF' (<*alzaprima* 'lever', lit. 'lift-press').

5.2   The integral and deverbal [N + A]$_A$ patterns

By far the most frequent head-final compounding pattern with a nominal non-head has
the structure [N + A]$_A$. The adjectival constituent to the right is the head of the structure,
while the non-head noun appears to its left (cf. Núñez Cedeño 1992: 134; Rainer 1993:
287, where these compounds are classified as exocentric). When used endocentrically,
the resulting compound is an adjective, with the nominal acting as a secondary predicate.
This pattern has two main subpatterns, which I shall call integral and deverbal.

The **integral** pattern, which is responsible for over 80% of the total number of [N + A]$_A$ compounds quantified, is made up of a nominal that denotes a body part and an adjective that modifies it: *carirredondo* 'round-faced', lit. 'face-round', *manilargo* 'generous [long-handed]', lit. 'hand-long'. The resulting adjective is used to modify a noun that has the body part in question as its inalienable possession. Thus, *carirredondo* is an adjective that can be used as a predicate to apply to someone who has a round face; *manilargo* to someone who has long hands, and so on. However, the syntactic dependencies are reversed in the compound: it is the adjective that constitutes the head, whereas the nominal acts as a secondary predicate that restricts its applicability, in a structural relationship traditionally referred to as the Greek accusative.

The **deverbal** subtype, which constitutes under 20% of all [N + A]$_A$ compounds, involves adjectives that are either verbal participles (*letraherido* 'literature lover', lit. 'letter-hurt', *viandante* 'pedestrian', lit. 'way-goer') or derived through suffixation from a verbal base (e.g., *vasodilatador* 'blood vessel-dilator' <*vasodilatador* 'dilate' vessels' lit. vessel-dilate'). The nominal can discharge a theta role assigned by the verb, or it may act as an adjunct (instrumental, locative, etc.). Deverbal compounds can be distinguished from integrals in that the noun internal to the compound and the noun to which the compound acts as a predicate do not hold a part-whole relationship. Thus, whereas *el hombre carilindo* 'the pretty-faced man', lit. 'the man face-pretty' implies *el hombre tiene la cara linda* 'the man has a pretty face', it does not follow from *el hombre vascohablante* 'the Basque-speaking man', lit. 'the man Basque-speaking', that **el hombre tiene el vasco hablante* 'the man has the Basque speaking'. Given this clear-cut structural difference, in each section that follows these two types of [N + A]$_A$ compounds are considered independently.

5.2.1 Structure of integral [N + A]$_A$ compounds: *Manirroto*

5.2.1.1 *Compound constituents*

It has been noted before (García Lozano 1993; Rainer 1993: 289; Zacarías Ponce de León 2009) that there are several semantic preferences and formal constraints on the nominal constituents in [N + A]$_A$ compounds. Semantically, they are limited to physical features, so that the resulting adjectives can only act as predicates of nominals that contain the feature in question (hence the name 'integral'). The body parts are limited to those of humans (*barbiespeso* 'thick-bearded', lit. 'beard-thick'), animals such as bovines (*cornicorto* 'short-horned', lit. 'horn-short'), equines (*boquimuelle* 'soft-mouthed', lit. 'mouth-soft'), birds (*alirrojo* 'red-winged', lit. 'wing-red'), and primates (*cariblanco* 'white-faced', lit. 'face-white'). A small number apply to common types of crops (*arisblanco* 'white-bearded [of wheat]', lit. 'edge-white', *granigrueso* 'thick-grained', lit. 'grain-thick'), and an even smaller number refer to inanimate geometric bodies (*troncocónico* 'with a conical body', lit. 'trunk-conical'). Apparent exceptions to the inalienable restriction are *paso* 'step', *capa* 'cape', *falda* 'skirt', and *franja* 'stripe' (e.g., *pasicorto* 'short-stepped', lit. 'step-short', *capipardo* 'poor peasant [brown-caped]', lit. 'cape-brown', *faldicorta* 'wearing a short skirt', lit. 'skirt-short', *franjirrojo* 'red-striped [of a soccer team]', lit. 'stripe-red'). However, these nouns still relate to an outward physical property, if not directly to the body.

An additional restriction is that not all body parts are possible first constituents, but only those that designate visible distinguishing features: *alicorto* 'short-winged', lit. 'wing-short', *boquiconejuno* 'cleft-lipped', lit. 'mouth-harelike', *dorsirrojo* 'red-backed', lit. 'back-red'. No examples are recorded with parts such as *seso* 'brain', *corazón* 'heart', or *pulmón* 'lung', although perfectly intelligible examples can be constructed: **sesiblando* 'soft-brained', lit. 'brain-soft' **corazoniduro* 'hard-hearted', lit. 'heart-hard' **pulmonigrande* 'large-lunged', lit. 'lung-large'. It is possible to find compounds with *ventri-* 'belly', in which the word is interpreted as the surface (e.g., *ventrinegro* 'black-bellied', lit. 'belly-black', *ventriblanco* 'red-bellied', lit. 'belly-white'), but not with the meaning of 'gut' (**ventrilleno* 'full-bellied', lit. 'belly-full'). The only apparent exception found in the database is *carniseco* 'thin [dry-fleshed]', lit. 'flesh-dry', which can still be understood as an external feature, since it refers to a property that is noticeable through the skin.

There are also formal constraints on the nominal constituent of integral compounds, such as their syllabic structure. Out of 56 recorded nominal stems in the database, only ten are shorter or longer than a two-syllable foot. Consider the one-syllable stems *casc-/cazc-* 'hoof' (*cascalbo* 'white-hooved', lit. 'hoof-white', *cazcorvo* 'curved-hooved'), *coll-* 'throat' (*collalbo* 'white-throated', lit. 'throat-white'), *cul-* 'buttocks' (*culcosido* 'badly sewn, patched together', lit. 'buttocks-sewn'), *faz-* 'face' (*fazferido* 'insulted', lit. 'face-hurt'), *man/mam-* 'hand' (*manvacío* 'empty-handed', lit. 'hand-empty'), *test-* 'head' (*testerido* 'crazy', lit. 'head-hurt'), and *toz-* 'head' (*tozalbo* 'white-headed', lit. 'head-white'). By contrast, *oreji-* 'ear' (*orejisano* 'not earmarked [of cattle]', lit. 'ear-healthy'), *espaldi-* 'back' (*espalditendido* 'fallen on the back', lit. 'back-fallen'), and *cabeci-* 'head' (*cabeciduro* 'hard-headed', lit. 'head-hard') are the only stems with three syllables. These odd-syllable stems are responsible for relatively few compounds each. By comparison, consider *cari-* 'face', which appears in 34 compounds, *barbi-* 'beard', present in 27, or *boqui-* 'mouth', in 25.

Additional evidence of the two-syllable preference is the fact that several of the abovementioned anomalous stems have more productive bisyllabic allomorphs: *casqui-* 'hoof' (*casquiblando* 'soft-hooved', lit. 'hoof-soft'), *culi-* 'buttocks' (*culibajo* 'with a low rump', lit. 'rump-low'), *cabiz-/cabez-* (*cabizbajo* 'dejected', lit. 'head-low'), *mani-* (*manirroto* 'generous', lit. 'hand-broken'). Moreover, occasionally a long stem is clipped to fit into a bisyllabic foot: *aris-* from *arista* 'grain beard', in *arisnegro* 'black-bearded [of wheat]', lit. 'beard-black'. As noted by García Lozano (1993: 208), only the overwhelming preference for bisyllabic stems can be satisfactorily adduced to explain the absence of numerous possible external physical features that would fit the semantic requirements of the compound pattern, such as *costilla* 'rib' or *piel* 'skin'.

Another formal constraint on the nominal stem is a preference for an open second syllable: *alicorto* 'short-winged', lit. 'wing-short', *carilargo* 'long-faced', lit. 'face-long', *cuellicorto* 'short-necked', lit. 'neck-short', *puntiagudo* 'pointy', lit. 'tip-sharp'. There are very few closed syllables, among which figure *faz-* 'face', *nariz-* 'nose', *cabez/cabiz-* 'head', *casc/cazc-* 'hoof', *aris-* 'grain beard'. In the diachronic sections we explore the historical dimension of these formal preferences.

The nominal constituent may appear in two different forms. In the first and most frequent configuration, it is a bare stem without its word class marker (WCM), which may or may not be accompanied by a linking vowel: *cul<u>c</u>osido* 'badly sewn, patched together', lit. 'buttocks-sewn' vs. *cul<u>i</u>bajo* 'with a low rump', lit. 'rump-low'. The vowel is not inserted simply to improve the phonotactic structure of the word, as evidenced by examples such as *cul<u>i</u>alto* 'with a high tail', lit. 'butt-tall' (cf. **culalto*). In the second alternative, the nominal appears in full form, complete with its word class marker: *<u>boc</u>arroto* 'talkative', lit. 'mouth-broken', *<u>nariz</u> romo* 'flat-nosed', lit. 'nose-flat'. In this case, it may also bear number inflection, although this option is marginal and histori-cally restricted: *<u>orejas</u> caído* 'with low ears', lit. 'ears-fallen' (cf. also the diachronic dis-cussion in Section 5.2.2.5).

The adjectival constituent in integral $[N + A]_A$ compounds may also have different types of morphological structure. It may be a simple stem: *boqui<u>blando</u>* 'of soft mouth [of a horse], lit. 'mouth-soft', *boqui<u>dulce</u>* 'of soft mouth [of a horse]', lit. 'mouth-sweet', *boqui<u>rrojo</u>* 'red-mouthed', lit. 'mouth-red'. It can also be structurally complex, if it is obtained through derivation from a nominal or verbal base: *boqui<u>conejuno</u>* 'with a cleft palate', lit. 'mouth-rabbit-ADJ SUFF',(← *conejo* 'rabbit') *boqui<u>hundido</u>* 'sunken-mouthed', lit. 'mouth-sunken' (← *hundir* 'to sink'), *caridoliente* 'showing pain', lit. 'face-hurting' (← *doler* 'to hurt').

5.2.1.2 *Compound structure*

Compounds of the type $[N + A]_A$ are related to phrasal structures such as those under-lined in (5). As evidence, note that all those phrases could be replaced by existing or potential compounds: *boquirrasgado* 'slit-mouthed', lit. 'mouth-slit', *boquiabierto* 'open-mouthed', lit. 'mouth-open', *bracilargo* 'long-armed', lit. 'arm-long'. The unacceptability of *bigoticerdoso* 'thick-mustached', lit. 'moustache-thick', *miradihosco* 'of sullen look', lit. 'look-sullen' and *coloripurpúreo* 'purple colored', lit. 'color-purple' is due to the structural and semantic restrictions discussed earlier.

(5) *un gigantón, <u>hosco de mirada, cerdoso de bigotes, rasgado y muy abierto de boca, purpúreo de color</u> y muy <u>largo de brazos</u>*

(1878, José María de Pereda, CORDE)

'a giant, diffident of look, thick of moustache, slit and open of mouth, purple of color, and very long of arms'

Unlike the compounds, the phrasal structure allows for independent modification of the two constituents (*muy abierto de boca* 'with a very open mouth', lit. 'very open of mouth', vs. **bracimuylargo* 'id.'). It also permits head coordination (*rasgado y muy abierto de boca* 'with mouth split and very open', lit. 'split and very open of mouth' vs. **boquirrasgadiabierto* 'id.').

Both in the phrses in (5) and in the compound, the adjective constituent is the head. For example, if used as a predicate to an external noun, the adjective exhibits full concord in number and, when applicable, in gender: *hombre carirredondo* 'round-faced man', lit. 'man-MASC SG face-round-MASC SG', *novilla corniancha* 'wide-horned heifer', lit. 'heifer-FEM SG horn-wide-FEM SG'. The compound-internal noun is therefore not the head: *carirredondo*-MASC vs. *cara*-FEM; *corniancha*-FEM vs. *cuerno*-MASC. By contrast, the semantic relationship between the two constituents is in conflict with the compound's headedness. For example, in *carirredondo* 'round-headed', lit. 'head-round' there is a modifying relationship between *car-* 'face' and *redond-* 'round'. The structural challenge is how to represent these conflicting dependencies simultaneously.

This is a complex matter, for which I can only provide a simplified account here. The explanation will make use of the fact that there is a semantic parallelism between the compound *carirredondo* 'round-faced', lit. 'face-round', and the syntactic phrase *redondo de cara* 'with a round face', lit. 'round of face'. In line with a long tradition, I propose that both of these structures have an underlying small clause (SC in the diagrams), which establishes a predicative relationship between the noun and the modifier. Following Stowell (1983), small clauses are defined as tenseless predications. In the cases at hand, the small clause is embedded in a prepositional or partitive phrase (PP).

(6)   a.

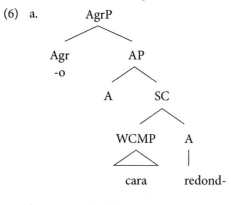

b.

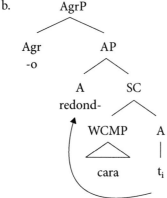

c.

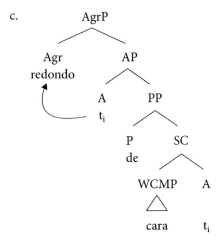

In a syntactic phrase such as *redondo de cara* 'with a round face', lit. 'round of face', an adjectival head selects the lower small clause, which contains the nominal in its full form (with WCM) and its adjectival predicate (6a). This adjective raises out of the small clause, by head-to-head movement, into the higher adjectival node, and then into the agreement phrase (AgrP) (6b, c). However, because only verbs and prepositions can assign case to nominals directly (Chomsky 1981), the preposition *de* must be inserted between the adjective head and the lower nominal in the SC. This late *de*-insertion is generally assumed when nouns act as complements to other nouns or adjectives, which can theta-mark them but not satisfy their case requirements.

The same structure is involved in the internal structure of the compound, with the adjective from the small clause raising to the adjectival position outside the small clause (7a, b). However, in this case the PP head is a linking element -*i*-, a type of particle we will assume does not discharge case. The lower nominal can therefore not appear in its full form, but as a bare N, *car*- 'face'. Devoid of case, the nominal will rise into the head of P and incorporate; however, the noun + linking vowel complex must further incorporate into the predicate through head-to-head adjunction, so that it becomes a sort of modifier (7c–e). This process is in line with Baker's (1988) proposal that if a nominal complement is not assigned case, then it must incorporate to the head to which it acts as a complement, as an alternative way to satisfy its visibility.

(7) a.

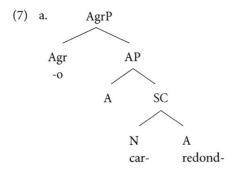

b.

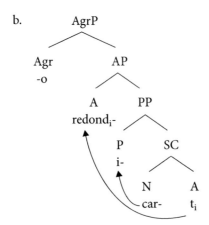

c.

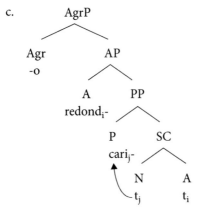

d.

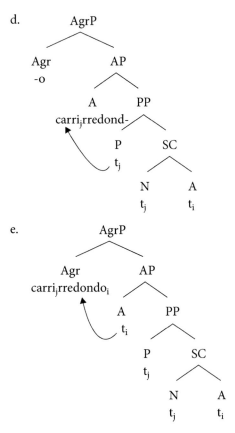

e.

Positing an underlying small clause is necessary to account for some restrictions in these structures. Small clauses are predicative structures, and as such, involve a single predicate. This accounts well for the fact that only one adjective may participate in both the syntactic construction and the compounded structure presented: *redondo de cara* 'round of face', *carirredondo* 'round-faced', lit. 'face-round'. If we were to propose that the noun and adjective are a head and an adjunct modifier, then this would predict that both the structure *redondo de cara* and the compound *carirredondo* could involve more than one modifier, as there is normally no limit to how many adjunctions can apply to a given head: *bonita cara redonda* 'beautiful round face', lit. 'beautiful face round', *bonita cara redonda morena* 'beautiful round dark face', lit. 'beautiful face round dark'. In the structure we are considering this is not the case. For example, whereas *niño de cara redonda* 'child with a round face', lit. 'child of face round', and *niño redondo de cara* lit. 'child round of face', are synonymous, *niño de cara redonda feliz* 'child with a happy round face', and *niño redondo de cara feliz* 'round child with a happy face' are not. In other words, only the SC predicate can undergo raising, whereas an adjunct cannot. Similarly, *niño de cara redonda feliz* has no compounded equivalent (*niño carirredondofeliz*). Assuming the existence of a small clause restricts the structure to one head and one non-head constituent, making the right predictions about both the phrasal and the compounded structures.

A final observation is in order: once the compound adjective has been formed, it holds a part-whole relationship with the external argument it modifies. In other words, there is a part-whole relationship between *niño* and *cara redonda*, on the one hand, and an argument-predicate relationship between *cara* and *redonda*, on the other. This suggests that the starting point of the predication with an integral adjective compound is also through a small clause, specifically, the so-called integral construction (Hornstein et al. 1994). However, this matter goes beyond the confines of compound formation, and will not be dealt with here.

5.2.1.3 *Compound meaning*

The types of semantic restrictions on the constituents discussed previously result in a pattern whose primary function is the external physical description of animates. From its earliest attestations in the 1200s, the pattern has been used in technical registers to describe humans and cattle, in the latter case both for work (livestock raising) and play (horse breeding and racing, bullfighting). More recently, its use in zoological nomenclature has given it a new vitality, especially in ornithology.

The meaning of these compounds is often literal, but there are also examples of metaphoric extension. In these cases, the semantic contribution of each constituent is blurred, and the compound can no longer be said to be a *bona fide* integral, since it will fail the usual identification test: *el hombre alicaído* 'the depressed [wing-droopy] man' → **el hombre tiene alas (caídas)* 'the man has droopy wings' (in the literal meaning). Some examples of semantic evolution will be discussed in the historical sections.

5.2.2 Diachrony of integral compounds

5.2.2.1 *Historical antecedents and comparative data*

Integral $[N + A]_A$ compounds have various counterparts in Indo-European patterns. Thus, there are integral compounds involving parts of the body, both in Sanskrit (e.g., *ugrá-bāhu* 'strong armed') and Greek (e.g., *ροδο-δάκτυλος* 'rodo-dáktylos, rose-fingered') (Fruyt 2005: 273), but unlike Spanish, their constituents appear in the order A + N. In Latin it is also the A + N order that prevails in descriptive adjectival compounds (e.g., MAGN-ANIM-US 'generous', lit. 'great-spirit SUFF', ALBI-CAPILLUS 'white-haired', lit. 'white hair'). The first constituent can be a numeral, a prefix, or even another noun: BI-CORN-IS 'two-horned', lit. 'two-horn-SUFF', IM-BERB-IS 'beardless', lit. 'PREF-beard-SUFF'. In other words, Latin exhibits compounds of a similar overall structure and semantics, but the difference in word order suggests that Spanish did not inherit the pattern itself from its ancestor.

In support of this hypothesis, note that few languages in Romance exhibit productive inherited adjectival patterns, either of the $[A + N + suff]_A$ or the $[N + A]_A$ structure. Thus, for example, there are no references to $[N + A]_A$ compounds in descriptions of Portuguese, French, or Romanian. Italian examples are provided in Dardano

(1988: 53) but not in Scalise (1992), which seems to suggest that in this language they are not productive either. Catalan is the only other Romance language that behaves like Spanish in terms of [N + A]$_A$ compounding. A [N + A]$_A$ pattern is mentioned in Gràcia & Fullana (1999: 247–49). Hualde (1992: 364) and Mascaró (1986: 64) not only include it but distinguish integral compounds from their deverbal counterparts, as I have here. However, Spanish and Catalan differ in terms of the morphological structure of the compound constituents. Whereas in Spanish compounds the nominal non-head generally appears in stem form, in Catalan it is indistiguishable from the singular lexeme: *un ocell alallarg* 'a long-winged bird', lit. 'a bird-MASC SG wing-FEM SG-long-MASC SG', *un home camacurt* 'a short-legged man', lit. 'a man-MASC SG leg-FEM SG short-MASC SG' (Gràcia & Fullana 1999: 248). This issue will be taken up in Section 5.2.2.5.

In Spanish, the first attestations appear quite early in the database, but they are not as early or as abundant as the [Adv + X]$_X$ patterns (Chapter 4). In the first period there are several patterns in competition, including one with full nominal non-head (*sanguine-mixto* 'of mixed blood', lit. 'blood-mixed, [1056]). There are also several options without a word class marker, including with bare stems (*tiestherido* 'crazy', lit. 'head-hurt' [1246–1252]), with bare stems + linking vowel (*barbirrapado* 'clean shaven', lit. 'beard-shaved' [c. 1280], *cuellealuo* 'white-throated', lit. 'throat-white'[1330–1343]), or with more drastic losses (*racorto* < *rabo* + *corto* 'short-tailed', lit. 'tail-short' [1250]). The alternative Latin pattern with internal structure [A + N]$_A$ (*conirrostro* 'of conical face', lit. 'conical-face' [1925], *tenuirrostro* 'of soft face', lit. 'soft-face' [1925]) appears rarely, late, and in restricted formal contexts, which indicates that it has not become productive in Spanish.

5.2.2.2 *Frequency and productivity*

If we consider absolute frequency, the numbers of [N + A]$_A$ compounds start out low but surge in the 1500s, followed by continued increases virtually every century. If considered in relative terms, the frequency also spikes in the 1500s, then increases even more in the 1600s to reach its peak, and then remains just under 10% for the remainder of the centuries considered (Table 5.4).

Table 5.4 [N + A]$_A$ integral compounds attested by century, as totals and as a percentage of all compounds

	[N + A]$_A$	All compounds	[N + A]$_A$ as % of all compounds
1000s–1200s	9	349	2.6
1300s	7	434	1.6
1400s	21	709	3.0
1500s	94	1073	8.8
1600s	121	1237	9.8
1700s	124	1360	9.1
1800s	167	1842	9.1
1900s–2000s	208	3005	6.9
Total	287	3451	8.3

If we consider the ratio of new-to-old compounds for each century, the 1400s and 1500s emerge as the two most productive (Table 5.5). In each of those centuries, the percentage of new compounds is 66% and 78% of all [N + A]$_A$ compounds, respectively. The pace slows down after that, although in almost every century between the 1600s and the 1900s at least 20% of these compounds are new. Some exemplars are rare, with several having only one attestation (e.g., *boquihendido* [1527], *capialzo* [1591], *boquisumido* [1599], *barbiblanco* [1605], *cariescrito* [1729], *cabecicaído* [1880–1881]), and others stretch over a period of a few centuries (*patimacizo* [1495–1737]). Additionally, some thirty compounds documented after 1700 only appear in Academic dictionaries (e.g., *vetisesgado* 'with slanted stripes', lit. 'stripe-slanted', *pernituerto* 'with a twisted leg', lit. 'leg-twisted'), which possibly skews the numbers slightly. However, the fact that transient or artificial compounds are transparent speaks to the pattern's vitality. The surge in [N + A]$_A$ happens simultaneously with the selection of one single structural pattern over several alternatives and the disappearance of forms whose nominal non-head appeared as a full lexeme in favor of those in which it is a bare stem. For example, *bocarroto* 'of broken mouth [of a horse]', lit. 'mouth-broken' [1246–1252], disappears in favor of *boquirroto* 'id'. [1508].

Compared to the other head-final adjectival compound patterns we have seen ([Adv + A]$_A$), those with the structure [N + A]$_A$ appear less frequently during the earlier periods, but they undergo a massive surge after the 1400s. Recall from Chapter 4 (Table 4.5) that [Adv + A]$_A$ compounds exhibit high productivity early on, but once they stop being productive, they never again regain momentum.

5.2.2.3 *Inseparability of constituents*

Integral [N + A]$_A$ compounds fall under the traditional category of 'proper' or perfect compounds: their internal structure is incompatible with sentence syntax, so they must be created by processes different from the juxtaposition of preexisting syntactic phrases, or 'agglutination' (Fruyt 1990). As expected, their constituent order is fixed and inversions are unattested: *boquiabierto* 'open-mouthed', lit. 'mouth-open' vs.

Table 5.5 Productivity of [N + A]$_A$ compounds attested by century

	Carried over	Lost	New	Total	Productivity Ratio
1200s	1	(1)	8	8	NA
1300s	8	(4)	3	7	−0.14
1400s	7	(1)	15	21	0.67
1500s	21	(3)	76	94	0.78
1600s	94	(15)	42	121	0.22
1700s	121	(24)	27	124	0.02
1800s	124	(4)	47	167	0.26
1900s–2000s	167	(27)	68	208	0.20

*abierto boca, *abierto boqui. Neither are there any attested insertions of extraneous material between constituents: *boca muy abierto, *boqui muy abierto 'mouth very open'.

5.2.2.4 Orthographic representation

The use of bare nominal stems as first elements is normally enough for a writer to interpret the complex as a single word and spell it accordingly. In the earlier periods exceptions exist, but a thorough examination of the data in CORDE found only 15 such tokens. Most of them are single occurrences and all but two are recorded before 1700, e.g., cabez colgado 'with head hanging', lit. 'head-hanged' [c. 1471], culi roto 'with broken butt', lit. 'butt-broken' [1519], cari redondo 'round-faced', lit. 'face-round' [1575, 1601]. When the nominal appears in full form, its separate spelling seems less surprising, given that it reflects its greater prosodic and morphological independence: boca abierto 'open-mouthed', lit. 'mouth-open' [ad 1300], nariz romo 'flat-nosed', lit. 'nose-flat' [1495]. By contrast, two-word spelling is almost inevitable in the rare cases when the nominal constituent appears in its fully inflected form (8).

(8)   eran estos todos quatro como duna hedad mancebiellos barbas punientes.
                                                    (c. 1280, Alfonso X, CORDE)
           'all those four were of the age where they were starting to grow a beard
                                                    (lit. 'young men beards growing')'.

[N + A]$_A$ compounds may also appear hyphenated, an option that is in fact more frequent than two-word spelling. The dating of spelling variants suggests that hyphenated forms are normally an orthographic innovation of the 19th century, rather than an intermediate stage towards compoundhood. For example, in compounds with the nominal element boqui- 'mouth', most hyphenated forms are dated in the 1800s and have earlier unhyphenated renderings: boquiconejuno [1572] vs. boqui-conejuno [1889]; boquifruncido [1580–1627] vs. boqui-fruncida [1881]; boquirrasgado [1600] vs. boqui-rasgada [1881]; boquirrubio [1580–1627] vs. boqui-rubio [1890].

5.2.2.5 Evolution of formal features

Most of the changes in this class affect the phonological or morphological structure of the nominal. First, consider the restrictions on syllable structure identified in Section 5.2.1.1. As far as the syllable count is concerned, there seems to be little overall difference over time in the preference for two-syllable stems, which total over 90% for all periods (Table 5.6). The irregular one- and three-syllable stems are and remain scarce throughout.

Table 5.6 Syllable count for nominal constituent in [N + A]$_A$ integral compounds

	One-syllable stem	Two-syllable stem	Three-syllable stem	Totals
1000s–1500s	3.8% (4)	93.3% (97)	2.9% (3)	100% (104)
1600s–1900s	3.7% (7)	92.9% (170)	3.3% (6)	100% (183)
Total	3.8% (11)	93.0% (267)	3.1% (9)	100% (287)

This issue can be examined in a slightly different way, however. New lexemes created with the same stem over time show a growing tolerance for three-syllable first constituents. Compare, for example, the allomorphy of *cabez-* 'head', for which first attestations of the bisyllabic closed stem precede those of the three open-syllable allomorph by some two hundred years: e.g., *cabizcaído* [1445–1519], *cabezbaxo* [1514–42], *cabezmordido* [1517], against *cabeciancho* [1729], *cabecijunto* [1729], *cabecicaído* [1880–1881].

It is less clear whether one-syllable stems become more or less acceptable over time. For *cul-/culi-* 'buttocks' there is indeed a replacement of the monosyllabic stem by its two-syllable allomorph, made by stem and linking vowel: *culcosido* [1626–1628] vs. *culinegro* [1899], *culiblanco* [c. 1920], and so on. A similar process can be noted for *ra(b)-/rabi-* 'tail': *racorto* [c. 1250] vs. *rabiahorcado* [1498], *rabicano* [1561], and later ones. However, in other cases both types of stems coexist over the centuries: *casc/cazc-* vs. *casqui-* 'hoof': *cazcorvo* [1495], *cascalbo* [1899] vs. *casquiacopado* [1564], *casquiderramado* [1564]; and *coll-/cuelli-* 'neck': *collalba* [1927] vs. *cuellierguido* [1550–1580], *cuellirrojo* [1973].

Tolerance for a closed final syllable in the nominal stem decreases, with 12 examples (out of 102, or 11.7%) occurring before the 1600s, and nine (out of 185 compounds, or 4.9%) after that; e.g., *cazcorvo* [1495], *cascalbo* [1899]. Often, the consonant-final stem is resyllabified, shortened, or subject to haplology, which prevents word-internal consonant clusters: *tozalbo* (< *tozo* 'head' + *albo* 'white'), *racorto* (< *rabo* 'tail' + *corto* 'short'), *cejunto* (< *ceja* 'eyebrow' + *junto* 'together').

Let us now turn to the morphological structure of the first constituent, which, as stated earlier, may be a full lexeme or a bare stem, with or without a linking vowel. Over time, there is a decrease in the full nominals in non-head position, from almost 30% before 1500 to virtually none after that (Table 5.7). The use of stems increases concomitantly until it becomes virtually obligatory, with the use of bare stems without a linking vowel decreasing to under 10% by the 1700s. In other words, insertion of -*i*- has become the preferred strategy for $[N + A]_A$ compound creation.

Even making allowances for the scarcity of data for the earlier periods, the generalization of nominal stems in $[N + A]_A$ compounds happens quite suddenly around the end of the 15th century (cf. Munthe 1889 for similar observations). This quick process was preceded by a period of instability and variation. We have evidence of this in

Table 5.7 Morphological structure of nominal constituent in $[N + A]_A$ integral compounds

	Full lexeme (n)	Stem (n)	Stem + linking vowel (n)	Totals (n)
1000s–1400s	29.6% (8)	22.2% (6)	48.2% (13)	100% (27)
1500s–1600s	0% (0)	4.2% (5)	95.8% (113)	100% (118)
1700s–1900s	3.5% (5)	7.1% (10)	89.4% (127)	100% (142)
Totals	4.5% (13)	7.3% (21)	88.2% (253)	100% (287)

Nebrija's *Vocabulario* (1495?), where fully inflected nouns in compounds such as *na-riz aguileño* 'aquiline-nosed', lit. 'nose-aquiline', *nariz romo* 'flat nosed', lit. 'nose-flat', and *orejascaido* 'with droopy ears', lit. 'ears-fallen', are attested alongside nominal stems with or without a linking vowel: *cabezcaído* (< *cabeza* + *caído*), *cejunto* (< *ceja* + *junto*), *patihendido* (< *pata* + *i* + *hendido*), *patimacizo* (< *pata* + *i* + *macizo*). The examples of full noun incorporation cannot be simply dismissed as Nebrija's creativity gone awry; rather, they must be taken as evidence of the existence of several competing compounding mechanisms.

5.2.2.6 *Evolution of meaning*

The typical semantic evolution of $[N + A]_A$ compounds can be traced in the case of frequent exemplars. Unsurprisingly, literal meanings tend to precede metaphoric values. When figurative meanings are developed, they may replace the literal meaning or both may coexist for centuries. Consider the case of *peliagudo* (< *pelo* 'hair' + *agudo* 'pointy'), illustrated in (9).

(9) a. *deuese guardar lo/mas que pudiere de toda carne salada acecinada & pe-liaguda*   (1542, Ruy Díaz de Isla, CORDE).
'he must stay away from all salted, dried, and bristly meat'

b. *Cubren pieles de Pantera,/que son forros peliagudos,/lo que fuera horror de todos/a descubrirse desnudo.*
(1624, Alonso de Castillo Solórzano, CORDE)
'they cover in panther skins, which are hairy covers, what would horrify everyone if it were visible'

c. *[...] todos eran peliagudos y nariagudos, mañosos, sagaces y políticos.*
(1657, Baltasar Gracián, CORDE)
'they were all wily and big-nosed, artful, cunning, and politic'.

d. *He compuesto/negocios más peliagudos/que éste en menos de dos credos.*
(1787, Tomás de Iriarte, CORDE)
'I have fixed more complicated affairs than these in a jiffy'.

The compound *peliagudo* is first applied literally to something covered in fur, to mean 'hairy, bristly' (9a, b). Later examples are less clear, and can be understood literally and figuratively (*peliagudos y narigudos* 'hairy and big-nosed' or 'wily and big-nosed'), when applied to humans (9c). When their meaning is extended to apply to abstract inanimates, the process of semantic shift is complete (9d). By contrast, in the case of *cabizbajo* (< *cabeza* 'head' + *bajo* 'low'), both direct and metaphoric meanings coexist over the life of the lexeme (10a–d).

(10) a. *los thebanos acusaban a Panículo que escopía mucho; los lacedemonios decían de Ligurguio que andaba <u>cabizbajo</u>; los romanos criminaban a Scipión que dormía roncando*   (1521–1543, Fray Antonio de Guevara, CORDE) 'The Thebans accused Panniculus of spitting too much; Lacaedemonians said that Lygurge walked with his head down; the Romans accused Scipio of snoring in his sleep'.

    b. *Los siete reyes tristes le ha mostrado,/llorosos, <u>cabizbajos</u> y cuitados*
          (1549, Jerónimo de Urrea, CORDE)
'He has shown him the seven sad kings, weepy, depressed and saddened'

    c. *Caminaba con las manos en los bolsillos de sus raídos jeans, encorvado, <u>cabizbajo</u>.*
          (1974, Ernesto Sábato, CORDE)
'He walked with his hands in the pockets of his ragged jeans, hunched over and looking down'.

    d. *Y salimos de la bodega, Álvaro despidiendo chispas de energía, yo <u>cabizbajo</u> y callado.*   (ad 1973, Pablo Neruda, CORDE)
'And we left the store, Alvaro brimming with energy, and I depressed and silent'.

Exceptionally, the earliest attestations of a compound may be metaphorical, with no literal counterpart (cf. *manilargo* < *mano* 'hand' + *largo* 'long' + *corto* 'short' in 11a–c). This may be due to lack of documentation of an earlier literal meaning or to the fact that the compound originated in an older figurative phrase that is no longer current. It is not surprising that a basic lexeme like *mano* 'hand', combined with an adjective like *largo* 'long' should result in a profusion of metaphoric meanings.

(11) a. *Envió a pedir un macho prestado cierto caballero a otro que era anciano y demasiado de guardoso, y como no se le diese, enviándole a decir que no era a propósito para camino por ser muy nuevo y pasicorto, respondió: "No es sino porque es su amo viejo y no <u>manilargo</u>".*   (1596, Juan Rufo, CORDE)
'A certain gentleman asked an old and stingy man for a mule. The latter wouldn't lend it, saying that it would be of no use, because it was too young and short-legged. The first man then said: "The problem is really that its owner is too old and not generous"'.

    b. *caballero arruinado que por nada en el mundo quería separarse de un antiguo mayordomo excesivamente <u>manilargo</u>.*
          (1897, Angel Ganivet, CORDE)
'an impoverished gentleman who wouldn't for anything in the world get rid of his old thieving butler'.

c. *Las mamás, que hoy pecan de consentidoras, eran por entonces todavía ma-*
   nilargas, y aquello de que la letra con sangre entra no había perdido todo su
   prestigio.   (1871, José Tomás de Cuéllar, CORDE)
   'Mothers, who are now excessively permissive, in those days were still not
   averse to punishing children, and "spare the rod, spoil the child" was still
   in vogue.'

5.2.2.7 *Endocentric and exocentric uses*

Here we consider whether [N + A]$_A$ compounds are used endocentrically, as adjectives, or reclassified under other grammatical categories with any systematicity. The
majority fall under the first category. However, like all adjectives, they may be nominalized quite freely (*el niño pelirrojo* 'the red-haired child' → *el pelirrojo* 'the red-head')
without any additional suffixation.

   There is a small group of compounds in this class, notably in zoological nomenclature, which has been recategorized permanently into the nominal category. The path
followed is elision, from a nominal phrase whose adjectival compound modifies the
noun to one where it replaces it: *charrán patinegro* 'snowy plover [bird]', lit. 'plover
foot-black' > *patinegro* 'id.', lit. 'foot-black'. In some cases, there is evidence that the
process is happening gradually, with the result that there is still some variation. Consider the Spanish word for the bar-tailed godwit (L. Limosa lapponica). The most
widely attested variant in Google is *aguja colipinta* lit. 'godwit tail-striped' (205 hits),
with an elided counterpart *colipinta* appearing as a less frequent (probably newer) alternative (70 hits).

(12) a. *Este año se ha llevado a cabo por primera vez el seguimiento de la Aguja*
        Colipinta (Limosa lapponica baueri) en su viaje a través del Pacífico, desde
        Alaska hasta Nueva Zelanda, pasando por China.   (7.11.08, Google)
        'This year for the first time the bar-tailed godwit (lit. 'tail-painted godwit')
        (*Limosa lapponica bauer*) has been followed on its journey across the Pa-
        cific, from Alaska to New Zealand, flying over China.'

    b. *Bonita luz y definicion de la colipinta y su espectro*   (7.11.08, Google)
       'Good lighting and definition of the bar-tailed godwit and its spectrum'

5.2.3 Structure of deverbal [N + A]$_A$ compounds: *Insulinodependiente*

5.2.3.1 *Constituents*

In deverbal [N + A]$_A$ compounds, it makes sense to start by describing the deverbal
adjective, since this constituent determines the selection and interpretation of the
noun. As noted earlier, the adjective may be a present participle: *fehaciente* 'trustworthy', lit. 'faith-making' (*haciente* 'making/maker' ← *hacer* 'to make'), *toxicodependiente*
'addicted to toxic substances', lit. 'toxic-dependent' (*dependiente* 'dependent' ← *depend-*
er 'to depend'), *castellanohablante* 'Spanish-speaking' (*hablante* 'speaking/speaker' ←

hablar 'to speak'). It may also be a past participle: *aguallevado* 'canal cleaning operation', lit. 'water-taken' (*llevado* 'taken' ← *llevar* 'to take'), *manumiso* 'freed slave', lit.
'hand-put' (*miso* irregular participle of *meter* 'to put'). Finally, it may be derived from
a verbal base through agentive suffixation: *vasodilatador* 'blood vessel dilator' (*dilatador* 'dilator' ← *dilatar* 'to dilate').

The verbal base from which the adjective is derived and the non-head nominal
have a similar relationship to that which holds in the $[V + N]_N$ pattern of *sacacorchos*
'corkscrew', lit. 'remove-corks'. Thus, the same type of verb phrase is the source of the
adjective *viandante* 'pedestrian', lit. 'way-walker' and *andarríos* 'white wagtail', lit.
'walk-rivers'. However, the two compound patterns differ in the types of verbal bases
they will accept. There is no restriction on the verbal bases from which deverbal adjectivals are derived. In fact, they run the gamut from states (*causahabiente* 'assign', lit.
'right-holder'), to activities (*viandante* 'pedestrian', lit. 'way-goer'), accomplishments,
and achievements (*cabopreso* 'contained, surrounded', lit. 'top-held'). By contrast, states
are barred from appearing in the $[V + N]_N$ pattern (Chapter 7, Section 7.1.1.1).
Compare, for example, *toxicodependiente* 'toxic-dependent', *poderdante* 'grantor', lit.
'power-giver', *castellanohablante* 'Castilian speaker', with the ungrammatical **depende-
tóxicos* 'toxic-dependent', lit. 'depend-toxics', *dapoder 'grantor', lit. 'give-power', **habla-
castellano* 'Castilian speaker', lit. 'speak-Castilian'.

The non-head nominal may be a complement required to discharge a theta role of
the verb: *habla vasco* 'speaks Basque' → *vascohablante* 'Basque speaker' (direct object);
depende de la insulina 'depends on insulin' → *insulinodependiente* 'insulin-dependent'
(obligatory prepositional object). It may also act as an adjunct: *escribe a mano* 'writes
by hand' → *manuscrito* 'hand-written' (manner), *anda por la vía* 'walks on the road' →
viandante 'pedestrian' (locative).

As in integral $[N + A]_A$ compounds, there is an asymmetry in the internal structure of the first and second constituents. The head on the right appears in its full-
fledged form, complete with word class marker, and acts as the locus of inflectional
suffixation: *compuestos vasodepresores* 'vessel-depressing compounds', lit. 'compound-
MASC PL vessel-depressing-MASC PL', *medicaciones vasodepresoras* 'vessel-depressing
medications', lit. 'medication-FEM PL vessel-depressing-FEM PL'. By contrast, the non-
head nominal is invariable in number, even when a plural interpretation is semantically unmarked: *vasodepresor* vs. *vasosdepresor 'blood vessel depressor' (cf. Eng.
sandwich-maker).

The non-head noun may appear as a full lexeme or as a bare stem, with or without
a linking vowel. For example, *mano* 'hand' normally appears in a combining form:
manumiso 'freed slave', lit. 'hand-put', *mantenido* 'maintained', lit. 'hand-held'. In compounds modeled on learned patterns the first constituent also appears in bare form,
with the Latinate linking vowel -*i*-: *armipotente* 'powerful in arms', lit. 'arm-powerful'

(cf. *arma* 'arm').[2] Other first constituents have a linking vowel *-o-* instead: *catalano-hablante* 'Catalan-speaking', *insulinodependiente* 'insulin-dependent' (cf. *catalánø*, *insulina*). In other cases it is harder to decide whether the first constituent is a full form or a stem. In some compounds, such as *castellanohablante* 'Castilian-speaking' and *pampringada* 'smeared with bread', lit. 'bread-smeared', it is reasonable to propose that the first constituent is a bare form, although it is no different from the free form (*castellano*, *pan*). However, there is a small set of examples in which the word class marker is unquestionably present: *cuentadante* 'trustee', lit. 'account-giver', *causahabiente* 'assign', lit. 'right-holder'. They constitute a minority, however, and are circumscribed to legal language, so it seems safe to assume that the unmarked situation is for the word class marker to be absent.

5.2.3.2 *Compound structure*

The head status of the adjectival constituent in deverbal $[N + A]_N$ can be shown through concord: *poblaciones vascohablantes* 'Basque-speaking populations', lit. 'population-FEM PL Basque-speaking-FEM PL', *niños teleadictos* 'children addicted to television', lit. 'children-MASC PL TV-addicted-MASC PL' (cf. *vasco*-MASC SG; *tele*-FEM SG). The nominal is incorporated into the adjectival head via an intermediate prepositional phrase (13). Similarly to what happens in integral compounds, if the noun appears as a bare nominal head, it must incorporate into the prepositional head, occupied by a linking vowel that is not a case assigner (*-o-*, *-i-*, or *-ø-*). The noun + interfix complex (*catalano-*), still caseless, must incorporate into the higher adjectival head to satisfy the visibility condition. In contrast, when the head is occupied by a partitive preposition, it must select a word class marker phrase that can receive case (14). In both situations, the adjective head *hablante* 'speaker' must raise to AgrP in order to satisfy concord. The difference lies in the fact that in the phrasal structure it raises by itself, whereas in the compounded structure, it does so together with the entire incorporated structure (*catalan-o-hablante*).

(13)

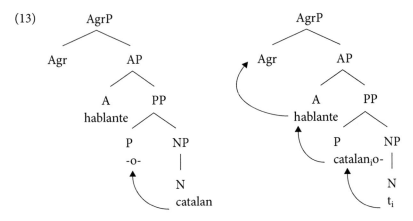

---

2. They are included in this database because their stems are not obligatorily bound: *arma* 'arm', *tiple* 'treble', *tono* 'tone'.

(14)

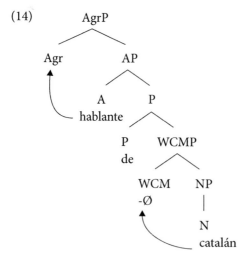

5.2.3.3 Compound meaning

Because any verb can be used to derive adjectival heads, there are few a priori limitations in the meanings and semantic fields for deverbal $[N + A]_A$ compounds. However, these compounds tend to distribute themselves in specific semantic fields according to historical period. Older compounds appear both in the technical terminology of menial labor such as construction and cooking (*terrapleno* 'embankment', lit. 'earth-filled', *salcocho* 'cooked with salt', lit. 'salt-cooked'), and in the higher arts of law and religion (*fementido* 'deceitful', lit. 'faith-lied', *senadoconsulto* 'senate consult', *manumiso* 'freed slave', lit. 'hand-put'). In the later periods, the overwhelming majority of compounds in this class appear in scientific discourse: *vasoconstrictor* 'vasoconstrictor', lit. 'blood vessel-constrictor', *acidorresistente* 'acid-resistant', *gallegohablante* 'Galician speaker'.

5.2.4 Diachrony

5.2.4.1 Historical antecedents and comparative data

Deverbal adjectival compounds have antecedents in the Indo-European languages. Whitney (1941 [1879]: 490) describes them for Sanskrit among the class of dependent adjective compounds, stating that the first member is in a case relation with the head (e.g., locative in *sthālīpakva* 'cooked in a pot', lit. 'pot-cooked'). In Greek they are also present, and again, their nominal first constituents may take on several syntactic cases (e.g., dative in ἀηῒ-φιλος 'arēï-philos, beloved of Ares', lit. 'dear to Ares', genitive in διόσ-δοτος 'diós-dotos, god-given') (Debrunner 1917: 34). In Latin these compounds are often related to the $[N + V]_V$ pattern, either because they derive from it, or on the contrary, because they are their source through derivation. For example, MANŪ MISSUS 'freed slave', is the source of MANŪMITTĔRE 'set free' and MANŪMISSOR 'emancipator', according to Klingebiel (1989: 39).

A review of comparative evidence from the Romance family reveals that deverbal adjectival [N + A]$_A$ compounds are frequently absent from contemporary descriptions. There are some notable exceptions to this, such as Hualde (1992: 364) and Mascaró (1986: 64), both of whom present examples for Catalan. The deverbal pattern is better illustrated in historical accounts, such as Klingebiel (1989), who musters examples from a variety of sources and Romance varieties (especially eastern Iberia and southern France), such as Bearnais-Catalan *cap-pelat* 'bald', lit. 'head-bald', Old French *champcheü* 'fallen on the battlefield', lit. 'field-fallen', French *vermoulu* 'worm-eaten', *crouste-levé* '[of bread] with separated crust', lit. 'crust-raised', *lettre-féru* 'learned', lit. 'letter-hit', Italian *cap-aguto* 'sharpened', lit. 'head-sharpened'.

Deverbal [N + A]$_A$ compounds in Spanish are documented from the earliest times in the databases available starting before the 1000s, and continuously through the 1100s and 1200s (15).

(15)   Early attestations of [N + A]$_A$ compounds in Spanish

   a.   *concedimus [...] IIIIor capudmasos in castro [...]; unum de isis capudmasis est ubi dicitur ad Pares altas*   (863, Obarra, LHP)
   'we grant [...] four homesteads in the fortification [...]; one of those homesteads is in the place called Pares Altas'

   b.   *damus [...] totum jus atque plenum dominium sicut nos abemus in Uilla uerde in homicidijs et in calumpniis et in manpuesta [...]*
                    (1146, *Carta de donación*, CORDE)
   'we give [...] all rights and dominion that we have in Villaverde by virtue of pecuniary damages for homicide and calumny and taxes'

   c.   *[...] non puede ser medido nin cabopreso por fecho nin por forma.*
                    (c. 1252–1270, Alfonso X, CORDE)
   'it cannot be measured or contained in fact or in form'

5.2.4.2 *Frequency and productivity*

The database has a total of 62 examples of deverbal [N + A]$_A$ compounds (or 1.8%). Their frequency is low throughout history, in a situation reminiscent of the [N + V]$_V$ compounds to which they are related (Section 5.1.2.2). The 1800s and 1900s have seen an increase in new compounds created with this pattern, resulting in a doubling of their number since the 1700s. Yet, their relative frequency has been cut almost by half over the centuries (Table 5.8). This distances them from the [N + A]$_A$ integrals discussed in Section 5.2.2.2, which had a sudden spike after the 1400s.

The productivity of this pattern is modest for most of the period under study. It exhibits small gains until the 1800s and a sudden spike after that (Table 5.9). This increase in the modern period is due to the fact that some adjectives constitute small pockets of local productivity (*dependiente* 'dependent', in *toxicodependiente* 'toxic-dependent', *hablante* in *castellanohablante* 'Castilian speaking').

Table 5.8 [N + A]$_A$ deverbal compounds attested by century, as totals and as a percentage of all compounds

	Deverbal [N + A]$_A$	All compounds	Deverbal [N + A]$_A$ as % of all compounds
1000s–1200s	8	349	2.3
1300s	7	434	1.6
1400s	9	709	1.3
1500s	15	1073	1.4
1600s	17	1237	1.4
1700s	23	1360	1.7
1800s	28	1842	1.5
1900s–2000s	55	3005	1.8
Total	62	3451	1.8

Table 5.9 Productivity of [N + A]$_A$ deverbal compounds attested by century

	Carried over	Lost	New	Total	Productivity Ratio
1200s	2	(1)	6	7	NA
1300s	7	(1)	1	7	0.00
1400s	7	(1)	3	9	0.22
1500s	9	(0)	6	15	0.40
1600s	15	(0)	2	17	0.12
1700s	17	(0)	6	23	0.26
1800s	23	(2)	7	28	0.18
1900s–2000s	28	(2)	29	55	0.49

The compounds in this category tend to be quite stable, like the related [N + V]$_V$ type. Only nine out of the 56 were lost over history (a little under 16%), for example: *cabopreso* [1208], *tiplisonante* [1630–1655], *ondisonante* [c. 1798–1809]. By contrast, almost twice as many integral compounds were lost over history relative to their total number.

5.2.4.3 *Inseparability of constituents*
The compounded status of the constituents can be shown by the impossibility of insertions between them, as well as by the non-attestation of examples with inverted order: *viandante* 'pedestrian', lit. 'way-goer' vs. *andantevía. In most cases, the inversion would only be possible with the additional insertion of a preposition: *acidorresistente* 'acid-resistant' > *resistente a ácidos* 'resistant to acids'.

5.2.4.4 *Orthographic representation*

Deverbal compounds can be spelled as a unit, and indeed over half of them exhibit no spelling variation. The remainder shows some degree of oscillation, with two-word and hyphenated spelling alternants. However, these do not reflect an increasing level of agglutination of syntactic heads into a single unit, or a generalized gradual transition from two- to one-word spelling over time (unlike, for example, the [Adv + A]$_A$ compounds in Chapter 4, Section 4.2.2.3). Unitary spelling tends to be attested before or at the same time as two-word spelling: *fementido* [1246–1252] vs. *fe mentida* [ad 1400]; *salpicado* [1448] vs. *sal picado* [1615]; *cabopreso* [c. 1252–1270] vs. *cabo preso* [1208]; *causahabiente* vs. *causa habiente* [both 1861]. This suggests that two-word spellings reflect the writer's recognition that both constituents retain prosodic and semantic independence, rather than a gradual agglutination.

5.2.4.5 *Evolution of formal features*

Let us turn to the history of deverbal compounds in terms of the evolution of their internal structure. Unlike integral [N + A]$_A$ compounds, the nominal non-head in deverbals has no phonological restrictions in syllabic structure or count. Consider, for example, *insulinodependiente* 'insulin dependent', whose two constituents are four syllables long. Deverbal [N + A]$_A$ compounds are also different from integrals in terms of the form taken by the non-head nominal. For one thing, nominals in full form do not disappear over time (Table 5.10). The last period in fact exhibits a surge in their occurrence, due to the frequent presence of nouns of ambiguous form (e.g., *castellanohablante* 'Castilian-speaking' [1980], analyzable as *castellan-o-hablante* or *castellanohablante*) and to a growing tolerance for full forms (*cuentadante* 'trustee', lit. 'account-giver' [1869]). Moreover, in cases in which linking vowels are present, the formant can be an *-i-* (e.g., *armipotente* 'powerful in arms', lit. 'arm-powerful' [1615]), and in the later period also an *-o-* (*insulinodependiente* 'insulin dependent' [1987]). In other words, the preference for stem forms is lost over time, in a pattern strikingly different from that of integral [N + A]$_A$ compounds.

   To illustrate the formal evolution of constituents, we turn to a brief case study of two common deverbal adjectives that have become increasingly frequent in [N + A]$_A$ compounds, i.e., *hablante* and *parlante* 'speaker/speaking'. According to data in CORDE/CREA, *parlante* participates in compounding earlier, with four out of its total

Table 5.10 Morphological structure of nominal constituent in [N + A]$_A$ deverbal compounds

	Full lexeme (n)	Stem (n)	Stem + linking vowel (n)	Totals (n)
1000s–1400s	50% (6)	33.3% (4)	16.7% (2)	100% (12)
1500s–1700s	37.5% (3)	25% (2)	37.5% (3)	100% (8)
1800s–1900s	64.3% (27)	7.1% (3)	28.6% (12)	100% (42)
Totals	58.1% (36)	14.5% (9)	27.4% (17)	100% (62)

14 compounds appearing in the 1800s: *latini-parlante* [1879], *galiparlante* [1880–1881], *anglo-parlante* [1886], *hispano-parlante* [1886]. For their part, compounds with *hablante* first appear in the mid-20th century (*hispano-hablante* [1950]), and soon start to replace *parlante* compounds in popularity, accounting for 60% of compounds after their first attestation. Although *parlante* retains a certain combinatorial advantage when the languages are designated with learned or semi-learned stems, this preference is not categorical: *germanohablante* and *alemano-parlante* 'German speaker'. In fact, the two adjectives show considerable freedom to combine with any nominal stem: *hispanohablante*, *hispanoparlante* 'Spanish speaker', *quechua hablante*, *quechuaparlante* 'Quechua speaker'.

The linking vowel *-i-*, popular in the earlier compounds (*latin i-parlante* 'Latin speaker', *gali-parlante* 'French speaker'), is gradually dropped in favor of *-o-* in later ones (*angloparlante* 'English speaker', **angliparlante*; *catalanohablante* 'Catalan speaker', **catalanihablante*; *valencianoparlante* 'Valencian speaker', **valencianiparlante*). Ambiguous cases like the last example provide a possible path to the reanalysis of the first noun as stem + word class marker rather than stem + linking vowel (*valencian-o-parlante* or *valenciano-parlante*). Adding to this ambiguity is the need to create compounds to designate speakers of languages whose name lacks an overt word class marker: *aymara-ø hablante*, *guaraní-ø hablante*. Late examples suggest that some speakers have reanalyzed the first nominal as a full lexeme (16).

(16)   *en respuesta al desamparo que los "Español-hablantes" venimos padeciendo desde que tenemos nuevo gobierno municipal y para evitar que el idioma español desaparezca de esta tierra [...] se pasó a una forma más respetuosa con la Constitución, como era la bilingüe, que contentaba tanto a españoles-hablantes como a gallego-hablantes*   (2001, *Faro de Vigo*, CREA)
'as a response to the lack of protection that we Spanish speakers have been suffering since we have had a new municipal government, and to prevent the disappearance of the Spanish language from this land [....] a more respectful version of the constitution was passed, which was bilingual and satisfied both Spanish speakers and Galician speakers'

5.2.4.6 Endocentric and exocentric uses

Like other adjectival compounds, deverbal compounds are occasionally recategorized as nominals: *manuscrito* 'hand-written', also 'manuscript'. Typically, it is the older compounds in this class that undergo permanent reassignment to the nominal class and have no adjectival meaning: *caputmasso* 'homestead', lit. 'head-stayed' [1044], *mampuesta* 'line of rubblework', lit. 'hand-put' [1146], *terraplen(o)* 'embankment', lit. 'earth-filled' [1527–1550].

5.2.4.7 Evolution of meaning

Deverbal $[N + A]_A$ compounds are in general more semantically stable than their integral counterparts. Many of them are semantically opaque from the start, since they are inherited from Latin as specialized technical terms, whose meanings they retain. In other compounds, the original meaning tends to last and develop few metaphoric extensions, even in words with quite long histories. Take, for example, the case of *viandante* 'pedestrian', lit. 'way-walker', which has used for over 700 years as an adjective with the meaning 'on foot', and as a noun meaning 'pedestrian' (17a, b), only very sporadically stretched to mean 'wandering' (17c).

(17) a. *del danno que el <u>uiandante</u> recibe en alguna puente.*
>   (1310, *Leyes de estilo. Esc Z. III. 11*, CORDE)
>   'On the injury that a pedestrian may receive when crossing a bridge'.

   b. *preguntó al hermitaño quién era aquel su huésped. & él le dixo un cavallero <u>viandante</u> que llegara allí por su desaventura*
>   (1300–1305, *Libro del Cavallero de Cifar*, CORDE)
>   'The hermit asked who his guest was, and he told him that it was a wandering knight who had arrived there due to a misfortune'

   c. *No dió lugar a esto otro pintor <u>viandante</u> y desharrapado que llegó por aquel tiempo a Sevilla*   (1724, Antonio Palomino y Velasco, CORDE)
>   'This did not happen because of another wandering and tattered painter who arrived from Seville at the time'

5.2.5 Special cases: Toponymic compounds

Among the compounds that appear to have the $[N + A]_A$ structure are 'toponymic ' compounds, in which the non-head nominal is a cardinal point or location in full or reduced form (e.g., *norte/nor-* 'north'), and the head is a place-name restricted in extension by the non-head: *survietnamita* 'South Vietnamese', *norteafricano* 'North African', *extremo-oriental* 'Far Eastern', *centroasiático* 'Central Asian' (Val Álvaro 1999). Although superficially they parallel the other subclasses of $[N + A]_A$ discussed, their internal structure is different. Unlike integral compounds, the noun they modify does not contain the incorporated non-head in a part/whole relationship: *hombre norteamericano* 'North American man' → **hombre que tiene el norte americano* '* man who has an American north'. Unlike deverbal compounds, their head adjective is not deverbal: *el hombre norteamericano* > **el hombre americanea el norte* '*the man americans$_V$ the north'.

These compounds are in fact the adjectival derivation of a placename, in which the nominal non-head is incorporated into the head at the time of adjectival suffixation: *Vietnam del Sur* 'Vietnam of the South' → *Sur-Vietnam* 'South Vietnam' → *survietnamita* 'South Vietnamese'. Because the intermediate incorporation $[N + N]_N$ is not attested independently, the $[[N + N]_N + \text{SUFF}]_A$ compound is parasynthetic, i.e., it undergoes simultaneous compounding and suffixation. However, it is still licit to include them as compounds because the two constituents exist independently (*sur* 'South', *vietnamita* 'Vietnamese') and the possibility of decomposing the complex form still exists.

The historical data corroborate that these compounds are independent from integrals and deverbals. They are a contemporary phenomenon, starting in the

19th century and becoming more frequent in the 20th, as it becomes necessary to name portions of locations separately. The earliest ones, not surprisingly given the political history of Spain, are *sudamericano* 'South American' [1811], *norteamericano* 'North American' [1824], and *centroamericano* 'Central American' [1867]. The secessionist wars of the 20th century led to several new names for the broken-off portions of larger land masses: *norirlandés* 'Northern Irish' [1977]. These compounds appear in spelling variants, with two-word and hyphenated forms alternating with one-word forms: *los indios norteamericanos* 'North American Indians' [1824], *agente norteamericano* 'North American agent' [1853], *la escuadra norte americana* 'the North American fleet' [1899]. It should be noted that, because of their special structural features, these compounds are not included in any quantitative analysis in the book.

5.3   The deverbal [N + N]ₙ pattern: *Maniobra*

There are several kinds of compounds with a nominal head on the right (e.g., *argentpel* 'thin layer of tin covered in silver', lit. 'silver-skin', *vitaminoterapia* 'vitamin therapy'). In this section, I limit the description to compounds whose nominal heads are clearly deverbal and hold with their non-head the same head-complement or head-adjunct relationship as the original verb: *dilatar los bronquios* 'dilate the broquial tubes' → *broncodilatador* 'bronchodilator'. These [N + N]ₙ final-head compounds with deverbal heads tend to be abstract, typical of scientific and legal discourse in all historical stages: *causahabiente* 'assign', lit. 'right-holder', *drogodependencia* 'drug dependence'. Other head-final nominal compounds are dealt with together with their head-initial mirror image pattern in Chapter 6, Section 6.2.

5.3.1   Structure

5.3.1.1   *Constituents*
In deverbal [N + N]ₙ compounds, the rightmost head is structurally derived through suffixation. The suffix may be applied to a pre-existing compound of another class, such as [N + V]ᵥ: *manumitir* 'to free [a slave]' lit. 'to hand-put'→ *manumisión* 'freedom [of a slave]', lit. 'hand-putting'; *mantener* 'to maintain,' lit. 'to hand-hold'→ *mantenimiento* 'maintenance', lit. 'hand-holding'. In other cases, there is no compound precursor for the deverbal [N + N]ₙ, suggesting that derivation and compounding operate simultaneously: *misacantano* 'priest who can say mass', lit. 'mass-singer'. Like for non-deverbal compounds, there is a difference in the morphological complexity of head and non-head, since the non-head is normally a non-derived nominal stem that cannot accept inflection of number and whose gender is not percolated to the entire compound: *la captenencia* 'the-FEM SG protection-FEM SG' (cf. *el cabo* 'the-MASC SG head-MASC SG', *la tenencia* 'the-FEM SG holding-FEM SG'). As already noted for the [N + V]ᵥ pattern, there are some high-frequency non-heads, such as *mano* 'hand' or *cab/cap* 'head'.

5.3.1.2 *Compound structure*

Like compounds with the structure $[Adv + N]_N$ (Chapter 4, Section 4.3), $[N + N]_N$ compounds with deverbal nominals are not the result of a process of compounding *per se*. Rather, they are the product of suffixation on a compounded base, which itself involves a verb and its complement (18). We will assume, as before, that only word class marker phrases (WCMP) are capable of receiving case from the verbal head. The absence of that projection forces the nominal to incorporate into the verbal head as a modifier (Baker 1988) (18a-c). The noun-verb complex is then raised into the suffix head.[3]

(18) a.

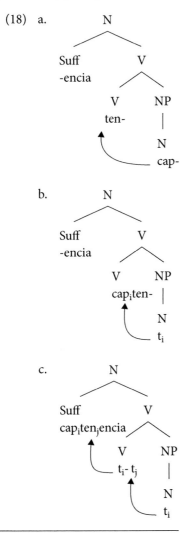

b.

c.

---

3.   It is harder to account for the exact function of the linking vowel in the derivation, for those deverbal compounds that have it. For the purposes of simplification, here I will assume that they are just variants of the bare forms, and I submit the same derivation for cases such as *manirrotura* 'excessive generosity', lit. 'hand-breaking' as for those without linking vowels.

5.3.1.3 *Compound meaning*

The head and non-head in deverbal $[N + N]_N$ compounds are often in the same kind of configuration as the $[N + V]_V$ compounds to which they are related. This may be a head-complement configuration (*poderdante* 'assign', lit. 'power-giver' → *dar un poder* 'to give a power [of attorney]'), as well as head-instrumental and head-locative (*viandante* 'pedestrian', lit. 'path-walker' → *andar por la vía* 'walk along the path', *manutenencia* 'maintenance', lit. 'hand-holding' → *tener con la mano* 'hold in the hand'). As the last example shows, however, most compounds in this class are old, so that their semantic transparency has been lost.

5.3.2 Diachrony

5.3.2.1 *Historical antecedents and comparative data*

The nominalization of $[N + V]_V$ verbal locutions is attested for Latin: MANŪMITTO 'free a slave' > MANŪMISSIŌ 'emancipation' (Bader 1962: 296–97). It is not mentioned in other compendia of Romance compounding, possibly due to its low productivity and to the fact that this structure straddles compounding and derivation. In Spanish, the deverbal $[N + N]_N$ head-final pattern is attested from the earliest stages in the texts consulted (19).

(19) Early attestations of deverbal $[N + N]_N$ compounds in Spanish

    a. *Fue villán e sobervio, de mala <u>captenencia</u>, díssol' palabras locas de fea parecencia*   (c. 1230, Berceo, CORDE)
        "He was mean and arrogant, of little care,/he said crazy ugly things to him"

5.3.2.2 *Frequency and productivity*

Most of the examples of $[N + N]_N$ head-final deverbal compounding appear in the very early periods. Their increase in absolute terms is very small, with long stretches during which numbers remain stagnant or even dip slightly (Table 5.11). The relative frequency of the pattern decreases even more steeply over the centuries, from a high of 5.7% in the earliest period to a low of 1%. It is also interesting to contrast deverbal $[N + N]_N$ compounds with their non-deverbal counterparts, from which they differ in two ways: they have a lower frequency (1% of the total database against 9.5%) and in the fact that they exhibit quite a different distribution over time (see Chapter 6, Section 6.2.2.2).

Let us now turn to pattern productivity, measured in terms of the ratio of new to old compounds per century. Table 5.12 shows that, aside from the inherited compounds attested in the earlier centuries, deverbal $[N + N]_N$ are of very negligible productivity. In most centuries there is either no increase or a net decrease in total numbers of new compounds (cf. 1400s–1600s, 1900s). Only the 1700s and 1800s exhibit moderate productivity, with new compounds constituting around 10% of their total. Compounds in this class are also quite likely to fall out of use, with negative productivity ratios in several centuries.

Table 5.11 Deverbal [N + N]$_N$ head-final compounds attested by century, as totals and as a percentage of all compounds

	Deverbal [N + N]$_N$	All compounds	Deverbal [N + N]$_N$ as % of all compounds
1000s–1200s	20	349	5.7
1300s	23	434	5.3
1400s	25	709	3.5
1500s	24	1073	2.2
1600s	22	1237	1.8
1700s	24	1360	1.8
1800s	27	1842	1.5
1900s–2000s	29	3005	1.0
Total	45	3451	1.3

Table 5.12 Productivity of deverbal [N + N]$_N$ head final compounds attested by century

	Carried over	Lost	New	Total	Productivity Ratio
1200s	2	(0)	18	20	NA
1300s	20	(3)	6	23	0.13
1400s	23	(2)	4	25	0.08
1500s	25	(5)	4	24	−0.04
1600s	24	(3)	1	22	−0.09
1700s	22	(1)	3	24	0.08
1800s	24	(0)	3	27	0.11
1900s	27	(2)	4	29	0.07

5.3.2.3 *Inseparability of constituents*

The order of nominal constituents inside a [N + N]$_N$ deverbal compound is incompatible with the word order of Spanish syntax. There is no evidence that constituents were ever separable, either by insertions or by independent modification: *droga terrible dependencia* 'terrible drug dependence', lit. 'drug terrible dependence;' *mucho poderdante* 'grantor of much power', lit. 'a lot power-giver'. The reversal of constituents is not recorded either: *casateniente* 'homesteader', lit. 'house-holder' vs. *tenientecasa* lit. 'holder house'.

5.3.2.4 *Orthographic representation*

In general terms, [N + N]$_N$ deverbal compounds compounds are spelled together, further evidence of their unitary status. A few newer compounds have alternative two-word or hyphenated spellings: *broncodilatador ~ bronco-dilatador ~ bronco dilatador*

Table 5.13 Morphological structure of nominal constituent in [N + N]$_N$ deverbal head-final compounds

	Full lexeme (n)	Stem (n)	Stem + linking vowel (n)	Totals (n)
1000s–1400s	13.3% (4)	76.7% (23)	10% (3)	100% (30)
1500s–1700s	12.5% (1)	25% (2)	62.5% (5)	100% (8)
1800s–1900s	42.9% (3)	0% (0)	57.1% (4)	100% (7)
Totals	17.8% (8)	55.5% (25)	26.7% (12)	100% (45)

'bronchodilator' (cf. the similar pattern in non-deverbal [N + N]$_N$ head-final compounds in Chapter 6, Section 6.2.2.4).

5.3.2.5 *Evolution of formal features*
The most salient feature that has undergone changes over time in deverbal [N + N]$_N$ head-final compounds is the internal structure of the non-head nominal, which can appear as a full noun, as a bare stem, or as a stem with a linking vowel. To explore this, the internal structure of new compounds was considered by century (Table 5.13). In compounds created in the early periods, between the 1000s and the 1400s, stems are much more frequent than full words (26 vs. 4, or 87% vs. 13%). Among the stems, those without linking vowels are more frequent. The preference for stems is maintained in the following period (1500–1799), with the linking vowel having generalized to most stems. In the later periods, this tendency is reversed, with full forms becoming more frequent in new compounds than at any point before. On closer inspection, this surge is caused mostly by the presence of ambiguous forms as non-heads.

5.3.2.6 *Endocentric and exocentric uses*
The [N + N]$_N$ head-final pattern is robustly endocentric, with virtually none of its exponents having shifted grammatical category. The only doubtful cases are those where the deverbal head could be classified as a noun or as an adjective, such as *viandante* 'pedestrian', lit. 'way-walker' (recall the examples in (17)). However, this ambiguity is present in the deverbal suffixes themselves, and is not a product of the compounding process. When classifying data, compounds whose head could be interpreted as nominal or adjectival were placed where they seem to fit best, according to their meanings and distributional frequencies.

5.4 Summary of chapter

This chapter has dealt with the second class of head-final compound patterns of Spanish. These are three related patterns with a nominal non-head, combined with a verbal, adjectival, or deverbal nominal head. Of the three, those with the form [N + V]$_V$ (e.g., *maniatar* 'tie by the hands', lit. 'hand-tie') are very rare and appear early. The nominal class (e.g., *maniobra* 'maneuver', lit. 'hand-work') is small, and like the [Adv + N]$_N$ compounds presented in Chapter 4, it is related to the verbal class through suffixation. By contrast, [N + A]$_A$ compounds are much more frequent than either of the other classes and are produced over a longer period, very much like the [Adv + A]$_A$ pattern in Chapter 4. The [N + A]$_A$ class is also more complex, with several subtypes. Among them is a large class of integrals (e.g., *manirroto* 'generous', lit. 'hand-broken'), which peaks in the 1400s and 1500s, and a smaller class of deverbals (e.g., *vascohablante* 'Basque speaker'), which is less semantically homogeneous and more evenly spread over historical periods. The adjectival class is also the only one to have retained an observable degree of productivity in contemporary Spanish.

CHAPTER 6

Endocentric compounds with nominal heads and nominal/adjectival modifiers

Pájaro campana, pavipollo, avetarda, falsa abeja

This chapter describes the structure and evolution of Spanish compounding patterns whose head constituent is a nominal, modified by either another nominal or an adjective. Since the head can appear first or last, this yields a total of four possible patterns (Table 6.1). All four have moderate to high productivity over the centuries. Those with adjectival non-heads have syntactic parallels, from which they are sometimes hard to distinguish unequivocally. Numerous tests have been designed to do so, but even then, the nature of historical data sometimes precludes their systematic application, resulting in some uncertainty in the demarcation of these classes, as shall be discussed in the relevant sections.

6.1 The head-initial $[N + N]_N$ pattern: *Pájaro campana*

The $[N + N]_N$ pattern has a head nominal on the left, followed by another nominal, which acts as its non-head modifier. There are two main types of semantic relationships between the nouns. One possibility is a vaguely 'prepositional' relationship in cases such as the genitive/possessive implicit in *bocacalle* 'intersection', lit. 'mouth-street' (*boca de calle* 'mouth of street'), or in examples such as *aguamanos* 'wash basin', lit. 'water-hands', whose second term indicates the purpose (*agua para manos* 'water for hands'). Alternatively, the non-head nominal can have an identificational predicative relationship with its head, in cases such as *hombre araña* 'spider man', lit. 'man-spider' (man like a spider) or *pájaro campana* 'bellbird', lit. 'bird bell' (bird that sounds like a bell).

Table 6.1 Endocentric patterns with nominal heads in Spanish

Pattern	Example	Found in →
Head-initial $[N + N]_N$	*pájaro campana* 'bellbird', lit. 'bird bell'	Chapter 6, Section 6.1
Head-final $[N + N]_N$	*pavipollo* 'turkey chick'	Chapter 6, Section 6.2
$[N + A]_N$	*avetarda* 'bustard', lit. 'bird-slow'	Chapter 6, Section 6.3
$[A + N]_N$	*falsa abeja* 'bee fly', lit. 'false bee'	Chapter 6, Section 6.4

Head-initial [N + N]$_N$ compounds are frequent in colloquial registers typical of every-day language. They tend to be concrete and include names for animals and plants, as well as man-made objects and tools: *perro salchicha* 'dachshund', lit. 'dog sausage', *malvarrosa* 'hollyhock', lit. 'mallow rose', *filoseda* 'filoselle', lit. 'thread-silk', *carro tanque* 'tank', lit. 'car tank', *cierre relámpago* 'zipper', lit. 'zipper lightning'. Even in recent centuries, the pattern has seldom strayed from the concrete, and only a handful of head-initial [N + N]$_N$ compounds are abstract or belong to scientific or technical registers: *política-ficción* 'fake politics', lit. 'politics fiction', *año-luz* 'light year', lit. 'year-light'.

The vast majority of these compounds is endocentric, i.e., the [N + N] complex denotes a subset of the items denoted by the head, e.g., an *hombre araña* is some type of *hombre* 'man', and so on. However, sometimes a possessive relationship holds between the compound constituents and the denotatum, resulting in an exocentric [N + N]$_N$ compound. Thus, for example, a *puntapié* 'kick', lit. 'point-foot' is not a type of point but a type of blow, given with the tip of the foot, and *ajoarriero* 'type of stew', lit. 'garlic-muleteer', is not a type of garlic but a type of food that contains garlic among its ingredients.

6.1.1 Structure

6.1.1.1 *Constituents*

The constituents in [N + N]$_N$ compounds can be any type of nominal, including mass (*aguamiel* 'mead', lit. 'water-honey'), count (*silla poltrona* 'armchair', lit. 'chair sofa'), animates (*pejesapo* 'frogfish', lit. 'fish-frog' < *peje* var. of *pez* 'fish'), or humans (*hombre rana* 'frogman', lit. 'man frog'). Abstract nouns are possible but very infrequent for all historical periods, with the notable exception of color names (*verde esmeralda* 'emerald green', lit. 'green emerald'). As the previous examples show, the nouns involved also tend to be derivationally simple, with very few exceptions, and those mostly in the latest periods (e.g., *mecánico dentista* 'dental technician', lit. 'mechanic dentist'). The constituent lexemes tend to correspond for the most part to non-technical registers, and the resulting compounds are also colloquial. In this regard, there are a few changes in the last two centuries, with the incorporation of some technical compounds such as *molécula gramo* 'gram molecule', lit. 'molecule gram' or *célula huevo* 'zygote', lit. 'cell egg'.

The nominal constituents in head-initial [N + N]$_N$ compounds can both be full nouns, but the head can also appear without its word class marker, with or without a linking vowel: *sauzgatillo* 'chaste tree [Vitex agnus-castus L.]', lit. 'willow-trigger' (cf. *sauce*), *palabrimujer* 'man who sounds like a woman', lit. 'word-woman' (cf. *palabra*). Yet, these are a minority of all [N + N]$_N$ compounds, amounting to less than 8% of the total. The head constituent percolates its gender features to the entire compound: *la sal amoníaco* 'the ammonia salt', lit. 'the-FEM salt-FEM ammonia-MASC', *el verdemontaña* 'the mountain green', lit. 'the-MASC green-MASC mountain-FEM'. Only occasionally do we find exceptions: *el varapalo* 'the stick', lit. 'the-MASC stick-FEM pole-MASC'. The plural marking on [N + N]$_N$ compounds is more complex and exhibits variation over time, so it will be dealt with in the diachronic section.

6.1.1.2 *Compound structure*

All head-initial [N + N]$_N$ compounds have in common the fact that they denote a subset of the head. For instance, *pez espada* 'sword fish', lit. 'fish sword' is a kind of fish, *canción protesta* 'protest song', lit. 'song protest' is a kind of song. However, the semantic contribution of the second constituent depends on whether its relationship with the first one is identificational or partitive/prepositional. This suggests that the surface structure [N + N]$_N$ corresponds to at least two distinct internal structures, which I present in turn (cf. also Hualde 2006/2007, for a similar two-way distinction in [N + N]$_N$ compounds).

In the identificational pattern, the secondary nominal modifies the noun in a manner similar to an adjective, hence the quotes around the higher node in (1). Note that in the diagram the structures have been simplified by obviating the word class marker phrase and head that are arguably present.

(1)

Modification establishes a similar relationship between the denotation of the head nominal (a primary predicate) and the secondary predicate, regardless of whether it is an adjective (as in *pejeverde*) or a second nominal (as in *peje araña*). However, the [N + N]$_N$ configuration is semantically more complex than that of [N + A]$_N$. In the latter there is a semantic relationship of theta-identification between the nominal argument and its adjectival modifier, which means that the referential variable position of the adjective is identified with the corresponding position within the nominal. In [N + N]$_N$ identificational compounds the same process is arguably impossible, since both nominals have referential variables that define mutually exclusive sets. Thus, whereas the denotation of *pejeverde* 'ornate wrasse', lit. ' fish green' can be defined through the intersection of the set *peje* 'fish' and the set *verde* 'green' (something that is a fish and is green, in some sense), a similar operation cannot be proposed for *peje araña* 'spider fish', lit. 'fish spider', since the two sets are mutually exclusive. At this point this matter will remain unresolved, but it bears some degree of resemblance with the situation that Higginbotham refers to as autonymous theta-marking, i.e., cases like *little elephant* or *giant spider*, where theta identification cannot operate as the addition of two predicates (a little elephant is not 'something that is an elephant and that is little', but 'something that is small for an elephant'). In the case at hand, a *peje araña* 'ornate wrasse', lit. 'fish spider' is something that is spider-like for a fish, but not a spider proper.

In the partitive pattern, I argue that the non-head nominal is related to the head through an intermediate prepositional phrase with a null head. There is evidence for this in the fact that some of these compounds alternate with [N + prep + N] sequences: *dulce de leche* 'crème caramel', lit. 'paste of milk' > *dulceleche* 'id.', lit. 'paste milk'. Moreover, in some cases the prepositional formant has not been lost but trapped between the first and second nominals (e.g., *hijodalgo* 'nobleman' < *hijo + de + algo* 'son of something'). I will assume that the null preposition has a theta grid with a two-place argument structure and a corresponding theta grid with a relational theta role and a theme role (Saint-Dizier 2006: 6). It discharges the theme role on the lower nominal, while its relational role is theta-identified with the referential variable of the head nominal. Thus, the entire [N + N]$_N$ compound has only one referential variable, i.e., that of the higher nominal. The secondary nominal is subsumed into the secondary predicate as a partitive (2).

(2)

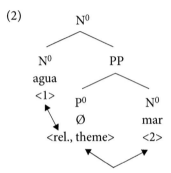

Head-initial [N + N]$_N$ compounds can also appear as exocentric possessives (i.e., *bahuvrihi*), to denote the whole of which they are a part. Consider, for example, *puntapié* 'kick', lit. 'point-foot', a blow given with the point of the foot, rather than the point of the foot itself, *balonmano* 'handball', lit. 'ball-hand', a sport that involves a ball thrown with the hand, rather than the name for a kind of ball, or *caravinagre* 'sullen person', lit. 'face-vinegar', in which features of the face are used metonymically, to denote those of the entire person. These [N + N]$_N$ compounds have more internal structure than those presented earlier; in particular, they require a head external to the two constituents, which I represent as a null word class marker head (3).

(3)

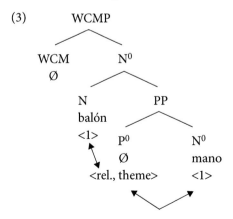

6.1.1.3 *Compound meaning*

[N + N]$_N$ compounds typically denote a subset of the head, restricted by the presence of the non-head nominal. For example, *coche restaurante* 'restaurant car', lit. 'car res-taurant' is not any type of car, but the car on a train where food is served, and *coche cama* 'sleeper car', lit. 'car bed' is a different type of car, where passengers sleep. Seman-tic specialization tends to occur, however, so that other possible meanings are nor-mally eliminated. Thus, a *coche restaurante* is not a free-standing vehicle out of which meals are served, nor is it a car that belongs to a restaurant to be used for deliveries.

The subset-superset semantic relationship described above is most frequent in the newer compounds: *ciudad dormitorio* 'bedroom community', lit. 'city bedroom' [1968] *hora punta* 'rush hour', lit. 'hour point' [1968], but even some old compounds have re-mained transparent after centuries of existence: *cuerno cabra* 'goat horn', lit. 'horn goat' [1250], *piedrazufre* 'sulphur', lit. 'stone sulphur' [1223]. Predictably, though, in the earliest examples the semantic relationship between head and compound may be obscured through semantic narrowing, metaphor, or metonymy: *maestrescuela* 'ecclesiastic in charge of teach-ing religion', lit. 'master-school', *aguapié* 'poor quality wine', lit. 'water foot', *mancuadra* 'oath of calumny, sworn by four parties', lit. 'hand-square'. Phonetic erosion can also make one or both lexemes unrecognizable, obscuring the semantic motivation behind the compound: *feligrés < feliglesie* 'parishioner', lit. 'faithful church' (cf. *fiel* 'faithful' and *iglesia* 'church').

6.1.2 Diachrony

6.1.2.1 *Historical antecedents and comparative data*

Compounds made up of two nominals whose first term is the head are included in some accounts of Latin compounding. However, they are generally described as juxtaposed groups, whose postposed non-head appears with various case markings that are not lost (Bader 1962: 309): PATER FAMILIĀS 'father of the family'. De Dardel (1999) traces the his-tory of what he calls 'governed' [N + N]$_N$ compounds (*composés rectionnels*) in Early Romance, proposing that they do not all have the same historical depth. He argues, on the one hand, for a very ancient Indo-European origin for compounds whose non-head appears in stem form, with no interfixes and no case marks (e.g., *aguamanos* 'wash basin', lit. 'water-hands'). On the other hand, he proposes that other compounds come from antecedents with explicit case marking, such as the Latin genitive (e.g., COMES STABULI 'count of the stables' > *condestable* 'military chief') or the Early Romance genitive/dative, present in continental Romania, but not in Iberia (e.g., Fr. *cuisse-madame* 'type of pear', lit. 'thigh-lady'). According to this author, head-initial [N + N]$_N$ compounds belong to a non-learned tradition (e.g., the toponym *Fuentidueña*, lit. 'fountain-woman').

In keeping with their early appearance in Latin and Romance, head-initial [N + N]$_N$ compounds are documented for all the languages in the Romance family. For example, for Portuguese, see Villalva (1992: 207), for Catalan, Hualde (1986: 69; 1992: 363), for French, Zwanenburg (1990a: 135; 1990b: 74; 1992: 224), Spence (1980: 34), and Picone (1996: 163–69), for Italian Scalise (1992: 177), for Sardinian, Loi Corvetto

(1988: 858), and for Romanian Mallinson (1986: 329). In Spanish also, head-initial compounds with the structure [N + N]$_N$ are attested in all general descriptions and are found from the earliest periods (4).

(4)   Early attestations of head-initial [N + N]$_N$ compounds in Spanish
   a.   *et si firmar nonchelo podiere, faga manquadra con un vecino*
                           (c. 1129, *Fuero de Medinaceli*, CORDE)
         'and if he cannot sign it, he must swear an oath of calumny with a neighbor'

   b.   *Et mando que trayades argenpel e orpel e cintas en coberturas e en per-*
         puntes   (1252, *Actas de las Cortes de Alcalá de Henares [Documentos de*
         Alfonso X dirigidos a Castilla la Nueva], CORDE)
         'And I order that you wear silver ornaments, gold ornaments, and ribbons
         on your coverings and on your stitches'

6.1.2.2 *Frequency and productivity*

Head-initial [N + N]$_N$ compounds are abundant in the database, with a total of 404 different examples altogether (11.7% of the total) (Table 6.2). Their absolute frequency is high from the earliest periods documented, evidence of their presence in the inherited Romance lexicon. These figures grow quickly in the earlier centuries, with large increases between the 1300s and 1400s, and more moderate growth after that. The last two centuries again experience staggering growth, with around 100 new compounds per century. The percentage of head-initial [N + N]$_N$ with respect to the total number of compounds remains relatively stable at slightly over 10% throughout the centuries, which means that their rate of growth keeps pace with that of compounding in general.

The productivity of the head-initial [N + N]$_N$ pattern is constant over the entire period studied, with new compounds accounting for around 30% of all compounds in any given period. The only exceptions are the 1600s and the 1700s, when pattern productivity dips noticeably, due both to fewer creations and to losses.

Table 6.2 Head-initial [N + N]$_N$ compounds attested by century, as totals and as a percentage of all compounds

	Head-initial [N + N]$_N$	All compounds	[N + N]$_N$ as % of all compounds
1000s–1200s	32	349	9.2
1300s	44	434	10.1
1400s	71	709	10.0
1500s	104	1073	9.7
1600s	129	1237	10.4
1700s	140	1360	10.3
1800s	220	1842	11.9
1900s–2000s	357	3005	11.9
Total	404	3451	11.7

Table 6.3 Productivity of head-initial $[N + N]_N$ compounds attested by century

	Carried over	Lost	New	Total	Productivity Ratio
1200s	3	(0)	29	32	NA
1300s	32	(5)	17	44	0.27
1400s	44	(2)	29	71	0.38
1500s	71	(5)	38	104	0.32
1600s	104	(5)	30	129	0.19
1700s	129	(16)	27	140	0.08
1800s	140	(3)	83	220	0.36
1900s–2000s	220	(11)	148	357	0.38

6.1.2.3 *Inseparability of constituents*

The order of nominal constituents inside head-initial $[N + N]_N$ compounds is compatible with the word order of Spanish syntax. It is possible to find phrasal sequences where a nominal is followed by another noun that acts predicatively: *problema clave* 'key problem', lit. 'problem key', *sector servicios* 'service sector', lit. 'sector services' (Bisetto & Scalise 1999: 39–40; Rainer 1993: 247–50; Rainer & Varela 1992). However, cases like these can be distinguished from authentic compounds because they fail the inseparability test (cf. *problema muy clave* 'very key problem', lit. 'problem very key') and/or can undergo head deletion under coordination (cf. *sector agricultura y servicios* 'service and agriculture sector', lit. 'sector agriculture and services'). Constructions with two nominals were not included in the final compound listing if they consistently failed either of these tests in the data.

At least some of the compounds in the $[N + N]_N$ class were formed through agglutination of phrases, i.e., the univerbation that comes as a result of frequent collocation of constituents, sometimes accompanied by the gradual stripping away of non-lexical material over the centuries. This is suggested by the fact that first attestations for $[N + N]_N$ compounds are in some cases preceded by corresponding $[N + de + N]$ phrases, as shown by several of the example sequences presented in Table 6.4 (cf. also discussion in Chapter 1, Section 1.5.4). This is not to say that all compounds in the class were created through this same process. Table 6.4 shows that for some combinations (e.g., *casa cuna*), the sequence of structures seems to be reversed, with $[N + de + N]$ actually following the compound. Moreover, for a vast majority of compounds, no phrasal antecedents can be found. Even allowing for some documentary gaps, there is no reason to believe syntactic precursors always exist, especially for identificational compounds, which have no underlying preposition.

Table 6.4 First attestations for [N + de + N] phrases and related [N + N]$_N$ compounds

Compound constituents	First attestation [N + de + N]	First attestation [N + N]$_N$
baño maría	1710	1791
boca calle	1545 – 1565	1571
boca jarro	c. 1791	1891
boca llave	1629	1851–1855
boca mina	1954	1640
cartón piedra	1951	1872 – 1878
casa cuna	1972	1869
pedo lobo	1926	1965
tela araña	1376 – 1396	1379 – a 1425

6.1.2.4 *Orthographic representation*

As mentioned in Chapter 3 (Section 3.2.3), spelling can be evidence of stress, which in turn can be symptomatic of compound status. However, it should also be remembered that unitary spelling is not invariably used to represent the de-stressing of one constituent, and, in turn, this de-stressing is not always present in compounds. This section briefly explores the stress properties of head-initial [N + N]$_N$ compounds, as described in contemporary accounts. After that, I show how these properties have evolved, insofar as this evolution can be traced using the written medium.

Hualde (2006/2007) notes that head-initial [N + N]$_N$ compounds are generally stressed on both constituents. This is invariably true of the kinds of identificational endocentric compounds: *hómbre rána* 'frog man', lit. 'man frog', *cása jardín* 'garden house', lit. 'house garden'. By contrast, compounds with a partitive/prepositional relationship between constituents may undergo de-stressing, although not all of them do. For example, consider *camión cisterna* 'tanker truck', lit. 'truck watertank' and *telaraña* 'spiderweb', lit. 'cloth spider', in both of which a prepositional relationship holds between the head and non-head (i.e., *camión con cisterna* 'truck with a watertank', *tela de araña* 'cloth of spider'). In spite of this structural similarity, only the later compound undergoes de-stressing of the first constituent: cf. *camión cistérna* vs. **camion cistérna*, and *telaráña* vs. *télaráña*. Hualde proposes that compounds that do not undergo de-stressing are structurally different from those that do. In particular, he suggests that all compounds with de-stressed first constituents are 'word level' compounds, whereas those with stressed first constituents are 'phrasal', and have a null preposition between first and second constituent: [N[ø[N]]]. However, under this hypothesis, identificational compounds of the type *hombre araña* must also be prepositional, which has little semantic justification. I will thus continue to assume that head-initial [N + N]$_N$ compounds can have the two structures proposed in 6.1.1.2, and that these structures are largely independent of their stress properties.

Table 6.5 First attestations for two-word and one-word spellings for head-initial $[N + N]_N$ compounds

	First attestation Two-word spelling	First attestation One-word spelling
agua + pié	1263	c. 1352
capa + piel	c. 1234–1275	1886
piedra + azufre	c. 1414	1250
sal + gema	c. 1250	1344
piedra + imán	1406–ad 1435	1551
agua + mar	c. 1754	–
boca + llave	1851–1855	1851–1855
bono + metro	1989	1986

In historical perspective, the appearance of $[N + N]_N$ compounds spelled as a unit after or concurrently with two-word spelling is consistent with a process of gradual de-stressing of the first constituent, as the compound lexicalizes. Table 6.5 offers some examples of the first attestations of one- and two-word spellings of $[N + N]_N$ compounds from different historical periods. The expected trend for two-word spelling to precede one-word spelling is confirmed in most, but not all, compounds. Note that all the examples of spelling alternation correspond to the prepositional/partitive type of $[N + N]_N$ compound. This reinforces the idea that de-stressing is only available to compounds with that type of internal structure, and is impossible for identificational endocentric $[N + N]_N$ compounds of the type *hombre araña* 'spiderman', lit. 'man spider'.

Hyphenated forms provide evidence of compounding without clearly indicating de-stressing. It is thus possible for both identificational and prepositional $[N + N]_N$ compounds to be represented with hyphens. Compare, for example, the identificational *azul-cielo* 'sky blue', lit. 'blue sky' [1852], with the prepositional *año-luz* 'light year', lit. 'year-light' [1957–1974]. Hyphenated forms are restricted to the 19th and 20th centuries, however, and are not used reliably or frequently enough to offer more than ancillary evidence of compound status.

6.1.2.5 *Evolution of formal features*

As noted earlier, the first nominal in $[N + N]_N$ compounds may appear in full form or as a bare stem. In this section we consider whether there have been any changes over time in the preference for those two morphological configurations. Because there are so few cases in which the first constituent appears in bare form, stems and stems augmented by linking vowels are considered together, and tabulated against compounds whose first constituent appears as a full lexeme. As Table 6.6 shows, over time, first constituents are less likely to appear in stem form. This is a pattern completely unlike that of nominals in $[N + A]_A$ compounds. In $[N + N]_N$ compounds, the nominal is the head, whereas in $[N + A]_A$ it is the non-head. The internal morphological structure of the nominal is therefore related not simply to its position in the compound, but, crucially, to its hierarchy within the compounded structure, a matter to which I return in Chapter 9.

Table 6.6 Morphological structure of leftmost constituent in head-initial $[N + N]_N$ compounds

	Full word (n)	Stem (n)	Totals (n)
1000s–1400s	91% (71)	9% (7)	100% (78)
1500s–1600s	83.8% (57)	16.2% (11)	100% (68)
1700s–1900s	97.3% (251)	2.7% (7)	100% (258)
Totals	93.8% (379)	6.2% (25)	100% (404)

If the first nominal in a compound has no word class marker, then the inflection on the entire compound will attach to the compound's rightmost edge. However, if, as is the case for the majority of head-initial $[N + N]_N$ compounds, the leftmost head appears in full form, then the position of inflectional marking needs to be considered in greater detail. On the one hand, because the head is usually the locus of inflection (Zwicky 1985), plural marking should attach to the first nominal. On the other, because inflection tends to appear on the rightmost edge of a word, plural marks could appear on the non-head noun as well as or instead of on the head nominal. Although frequent gaps in the data make this hard to document in diachronic corpora, there is some contemporary evidence of a shift in the locus of inflection from the first to the second nominal.

Table 6.7 presents the frequencies of inflectional markings for several head-initial $[N + N]_N$ compounds found in Google (3.6.09), tabulated according to their locus of inflection. The most common possibilities are for inflection to be on the first constituent or on the rightmost edge, whereas marking on both constituents appears to be transitional. Moreover, the percentages suggest that the direction of change is the one proposed previously. The rightmost edge appears as the endpoint, so that when inflection appears there, alternatives disappear and the position of inflection becomes categorical (cf. *bocallaves* 'keyholes', lit. 'mouth-keys', *autobombas* 'fire trucks', lit. 'car-pumps', *malvarrosas* 'hollyhocks', lit. 'mallow roses').

Table 6.7 Frequency of plural inflection on $[N + N]_N$ head-initial compounds

	$[N = s + N]_{Npl}$ (n)	$[N = s + N = s]_{Npl}$ (n)	$[N + N = s]_{Npl}$ (n)	Totals
pez + espada	81.5% (10600)	16.7% (2170)	1.9% (243)	13013
casa + cuna	77.2% (53500)	9.8% (6800)	13% (9030)	69330
hombre + lobo	52% (199000)	18.1% (69100)	29.9% (114400)	382500
coche + cama	50.6% (7260)	35% (5010)	14.4% (2070)	14340
palo + rosa	17.6% (156)	30.3% (269)	52% (462)	887
boca + llave	0.3% (33)	2.4% (317)	97.3% (12760)	13110
auto + bomba	0.3% (2940)	0.5% (4030)	99.2% (856940)	863910
malva + rosa	0.2% (407)	0.4% (781)	99.4% (190000)	191188

6.1.2.6 *Exocentric and endocentric uses*

Head-initial $[N + N]_N$ compounds can be endocentric or exocentric, with a few having both types of interpretations. For example, *calvatrueno*, lit. 'bald patch – thunder' can mean both a large bald patch covering the entirety of the head (endocentric) or a crazy young man (exocentric). Yet, when seen in quantitative terms, endocentric compounds are overwhelmingly more frequent, making up over 95% of head-initial $[N + N]_N$ compounds. Historically, exocentric $[N + N]_N$ compounds do not appear to be an offshoot of the endocentric ones, but rather, both have been available all through the history of the language. Examples of exocentric $[N + N]_N$ compounds are documented from the earliest periods and at regular intervals over the centuries: e.g., *mancuadra* 'agreement', lit. 'hand-square' [c. 1129], *puntapié* 'kick', lit. 'point-foot' [1528], and so on.

6.1.3 Special cases

Borrowing may be responsible for the appearance in Spanish of forms whose internal structure can be interpreted partially as $[N + N]_N$, even when one constituent lacks independent existence. Thus, for example, only the first constituent is native and transparent in *avestruz* 'ostrich' < *ave* 'bird' + Old Sp. *estruz* < Old. Occ. *estrutz* < Lat. STRŪTHIO, -ŌNIS < Gr. στρουθίων, -ωνος 'stroythion, -onos', itself a compound of στρουθός 'stroythos', 'sparrow' and κάμηλος 'kamelos', 'camel' (Corominas & Pascual 1980–91: vol. 1, 421).

Further evidence of the reality of the $[N + N]_N$ compound pattern, if any was needed, is the fact that folk etymologies in some of the historical dictionaries are based on the imposition of this pattern on opaque forms. Thus, for example, when Covarrubias proposes that the probable origin for the word *buchorno* (i.e., *bochorno*) 'hot humid weather' is *boca de horno* 'mouth of oven' he may be mistaken, but he provides evidence of the reality of $[N + N]_N$ compounds (cf. Corominas & Pascual 1980–91: vol. 1: 607, where the origin is traced back to Lat. VŬLTŬRNUS 'southerly wind').

6.2 The head-final $[N + N]_N$ pattern: *Pavipollo*

This section deals with head-final compounds whose head is a non-deverbal noun (for $[N + N]_N$ head-final compounds with deverbal heads, cf. Chapter 5, Section 5.3). Head-final $[N + N]_N$ compounds fall into two main stylistic and semantic classes, which correspond to two distinct historical layers. The first layer is very old, and can be traced to Latin and early Romance (de Dardel 1999). These early head-final [N + N] $_N$ compounds are concrete terms typical of everyday language and manual labor. They include names for animals and animal body parts, plants, man-made objects and tools: *maristela* 'starfish', lit. 'sea-star' [1379–1425], *pavipollo* 'young turkey, turkey chicken' [1781–1784], *pezuña* 'hoof', lit. 'foot-nail' [c. 1450–1470], *cabrahígo* 'wild fig', lit.

'goat-fig' [1379–1384], *argentpel* 'thin layer of tin', lit. 'silver-skin' [1252], *gallipuente* (< *callipuente*) 'hanging bridge', lit. 'street bridge' [ad 1605].

The second group of [N + N]$_N$ compounds, responsible for the expansion in the use of the non-verbal pattern in the last century, owes its existence to two tendencies of the Spanish lexicon in the 20th century. The first is the importation of technical and non-technical vocabulary from languages such as English, whose compound constituent order is head-final (*tour operador* 'tour operator'). The second is the incorporation into everyday language of technical terminology that retains learned word order (*avifauna* 'bird species', lit. 'bird-fauna'), as well as the modeling of semi-technical or commercial terminology on learned patterns (*aerosolterapia* 'aerosol therapy', *buhobús* 'night bus', lit. 'owl-bus'). As would be expected, this layer of compounds is made up in large part of innovative abstract nouns that belong in scientific and technical fields: *sueroterapia* 'serum therapy', *servosistema* 'service system', lit. 'servo-system'. The increased impact of technology on everyday life has contributed to the generalization of head-final patterns in colloquial language.

6.2.1 Structure

6.2.1.1 *Constituents*
In head-final [N + N]$_N$ compounds, both nouns tend to be morphologically simple: *cabrahígo* 'wild fig', lit. 'goat-fig', *ranacuajo* 'tadpole', lit. 'frog-clot'. The non-head nominal, in particular, is hardly ever complex: *oropel* 'gold leaf', lit. 'gold-skin', *casamuro* 'wall', lit. 'house wall', (but cf. *platinocianuro* 'platine-cyanide', lit. 'platinum-cyanide' where *platino* 'platinum' ← *plata* 'silver'). The head may sometimes exhibit derivational suffixation, especially when a [N + N]$_N$ compound serves as the base for another: *cabrahígo* 'wild fig', lit. 'goat-fig' → *cabrahigal* 'grove of wild fig trees', lit. 'goat-fig tree grove'.

The rightmost head is the only locus of number and gender inflection: *buhobús* 'owl-bus-SG' → *buhobuses* 'owl-bus-PL'. The entire compound receives its gender specifications from the rightmost head constituent: *el gutiámbar* 'the gamboge', lit. 'the-MASC drop-FEM amber-MASC' (cf. *la gota* 'the drop-FEM', *el ámbar* 'the amber-MASC'), *la aerosolterapia* 'the-FEM aerosol therapy-FEM'. (cf. *el aerosol* 'the-MASC aerosol-MASC', *la terapia* 'the-FEM therapy-FEM'.).

Whereas head constituents always appear with their word class marker – referability being a prerequisite for further inflectional attachment – non-heads vary a great deal in this respect. Around 40% of them appear in bare form or with some kind of a linking element: *gat-uña* 'restharrow', lit. 'cat-nail' (cf. *gat-o*), *gom-o-rresina* 'gum-resin' (cf. *goma*), *corn-i-cabra* 'turpentine tree', lit. 'horn-goat' (cf. *cuern-o*). The remainder exhibit full forms (e.g., *casapuerta* 'door house', cf. *cas-a*) or forms that are ambiguous (*ozonoterapia* 'ozone therapy', analyzable as *ozono-terapia* or *ozon-o-terapia*). The issue of bare forms vs. full lexemes will be considered in its historical perspective in Section 6.2.2.5.

Finally, several non-heads and heads appear repeatedly in pockets of productivity that create families of related compounds. Consider, for example, heads such as *manía* 'mania, addiction' (*cocainomanía* 'cocaine addiction', *opiomanía* 'opium addiction', and neologisms such as *demoniomanía* 'demonic possession', lit. 'devil-mania', *faxmanía* 'addiction to sending faxes', lit. 'fax-mania'), and *terapia* 'therapy' (*farmacoterapia* 'medicine-therapy', *hormonoterapia* 'hormone therapy', *laserterapia* 'laser therapy', *fangoterapia* 'mud therapy', *musicoterapia* 'music therapy'). There are also frequent non-heads such as *video* (*videotexto* 'video-text', *videoportero* 'intercom', lit. 'video-doorman', *videojuego* 'videogame'), *radio* (*radionovela* 'radio soap opera', *radiopatrulla* 'patrol car', lit. 'radio-patrol', *radiodifusión* 'broadcasting', lit. 'radio-dissemination'), *auto* 'car' (*autoventa* 'sale out of a car', lit. 'car-sale', *autocarril* 'car lane', *autorradio* 'car radio').

6.2.1.2 *Compound structure*

In [N + N]$_N$ head-final compounds the relationship between both nominals is of the kind that in syntax would be associated with the range of uses of the preposition *de* 'of'. Thus, *gomorresina* is *resina de goma* 'resin made with gum', *bronconeumonía* is *neumonía de los bronquios* 'pneumonia affecting the bronquial tubes', *gelatinobromuro* is *bromuro de/con gelatina* 'bromide with gelatin'. I will assume that the head nominal selects a prepositional phrase that in turn selects the non-head. The PP head is either empty or filled with the linking vowel, but crucially, not with a preposition. The lower nominal in bare form incorporates into the PP head, and then, into the higher nominal, thus circumventing the case requirements of the visibility condition (cf. Chapter 5, Section 5.1.1). Like in the [N + V]$_V$ compounds discussed in Chapter 4, the non-head acts as a modifier to the head.

(5) a.

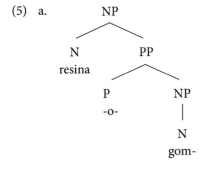

b.

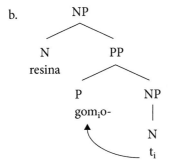

c.

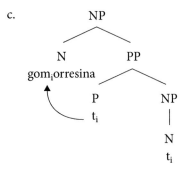

The analysis of noun-to-noun incorporation presented here hinges on the assumption that a nominal without its word class marker projection is incapable of receiving case from a higher head. If this is so, then we expect all incorporating nominal non-heads to appear in their bare form. However, as the reader will recall, there are in fact head-final [N + N]$_N$ compounds whose non-head appears in a form that is compatible with an analysis as noun + word class marker, and should therefore preclude incorporation: *buhobús* 'late bus', lit. 'owl-bus' (cf. *búho* 'owl'). I will deal with this issue by assuming that the presence of the word class marker as a prerequisite for case assignment is a historical development. Many of the earliest compounds, inherited from Latin, do not conform to it: *orofrés* 'gold-ribbon' (cf. *or-o* 'gold') [c. 1240], *cabrahígo* 'wild fig', lit. 'goat fig' [1379–1384] (cf. *cabr-a* 'goat'). By contrast, very innovative forms pass the requirement by exhibiting non-heads that are ambiguous in morphological structure. Consider, for example, *fangoterapia* 'mud therapy', analyzable as *fango-terapia* or as *fang-o-terapia*. Note that one argument in favor of this analysis is that, even in a form compatible with a stem + WCM analysis, the preposed nominal is incapable of bearing plural marks, which it could if it were placed after the nominal (**librosfórum*, **buhosbús*, vs. *fórum de libros*, *bus para búhos*). This can be accounted for straightforwardly if we assume that there is no word class marker present in the first constituent, but remains mysterious otherwise. The historical details of this evolution will be considered in Section 6.2.2.5.

6.2.1.3 *Compound meaning*
Even in the more transparent compounds, the relational predication established by the [N + N] template can be used in a number of different ways. Compare, for example, *ferrobús* 'local train', lit. 'iron-bus', whose non-head invokes the material composition of the head (*bus hecho de hierro* 'bus made of iron'), with *trolebús* 'trolley bus', where it denotes one of its component parts (*bus con troles* 'bus with trolleys'), and *buhobús* 'late night bus', lit. 'owl bus', where it metaphorically gives information about the schedule of the route (*bus para búhos* 'bus for owls'). Other, non-exhaustive, meanings include goal (*autocarril = carril para autos* 'car lane'), reason (*litisexpensas = expensas por la litis* 'court costs', lit. 'suit expenses'), and presentation (*gutiámbar = ámbar en gotas* 'gamboge', lit. 'amber in drops').

6.2.2 Diachrony

6.2.2.1 *Historical antecedents and comparative data*

Head-final [N + N]$_N$ patterns are better documented for historical languages than their head-initial counterparts. For example, they are present in Greek (e.g., ἀκρόπολις 'akró-polis', 'citadel', lit. 'extremity-city') (Schwyzer 1953 [1938]: 428) and Sanskrit (e.g., *rājadanta* 'king-tooth') (Whitney 1941 [1879]: 495). Latin also offers abundant and well-documented examples of head-final [N + N]$_N$ patterns with a partitive relationship between constituents (Bader 1962: 308; Fruyt 2002; 2005: 266; Oniga 1992: 102): CAPRI-FICUS 'wild fig', lit. 'goat-fig', MUS-CERDAE 'mouse droppings'. Authors generally distinguish proper or true compounds, whose preposed non-head nominal appears without any case marking (Bader 1962: 316–22), and juxtaposed or 'false' compounds, whose non-head may appear with various case markings, evidence of a phrasal origin (Bader 1962: 296–97). For de Dardel (1999), early Romance head-final [N + N]$_N$ compounds belong to two distinct historical layers. The older ones are prolongations of the Classical Latin pattern (e.g., Lat. PEDIS UNGULAM 'foot nail' > Sp. *pezuña* 'hoof'), whereas the newer ones are popular and exhibit no overt case marks (e.g., Lat. CATTAM UNGULAM 'cat nail' > Sp. *gatuña* 'restharrow').

Head-final [N + N]$_N$ compounds are very seldom mentioned in panoramic contemporary studies of compounding in the Romance languages. Mascaró (1986: 74) and Picone (1996: 172–73) are exceptions, since they include some examples for Catalan and French, respectively. Other authors only mention head-final nominal [N + N]$_N$ compounds in the learned and semi-learned categories, such as Port. *herbívoro* 'herbivore', Fr. *agriculture*, It. *ferrovia* 'railroad', lit. 'iron-way', Cat. *gammaglobulina* 'gammaglobulin'. By contrast, Spanish examples can be found from the earliest periods (6), even if in some cases phonetic changes and lexical losses would obscure the relationship between lexemes and compound.

(6) Early attestations of head-final [N + N]$_N$ compounds in Spanish
  a. *Et mando que trayades* _argenpel_ *e* _orpel_ *e cintas en coberturas*
     (1252, *Actas de las Cortes de Alcalá de Henares [Documentos de Alfonso X dirigidos a Castilla la Nueva]*, CORDE)
     'And I order that you wear silver ribbons, gold ribbons, and sashes in the coverings'
  b. *Aquí tanne Dauid los periglos que suellen acaescer a los romeros por los* _agua duchos_ *de las pluuias*
       (c. 1240–1272, Hernán el Alemán, *Traslación del Psalterio*, CORDE)
       'Here David sang about the perils that rain floods may present for pilgrims'

Over time some of these early compounds have become completely opaque, but how compositional they were in the earliest periods under consideration is less obvious. For example, *aguaducho* 'water conduit' may have been formally transparent for quite some time, although its head *ducho* 'duct' very seldom appears in isolation. Yet, the rare cases where it does appear as a free form constitute evidence for compositionality: e.g., *vna heredat que es en Merezilla a la calleja de Pertecedo; que tien por costaneras: de la vna parte, la carrera antigua e ducho de la mier* 'a plot that is in Merezilla in the street of Pertecedo, which has as its limits, on one side, the old road and the water conduit of the swamp...' (1459, *Venta de heredad [Colección diplomática de Santa Catalina del Monte Corbán]*, CORDE). Additionally, the earliest documentations of *aguaducho* are consistently spelled as two words (6b). Finally, one can cite the relatively late occurrence of the equivalent learned form *aguaducto* [1605].

6.2.2.2 *Frequency and productivity*

Head-final $[N + N]_N$ compounds are abundant, with a total of 327 different examples in the database (9.5%). There is a non-negligible number of inherited forms in the earliest period, with steady but modest gains until the 1500s. After that, numbers flatline and the relative frequency of the pattern dips. Surprisingly, in the 20th century there is a sudden spike as the number of compounds more than triples from the previous period. As a consequence, the head-final $[N + N]_N$ pattern doubles in relative frequency from the earliest to the latest period.

Let us now turn to pattern productivity, measured in terms of the ratio of new to old compounds per century (Table 6.9). After the initial period, which shows the effect of the inherited examples on the totals, there is a period of high productivity in the 1400s and 1500s, when new compounds account for between 50% and 30% of the total for each century, respectively. After that come two centuries during which the pattern ceases to be productive, with ratios of new compounds of under 10%. In the 1800s the ratio picks up again, with new compounds constituting around one third of the total. Finally, the 1900s see a spectacular surge, with over two new compounds for every one carried over from the previous century. The pattern is also quite prone to losses, as words fall out of use throughout its history at different rates.

Table 6.8 Head-final $[N + N]_N$ compounds attested by century, as totals and as a percentage of all compounds

	Head-final $[N + N]_N$	All compounds	$[N + N]_N$ as % of all compounds
1000s–1200s	17	349	4.9
1300s	18	434	4.1
1400s	34	709	4.8
1500s	48	1073	4.5
1600s	47	1237	3.8
1700s	48	1360	3.5
1800s	72	1842	3.9
1900s–2000s	301	3005	10.0
Total	327	3451	9.5

Table 6.9 Productivity of head-final [N + N]$_N$ compounds attested by century

	Carried over	Lost	New	Total	Productivity Ratio
1200s	6	(1)	11	16	NA
1300s	16	(5)	7	18	0.11
1400s	18	(0)	16	34	0.47
1500s	34	(2)	16	48	0.29
1600s	48	(8)	7	47	−0.02
1700s	47	(5)	6	48	0.02
1800s	48	(2)	26	72	0.33
1900s–2000s	72	(3)	232	301	0.76

6.2.2.3 *Inseparability of constituents*

The compound status of head-final [N + N]$_N$ compounds is not normally in doubt, because the order of constituents is incompatible with the word order of Spanish syntax. In other words, today this pattern cannot be formed through the gradual agglutination of syntactic phrases. None of these compounds have precursors whose two nominals could be interpreted as separable, i.e., with elements inserted between the two constituents. This is true both in cases in which the first nominal appears in stem form: *vitamino efectiva terapia* 'effective vitamin therapy', lit. 'vitamin effective therapy'; and when it appears as a full-fledged lexeme: *agua gran ducto* 'large water pipe', lit. 'water great pipe'. Moreover, constituents in these [N + N]$_N$ configurations cannot receive independent modification: *fresca aguaducto* 'duct for fresh water', lit. 'fresh water duct', *respiratorio organoterapia* 'therapy of a respiratory organ', lit. 'respiratory organ therapy'. Their non-head/head order is also stable, with no compounds exhibiting reversal of constituents: *organoterapia* 'organ therapy' vs. *terapiaórgano* 'id.', lit. 'therapy organ' (but cf. *lobombre* 'werewolf', lit. 'wolf man' vs. *hombre lobo* 'id.', lit. 'man wolf').

6.2.2.4 *Orthographic representation*

In general terms, these compounds are spelled as one word, further evidence of their unitary status. In fact, only a tiny minority (less than 2%) appear only in two-word or hyphenated spelling, without one-word alternants: e.g., *aguja paladar* 'silver scabbardfish [Lepidopus caudatus L.]', lit. 'needle palate', *sangre lluvia* 'menstrual bleeding', lit. 'blood rain', *cóctel-bar* 'cocktail bar'. One-word spellings may alternate with two-word and hyphenated forms, depending on factors such as the time depth of the compound and the internal structure of its first constituent. Compounds from the earlier periods are spelled more frequently as one word than two. Consider, for example, the unitary spelling of the alternants of *aurifreso* [1050], *orfres* [1252], *orofresa* [1542], *orifrés* [1886] 'gold ribbon'. Newer compounds tend to present a wider array of possibilities: *videoconferencia* ~ *video-conferencia* ~ *video conferencia* 'video conference'; *radioyente* ~ *radio-oyente* ~ *radio oyente* 'radio listener'. However, no compounds, either old or new, are spelled as two words if the first constituent is unambiguously a stem: *cosmo-visión* ~ *cosmo-visión* vs. **cosmo visión*.

6.2.2.5 *Evolution of formal features*

The most salient feature that undergoes changes over time in head-final $[N + N]_N$ compounds is the internal structure of the non-head nominal, which can be a full noun, a bare stem, or a stem with a linking vowel. However, there is some ambiguity because more than half of the non-head nominals can be considered either full words or stems with a linking vowel (*radio-* vs. *radi-o*, *auto-* vs. *aut-o*, etc.). Table 6.10 explores the evolution of the morphological makeup of constituents in global terms by considering the internal structure of new compounds.

For compounds created between 1000 and 1499, preposed non-heads tend to appear as full forms more frequently than as stems. Thus, for example, compounds such as *aguaducho* 'water conduit', lit. 'water-duct' and *orofrés* 'gold-ribbon' are more frequent than those with the structure of *argentpel* 'thin layer of tin covered in silver', lit. 'silver-skin'. The latter, in turn, are as frequent as those with linking vowels, such as *aurifreso* 'gold-ribbon'. However, the preference for stems increases to over 80% in compounds created in the following period (1500–1799), and the linking vowel has generalized to almost half of the stems in these new compounds. In the 1800s and 1900s the situation becomes more confusing, with the presence of 160 first constituents that can be interpreted either as full forms or as stems (e.g., *videojuego* 'videogame', *reflejoterapia* 'reflexotherapy'). If they are counted as full lexemes, then they constitute a reversal of the tendency shown in the previous period: full lexemes become more frequent than stems in the non-head nominal. However, if those ambiguous forms are classified as stems (e.g., in a case like *laser-terapia* 'laser therapy',) or as stems with a linking vowel (e.g., in a case like *radi-o-terapia* 'radio therapy'), as has been done in Table 6.10, then the tendency of the previous period is maintained and deepened. By the 20th century, stems are overwhelmingly preferred over full words in preposed non-head nominals. It could be argued that the presence of ambiguous constituents could be the beginning of a reversal of the previous preference for bare stems. This is indeed true. However, for the process of reversal to be unequivocal, the non-head nominal should be able to exhibit plural marks as well (e.g., *tour operador* 'tour operator' > *tours operador* 'tours operator'). Since there is no indication that this is the

Table 6.10 Morphological structure of nominal constituent in head-final $[N + N]_N$ compounds

	Full lexemes (n)	Stem (n)	Stem + linking vowel (n)	Totals (n)
1000s–1400s	50% (20)	25% (10)	25% (10)	100% (40)
1500s–1700s	14.3% (4)	46.4% (13)	39.3% (11)	100% (28)
1800s–1900s	7.3% (19)	12.7% (33)	80% (207)	100% (259)
Totals	13.2% (43)	17.1% (56)	69.7% (228)	100% (327)

case, it is preferable to assume that these first constituents are indeed stems. The pattern presented here is different from that seen in head-initial $[N + N]_N$ compounds in 6.1.2.5, where compounds always exhibit a preference for a full nominal in leftmost position, and where this preference increases gradually over the centuries.

6.2.2.6 *Endocentric and exocentric uses*
The head-final $[N + N]_N$ pattern is robustly endocentric, with very few exponents exhibiting grammatical recategorization or metonymic shifts (but cf. a counterexample such as *gallocresta* 'wild clary', lit. 'rooster-comb').

6.3 The $[N + A]_N$ pattern: *Avetarda*

The last two sections of this chapter deal with structurally asymmetrical compounds with nominal heads and adjectival non-heads. Since these compounds are created through the agglutination of syntactic phrases, they are the hardest to distinguish from non-compounded phrases. The problem cannot be solved by consulting lexicographical sources alone, since these works list multi-lexeme items with specialized meaning, regardless of whether they are also structurally atomic. For our purposes, several tests were carried out to check the structural and semantic stability of each compound (cf. Chapter 3, Section 3.2.2.4.1 for details). It must be noted, however, that given the very nature of these lexemes, it is impossible to produce a definitive list, since what is a compound for some speakers may not be for others.

This section deals with compounds with nominal heads and adjectival non-heads whose head appears before its modifier (for compounds with preposed adjectivals, cf. 6.4). $[N + A]_N$ compounds are very frequently used to denote concrete items such as animals, plants, and minerals: *avucasta* 'bustard', lit. 'bird-chaste', *león pardo/leopardo* 'leopard', lit. 'lion brown', *alga marina* 'sea algae', lit. 'algae sea-ADJ SUFF', *hierbabuena* 'mint', lit. 'herb-good', *piedra preciosa* 'precious stone', lit. 'stone precious', *aguamarina* 'aquamarine', lit. 'water sea- ADJ SUFF'. They are also used to denote man-made products and objects: *vinagre* 'vinegar', lit. 'wine-sour', *goma arábiga* 'gum arabic', *casa rodante* 'camper', lit. 'house wheel- ADJ SUFF'. They can name humans and body parts: *marimandona* 'bossy woman', lit. 'Mary-bossy', *guardiacivil* 'policeman', lit. 'guard civilian', *cuero cabelludo* 'scalp', lit. 'skin hairy'. In the earlier periods they are also frequent in the religious and legal lexicon: *agua bendita* 'holy water', lit. 'water blessed', *disanto/día santo* 'holiday', lit. 'day holy', *cosa juzgada* 'res judicata', lit. 'thing judged'. However, these uses become less frequent in the later centuries, something that distinguishes $[N + A]_N$ compounds from their $[A + N]_N$ counterparts, common in academic registers all through their history.

$[N + A]_N$ compounds are overwhelmingly endocentric, so that, for example, a *puerco montés* 'wild boar', lit. 'pig hill-ADJ SUFF' is a type of *puerco*. A small number appear in metonymic or metaphoric uses, such as *piel roja* 'redskin', lit. 'skin red' (not a kind of *piel*) *marimorena* 'upheaval', lit. 'Mary-dark' (not a kind of *María*, i.e., woman).

6.3.1   Structure

6.3.1.1   *Constituents*

The first constituent in [N + A]$_N$ compounds is the head, which can be a mass noun (*argent vivo* 'mercury', lit. 'silver live', *aguardiente* 'brandy', lit. 'water burning'), a countable noun (*bancarrota* 'bankruptcy', lit. 'bench-broken', *paloblanco* 'Willard's acacia', lit. 'stick-white'), or a noun designating animates (*mosca muerta* 'insignificant person, i.e., dead fly' lit. 'fly dead', *perro caliente* 'hotdog', lit. 'dog hot'), and humans (*mozalbete* 'young man', lit. 'youth-white-DIM SUFF'). Abstract nouns are not frequent in [N + A]$_N$ for any historical period, although there are isolated examples (*fe católica* 'Catholic faith', lit. 'faith Catholic').

The vast majority of nouns in [N + A]$_N$ compounds appear in full form: *sangregorda* 'bore', lit. 'blood fat', *caña melar* 'sugar cane', lit. 'cane honey-ADJ SUFF' A small minority of compounds (6.2%), mostly from the early periods, appears with nominals in stem form: *avucasta* 'bustard [bird]', lit. 'bird chaste', *manvacía* 'empty hand', lit. 'hand-empty'. When accompanied by a word class marker, nouns are also the locus of inflection for the entire compound and are responsible for the concord features on the adjectival constituent: *la tinta china* 'the-FEM SG ink- FEM SG Chinese- FEM SG' vs. *las tintas chinas* 'the-FEM PL ink-FEM PL Chinese- FEM PL'. However, over time this inflection tends to be lost, so that the adjectival non-head may end up being the only constituent that exhibits inflection for the entire compound (*guardias civiles* 'policemen', lit. 'guard-MASC PL civilian- MASC PL' > *guardiaciviles* 'id'. lit. 'guard-MASC SG civilian-MASC PL').

Postposed adjectives in [N + A]$_N$ compounds are of the same types that would be found in that position in syntax. They include descriptive adjectives of color, size, texture, and so on (*huevomol* 'type of dessert', lit. 'egg soft', *fiebre amarilla* 'yellow fever', lit. 'fever yellow'), and relational adjectives (*defensa personal* 'personal defense', lit. 'defense personal', *caja registradora* 'cash register', lit. 'box register-ADJ SUFF', *crema pastelera* 'pastry filling', lit. 'cream cake-ADJ SUFF') (cf. Bosque & Picallo 1996, for a discussion of postnominal adjectives).

Structurally, a vast majority of adjectives in [N + A]$_N$ are simple stems, with no derivational suffixation: *cabeza dura* 'stubborn person', lit. 'head hard', *aguamala* 'jellyfish', lit. 'water bad'. There are also deverbal and denominal adjectives: *papel pintado* 'wallpaper', lit. 'paper painted' (< *pintar* 'to paint'), *oso hormiguero* 'anteater', lit. 'bear ant-ADJ SUFF' (< *hormiga* 'ant'). A few of the adjectives in [N + A]$_N$ can also appear in [A + N]$_N$. Consider, for example, *franco* 'free, frank' in *francotirador* 'sniper', lit. 'free shooter', and *puerto franco* 'free port', lit. 'port free', or *doble* in *doblemano* 'two-way street', lit. 'double hand', and *pasodoble* 'dance', lit. 'step-double'. However, once compounded, a noun-adjective sequence is not amenable to changes in the order of its two constituents: *francotirador* 'sniper', lit. 'free shooter' vs. **tirador franco*, *puerto franco* 'free port' vs. **franco puerto*.

6.3.1.2 *Compound structure*

The internal structure of [N + A]$_N$ compounds mirrors that of [A + N]$_N$ compounds (cf. (7) and (12)). [N + A]$_N$ compounds may be exocentric, designating a whole by denoting one of its parts. The structural configuration in that case can be represented as in (8), with an empty word class marker head in the internal structure.

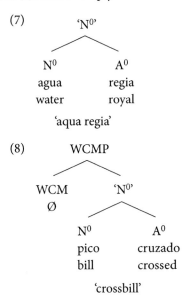

(7)   'N^0'

N^0 A^0
agua   regia
water   royal

'aqua regia'

(8)   WCMP

WCM   'N^0'
Ø

N^0 A^0
pico   cruzado
bill   crossed

'crossbill'

6.3.1.3 *Compound meaning*

Modification of the kind that holds between the noun and the postposed adjective can be viewed as a relationship of coordination between the denotation of a nominal (itself a predicate) and the secondary predicate that the adjective introduces. Recall that this thematic relationship is known as theta identification, since the position in the adjective that corresponds to its referential variable is identified with the corresponding position within the nominal (9), and the adjective, which lacks its own denotation, piggybacks onto whatever role the nominal performs, be it argumental or predicative. Thus, *hierbabuena* 'mint', lit. 'herb-good' is a type of *hierba*, and so on. Like all compounds, [N + A]$_N$ can become opaque over time through metaphoric or metonymic interpretations, in which case the set-superset relationship between the nominal head and the compound may be lost. Consider, for example, *tiovivo* 'merry-go-round', lit. 'uncle living', not a type of *tío*, or *montepío* 'pawnshop', lit. 'mount-pious', not a type of *monte*.

(9)   N

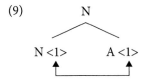

N <1>   A <1>

6.3.2 Diachrony

6.3.2.1 *Historical antecedents and comparative data*

Compounds with the structure $[N + A]_N$ are not documented for Sanskrit in Whitney (1941 [1879]) or for Greek in Schwyzer (1953 [1938]), but they do appear in Latin, where according to Bader, they constitute calques from Greek or late formations (e.g., EQUIFER 'wild horse', lit. 'horse-wild', NARDOCELTICUM 'Celtic nard', lit. 'nard Celtic'). Moreover, the *bahuvrihi* type of $[N + A/A + N]_N$ compound is said to be the earliest type found in Indo-European (Kastovsky 2009: 339).

In the Romance languages, the $[N + A]_N$ compounding pattern is attested in a wide array of descriptions. There are references to the pattern and specific examples of its use in Portuguese (Alves 1986–1987: 56; Villalva 1992: 210), Catalan (Hualde 1992: 363; Mascaró 1986: 72), French (Spence 1980: 73; Zwanenburg 1990a: 135; 1990b: 74; 1992: 224), Italian (Dardano 1988: 59; Scalise 1992: 177), and Romanian (Mallinson 1986: 329). Several authors present both exo- and endocentric examples (Dardano 1988: 59; Mallinson 1986; Zwanenburg 1992: 224), but it is reasonable to assume that the process whereby the structure is allowed to be used exocentrically is common to more, possibly all, Romance languages.

$[N + A]_N$ compounds are attested in Spanish from the earliest periods recorded. Even at those early stages some already show signs of univerbation, such as lack of word class marker on the nominal constituent (10a) or unified spelling (10b), evidence of their very early creation.

(10) Early attestations of $[N + A]_N$ compounds in Spanish

 a. *Ego Mari Díaz e Ferrando Díaz e Petro Guigélmez somos fiadores de <u>man-común</u> de a tot omne qui ì deve heredar*
  (1201, *Carta de venta, Documentos del Archivo Histórico Nacional (1200–1492)*, CORDE)
  'I, Mari Díaz and Ferrando Díaz, and Petro Guigélmez are guarantors in common of any man who must inherit there'.

 b. *Item un <u>aguamanil</u> fecho commo leon.* (1275, *Inventario de bienes de la catedral [Documentos de los archivos catedralicio y diocesano de Salamanca]*, CORDE)
  'Item: a washbasin shaped like a lion'.

6.3.2.2 *Frequency and productivity*

$[N + A]_N$ compounds constitute one of the main types in the database, with a total of 396 examples altogether (over 10% of the total) (Table 6.11). Their relatively high weight in the earliest periods documented provides evidence of their frequent presence in the inherited Romance lexicon. Like their inverted $[A + N]_N$ counterparts, $[N + A]_N$ compounds increase their relative percentages slightly in the early centuries, peak in the 1400s, and start to decrease after that, as their absolute numbers fail to keep pace with the growth in the total number of compounds in Spanish.

Table 6.11 $[N + A]_N$ compounds attested by century, as totals and as a percentage of all compounds

	$[N + A]_N$	All compounds	$[N + A]_N$ as % of all compounds
1000s–1200s	65	349	18.6
1300s	95	434	21.9
1400s	161	709	22.7
1500s	204	1073	19.0
1600s	226	1237	18.3
1700s	241	1360	17.7
1800s	295	1842	16.0
1900s–2000s	367	3005	12.2
Total	396	3451	11.5

Table 6.12 Productivity of $[N + A]_N$ compounds attested by century

	Carried over	Lost	New	Total	Productivity Ratio
1200s	3	(0)	62	65	NA
1300s	65	(1)	31	95	0.32
1400s	95	(0)	66	161	0.41
1500s	161	(4)	47	204	0.21
1600s	204	(6)	28	226	0.10
1700s	226	(10)	25	241	0.06
1800s	241	(1)	55	295	0.18
1900s–2000s	295	(7)	79	367	0.20

Table 6.12 summarizes the findings on the productivity of $[N + A]_N$ compounds. After the initial period, the 1300s and 1400s exhibit quite high productivity, with the percentage of new compounds at or above 30% of the total for each of these centuries. After that, the ratio of new to old compounds decreases though the 17th century and only picks up slightly in the later periods. Overall, this is quite a stable pattern, with few losses per century. With some minor differences, this pattern's productivity resembles that of $[A + N]_N$ compounds presented in 6.4.2.2.

6.3.2.3 *Inseparability of constituents*
It is widely recognized that it is difficult to establish the compound status of both $[N + A]_N$ and $[A + N]_N$ compounds (cf. discussion in Martinell Gifre 1984; Rainer 1993: 294). Since these compounds have an internal structure compatible with sentence syntax, it is not always clear that they are not simply lexicalized phrases with stable idiomatic meaning. Since the majority of the compounds in this class seem to

originate in these phrases, it is hard to draw the line between the two categories. The task of establishing whether a given [N + A] sequence is in fact a compound is therefore quite complex, and individual cases fall along a continuum, from those that are highly compounded (syntactically atomic, semantically non-compositional), to those that are less so, on either semantic or syntactic terms.

By following the criteria introduced in Chapter 2, the list of possible compounds can be narrowed down to those that exhibit formal fixity (stable word order, no insertions of extraneous material, etc.), semantic stability, and a threshold frequency consistent with lexicalization. That said, compoundhood must be considered a gradient measure, based not on the absolute absence of clearly phrasal counterexamples, but on their low frequency. For example, the sequence *caballero aventurero* 'knight errant', lit. 'knight adventuresome', appears in CORDE with the same form and meaning in 67 instances, so it is included as a compound in spite of 5 counterexamples (of the kind in 11a, b).

(11) a. *Allí fue luego presentada al emperador, de parte de todos los <u>caballeros aventureros y errantes</u>, una carta*
                                  (1552, Juan Cristóbal Calvete de Estrella, CORDE)
    'Immediately, a letter was presented to the emperor, on behalf of all the knight errants'.

    b. *Salga, pues, nuevamente a la luz del mundo el gran Don Quijote de la Mancha, si hasta hoi <u>cavallero desgraciadamente aventurero</u>, en adelante por U. E. felizmente venturoso.*   (1737, Gregorio Mayans y Siscar, CORDE)
    'Let the great Don Quixote de la Mancha come back to public light; if until now an unfortunately errant knight (lit. 'knight unfortunately adventuresome'), from now on, happily fated thanks to Your Excellency'.

It can also be tricky to ascertain the semantic stability of $[N + A]_N$ compounds. For example, whereas *bala perdida* 'loose cannon', lit. 'bullet lost', is attested as early as 1781, it is not until the 1900s that it acquires its metaphorical meaning of 'reckless person'. However, because it proved impractical to ascertain the vagaries of meaning for each $[N + A]_N$ compound, in general the first date of attestation of the [N + A] complex was used as its starting point, even if its meaning was still not stabilized.

6.3.2.4 *Orthographic representation*

The only $[N + A]_N$ compounds that are always spelled as one word, independently of their historical depth, are those whose nominal head appears without a word class marker: *manizquierda* 'left hand', lit. 'hand left' [1427–28], *mozalbillo* 'young man', lit. 'youth white-DIM' [1540 – c. 1577], *marimandona* 'bossy woman', lit. 'Mary bossy' [1911]. All other $[N + A]_N$ compounds, in keeping with their gradual emergence from phrases, can vacillate between one- and two-word spellings and, sometimes hyphen

Table 6.13 First attestations for two-word and one-word spellings for [N + A]$_N$ compounds

	First attestation Two-word spelling	First attestation One-word spelling
guardia + civil	1849	1940
verde + gay	1441	1406–1435
agua + fuerte	ad 1429	1580 – ad 1627
campo + santo	ad 1582	1326
agua + marina	1579	1515
mata + parda	1575–1580	1962
palo + santo	1527–1550	1605
zarza + perruna	1606	1962
cara + dura	1876	1611
paso + doble	1845	1871

ated alternants: *aguardiente ~ agua ardiente* 'brandy', lit. 'water burning', *ajo blanco ~ ajo-blanco ~ ajoblanco* 'type of sauce', lit. 'garlic-white'. In general, two-word spelling precedes one-word spelling, but this sequence is less clear than for [A + N]$_N$ compounds (cf. Section 6.4.2.4). In six of the ten representative examples in Table 6.13, two-word spelling precedes one-word spelling, in one they are simultaneous, and in the remaining three one-word spelling is attested earlier than two-word spelling, against expectations.

6.3.2.5 *Evolution of formal features*

[N + A]$_N$ compounds may present the nominal constituent in full form or as a bare stem, lacking its word class marker. As shown in Table 6.14, all through history [N + A]$_N$ compounds have an overwhelming preference for the nominal to appear as a full lexeme (>90%). This preference has become virtually categorical in the last two centuries, with almost 98% of new compounds exhibiting full lexemes as their head nominals. The pattern of growing intolerance for nominal stems is parallel to that noted for [N + N]$_N$ head-initial compounds (Section 6.1.2.5).

Table 6.14 Morphological structure of leftmost constituent in [N + A]$_N$ compounds

	Full lexeme (n)	Stem (n)	Totals (n)
1000s–1400s	93.2% (151)	6.8% (11)	100% (162)
1500s–1700s	92% (92)	8% (8)	100% (100)
1800s–1900s	97.8% (131)	2.2% (3)	100% (134)
Totals	94.4% (374)	5.6% (22)	100% (396)

Table 6.15 First attestations of [N + A]$_N$ compounds with and without internal plural concord

	First attestation [N = s + A = s]$_{Npl}$	First attestation [N + A = s]$_{Npl}$
casa + fuerte	1300–1305	1461
foto + fija	1984	1986
guardia + marina	1748	1881
guardia + civil	1849	1940
paso + doble	1845	1889

In the majority of [N + A]$_N$ compounds whose nominal head appears in its full form, the head can be expected to be the locus of gender and number inflection, while the postposed adjective exhibits internal concord marks: *perros calientes* 'hot dogs', lit. 'dog-MASC PL hot- MASC PL', *montañas rusas* 'roller coasters', lit. 'mountain-FEM PL Russian-FEM PL'. The internal number concord may disappear from the first constituent, a historical sequence that can be corroborated by looking at first attestations (Table 6.15). An important observation is that in [N + A]$_N$ compounds it is the head that loses number inflection, now found only on the rightmost margin. However, the process of loss of this intermediate inflection is harder to trace with the extant data, since there are few compounds that exhibit all the possible inflectional marking combinations.

6.3.2.6 Exocentric and endocentric uses

As anticipated in Section 6.3.1, [N + A]$_N$ compounds, like their head-final counterparts, can be endocentric or exocentric (e.g., *brazo derecho* 'right-hand man', lit. 'arm right'), but endocentric compounds constitute the vast majority of [N + A]$_N$ head-initial compounds (95%). Exocentric uses are attested from the earliest periods and do not seem to be a later development.

6.4 The [A + N]$_N$ pattern: *Falsa abeja*

This last section deals with the remaining compounds with nominal heads and adjectival non-heads, i.e., [A + N]$_N$ compounds whose nominal head appears second, while the preposed non-head acts as its modifier. These compounds tend to be endocentric. For example, *malparto* 'miscarriage', lit. 'bad-birth', is a kind of *parto* 'birth', and a *nuevo rico* 'upstart', lit. 'new rich', is a kind of *rico* 'rich person'. There are also some exocentric or metonymic compounds, such *pocachicha* 'small thin man', lit. 'little-flesh' and *purasangre* 'thoroughbred [horse]', lit. 'pure blood'.

[A + N]$_N$ compounds are found in a full range of registers, from the colloquial to the academic. They can denote concrete items such as animals, plants, and man-made objects: *purasangre* 'thoroughbred', lit. 'pure-blood', *gordolobo* 'mullein [Verbascum L.]', lit. 'fat wolf', *terciopelo* 'velvet', lit. 'third-hair'. They are also used to name humans and body parts: *ricohombre* 'nobleman', lit. 'rich-man', *duramadre* 'dura mater, outermost meningeal layer' lit. 'hard mother'. Finally, they can be abstract terms for time periods (*medianoche* 'midnight', lit. 'half night'), feelings (*vanagloria* 'vainglory'), ideas or theories (*librepensamiento* 'free thinking', lit. 'free thought', *nacionalsocialismo* 'national socialism').

6.4.1 Structure

6.4.1.1 *Constituents*

The first constituent in $[A + N]_N$ is the non-head adjective. In general, prenominal adjectives are the same that would be found in that position in syntax. They include ordinals and other types of weak quantifiers (*quintaesencia* 'quintessence', lit. 'fifth-essence', *mediafuente* 'tray', lit. 'half-tray', *doblemano* 'two-way [street]', lit. 'double-hand'), some qualifying adjectives (*buen varón* 'common groundsel [Senecio vulgaris L.]', lit. 'good man', *bellasombra* 'ombu [Phytolacca dioica L.]', lit. 'good shade'), and some that denote dimensions (*altocúmulo* 'high cumulus cloud', lit. 'high-cumulus', *granguardia* 'grand guard', lit. 'large guard').

In the majority of compounds (80%), the preposed adjective appears in full form and exhibits gender concord with the nominal: *altavoz* 'loudspeaker', lit. 'high-FEM SG voice-FEM SG'. However, there is a sizeable minority of compounds whose adjective appears as a reduced base lacking a word class marker, with or without a linking vowel: *justiprecio* 'fair value', lit. 'fair price' (cf. *justo* 'fair-MASC SG') *duraluminio* 'hard aluminum', (cf. *duro*) *maloclusión* 'malocclusion', lit. 'bad-occlusion' (cf. *mala*). Plural concord marks can also be lost over time: *medias lunas* 'croissants', lit. 'half-FEM PL-moon-FEM PL' > *medialunas* 'id.', lit. 'half-FEM SG-moon FEM PL'. This issue will be discussed at length in the historical section, since concord loss is a function of lexicalization over time.

The nouns in $[A + N]_N$ compounds can be of any type, including mass nouns (*liquidámbar* 'liquid-amber', *amargamiel* 'climbing nightshade', lit. 'bitter-honey', *altamar* 'high seas', lit. 'high sea') and countable nouns (*falsarrienda* 'checkrein', lit. 'false-rein', *malalengua* 'gossipmonger', lit. 'bad-tongue'), and to a lesser extent, nouns denoting humans (*pequeñoburgués* 'petit burgeois', lit. 'small-burgeois', *gentilhombre* 'gentleman'). Abstract nouns are infrequent in the earlier periods, but become more prevalent in later $[A + N]_N$ compounds (*nacionalsocialismo* 'national socialism'). As the head of the compound, the nominal is responsible for any concord features on the adjectival constituent and is also the locus of inflection for the entire lexeme: *el gentilhombre* 'the-MASC SG gentle-man- MASC SG' vs. *los gentilhombres* 'the- MASC PL gentle-man- MASC PL'.

6.4.1.2 *Compound structure*

The internal structure of $[A + N]_N$ compounds is parallel to that of nominal phrases with preposed adjectives. It has been a matter of much debate what this structure may be for Spanish (cf. for example, Bernstein 1993; Cinque 1994). Although this will not be solved here, it should be noted that the fact that both A + N and N + A orders are possible in compounding, coupled with the absence of specifier positions, favors an account of adjective position in noun phrases that does not invoke specifiers. The entire issue will be greatly simplified here by assuming that a modification relationship holds between head and non-head in [A + N]$_N$ (12). This relationship will be assumed to be a mirror image of that which holds between the noun and adjective in [N + A]$_N$ compounds.

(12)

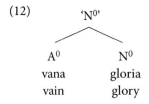

For the minority of compounds in this class that are exocentric, a different internal structure must be proposed. As was done earlier for [N + N]$_N$ exocentric compounds of the type *puntapié* 'kick', lit. 'point-foot', the presence of an empty word class marker head will be invoked, which adds more internal structure to account for this secondary interpretation (13).

(13)

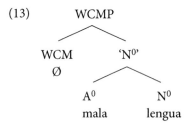

6.4.1.3 *Compound meaning*

Like their head-initial counterparts, compounds of the structure [A + N]$_N$ involve modification, with theta identification of the adjective and the noun (14). Thus, for example, *bajamar* 'low tide', lit. 'low-sea' is a type of *mar*, *medio relieve* 'mid-relief', lit. 'half-relief' is a type of *relieve*, and so on. Again like their head-initial counterparts, [A + N]$_N$ can become opaque over time through metaphoric or metonymic interpretations. Consider, for example, *terciopelo* 'velvet', lit. 'third-hair', no longer a type of *pelo*, or *bellasombra* 'ombu [Phytolacca dioica L.]', lit. 'good-shade', not a type of *sombra*.

(14)

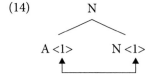

6.4.2   Diachrony

6.4.2.1   *Historical antecedents and comparative data*

The [A + N]$_N$ pattern has antecedents in Greek (Schwyzer 1953 [1938]) and Sanskrit (e.g., *nīlotpala* 'blue lotus') (Whitney 1941 [1879]: 494), as well as in Latin (e.g., DULCIRĀDĪX 'liquorice', lit. 'sweet-root'), where many, but not all of the compounds originated in juxtapositions (Bader 1962: 322). Bader claims that in Latin these compounds are frequently artificial creations of the language of comedy (e.g., PERENNISERUUS 'eternal slave'), whereas their use in familiar and technical lexicons is limited and comes late (e.g., UĪUERĀDĪX 'live plant').

By contrast, the [A + N]$_N$ compounding pattern is well attested in descriptions of all languages in the Romance family, including Portuguese (Villalva 1992: 210), Catalan (Mascaró 1986: 72), French (Spence 1980: 73; Zwanenburg 1990a: 135; 1990b: 74; 1992: 224), Italian (Dardano 1988: 59; Scalise 1992: 177), and Romanian (Mallinson 1986: 329). Although only some of these authors provide explicit endo- and exocentric examples (Mallinson 1986; Zwanenburg 1992), in fact all Romance languages allow for both uses of the pattern. In Spanish, the [A + N]$_N$ endocentric pattern is well attested from the earliest periods, as seen in (15).

(15)   Early attestations of [A + N]$_N$ compounds in Spanish
   a.   *De periurio et falsario [falso testimonio].*
        (c. 950–1000, *Glosas silenses*, CORDE).
        'On perjury and false testimony'.
   b.   *Et si lo non fizo por sanna o por mala voluntad, peche el omezillo*
        (c. 1196, *Fuero de Soria*, CORDE)
        'And if he did not do it with animosity or ill-will, he must pay for the homicide'.
   c.   *Fue ya la media noch e el Sennor mato al mayor fijo*
        (c. 1200, *La Fazienda de Ultra Mar*, Almerich, CORDE)
        'It was midnight and the Lord killed the eldest son'.

6.4.2.2   *Frequency and productivity*

[A + N]$_N$ compounds are quite frequent in the database, with a total of 233 examples altogether (6.8% of the total) (Table 6.16). Their relative frequency is even higher in the earliest periods documented, evidence of their presence in the inherited Romance lexicon. Relative percentages grow slightly in the early centuries, peak in the 1500s, and start to decrease after that, as their increase in frequency fails to match the growing overall number of compounds.

Table 6.17 shows that the productivity of the [A + N]$_N$ pattern has been uneven over time. The initial period shows the effect of the inherited examples on the totals, followed by high productivity in the 1400s and 1500s, as the percentage of new

Table 6.16 $[A + N]_N$ compounds attested by century, as totals and as a percentage of all compounds

	$[A + N]_N$	All compounds	$[A + N]_N$ as % of all compounds
1000s–1200s	32	349	9.2
1300s	39	434	9.0
1400s	63	709	8.9
1500s	96	1073	8.9
1600s	107	1237	8.6
1700s	116	1360	8.5
1800s	140	1842	7.6
1900s–2000s	209	3005	7.0
Total	233	3451	6.8

Table 6.17 Productivity of $[A + N]_N$ compounds attested by century

	Carried over	Lost	New	Total	Productivity Ratio
1200s	5	(0)	27	32	NA
1300s	32	(1)	8	39	0.18
1400s	39	(1)	25	63	0.38
1500s	63	(4)	37	96	0.34
1600s	96	(3)	14	107	0.10
1700s	107	(2)	11	116	0.08
1800s	116	(3)	27	140	0.17
1900s–2000s	140	(10)	79	209	0.33

compounds reaches 40% of the total. After that, the ratio of new to old compounds decreases, and only picks up slightly in the 20th century. Overall, this is quite a stable pattern, with few losses per century.

6.4.2.3 *Inseparability of constituents*

When it comes to determining whether the compound constituents are inseparable or not, $[A + N]_N$ compounds present the same challenges as $[N + A]_N$, and for the same reasons, viz., that there is no easy way to distinguish lexicalized phrases from compounds on merely structural or semantic grounds. Recall that a number of formal criteria were incorporated into the search in order to ensure internal cohesiveness in all the lexemes included. However, counterevidence is inevitable and it does not seem reasonable to exclude all cases that exhibit it. Consider, for example, the sequence *alta mar* 'open sea', lit. 'high sea'. The CORDE/CREA databases include 1149 such sequences, of which 78 are spelled as a unit, *altamar*, and all of which have the same meaning

(16a, b). In light of that, it seems safe to ignore the fact that the same meaning can be conveyed by the inverted sequence *mar alta*, a variant that appears 63 times in the database, i.e., less than 10% (16c). This alternative never prospered, as shown by its low numbers, by the fact that it does not exhibit any unified spelling variants, and by its absence in the contemporary CREA database.

(16) a. *Segun dizen/los sabios nunca cahe la/njebe en alta mar.*
           (c. 1223, *Semejanza del mundo*, CORDE)
           'According to what the wise men say, it never snows into the high seas'.

      b. *Et desi tomaron/a Affla & a sos fijos con/ell. & echaron los en ell altamar.*
           'And they took Affla and his sons and they tossed them in the high seas'.
           (1270–1284, Alfonso X, CORDE)

      c. *los delas naues estauan en la mar alta por que sy les vinjese viento que pud-iesen fuyr o que pudiesen pelear.*
           (c. 1340–1350, Fernán Sánchez Valladolid, CORDE)
           'those on the ships were out at sea so that they could escape if they had winds, or they could fight'.

The above example illustrates the complexities inherent to distinguishing compounds from parallel phrases when the meaning stays constant. It is an even more complicated matter to distinguish phrases from compounds when meaning changes over time. Consider, for example, the evolution of the [A + N] complex *mala sangre*, lit. 'bad blood', whose early meanings include 'bad blood' in a literal medical sense (17a), and metaphorically, to mean 'bad lineage, bad parentage' (17b). Later on, we find other metaphoric meanings, such as 'worry' (17c) and 'bastard' (17d). Unitary spelling (17d) is also an indication of de-stressing, which one would expect as a consequence of com-pounding (for discussion, cf. Chapter 3, Section 3.2.3).

(17) a. *Empero si fallaren enel estomago malos humores:/engendran mala sangre & ventosidad & finchazon/y engendran piojos enel cuerpo.*
           (c. 1381–1418, Juan de Burgos, CORDE)
           'However, if there are bad humors in the stomach, they engender bad blood, and flatulence, and bloating, as well as lice in the body'.

      b. *E Adam sabié cómo eran ellas de mala sangre e malas por sí*
           (c. 1275, Alfonso X, CORDE)
           'And Adam knew that they were of bad lineage and bad themselves'

      c. *No quiero hacerme mala sangre ni quiero saber nada con los porteños*
           (1903, Pastor Servando Obligado, CORDE)
           'I do not want to worry (lit. 'cause myself bad blood') nor do I want to know anything about the people from Buenos Aires'.

d. *Eres de lo peorcito... ¿Sabes?... ¡De lo peorcito!... Criminal, <u>malasangre</u> y*
   ahora cantante...   (1991, Rodolfo Santana, CREA)
   'You are so bad... You know? So bad! A criminal, a bastard, and now, a
   singer...'

In other words, *mala sangre* 'bad blood' is a compound starting at some point after it
is first attested and in at least some of its meanings; the problem is when to date its
first compounded attestation. In general, in this work the first date of attestation of
the [A + N] complex is considered the first attestation of the compound, unless a totally compositional interpretation precludes this. This decision is based on the hypothesis that written evidence of compoundhood would come late, and because a
case-by-case investigation of semantic stabilization is not possible, given the size of
the database.

6.4.2.4 *Orthographic representation*

The only compounds in the $[A + N]_N$ class that are invariably spelled as one word
are those whose preposed adjective appears without its word class marker. This
observation holds regardless of the historical depth of the compound, demonstrat-
ing that the absence of the word class marker is always concomitant with prosodic
dependence: *blanquibol* 'white lead', lit. 'white clay' [1495], *justiprecio* 'fair price', lit.
'just price' [1785], *duraluminio* 'durable tin', lit. 'hard tin' [1946]. For all other
$[A + N]_N$ compounds, variable spelling is the norm, as one would expect from their
gradual emergence from parallel phrases. The alternatives may include one- and
two-word spelling, as well as hyphenated forms: *pia madre ~ piamadre* 'pia mater',
salvo conducto ~ salvo-conducto ~ salvoconducto 'safe conduct'. The tendency is for
increased one-word spelling over time. In four of the eight compound lexemes presented in Table 6.18, one- and two-word spellings are roughly simultaneous, whereas in the remaining four two-word spellings precede one-word variants by at least
a century.

Table 6.18 First attestations for two-word and one-word spellings for $[A + N]_N$ compounds

	First attestation Two-word spelling	First attestation One-word spelling
medio + día	1223	c. 1250
mal + fado	c. 1230	c. 1250
media + luna	1411–1412	1645
falsa + rienda	1441	1627
mal + parto	c. 1481–1502	1825
libre + pensador	1861	1869
corto + circuito	c. 1870–1905	1923–1974
franco + tirador	1910	ad 1936

6.4.2.5 *Evolution of formal features*

In this section we consider changes in the morphological structure of the adjectival constituent over time, in particular, its appearance in lexeme or bare stem form. As shown in Table (6.19), $[A + N]_N$ compounds have a marked preference for the preposed adjective to appear in full form (almost 80% overall). However, over time, as the lexicon is enriched with technical and semi-technical vocabulary, tolerance increases for adjective stems, so that in the latter centuries, their percentage reaches almost 30%: *cristian o-democracia* 'Christian democracy', (cf. *democracia cristiana* vs **cristiana-democracia* 'id.'), *inmun-o-terapia* 'immune therapy' (cf. *terapia inmune* vs. **inmune-terapia* 'id.').

The pattern of increased tolerance for stems contrasts with other head-final compounds presented in this chapter, such as head-final $[N + N]_N$ compounds (Section 6.2.2.5, Table 6.10). Both of these types of head-final compounds ($[A + N]_N$ and $[N + N]_N$) share the fact that the rate of use of preposed non-head stems increases over time. However, the increase for $[N + N]_N$ compounds goes from 50% to over 90% in the period under study (e.g., *ajipuerro* 'wild leek', lit. 'garlic-leek'), while for $[A + N]_N$ compounds the occurrence of forms with stems grows from under 10% to a little over 30% (e.g., *altiplano* 'meseta', lit. 'high-plain'). In other words, preposed non-head nouns and preposed non-head adjectives exhibit different morphological evolutions: while the former become increasingly less likely to appear with their word class marker, the latter continue to appear in full form most of the time. This shows that the morphological make-up of constituents is determined not just by their position or their headedness status but also by their lexical category.

In $[A + N]_N$ compounds whose adjective exhibits a word class marker, the latter may be the locus of further gender and number inflection. In principle, and given the phrasal origin of these compounds, the adjective can be expected to exhibit concord with the noun, as it would in syntax: *bellas artes* 'fine arts', lit. 'beautiful-FEM PL art-FEM PL', *libres pensadores* 'free-MASC PL thinkers-MASC PL'. However, the passage of time may erode the internal number concord on the non-head, as apparent from the increasing presence of alternants whose adjective exhibits no number concord. Table 6.20 shows that forms without plural marking on the adjective appear simultaneously or later than those with it. Loss of internal concord is also apparent in contemporary data as compounds acquire idiomatic meaning. For example, in Google the plural for *salvo conducto* 'safe conduct' appears as *salvos conductos* 629 times, barely 1% of the

Table 6.19 Morphological structure of leftmost constituent in $[A + N]_N$ compounds

	Full lexeme (n)	Stem (n)	Totals (n)
1000s–1400s	93.8% (61)	6.2% (4)	100% (65)
1500s–1700s	87.9% (51)	12.1% (7)	100% (58)
1800s–1900s	69.1% (76)	30.9% (34)	100% (110)
Totals	80.7% (188)	19.3% (45)	100% (233)

Table 6.20 First attestations of [A + N]$_N$ compounds with and without internal plural concord

	First attestation [A = s + N = s]$_{Npl}$	First attestation [A + N = s]$_{Npl}$
medio + día	1272	c. 1499–1502
salvo + conducto	1566	c. 1550
media + luna	1428	1958
falsa + rienda	1441	1627
mal + parto	ad 1598	1842
libre + pensador	1861	1869
medio + hermano	1624	1648
pequeño + burgués	1909	1925

55,950 hits for *salvoconductos/salvo-conductos*. Other examples, such as *mediodía* 'midday', lit. 'half day' exhibit only the plural form *mediodías*, whereas *medios días* is only interpretable as 'half days'.

6.4.2.6 *Endocentric and exocentric uses*

As stated in Section 6.4.1, [A + N]$_N$ compounds can be endocentric or exocentric, but when seen in quantitative terms, endocentric compounds are overwhelmingly more frequent, making up 95% of [A + N]$_N$ compounds. Historically, exocentric [A + N]$_N$ follow endocentrics by some centuries, with the first clear example (*malavés* 'barely', lit. 'bad-time') attested in the 1400s. Yet, it is hard to be definitive, given the low overall percentages of exocentric compounds in this class.

6.5 Summary of chapter

Hierarchical compounds with a nominal head and a nominal or adjectival non-head are frequent throughout the history of the language, and taken together account for close to 40% of all compounds for all periods. In these compounds, the head nominal is theta modified by its non-head. Compounds with head-initial configurations are more frequent throughout history than their head-final counterparts, i.e., [N + A]$_N$ and head-initial [N + N]$_N$ have higher frequencies than their mirror compounds for any period considered. Additionally, those with [N + N] structure, both head-initial and head-final, increase in frequency over time, whereas compounds that combine nouns and adjectives decrease over the same period. In all the compound patterns studied in this chapter, when the head precedes the non-head, its status as the locus of inflection tends to be eroded over time.

CHAPTER 7

Exocentric patterns

Cuajaleches, mil leches

In all the patterns presented so far, one of the two compound constituents can be identified as the head, from which the compound inherits its syntactic properties and often also its semantic specifications. However, it is also true that in most compound classes seen so far, a subset of tokens 'jump' grammatical category, exhibiting distributional properties incompatible with those of the head constituent. In those cases, the resulting compound is said to be exocentric. In Spanish this conversion process can lead to the recategorization of any compound as a nominal (*bienestar* 'welfare', lit. 'well-be', *subibaja* 'see-saw', lit. 'go up-go down'), or of nominal compounds as adjectives (*muy cararrota* 'very cheeky', lit. 'very face-broken').[1]

In addition to these sporadic examples of exocentricity, some productive and stable compound patterns of Spanish are *always* exocentric, i.e., neither of their constituents is ever the head of the compound. In all cases of exocentric patterns, the resulting compound is a noun. Consequently, rather than proposing ad hoc conversion for each compounded token, it is more theoretically sound to incorporate the process of conversion or ø-derivation into the pattern itself. In Chapter 2, Section 2.4.1.2, it was proposed that the first merge operation between constituents is followed by a second merge with an empty (unpronounced) head, which corresponds to the WCM and is responsible for the conversion of the compound. In Spanish the two most common exocentric compounding patterns are $[V + N]_N$ and, to a much lesser extent, $[Q + N]_N$ compounds (Table 7.1). Each one of them will be considered separately.

Table 7.1 Exocentric compounds in Spanish

Pattern	Example	Found in →
$[V + N]_N$	*cuajaleches* 'yellow bedstraw [Galium verum L.]', lit. 'curdle-milk'	Chapter 7, Section 7.1
$[Q + N]_N$	*mil leches* 'mongrel animal', lit. 'thousand milks'	Chapter 7, Section 7.2

---

1. Of course, these examples are not exclusive to compounding, since they can affect other non-compounded lexemes (*el fumar* 'smoking-N' lit. 'the to-smoke', *el mañana* 'the future', lit. 'the tomorrow', *la loca* 'the crazy woman', lit. 'the crazy').

7.1   The [V + N]$_N$ pattern: *Cuajaleches*

Compounds formed by a verbal stem and a complement (normally a noun) (e.g., *saca-corchos* 'corkscrew', lit. 'pull-corks') are without a doubt, the largest class of possessive or *bahuvrihi* compounds in Spanish. In fact, as we shall see later, they constitute the most productive and studied compound pattern of the entire Romance family. Although the pattern also exists in English (e.g., *pickpocket, breakwater*, etc.) its appearance is generally attributed to borrowing from French followed by modest productivity (Nevalainen 1999). The verb and its object together constitute a predicate; the resulting nominal compound is generally interpreted as the agentive of the predicate in question. Thus, for example, *sacacorchos* 'cork-screw', lit. 'pull-corks' is an instrument that pulls out corks from bottles, *aguafiestas* 'party pooper', lit. 'water-parties' is someone who spoils the enjoyment of others by raining on their party, metaphorically speaking. These compounds are exocentric because the verb does not percolate its categorial features to the entire compound, although there is a hierarchical dependency internal to the compound, with the head verb governing a complement. The nominal can also be discarded as the head because it does not determine the number or gender of the whole (e.g., *el aguafiestas* 'the party-pooper-MASC SG', vs. *las fiestas* 'the parties -FEM PL').

7.1.1   Structure

7.1.1.1   *Constituents*

The first constituent in [V + N]$_N$ compounds is a verb stem, which normally appears with its accompanying theme vowel (the verbal equivalent of the nominal WCM): *mata̠buey* 'umbelliferous plant', lit. 'kill-ox', *mete̠muertos* 'prop man', lit. 'put-dead people', *suple̠faltas* 'substitute', lit. 'make-up-absences' (cf. *mata̠r, mete̠r, supli̠r*). In some compounds the theme vowel may be replaced by a linking element of some kind: *bati̠cor* 'pain', lit. 'beat-heart' (cf. *bate*); or it may be fused with the initial vowel of the following constituent: *chafalmejas* 'bad painter', lit. 'spoil-clams' (< *chafa* + *almejas*). The verb appears with its theme rather than as a bare stem, as evinced in the fact that in most stem-changing verbs the irregularity is present in the compound: *ciegayernos* 'something that looks more valuable than it is', lit. 'blind-sons-in-law' (cf. *cegar*), *revientacaballo* 'bellflower', lit. 'break-horse' (cf. *reve̠ntar*) *desuellacaras* 'clumsy barber', lit. 'skin-faces' (cf. *deso̠llar*). There are very few exceptions: *torcecuello* 'wryneck [genus Jynx L.] lit. 'twist-neck' (cf. *to̠rcer*, 3 SG PRES *tue̠rce*), *volapié ~ vuelapié* 'bullfighting stroke', lit. 'fly-foot' (cf. *vo̠lar*, 3 SG PRES *vue̠la*).[2]

---

2.   Under the assumptions of this work, the stem status of the verb is a theoretical given. This allows us to obviate arguments in favor of possible conjugated forms, such as the imperative or the third person singular, which has been a traditional staple of previous works (cf. Darmesteter 1967 [1874]: 169–204; Kastovsky 2009: 336; Lloyd 1968; Rainer 1993: 265–268, for some examples and details of these two positions).

Table 7.2 Examples of verb Aktionsart in [V + N]$_N$ compounds

Type of verb	Example verb	Example compound
activity	*correr* 'to run'	*correcaminos* 'road-runner', lit. 'run-roads'
	vagar 'to wander'	*vagamundos* 'globe-trotter', lit. 'wander-worlds'
	rascar 'to scratch'	*rascacielos* 'sky-scraper', lit. 'scrape-skies'
achievements	*atajar* 'to catch'	*atajasolaces* 'party pooper', lit. 'catch-solace'
	atrapar 'to trap'	*atrapamariposas* 'butterfly net', lit. 'trap-butter-flies'
	reventar 'to burst'	*[a] reventacinchas* 'at breakneck speed', lit. 'at break-saddle girths'
accomplishments	*calentar* 'to heat up'	*calientaplatos* 'plate warmer', lit. 'warm up-plates'
	cumplir 'to accomplish'	*cumpleaños* 'birthday', lit. 'accomplish-years'

The verb itself can belong to several classes as defined by their Aktionsart properties, including activities, achievements, and accomplishments (Table 7.2). Among the most frequent verbs in [V + N]$_N$ compounds, the most prevalent are activities (*guardar* 'to keep, protect', 78 tokens, *portar* 'to hold, carry', 53), and achievements (*matar* 'to kill' 56, *sacar* 'to remove', 32, and *cortar* 'to cut', 29). Stative verbs are virtually barred from appearing in [V + N]$_N$ compounds, with a few exceptions such as *saber* 'to know' (i.e., *sabelotodo* 'know-it-all').[3]

If considered from the point of view of their argument structure, rather than their semantic features, the verbs permitted in [V + N]$_N$ compounds form a rather well defined class (Table 7.3). The overwhelming majority of them are transitive, although unergative verbs are also possible, as long as the implicit object appears as the overt direct object of the compound. Unaccusative verbs, which do not have an agentive subject, are only possible if they can be interpreted as having undergone causativization. Consider, for example, the compound *ardeviejas* 'spiny shrub', lit. 'burn-old women'. The argument structure of *arder* 'to burn-UNACC' normally does not include an agentive subject: *La capilla ardió toda la noche* 'The chapel burned all night', vs. **Juan ardió la capilla* 'Juan burned the chapel', *Juan hizo arder la capilla* 'Juan burned [lit. made burn] the chapel'. However, in the compound, *arder* must be interpreted as 'to burn-ACC'. Similar examples include *tardanaos* 'remora', lit. 'delay-vessels', (< *tardar* 'to take long', but here 'to delay'), *crecepelo* 'hair lotion', lit. 'grow-hair' (< *crecer* 'to grow-UNACC' but here 'to grow-ACC'), *rabiazorras* 'easterly wind', lit. 'anger-vixens'

---

3. The only other exceptions are rare archaisms or borrowings that are not entirely transparent: *oroval* 'winter cherry, [Withania somnifera L.]', lit. 'gold-is worth', *estafermo* 'revolving dummy', lit. 'is-firm' (< It. *stafermo* 'id.'). The pattern of *tente-* (e.g., *tentetieso* 'roly-poly', lit. 'hold-yourself-still'), is not truly a compound as defined in this work since it includes functional constituents (i.e., the pronoun *te* 'you DIR OBJ').

Table 7.3 Examples of verb argument structure in [V + N]$_N$ compounds

Type of verb	Example verb	Example compound
Transitive	*matar* 'to kill'	*matarratas* 'rat poison', lit. 'kill-runs'
	portar 'to hold'	*portacartas* 'letter holder', lit. 'hold-letters'
Unergative	*correr* 'to run'	*correcalles* 'hopscotch', lit. 'run-streets'
	vagar 'to wander'	*vagamundos* 'globe-trotter', lit. 'wander-worlds'
Unaccusative	*crecer* 'to grow'	*crecepelo* 'hair lotion', lit. 'grow-hair'
	tardar 'to take long'	*tardanaos* 'remora', lit. 'delay-vessels'
Non-lexical	*poder* 'to be able'	**puedemilagros* 'miracleworker', lit. 'can-miracles'
	tener 'to have'	**tienemiedo* 'scaredy-cat', lit. 'have-fear'
	estar 'to be'	**estáloco* 'crazy person', lit. 'is-crazy'

(< *rabiar* 'to be angry' but here 'to anger'). Finally, and as predicted by the overarching theory of compounding presented in Chapter 1, non-lexical verbs are barred from [V + N]$_N$ compounds, even in cases that would be perfectly semantically interpretable.

Virtually all the compounds in this class (over 99%), have a noun as their second constituent. Because normally [V + N]$_N$ compounds denote an entity involved in habitual or repetitive activities, when the nominal is countable it tends to appear in plural form: *guardajoyas* 'jewel cabinet', lit. 'keep-jewels' *guardapiés* 'long women's dress', lit. 'protect-feet'. Uncountable collective nouns are often singular: *guardapolvo* 'tunic', lit. 'guard-dust', *guardarropa* 'closet', lit. 'keep-clothes'. However, there can be quite a bit of variation in a given compound with no apparent semantic consequences: e.g., *guardamonte ~ guardamontes* 'croup blanket', lit. 'guard-bush(es)'. Occasionally, a nominal appears in singular form but must be interpreted as plural: e.g., *guardallama* 'flame protection', lit. 'guard-flame'. By contrast, an uncountable noun can appear in plural form: e.g., *guardalodos* 'mud-guard', lit. 'guard-muds'). The presence of plural *-s* is favored because it acts not as a plural to the noun, but rather, as an aspectual mark to the entire predicate. It conveys iteration of the event and is thus well suited to designate items characterized by habitual use or function. Retention of final *-s* is at odds with the standard structure of Spanish nouns, few of which end in *-s* in the singular, and with the phonotactics of many Spanish dialects, which favor open syllables. The historical outcome of the tension between these two opposing forces will be discussed in Section 7.1.2.5.

The noun constituent appears almost categorically in full lexeme form, but devoid of determiners. Exceptions can be counted on one hand and are the result of folk etymology or of lexicalization of syntactic phrasal formulas, and thus, not true exponents of the pattern: *besalamano* 'short note', lit. 'kiss-the-hand', (< *besa la mano de Vuestra Merced* 'kisses the hand of Your Mercy', an archaic valediction in formal notes).

The very few compounds with non-nominal second constituents exhibit adverbial complements instead: *catalejo* 'looking glass', lit. 'see-far', *cantaclaro* 'outspoken person', lit. 'sing-clearly'), and the occasional prepositional phrase or nominalized adjective (e.g., *cenaaoscuras* 'cheapskate', lit. 'dine-in-darkness', *urdemalas* 'schemer', lit. 'plot-bad ones'). To be absolutely precise, these compounds should be characterized as [V + Adv]$_N$, but this group is small and their behavior is otherwise so similar to that of [V + N]$_N$ that the latter label will be used to refer to both types of compounds indistinctly.

Finally, it should be noted that a few [V + N]$_N$ compounds (around 15) never appear as nouns in isolation but rather, as prepositional complements in adverbial phrases or longer idiomatic expressions: *a rajatabla* 'strictly', lit. 'of break-plank', *a quemarropa* 'from close range', lit. 'of burn-clothes', *de repicapunto* 'carefully', lit. 'of pick-point', *puerto de arrebatacapas* 'den of thieves', lit. 'port of steal-capes'. In the following section, I discuss the syntactic and semantic relationship between the verb and its different types of complements.

7.1.1.2 *Compound structure*

From the earliest accounts (Diez 1973 [1874]: 403; Meyer-Lübke 1923 [1895]: 630), it has been observed that [V + N]$_N$ compounds have the structure of a verb phrase, with the verb governing the noun. The structure proposed in (1) is therefore based on a merge operation between the verb and the noun to form a bare verb phrase, which is later merged with a WCM head, resulting in a nominal compound. The diagram represents the nominal constituent in all its possible complexity, as a noun with its WCM and in plural form. The verb, in turn, also exhibits a theme vowel as head of the theme phrase (ThP) and a nominalizing (but overtly null) WCM.

(1)

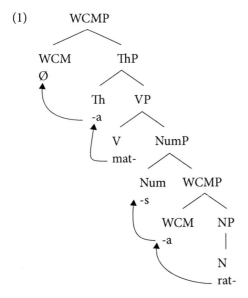

The nominal always occupies the position of the 'first sister' of the noun, which in most cases means that it is interpreted semantically as the verbal theme: *matarratas* 'rat killer', lit. 'kill-rats', *guardarropa* 'closet', lit. 'keep-clothes', *pelagatos* 'poor person', lit. 'skin-cats'. However, if the verb is not transitive but a verb of motion, then it discharges a locative theta role on the noun: *andarríos* 'white wagtail', lit. 'go-rivers', *trotaconventos* 'match-maker', lit. 'trots-convents'. Note that the verb-complement structure is possible in Spanish syntax to express the same theta role: *he andado muchos caminos* 'I have walked many paths', *nadé todo el ancho del río* 'I swam the entire width of the river'. Consequently, no additional structure will be posited in addition to that presented in (1). Whatever makes possible the existence of non-prepositional locative complements in syntax will be assumed to be at work in these cases.

In contrast, adverbials in [V + Adv]$_N$ are always place or manner adjuncts: *saltatrás* 'dark child of mixed-race parents', lit. 'jump-backwards', *armatoste* 'bulky object', lit. 'assemble-fast'. They can be represented by a structure that includes an adverbial phrase adjoined to the verb in parallel fashion (2). The type of relationship that must be posited in those cases is therefore the weaker association of modification (recall Chapter 2, Section 2.2.2), followed by the merger with the higher WCM node. Recall that although on the surface these structures are indistinguishable, the simple quotes ('VP') represent the fact that no theta role is dispensed by the verb to the non-head element.

(2)

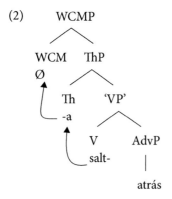

There are very few exceptions to the general pattern, which can be considered oddities and will not be given a separate structural representation. These include cases where the nominal is interpretable as the subject in some intransitive verbs (e.g., *tornaviaje* 'return trip', *andaboba* 'card game', lit. 'go stupid', *cantarrana* 'toy that makes a frog-like noise', lit. 'sing-frog') or has some other thematic role (e.g., *guardapolvo* 'dust cover', lit. 'guard-dust', cf. *guarda del/contra el polvo* 'guards from/against dust').

7.1.1.3   *Compound meaning*
Two semantic issues will be considered in this section. The first is the type of meanings that [V + N]$_N$ compounds convey. It has been observed before that [V + N]$_N$ compounds are used for several specific semantic functions (Lang 1990: 77; Lloyd 1968: 20–30; Rainer 1993: 276–78). When applied to humans, compounds in this class tend to denote occupations that are considered menial in themselves (e.g., *aparcacoches* 'valet', lit. 'park-cars', *mercachifles* 'peddler', lit. 'sell-whistles') or are treated disparagingly

(e.g., *cagatinta* 'office employee', lit. 'shit-ink', *matasanos* 'quack doctor', lit. 'kill-healthy ones'). They may also be used to highlight behavioral characteristics in mocking terms: *chupacirios* 'pious', lit. 'suck-candles', *aguafiestas* 'party pooper', lit. 'water-parties', *calientabraguetas* 'cock-teaser', lit. 'heat-zippers'. The second possible meaning for [V + N]$_N$ compounds is names of plants and animals (especially birds and insects), which are thus characterized by some salient permanent property or habitual behavior: *mirasol* 'sunflower', lit. 'look-sun', *matalobos* 'aconite', lit. 'kill-wolves', *picaflor* 'hummingbird', lit. 'peck-flower', *cagaaceite* 'missel thrush', lit. 'shit-oil', *saltamontes* 'grasshopper', lit. 'jump-hills'. Finally, this type of compound can be used to designate inanimate objects, mostly instruments or receptacles. Thus, *abrebotellas* 'corkscrew', lit. 'open-bottles', *alargavistas* 'telescope', lit. 'lengthen-views', and *apagavelas* 'candle snuffer', lit. 'blow out-candles', *fijapelo* 'hairspray', lit. 'fix-hair', are examples of instruments or products created for a specific purpose, with the verb and nominal theme designating that purpose. An example such as *guardarropa* 'wardrobe', lit. 'keep-clothes' designates a receptacle, as do *guardajoyas* 'jewel box', lit. 'keep-jewels' and *portadocumentos* 'wallet', lit. 'hold-documents'.

Another semantic issue has to do with the possible interpretations of the verb-noun combination, which range from literal to metaphoric. Here, too, the properties of the denotation influence interpretation. For example, in the designation of man-made instruments and products, meaning is straightforward, as in *exprimelimones* 'juicer', lit. 'press-lemons' or *lavavajilla* 'dishwasher', lit. 'wash-dishes'. Once created they tend to specialize, so that *lavavajilla* 'dishwasher', lit. 'wash-dishes' has come to refer mainly to the machine, rather than the detergent or the person involved in the process. When applied to animates that were not simply created with one purpose in mind, however, [V + N]$_N$ compounds tend to highlight a part of the denotation that is used metonymically to refer to the whole. For example, a *correcaminos* 'road runner', lit. 'run-road' is a bird so called because its salient feature is that it runs instead of flying. In the case of human denotata, compounds tend to be even more indirect and metaphoric. For instance, *chupasangre* 'mooch', lit. 'suck-blood' denotes someone who takes advantage of others, through the metaphor of parasitic behavior. Similarly, *huelebraguetas* 'private detective', lit. 'smell-zippers' or *lameculos* 'brown noser', lit. 'lick-asses' apply to their denotation in non-literal ways. These metaphoric designations can involve exaggeration, as in *tragaldabas* 'glutton', lit. 'swallow-door-knockers', or irony, contradiction, and humor, as in *rompetechos* 'short person', lit. 'break-ceilings' or *quitapenas* 'knife', lit. 'remove-pains'. Some compounds even incorporate pre-existing stock metaphors, such as *metepatas* 'awkward person', lit. 'put-feet', created on the basis of the metaphoric expression *meter la pata* 'to put one's foot in it'. Diachronic semantic shifts can completely obscure the original relationship between the [V + N] predicate and the compound's current meaning. Thus, it may have been clear at some past period of the Spanish language what the relationship was between the form and the meaning of *matasuegras* 'noise maker, party blower', lit. 'kill-mothers-in-law', but present speakers are unaware of it. The issue of the evolution of $[V + N]_N$ compound meanings is further discussed in Section 7.1.2.6.

7.1.2 Diachrony

7.1.2.1 Historical antecedents and comparative data

It has been noted before that $[V + N]_N$ is not a pattern prevalent in classical Latin (Bader 1962: 143; Lloyd 1968: 11). Among the scarce examples are the following: LAU-DICENUS 'parasite', lit. 'borrow-dinner', UERTIPEDIUM 'sacred plant', lit. 'turn-feet', epithets such as VERTICORDIA 'Venus', lit. 'turn-heart', and some proper names such as VINCELŪNA and VINCEMALUS). In light of this, its productivity in all the modern Romance is puzzling, and two main theses have been proposed to account for this. According to the first one, $[V + N]_N$ compounds in Romance were an independent development in the daughter languages (Diez 1973 [1874]: 630). According to this view, Latin $[V + N]_N$ compounds disappeared without a trace in Romance (Lloyd 1968: 11), and their scarcity could be related to their anomalous structure, since their head-complement order goes counter the structure of the language (Bader 1962: 143–44). According to the second hypothesis, $[V + N]_N$ compounding is indeed a Latin development that spread to all the Romance languages (Bork 1990 and discussion therein). The first argument for this view is that without a prior common model, it is hard to explain how all the Romance languages started to make verb-complement compounds simultaneously and to use them in similar semantic fields. This view is strengthened by the fact that several $[V + N]_N$ compounds have exact structural and semantic parallels in several Romance languages. Consider, for example, Sp. *pasatiempo* 'pastime', with reflexes in at least six varieties: Old Catalan *passatemps* [1388], Middle French *passe-temps* [1443], Old Spanish *passatiempo* [1490], Old Italian *passatempo* [15th century], Old Portuguese *passatempo* [15th century], and Old Occitan *passatemps* [not dated] (Bork 1990: 128). This is expected if the forms have a common ancestor in Latin, but a mysterious coincidence otherwise. Moreover, Bork sees the documented existence of at least 16 examples of $[V + N]$ compounds in Latin in a variety of styles as evidence of the pattern's vitality (Bork 1990: Ch. 4), while its relative scarcity may be due to stylistic reasons or to the competition from inverted $[N + V]$ patterns. Bork relates the presence of $[V + N]_N$ compounds in Latin to the influence of Greek (Bork 1990: Ch. 5). He claims that these Greek-influenced Latin compounds with head-complement order must have been more frequent in the spoken language by the time they started to be seen in texts of the 4th century. Their increased frequency could have been fueled by a general word order shift in late Latin and early Romance syntax.

As stated above, then, $[V + N]_N$ compounds are reported for all languages of the Romance family, where they occupy a preeminent position as a large productive class. They are described in general accounts of Romance compounding, and have also been treated specifically in numerous studies for Portuguese (Alves 1986/1987: 56; Eliseu & Villalva 1992; Villalva 1992: 211), Catalan (Hualde 1992: 362; Mascaró 1986: 58),

French (Bennett 1977; Spence 1980: 6; Zwanenburg 1990: 136; 1992: 224, 233), and Italian (Bisetto 1994; Dardano 1988: 59; Scalise 1992: 177; Vogel & Napoli 1992). The only exception is Romanian, where the pattern is reported to be unproductive (Mallinson 1986: 329; Lloyd 1968: 7, ftn. 4), but cf. also Giurescu (1975: 68) where no such mention is made.

In Spanish, the first attestations of $[V + N]_N$ compounds appear in the earliest textual sources available (3). The relationship between constituents continues to be transparent almost a thousand years later, even where the compound itself no longer has common currency. Thus, for example, *cubrepán* 'bread cover', lit. 'cover-bread' is not a current everyday term in Spanish, but it is clearly some kind of instrument used to cover bread.

(3)   Early attestations of $[V + N]_N$ compounds in Spanish

a.   *Otro ssi non aya montadgo [...] nj por forquiella njn por forgunero njn por* <u>*cubre pan*</u>.   (c. 1196, *Fuero de Soria*, CORDE)
'Moreover, no tax should be levied [....] on the fork or on the oven poker or on the bread-cover'.

b.   *Entre las animalias dell aer e las de la tierra fallamos otrossí por dichos de los omnes que se fazen mezclas, ca ell avanto, que es ave a que llaman otra guisa* <u>*quebrantahuessos*</u>, *que yaze con la raposa e empréñala [..]*
(c. 1275, Alfonso X, *General Estoria*, CORDE)
'According to what many people say, among the animals of air and land we also find mixed breeds, since the vulture, a bird also called *quebranta-huessos* (lit. 'break-bones') mates with the vixen and impregnates it'.

c.   *sus fijas delas quales estamos/muy mal casados et por/*<u>*torna bodas*</u> *nos fizo este mal.*   (c. 1270–1284, Alfonso X, CORDE)
'His daughters, with whom we are unfortunately married and after the wedding (lit. 'in turn-wedding') he harmed us thus'.

Interestingly, among these early attestations several show the vitality of the pattern not in the coinage of a lexeme but in its use to reanalyze an opaque form, so that it becomes fully or partially motivated for Spanish speakers. Strictly speaking, these are not examples of word formation through the $[V + N]_N$ pattern, but they are equally strong evidence of its reality. This is the case of *tragacanto* 'tragacanth' (var. of *tragacanta* < Gr. τραγαχανθα 'tragakanta, thorn of he-goat' according to Corominas & Pascual (1980–91: vol. 5, 584), and of the partial reanalyses of Old Cast. *matafalúa, matahalúa* 'aniseed' < Old Cast. *batafalua* < Hisp. Arab. *al-ḥábbaᵗ al-ḥulûwa* 'the sweet grain' (Corominas & Pascual 1980–91: vol. 3, 877); and *guardamecir*, a var. of *guadamecí* 'decorated leather' < Arab. *ǧild gadāmasî* 'leather from Gadames' (Corominas & Pascual 1980–91: vol. 3, 233–34). In the two latter examples, a verbal constituent is discernible but the complement is semantically opaque. Both of these forms show evidence of their reanalyzed origin in their high variability (e.g., *matafalúa, matalaúga, matalahúga, matalahúva,* and *guardameçir, guardameçil, guadameçi, guadamesçi, guadamenci*).

Another such example is *sabihondo* 'egghead', lit. 'know-deep' (vars. *sabiondo, sabijondo*), which several etymologists agree is not an instance of [V + N]$_N$ compounding but the result of suffixation of *-(i)ondo* to the verbal base *saber* 'to know' (Corominas & Pascual 1980–91: vol. 5, 114–15; Pharies 1991; 2002: 435). However, the presence of spellings such as *sabijondo* strengthens the view that the lexeme was reinterpreted through folk etymology as a verbal base and an adverbial *hondo* 'deep', an instantiation of the [V + N]$_N$ compounding pattern, possibly because the suffix *-(i)ondo* was only marginally productive.

7.1.2.2 *Frequency and productivity*

The [V + N]$_N$ pattern is far and away the most frequent in Spanish, represented by an overall total of 961 examples (27.8% of all compounds in the database). As Table 7.4 shows, its beginnings are modest, less robust than those of many other compounding patterns, including some head-final patterns such as [Adv + A]$_A$, and head-initial patterns such as [N + N]$_N$ and [N + A]$_N$. However, it exhibits an early expansion between the 1300s and the 1400s and steady gains over time, especially in the 1500s and later centuries. When considered in terms of relative frequency, the percentages of [V + N]$_N$ over the total number of compounds doubles between the 1300s and the 1400s, and continues to grow steadily every century.

The productivity of this pattern has also been quite high throughout history, especially in the 1400s, the 1500s, the 1800s, and the 1900s (Table 7.5). Impressive gains in each one of those centuries, in the hundreds of tokens, are reflected in high ratios of new-to-old compounds. However, [V + N]$_N$ compounds are also lost at quite high rates, which shows that the pattern not only augments the word stock permanently but is also a source of short-lived coinages. Examples of infrequent lexemes can be found in

Table 7.4 [V + N]$_N$ compounds attested by century, as totals and as a percentage of all compounds

	[V + N]$_N$	All compounds	[V + N]$_N$ as % of all compounds
1000s–1200s	11	349	3.2
1300s	19	434	4.4
1400s	75	709	10.6
1500s	169	1073	15.8
1600s	237	1237	19.2
1700s	292	1360	21.5
1800s	462	1842	25.1
1900s–2000s	837	3005	27.9
Total	961	3451	27.8

Table 7.5 Productivity of [V + N]$_N$ compounds by century

	Carried over	Lost	New	Total	Productivity Ratio
1200s	2	(0)	9	11	NA
1300s	11	(3)	11	19	0.42
1400s	19	(2)	58	75	0.75
1500s	75	(9)	103	169	0.56
1600s	169	(12)	80	237	0.29
1700s	237	(41)	96	292	0.19
1800s	292	(17)	187	462	0.37
1900s–2000s	462	(40)	415	837	0.45

every century, as illustrated by *guardacós* 'keeper', lit. 'keep-things' [c. 1260], *a rozapoco* 'superficially', lit. 'rub-little' [1330–1343], *rompenecios* 'freeloader', lit. 'break-fools' [1499–1502], *aferravelas* 'furling line', lit. 'grab-sails' [1519–1547], *cardaestambre* 'carder', lit. 'card-thread' [1737], and *baticabeza* 'chick beetle', lit. 'beat-head' [1893]. Even allowing for the fact that infrequent words are poorly documented and may have had a longer span than the data show, the cumulative evidence points to a pattern often used for fleeting neologisms.

7.1.2.3 *Inseparability of constituents*
The constituents of [V + N]$_N$ compounds are syntactically inseparable. There are a few cases where a determiner or a preposition precedes the nominal, but this inserted element is also a constituent that may not be eliminated: *matalaúva* 'aniseed', lit. 'kill-the-grape'. I have found no attestation of a [V + N]$_N$ compound created by stripping off pre-existing non-lexical material: *matalaúva* > **mataúva*; *cazalaolla* > **cazaolla*. Conversely, there are no attested cases where an extraneous non-lexical constituent appears between the verbal and nominal stems of a regular [V + N]$_N$: *sacacorchos* 'corkscrew', lit. 'remove-corks', vs. **sacaloscorchos* 'id.', lit. 'remove the corks'. This is so even in cases where the determiner would be warranted syntactico-semantically. For example, although abstract nouns such as *paz* 'peace' and unique definite descriptions such as *sol* 'sun' normally require determiners in Spanish syntax, they both appear in bare form in the compounds *portapaz* 'plate that carries the image presented to be kissed by the pious at mass', lit. 'carry-peace', and *tornasol* 'sunflower', lit. 'turn-sun' (cf. **portalapaz*, **tornaelsol*).

7.1.2.4 *Orthographic representation*
Compounds of the [V + N]$_N$ pattern are represented with unitary spelling in most lexicographical and textual databases, for all periods. Although a minority (around 10%) also exhibits two-word or hyphenated variants, there is no discernible gradual progression from two-word to one-word spelling over time: *quitasol* 'parasol', lit.

'remove-sun', [1535–1557], *quita sol* [1625], *quita-sol* [1710]; *pararrayo* 'lightning rod', lit. 'stop-lightning bolts' [c. 1806], *para rayo* [1870], *para-rayo* [1881]. Hyphenated alternatives seem to peak during the latter part of the 19th century, possibly as part of a more general experimental orthographic trend (maybe influenced by French patterns). The above suggests that the two-word spellings are not necessarily older, as one would expect if the compound pattern had grown out of the juxtaposition of a syntactic verbal phrase.

7.1.2.5 *Evolution of formal features*

The hallmark of this pattern is its structural stability: all through history, it has contained a verb followed by the theme or locative complement subcategorized by the verb. In the vast majority of these compounds, the verb precedes its complement, as it would in sentence syntax. The form of the constituents also remains stable over the centuries, with the verb appearing almost invariably as a stem with a theme vowel. Consider, for example, *torna* 'turn', found in the same form in *tornaboda* 'day after the wedding, lit. turn-wedding' [1270–1284] and in *tornarratas* 'door against rats, lit. turn (away)-rats' [1949]. There are a few systematic exceptions, such as compounds with *batir* 'to beat', which appear with a linking vowel -*i*- instead of the expected -*e*. Yet, this anomaly is not attributable to phonetic changes, since *bati*- is preferred all through history: e.g., early *baticor* 'sorrow, lit. beat-heart' [1240–1250], *batifulla* 'metal worker, lit. beat-leaf' (Cat. *fulla* 'leaf') [1475], and late *baticulo* 'type of rope used in sailing', lit. 'beat-behind' [ad 1540], *baticabeza* 'chick beetle, lit. beat-head' [1893], *batifondo* 'racket, lit. beat-back' [1970] (cf. Rainer 1993: 266).

Phonetic change affects compounds more frequently when the nominal starts with a vowel, since this results in a sequence of two vowels that is prone to reduction or loss: *pujavante* 'horseshoe cutter' < *puja* 'push' + *avante* 'ahead'; *tornaire* 'type of woven material' < *torna* 'turn' + *aire* 'air'. However, the history of this process is hard to trace, since only occasionally do we find both forms in the database. Additionally, in several pairs the order of attestation is not what one would expect from phonetic erosion: *abrojo* [1250] ~ *abreojo* [c. 1482–1500] 'bur', lit. 'open-eye', *tragaldabas* [1727–1728] ~ *traga-aldabas* [1863] 'glutton', lit. 'swallow-door-knockers'. The fact that the form with a hiatus often comes later suggests a process of recovery of constituents that had been welded together for centuries.

The nominal constituent is quite stable, always appearing in full form. As stated earlier, however, there is variability in the occurrence of the plural marker. When the $[V + N]_N$ contains a countable noun, earlier allomorphs tend to favor the presence of the plural, which results in a generic interpretation (e.g., *sacacorchos* 'corkscrew', lit. 'remove-corks', *escarbadientes* 'toothpick', lit. 'pick-teeth'). As the compound becomes older, the final plural mark tends to be lost. This is apparent in the fact that older compounds tend to exhibit a higher percentage of -*s* loss at a given point in time than newer ones. Thus, for example, *un escarbadiente* [1578] has 1,970 hits in Google against 5,920 for *un escarbadientes* (a ratio of 1 to 3). By contrast, the newer compound

Table 7.6 First attestations of $[V + N]_N$ compound alternants with plural and singular nominal constituents

	First attestation Singular nominal	First attestation Plural nominal
Countable nouns		
cubrecama(s)	1907	1969
engañapastor(es)	1958	c 1535–1575
escarbadiente(s)	1960	1578
matarrata(s)	–	1876–1880
pasamano(s)	1493–1564	1867
sacabocado(s)	1592	1652
sacacorcho(s)	1987	1889
tapaboca(s)	1587	1820–1823
Mass nouns		
buscavida(s)	c. 1617	1847
cascarrabia(s)	–	ad 1688
catavino(s)	1981	1615
cuajaleche(s)	1797	1962
guardafuego(s)	1770	1972
matafuego(s)	–	1944–1949
sacadinero(s)	1487	1913

sacacorchos [first att. 1889], seems to be at a more incipient stage of the process, with *un sacacorcho* exhibiting only 898 hits against 17,800 for *un sacacorchos* (a ratio of 1 to 20) (Google, 11.22.08). However, as Table 7.6 shows, not all countable nouns exhibit plural forms before they appear as singulars in the historical data. Thus, while *engaña-pastores* precedes *engañapastor* 'goatsucker', lit. 'fool-shepherd(s)', *tapaboca* 'muffler', lit. 'cover-mouth' precedes *tapabocas*. More puzzling perhaps are the $[V + N]_N$ compounds with uncountable nouns whose nominal appears in the plural, since this plural is unwarranted on semantic grounds: *cascarrabias* 'grumpy person', lit. 'break-rage-PL'. The pluralization of mass nouns is a topic that deserves further study.

Let us close this section with a note concerning an alternative type of compound that exhibits the same constituents in reverse order, i.e., $[N/Adv + V]_N$: *maltrabaja* 'lazy person', lit. 'badly-work', *gatatumba* 'simulation', lit. 'cat-topple', *[a] mocosuena* 'as it sounds', lit. '[of] snot-sound'. This secondary pattern, which amounts to no more than 1% of the total, represents an older word order. About half of the first attestations are dated before the 1700s, and only one is first attested in the 1900s, possibly due to lack of earlier documentary sources rather than modern creation of the pattern. Folk etymology can be a source for some of these inverted compounds, since compound meaning cannot be transparently derived from the meaning of constituents in a complement-head configuration. For example, in the case of *milsana* 'milefolium', Corominas suggests the etymology to be **milfolla* 'milefolium', where the second part was identified as the verb *afollar* 'to hurt', and later changed to *sanar* 'to cure' to avert bad luck and guarantee the curative properties of the plant (Corominas & Pascual 1980–91: vol. 4, 75–76). Interestingly, the inverted pattern has been documented in other Western Romance varieties such as Catalan, Occitan, and Gascon (Klingebiel 1988; 1994). This author observes that some [N + V]$_N$ compounds later developed counterparts in the [V + N]$_N$ compound class: Cat. *camalliga/lligacama* 'garter', lit. 'leg-bind/bind-leg', Cat. *feina-fuig* 'lazy', lit. 'work-flee', vs. Occ. *fuglòbra* 'id.', lit. 'flee-work'.

7.1.2.6 *Evolution of meaning*

Some accounts have suggested that over history [V + N]$_N$ compounds underwent a gradual semantic shift, from nicknames to pseudo-names, to satirical appellations, to pejorative names for professions, and finally, non-pejorative names and designations of instruments (Spitzer 1951; Lloyd 1968). However, like Bork (1990), I found that the meanings of [V + N]$_N$ compounds – defined in broad semantic classes as inanimate, animate, human, and a miscellaneous class including abstracts – were surprisingly stable, with all uses possible from their earliest attestations and few changes over time, other than in relative frequency. Thus, among the earliest examples there were man-made utensils (*cubrepán* 'bread cover', lit. 'cover-bread' [c. 1196]) and flora/fauna (*quebrantahuesos* 'vulture', lit. 'break-bones' [c. 1275]).[4] The first cases of humorous human characterization follow a little later (*trotaconventos* 'match-maker', lit. 'trot-convents' [1330–1343]), and perhaps not surprisingly, they tend to appear in creative fiction. Over the centuries, each one of the semantic categories adds more members, with the balance between the various meanings shifting somewhat, as shown on Table 7.7, which focuses on three periods (1100s –1300s, the 1600s, and 25% of the data from the 1900s). In the initial period the most frequent semantic functions documented are designations for natural phenomena and man-made instruments. In the 1600s, the pattern continues to be used to name instruments and to a certain extent nature, but its most prevalent semantic function is to designate humans, either humorously or disparagingly: *azotacalles* 'gadabout', lit. 'hit-streets' [1601], *lameplatos* 'servant who attends the table', lit. 'lick-plate' [1617] (for a similar pattern in French, Bierbach 1983). Finally, in the selection of 20th century examples, the most prevalent new [V + N]$_N$ compounds are names of natural phenomena (*chuparrosa* 'hummingbird', lit. 'suck-rose' [1955 – 1980]), and, maybe not surprisingly, novel instruments (*exprimelimones* 'lemon squeezer', lit. 'squeeze-lemons' [1958]).

The lexical evolution of [V + N]$_N$ compounds can also be analyzed by looking at the history of a specific verbal constituent. The most frequent verbs are probably the most interesting, since large overall numbers of compounds correlate with early appearance of a verb in [V + N]$_N$ compounds, and thus, with a longer historical span. Consider, for example, the three most frequent verbs *guardar* 'to keep', *matar* 'to kill', and *portar*

---

4.   As previously noted in Chapter 1, Section 1.6.2, I exclude proper names from consideration.

Table 7.7 Semantic fields of [V + N]$_N$ compounds in three historical periods

	Inanimates	Non-human animates	Humans	Others
1100s–1300s	33.3% (8)	37.5% (9)	4% (1)	25% (6)
1600s	31.6% (24)	6.6% (5)	42.1% (32)	19.3% (15)
1900s	36% (36)	32% (32)	22% (22)	10% (10)

'to carry', first attested in compounds in the 1100s, 1200s and 1400s, respectively. The semantic nature of the verbs tends to determine the types of meanings of the compounds. For example, both *guardar* and *portar* are used mainly to generate names of objects or locations (*guardasol* 'parasol', lit. 'protect-sun', *portaleña* 'firewood holder', lit. 'hold-firewood') and occasionally to name humans (*guardametas* 'goalie', lit. 'protect-goals', *portaestandarte* 'flag bearer', lit. 'carry-emblem'). Neither is used to denote flora or fauna nor with metaphoric meanings. By contrast, compounds with the verb *matar* convey a wider array of meanings, including several figurative uses made possible by the greater semantic range of the verb itself: *matarratas* 'rat poison', lit. 'kill-rats', *matacandiles* 'candle snuffer', lit. 'kill-candles', *matasellos* 'rubber stamp', lit. 'kill-stamps', *matasuegras* 'noise maker, party blower', lit. 'kill-mothers-in-law'.

7.1.2.7 *Endocentric and exocentric uses*
The totality of the compounds in this class are exocentric, since neither of the two overt constituents is the head of the entire complex. This supports the proposal that the V + N predicate is in fact selected by an empty WCM head, responsible for its nominal properties. Further category reassignment is undocumented. However, [V + N]$_N$ can be used as adjectives, and as such appear in positions where nominals would be impossible, such as predicates with *estar* or *andar* 'to be in a temporary state' (4a, b), with degree phrases (4a), or as modifiers to nouns (4c).

(4) a. *lo que pasa es que Microsoft anda muy rompebolas con la seguridad*
                                                              (11.11.08, Google)
         'the problem is that Microsoft is getting very picky (lit. 'very break-balls')
         about security'.

     b. *Acá en Tandil con lo que están rompebolas es con el casco y el carnet.*
                                                              (11.11.08, Google)
         'Here in Tandil they are being insistent (lit. 'break-balls') when it comes to
         requiring a helmet and licence'.

     c. *Si tenés un viejo rompebolas es preferible [trabajar para] un extraño*
                                                              (11.11.08, Google)
         'If you have an annoying (lit. 'break-balls') old man, [working for] a
         stranger is better'

7.1.2.8 *Special cases*

One last point of interest regarding [V + N]$_N$ compounds is the fact that the database exhibits several examples of borrowing from other Romance languages, sometimes with some degree of reanalysis. This is not surprising, given the complete parallelism of the language family with regard to this compound pattern. This structural identity, coupled with the frequent use of cognate stems, makes these words more likely to be borrowed and easier to understand in the recipient language. Borrowed [V + N]$_N$ are easiest to detect if they retain phonological or morphological features of their source language or if the reanalysis is partial. Thus, for example, they may show distinctive phonetic shape: *cagafogo* 'Portuguese galleon', lit. 'shit-fire', according to Covarrubias, so called because of its artillery (cf. Port. *fogo* 'fire' vs. Sp. *fuego* 'id.'), *botafumeiro* 'thurible', lit. 'toss-smoke' (cf. Gal. *fumeiro* 'smoke' vs. Sp. *humero* 'id.'). Borrowed [V + N]$_N$ compounds may also have morphological marks different from those of Spanish: *saltimbanqui* 'clown' (< It. *saltimbanchi* 'clown', lit. 'jump-embankments'). In some cases, partial reanalysis results in compounds that are totally or partially opaque: Fr. *tirebouchon* 'corkscrew', lit. 'pull-corks' > *tirabuzón* 'corkscrew', lit. 'pull-mailboxes' (Bork 1990: 147–48). Without painstaking etymological work, it is a great deal harder to identify compounds calqued on other Romance languages if Spanish stems have been substituted for those in the source language.

7.2 The [Q + N]$_N$ pattern: *Mil leches*

Compounds formed by a weak quantifier (normally a numeral) and a nominal (e.g., *milpiés* 'millipede', lit. 'thousand-feet') are a small subset of possessive or *bahuvrihi* compounds in Spanish. The resulting nominals denote an individual characterized as possessing the particular feature in the quantity specified. These compounds are exocentric because neither the numeral nor the plural nominal constituent is in fact the head of the compound, as evinced by their concord features: *el milpiés* 'the millipede', lit. 'the-MASC SG thousand-feet'. The main variation on this type is made up of compounds whose head is actually the non-numeral, with a numeral modifier: *diezañal* 'ten-year old', lit. 'ten-year-ADJ SUFF' (cf. *añal* 'yearling'), *dosalbo* 'horse with two white legs', lit. 'two-white' (cf. *albo* 'white').

7.2.1 Structure

7.2.1.1 *Constituents*

The first constituent in [Q + N]$_N$ compounds is a weak quantifier: *cientopiés* 'centipede', lit. 'hundred-feet', *milamores* 'red valerian [Centrantus ruber L.]', lit. 'thousand-loves', *poca vergüenza* 'shameless person', lit. 'little shame'. Only certain digits, some with traditionally symbolic value, are attested in the existing compounds: two (*dos piezas* 'two-piece swimsuit', lit. 'two pieces'), three (*tres sietes* 'twenty-one [card game]', lit. 'three sevens'), four (*cuatro ojos* 'person who wears glasses', lit. 'four eyes'), five (*cinco negritos* 'lantana [Lantana camara L.]', lit. 'five-little blacks'), seven (*sietemachos* 'brave man', lit. 'seven-males'), ten (*diez cuerdas* 'musical instrument', lit. 'ten strings'), forty (*cuarenta horas* 'quadraginta [religious celebration]', lit. 'forty hours'), one hundred (*ciempiés* 'centipede', lit. 'one hundred feet'), and one thousand (*milhombres* 'man-eating woman', lit. 'thousand-men'). Note that only simplex number constituents are possible: **treinta y tres pies* 'thirty-three feet'. A few compounds have a first constituent that is not a numeral, but can still be considered a weak quantifier, in the sense that it cannot be used with a distributive meaning: *todos santos* 'all saints' day', lit. 'all saints' (i.e., all saints together, rather than severally).[5]

The second constituent is a noun, normally in the plural, although the final *-s* can be absent if the compound itself was created through folk etymology or underwent phonetic erosion over time: *milhoja* 'millefeuille', lit. 'thousand leaf' < *milhojas* 'id.'; *milgrana* 'persimmon' < Lat. MILLE GRANA 'thousand grain' (cf. discussion in Corominas & Pascual 1980–91: vol. 3, 197–198). Compounds in the $[Q + N]_N$ class whose non-numeral is singular (e.g., *tresnieto* 'great-grandson', lit. 'three-grandson') have a different internal structure, as shown below.

7.2.1.2 *Compound structure*

In compounds with a plural nominal, the relationship between the two constituents is one of head and complement, with the quantifier selecting the noun (5). The numeral Quantifier Phrase (QP) is then selected as a complement by a WCMP head, which nominalizes the entire construction and permits further morphological suffixation such as number and gender.

(5)

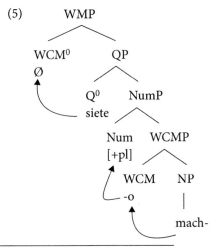

---

5. The distributive and non-distributive uses of *todos* 'all' can be demonstrated with semantic contrasts such as: *Todos los hombres cantaron la canción* 'All the men sang the song', interpretable as 'all of them together', 'each man in turn', or 'all the men in any and all possible groupings'. Only the first of those interpretations is possible in compounds: e.g., a *vehículo todo-terreno* 'all-terrain vehicle', can be driven on any type of terrain at any time. For more on the distinction between weak and strong quantifiers, cf. Chapter 1, Section 1.2.4.2.

A different construction must be posited for cases in which the nominal appears in the singular. In these cases, the rightmost nominal is the head of the construction, as shown by the fact that it is responsible for the agreement features of the compound: *el tresnieto* 'the great-grandson', lit. 'the-MASC SG three-grandson', *la tresnieta* 'the great-granddaughter', lit. 'the-FEM SG three-granddaughter'. To account for the multiplication interpretation (*tresduplo* = *duplo de tres* 'triple = double of three', *tresnieto* = *nieto por tres* 'great-grandson = grandson three times', parallel to *tres mil* = *mil por tres* 'three thousand = a thousand by three'), I propose that the numeral is in fact selected by a lower prepositional phrase with a null head (6).

(6)

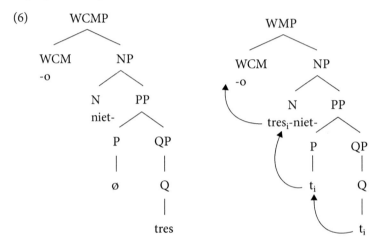

7.2.1.3 *Compound meaning*

Like other *bahuvrihi* compounds, exocentric [Q + N]$_N$ denote a class of individuals that possess the feature specified in the quantity specified. The pattern is used to create common names for animals and plants: e.g., *sietecolores* 'many-colored rush-tyrant [Tachuris rubrigastra L.]', lit. 'seven-colors', *ciempiés* 'centipede', lit. 'hundred feet'. There are also compounds in this class that denote man-made objects such as clothes, instruments, and so on: e.g., *diez cuerdas* 'musical instrument', lit. 'ten strings', *dos piezas* 'bikini', lit. 'two pieces'. There are also cases of metaphoric use, where the relationship between the numeral expression and the referent is blurred: *milamores* 'red valerian [Centrantus ruber L.]', lit. 'thousand-loves', *cinconegritos* 'lantana [Lantana camara L.]', lit. 'five-little blacks'. Generally speaking, these compounds correspond to the colloquial register, so when used to denote a human type, they tend to be humorous or pejorative: *cuatro ojos* 'person who wears glasses', lit. 'four-eyes', *poca vergüenza* 'shameless person', lit. 'little-shame', *milhombres* 'man-eating woman', lit. 'thousand-men'. By contrast, in endocentric [Q + N]$_N$ compounds no part-whole relationship holds. In that pattern, it is the nominal head that percolates its semantic features to the whole, with the numeral modifying it. Thus, for example, a *tresnieto* 'great grandchild' is in essence a *nieto* 'grandchild' but one that is three rather than two generations removed from the ancestor; *todopoder* 'omnipotence', lit. 'all-power' is power without limit.

7.2.2 Diachrony

7.2.2.1 Historical antecedents and comparative data

Compounds with the structure [Q + N] in which a numeral governs the following nominal are known in the Indo-European family. For example, they are present in Sanskrit, where they are known as *dvigu*, a name that is in itself a representative example with the modifying meaning 'worth two cows', lit. 'two-cows'. They are also documented in Greek, with forms such as δι-ώβολος 'di-óbolos' 'having two obol-pieces', lit. 'three-obols' (Debrunner 1917: 44). In Latin, they are present both as juxtaposed formations, such as DUAPONDŌ 'weighing two pounds', lit. 'two-pounds' (Bader 1962: 298), and exceptionally, as authentic compounds, such as TRITECTUM 'third floor' (Bader 1962: 324). It is a matter of some discussion whether this pattern is endo- or exocentric (cf. Clackson 2002: 165). As seen earlier, the disagreements among scholars may be due, at least in part, to the fact that compounds with the same surface pattern $[Q + N]_N$ may have both possible internal structures (represented in diagrams (5) and (6) above).

In the Romance languages, however, the $[Q + N]_N$ pattern does not command as much attention as $[V + N]_N$, possibly due to its greatly restricted usage. In the works consulted, there are references to this type of compound only in Mascaró's description of Catalan, where they are considered together with the $[A + N]_N$ (1986: 72), and very briefly for French in Spence (1980: 74).

The first attestations in the Spanish corpus appear in the 1200s: *todos santos* 'all saints' day', lit. 'all saints' [1252–1284], *sietecueros* 'castin leatherjacket, [Oligoplites saliens L.]', lit. 'seven hides' [1880–1882], *cientopiés* 'centipede', lit. 'hundred-feet' [1513]. The endocentric $[Q + N]_N$ pattern emerges simultaneously with the exocentric pattern: *trasmacho* (var. of *tresmallo*) 'net made with three nets', lit. 'three net' [1251–1284], *tres duplo* 'triple', lit. 'three double' [1254–1260], *tresabuelo* 'great-grandfather', lit. 'three grandfather' [c. 1250–1260].[6] This second head-final endocentric pattern is rather frequent during the earliest period, but all but one of the forms are recorded in the 1200–1300 period, and no neologisms are recorded after the 1400s.

7.2.2.2 Frequency and productivity

Because neither the endocentric nor the exocentric $[Q + N]_N$ patterns are very frequent, in what follows they are grouped together, for an overall total of 47 examples in the entire database (1.4%). The number of examples increases slightly over the centuries, especially in the latter period (Table 7.8), but when considered in terms of relative frequency, their percentages in fact decrease gradually from a high of 3.4% to a low of 1.2%.

---

6. In the case of forms such as *tresabuelo* 'great-grandfather', one cannot discard interactions between the preposition *tras* 'behind' and the numeral (cf. discussion under *tras* in Corominas & Pascual 1980–91, vol. 5, 606).

Table 7.8 [Q + N]$_N$ compounds attested by century, as totals and as a percentage of all compounds

	[Q + N]$_N$	All compounds	[Q + N]$_N$ as % of all compounds
1000s–1200s	12	349	3.4
1300s	13	434	3.0
1400s	16	709	2.3
1500s	16	1073	1.5
1600s	17	1237	1.4
1700s	18	1360	1.3
1800s	20	1842	1.1
1900s–2000s	37	3005	1.2
Total	47	3451	1.4

Table 7.9 Productivity of [Q + N]$_N$ compounds by century

	Carried over	Lost	New	Total	Productivity Ratio
1200s	1	(0)	11	12	NA
1300s	12	(0)	1	13	0.08
1400s	13	(1)	4	16	0.19
1500s	16	(2)	2	16	0.00
1600s	16	(2)	3	17	0.06
1700s	17	(3)	4	18	0.06
1800s	18	(1)	3	20	0.10
1900s–2000s	20	(1)	18	37	0.46

The productivity of this pattern over time has remained quite modest, with few neologisms except in the final period, and gradual losses that keep the ratio of new to old compounds very low (Table 7.9).

7.2.2.3 *Inseparability of constituents*

[Q + N]$_N$ compounds have a structure that exactly parallels syntax (e.g., *tengo cinco hermanos* 'I have five brothers'). It therefore makes sense to look for signs of a possible origin of [Q + N]$_N$ compounds in syntactic phrases. If that were the case, we would expect at least some syntactic precursors to those compounds that would exhibit phrasal properties such as insertions between the numeral and the nominal. However, no such insertions are attested when the numeral + noun complex is interpreted as a compound: *pequeño sietecolores* 'small many-colored rush-tyrant', lit. 'small seven-colors', vs. *siete pequeño colores* 'seven small colors'; *milamores* 'red valerian, [Centrantus ruber L.]', lit. 'thousand-loves' vs. *mil grandes amores* 'a thousand great loves'.

7.2.2.4 *Orthographic representation*

Compounds with numerals exhibit considerable spelling variation. Some present both one- and two-word spelling: *siete machos* ~ *sietemachos* 'brave man', lit. 'seven-males', *cuatro ojos* ~ *cuatroojos* ~ *cuatrojos* 'person with glasses', lit. 'four-eyes', *ciento pies* ~ *cientopiés* 'centipede', lit. 'hundred-feet'. Others are attested only in two-word spellings (*tres duplo* 'triple', lit. 'three double'). The only cases in which two-word spelling was impossible were compounds in which the digit appeared in stem form: *cuatrirreactor* 'four engine vehicle', lit. 'four reactor' (cf. *cuatro* 'four'). This suggests that the number is in general prosodically and semantically discernible for writers well after the process of compounding has been completed.

7.2.2.5 *Evolution of formal features*

This compound class is so small and diverse that very few general observations can be made about their evolution. As noted, endocentric $[Q + N]_N$ compounds disappear early on: *tresduplo* [1313], *tresnieto* [1246–1252], *trestanto* [1385]. For the exocentric pattern, the most notable changes over time include the loss of the plural mark, as they become semantically opaque: *milhojas* > *milhoja* 'millefeuille', lit. 'thousand-leaves/leaf'. Another development is the increased use of stems instead of lexemes in new creations: *cuatrirreactor* 'four engine [vehicle]', lit. 'four-reactor', [1983], *cuatrimotor* 'four engine vehicle', lit. 'four engine' [1956], *cuatricolor* 'four-colored', lit. 'four-color' [1975].

7.2.2.6 *Endocentric and endocentric uses*

When $[Q + N]_N$ compounds are structurally exocentric, no further changes in headedness occur. As for the head-final endocentric numeral compounds, they are so few and disappear so early that no generalizations are warranted about their category changes.

7.2.2.7 *Special cases*

The totals of numeral compounds grow if we add some related cases, such as $[Q + A]_A$: *dosalbo* '[horse] with two white legs', lit. 'two-white', *tresdoblado* 'tripled', lit. 'three-doubled'; $[Q + prep + N]_N$: *cincoenrama* 'creeping cinquefoil [Potentilla reptans L.]', lit. 'five-in-branch'; and $[Q + V]_V$: *cuatrodoblar* 'to multiply by four', lit. 'four-double'. The only minimally productive pattern of these, $[Q + A]_A$, is most often used to create adjectives that predicate about time, in years or months: *cadañera* '[female] that has offspring every year', lit. 'every-year-ADJ SUFF', *cincuentañal* 'fifty-year-old', lit. 'fifty-year-ADJ SUFF'. These forms are created by parasynthesis, i.e., adjectival suffixation simultaneous with nominal compounding: $[[Q + N]_N \text{ suff}]_A$: $[[\text{siete} + \text{mes}] + \text{-ino}]_A$ 'premature infant born at seven months of gestation', lit. 'seven-month-ADJ SUFF'.

7.3 Summary of chapter

This chapter has dealt with two main compounding patterns, $[V + N]_N$ and $[Q + N]_N$, which share the property of being exocentric. In both of them, the relationship between the internal verbal or numeral constituent and the accompanying nominal is one of head-complement. The fact that this internal head does not pass on its features to the compound as a whole is accounted for by positing an empty WCM head, responsible for the nominal features of the complex. One difference between both patterns is the existence, for $[Q + N]_N$, of some early endocentric examples. No such cases exist for $[V + N]_N$, which appears as one of the most structurally stable and semantically transparent compounding patterns in the language. Another difference is in their productivity: whereas $[Q + N]_N$ compounds are marginal, $[V + N]_N$ are one of the main patterns of modern Spanish. As far as their meanings are concerned, like all lexemes, these undergo different types of semantic shifts over their history. As a result, it may very well happen that knowledge of the meaning of the constituent parts tells us nothing about the meaning of the whole.

CHAPTER 8

Concatenative compounds

Ajoqueso, agridulce, subibaja, dieciséis

This chapter deals with compounds with hierarchically identical constituents, referred to as dvandvas in the Sanskrit tradition and with a variety of other names in many accounts (e.g., co-compounds, copulative, binominals, etc.) (cf. discussion in Bauer 2008 and Wälchli 2005). In Spanish the two largest groups are made up of two nouns or two adjectives. These nominal and adjectival concatenative patterns have several subtypes each, which are discussed in Section 8.1 and 8.2, respectively. A much smaller group is made up of two concatenated verbs; this is an exocentric class, because the resulting compound is always nominal (Section 8.3). Finally, there are complex additive numerals, which are possibly the clearest example of a productive class, since they are infinite by definition (Section 8.4) (Table 8.1).

8.1 The $[N + N]_N$ concatenative pattern: *Ajoqueso*

Concatenative compounds made up by stringing together two (or more) nominals are well attested, with 182 exemplars, or about half the concatenative compounds in the database. They come in the three main subtypes described in Chapter 2, namely identificational compounds, whose constituent nouns are coextensional (e.g., *actor-bailarín* 'actor-dancer'), additive compounds, whose the constituents have non-overlapping denotation (e.g., *[relaciones] madre-niño*, 'mother-child [relations]'), and hybrid dvandvas, compounds that "blend" or combine semantic features of the relevant portions of the constituent denotation into a novel denotation (e.g., *centro-derecha* 'center-right').

Table 8.1 Concatenative patterns in Spanish

Pattern	Example	Found in →
$[N + N]_N$	*actor-bailarín* 'actor-dancer'	Chapter 8, Section 8.1
	amor-odio 'love-hate'	
$[A + A]_A$	*tontivano* 'stupid and vain', lit. 'stupid-vain'	Chapter 8, Section 8.2
$[V + V]_N$	*duermevela* 'light sleep', lit. 'sleep-wake'	Chapter 8, Section 8.3
$[Q + Q]_Q$	*dieciséis* 'sixteen', lit. 'ten-and-six'	Chapter 8, Section 8.4
	treinta y tres 'thirty-three', lit. 'thirty-and-three'	

8.1.1 Structure

8.1.1.1 *Constituents*

The nouns that participate in [N + N]$_N$ compounding must be of the same sort, or more specifically, they must be predicates that can apply simultaneously to the very same argument. They may be both abstract nouns (*tecno-pop* 'techno-pop', *usufruto* 'usufruct', lit. 'use-enjoyment'), uncountable nouns (*ajolio* 'sauce with garlic, oil, and other ingredients', lit. 'garlic-oil'), inanimate count nouns (*falda pantalón* 'skort', lit. 'shirt-trousers', *radio despertador* 'radio alarm clock', *mueble bar* 'cocktail cabinet', lit. 'furniture-bar'), animates (*gallipavo* 'American turkey', lit. 'rooster-turkey'), or humans (*cantautor* 'singer-songwriter', lit. 'singer-author'). Concatenatives with nominals of mismatched semantic structure or dimensions – in the sense of Muromatsu (1998) or Uriagereka (2008) – are not attested and are virtually impossible to interpret, even when they might have a reasonable denotation (**radio-conferencia* 'radio-conference', **madre coloquio* 'mother-colloquium').

In terms of form, the last noun in the compound appears as a complete lexeme, hosting the WCM and further inflection of the whole expression: *ajoqueso* 'sauce with cheese, garlic, and other ingredients', lit. 'garlic-cheese', *moquillanto* 'sobbing', lit. 'snot-weeping' *mortinatalidado* 'death rate and birth rate', lit. 'death-birth rate'. As the previous examples show, the first nominal can exhibit a number of possible structures. The vast majority appear in full form, with their WCM. Consider, for example: *urogallo* 'capercaillie [Tetrao urogallus L.]', lit. 'bull-rooster' (cf. *uro* 'type of bull'), *disco-pub* 'discotheque and pub' (cf. *disco*), *bragapañal* 'pull-up diaper', lit. 'panty-diaper' (cf. *braga*), *zapapico* 'pickaxe', lit. 'spade-pick' (cf. *zapa*). A minority of first constituents appear as bare stems, lacking their WCM and sometimes followed by a linking vowel: *pasitrote* 'short trot', lit. 'step-trot' (cf. *paso*), *doncellidueña* 'woman who marries late in life', lit. 'maiden-woman' (cf. *doncella*), *tablestaca* 'sheet pile', lit. 'plank-stake' (cf. *tabla*). Finally, there are some [N + N]$_N$ concatenative compounds whose first nominal is missing segments beyond the WCM or lacks nominal suffixation altogether: *tractocamión* 'tractor-truck' (< *tractor* + *camión*), *mortinatalidad* 'mortality and birth rates', lit. 'death-birth rate' (< *mortalidad* + *natalidad*). Absence of nominal suffixation in the first constituent often involves two nouns with the same suffix: *rectocolitis* (< *rectitis* + *colitis*).

8.1.1.2 *Compound structure*

Concatenative, [N + N]$_N$ compounds exhibit the three distinct structural possibilities as noted in Chapter 2, Section 2.3: there are identificational compounds, additive compounds, and hybrid dvandvas. In the following sections we deal with the structure and semantics of each subtype separately.

8.1.1.2.1 *Structure and meaning of identificational concatenative compounds.* Recall from Chapter 2, Section 2.3, that in identificational compounds not only are the constituents

syntactically equivalent, but they are also identificational predicates that hold of the same individual, as non-restrictive appositions of the type *Guillermo, mi único hermano* 'Guillermo, my only brother' (Fuentes Rodríguez 1989; Guelpa 1995). The underlying relationship can be tested by inverting the constituents, which should not affect compound meaning (*bailarín-actor = actor-bailarín*, but cf. Brucart 1987: 507).[1]

The structure of identificational compounds is represented in (1) in a somewhat simplified form. The diagram represents a series of nominal heads joined by simple concatenation. At issue is how to represent the theta-identification that holds between each one of the constituents in the series and the others, i.e., the compound as a whole. Since the compound and its constituents are of the same grammatical category and hierarchical level, I will assume that they are adjoined to each other, adjunction being the only structure that allows addition of constituents without increasing the level of embeddedness. Each one of the constituents in the series acts as an argument and as a modifier to the others in a relationship of theta-identification (hence the reversibility of the structure) (2). For this to be possible, they must have the same referential variable, which will later be bound by the quantifier or verb outside the compound. This syntactic structure accounts for the fact that for identificational nominal compounds to be interpretable, one single entity must have the features assigned by both constituents. This is because although there are two nouns, there is only one referential variable.

(1)

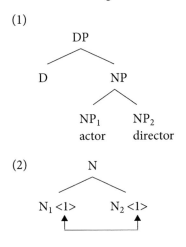

(2)

---

1. In strictly semantic terms, the constituents should be reversible both in identificational compounds and in apposition. For example, *mi único hermano, Guillermo* 'my only brother, Guillermo' and *Guillermo, mi único hermano* 'Guillermo, my only brother', are denotationally equivalent. However, the order in which they are presented is of pragmatic relevance, since their presuppositions are different. Of the two presentations above, the first would be used if the speaker assumes the addressee does not know the brother's name, but knows about his existence. The second one, on the other hand, assumes the addressee has met Guillermo, but does not know the relationship he has with the speaker.

Any number of nouns can be lined up in the iterative structure (Olsen 2001: 2, for Sanskrit). However, the lexicographical database has no lexicalized identificational compounds with more than two nominals, and very few examples with more heads are found in CORDE/CREA (3).

(3)   [...] *en la casa-tienda-taller de Pascual Orquín, que carecía de antecedentes al-fareros, se producía alfarería tradicional y lozas con vista al turismo.*

(1997, Natacha Seseña, CREA)

'[...] in the house-shop-workshop owned by Pascual Orquín, who had no background as a potter, they were producing traditional pottery and tiles for sale to tourists'.

In the simplified structure presented in (1) above, it is not clear where to place the heads of the functional categories of WCM, gender, and number. In principle, they could be within each compound constituent, and thus lower than the concatenation, or, on the contrary, higher than the concatenation, affecting all constituents simultaneously through copies. The data suggest, in fact, that the various functional heads occupy different positions with respect to the concatenated structure, and that their specific position depends, at least in part, on whether the compound designates a human or a non-human.

Let us begin with the case of compounds that designate a human and whose two constituents share the same gender specification: *actor bailarín* 'actor-MASC SG dancer-MASC SG', *actores bailarines* 'id.-MASC PL', *actriz bailarina* 'id.-FEM SG', *actrices bailarinas* 'id.-FEM PL' (cf. **actriz-bailarín* 'actor-FEM SG dancer-MASC SG'). This suggests that they share a single gender node, as represented in (4), and any higher node, such as NumP and DP.

(4)

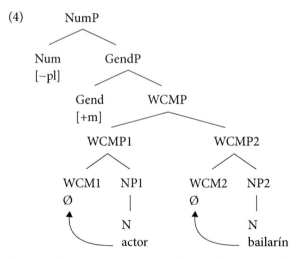

In the case of inanimates there can be a gender mismatch between the two constituents: *sofá-cama* 'sofa-MASC-bed-FEM'. This suggests that in those cases the concatenation involves the GendP nodes, which accounts for the fact that they may differ in gender, but normally not in number (5). In those cases the compound inherits its gender features from the first constituent, suggesting that adjacency is the principle at work in gender assignment (6).

(5)

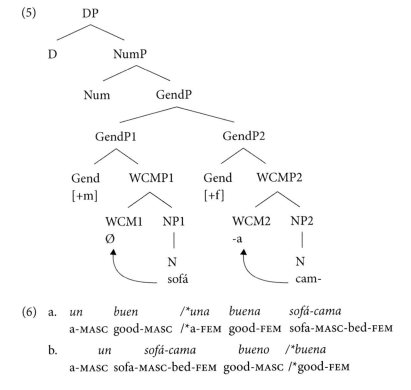

(6) a. *un   buen   /*una   buena   sofá-cama*
         a-MASC good-MASC /*a-FEM good-FEM sofa-MASC-bed-FEM

     b.   *un   sofá-cama   bueno /*buena*
         a-MASC sofa-MASC-bed-FEM good-MASC /*good-FEM

8.1.1.2.2 *Structure and meaning of additive compounds.* Nominal additive compounds are generally not represented in dictionaries, given their high productivity and non-lexicalized nature. Recall from Chapter 2 that in Spanish these compounds act as a dependent to an external nominal head: *(rivalidad) ciudad-campo* 'city-country (rivalry)', lit. '(rivalry) city-country', *(relaciones) madre-niño* 'mother-child (relationship)', lit. '(relationship) mother-child', *(colección) primavera-verano* 'spring-summer (collection)', lit. '(collection) spring-summer', *(coordenadas) espacio-tiempo* 'time-space coordinates', lit. '(coordinates) space-time'. The proposed structure in this case involves the coordination of the two constituents with a null conjunct, and the compound itself results from deletion (cf. (7), repeated from Chapter 2).

(7)   NumP

```
            NumP
          /       \
       Num       WCMP_conj
      [+pl]     /        \
          WCMP           W̶C̶M̶P̶
         /    \         /     \
      WCM    NP      W̶C̶M̶    N̶P̶
      -a    /  \     -̶a̶    /   \
    coordenad- WCMP  c̶o̶o̶r̶d̶e̶n̶a̶d̶- WCMP
              /\             /\
          espacio         tiempo
```

Just as identificational compounds, additive dvandvas can have more than two heads (for English, cf. examples in Olsen 2001). Although binomial structures are the most frequent, theoretically an infinite number of constituents could be strung together: *colección primavera-verano-otoño* 'spring-summer-fall (collection)', lit. '(collection) spring-summer-fall'. This fact can also be accounted for by the coordination analysis: just as coordination is iterative in syntax, so it is at the level of compounding.

8.1.1.2.3 *Structure and meaning of hybrid dvandvas.* It has already been stated that these are the most peculiar concatenative compounds, since they involve the blend of features of two constituents to create a new denotation: *centro-derecha* 'center-right', *gallipavo* 'American turkey', lit. 'rooster-turkey'. Recall also that the structure proposed in Chapter 2 involves a conjunction even before the predicates acquire any referential properties, that is, before the attachment of the WCM (8).

(8)   GendP

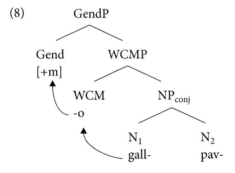

In many hybrid compounds the first constituent has a linking vowel in lieu of a WCM (*gallipavo* 'American turkey', lit. 'rooster-turkey', *arquimesa* 'desk', lit. 'chest-table'). This is a structural feature that singles them out from other concatenative compounds, which do not exhibit this morphological characteristics. When the leftmost noun appears in bare form, it is the rightmost constituent that determines gender: *el capisayo* 'the-MASC cape-FEM cloak-MASC'.[2] There are also hybrid compounds whose two constituents may exhibit their own WCM. In these cases, if there is a gender mismatch between the constituents, it is the leftmost noun that dictates the gender of the whole: *la falda pantalón* 'the-FEM skirt-FEM trousers-MASC'. In other words, gender assignment is ruled by adjacency.

Because the individuation that takes place through the attachment of the WCM follows the conjunction of both noun heads, these compounds involve coordination of two sets of semantic features without defining two separate entities. The semantic interpretability of these compounds depends on the two constituents being understood as compatible. For example, *sureste* 'southeast' is a possible hybrid dvandva because *sur* 'south' and *este* 'east', while contrasting, are still compatible; by contrast, *surnorte 'southnorth' is not a possible hybrid dvandva, given that the semantic features of *sur* 'south' and *norte* 'north' cancel out. If the features can be somehow reconciled (say, through partial or alternating predication), then they can be interpreted even when antonymous: *amor-odio* 'love-hate'.

8.1.2 Diachrony

8.1.2.1 *Historical antecedents and comparative data*

Concatenative compounds involving nominals are ancient, as evinced by the fact that they are recorded for a variety of historical languages, including Sanskrit, Greek, and Latin. In Sanskrit they are numerous and may be plural, dual or neuter singular nouns: *ajāváyas* 'goats and sheep' (plural), *keçaçaçmacrú* 'hair and beard' (neuter collective) (Fruyt 2002: 278; Olsen 2001: 281; Whitney 1941 [1879]: 480). Nominal concatenative compounds are also present in Greek (Debrunner 1917: 40; Fruyt 2002: 278; Schwyzer 1953 [1938]): ἀνδρό-γυνος 'andró-gynos, hermaphrodite', lit. 'man-woman' and ἀνδρό-γυνον 'andró-gynon, couple', lit. 'man-woman', γυνανδρος 'gyn-andros, feminine, virago', lit. 'woman-man'. Authors normally underscore the scarcity of this type of compound in Latin as compared to Sanskrit (Bader 1962: 333; Fruyt 1990: 201; 2002: 263; 2005). Yet, examples, sometimes modeled on Greek, are found to designate hybrid fauna and flora (e.g., PORCOPISCIS 'dolphin', lit. 'pig-fish', NUCIPRŪNUM 'prune-nut'), foods (e.g., OXYPIPER 'vinegar and pepper'), functions (e.g., COMITOTRIBŪNUS 'count-tribune'), hybrid ethnicities (e.g., CELTIBĒRĪ 'Celtiberian'), and winds (e.g., AUSTRO-AFRICUS 'Southern-African').

In the Romance family, [N + N]$_N$ concatenative compounds have been documented for most varieties, such as Portuguese (Villalva 1992: 207, 210), Catalan (Mascaró

---

2.   Some compounds in this category oscillate. For example, a Google search yields 794,000 examples of *el centro-derecha* and 495,000 of *la centro-derecha* 'the-MASC/FEM center-MASC. right-FEM' for the political party that is right of center. This suggests that in the case where the compound is assigned feminine gender the *-o* in *centro* is better interpreted as a linking vowel, not a WCM.

1986: 73), French (Spence 1980: 85; Zwanenburg 1992: 224), Italian (Dardano 1988: 60; Scalise 1992: 180, 183), and Romanian (Mallinson 1986: 330). In Spanish, the first attestations of $[N + N]_N$ concatenative compounds date back to the earliest period for which data are available (9). The pattern thus shows evidence of its antiquity, since its earliest tokens are inherited from Latin via Romance (cf. Section 8.2.2 for a similar development for adjectival concatenative compounds).

(9)   Early attestations of Spanish $[N + N]_N$ concatenative compounds
   a.   *por la muert del marido o de la muiller se gana <u>usofructo</u> por este fuero al qui finqua biuo*   (c. 1250, *Vidal Mayor*, CORDE)
       'through the death of the husband or the wife, the surviving spouse retains usufruct by virtue of this charter'.

   b.   *Otrossil damos en Sevilla unas <u>casas tiendas</u> a la collaçion de sancta Catherina, que fueron de Marina Perez*   (1283, *Carta de donación [Documentos de Alfonso X dirigidos a Andalucía]*, CORDE)
       'Moreover, we bequeath some house-stores in Seville that used to belong to Marina Pérez, to the parish lands of Saint Catherine'

8.1.2.2 *Frequency and productivity*

There are 182 nominal concatenative compounds in Spanish, for all periods considered (5.3% of the database). Regular increases in the numbers of attested $[N + N]_N$ compounds over the centuries keep the relative frequencies growing at a modest pace until the 1700s (Table 8.2). When considered against other concatenatives, the nominal pattern slightly outnumbers adjectivals until the 1500s. However, in the later periods adjectival concatenatives catch up in relative frequency, so that by the end of the 1900s adjectival compounds are slightly more frequent than nominals (cf. Table 8.2 and 8.6).

Table 8.2 $[N + N]_N$ concatenative compounds attested by century, as totals and as a percentage of all compounds

	Concatenative $[N + N]_N$	All compounds	Concatenative $[N + N]_N$ as % of all compounds
1000s–1200s	8	348	2.3
1300s	14	434	3.2
1400s	35	709	4.9
1500s	70	1073	6.5
1600s	80	1237	6.5
1700s	86	1360	6.3
1800s	99	1842	5.4
1900s–2000s	164	3005	5.5
Total	182	3451	5.3

Table 8.3 Productivity of $[N + N]_N$ concatenative compounds by century

	Carried over	Lost	New	Total	Productivity Ratio
1200s	0	(0)	8	8	NA
1300s	8	(1)	7	14	0.43
1400s	14	(0)	21	35	0.60
1500s	35	(1)	36	70	0.50
1600s	70	(3)	13	80	0.13
1700s	80	(5)	11	86	0.07
1800s	86	(6)	19	99	0.13
1900s–2000s	99	(2)	67	164	0.40

As far as productivity is concerned, the $[N + N]_N$ pattern has high ratios of new to old compounds in every century between 1200 and 1500 (Table 8.3). This initial surge then slows down, only to pick up again in the last century. These compounds appear quite stable for most periods, but they experience increased losses in the latter centuries (1700–2000), with the 1700s seeing half as many compounds lost as created. Some of these losses are short-lived jocular formations: *doncellidueña* 'woman who marries late in life', lit. 'maiden-woman' [att. 1732–83] or *demonichucho* 'demon', lit. 'demon-dog' [c. 1626–28].

8.1.2.3 *Inseparability of constituents*
Constituent inseparability can be measured by whether elements extraneous to the compound can appear between its parts. There is no evidence, either synchronic or diachronic, that the two nouns in $[N + N]_N$ concatenative compounds can be separated or modified independently: **cúmulo-un-nimbo* 'cumulus – a -nimbus', **agua-sucia-miel* 'dirty water and honey mixture', lit. 'water-dirty-honey'.

8.1.2.4 *Orthographic representation*
Like in other concatenative compounds, the spelling of $[N + N]_N$ depends somewhat on their surface structure. Compounds whose first constituent is a bare noun or appears with a linking vowel normally do not exhibit two-word alternatives: *pasitrote* 'short trot', lit. 'step-trot' (cf. *paso*), *pinabeto* 'Mexican white pine', lit. 'pine-spruce' (cf. *pino*), though a few isolated hyphenated examples exist: *sopi-caldo* 'thin broth', lit. 'soup-broth' [1863]. As one could expect, when the loss is greater than the WCM, the tendency for unitary spelling is maintained. Thus, for example, *cantautor* 'singer-songwriter', lit. 'singer-author' (< *cantor* + *autor*), *rectocolitis* (*rectitis* + *colitis*), and *mortinatalidad* (< *mortalidad* + *natalidad*) are virtually always spelled as one word (Google, 10.01.08).

The situation is a lot more variable for the majority of $[N + N]_N$ concatenative compounds, whose two constituents retain their WCM (Table 8.4 with data from Google 10.01.08). However, by and large, the compounds that are interpretable as hybrids (i.e., as new mixed denotations) appear in one-word spelling. Consider, for example, *zapapico* 'pickaxe', lit. 'spade-pick' and *urogallo* 'capercaillie [Tetrao urogallus L.]'

Table 8.4 Attestations of one-word and two-word spellings for concatenative $[N + N]_N$ compounds with full word first constituents

	One-word spelling		Two-word spelling (incl. hyphen.)	
uro + gallo	99.9%	(112,000)	0.1%	(68)
zapa + pico	98.2%	(9,060)	1.8%	(166)
cúmulo + nimbo	88.8%	(5,420)	11.2%	(681)
agua + miel	73%	(52,400)	27%	(19,400)
caza + bombardero	67.8%	(21,200)	31.8%	(9,870)
cilindro + eje	42.8%	(2,390)	57.2%	(3,190)
sofá + cama	4.3%	(64,500)	95.7%	(1,440,000)
pleito + homenaje	1.2%	(146)	98.8%	(12,400)
braga + pañal	0.9%	(9)	99.1%	(1,010)
beca + salario	0.4%	(8)	99.6%	(2,020)

lit. 'bull-rooster', unattested as two words. Those with identificational interpretation (i.e., two independent denotations) tend to appear more frequently in two-word spelling. Thus, for example, *pleito homenaje* 'homage', lit. 'praise homage', *braga pañal* 'pull-up diaper', lit. 'panty-diaper', and *beca salario* 'assistantship', lit. 'scholarship salary' are virtually unattested in one-word spelling. For additive dvandvas (*relación madre-niño* 'mother-child relation', lit. 'relation mother-child') separate orthographic representation is quite categorical.

8.1.2.5 *Evolution of formal features*
There are four aspects related to the formal features of these compounds that are worth studying in diachronic perspective. One is the morphological structure of the first constituent, the second is its capacity to bear inflectional marks, the third is the existence of alternants with overt coordination, and the last one is the reversibility of constituents. These are dealt with in order in this section.

As stated earlier, the morphological structure of the first constituent can include a stem accompanied by its WCM or a bare stem, with or without a linking vowel. In this section we explore whether there has been an evolution from one to the other over time, by considering a few compounds that have enough historical depth to exhibit morphological changes. From the available evidence, the conclusion is that the shift from full forms to bare forms is more likely to occur in hybrid compounds, whereas identificational compounds are resistant to this change. Consider, for example, the hybrid compound *capisayo* 'cape', lit. 'cape-cloak' (vars. *capa sayo, capassayo, capissayo,* and *capisayo*). The earliest first attestations present some variability in first constituent structure: *capassayo* [1406 – ad 1435], *capa sayo* [1582–83], *capissayo* [ad 1440], *capisayo* [1467–1482]. However, forms with the intermediate word class marker are not attested again, whereas *capisayo* is in continued use until the 20th century. For their part, early compounds with a clear identificational interpretation have resisted the reduction of first constituents to stem form. Consider *pleito homenaje* 'homage', lit. 'praise homage' [1304], which has never given rise to variants with a first constituent in stem form.

Let us now turn our attention to the issue of internal inflection and its possible changes over time. As one might expect, first nominals that appear in bare form are barred from exhibiting any further inflection: *gallipavos* vs. *gallispavos*, *carricubas* vs. *carriscubas*, *tractocamiones* vs. *tractoscamiones*. By contrast, for compounds whose two constituents appear in full form there is a whole range of possibilities. Some compounds always lack intermediate inflection (*urogallos* vs. *uros gallos*; *zapapicos* vs. *zapas picos*), while others always have it (*becas salarios* vs. *becasalarios*) (Table 8.5).

The pattern that emerges coincides with the findings of constituent inseparability. For compounds that have a clear hybrid interpretation, i.e., those whose two constituents combine their features in a new denotation, the rate of inseparability is high, sometimes categorical. For example, the impossibility of inserting plural markings between the constituents in *urogallo* and *zapapico* matches their interpretations as hybrid animals or objects. By contrast, the continued possibility of inserting plural inflection in both constituents of *pleito homenaje* agrees with the fact that it is an identificational compound. The incidence of intermediate plural marking therefore matches the interpretation of a given concatenative $[N + N]_N$ as a hybrid dvandva or as an identificational compound. Examples that are more ambiguous and capable of having both interpretations often fall in the middle. For example, *sofá cama* 'sofa-bed' can be interpreted identificationally, as a sofa and a bed simultaneously, or as a hybrid dvandva, i.e., a new type of furniture piece with some of the features of a sofa and some of the features of a bed, but strictly speaking, neither. Consequently, its rate of plural marking falls somewhere in the middle.

The evolution of internal plural marking also provides evidence for growing inseparability of constituents in hybrid compounds. For example, the plural of *puerta ventana* 'bay window', lit. 'door-window', is first attested with number marking on both constituents, as *puertas ventanas* [ad 1492]. This form continues to be used into the present, but now exhibits alternants without internal plural, *puerta-ventanas* [1964–1967].

Table 8.5 Internal number inflection in representative concatenative $[N + N]_N$ compounds

	Uninflected first constituent	Inflected first constituent
uro + gallo	100% (15,600)	0% (0)
zapa + pico	99.9% (85,754)	0.1% (7)
cúmulo + nimbo	89.4% (9,385)	10.6% (1,109)
braga + pañal	88.2% (360)	11.8% (48)
caza + bombardero	81.6% (56,810)	18.4% (12,831)
cilindro + eje	60.1% (1,612)	39.9% (1,072)
sofá + cama	55.8% (76,550)	44.2% (60,607)
pleito + homenaje	28% (120)	72% (308)
beca + salario	0.5% (4)	99.5% (864)

These two alternatives are possible because the compound has two distinct interpretations. If it is interpreted as a hybrid, with features of both a door and a window, then *puerta-ventanas* appears as the most likely plural. If the compound is interpreted as both a door and a window, then both constituents will be pluralized (*puertas ventanas*). By contrast, in the case of *casa tienda* 'house-store', the double plural prevails all through history, *casas tiendas* [first att. 1283]. This corresponds well with the fact that hybrid interpretation is unavailable for this compound. A *casatienda* is generally not thought of as a building that has some features of a house and some of a store, but rather, as a construction housing both a store and a residence. Similarly, in a compound like *pleito homenaje* [1304], it is the form with double pluralization that prevails to the present. The opposite structural possibility, i.e., absence of rightmost inflection and presence of internal inflection, is never attested for $[N + N]_N$ concatenatives, setting them apart from the head-initial $[N + N]_N$ pattern (cf. Chapter 6, Section 6.1.2. 5, Table 6.7).

Let us now consider the relationship between concatenative $[N + N]_N$ compounds and idiomatic N + N strings with overt coordination. If it is found that there is frequent alternation between these two types of constructions, this could potentially weaken the lexical status of $[N + N]_N$ compounds. It would mean that they are somehow reduced syntactic phrases. The first observation is that there are quite a few coordinated phrases with the structure [N + coordination + N]. There is generally no doubt that these coordinated strings are listemes in their own right (cf. Chapter 1, Section 1.2.1), because their meaning is stable and impossible to deduce from the parts: e.g., *duelos y quebrantos* 'type of stew', lit. 'pains and sufferings' or *punto y coma* 'semicolon', lit. 'point and comma'. There is an etymological relationship between some of these idiomatic coordinations and *bona fide* compounds, with or without a linking vowel (Table 8.6). In most cases, the earliest form appears with overt coordination, and over time spawns alternants with a word-internal linking vowel or with juxtaposed constituents.

In spite of the evidence for an etymological relationship between coordinated phrases and concatenative nominal compounding, it would be unfounded to assume phrasal origin for all the compounds in this class. The majority of [N + coordination + N] phrases continue to be phrasal and have not given way to compounded forms. Conversely, most concatenative nominal compounds cannot be traced back to coordinated phrases.

Table 8.6 First attestation of some [N + coord + N] phrases and equivalent concatenative $[N + N]_N$ compounds

	Overt coordination	Compound
jaque + mate	jaque y mate [1580]	jaque mate [1799–1815]
pan + quesillo	pan y quesillo [1535–1557]	paniquesillo [1611]
cabo + quinal	cab & quinal [1283]	cabo quinal [1276]
punto + aparte	punto y aparte [1895]	punto aparte [1893]
arte + maña	arte y maña [1499]	artimaña [1528]
cal + canto	cal e canto [1345]	calicanto [1554]

To end this section, I will briefly consider the issue of reversibility of constituents. If this were proven to be frequent, then it would conspire against the compounded status of concatenative compounds. But this is not the case; in fact, very few compounds in this class have inverted counterparts: *nabicol* 'type of cabbage', lit. 'turnip-cabbage' [1913] vs. *colinabo* 'id'. [1933]. Inversion of constituents is slightly more frequent in overtly coordinated phrases: *cala y cata* [1549] vs. *cata y cala* [1574] 'test of a product', lit. 'cut and test', and *daños y perjuicios* 'damages and losses', lit. 'damages' [1490] vs. *perjuicios y daños* 'id'. [1714]. This is not surprising, since overt coordination signals a looser relationship between the two nouns than what would be found in an authentic compound.

To summarize this section, the evolution of their formal features shows that concatenative [N + N]$_N$ are *bona fide* compounds. Although some of them are related to phrases, when they become compounded they reject the overt functional category and their constituent order becomes fixed. Moreover, hybrid dvandvas exhibit a cluster of additional features of inseparability, such as the presence of a first constituent that is in stem form and incapable of bearing any plural inflectional marks. Identificational concatenative compounds are resistant to these additional measures of fusion, thus providing a structural correlate to their structural differences with hybrids.

8.1.2.6 *Endocentric and exocentric uses*

Concatenative [N + N]$_N$ compounds are always endocentric, i.e., not reassigned to other grammatical classes, even over time. Occasionally, a [N + N]$_N$ compound is used as an adjective, in cases such as *un alemán rosacruz* 'a Rosacrucian German' (*rosacruz* < *rosa* 'rose' + *cruz* 'cross'), or *muy marimacho* 'very tomboyish' (*marimacho* < *María* 'woman, girl' + *macho* 'male'). However, these are not exceptional in any way, since Spanish allows that type of adjectival use of nouns more generally. The class of concatenative nominals therefore exhibits a high degree of stability.

A few concatenative [N + N]$_N$ compounds undergo a process of radical semantic displacement, in which the meaning of the compound is metonymic rather than the result of operations on the meanings of the constituents. For example, games may be named after some of their properties: *cabo quinal* 'card game', lit. 'end-thick cord'. A ticket may be named after the types of public transportation it is valid on: *metrobús* 'ticket for underground and bus', lit. 'underground-bus', and a mixed drink may be given a metaphorical name after the look of the resulting mix: *solisombra* 'mixture of cognac and anise', lit. 'sun-and-shade'. None of these examples constitute grammatical category changes, but the semantic change is radical enough that by some definitions, they may be considered exocentric.

8.1.2.7 *Special cases*

Additional evidence for the concatenative [N + N]$_N$ pattern can be gleaned from etymologies provided by early lexicographers. Although their accounts are often fanciful, they underscore the psychological reality of the concatenative template in the interpretation of complex forms. For example, when accounting for the word *leopardo*, *Autoridades* reports the following: *Animal, que algunos quieren sea hijo de Pardo y de Leona, aunque otros son de sentir que procede de León y Panthera* 'an animal that some think is the offspring of a <u>wild cat</u> and a <u>lioness</u>, whereas others believe it comes from crossing a <u>lion</u> and a <u>panther</u>' (Real Academia Española 1734: vol. 3, 386). Biological inaccuracies notwithstanding, the semantic link suggested between the purported constituents and the whole corresponds to those of a blend of semantic features. The creature is supposed to be a hybrid, and so is the etymology of its designation. As for *argamasa*, *Autoridades* again suggests its possible origin thus: *Parece viene de la voz Latin Argilla, especie de tierra, y del nombre Massa, porque con el agua que se le echa se hace como una Massa* 'it seems to come from the Latin word *argilla*, a kind of soil, and from the word *massa* [mass] because when you add water it turns into a paste' (Real Academia Española 1726: vol. 1, 385).

Covarrubias is also quite creative in his etymological accounts of apparent compounds, venturing that *cachos y vasos* 'pieces and glasses' is a possible origin for *cachivaches* 'knick-knacks' and *capa y arzón* 'cape and straps' as the likely source for *caparazón* 'turtle shell, caparace' Corominas and Pascual do not entirely agree with these proposed etymologies. For example, for *cachivache* they do accept that the first element may be *cacho* 'piece', but they propose that the second is not a pre-existing lexeme such as *vaso* 'cup' or *bache* 'hole', but a reduplicative echo of the first one (< *cachi-bachi*), with a consonantal change to indicate the mixed up nature of *cachivaches* (cf. the semantic and formal parallels with Eng. *knick-knacks*) (Corominas & Pascual 1980–91: vol. 1, 726). As for *caparazón*, they do not entirely discard the possibility that the first constituent may be *capa*, but they are skeptical, and they do not venture any likely etymology for the second element (Corominas & Pascual 1980–91: vol. 1, 830).

8.2 The [A + A]$_A$ concatenative pattern: *Agridulce*

Concatenative compounds created by stringing together two adjectives are numerous (195, or about half of all concatenatives). The adjectives involved in this type of compounding fall into distinct structural, semantic, and stylistic classes. Among the nontechnical compounds, which are the oldest, the most frequent combinations create adjectives that denote mixed origin (e.g. *austrohúngaro* 'Austro-Hungarian'), a color combination (e.g., *rojiazul* 'red-and-blue'), or the mixture of other properties (e.g., *anchicorto* 'wide and short', lit. 'wide-short', *loquitonto* 'crazy and stupid', lit. 'crazy-stupid'). Among the more modern coinages, there are descriptive adjectives used in anatomy, physiology, chemistry, philosophy, and other technical fields (e.g., *fibrocartilaginoso* 'fibrous cartilaginous', *alcalinotérreo* 'alkaline-terreous', *marxista-leninista* 'Marxist-Leninist').

8.2.1 Structure

8.2.1.1 *Constituents*

The adjectives that participate in concatenative compounding must be of the same sort, in the sense that they must be applicable to the same aspect of the same argument. For example, if one of them is a color adjective, then so is the other one (*rojiazul* 'red-and-blue'); if one is a dimension predicate, so must the other (*anchicorto* 'wide-short'); and if one is an abstract predicate, the other is, too (*tontivano* 'stupid and vain', lit. 'stupid-vain'). Concatenatives of the type *rojidulce* 'red and sweet' or *negriancho* 'black and wide' are unattested in the lexicographical sources, even if in principle they could be interpreted and do not strike the native speaker as particularly deviant. Compounds that concatenate highly disparate adjective sorts are simply malformed: **tontifrancés* 'silly-French'. This is because concatenative adjectives create a complex predicate that must be attached as a unit at the same level in the eventive structure of a nominal, or it will give rise to ungrammaticality through zeugma effects, i.e., the coordination of non-parallel structures. In other words, the constituents in a concatenative $[A + A]_A$ compound must be capable of occupying the same position in a sequence of modifiers. For example, the ungrammatical combination of two constituents in **tontifrancés* 'silly-French' is mirrored in sentence syntax by the impossibility of inverting the relative position of those two adjectives in a noun phrase: *tonto chico francés* 'silly French kid', lit. 'silly kid French' vs. **francés chico tonto* 'id.', lit. 'French kid silly'.

In terms of form, the last adjective always appears as a complete lexeme, and hosts concord inflection for the whole: *tontivano, tontivana, tontivanos* 'stupid and vain-MASC SG/FEM SG/MASC PL'. By contrast, the first adjective exhibits several possible structures. In a few compounds it appears in full form or at least in a form that is ambiguous: *contencioso administrativo* 'contentious administrative', *demócrata-cristiano* 'Christian democrat', lit. 'democrat-christian', *tupí-guaraní* 'Tupi-Guarani'. In some of these compounds the first adjective can host further suffixation of gender (e.g., *amaro̲dulce* vs. *amara̲dulce* lit. 'sour-MASC/FEM-sweet') and number (e.g., *marxistas̲-leninistas̲* lit. 'Marxist-PL-Leninist-PL', *contenciosas̲ administrativas̲* 'contentious-FEM PL administrative-FEM PL). The first member can also appear in bare form, sometimes followed by a linking vowel: *celtíbero* 'Celtiberian' (cf. *celta*), *blanquirrojo* 'white and red' (cf. *blanco*), *[relaciones] hispanoeuropeas* 'Hispanic-European [relations]' (cf. *hispanas*). There are some compounds in this class whose first adjective appears in a form that is even further reduced. This is because when the base is morphologically complex it may lose its adjectival suffixation. The second adjective may have the same suffix as the first: *fibrocartilaginoso* 'fibrous cartilaginous' (< *fibroso* + *cartilaginoso*), *mineromedicinal* 'mineral-medicinal' (< *mineral* + *medicinal*), *iberoatlántico* 'Iberian-Atlantic' (< *ibérico* + *atlántico*). However, both adjectives in isolation may differ in derivational suffixation, without this impeding the reduction: *austrohúngaro* 'Austro-Hungarian' (< *austríaco* + *húngaro*).

8.2.1.2 *Compound structure*

Compounds with the structure $[A + A]_A$ exhibit a simple concatenation that can be represented with a flat structure (10). Like other concatenative classes, $[A + A]_A$ compounds with multiple iterations are not attested in the lexicographical sources, but the potential for such creations exists and emerges sporadically (cf. 11).

(10)

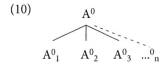

(11)   a.   *Os tendrán por pozos de ciencia <u>poético-trágico-cómico-grecolatino-ángli-co-itálico -gálico-hispánico-antiguo-moderno</u> (sic); (¡fuego, y qué tirada!) y pobre del autor que saque su pieza al público sin vuestra aprobación.*
               (1772, José Cadalso, CORDE)
               'They will think of you as wells of <u>poetic-tragic-comic-Graeco-Roman-Anglian-Italic-Gallic-Hispanic-ancient-modern</u> knowledge (what a mouthful!), and woe to the poor author who shows his play to the public without your approval'.

         b.   *[...] e iniciar alegremente tu nueva aventura con esa esquiadora <u>franco-austro-polaca</u> que rueda por las laderas*
               (1992, Santiago Moncada, CREA)
               '[...] and to happily start your new affair with that French-Austrian-Polish skier who slides down the slopes'

         c.   *Pude distinguir los diferentes efluvios que transportaba el aire, escuchar una gama de innumerables ruidos, ver insospechados detalles, sentir el poder de mis mandíbulas. Antes de aquello había sido casi un <u>ciego-sordo-mudo</u> sin olfato.*
               (2001, Alejandro Jodorowsky, CREA)
               'I managed to distinguish the various smells that wafted through the air, hear the full range of sounds, see minute details, feel the power of my jaws. Before all that, I had been almost a blind-deaf-dumb [person] with no sense of smell'.

Normally, the entire compound has a single locus for gender/number concord. This suggests that the compounded adjective is formed by concatenation of adjectival stems before selection by higher concord nodes, just as we supposed for hybrid dvandvas in Section 8.1.1.2.3 (12). In adjectives whose bases are morphologically derived, it could be argued that derivation follows concatenation of two bare stems (13).

(12)

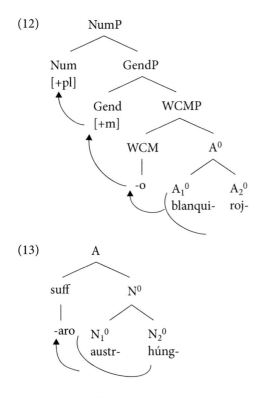

(13)

8.2.1.3 *Compound meaning*

There are several possible ways of interpreting the relationship between the adjectives as predicates of the same external nominal head. In all these interpretations, the features of the two predicates are added, but this addition may take on different guises and may even be dependent on individual interpretation and contextual clues (14).

(14)		compound	literal gloss	meaning
	a.	*sordo mudo*	deaf-mute	deaf-mute
		ético-moral	ethical-moral	ethical-moral
		angoleño-cubano	Angolan-Cuban	Angolan-Cuban
		marxista-leninista	Marxist-Leninist	Marxist-Leninist
	b.	*rojinegro*	red-black	red and black
		verdiblanco	green-white	green and white
		albiazul	white-blue	white and blue
	c.	*paterno-filial*	father-ADJ-son-ADJ	[of] father-son
		greco-turco	Greek-Turkish	Greek-Turkish

The examples in (14a) present what is normally the most straightforward situation: the features associated with the two adjectives are mixed to form a new predicate that applies additively to the entire argument. Thus, someone who is *angoleño-cubano*

'Angolan-Cuban' is both Angolan and Cuban, someone who is *sordomudo* is both deaf and mute, and so on. It is possible, of course, to come up with ambiguous cases. For example, *marxista-leninista* could be interpreted in many different ways. It could be considered disjunctive, i.e., a predicate that could be applied to someone or something whose political ideas are alternatively Marxist and Leninist. This interpretation is possible under the assumption that the sets of ideas of each one of these political philosophies are incompatible and cannot be professed simultaneously. Consider the two following examples: (i) *Pepe es castrista-marxista*. 'Pepe is Castrist-Marxist' and (ii) *Pepe es castrista-franquista*. 'Pepe is Castrist-Franquist'. Although at first blush it seems clear that *castrista-marxista* is additive and *castrista-franquista* is disjunctive, in fact the interpretation hinges on the degree to which the speaker thinks the ideas of Fidel Castro are compatible with those of Karl Marx and with those of Francisco Franco. In other words, for someone who thinks Castro is a faithful follower of Marxist principles, it will be natural to interpret *castrista-marxista* additively. Although the specifics of Pepe's philosophy are not absolutely clear, in this interpretation they are some blend of those of Castro compatible with those of Marx. By contrast, if the speaker considers that Castro has betrayed the ideals of Marx, then Pepe's being *castrista-marxista* can only mean that he is one or the other, i.e., that he wavers between being a believer in Castro's policies and being a Marxist. The complete reverse obtains with (ii). In its most salient reading, this compound would be disjunctive, since for most people Castro and Franco are at opposite ends of the political spectrum: Pepe's political affiliations would alternate between the two. However, if someone considered Castro and Franco as not incompatible, the notion of *castrista-franquista* may well be entertained as an addition of some features of both of the constituent adjectives.

By contrast, the concatenatives in (14b) do not add their features outright, but rather apply them distributively to portions of the argument. That is true of color blends, which are not hues of either color but rather a distributive attribution of two different colors. For example, a tee-shirt that is *albiazul* 'white-blue' is not a light blue color all over, but rather, has white and blue portions.[3] Finally, the examples in (14c) recall the nominal examples of the type *relación madre-niño* 'mother-child relationship', lit. 'relationship mother-child'. In them, the distributive predication is tied to the semantic structure of an external nominal that defines 'sides', each modified independently. Thus, if the noun is *interinfluencias* 'mutual influences', two modifiers will be needed to cover the spaces it defines.

---

3.   Why this partial attribution is favored or even possible is a problem I will not attempt to address, but it is clearly connected to general properties of coordinated predicates in syntax (cf. i, where in the most salient reading, the attributes are assumed to apply to distinct fractions of the U.S. population, not to all the individuals in the subject DP simultaneously).

(i)   *Los americanos son blancos, negros, latinos....*
      'Americans are white, black, Latino ...'

8.2.2 Diachrony

8.2.2.1 *Historical antecedents and comparative data*

Like nominal concatenative compounds, [A + A]$_A$ compounds are documented since antiquity. In Sanskrit, although they are less frequent than their nominal counterparts, some examples are present nonetheless: *çulkakṛṣṇa* 'light and dark' (Olsen 2001: 281; Whitney 1941 [1879]: 480– 487). In Greek they are recorded by Fruyt (2002: 278) and Debrunner (1917: 40): *χλωρό-μελας* 'chlōro-melas, light and dark', *γλυκύ-πικρος* 'glykú-pikros, bittersweet'. Bader (1962: 333–34) mentions several examples for Latin, while recognizing their scarcity and low productivity until later periods: NIGROGEM-MEUS 'bright and somber', DULCACIDUS 'sweet and sour'.

Concatenative compounds made up of two adjectives are found in many languages in the Romance family. They are reported explicitly in descriptions of Portuguese (Alves 1986–1987: 56; Villalva 1992: 210), Catalan (Mascaró 1986: 73), French (Zwanenburg 1990: 135; 1990: 74), Italian (Dardano 1988: 59; Scalise 1992: 177), and Romanian (Mallinson 1986: 330). In Spanish, first attestations of [A + A]$_A$ compounds date back to the earliest period for which data are available (15), with examples inherited from Latin via early Rromance.

(15) Early attestations of Spanish concatenative [A + A]$_A$ compounds

   a. *Ego Ferdinandus ... una pariter cum coniuge mea Santia regina, tibi Aurio-li abati ... offerimus <u>sacrosanto</u> altario vestro ad integrum*

        (1046, *Fernando I concede a Arlanza la tercia que le corresponde en Castrillo Solarana*, CORDE)

        'I, Ferdinand, party of the first part, together with my spouse Santia Regina, offer you, abbott Aurioli, your holy altar in its entirety'

   b. *& deue comer las uiandas frias tal commo carne de bezezerro (sic) & cala-baças con uinagre pollos engrossados & de la fructa maçanas agras & çiru-elas & milgranas <u>agras dulçes</u>*   (c. 1250, *Poridat de poridades*, CORDE)

        'And he must eat cold victuals such as calf meat and pumpkins with vinegar, fattened chicken, and fruit such as sour apples and plums and sweet-sour pomegranates'

8.2.2.2 *Frequency and productivity*

[A + A]$_A$ compounds show low frequencies in the early periods, with numbers comparable to those of [V + V]$_N$ compounds. However, in the later periods (1800–2000), there is dramatic jump in the absolute totals for [A + A]$_A$ compounds resulting in an increase in their relative share among all compounds, from 2.9% to almost 6% (Table 8.7).

Table 8.7 Concatenative [A + A]$_A$ compounds attested by century, as totals and as a percentage of all compounds

	Concatenative [A + A]$_A$	All compounds	Concatenative [A + A]$_A$ as % of all compounds
1000s–1200s	10	349	2.9
1300s	11	434	2.5
1400s	12	709	1.7
1500s	20	1073	1.9
1600s	22	1237	1.8
1700s	30	1360	2.2
1800s	77	1842	4.2
1900s–2000s	182	3005	6.1
Total	195	3451	5.7

Table 8.8 Productivity of concatenative [A + A]$_A$ compounds by century

	Carried over	Lost	New	Total	Productivity Ratio
1200s	1	(0)	9	10	NA
1300s	10	(1)	2	11	0.09
1400s	11	(0)	1	12	0.08
1500s	12	(0)	8	20	0.40
1600s	20	(3)	5	22	0.09
1700s	22	(2)	10	30	0.27
1800s	30	(2)	49	77	0.61
1900s–2000s	77	(5)	110	182	0.58

The higher share of [A + A]$_A$ compounding is linked to its increased productivity over time. With the exception of the 1600s, the ratio of new to old compounds becomes higher with every century (Table 8.8). In the 1800–2000 period, in particular, the number of compounds in this class almost doubles every hundred years. These compounds also appear to be quite stable: once formed, very few of them are lost.

8.2.2.3 *Inseparability of constituents*
The issue of whether the two constituents are inseparable or not can be analyzed from two different perspectives. First, one should consider whether elements extraneous to the compound are permissible between the constituents. The answer is no; there are no counterexamples of the type *verdi-muy-negro* 'green-very-black', *blanqui-poco-azul* 'white-somewhat-blue', *maníaco-extremadamente-depresivo* 'maniac-extremely-depressive'. In other words, modification does not affect the adjectives independently. In fact, it modifies the concatenation, rather than either or both of the concatenated constituents:

muy verdinegro = con muchas partes verdes y muchas partes negras 'very green-black = with many green sections and many black sections', *extremadamente maniacodepresivo = con fluctuaciones extremas entre lo maníaco y lo depresivo* 'extremely maniacal-depressive = with extreme mood swings between manic and depressive poles'.

The second aspect to consider is whether the inflectional suffixation of the whole is only possible on the rightmost edge, or whether it may also have exponents on the first adjective. In this regard, [A + A]$_A$ compounds do not have uniform behavior. On the one hand, compounds that lack a WCM in the first constituent are barred from any further inflection on it: *blanquiazules* vs. **blanquisazules, tontilocos* vs. **tontislocos*. Compounds whose first constituent appears shortened and without adjectival suffixation are incapable of exhibiting intermediate inflection: *toracolumbares* vs **toracoslumbares, infecto-contagiosas* vs. **infectos contagiosas*.

Even when the first constituent can be interpreted as a free form, there is a general preference for leaving it uninflected (Table 8.9 based on data from Google 9.20.08). This preference is almost categorical for some of the compounds studied (*azulgranas* vs.*??azules granas*) and less so for others (*contencioso administrativos* vs. *contenciosos administrativos*). In fact, the behavior of concatenative adjectives with respect to inflection is comparable to that of nominal hybrid dvandvas. This strengthens the hypothesis that their internal structure is that of two concatenated predicates prior to any inflection, as suggested in (12).

An analysis of the older compounds in the [A + A]$_A$ concatenative class makes it possible to draw some tentative conclusions about the evolution of intermediate inflectional markers. For illustrative purposes, let us consider the very old compound *agridulce* 'bitter-sweet' (vars. in CORDE: *agrodulce, agredulce*, and *agriodulce*). The earliest variant to appear, *agrodulce* (as the feminine plural *agras dulces* [c. 1250]), continues to exhibit totally or partially inflected forms throughout the following three centuries (*agradulce* until 1541, *agradulces* and *agrasdulces* until 1598). The variant with first constituent *agre* exhibits a few sporadic uninflected tokens between 1529 and 1607,

Table 8.9 Percentages and totals of double and simple inflection in plural [A + A]$_A$ compounds

Compound	Uninflected first constituent	Inflected first constituent
azulgrana	99.9% (172,264)	0.1% (40)
sacrosanto	99.7% (28,778)	0.3% (73)
sordomudo	87.7% (184,800)	12.3% (25,821)
alcalinotérreo	88.4% (8,990)	11.5% (1,175)
contencioso administrativo	71.1% (88,100)	28.9% (35,760)
castellano leonés[4]	71.1% (84,900)	28.9% (34,439)

---

4.   It should be noted that Google searches do not automatically discard items separated by a comma (e.g., *castellanos leoneses* from *castellanos, leoneses*), which may have inflated the numbers of double inflection in Table 8.9.

whereas the allomorph *agrio* makes a slightly later and equally fleeting appearance [1615–1629], in forms inflected for gender and/or number (*agriadulce* [c. 1607], *agrias dulces* [1609], *agriasdulces* [ad 1613]). However, by the mid-1500s a competing allomorph *agri-* emerges (*agridulce* [1576–77]) and becomes virtually the only form attested by the mid 1600s. Thus, there is a shift from full word first constituents (*agro*, *agre*, *agrio*), to distinctly bare forms (*agri-*), with a concomitant loss of inflection in the first adjective (**agrisdulces*).[5]

Not all the compounds in the [A + A]$_A$ class have as many variants or show the disappearance of intermediate inflection. For example, [A + A]$_A$ *sordomudo* 'deaf-mute' lacks an unambiguous bare stem alternative of the type **sordimudo*. A possible explanation could be based on the different semantics of each [A + A]$_A$ compound: whereas *agridulce* 'bitter-sweet' is of the distributive kind, i.e., the compound adjective implies some sweet and some bitter components, *sordomudo* 'deaf mute' is additive, i.e., the adjective simply adds the features of both constituents and applies them to the totality of the argument.

I would like to close this section with a brief discussion of the possible relationship between [A + A]$_A$ concatenative compounds and syntactic phrases of the type [A + coord. + A]. In particular, it is of interest to establish whether the origin of [A + A]$_A$ compounds could be the agglutination of frequent phrases, or whether they are created with no intermediate phrasal stage. The data suggest quite clearly that it is the second option. There are a few cases in which compounds have parallel phrases, and their relative dates suggest a possible etymological relationship: *sordo y mudo* 'deaf and dumb' [1580] > *sordomudo* 'id'. [1793], *claro y oscuro* 'chiaroscuro', lit. 'clear and dark' [1580] > *claroscuro* 'id'. [1780]. However, in some other pairs the compound is attested before the phrase: *sacrosanto* 'holy', lit. 'holy-saintly' [1046] and *santo y sagrado* 'saintly and holy' [c. 1275]; *contencioso administrativo* 'contentious administrative' [1840] and *contenciosos y administrativos* [1950 –1967]. More importantly, most [A + A]$_A$ compounds do not have a phrasal precursor of the structure [A + coordination + A], and conversely, several frequent conjoined adjectival phrases do not yield *bona fide* compounds. For example, *sano y salvo* 'safe and sound' [c. 1218–1250], has no counterpart *sanosalvo* (cf. also *hecho y derecho* 'mature', lit. 'built and straight'; *contante y sonante* 'in cash', lit. 'counting and sounding').

8.2.2.4 *Orthographic representation*

As pointed out earlier, the constituents in [A + A]$_A$ compounds have several different surface structures. This in turn has consequences for their orthographic representation. Compounds whose first constituent is bare and appears with the linking vowel *-i-* are the least likely to be spelled separately, although some isolated hyphenated

---

5.   Although social or regional variation cannot be discarded as a possible reason for the profusion of forms, the historical progression seems clear enough from the data available. A bigger study, considering more compounds of this type, would be highly desirable.

examples exist: *verdi-negros* [1573], *verdi-roja* [1799–1815]. In general, however, these compounds are consistently spelled as one word throughout their history. For example, *altibaxo/altibajo* 'ups and downs', lit. 'high-low' has only one-word attestations in CORDE (196 tokens from 1330–1334 to 1975).

Spelling variants are more frequent in compounds with the linking vowel -*o*-. In these cases, both hyphenated and two-word spellings are attested as alternatives to one-word representation: *celtohispano* ~ *celto-hispano* 'Celto-Hispanic', *cerebroespinal* ~ *cerebro-espinal* 'cerebral-spinal', *fibrocatilaginoso* ~ *fibro cartilaginoso* 'fibrous cartilaginous', *hispanomusulmán* ~ *hispano-musulmán* ~ *hispano musulmán* 'Hispanic-Muslim'. It is tempting to propose an orthographic evolution from two-word, to hyphenated, to one-word representation, but lack of historical depth for most of these compounds makes it impossible to know for sure.

As seen earlier, compounds whose first constituent is a full lexeme with a WCM and gender/number inflection are a great deal less frequent. When they do occur, they are often represented by hyphenated or two-word spellings. For example, a search in Google (9.18.08) of the possible spellings of *contencioso administrativo* 'contentious administrative' for all gender and number combinations recovered fewer than 1% of occurrences spelled as one word (e.g., *contenciosasadministrativas*).

One final comment regards the presence of the hyphen in [A + A]$_A$ compounds. This orthographic device is recorded for the first time in a lexicographical source in the 1700s (*céfalo-faríngeo* 'cephalic-pharyngeal', *Autoridades* 1729), and a little later in CORDE (*épico-burlesco*, [1778–1822]). It becomes more frequent in the 1800s and continues to be quite widespread throughout the 1900s.

8.2.2.5 *Endocentric and exocentric uses*
Compounds created through concatenation of two adjectives are adjectival, and as such, they readily nominalize in the right kind of syntactic context (cf. 16 a,b).

(16) a. *La guardameta* <u>albiceleste</u>, *Mariela Antoniska, impidió con sus atajadas lo que pudo ser una goleada.* (21.09.2000, *El Nuevo Herald*, Miami, CREA)
'The Argentine (lit. 'white-blue') goalie, Mariela Antoniska, stopped with her saves what could have been a thrashing'.

   b. *Los* <u>albicelestes</u> *son claros favoritos ante un equipo como el boliviano.*
(22.01.1997, *El Observador*, Montevideo, CREA)
'The Argentines (lit. 'white-blues') are the clear favorites in a match against the Bolivian team'.

A very tiny subset of [A + A]$_A$ compounds are permanently reassigned to the lexical class of nouns, and have no possible adjectival use. Among them are *altibajo* 'vicissitudes', lit. 'high-low', *claroscuro* 'chiaroscuro', lit. 'clear-dark', *cochifrito* 'stew', lit. 'cooked-fried', *altiplano* 'meseta', lit. 'high-flat'.

8.2.2.6 *Special cases*

Some [A + A]$_A$ compounds are borrowed from other Romance languages (e.g., *claroscuro* 'chiaroscuro', lit. 'clear-dark' < It. *chiaroscuro*), but their structure in the lending languages is transparently parallel.

8.3 The [V + V]$_N$ concatenative pattern: *Subibaja*

Concatenative compounds made with two verbs are the smallest concatenative pattern. The two verbs can have mainly three types of relationships: identity (through reduplication: *picapica* 'magpie', lit. 'peck-peck', or synonymy: *arrancasiega* 'act of harvesting short crops', lit. 'mow-pull'); antonymy (*ciaboga* 'turn-around', lit. 'row backward-row forward', *vaivén* 'oscillation', lit. 'go-come', *subibaja* 'see-saw', lit. 'go-up-go-down'); or simple listing (*picaraña* "pickaxe", lit. 'peck-scratch', *tiramira* 'line, series', lit. 'throw-look'). They are categorically exocentric, since the resulting compound is never verbal, but nominal.

8.3.1 Structure

8.3.1.1 *Constituents*

In [V + V]$_N$ compounds both constituents are verb stems with the verbal theme vowel (*cuec-e-call-a* 'secretive person', lit. 'cook-be silent'). Occasionally, one of the verbs lacks its theme (*cant-implor-a* 'water bottle', lit. 'sing-implore') or appears in its base form with no vocalic changes (*dorm-i-vel-a, duerm-e-vel-a* 'light sleep', lit. 'sleep-wake'). In the majority of cases, the two verbs are simply juxtaposed, but an occasional example exhibits an overt coordinative element, suggesting a more complex internal structure: (*de*) *quita-i-pón* 'removable', lit. '(of) remove-and-put', *tira y afloja* 'scuffle', lit. 'pull-and-loosen'.

The types of verbs represented include states (*callar* in *callacuece* 'secretive person', lit. 'be silent-cook'; *velar* in *duermevela* 'light sleep', lit. 'sleep-wake'), activities (*mirar* in *tiramira* 'line, series', lit. 'throw-look', *comer* in *comecome* 'itch', lit. 'eat-eat'), achievements (*ganar* in *ganapierde* 'losing game', lit. 'win-lose'), and accomplishments (*cocer* in *callacuece* 'secretive person', lit. 'be silent-cook'). In cases in which the verbs in the concatenation are synonyms or antonyms, they share aspectual properties, but when they are simple concatenated lists, they do not need to. Consider, for example, *tiramira* 'line, series', lit. 'throw-look', where *tirar* is an achievement and *mirar* an activity, or *saltaembarca* 'head cover', lit. 'jump-board', where *saltar* is an activity and *embarcar* an achievement with a clear endpoint. In this regard, note the difference between [V + V]$_N$ and the other classes of concatenatives, which do not tolerate these aspectual mismatches. The reason for this, I surmise, is that in the nominalization process the issue of whether they constitute parallel predicates or not becomes a moot point, since they will not act as predicates outside the compound itself but will be bound within the compound structure by the WCM.

8.3.1.2 *Compound structure*

Compounds with the structure $[V + V]_N$ exhibit a simple concatenation, either of identical bases (in the case of reduplication) or of different bases (in all the others). This can be represented with a flat structure (17). It is interesting that in spite of the potential for listings or reduplications to iterate beyond the first pair of constituents, $[V + V]_N$ compounds do not do so, at least in the lexicalized items found in lexicographical sources.

(17)

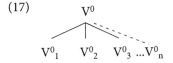

The verbal constituents do not percolate their grammatical category to the whole, as demonstrated by the fact that the entire compound is not a verb. Therefore, a higher nominal phrase is posited that selects the concatenated pair as its complement. Because it has no overt manifestation, in the diagram it is represented with an empty category ø (18). The WCMP is later selected by gender and number inflectional heads.

(18)

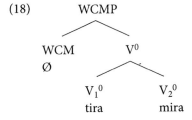

8.3.1.3 *Compound meaning*

Like other concatenative compounds, those made up of verbal constituents have a number of different possible meanings. Because of the looseness of the semantic connection between their parts, compound interpretation often depends on the actual verbs concatenated. When the two have the same denotation, through reduplication or synonymy, their added meaning is intensive: *picapica* 'magpie', lit. 'peck-peck', *come-come* 'itch', lit. 'eat-eat', *tejemaneje* 'intrigue', lit. 'weave-handle', *arrancasiega* 'act of harvesting short crops', lit. 'mow-pull'. When the constituents have opposite semantics, then they can only denote an event or instrument involving an alternation: *subibaja* 'see-saw', lit. 'go up-go down', *(de) quitaipón* 'removable', lit. '(of) remove-and-put', *ganapierde* 'losing game'. (cf. concatenative $[N + N]_N$ examples such as *amor-odio* 'love-hate'). Finally, when the two verbs are not opposites, they act as a label for a more general denotation: *saltaembarca* 'head cover', lit. 'jump-board', *cantimplora* 'water bottle', lit. 'sing-implore', *cortapisa* 'limitation', lit. 'cut-step on'.

8.3.2 Diachrony

8.3.2.1 *Historical antecedents and comparative data*

It has been stated that [V + V] compounding is an innovation in the Indo-European languages, since there are no examples documented even in Sanskrit, whose other concatenative compound patterns are very productive (Kastovsky 2009: 338; Whitney 1941 [1879]). An exception is Armenian, which exhibits nominal compounds made up of verbal stems, such as *tor-ow-ber* 'agitation', lit. 'bring-and-carry' (Olsen 2002: 235). In the remainder of the historical Indo-European languages, it is generally accepted that they are nonexistent, and the origin of [V + V]$_V$ in Modern Greek, for example, is a matter of much recent discussion (Kiparsky 2009, Nicholas & Joseph 2009, Ralli 2009). In the Romance tradition, concatenative compounds made up of two verbs are also a great deal less frequent than their nominal and adjectival counterparts, so they are sometimes overlooked in panoramic studies of the compounding process. However, they do appear in descriptions of Italian and Portuguese (Scalise 1992: 180; Villalva 1992: 211, respectively). In his description of Catalan, Mascaró refers explicitly to [V + V]$_N$ compounds with two distinct verbs and to reduplicatives (Mascaró 1986: 73–74).

For Spanish, the [V + V]$_N$ pattern is also a rarity, and as such has received less attention than its nominal and adjectival counterparts. However, there has been at least one detailed descriptive study of the reduplicative pattern of [V + V]$_N$ compounding (Pharies 1986: 144–46), which provides evidence of the generality and geographic spread of the process, and some theoretical treatments (Piñeros 1998). Up until now, however, I know of no account that has specifically targeted their diachrony.

The infrequency of the verbal concatenative pattern may be partly responsible for its rather late appearance in the databases (19). The late emergence of these compounds in the data could also be partially the result of their playful or colloquial register, since those types of discourse are not well represented in early texts. In other words, it seems plausible that [V + V]$_N$, especially reduplicatives, have been present in Romance since early times, without leaving any textual vestiges.

(19) Early attestations of Spanish concatenative [V + V]$_N$ compounds

    a. *Vistía una saya de pura cordura,/la su <u>cortapisa</u> era lealtad,/el su chapirete era fermosura,/el su noble manto muy grant onestad*

                              (ad 1435, Pero Vélez de Guervara, CORDE)

       'She wore a skirt of pure good sense, her overskirt was loyalty, her hood was beauty, and her noble cape was great honesty'

    b. *Acordó remifasol/a jugar la badalassa,/y el juego de <u>passa passa</u>/púsose detrás del sol*   (1481–1496, Juan del Encina, CORDE)

       'Re-fa-mi-sol agreed to play the badalassa [?] and the game of pass-pass hid behind the sun'

c. *alcançaron al romper de la puerta segunda, cuando fue quebrada con los vaivenes.* (1427–28, Enrique de Villena, CORDE)
'they managed to break the second door, when it was splintered by the back-and-forth movements'.

8.3.2.2 *Frequency and productivity*

The total number of $[V + V]_N$ is very small when compared to concatenatives with nominal and adjectival stems (30, or under 1%). This low overall frequency is true all throughout history, and especially obvious in the later periods, when the other concatenative patterns exhibit increases with no parallels in this class (Table 8.10).

In terms of the neologistic use of the $[V + V]_N$ pattern, after a protracted period of latency during which it does not appear reflected in the data, there are examples in the 1400s and 1500s, followed by a period of relative stability and modest productivity until the 1900s (Table 8.11). The compounds created with this pattern exhibit resilience, however, in that virtually none of them are lost over time.

Table 8.10 $[V + V]_N$ concatenative compounds attested by century, as totals and as a percentage of all compounds

	Concatenative $[V + V]_N$	All compounds	Concatenative $[V + V]_N$ as % of all compounds
1000s–1200s	1	349	0.3
1300s	1	434	0.2
1400s	6	709	0.8
1500s	15	1073	1.4
1600s	16	1237	1.3
1700s	18	1360	1.3
1800s	22	1842	1.2
1900s–2000s	28	3005	0.9
Total	30	3451	0.9

Table 8.11 Productivity of $[V + V]_N$ compounds by century

	Carried over	Lost	New	Total	Productivity Ratio
1200s	0	(0)	1	1	NA
1300s	1	(0)	0	1	0.00
1400s	1	(0)	5	6	0.83
1500s	6	(0)	9	15	0.60
1600s	15	(0)	1	16	0.06
1700s	16	(2)	4	18	0.11
1800s	18	(0)	4	22	0.18
1900s–2000s	22	(0)	6	28	0.21

8.3.2.3 *Inseparability of constituents*

Regardless of their spelling, there are no [V + V]$_N$ compounds in which either of the two constituents can be modified independently of the other: *ciaboga rápido* "fast turn-around', lit. 'row backward-row forward fast'. Moreover, no extraneous element is ever found between the two verbs in the nominal compound: *picamuchopica* lit. 'peck-a lot-peck'. In other words, when they appear inside a concatenative compound, the two verbal stems are syntactically inert.

The presence of an overt coordinative element is not frequent in [V + V]$_N$, although it is not impossible: *tira y afloja* vs. *tirafloja* 'struggle', lit. 'pull and release'. There are a few instances in which the coordination has been incorporated into the compound in spelling (e.g., *vaivén* 'oscillation', lit. 'come-and-go') and others in which the theme vowel of the first verbal constituent has been replaced by a linking vowel that could be interpreted as a coordinative conjunction (*metisaca* vs. *metesaca* '[in bullfighting] imperfect thrust of the sword', lit. 'insert-remove').

8.3.2.4 *Orthographic representation*

[V + V]$_N$ compounds normally appear spelled as an orthographic unit, which suggests word stress and compound status. In some cases, two-word spelling precedes one-word forms, with intermediate hyphenated forms: *pasa pasa* > *pasapasa* 'children's game', lit. 'pass-pass'. Yet, in many other examples several attested orthographies show no obvious progression towards unitary representation (Table 8.12). This may be attributable to the low frequency of these compounds, which makes it difficult to ascertain trends clearly. For example, in *metesaca* '[in bullfighting] imperfect thrust of the sword', lit. 'put-remove', the one-word spelling is attested a century before any alternative. The three orthographic representations may co-occur and compete, or appear in any order (e.g. *picapica* 'magpie', lit. 'peck-peck'). The absence of a clear orthographic progression in [V + V]$_N$ concatenative compounds suggests that they do not always originate from the agglutination of juxtaposed phrases but are the result of independent compounding mechanisms.

Table 8.12 First attestation of spelling variants for some frequent [V + V]$_N$ compounds (data from CORDE, CREA, and Covarrubias (1611))

	Two-word spelling	Hyphenated	One-word spelling
bullebulle	1834	1849	1773
cortapisa	c. 1495	–	ad 1435
duermevela	1993	1874	1825
metesaca	1995	2001	1909 *metisaca*, 1994
pasapasa	1481–1496	1527–1550	1554
picapica	1944	1872	1962
tejemaneje	ad 1800	1851	1828–1870

8.3.2.5 Endocentric and exocentric uses

In the entire dataset, there is only one example of an endocentric compound with two verbs, e.g., *cascamajar* 'to crush', lit. 'chip-break'. The remainder are nominalized, and thus, exocentric. In a few cases, the nominal compound appears as the complement to a preposition in a longer phrase: *de quitaipón* 'removable', lit. 'of remove-and-put'.

8.4 The [Q + Q]$_Q$ concatenative pattern: *Dieciséis*

The last type of concatenative compound considered in this chapter is made up of two numerals, whose meaning is very literally the added meaning of the two conjuncts. The process can be reiterated as many times as needed to name any number by concatenating hundreds, thousands, and so on.

8.4.1 Structure

8.4.1.1 Constituents

In Spanish [Q + Q]$_Q$ compounds are made up of two numerals strung together in decreasing order. At the lowest end, one of the numerals is in the tens and the other one in the units: *veinticinco* 'twenty-five', *sesenta y siete* 'sixty-seven'. Larger numbers are obtained by concatenating hundreds, thousands, and the like: *ciento treinta y cinco* 'one hundred and thirty-five', lit. 'hundred-thirty-and-five', *mil ciento veinticinco* 'one thousand one hundred and twenty-five', lit. 'thousand hundred twenty-and-five'.

As the above examples show, there is an overt marking of concatenation in the tens (*veinticinco*, *treinta y cinco*), but mere juxtaposition in numerals over a hundred (*ciento treinta*, *mil ciento veinticinco*). In the tens there are two possible realizations, one being the careful pronunciation reflected in the spelling of numerals higher than thirty: *treinta y tres* 'thirty-three', lit. 'thirty-and-three' and another, exhibited in the twenties (*veintitrés* 'twenty-three' < *veinte y tres* 'twenty and three') and in the colloquial pronunciation of all tens ([treįntįtrés] < *treinta y tres* 'thirty and three'). The linking vowel is simply an alternative rendering of the coordinating conjunction.

8.4.1.2 Compound structure

In [Q + Q]$_Q$ compounds it cannot be claimed that both orderings of constituents are identical, because there is a big difference between *ciento dos* 'one hundred and two', lit. 'hundred two' and its reverse, *doscientos* 'two hundred', lit. 'two hundreds'. Therefore, it makes sense to propose coordination with conjunct reduction for the first structure, and a hierarchical internal structure for the second. Thus, *ciento dos estudiantes* 'one hundred and two students', lit. 'hundred two students' is the result of the reduction of *cien(to) estudiantes y dos estudiantes* 'hundred students and two students' (20). By contrast, *doscientos estudiantes* 'two hundred students' requires an operation between the two numeral heads that yields a multiplicative meaning (cf. 21, where, for the sake of brevity, number agreement on the lower phrase has been omitted). In the first structure, there are two numeral heads, one deleted under coordination, whereas in the second there is only one.

(20)

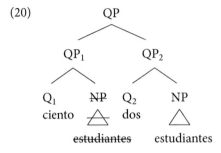

(21)

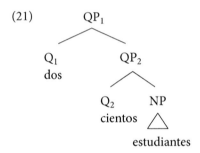

8.4.1.3 *Compound meaning*

Compound numerals are completely transparent: they can only mean the addition of the tens and units involved, or of the hundreds and tens, and so on, and their internal structure is always recoverable from the compound. In the case of multiplicative compounds, again there is only one possible semantic interpretation for each compounded structure. This is not to say that all figures are named with transparently compounded structures, though. For example, *quinientos* 'five hundred' is not created through the compounding of two numerals *cinco* 'five' and *ciento* 'hundred'. For numeral combinations used to name entities other than numbers, cf. Section 8.4.2.5.

8.4.2 Diachrony

8.4.2.1 *Historical antecedents and comparative data*

The concatenative nature of numerals is noted by several authors when describing Indo-European compounding. For example, they are described for Sanskrit in Whitney (1941 [1879]: 488), and for Greek in Schwyzer (1953 [1938]: 428) and Debrunner (1917: 40). Fruyt (2002) mentions numeral formation in Latin, classifying it under agglutination rather than *dvandva* formation proper, whereas Bader does not make that distinction (Bader 1962: 343). Interestingly, the formation of numbers has not been addressed as a special case of copulative compounding in virtually any description of modern Romance compounding, the sole exception being Mascaró (1986: 47), who does refer to Catalan numerals as a special case of compounding.

Spanish numerals come directly from Latin, and as one could expect, they are attested from the earliest documents, in forms that closely match their modern counterparts (cf. 22 for structural variants).

(22)   Early attestations of Spanish $[Q + Q]_Q$ compounds

    a.   *por tierra andidiste treinta e dos años, Señor spirital,/mostrando los miráculos, por én avemos qué fablar.*   (*Poema de Mio Cid*, CORDE)
        'you were on earth for thirty-two years, spiritual Father, showing the miracles that we talk about'.

    b.   *Fecha la carta a ueynte e nueue dias del mes de marzo hera de mill e treçientos e treinta e siete años.*   (1299, *Carta de concierto [Colección documental del archivo municipal de Hondarribia]*, CORDE)
        'This letter was given on the twenty-ninth (lit. 'twenty and nine') day of the month of March of the year one thousand three hundred and thirty seven (lit. 'thousand and three hundred and thirty and seven').

    c.   *esto que sea ante que passen ueyntiquatro horas.*
                                  (c. 1250, Alfonso X, *Lapidario*, CORDE)
        'this should be done before twenty-four hours go by'

8.4.2.2 *Frequency and productivity*

The issue of frequency is a moot point in the case of compounded numerals, since the category is and has always been infinite by definition. Numerals are boundless at any given time. As a consequence, their quantities cannot be computed for any period, nor would it make sense to factor them into the calculations of total compound frequency.

8.4.2.3 *Inseparability of constituents*

Let us now consider whether the two constituent lexemes can be separated by any extraneous element. In that regard, all through history, numbers that constitute a given figure have appeared together: *cincuenta y cuatro policías* 'fifty-four policemen', lit. 'fifty and four policemen'. Forms such as **cincuenta policías y cuatro* 'id.', lit. 'fifty policemen and four' or **cincuenta policías y cuatro policías* 'id.', lit. 'fifty policemen and four policemen' are unattested, even if the second one at least is grammatical (cf. *cincuenta policías de civil y cuatro policías uniformados* 'fifty plainclothes policemen and four uniformed policemen'). The only exception I have found in text is *las mil noches y la noche* 'one thousand and one nights', lit. 'one thousand nights and the night', a calque on the original Arabic numerical system.

The presence of overt coordination between numeral conjuncts is quite variable over time. Unlike most other concatenative compounds analyzed in this chapter, variants with overt coordination tend to prevail for numerals between twenty and

Table 8.13 Examples of numeral compounds with tens and units (from CORDE and Google)

	Juxtaposed forms	Coordinated forms	Linking vowel
veinte	ueynte cinco [1270]	ueynte e çinco [1268]	ueyntiun [c. 1250]
	veinte cuatro [1729]	veinte y dos [1856]	veintidós [2008]
treinta	treynta seys [1280]	treynta & quatro [1196]	treinticinco [1546]
	treinta una [1843]	treinta y nueve [2008]	treinticinco [2002]
setenta	setenta dos [1280]	setaenta & nueue [1270]	unattested
	setenta tres [1866]	setenta y cinco [2008]	

ninety-nine. Forms without coordination are attested, but they are very sporadic and tend to disappear (cf. Table 8.13, under *Juxtaposed forms*). In numbers between twenty-one and twenty-nine the linking vowel is the most common option, whereas after thirty forms with overt coordination are preferred. The higher the ten (and possibly the smaller its number of overall tokens), the less frequent alternants with a linking vowel are. Conversely, for the twenties it is the forms with overt coordination that tend to disappear over time. These developments seem to owe much to prescriptive pressure, however, as the spoken samples in (23) suggest.

(23)   Data from Corpus del Español (Davies 2002)

    a.   *[...] y tiene veinte y seis hijos en distintas mujeres*

                              (1900s, Habla culta de Caracas, M-10)

      'and he has twenty-six (lit. 'twenty and six') children with different women'

    b.   *estoy ya en una rutina de trabajo muy clave para nosotros, que es la vista a los treinta dos estados en la República Mexicana*

                            (August 11, 1999, Interview with Vicente Fox)

      'I'm in a new working routine that is very important for us, a review of the thirty-two states of the Mexican Republic'

    c.   *En Cuba yo tenía un... Chevrolet cincuentidós muy bonito muy bien arregladito muy lindo en el año cincuenticinco* (Habla culta de La Habana, M-10)

      'In Cuba I had a very pretty fifty-two Chevrolet, very nicely fitted and decorated in the year fifty-five'

Numerals that combine hundreds or thousands evolve in the opposite direction. The earliest attestations include overt coordinates (spelled as *e*, *y*, or *&*) as well as simple juxtaposition, but coordinated forms disappear over time without ever giving way to linking vowel (Table 8.14).

Table 8.14 Examples of numeral compounds with hundreds and thousands (from CORDE and Google)

	Juxtaposed forms	Coordinated forms	Linking vowel
ciento	ciento dos [1272]	ciento e uno [1275]	Unattested
	ciento dos [2008]	ciento y cincuenta [1898]	
mil	mil trezientos [1288]	mil e ciento [1270]	Unattested
	mil trecientos [2008]	mil e quinientos e nobenta e dos [1621]	

8.4.2.4 *Orthographic representation*

Numeral compounds are generally represented in as many words as there are units, tens, hundreds, thousands, and so on. Thus, for example: *trescientos cuarenta y cinco* 'three hundred forty-five', *doce mil cuatrocientos sesenta y dos* 'twelve thousand four hundred and sixty-two'. Given space constraints, I will restrict my observations here to the orthographic representation of the tens.

Spanish orthographic rules state that the twenties are to be spelled as a unit (*veintitrés* 'twenty-three'), whereas higher tens are two words separated by the coordinating conjunction (*treinta y cinco* 'thirty five', lit. 'thirty and five'). These rules reflect the fact that lower tens have more tokens in discourse, and thus are more often said together, with the consequent accentual weakening of the first constituent, loss of the final vowel, and fusion with the coordinating conjunction. The difference also seems motivated at least partly by phonetics: the mid-vowel (veint*e*) seems more likely to be lost in contact with a high vowel ([e*i̯*] > [i]), whereas the low vowel (cuarent*a*, sesent*a*, etc.) is more resistant. At no point in history does the hyphen seem to have been used to join the parts of complex numbers: **cincuenta-y-tres*.

8.4.2.5 *Endocentric and exocentric uses*

The overwhelming majority of $[Q + Q]_Q$ compounds are endocentric. There are only a few exceptions in which the resulting numeral is reassigned to the nominal class: *veinticuatro* 'alderman in Seville', lit. 'twenty-four'.

8.5 Summary of chapter

This chapter has described the four types of compounding in Spanish that exhibit no hierarchical relationship between constituents. The two main patterns used to create new lexical items combine two nominal or two adjectival constituents. Additional patterns involve the concatenation of verbs and numerals. Concatenative compounds are recorded early in Spanish, which allows us to conclude that they are an inheritance from Latin via early Romance. The only exception to this is the pattern $[V + V]_N$, a class that is scarce and tends to appear only in informal registers and is possibly not inherited (cf Ralli 2009 for a similar conclusion for Greek $[V + V]_V$ compounds).

In nominal and adjectival concatenative patterns, the two constituents must be of the same sort, i.e., they must share featural semantic properties (abstractness, animacy, etc.), because they form a complex predicate that must be applicable to a single argument. Each of the lexical categories of concatenative compounds has several possible internal structures. Among the nominal concatenative compound patterns that are recorded in dictionaries, some are identificational, when both constituents apply independently to the argument. Others are hybrid, when the two constituents blend a portion of their semantic features into a new denotation that has some (unspecified) features of each constituent. These differences have structural consequences. For example, in hybrid compounds the first constituent may exhibit a linking vowel instead of its WCM, and concord features have a tendency to be present only on the rightmost edge. By contrast, identificational concatenative compounds tend to present the first constituent in full form consistently over time, and both constituents show gender/number marks. In the case of adjectival concatenative compounds, the main issue is whether the adjectival constituents apply simultaneously or distributively to their argument.

The class of compounds created by concatenating two verbs is unique in several ways. It is a very marginal class, with few exemplars, and it is exocentric, i.e., the resulting compound is not a verb but a noun, suggesting that there is additional structure involved. Moreover, unlike nominal and adjectival concatenative compounds, the two verbs need not be of the same sort. Finally, numerical compounds are the most straightforward, because their structural differences have a clear semantic correlate. In particular, when the numbers are added, the structure is simply coordinative and the number is really the result of deleting a nominal head (*ciento hombres y dos hombres* > *ciento dos hombres* 'a hundred and two men', lit. 'hundred two men'), but when they are multiplied (*doscientos* 'two hundred', lit. 'two hundreds') there are further layers of structure and only one nominal head.

CHAPTER 9

Historical developments
in Spanish compounding

So far, this book has presented a theory of compounding and illustrated it specifically with Spanish. It has proposed that compounding is the combination of constituents following a set of operations that are essentially syntactic. However, it has also been proposed that there is a difference between sentence syntax and word syntax of the kind that results in compounds, namely, the absence of functional heads (in a modified version that defines functional heads in terms of binary features as [+F, –L], cf. Chapter 1 Section 1.2.5). This difference is linked to the absence of specifier positions in compounding, with its concomitant restriction to two hierarchical configurations (head-complement and head-adjunct) and one non-hierarchical configuration (head-head).

After the theoretical groundwork was laid, individual compounding patterns were presented in related groups, based on certain common features, including their head-edness, the type of relationship that holds between the constituents, and the types of constituents involved, as illustrated in Table 9.1. The compounds in Chapters 4 through 7 share the feature that their compound constituents are in a hierarchical relationship, whereas in Chapter 8 the structure is flat and all constituents are of the same rank. In Chapters 4 through 6 and in Chapter 8, compounds are endocentric, i.e., one of the

Table 9.1 Summary and examples of compound types

	Hierarchical relations	Headedness	Head position	Example compound patterns
Chapters 4/5	Hierarchical	Endocentric	Final	$[Adv + A]_A$ *maleducado* 'ill-bred', lit. 'badly-educated' $[N + V]_V$ *maniatar* 'tie by the hand', lit. 'hand-tie'
Chapter 6	Hierarchical	Endocentric	Initial/Final	$[N + A]_N$, $[A + N]_N$ *hierbabuena* 'mint', lit. 'herb-good'
Chapter 7	Hierarchical	Exocentric	Initial	$[V + N]_N$ *matamoscas* 'fly-swatter', lit. 'kill-flies'
Chapter 8	Non-hierarchical	Endocentric	NA	$[A + A]_A$ *blanquinegro* 'black and white', lit. 'white-black'

constituents is the head and percolates features to the entire compound, whereas the other one is a non-head element. By contrast, in Chapter 7 the head is neither of the overt constituents, but rather, a null nominalizing element outside the compound. Then there is the issue of head position: in Chapters 4 and 5, compounds are head-final, in Chapter 7 they are mostly head-initial, and in Chapter 6 there are some head-initial and some head-final patterns. Within each chapter, patterns have been arranged for convenience according to the lexical category of their constituents.

Each individual compound description also represents a first attempt to corroborate certain predictions of the theory. Let us recall two cases. First, it follows from the theory that non-head constituents in compounding will only be capable of occupying complement or adjunct/modifier positions. Indeed, those two are the only categories needed to account for all the different hierarchical compound structures found in Spanish. For example, in $[V + N]_N$, the nominal acts as a complement to the verbal head, whereas in $[Adv + V]_V$ the adverbial non-head is an adjunct. Second, it is predicted that productive compounding will not involve categories such as determiners or verbs inflected for tense/mood/person. This prediction is borne out in the data. One after another, the examples of lexicalized compounding culled from the dictionaries and databases exhibit these categorial restrictions. Complex lexemes in violation of these principles are so few as to be negligible.

9.1 Introduction

The time has come to consider the historical implications of the theory more closely. Briefly put, if compounds are indeed formed through the application of a limited syntax of the type described in Chapter 1, then the combinations of lexemes that yield compounds can be expected to reflect changes in sentence syntax over time. For example, if there are changes in the order of phrasal constituents, speakers should eventually realign compound constituents to fit the new order. Any deviations from the expected order should be explainable by invoking clearly defined differences between the constituents manipulated by syntax and by compound formation.

This chapter starts by considering the issue of word order in Spanish syntax and compounding, with the aim of establishing parallels between the two. It shows that, although there is a time lag between syntactic re-parametrization and its instantiation within compounds, it is indeed the case that both eventually align. However, matters are not as straightforward as they might seem when considered globally. As Section 9.4 shows, a couple of head-final patterns exhibit increased frequency over time, rather than disappearing as would have been expected. This apparent violation of syntax-compounding symmetry is explainable by invoking specific morphological properties of the constituents of these compounds, which distinguish them from their syntactic counterparts and force rearrangements in the surface order.

The second issue addressed in this chapter is the unprecedented productivity of $[V + N]_N$ compounds, which goes from being a marginal pattern in Latin to being the most frequent in Spanish (Section 9.5), with over twice as many compounds as the second most frequent pattern in the sample. Explaining this increase is a matter of theoretical interest because it is a test case of the influence of syntactic change on compounding change. At first glance the explanation may seem straightforward: since the order of constituents in $[V + N]_N$ compounds is parallel to VO syntax, it follows that once the Romance varieties became solidly head-initial at the sentential level, head-initial compounding patterns would be favored. However, $[V + N]_N$ compounds increased their frequency significantly more than other head-initial compounds, so this cannot be the whole story. In Section 9.5.3 I sketch a possible explanation for this increase in frequency, taking into account the process of natural language acquisition and its impact on language change.

Other global trends of Spanish compounding over the centuries are addressed, too, some of which were not anticipated and are not explainable by the properties of the theoretical framework presented in Chapter 1. For example, Section 9.6 considers the relative frequencies of the various lexical classes of compounds (nominal, adjectival, and verbal), to see whether their weights over the centuries have changed. It is shown that noun formation comes to dominate compounding, for reasons that at this point remain unclear. Another issue explored is whether there have been any changes in the endo-/exocentricity of Spanish compounds (Section 9.7), and in particular, whether it can be confirmed that endocentric compounds have precedence over exocentrics. We will see that there is some support for this view, and discuss some reasons why this might be so. The chapter ends with a discussion of other matters of theoretical import that remain to be dealt with in future work.

9.2 Counting frequency or productivity?

Before moving on to the more theoretically substantive discussion, some methodological decisions must be made regarding the treatment of the data. Because one objective of this work is to establish whether a compound pattern becomes more or less frequent from one period to the next, the issue of measuring and comparing compound frequency is addressed for the first time in Chapter 3 (Section 3.4.1). It is noted that considering raw frequency of compound exemplars would not be a meaningful measure, given the differences in the sizes of the databases available for each century. A compound pattern can appear to be growing if it has 100 compounds in one period and 200 in the next, but this may not represent meaningful growth if the database from which compounds are obtained is in fact ten times larger for the second period. To correct for this, instead of measuring raw totals, frequency is established *relative* to the total number of compounds for the same century. The assumption is that, if all compounding patterns have an equal chance of being represented in the database at a given period, and if the size of the databases for two periods differs by factor x, then the frequency of a stable compound pattern can be expected to differ by that same factor. When considered relative to the total number of compounds for both periods, the effect of factor x will be cancelled out. If all patterns grow at the same rate as a result of the availability of more data, then no observable increase should be noted. Relative frequency of a pattern only increases if the pattern grows *at a greater rate* than the others.

Another methodological issue related to the quantification of compounds is the distinction between frequency and productivity. Recall that, when quantifying frequency, a compound is counted in all the historical periods in which it is attested. This is established explicitly, by verifying that it appears in texts and/or lexicographical sources, or implicitly, by showing that it appears over a span of time, even if it is not verifiably attested in every century. For its part, productivity is measured as the ratio of new compounds generated by a pattern in a given century against the total of previously existing compounds with that pattern. Frequency thus measures how often a pattern is present in the language at any given time, whereas productivity is a measure of how much of that frequency is due to new compounds.

Both types of measures can in principle be used, but in this chapter comparisons are established among compound patterns on the basis of their relative frequency, rather than their productivity. There are several advantages to doing this. First, the measures of frequency and productivity tend to be well matched, so both appear to be valid ways of reporting information. In other words, it does not happen that a pattern loses frequency over time while gaining productivity or vice versa. When the percentage of *all* compounds created with a pattern over a given period is compared against the percentage of *new* compounds created with the same pattern over the same period, the general trend is the same. A compounding pattern's increased or decreased productivity leads to its increased or decreased frequency.

As an example, consider Table 9.2. Note that the initial percentages are identical in both columns for each pattern, because they are the sum total of all compounds attested with that pattern until the end of the 1200s. After that, although the figures on either column for a single pattern diverge, their tendencies are parallel. Put differently, the slopes of the curves are not identical, but their overall direction is. In an increasingly productive pattern, such as $[V + N]_N$, percentages go up both as a ratio of all existing compounds and as a ratio of all new compounds. For instance, $[V + N]_N$ compounds constitute about 10% of all the compounds attested in the 1400s, but they are 20% of all the new compounds. By the 1500s they constitute over 15% of all compounds, but by now 25% of the new compounds in the database are $[V + N]_N$. By contrast, in a pattern that becomes less productive, such as $[Adv + A]_A$, both columns show a drop in percentages.

Table 9.2 $[V + N]_N$ and $[Adv + A]_A$ compounds as a percentage of all compounds and as a percentage of new compounds over time

	% $[V + N]_N$ *sacacorchos*		% $[Adv + A]_A$ *malcriado*	
	Total frequency	New compounds	Total frequency	New compounds
1000s–1200s	3.2	3.2	20.1	20.1
1300s	4.4	8.7	19.1	16.7
1400s	10.6	20.0	15.2	9.3
1500s	15.8	25.1	10.5	2.4
1600s	19.2	34.2	9.1	0.9
1700s	21.5	40.0	8.2	1.7
1800s	25.1	35.6	6.3	0.8
1900s–2000s	27.9	32.5	3.9	0.5

The second advantage of looking at frequency is that this measure is more 'conservative', usually showing smoother and more gradual increases or decreases, making general tendencies easier to identify and describe. It is clear why this should be so. At any given point, the total upon which frequencies are calculated is made up not just of new compounds from that century, but also of all the compounds carried over from previous centuries and still in active use. Even after speakers have stopped employing a compounding pattern to create new lexemes, they may continue to use older compounds that they learned as unanalyzed chunks. Whereas the *creation* of lexemes is dependent on an active word formation pattern, their *disappearance* owes more to the continued existence of whatever they denote, a non-linguistic factor. Additionally, productivity is more affected by gaps in lexicographical sources, resulting in more haphazard fits and starts. This is partly because, as a measure of new compounds, productivity may be more affected by poor records for a given century, unrelated with an actual drop in pattern use.

For illustrative purposes, again consider Table 9.2. In the $[V + N]_N$ pattern, the increase in percentage is much more marked in the column that counts new compounds than in the one that quantifies totals. As a percentage of new compounds, $[V + N]_N$ compounds reach virtually 40% in the 1700s, whereas as a percentage of all compounds, they constitute a little under 30% of the total at their highest point in the 1900s. Additionally, the percentage of new $[V + N]_N$ compounds does not grow gradually, but doubles between the 1300s and the 1400s and continues to grow until it reaches its peak in the 1700s, to taper off later. In similar but inverted fashion, for the $[Adv + A]_A$ pattern the decrease is more gradual when one considers totals than when only new compounds are counted. For new compounds, the $[Adv + A]_A$ pattern is still measurably productive in the 1300s and 1400s, but it decreases drastically in the 1500s and stops being used after that. The difference between the two measures shows that existing compounds with the structure $[Adv + A]_A$ continued to be in use well after the pattern had been lost. This in turn helps explain why $[V + N]_N$ total percentages are lower than their percentages among new compounds. As time goes by, some patterns stop being acquired by children learning the language, because they have structural features that make them incompatible with the rest of the grammar. However, there is still a sufficiently large number of compounds with that pattern that are learned piece-meal and counted as compounds in a given period, masking this lack of productivity.

In what follows, therefore, comparisons between compound types are established as a measure of relative frequency per century. There have been a few instances, how-ever, where it is illuminating to present measures of productivity, in which case both are included.

9.3 Word order in syntax and in compounds

9.3.1 VO in Spanish syntax

This section shows how changes in the word order of compound constituents mirror those that happened in sentence syntax. It begins by showing what the syntactic changes were, and then how they were accompanied by changes in the order of com-pound constituents. The syntactic change in question is the well documented replace-ment of OV order by VO, which had started in Latin itself and continued in Romance (Adams 1976; Hinojo-Andrés 1988; Lehmann 1972; Marouzeau 1953; Vennemann 1974). Although this is not the place for a thorough analysis of this shift and its com-plexities, Table 9.3 provides some figures to illustrate the process of OV-to-VO shift in Latin. Note that in some instances, there are large differences in the rates of verb-final clauses that are not related to any diachronic difference but to stylistic preferences of the authors (cf. Cicero and Caesar), but on the whole, there is a general tendency to decrease the rate of verbs placed at the end of the clause. In Medieval Spanish we lack data classified by clause type, but there is every indication that the process of OV-to-VO shift continued, with a total of 28% of verb-final clauses in a selection of texts dated until the period of Alfonso X, i.e., the late 1200s (Hinojo-Andrés 1988: 444).

Table 9.3 Percentage of verb-final main and subordinate clauses in Latin texts (data from Bork 1990: 373)

Text	% Verb final clauses	
	Main clause	Subordinate clause
Caesar *De bello gallico* (50–40 BC)	84%	93%
Cicero *De re publica* (54–51 BC)	35%	61%
Seneca *Epistulae morales* (64 AD)	58%	66%
Itinerarium Egeriae (Peregrinatio Aetheriae) (c. 385)	25%	37%

9.3.2 Constituent order in compounds

Let us now turn to the effect that this syntactic change had on compounding. Naturally, the comments that follow only apply to compounds that have a hierarchical relationship between their constituents, so concatenatives will not be considered in the discussion. As expected, head-initial compounds and head-final compounds invert their frequencies over time: head-initial patterns go from around one-third to around two-thirds of the total, whereas head-final compounds undergo a concomitant reduction (Table 9.4). Yet, if we compare these totals to what we know about word order in Spanish syntax, the percentages of head-final compounds show a greater retention of the head-final order, with head-initial patterns overtaking head-final patterns for the first time in the 1500s. Head-final compounds do not drop to 28%, the figure for syntactic phrases in the 1200s, even in the latest periods documented. This seems to confirm Clackson's description of compounding as 'the museum of a language's history' (2002: 165). However, if we compare the percentage of head-final clauses in Spanish with that of *new* compounds per century, then the percentages of head-final compounds align much more closely with the data from syntax (Table 9.5). In this case, the drop in head-final compounds occurs earlier, with head-initial compounds overtaking head-final compounds as early as the 1300s, and showing faster overall losses. It seems, then, that the general word order shift was almost as fast in compounding as it was in syntax. The lag observed for compounds on Table 9.4 can be accounted for by the fact that lexemes have a longer shelf-life than syntactic constructions. But compound patterns that do not align with general syntactic parameters do eventually disappear, as no new compounds are created using the old patterns and the old – possibly less frequent – compounds are sometimes recreated by speakers following the new word order, a matter to which we return shortly.

Table 9.4 Totals and percentages of all head-initial and head-final compounds over time (n = 3044)

	Head-initial	%	Head-final	%
1000s–1200s	120	36.4	210	63.6
1300s	171	41.9	237	58.1
1400s	323	49.2	333	50.8
1500s	493	50.9	475	49.1
1600s	609	54.4	510	45.6
1700s	691	56.4	535	43.6
1800s	997	60.6	647	39.4
1900s–2000s	1598	60.7	1033	39.3
Total	1808	59.4	1236	40.6

Table 9.5 Totals and percentages of new head-initial and head-final compounds over time (n = 3044)

	Head-initial	%	Head-final	%
1000s–1200s	120	36.4	210	63.6
1300s	60	51.3	57	48.7
1400s	157	59.7	106	40.3
1500s	190	53.2	167	46.8
1600s	141	65.6	74	34.4
1700s	151	70.2	64	29.8
1800s	329	72.8	123	27.2
1900s–2000s	660	60.3	435	39.7
Total	1808	59.4	1236	40.6

Taken together, the retention of compounds with old word order followed by the eventual shift of the constituents provide support to 'horserace' models of compound processing and retrieval (Anshen & Aronoff 1999; Libben 2005). This type of model is an alternative to others that maximize storage and minimize the need for computation – i.e., compounds are kept in the lexicon as units, as are the individual lexemes that are their constituents – and those that maximize storage efficiency by relying heavily on computation – i.e., compounds are not stored in the lexicon at all, so that processing and retrieval requires the cooperation of combining the two constituents. The horserace model is a third alternative, based on maximizing opportunity. The compound and its constituents are all represented in the lexicon, with links between them. This redundant system is inefficient, but by permitting the simultaneous computation of a compound and its direct retrieval it provides the fastest route to interpretation.

As stated above, the historical data support this. The fact that compounds survive longer than the syntactic operations through which they were created in a previous historical period supports the view that they must be stored and accessed directly as unanalyzed units. Otherwise, they would disappear after they stopped being generated syntactically. The fact that they are eventually lost or remodeled shows that complex words are not just isolated stored lexemes, but that speakers seek to motivate them through their grammar. When the stored constituents and the stored compounds are linked through operations that have no contemporary reality for the speaker, the compound is an oddity, and it is vulnerable to reanalysis.

9.3.3 Effect of the OV-to-VO shift on compound patterns

The shift from head-final to head-initial affected some compound patterns very directly. For example, in compounds created through 'agglutination', i.e., the univerbation of frequent lexicalized phrasal sequences, the loss of the syntactic verb-final order quickly bled the feeding phrasal pattern. Thus, for example, $[Adv+V]_V$ and $[N + V]_V$ compounds (e.g., *malograr* 'to spoil', lit. 'to badly-achieve', *mantener* 'to maintain', lit. 'to hand-hold') disappeared quickly. This also affected some allied patterns such as $[Adv + N]_N$ and $[N + N]_N$ deverbals (e.g., *malogramiento* 'spoilage', lit. 'badly-achieve-ment', *mantenimiento* 'maintenance', lit. 'hand-holding'), which depended on new verbal bases as their input, and possibly also $[Adv + A]_A$ (e.g., *maleducado* 'ill-bred', lit. 'badly-educated'). Although the initial percentage for each of these patterns is different, as a group they all undergo comparable, sometimes quite drastic, drops in frequency (Figure 9.1).

Conversely, compounds that were in line with the new word order were favored by its generalization. Consider the patterns presented in Figure 9.2, all of which show head-initial constituent order. On the whole, these patterns either maintained stable levels of frequency over the centuries or exhibited increases in their frequency relative to all patterns. Head-initial $[N + N]_N$ patterns had the advantage of their constituent order to support their stability and retention over the centuries, while $[V + N]_N$ compounds established themselves as the most productive in the Spanish language. Head-complement $[Q + N]_N$ compound patterns exhibited overall losses, but their initial and final frequencies were both quite negligible, so it seems valid not to count them as counterexamples.

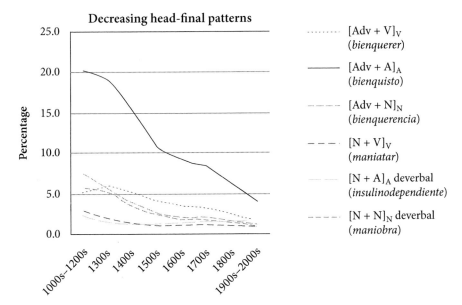

Figure 9.1 Percentage of head-final patterns that decrease in relative frequency over time

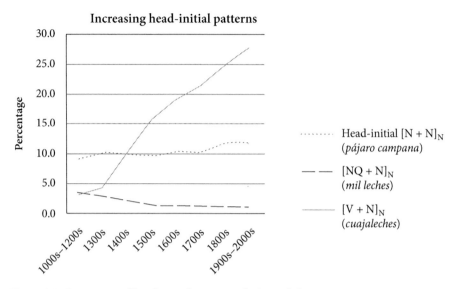

Figure 9.2 Percentage of head-initial compounds that exhibit increases over time

9.3.4 Effect of constituent order changes on individual compounds

Looking at global shifts in compound headedness is not the only way to ascertain the increase in the preference for head-initial over head-final compounds. Specific compounding patterns can also be considered to obtain more fine-grained evidence. For example, $[V + N]_N$ compounds can be compared against their small number of inverted counterparts ($[N + V]_N$, *maltrabaja* 'lazy person', lit. 'badly-work') that are not quantified in the data due to their low frequency. Head-final compounds may exhibit later head-initial counterparts, with or without the same meaning: *malqueda* 'irresponsible person', lit. 'badly-stay', vs. *quedamal* 'irresponsible person', lit. 'stay-badly', *gatatumba* 'simulation', lit. 'cat-tip' vs. *tumbagatos* 'cat killer', lit. 'tip-cats' (cf. examples 1a, b and c, d respectively). All this suggests that the head-final compounds came early – possibly even earlier than their first attested forms – and that at least some of them were recreated by native speakers on the basis of the newer pattern (for additional comparative evidence, cf. Klingebiel 1988).

(1)   a.   *bajó la tal con la boca llena de malicias, tratando al marido de malqueda y de holgazán.*   (1984, Ramón Ayerra, CREA)
"She [Petronila] went down spewing out insults, calling her husband irresponsible and lazy".

   b.   *Mentira es un vato quedamal por eso tiene muchas calificaciones negativas.*
                                                              (5.4.09, Google)
'That's not true. He is an irresponsible dude, that's why he has so many bad ratings'.

    c. *[...] tú has de hacer la <u>gatatumba</u> y el agachapanza. Quiero decir que te has de mostrar convencido de sus razones, rendido a sus consejos, dócil a sus instrucciones, oyéndole en lo exterior con mucha humildad, respeto y reverencia, pero allá dentro de tu corazón has de estar bien resuelto a reírte y a hacer burla de todo cuanto te dijere.*   (1758, José Francisco de Isla, CORDE) 'You should use simulation (lit. 'cat-tip') and flattery. I mean that you should agree with his views, follow his advice, obey his instructions, and pretend to listen to him with great humility, respect, and reverence, but your heart must be resolved to laugh and make fun of whatever he says'.

    d. *dice que nunca habia matado un gato [...] pero si quedo como anecdota, y ahora se le conoce como el "<u>tumbagatos</u>".*

        (5.4.09, Google; no stress marks in the original) 'He says he had never killed a cat, [...] but the anecdote stuck, and now he is known as the catkiller (lit. 'tip-cats').

Speakers also inverted the word order of constituents in other compound patterns, so that popular inherited head-final [N + N]$_N$ compounds became head-initial, possibly as native speakers reorganized the constituents on the basis of their head-initial syntax. For example, head-final *maristela* 'starfish', lit. 'sea-star' is attested earlier and has a briefer span of use [1379 – 1539] than its head-initial counterpart *estrellamar* (vars. *estrella mars, estrella maris*) [1452–1997]. Similar tendencies can be shown for the pair *gatuña* 'restharrow', lit. 'cat-nail' [1549–1962] and *uñagata* 'id.', lit. 'nail-cat' [1962–1986]; and for *gallocresta* 'wild sage', lit. 'rooster-comb' [c. 1300 – 2000] and *crestagallo* 'id.', lit. 'comb-rooster' [Google, 5.26.09] (for discussion cf. de Dardel 1999).

    In the examples above, the order of constituents is affected, while the meaning remains the same. There are other cases in which it seems that speakers do not rearrange constituents but take a head-final compound to be head-initial, bringing about a difference in meaning. That is the case, for example, of *autoescuela*, lit. 'car-school', first attested to mean 'driving school' (head-final), and later 'training car' (head-initial), a shift with gender assignment consequences: *la autoescuela* 'the driving school', lit. 'the-FEM car-MASC-school-FEM' vs. *el autoescuela* 'the training car', lit. 'the-MASC car-MASC-school-FEM'. There are also marginal cases where the dating is reversed, however, such as the pair *puercoespín* 'porcupine', lit. 'pig-thorn' [1348 – 2000] and the head-final compound *espinpuerco* 'id.', lit. 'thorn-pig' [1611]. Finally, there are cases in which the reverse order brings about a difference in meaning and that therefore have no bearing on the topic at hand. That would be the case of *malvarrosa* 'hollyhock', lit. 'mallow-rose', and *rosa malva* 'pink color', lit. 'rose mallow'. In sum, the preference for head-initial patterns has led to the structural reanalysis or semantic reinterpretation of some compounds whose constituents were in the opposite order.

9.3.5 Unchanged patterns

Let us now turn to a group of compound patterns that remained largely unaffected by the changes in word order, since they did not contain the types of constituents that were directly involved in the OV-to-VO shift. These were patterns with nominal heads and adjectival non-head modifiers, in head-initial and head-final configurations ([N + A]$_N$ and [A + N]$_N$, respectively). The order of the adjective with respect to its nominal head in these cases was ruled by semantic factors that remained quite stable form Latin to Spanish. Throughout history, at least for the unmarked cases, adjectives whose purpose is to qualify are typically preposed, and those meant to discriminate are postposed (Hinojo-Andrés 1988: 446; Marouzeau 1953: 1–3). This resulted in no noteworthy changes over time in syntax, and as a consequence, the frequency of [N + A]$_N$ and [A + N]$_N$ compounding patterns with respect to each other remained quite stable over the centuries. This can be seen in Table 9.6, which quantifies the percentages of both [N + A]$_N$ and [A + N]$_N$ compounds with respect to each other. It can also be seen in Figure 9.3, where the graph shows the relative frequency of each of these patterns with respect to the total of all compound patterns; although their initial relative frequencies differ, they exhibit similar general trends.

   The stability is also reflected in the fact that speakers did not reverse the constituents in these compounds to make them align to a new syntactic word order. As an example, consider the compound *nacionalsocialismo* 'national socialism' [1946]. The constituents first appear as [A + N]$_N$, no doubt as a calque on the German word order. In spite of its slightly alien structure, this combination comes to be preferred to designate the right-wing Fascist ideology of Hitler (2a), whereas the opposite order, *socialismo nacional*, lit. 'socialism national', is only occasionally used as an alternative (2b). However, more often than not, the second option has a different meaning: it designates a form of socialism that deviates from Marxist orthodoxy because it has national, rather than international, goals.

Table 9.6 Relative frequency of head-initial and head-final noun-adjective compounds by century

	% [N + A]$_N$ (*hierbabuena*)	% [A + N]$_N$ (*buenamoza*)
1000s–1200s	67.0	33.0
1300s	70.9	29.1
1400s	71.6	28.4
1500s	68.0	32.0
1600s	67.9	32.1
1700s	67.5	32.5
1800s	67.7	32.3
1900s–2000s	63.7	36.3
Total	63.0	37.0

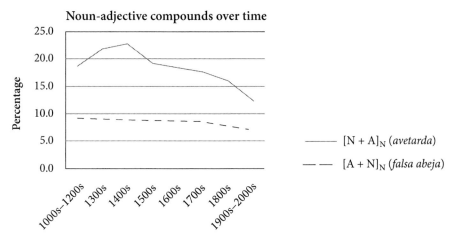

Figure 9.3 Relative frequencies of [N + A]$_N$ and [A + N]$_N$ compounds over time as a percentage of all compounds

In other words, the N + A order, which would have been more unmarked for Spanish, never prevailed for 'Nazism' and remained available to denote other ideologies.

(2) a. *El nacionalsocialismo nació en Alemania hacia 1919, y fue creado por el político austríaco Adolf Hitler.*   (5.5.09, Google, Wikipedia)
'National Socialism was born in Germany around 1919, and was created by Austrian politician Adolf Hitler'.

   b. *El que un trabajador pueda conseguir tener un coche a un precio ridículo al mes, se consiguió diseñando y creando el coche del trabajador, el famoso Volkswagen; pero aún iba el socialismo nacional más lejos.* (5.5.09, Google)
'The fact that workers could succeed in owning a car for a ridiculous monthy payment was made possible by designing and creating a car for the worker, the famous Volkswagen; but National Socialism (lit. 'socialism national') went further'.

   c. *Revolución permanente o socialismo nacional: este dilema se plantea no sólo ante los problemas de régimen interior de la Unión Soviética, sino ante las perspectivas de la revolución en Occidente y ante los destinos de la Internacional Comunista en el mundo entero.*   (5.5.09, Google)
'Permanent revolution or national socialism: that is the conundrum we face not just to solve the problems of the Soviet domestic regime, but also the future of the Western revolution and the fate of the Communist International worldwide'.

To summarize Section 9.3, OV-to-VO word order changes had almost immediate consequences for compounding constituent order. This is seen in the loss of certain patterns and in the retention and increased frequency of others. Moreover, patterns that were not directly involved in the OV-to-VO shift remained largely inert to it. The issue does not end here, however. In the next section I address the potential problem posed by a couple of compound patterns that appear to be robust counterexamples to the hypothesis presented.

9.4 Morphological structure and constituent order

9.4.1 Two productive head-final patterns

When discussing Table 9.5 it was observed that the rates of new head-final patterns drop overall over the centuries, but there are two unexplained spikes in the 1500s and the 1900s. On closer inspection, two head-final patterns, $[N + A]_A$ and head-final $[N + N]_N$, appear to be responsible for this. Unlike other head-final patterns, these two do not just limp along after the Middle Ages, but actually exhibit big gains over the centuries (Figure 9.4). The $[N + A]_A$ pattern (e.g., *aliblanco* 'of white wings', lit. 'wing-white') is almost single-handedly responsible for the increase in new head-final compounds in the 1500s, whereas the head-final $[N + N]_N$ pattern (e.g., *cóctel-bar* 'cocktail bar') exhibits a sharp increase in the last period, responsible for the spike in head-final patterns in the 1900s. These increases cannot be reconciled with the claim of an overall drop for head-final compounds, unless they can be linked to very specific differences in the internal structure of syntactic and morphological non-head constituents. In this section I show that this difference does exist, what it is, and how it has affected compounding.

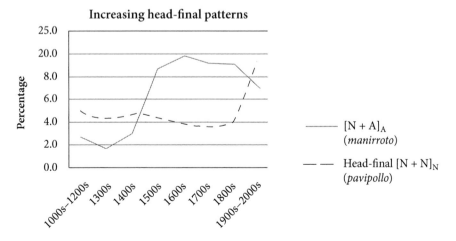

Figure 9.4 Percentage of $[N + A]_A$ and head-final $[N + N]_N$ compounds over time

In order to present the argument, it is necessary to take a step back and return to the issue of the internal morphological structure of nominal constituents in compounding. Recall that in previous chapters it was noted that nominal constituents in compound-initial position may appear with or without their final morpheme, the word class marker (WCM), which may or may not be replaced by a linking vowel. Here we return to this issue, with the purpose of establishing whether the loss or retention of word class markers is related to the status of the nominal constituent that hosts them. For this, I consider all compounds with preposed nominals, including head-initial patterns such as $[N + A]_A$, $[N + N]_N$ (e.g, *hierbabuena* 'mint', lit. 'herb-good', and *pájaro campana* 'bellbird', lit. 'bird bell'), and head-final compounds like $[N + A]_A$ (deverbals like *mantenido* 'maintained', lit. 'hand-held' and integrals like *carilindo* 'pretty-faced', lit. 'face-pretty'), $[N + V]_V$ (*maniatar* 'tie by the hands', lit. 'hand-tie'), and deverbal $[N + N]_N$ (*mantenimiento* 'maintenance', lit. 'hand-hold-N SUFF'). If the presence or absence of the word class marker is unrelated to the headedness status of the leftmost nominal constituent, then head-initial and head-final patterns should behave similarly. In other words, it should be equally likely for a leftmost head and for a leftmost non-head to appear in stem or in full form. In fact, it is shown that the loss or retention of word class markers does in fact correlate strongly with the headedness status of their host. When compounds are distinguished by the hierarchical properties of the preposed noun (head or non-head), the two groups behave in noticeably different ways. If the preposed nominal is a head, it exhibits a preference for full forms, which increases over time (Table 9.7). If it is a non-head, there is a gradual increase in the preference for stems over full forms. Preposed nominals in stem form constitute around 70% of the examples in the early compounds, but go up to over 90% in the 20th century.

Table 9.7 Percentages of preposed nominals in full lexeme and stem form, for head-initial and head-final patterns by century

	Preposed nominal head		Preposed nominal non-head	
	% Lexeme	% Stem	% Lexeme	% Stem
1000s–1200s	91.8	8.2	29.7	70.3
1300s	91.4	8.6	26.6	73.4
1400s	92.7	7.3	28.6	71.4
1500s	91.2	8.8	15.5	84.5
1600s	91.0	9.0	13.1	86.9
1700s	91.6	8.4	12.3	87.7
1800s	93.4	6.6	12.1	87.9
1900s–2000s	94.5	5.5	9.0	91.0
Total	94.1	5.9	10.2	89.8

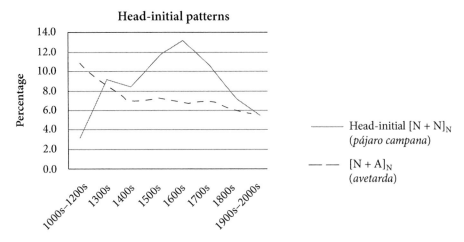

Figure 9.5 Percentage of preposed nominals that appear as stems in head-initial compounds over time

The percentages observed for head-initial patterns hold true for both $[N + A]_N$ (e.g., *hierbabuena* 'mint', lit. 'herb good') and head-initial $[N + N]_N$ compounds (e.g., *pájaro campana* 'bellbird', lit. 'bird bell'). With some fluctuation, this has been the case over the entire documented history of the two patterns (Figure 9.5). For head-initial $[N + N]_N$ compounds, heads show a small increase in their tendency to appear in stem form between the 1400s and the 1600s, but for the most part they remain under 10% of the total, and show a general downward trend. As for $[N + A]_N$ compounds, they exhibit a steady decrease in the presence of heads in stem form that results in a halving of their relative frequencies over time.

By contrast, head-final patterns with preposed nominals tend to exhibit more stems over time. This applies to most of the individual head-final patterns, but particularly to those that became more frequent over time, viz, $[N + A]_A$ and head-final $[N + N]_N$ compounds (Fig 9.6). Thus, the percentage of stems as leftmost non-head nominals in $[N + A]_A$ integral compounds (*carilindo* 'pretty-faced', lit. 'face-pretty') goes up from 60% to 98.1%. For head-final $[N + N]_N$ compounds (*vitaminoterapia* 'vitamin therapy') the use of stem-form non-heads goes from 58.8% to 87.2%. If we compare the trends presented in Figure 9.4 and those in Figure 9.6, it is apparent that there is a close connection between the increase in the use of stem forms and the increase in the use of the compound patterns themselves. For $[N + A]_A$ compounds this is evident in the spikes in both curves in the 1400s, whereas for head-final $[N + N]_N$ compounds the two curves show a similar increase in the 1900s.

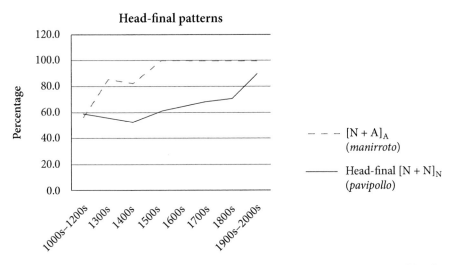

Figure 9.6 Percentage of preposed nominals that appear as stems in [N + A]$_A$ and head-final [N + N]$_N$ compounds over time

9.4.2 Morphological structure and individual compounds

The abovementioned tendency is noticeable in some [N + A]$_A$ compounds that have earlier alternants with full-fledged nominals and are superseded by newer forms whose preposed nominal appears in stem form. Consider the cases of *barbapuniente* [c. 1240–1250] vs. *barbiponiente* [c. 1499–1502] and *bocabierto* [c. 1240–1249] vs. *boquiabierto* [1533] (cf. also Chapter 5, Section 5.2.2.5). Other evidence of the phenomenon can be garnered from the head-final [N + N]$_N$ pattern, in examples such as *gallocresta* [c. 1300] vs. *gallicresta* [1494], *orofrés* [1240] vs. *orifrés* [1886], and *cabrahígo* [1379–1384] vs. *caprifigo* [1495]. In all those cases, the first attestations suggest that native speakers replaced a nominal non-head in full form by one in stem form, often with a linking vowel; some of these changes came about through the borrowing of Latinate forms.

To summarize the findings so far, two head-final compound patterns with nominal non-heads experience frequency increases over time. Those increases are accompanied by a growing preference for their preposed nominal non-head in stem form. Speakers have both created new compounds with preposed non-heads in stem form, and replaced full-fledged nouns by nominal stems in older compounds that did not comply with the structural restriction. Below it is shown that this difference can be invoked to account for the continued existence of some head-final patterns in compounding, in spite of the overall shift from head-final to head-initial word order.

9.4.3   The word class marker and constituent order

As was stated in Chapter 1, Section 1.2.4.3, if the non-head appears in stem form, lacking its word class marker, it is non-referable, and as such, incapable of occupying an
argument position and receiving case from a case assigner (cf. 3, for the derivation of
gomorresina 'gum-resin'). It must therefore incorporate into its head to satisfy the
visibility condition (3c). In other words, the non-head appears to the left of the head
because it has moved leftward past the head. Underlyingly, all productive Spanish
compound patterns are in fact head-initial.

(3)   a.

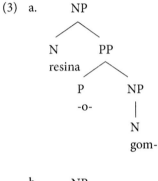

   b.

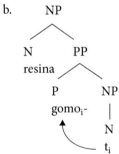

   c.

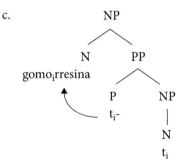

This proposal has the welcome consequence of helping to solve some vexing problems in
English compounding. I am referring in particular to the issue of head-final compounding patterns that seem to run counter to the order of their corresponding phrases. Thus,

for example, whereas word order in English is VO (*hang coats*), corresponding agentives are head-final (*coat-hanger*). It has long been accepted (Roeper & Siegel 1978) that *coat* incorporates into the verbal base, which in turn moves to an agentive head to result in the canonical order O-V-er. Yet it is not easy to justify why the noun should move. I argue that it moves for the same reason in English as it does in Spanish: it is a nominal stem, and cannot remain in postverbal position because it is incapable of bearing accusative case. Because English lacks the overt word class markers of Spanish, the difference between full forms and stems is hard to see. However, there is indirect evidence of their presence or absence. For example, the incorporated nominals cannot be inflected for number even if this would be semantically warranted (**coats-hanger*), which is easy to explain if we accept that these nominals are stems, and thus lack the WCM head selected by the NumP. So there is a morphological difference between the verbal phrase in the compound $[coat\text{-}hang]_{VP}\text{-}er]_{NP}$, involving a verbal head and a nominal stem, and the verbal phrase *hangs coats*, involving a verbal head and a full-fledged WCMP. The WCM head is responsible for the fact that the pure predicate *coat* is now an argument and can receive case.

In brief, word order in Spanish compounds results from the interaction of two conflicting demands. The first is the requirement for heads to be on the left, in keeping with Spanish syntax. The second is the requirement for NPs to be selected by WCM heads as a prerequisite for their availability for syntactic operations such as case assignment. Nominal stems that are devoid of their word class marker must incorporate, and that is how non-head nominals may appear on the left. They are there because they have moved from their underlying position to the right of the head.

9.5 The $[V + N]_N$ compound pattern

9.5.1 Productivity of $[V + N]_N$

By now it has become apparent that the exocentric $[V + N]_N$ pattern represented by compounds such as *sacacorchos* 'corkscrew', lit. 'remove-corks' is by far the most productive in modern Spanish (Figure 9.2), a generalization that can be extended to most other Romance languages. The increase in their frequencies is one of the contributing factors for the shift in head position from right to left. Yet, although some authors have shown that Latin had at least some $[V + N]_N$ compounds, the pattern was quite marginal. How did this unprecedented surge in productivity come about?

The first hypothesis that could be proposed is that in fact, $[V + N]_N$ compounds have always been popular in Romance, but the registers in which they were productive were just not as well documented as those where other types of compounds abounded. In this view, what we see as growth is no more than an illusion, created by the lack of accurate records for the early periods. There is no doubt some truth to this, especially when considering the earliest centuries. For example, there is evidence that $[V + N]_N$ compounds tend to be more frequent in the humbler registers of technical terminology rather than in the better documented lexicon of law and religion. Additionally, given the way the database was created, some of the earliest documented $[V + N]_N$ compounds in Early Romance were not included, because they were toponyms and patronyms (Lloyd 1968: 12–19). However, starting in the 1300s and 1400s, when there is good documentation from a multitude of sources, $[V + N]_N$ compounds still show a continued increase in relative frequency that regularly outstrips all other patterns. The assumption that $[V + N]_N$ compounds were undercounted in the earliest periods does nothing to explain these later increases in their frequency. A reasonable alternative is to posit that, if $[V + N]_N$ compounds appear to have increased in relative frequency, this is because they actually did grow at a disproportionate rate.

Why should this be so? One easily dismissed explanation is teleological or functional: the $[V + N]_N$ pattern was an ideal template to create new words because it was intrinsically useful as a neologistic tool. According to this view, the agentive/instrumental meaning of the pattern made it ideal in the face of an increasing need to name new man-made instruments and the like in an increasingly technological age. However, this is a *post facto* argument that holds little water on closer examination. For one thing, meanings conveyed by $[V + N]_N$ need not be conveyed by that compound pattern or by any compound pattern at all, for that matter. Compare, for example, *pelapapas* 'potato peeler', lit. 'peel-potatoes' against *pelador de papas* 'id.', lit. 'peeler of potatoes' (both profusely documented in Google, with over 99,000 and 60,000 hits, respectively). It is highly unlikely that potato peelers would have remained unnamed in the absence of $[V + N]_N$, since speakers see nothing wrong with a phrasal alternative. Moreover, other languages, just as pressed for neologisms, do not use the $[V + N]_N$ pattern at all or do so minimally. For example, English resorts to other productive mechanisms to name instruments/agents, such as the pattern O-V-er (cf. *potato-peeler*). In other words, the cause-consequence sequence suggested above is on its head. It was not the need for neologisms that caused the productivity of $[V + N]_N$, but the viability of the pattern that made it available for the naming of new agents/instruments.

Another unsatisfactory explanation is based on connectionist models and analogy. According to these explanations, the existence of many compounds with a given pattern would encourage speakers to generate more forms with the same pattern, by substitution of one or both of the lexemes in the template. However, the argument of analogy is contradicted by the facts. If it were true that the existence of compound exemplars were the sole cause of the production of new ones, then patterns that were more abundantly represented should be expected to yield more new exemplars in the following period. The argument that the rich get richer leaves unexplained how $[V + N]_N$, a marginal pattern before the 1200s, increased its share of compounding seven-fold in eight centuries, while patterns that had large shares early on have virtually disappeared. This is a devastating blow for an analogy-based model. Clearly, high productivity is not the consequence of the presence of exemplars but its cause (Anshen & Aronoff 1999).

Let us now explore another possibility, that somehow social changes were at the root of the generalization of $[V + N]_N$. According to this analysis, the pattern was more frequent in some groups of speakers than in others, and later social changes would have generalized it till it became the single most popular pattern of all. This is not an entirely implausible hypothesis, given the popular origin of [V + N]$_N$, as evinced by the types of meanings conveyed by these compounds. However, with the available documentation there is little indication that these compounds were used by a limited group of speakers first, and then adopted by others. Indeed, there is little indication that [V + N]$_N$ compounds have undergone any type of shift in their prestige, since they are still mostly used in the same types of registers and to convey the same types of meanings as they were in the earliest periods documented (cf. Chapter 7, Section 7.1.2). Moreover, the social explanation would work to explain the spread of the pattern from one group to another, but it would do nothing to account for how it had become established in the pioneer group in the first place.

This seems to have brought us back to square one. If we assume that [V + N]$_N$ compounds did not just constitute a large but undocumented class to begin with, and if we believe that the arguments of necessity or piecemeal analogy are fallacious, and the hypothesis of socially motivated change cannot be sufficiently supported, an alternative explanation must be found. I argue here that the increased productivity of [V + N]$_N$ compounds resulted from the interaction of the two features of Spanish discussed earlier (one syntactic, i.e., VO order, and one morphological, i.e., the presence of overt WCM heads) with the processes of natural acquisition of compounds by children.

9.5.2 The acquisition of agentive deverbal compounds

Research in lexical acquisition has shown that children who speak languages with VO order go through a developmental stage where they coin nominal compounds (both agentive and instrumental) with a V + N configuration. This is regardless of whether such compounds are a conventional mechanism of word formation available to adults, i.e., children coin them even in the absence of evidence in the input, producing ungrammatical forms. The process is well attested for English. Although in this language [V + N]$_N$ compounds are of limited productivity, it has been documented that in the process of acquisition of deverbal compounds with the structure O-V-er (e.g., *coat-hanger*, etc.) children go through several intermediate stages, between the ages of three and four, where they produce forms with the structure V-O (e.g., *hug-kids* 'someone who hugs kids', *bounce-ball* 'a boy who bounces balls') or V-er/ing-O (*washing-people* 'something that washes people', *giver-present* 'someone who gives presents') (Clark et al. 1986) (cf. Table 9.8). Since this is not an option in the adult grammar, the structure then needs to be unlearned, resulting in a phasing-out process that becomes complete around the end of the preschool years. Children who are acquiring agentive/instrumental compounds in French go through similar stages, but for them the process is completed at an earlier stage (though not necessarily at an earlier *age*), when they start producing [V + N]$_N$, the target adult form in French (Nicoladis 2007).

Table 9.8 Stages in the acquisition of agentive/instrumental deverbal compounds in English and French (data from Clark et al. 1986; Nicoladis 2007)

	English	French
Stage 1	Head-final [N + N]$_N$: *wash-man, cut-machine*	Head-initial [N + N]$_N$: *machine-boutons* 'button machine', lit. 'machine-buttons' Phrases: *machine à yeux* 'eye machine', lit. 'machine of eyes'
Stage 2	[V + N]$_N$: *hug-kids, bounce-ball* [V + suff + N]$_N$: *giver-present, breaking-bottle*	[V + N]$_N$: *vide-ordures* 'garbage chute', lit. 'empty-trash'
Stage 3	[N + V + suff]$_N$: *box-mower, wall-builder*	NA

Moreover, it has been shown that the presence of the [V + N]$_N$ pattern in the environment may affect the rate at which these forms are produced by children, so that even slightly higher frequencies of [V + N]$_N$ in the input may tilt the balance. For example, a comparative study showed that children exposed to a variety of English richer in [V + N]$_N$ than another variety produced significantly higher rates of those compounds than children who were acquiring a [V + N]$_N$-poor variety (Murphy & Nicoladis 2006). In other words, the existence of at least some V + N compounds encourages children to produce those forms.

9.5.3   Child acquisition and language change

A possible scenario for the spectacular increase in the number of [V + N]$_N$ compounds of Spanish over the course of its history can be formulated on the basis of the information presented in the previous section. Briefly, this is how it may have operated. In the passage from Latin to Hispano-Romance, as word order became increasingly more reliably VO, children who spoke the language followed the natural path indicated above in the process of generating agentive/instrumental deverbal compounds. Since they already had some exemplars in the language that they could use as models, and since those models were consistent with the underlying syntactic word order, it seems safe to assume that, like contemporary English- and French-speaking children, they favored the creation of novel [V + N]$_N$ compounds. These compounds appeared very early in acquisition and coincided with at least one target pattern, so they expanded their application, as each generation of children extended them to new uses. The pattern was not ungrammatical, so children lacked any evidence in the input that forced them to reevaluate or correct the hypothesis that led to the creation of [V + N]$_N$ compounds.

One question remains, though. English-speaking children eventually replace *hug-kids* with *tree-hugger* on the basis of available evidence in the input. It is not clear why in Spanish the existence of the older [N + V]$_V$ pattern, in particular in its deverbal [N + A]$_A$ and [N + N]$_N$ variants (e.g., *mantenido* 'maintained, supported', lit. 'hand-held', *lugarteniente* 'lieutenant', lit. 'place-holder'), and the inverted [N + V]$_N$ pattern (e.g., *malqueda* 'irresponsible person', lit. 'badly-look' and *misacantano* 'priest who can say mass', lit. 'mass-singer') did not impede the growth of the [V + N]$_N$ compounding pattern. After all, those patterns could very well be extended to verbs so that instead of *pelapapas* 'potato-peeler' we could have *papapelador* 'id.', lit. 'potato-peeler'. The acquisition of compounds by Spanish-speaking children of the past seems to be at odds with that of English-speaking children of today, which is problematic if we claim that the two processes are in some way related through acquisitional constraints. If children of VO languages have a tendency to produce [V + N]$_N$ compounds, as we have argued for the growth of the pattern in Spanish, then we need to account for the fact that English children eventually marginalize this word formation mechanism. By contrast, if we argue that the replacement seen in the acquisition of English compounds is due to some form of counterevidence in the input, then we need to explain how come Spanish-speaking children lacked any corrective data in the Old Spanish input.

It is easier to argue this with evidence from modern-day English speakers than with historical data, which is scanty at best. The question that I will attempt to answer is why a language with VO order like English, where children create V + N compounds very early and spontaneously, does not end up reversing compounds that violate this unmarked order, and instead continues to employ a pattern of word formation that seems to run against the grain. (For comparison, recall that this did happen with early deverbal compounds in Spanish, so that *malqueda* 'irresponsible', lit. 'badly-remains/looks' became *quedamal* 'id'. lit. 'remains-badly', and so on.) The answer, I think, lies in the disparities between English and Spanish in terms of their WCM heads, in particular, the fact that in Spanish they are overt, whereas in English they are not.

As was illustrated in Chapter 7 (repeated here as 4 for convenience), [V + N]$_N$ compounds have an underlying structure that includes a VP shell with its complement. The structure proposed is therefore based on a merge operation between the verb and a WCM head, resulting in a nominal compound. The nominal constituent is a full-fledged noun, accompanied by its word class marker, and very often in the plural form, which is evidence of the existence of a NumP. The verb, in turn, also exhibits a theme vowel (an AspP according to Ferrari-Bridgers 2005) and a nominalizing (but overtly null) word class marker.

(4)

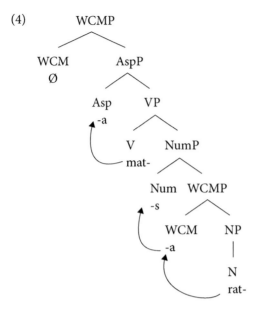

Note that this type of lexical structure is the most parallel to syntax, and it has been argued that this makes it the simplest form for children to attempt in word formation (Clark et al. 1986). As a result, in the process of creating agentive/instrumental deverbal compounds, this is predicted to be a favored structure for children of a VO language. We have evidence that English-speaking children use a structure parallel to (4) because in the early stages of acquisition of deverbal compounds the complement nominals may appear in full form, including number inflection (cf. the derivation of *hug-kids* in 5). However, fairly quickly children seem to replace this hypothesis with a new one, in which the lower nominal appears in bare form, even if the plural would be warranted semantically (a *bounce-ball* is someone who bounces many balls) (Clark et al. 1986: 13). A comparison of the two structures in (5) and (6) against the Spanish parallel in (4) shows what makes the English version ungrammatical: unlike Spanish, English has no overt formative for either the WCM head or the theme (or aspect) head. Now, it has been observed that phonologically null morphemes do not allow further derivational affixation (Myer's generalization), a fact that has been attributed to a violation of a parsing restriction (if there could be any number of zero morphemes, then the parser would have no way to recover them separately) Pesetzky 1996).[1]

The next stage involves the acquisition of the nominal formatives *-er/-ing*, which children seem to interpret as aspectual, given forms such as *giver-present* or *washing-people*. This yields the right derivational suffixation on the verb, avoiding the sequence of more than one zero morpheme, but the wrong word order (7).

---

1.   I wish to thank Juan Uriagereka for valuable discussion on this point.

(5)

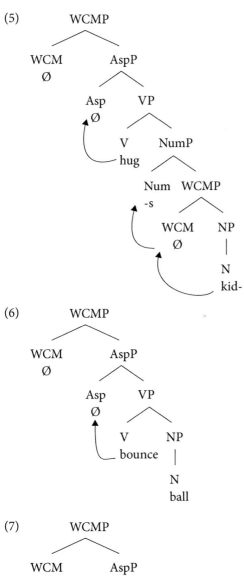

(6)

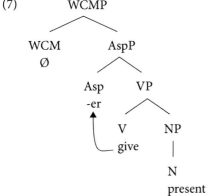

(7)

The structure in (7) assumes hypothesizing the existence of a WCM null head with the capacity to select an aspectual phrase as its complement and nominalize it. Children who speak Spanish receive ample evidence of the existence of nominalization of this kind in their language, since any AP can be turned into a referable expression: *un rojo* 'a Communist', lit. 'a red', *un loco* 'a crazy man', lit. 'a crazy', *un flaco* 'a thin man', lit. 'a thin', etc. (cf. Kornfeld 2009, for a proposal along these lines).[2] Children who speak English may very well assume that the same structure is possible, since positing it involves the simplest mechanism of word formation, which most closely parallels syntactic order. However, eventually they receive evidence that this type of structure is impossible in English, in the absence of structures such as *a red, a thin*, or *a crazy* in their input.[3]

For the right word order to be produced, children have to make another hypothesis, namely, that the bare nominal is incapable of remaining in place and still be assigned case from the verb, because it is not a referable expression and therefore cannot be an argument. In other words, they need to distinguish the nominal full forms that are used in syntactic phrases such as *gives presents* from the nominal stems used in word formation, such as *present-giver*, with very few overt clues to do so. This, of course, is unlike Spanish, where the difference is quite straightforward, since these two forms are overtly different in many contexts encountered in child language from a very early age (*cara* 'face', *car-ita* 'little face'). The fact that English-speaking children never incorporate nominals with plural inflection provides evidence that they reach this stage before they produce O-V-er compounds. The structure in (8) shows the resulting adult structure, where the nominalizing word class marker has been eliminated and the nominal stem has been incorporated to satisfy the visibility condition.

---

2.   This should not be equated with the *pro* proposed in Uriagereka (1988) for expressions such as *el rojo* 'the red one', lit. 'the red' (*el ø rojo*), *el de Parma* 'the one from Parma', lit. 'the from Parma' (*el ø de Parma*), *el que vino* 'the one who came', lit. 'the who came' (*el ø que vino*). There is a difference, only appreciable with the indefinite article, between *un rojo* 'a red person = a Communist' and *uno rojo* 'a red one'. In the first one the use of the indefinite article shows that *rojo* has indeed been nominalized: $[un[[rojo]_{Adj}]_{WCM}]_{DP}$. In the latter, the adjective continues to be an adjective and the overt indefinite pronoun *uno* 'one' occupies the head of NP: $[[[uno]_N]_D$ $rojo]_{Adj}]_{DP}$. The nominalizing WCM is not involved in expressions such as *el de Parma* or *el que vino*, as evidenced by the ungrammaticality of **un de Parma* 'a of Parma' and **un que vino* (cf. *uno de Parma* 'one from Parma' and *uno que vino* 'one who came').

3.   Clearly, there must be more to this, since English does allow compounds with empty heads of the type *redchest*, etc. The difference between those types of compounds and the unproductive *pickpocket* class needs to be considered in greater detail.

(8)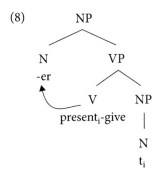

Some of the proposals above have consequences for the evolution of Spanish. Unlike the children who acquire English today, children acquiring Old Spanish had evidence that Spanish had a WCM head that could turn predicates (APs, VPs) into arguments. This gave them no reason to discard the construction in (4), once they had reached that stage in the evolution of their word formation patterns. This, coupled with the existence of some adult compound exemplars, cemented the pattern and allowed each generation to build on the previous one.

The clear morphological distinction between stems and words in Spanish was also behind the disappearance of alternatives such as the $[N + V]_N$ pattern (recall *misacantano* 'mass-singer'). For a speaker of Spanish, the presence of a word class marker on a nominal complement was a clear indication that the nominal was available for case assignment in situ, making incorporation into the verbal head an unjustifiable movement, violating economy in a minimalist sense. This led speakers to stop using patterns that had full forms to the left, and to invert them: *gatatumba > tumbagatos*. Another possibility, that of replacing the word class marker on the nominal by a linking vowel, would in theory have been available. However, linking vowels in Spanish seem to have been a later borrowing from Latin, imported as a stow-away in many learned complex words. As I showed earlier, the increase in their use actually made it possible for some head-final patterns such as $[N + A]_A$ to surge in the 1500s. However, it is possible that by that time the $[V + N]_N$ pattern was so well established that no competing alternatives were viable.

9.6 Relative frequency of compound patterns

Now that we have dealt with the very frequent $[V + N]_N$ compounding pattern and ventured an explanation of why speakers resorted to it increasingly over time, let us discuss the frequencies of the remaining patterns. It has been pointed out before that there are more compound nouns than verbs or adjectives across languages (Dressler 2005). This section provides confirmation that this is the case in Spanish, but it also shows that changes have occurred over time in this respect. Even if at this point no theoretical insights will come out of presenting this evolution, having a clear idea of the changes in compound lexical category may open up lines of inquiry.

In what follows the $[V + N]_N$ pattern will be excluded from consideration, since its productivity would skew the data. The first broad structural distinction is drawn between hierarchical compounds and non-hierarchical or concatenative compounds. All hierarchical and non-hierarchical compounding patterns other than $[V + N]_N$ are considered first, regardless of any structural differences within each set. Table 9.9 shows that the overwhelming majority of compounds in any given period are hierarchical, with concatenative compounds always constituting a small percentage of the total. However, concatenative compounds gain a bigger share of the total over the periods documented, a trend that is considered in greater detail below.

Let us first focus more specifically on hierarchical compounds by lexical category. As predicted, nominals are prevalent in the early stages and their frequencies increase over the centuries from 63.9% to over 70% of the total. (Recall that this figure excludes $[V + N]_N$ compounds, which increased even more.) Adjectival and verbal compounds have smaller shares early on, and lose ground over time (Table 9.10).

When considered in greater detail, these general trends are the result of averaging patterns that did not all evolve in the same way. For example, although it is true that both verbal patterns decrease their percentages in tandem (Figure 9.7), not all adjectival patterns do (Figure 9.8). As for the nominal patterns, a few of them are responsible for the general trends of the group, but several others are stable or even decrease slightly in frequency over time (Figure 9.9).

Table 9.9 Totals and percentages of hierarchical and concatenative compounds over time (n = 2490)

	Hierarchical	%	Concatenative	%
1000s–1200s	319	94.4	19	5.6
1300s	389	93.7	26	6.3
1400s	581	91.6	53	8.4
1500s	799	88.4	105	11.6
1600s	882	88.2	118	11.8
1700s	934	87.5	134	12.5
1800s	1182	85.7	198	14.3
1900s–2000s	1794	82.7	374	17.3
Total	2083	83.7	407	16.3

Table 9.10 Totals and percentages of hierarchical compounds over time, by lexical category (excluding [V + N]$_N$ compounds) (n = 2083)

	Verbal	%	Adjectival	%	Nominal	%
1000s–1200s	28	8.8	87	27.3	204	63.9
1300s	35	9.0	97	24.9	257	66.1
1400s	46	7.9	138	23.8	397	68.3
1500s	57	7.1	222	27.8	520	65.1
1600s	58	6.6	251	28.5	573	65.0
1700s	60	6.4	259	27.7	615	65.8
1800s	66	5.6	311	26.3	805	68.1
1900s–2000s	79	4.4	381	21.2	1334	74.4
Total	92	4.4	493	23.7	1498	71.9

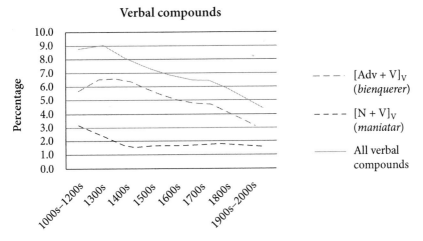

Figure 9.7 Relative frequency of verbal compound patterns over time as a percentage of all compounds

Let us now turn to the relative frequency of the various concatenative patterns (Figure 9.10). The adjectival and nominal concatenative compounds have both been fairly active over time, although the balance between them has shifted. After an early stage in which both lexical categories are quite even, nominal concatenatives gain ground over their adjectival counterparts between the 1300s and the 1600s. Adjectival compounds catch up in the 1900s, eliminating any difference in frequency between both classes. The (exocentric) [V + V]$_N$ pattern is and has always been marginal, staying at or below 10% of nominal concatenative compounds, which translates into under 2% of all compounds for all the periods studied.

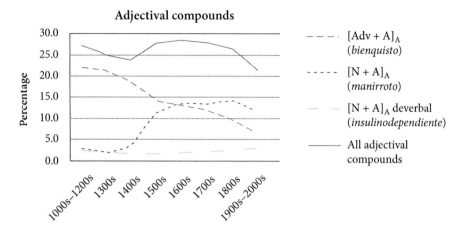

Figure 9.8 Relative frequency of adjectival compound patterns over time as a percentage of all compounds

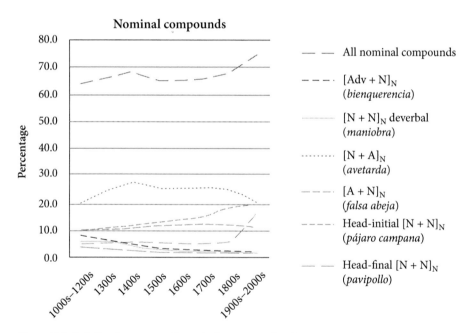

Figure 9.9 Relative frequency of nominal compound patterns over time as a percentage of all compounds

To summarize this section, over the entire period considered, hierarchical patterns are more frequent in the data, although concatenative compounds increase their share of the total. Within hierarchical patterns, nominal compounding is by far the most

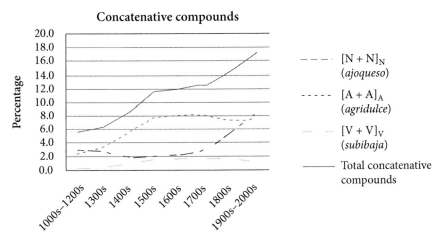

Figure 9.10 Relative frequency of concatenative compound patterns over time, as percentage of all compounds

frequent, and increasingly so, whereas adjectival and verbal compounding exhibits overall losses. Individual patterns within each lexical category may or may not follow the general trend for the group. Among concatenative compounds, adjectives and nouns have different evolutions, but in latter centuries they have reached similar frequencies. The theoretical significance of these shifts in frequency remains to be explained.

9.7 Endocentric and exocentric compounds

Another issue that deserves attention is whether there has been an increase or decrease over time in the endocentric and exocentric use of compound patterns and whether endocentric and exocentric uses of the same pattern appear in any specific historical order. It would be reasonable to expect endocentric structures to come first, and exocentric ones to be derivative, since the latter are structurally and semantically more complex. For example, a compound such as *cararrota* 'cheeky person', lit. 'face broken' contains an empty nominalizing head that selects the $[N + A]_N$ sequence as its complement (making it, in fact $[ø[N + A]_N]_{WCM}$). The empty head is responsible for the fact that the compound can be masculine even if the nominal in the compound is feminine: *Pedro es un cararrota* 'Pedro is a cheeky guy', lit. 'Pedro is a-MASC SG face-FEM SG-broken-FEM SG.' Semantically, they are more complex because they involve the notion of possessor, which is not stated overtly: *Pedro es un cararrota = Pedro tiene la cara rota* 'Pedro is a face-broken = Pedro has a broken face'. The data provide some support for the view that as a general rule exocentricity follows endocentricity.

The following discussion considers only compounding patterns that have exhibited at least some endocentric and some exocentric exemplars over time, because those are the only cases in which the question of a possible evolution from endocentricity to exocentricity makes sense. In other words, structurally exocentric compounds, such as $[V + N]_N$ (*sacacorchos* 'corkscrew', lit. 'remove-corks') or $[V + V]_N$ (*picapica* 'magpie', lit. 'peck-peck') in which the very pattern involves a lexical category shift (i.e., $[ø[V + N]_{VP}]_{WCM}$, $[ø[V + V]_{VP}]_{WCM}$), are not counted. Also excluded from consideration are patterns that were found not to present any exocentric uses. This group includes $[Adv + N]_N$ (*bienvenida* 'welcome'), and $[N + V]_V$ (*maniatar* 'tie by the hands', lit. 'hand-tie').

When the remaining patterns are considered together, the frequency of exocentric use among them is low and stable over time, never reaching 10% (Table 9.11).[4] In other words, the kinds of operations that result in exocentricity have applied infrequently and more or less evenly throughout the history of Spanish compounding.

When considered individually, compounding patterns tend to exhibit changes in their exocentric/endocentric use that cancel out when considered together as we did in Table 9.11. Because these increases or decreases tend to be small, it is not very profitable to show them in graph form. However, Table 9.12 shows examples of patterns that exhibit increases and decreases over time in the number of exocentric compounds generated, together with examples of each. Few clear general trends can be deduced from the data, but it appears that the larger compound classes are more prone to generating exocentric exemplars.

Table 9.11 Totals and percentages of endocentric and exocentric uses for all compounding patterns over time

	Endocentric	%	Exocentric	%
1000s–1200s	278	92.4	23	7.6
1300s	356	93.7	24	6.3
1400s	558	94.3	34	5.7
1500s	805	94.9	43	5.1
1600s	891	94.2	55	5.8
1700s	938	93.2	68	6.8
1800s	1220	93.4	86	6.6
1900s–2000s	1941	93.5	136	6.5
Total	2224	93.6	153	6.4

---

4.   For clarification, any compound that has exocentric and endocentric interpretations was counted as exocentric.

Table 9.12 Compound patterns that increase and decrease their exocentricity over time

Compound pattern	Example of exocentric use
Increased exocentricity	
$[N + A]_A$	*pechicolorado* 'redpoll, linnet' lit. 'chest-red'
$[N + A]_N$	*cabeza dura* 'stubborn person', lit. 'head-hard'
$[A + N]_N$	*malacabeza* 'reckless person', lit. 'bad-head'
Head-initial $[N + N]_N$	*cesta punta* 'jai alai, type of pelota', lit. 'basket point'
Decreased exocentricity	
$[Adv + A]_A$	*malentendido* 'misunderstanding', lit. 'badly-understood'
$[Adv + V]_V$	*bienhacer* 'well doing', lit. 'well-do'
$[N + A]_A$	*aguallevado* 'ditch cleaning by flushing', lit. 'water-taken'
Head-final $[N + N]_N$	*aguja paladar* 'garfish', lit. 'needle palate'
$[A + A]_A$	*altibajo* 'ups and downs', lit. 'high-low'

9.7.1 $[Q + N]_N$ compounds and exocentricity

There is one compounding pattern that does exhibit a marked trend towards increasing exocentric usage over time, namely $[Q + N]_N$. Recall from Chapter 7 that two distinct types of compounds have the overall structure of a numeral followed by a noun. In the first (exocentric) configuration, the numeral governs the nominal but does not percolate its lexical category to the entire compound (e.g., *sietemachos* 'brave man', lit. 'seven-males'). In the second (endocentric) pattern it is the nominal that acts as the head of the compound, with the numeral qualifying it in some way (e.g., *tresabuelo* 'great-grandfather', lit. 'three-grandfather'). Whereas both patterns are present all through history, only the exocentric $[Q + N]_N$ pattern can be used to create new compounds today. In this section we can quantify this evolution (Table 9.13). As the table shows, the total number of endocentric $[Q + N]_N$ compounds decreases over time, whereas that of exocentric compounds with the same surface structure increases steadily. As a consequence, the relative weight of the endocentric pattern shrinks to the point where it is almost negligible. On closer inspection, all ten of the endocentric compounds in the $[Q + N]_N$ class have first attestations on or before the 1400s, and eight of them had appeared by the 1200s, a sure measure of pattern obsolescence.

9.7.2 Endocentricity/exocentricity of individual compounds

Finally, it is worth looking at the fate of some individual compounds that have had both endocentric and exocentric acceptations over time. The question in this case is whether, as one might expect, endocentric interpretations preceded exocentric

Table 9.13 Totals and percentages of endocentric and exocentric $[Q + N]_N$ compounds by century

	Endocentric	%	Exocentric	%
1000s–1200s	8	66.7	4	33.3
1300s	9	69.2	4	30.8
1400s	9	56.3	7	43.8
1500s	8	50.0	8	50.0
1600s	7	41.2	10	58.8
1700s	5	27.8	13	72.2
1800s	5	25.0	15	75.0
1900s–2000s	5	13.5	32	86.5
Total	10	21.3	37	78.7

interpretations historically. This is not an easy matter to resolve, because few compounds have both endo- and exocentric interpretations, and their order relative to each other can only be established when both of these meanings are reasonably frequent. However, there is some confirmatory evidence that exocentric uses are indeed derivative. Consider, for example, *rabilargo* 'long-tailed', lit. 'tail-long', which is used as an adjective three centuries earlier than its first attested use as a noun, to designate a bird with a long tail, the azure-winged magpie (9a, b). Even if it does not shift its lexical category, a compound can become exocentric by shifting in meaning from a part to the whole that contains it. That must also have been the case of the compound *calvatrueno*, lit. 'bald head-thunder', originally used to designate someone's head, but eventually used for the entire individual (10a, b). Yet, the dates of first attestation are less distant in this case, making the sequence less clear.

(9) a. *de atrás le viene al galgo ser* rabilargo. (1655, Marcos Fernández, CORDE)
'It's in the blood of the greyhound to be long-tailed'.

b. *Sólo se oía el frenesí de las chicharras o de los* rabilargos *cantando entre la fronda* (1981, José Manuel Caballero Bonald, CREA)
'The only noise that could be heard was the buzzing of the cicadas and the azure-winged magpies singing in the bushes".

(10) a. *¡Qué Babilonia de lenguas avía formado la sobervia ignorante en el* calvatrueno *d'este probeto contra la gloria de la llaneza dulce y pareja!*
(1592, Francisco Agustín Tárrega, CORDE)
'What a confusion of languages had been amassed by ignorant pedantry in the crazy head of this old man, against the glory of sweet and even simplicity!'

b. '[*Epitafio*] El *calvatrueno que adornó a la Mancha/de más despojos que
   Jasón de Creta*.'   (1605, Miguel de Cervantes Saavedra, CORDE)
   '[Epitaph] The crazy man who adorned La Mancha of more spoils than
   Jason of Crete'.

To summarize this section, compound patterns exhibit different situations in terms of
their exo- and endocentricity. Apart from the few patterns that are always exocentric
and those that have never generated any exocentric examples, most compounding patterns exhibit at least some exocentric use (between 1% and 20% of all the compounds
they generate). Yet, no clear overall trend can be discerned towards a higher use of
exocentric compounds over time, as would have been expected from the fact that exocentrics are derivative and more complex. This could be simply because the newest
compounds are endocentric when they are created, so that the more productive patterns exhibit fewer exocentric compounds relative to the total. Finally, considering
endocentric and exocentric acceptations for a single compound lexeme provides some
evidence to support the hypothesis that endocentric acceptations precede exocentric
ones. The sole exception is constituted by $[Q + N]_N$ compounds, which have generated
increasingly more exocentric compounds over time. However, on closer inspection,
$[Q + N]_N$ compounds in fact represent two distinct sub-patterns, one endocentric but
obsolete, and another one exocentric and still vital.

9.8   Remaining questions for compounding and beyond

This book has sought to present an overall panorama of Spanish compounding over
the centuries of documented history, but as the first such attempt, it should not be
surprising that we have ended up with new questions. This section presents some of
the synchronic and diachronic descriptive issues that should be tackled next in the
study of Spanish compounding, because doing so could yield great dividends. This
section also presents some theoretical issues that are still unresolved, and it ends with
a proposal to extend the account applied in this chapter beyond compounding, to the
issue of language change more generally.

9.8.1 What are the prosodic properties of Spanish compounds?

From the descriptive point of view, one of the main limitations in the discussion of
Spanish compounding is the absence of a thorough and reliable description of their
stress patterns. Very few such studies exist (a notable exception being Hualde
2006/2007), and none have used experimental methods to ascertain the accuracy of
native speaker intuitions and any variability that may exist between patterns, speakers,
or dialectal varieties. The area of compound prosody is begging for fresh insights that
will help clarify, confirm, or correct many previous assertions, in particular, those related to the specific contribution of stress to the distinction between compounds and

phrases. In light of the controversy surrounding the status of prosody as a means to discriminate beween compounds and phrases in English, data from another language would help to shed new light on this old problem.

9.8.2 What is the status of linking vowels in compounding?

There are also some morphological aspects of compounding that deserve more focused attention than they have received in this book. Of particular interest are the linking vowels in compounds of the type *carilindo* 'pretty-faced', lit. 'face-pretty', *coliflor* 'cauliflower', lit. 'cabbage-flower', and *vitaminoterapia* 'vitamin therapy'. The semantic value of these linking vowels is not uniform. Whereas some are clearly coordinative in meaning and origin (*calicanto* 'masonry work' < *cal y canto* 'whitewash and pebble'), in other cases they are clearly not (*carilindo* *< *cara y lindo* 'face and pretty'). In the latter cases, the linking vowel seems to be merely a mark of the stem status of the morpheme to which it is attached. However, at this point it is not clear whether there has been any interaction over history between the two types of linking vowel, so that the appearance of one may have favored the occurrence of the other. Additionally, there is the issue of whether there is a simple rule that will account for the appearance of the *-o-* or *-i-* linking vowels in the cases where both can occur. These issues have a synchronic and a diachronic component which can be studied with the data collected for this book.

9.8.3 Do native speakers recognize the various types of concatenative compounds hypothesized?

Another area where fresh insights are needed is the description of certain compounding patterns of Spanish, such as concatenatives. Although recent work has helped clarify the different types of semantic relations that may exist between the constituents of these compounds (Bauer 2008), there has been no in-depth study of these patterns in Spanish. In particular, it must be determined whether the various categories established by linguists are indeed recognized by native speakers, and whether the semantic classification can be connected to formal features such as gender and number inflection. This will help clarify the various types of concatenative compounds of Spanish, and make it possible to tease apart the history of each pattern.

9.8.4 What happens to compound patterns in situations of language contact?

There is also much to be done to determine the possible regional and social variation of compounding. Recall that this book set out to be panoramic, and as such, it is based on general lexicographical sources that reflect Peninsular varieties better than American dialects. With the expansion of Spanish as a world language, compounding patterns and trends have been adopted and adapted in contact situations by speakers of a multitude of other languages, both European and indigenous. It is of interest to explore how compounding has fared under those conditions. Even in the limited dialectal data available so far, there are occasional hints that compounds have been built by mixing constituents of different languages, while at the same time respecting the combinatorial rules of Spanish. For example, *cidracayote* 'Asian pumpkin [Cucurbita ficifolia L.]', lit. 'gourd-white gourd [Sechium edule L.]' (< Sp. *cidra* + Nahuatl *chahuitli*), or *mangiamierda* 'shit-eater', lit. 'eat-shit' (< It. *mangiare* + Sp. *mierda*). In other words, these new complex lexemes have been created following the rules of Spanish compounding. An expanded analysis incorporating a broad spectrum of dialects may provide more evidence of how compounding is affected by contact, giving an idea not just of where Spanish has been, but also of where it is headed. Of particular interest are varieties of Spanish in regions and semantic fields where it comes in contact with languages with quite different compounding patterns (e.g., the United States, the Internet).

9.8.5 Why is hierarchical compounding always binary?

There are also theoretical questions worth addressing. One of the main generalizations that can be made on the basis of the data collected for this study is that compounding involves two constituents. This fact is mostly taken as a given and has been summed up theoretically in several different ways. For hierarchical compounding, it is generally assumed that a compound with more than two identifiable heads has been created recursively, i.e., by compounding a previously compounded constituent with a new one: [X[YZ]]. When a hierarchical compound has a head-complement internal structure, the binary nature of compounding seems to follow quite straightforwardly from syntactic principles. Thus, [saca[corchos]] 'corkscrew', lit. 'remove-corks' has two constituents for the same reason that [sacaste [el corcho]] 'you removed the cork' does. However, when the relationship between the constituents is head-adjunct, it is a great deal harder to account for. It is not clear why compounds such as *malvender* 'sell for a low price', lit. 'badly-sell' are licit, whereas **malprontovender* 'sell quickly and for a low price' is not, when both *vendimos mal* 'we sold badly' and *vendimos mal y pronto* 'we sold badly and quickly' are possible syntactic phrases. This also applies to adjectival modification: *hierbabuena* 'mint', lit. 'herb-good', vs. **hierbaverdebuena* 'herb-green-good' (cf. the phrases *hierba buena* 'herb good' and *hierba verde buena* 'herb green good'). In the past, all hierarchical compounds have been equated to head-complements by considering them all merge structures (Harley 2009; Moyna 2004; Roeper et al. 2003), but this does not seem justified on semantic grounds (cf. Chapter 2, Section 2.2). An alternative explanation may come from extending the notion of the syntactic small clause to the word domain, which would naturally account for the binary nature of compounds created through adjunction. Note that this type of structure would account theoretically for the description of certain types of compounds as 'embryonic relative clauses' (Kastovsky 2009: 333). The small clause configuration involves a simple form of non-tensed predication, and in that regard already shares some features with compounds. However, small clauses in the classical sense may involve functional categories, which I have claimed are barred from compounding. For the proposal of small clauses in compounding to work, the definition of small clause would have to be adapted to the sublexical level in ways to be determined.

9.8.6   Why is there a crosslinguistic preference for nominal compounding?

Another fact that requires theoretical attention is the overall preference for nominal compounding, a trend that is increasingly clear over time and that has not been satisfactorily explained by invoking specific morphological or syntactic parameters that could be behind it. It may be that the lexical category of productive compound patterns in a language is linked to other parameters, but it remains to be seen what those would be.

9.8.7   How can language acquisition data help explain language change?

Finally, I would like to expand on the issue of child acquisition and language change, which was invoked earlier to account for the increased productivity of $[V + N]_N$ compounds (Section 9.5). The reader will recall that explanations based on analogy were rejected, because they would have yielded the wrong results, favoring compounds that were better represented in the language at the expense of marginal patterns such as $[V + N]_N$. Explanations based solely on social factors, such as the generalization of $[V + N]_N$ compounds from some social groups to others, were also discarded simply because there was insufficient evidence that deverbal patterns were ever used by certain social groups but not by others or that $[V + N]_N$ compounds were subject to pressure from above or below. An explanation based on certain documented tendencies of child acquisition was favored instead. In what follows it is argued that incorporating language acquisition data into historical research would be useful beyond compounding.

Since the publication of Labov's seminal work in the sixties and seventies, sociolinguistics has been rightly considered one of the best explanatory tools available to account for language change (Labov 1965; 1975; 2001). Problems that were seemingly mysterious or intractable under the assumption that language was a monolithic entity have been illuminated by taking into consideration the variation of language across social groups and issues such as prestige relations between groups, contact with speakers of other dialects, and the like.

There is one aspect in which sociolinguistic explanations may prove to be incomplete, however. Sociolinguistic research has methodological constraints that restrict it to the language production of adults and older children, while excluding young children. From a sociological standpoint, this exclusion makes sense because very young children do not have a fixed and stable linguistic identity. Yet for historical research the absence of data from children is a gap, because there is every reason to believe that young children effect changes on the languages they acquire. We have evidence of this when children have had to create their own languages in situations of communicative crisis, such as creoles or deaf languages in new deaf communities (Bickerton 1984; Senghas 1995; Senghas & Coppola 2001). It seems reasonable to assume that whatever is at work in these extreme circumstances must also be in operation in some variant even when children acquire a full-fledged language (pace Aitchison 2001 [1981]: 201– 210). At least some language changes must be fashioned by speakers before they reach the age threshold that makes them reliable subjects of sociolinguistic research. Excluding data from small children from the study of language change is akin to trying to study language acquisition by considering only adult L2 learners. To be sure, some useful information will be obtained, but much will also be missed.

At first glance, studying child language in historical perspective may seem impossible. It is difficult enough to obtain data that reflect all adult social classes, but finding out how preliterate children spoke five hundred years ago appears impossibly elusive. My proposal, which I have illustrated with the study of $[V + N]_N$ compounds, is to take advantage of data from contemporary children who are acquiring languages that share features with the historical varieties under study. If there are universal tendencies in the acquisition of those features, it follows that these should emerge again and again when a child is faced with the task of acquiring them in any language. I like to think of the study of language change as trying to figure out what is inside a box by peering through a few small holes on its sides. Looking at authentic language acquisition data will not solve all our problems, but it opens another little hole to shed some new light on the dim interior of the box.

References

Academia Argentina de Letras. 2003. *Diccionario del habla de los argentinos*. Mexico, D.F.: Espasa Calpe Mexicana.

Adams, James 1976. "A Typological Approach to Latin Word Order". *Indogermanische Forschungen* 81.70–100.

Adelman, Allison. 2002. *On the Status of N–V Verbal Compounds in Catalan*. Swarthmore, Penn.: Swarthmore College Senior Thesis.

Aitchison, Jean. 2001 [1981]. *Language Change: Progress or Decay?* Cambridge & New York: Cambridge University Press.

Alemany Bolufer, José. 1920. *Tratado de la formación de palabras en la lengua castellana*. Madrid: Librería General de Victoriano Suárez.

Alonso Pedraz, Martín. 1986. *Diccionario medieval español: Desde las Glosas emilianenses y silenses (s. X) hasta el siglo XV*. Salamanca: Universidad Pontificia de Salamanca.

Alves, Ieda Maria. 1986/1987. "Aspectos da composição nominal no português contemporâneo". *Alfa* 30/31.55–63.

Anderson, Stephen. 1982. "Where's Morphology?" *Linguistic Inquiry* 13.571–612.

Anderson, Stephen. 1992. *A-Morphous Morphology*. Cambridge: Cambridge University Press.

Anshen, Frank & Mark Aronoff. 1999. "Using Dictionaries to Study the Mental Lexicon". *Brain and Language* 68.16–26.

Aronoff, Mark. 1992. *Morphology by Itself*. Cambridge, Mass. & London: MIT Press.

Aronoff, Mark & Kristen Fuderman. 2005. *What is Morphology?* Oxford: Blackwell.

Baayen, Harald & Rochelle Lieber. 1991. "Productivity and English Derivation: A corpus-based study". *Linguistics* 29.801–843.

Badecker, William & Alfonso Caramazza. 1998. "Morphology in Aphasia". *The Handbook of Morphology* ed. by Andrew Spencer & Arnold Zwicky, 390–405. Oxford: Blackwell.

Bader, Françoise. 1962. *La formation des composés nominaux du latin*. Paris: Éditions "Les Belles Lettres".

Baker, Mark. 1988. *Incorporation: A theory of grammatical function changing*. Chicago: University of Chicago Press.

Baker, Mark. 2003. *Lexical Categories: Verbs, nouns, and adjectives*. Cambridge: Cambridge University Press.

Barlow, Michael & Charles A. Ferguson, eds. 1988. *Agreement in Natural Language: Approaches, theories, and descriptions*. Stanford, Calif.: Center for the Study of Language and Information.

Bauer, Laurie. 2001a. "Compounding". *Language Typology and Language Universals* ed. by Martin Haspelmath, Ekkehard König, Wulf Oesterreicher & Wolfgang Raible, 695–707. Berlin & New York: Walter de Gruyter.

Bauer, Laurie. 2001b. *Morphological Productivity*. Cambridge: Cambridge University Press.

Bauer, Laurie. 2008. "Dvandva". *Word Structure* 1.1–20.

Bello, Andrés. 1928. *Gramática de la lengua castellana destinada al uso de los americanos*. Paris: A. Blot.

Benczes, Réka. 1995. "Creative Noun-Noun Compounds". *Annual Review of Cognitive Linguistics* 3.250–68.

Bennett, William. 1977. "Predicative Binomials in French". *Lingua* 41.331–342.

Benveniste, Émile. 1966. "Fondements syntaxiques de la composition nominale". *Problèmes de linguistique générale*, 145–162. Paris: Gallimard.

Bernstein, Judy. 1993. "The Syntactic Role of Word Markers in Null Nominal Constructions". *Probus* 5.5–38.

Bickerton, Derek. 1984. "The Language Bioprogram Hypothesis". *Behavioral and Brain Sciences* 7. 173–221.

Bierbach, Mechthild. 1983. "Les composés du type *portefeuille*: Essai d'analyse historique". *Travaux de linguistique et de littérature* 21.137–155.

Bisetto, Antonietta. 1994. "Italian Compounds of the *Accendigas* Type: A case of endocentric formation?". *Proceedings of the Workshop on Compound Nouns: Multilingual aspects of nominal composition* ed. by Pierrette Bouillon & Dominique Estival, 77–87. Geneva: Université de Genève.

Bisetto, Antonietta & Sergio Scalise. 1999. "Compounding. Morphology and/or Syntax?" *Boundaries of Morphology and Syntax* ed. by Lunella Mereu, 31–48. Amsterdam & Philadelphia: John Benjamins.

Blake, Robert. 1991. "Squeezing the Spanish Turnip Dry: Latinate documents from the early Middle Ages". *Linguistic Studies in Medieval Spanish* ed. by Ray Harris-Northall & Thomas Cravens, 1–14. Madison: Hispanic Seminary of Medieval Studies.

Bloomfield, Leonard. 1933. *Language*. New York: Henry Holt & Co.

Booij, Gert. 1996. "Inherent versus Contextual Inflection and the Split Morphology Hypothesis". *Yearbook of Morphology* ed. by Gert Booij & Jaap van Marle, 1–16. Dordrecht: Kluwer.

Bork, Hans Dieter. 1990. *Die lateinisch-romanischen Zusammensetzungen N + V und der Ursprung der romanischen Verb-Ergänzung-Komposita*. Bonn: Romanistischer Verlag.

Bosque, Ignacio & Carme Picallo. 1996. "Postnominal Adjectives in Spanish DPs". *Journal of Linguistics* 32.349–385.

Bresnan, Joan & Sam Mchombo. 1995. "The Lexical Integrity Principle: Evidence from Bantu". *Natural Language and Linguistic Theory* 13.181–254.

Brunet, Claude. 2005. Bene facere: Une ou deux lexies? *La composition et la préverbation en latin* ed. by Claude Moussy, 197–207. Paris: Presses de l'Université Paris-Sorbonne.

Bustos Gisbert, Eugenio de. 1986. *La composición nominal en español*. Salamanca: Ediciones Universidad de Salamanca.

Camacho, José. 1999. "How Similar are Conjuncts? Against asymmetric conjunction". *Formal Perspectives on Romance Linguistics: Selected papers from the 28th Linguistic Symposium on Romance Languages (LSRL XXVIII), University Park, 16–19 April, 1998* ed. by Jean-Marc Authier, Barbara E. Bullock & Lisa A. Reed (= *Current Issues in Linguistic Theory* 185), 73–88. Amsterdam & Philadelphia: John Benjamins.

Campos, Héctor. 1991. "Preposition Stranding in Spanish?" *Linguistic Inquiry* 22.741–750.

Chomsky, Noam. 1970. "Remarks on Nominalization". *Readings in English Transformational Grammar* ed. by Roderick Jacobs & Peter Rosenbaum, 184–221. Waltham, Mass., Toronto & London: Ginn and Company.

Chomsky, Noam. 1981. *Lectures on Government and Binding*. Dordrecht: Foris.

Chomsky, Noam. 1995. *The Minimalist Program*. Cambridge, Mass. & London: MIT Press.

Chomsky, Noam & Morris Halle. 1968. *The Sound Pattern of English*. New York & London: Harper & Row.

Chuchuy, Claudio. 2000. *Diccionario del español de Argentina*. Madrid: Gredos.

Cinque, Guglielmo. 1994. "On the Evidence of Partial N-movement in the Romance DP". *Paths Towards Universal Grammar: Studies in honor of Richard S. Kayne* ed. by Guglielmo Cinque, Jan Koster, Jean-Yves Pollock, Luigi Rizzi & Raffaella Zanuttini, 85–110. Washington, D.C.: Georgetown University Press.

Clackson, James. 2002. "Composition in Indo-European Languages". *Transactions of the Philological Society* 100.163–67.

Clark, Eve. 1998. "Morphology in Language Acquisition". *The Handbook of Morphology* ed. by Andrew Spencer & Arnold Zwicky, 374–389. Oxford: Blackwell.

Clark, Eve, Barbara Hecht & Randa Mulford. 1986. "Coining Complex Compounds in English: Affixes and word order in acquisition". *Linguistics* 24.7–29.

Company Company, Concepción. 2006. *Sintaxis histórica de la lengua española: Primera parte: La frase verbal (Vol. 1)*. Mexico, D.F.: Universidad Autónoma de México. Fondo de Cultura Económica.

Corominas, Joan & Antonio Pascual. 1980–1991. *Diccionario crítico español e hispánico*. 6 vols. Madrid: Gredos.

Covarrubias Orozco, Sebastián de. 2001 [1613]. *Suplemento al* Tesoro de la lengua española o castellana. Ed. by Georgina Dopico & Jacques Lezra. Madrid: Polifemo.

Covarrubias Orozco, Sebastián de. 2006 [1611]. *Tesoro de la lengua castellana o española*. Ed. by Ignacio Arellano & Rafael Zafra. Madrid: Centro para la Edición de Clásicos Españoles, Real Academia Española; Frankfurt am Main: Iberoamericana/Vervuert.

Dardano, Maurizio. 1988. "Italienisch: Wortbildungslehre/Formazione delle parole". *Lexikon der Romanistischen Linguistik, V: Italienisch, Korsisch, Sardisch/Italiano, corso, sardo* ed. by Günter Holtus, Michael Metzeltin & Christian Schmitt, 51–63. Tübingen: Max Niemeyer.

Dardel, Robert de. 1999. "Composés rectionnels nominaux nom + nom en protoroman". *Probus* 11.177–208.

Darmesteter, Arsène. 1967 [1884]. *Traité de la formation del mots composés dans la langue française comparée aux autres langues romanes et au latin. Deuxième édition, vue, corrigée, et en partie refondue, avec une préface par Gaston Paris (1894)*. Paris: Librairie Honoré Champion.

Davies, Mark. 2002-. *Corpus del español* (100 million words, 1200s–1900s). Available online at http://www.corpusdelespanol.org

Debrunner, Albert. 1917. *Griechische Wortbildungslehre*. Heidelberg: Carl Winter.

di Sciullo, Anna Maria & Edwin Williams. 1987. *On the Definition of Word*. Cambridge, Mass. & London: MIT Press.

Diez, Friedrich. 1973 [1874]. *Grammaire des langues romanes*. Paris: Franck.

Downing, Pamela. 1977. "On the Creation and Use of English Compound Nouns". *Language* 53.810–842.

Dressler, Wolfgang. 2005. "Compound Types". *The Representation and Processing of Compound Words* ed. by Gary Libben & Gonia Jarema, 38–62. Oxford: Oxford University Press.

Du Cange, Charles du Fresne. 1937 [1883–1887]. *Glossarium mediae et infimae latinitatis*. 10 vols. Paris: Librairie des sciences et des arts.

Dutton, Brian & Joaquín González Cuenca, eds. 1993. *Cancionero de Juan Alfonso de Baena*. Madrid: Visor.

Dworkin, Steven. 1994. "Progress in Medieval Spanish Lexicography". *Romance Philology* 47.406–425.

Eliseu, André & Alina Villalva. 1992. "*Tira-teimas*: entre morfologia e sintaxe". *Actas do VII Encontro da Associação Portuguesa de Linguística*, 16–140. Lisboa: Colibrí Artes Gráficas.

Emonds, Joseph. 1976. *A Transformational Approach to English Syntax: Root, structure-preserving, and local transformations*. New York: Academic Press.

Fabb, Nigel. 1998. "Compounding". *The Handbook of Morphology* ed. by Andrew Spencer & Arnold Zwicky, 66–83. Oxford: Blackwell.

Ferrari-Bridgers, Franca. 2005. "Italian [VN] Compound Nouns: A case for a syntactic approach to word formation". *Romance Languages and Linguistic Theory 2003: Selected papers from Going Romance 2003* ed. by Twan Geerts, Ivo van Ginneken & Haike Jacobs (= *Current Issues in Linguistic Theory*, 270), 63–79. Amsterdam & Philadelphia: John Benjamins.

Fruyt, Michèle. 1990. "La formation des mots par agglutination en latin". *Bulletin de la Société de Linguistique de Paris* 85.173–209.

Fruyt, Michèle. 2002. "Constraints and productivity in Latin nominal compounding." *Transactions of the Philological Society* 100 (3). 259–287.

Fruyt, Michèle. 2005. "Le statut des composés nominaux dans le lexique latin". *La composition et la préverbation en latin* ed. by Claude Moussy, 11–28. Paris: Presses de l'Université Paris-Sorbonne.

Fukui, Naoki & Margaret Speas. 1986. "Specifiers and Projection". *Papers in Theoretical Linguistics* ed. by Naoki Fukui, Tova Rapaport & Elizabeth Sagey, 128–172. Cambridge, Mass.: MIT Working Papers in Linguistics.

García Lozano, Francisco. 1993. "Los compuestos de sustantivo + adjetivo del tipo *pelirrojo*". *La formación de palabras* ed. by Soledad Varela, 205–214. Madrid: Taurus Universitaria.

Giegerich, Heinz 2009. "The English Compound Stress Myth". *Word Structure* 2.1–17.

Giurescu, Anca. 1975. *Les mots composés dans les langues romanes*. The Hague: Mouton.

Gleitman, Lila & Henry Gleitman. 1970. *Phrase and Paraphrase: Some innovative uses of language*. New York: W. W. Norton.

Goodall, Grant. 1983. "A Three-dimensional Analysis of Coordination". *Papers from the Nineteenth Annual Regional Meeting of the Chicago Linguistic Society* ed. by Amy Chukerman, Mitchell Marks & John F. Richardson, 146–154. Chicago: University of Chicago Press.

Gordon Peral, María Dolores. 2003. "Sebastián de Covarrubias ante la diversidad sociolingüística y estilística del español". *Zeitschrift für Romanische Philologie* 119.96–106.

Gràcia, Lluïsa & Olga Fullana. 1999. "On Catalan Verbal Compounds". *Probus* 11.239–261.

Gross, Gaston. 1988. "Degré de figement des noms composés". *Langages* 90.57–72.

Gross, Gaston. 1990a. "Définition des noms composés dans un lexique-grammaire". *Langue Française* 87.84–90.

Gross, Gaston. 1990b. "Les mots composés". *Modèles linguistiques* 12.47–63.

Guerrero Ramos, Gloria. 1995. *El léxico en el Diccionario (1492) y en el Vocabulario (¿1495?) de Nebrija*. Sevilla: Universidad de Sevilla & Ayuntamiento de Lebrija.

Gutiérrez, Juan. 2000. "La segunda edición del *Diccionario de uso* de María Moliner". *Lebende Sprachen* 45.31–36.

Haensch, Gunter. 2004. "Diccionario del español actual". *Lebende Sprachen* 49.92–93.

Hale, Kenneth & Samuel Jay Keyser. 1992. "The Syntactic Character of Thematic Structure". *Thematic Structure: Its role in grammar* ed. by Iggy Roca, 107–143. Berlin: Foris.

Hale, Kenneth & Samuel Jay Keyser. 1993. "On Argument Structure and the Lexical Expression of Syntactic Relations". *The View from Building 20: Essays in linguistics in honor of Sylvain Bromberger* ed. by Kenneth Hale & Samuel Jay Keyser, 53–109. Cambridge, Mass.: MIT Press.

Hale, Kenneth & Samuel Jay Keyser. 1997. "On the Complex Nature of Simple Predicators". *Complex Predicates* ed. by Alex Alsina, Joan Bresnan & Peter Sells, 29–65. Stanford: Center for the Study of Language and Information.

Halle, Morris & Alec Marantz. 1993. "Distributed Morphology and the Pieces of Inflection". *The View from Building 20: Essays in linguistics in honor of Sylvain Bromberger* ed. by Kenneth Hale & Samuel Jay Keyser, 111–176. Cambridge, Mass.: MIT Press.

Harley, Heidi. 2009. "Compounding in Distributed Morphology". Lieber & Štekauer, eds. 2009. 129–144.

Harris, James. 1991. "The Exponence of Gender in Spanish". *Linguistic Inquiry* 22.27–62.

Harris-Northall, Ray, & John Nitti, eds. 2003. *Peter Boyd-Bowman's Léxico hispanoamericano 1493–1993.* New York: Hispanic Seminary of Medieval Studies. CD-Rom.

Hernando Cuadrado, Luis Alberto. 1997. "El *Diccionario de Autoridades (1726–1739)* y su evolución". *Verba* 24.387–401.

Herrera, María Teresa. 1996. *Diccionario español de textos médicos antiguos.* Madrid: Arco Libros.

Higginbotham, James. 1985. "On Semantics". *Linguistic Inquiry* 16.547–593.

Hinojo Andrés, Gregorio. 1988. "Del orden de palabras en castellano medieval". *Actas del I Congreso Internacional de Historia de la Lengua Española* ed. by Manuel Ariza, Antonio Salvador & Antonio Viudas, 435–447. Madrid: Arco Libros.

Hornstein, Norbert, Sarah Rosen & Juan Uriagereka. 1994. "Integrals". *University of Maryland Working Papers in Linguistics* 2.70–90.

Hualde, José Ignacio. 1992. *Catalan.* London & New York: Routledge.

Hualde, José Ignacio. 2006/2007. "Stress Removal and Stress Addition in Spanish". *Journal of Portuguese Linguistics* 5.2/6.1. 59–89.

Jackendoff, Ray. 1977. *X-bar Syntax.* Cambridge, Mass.: MIT Press.

Kasten, Lloyd & Florian Cody. 2001. *Tentative Dictionary of Medieval Spanish.* New York: Hispanic Seminary of Medieval Studies.

Kasten, Lloyd & John Nitti. 2002. *Diccionario de la prosa castellana de Alfonso X el Sabio.* New York: Hispanic Seminary of Medieval Studies.

Kastovsky, Dieter. 2009. "Diachronic Perspectives". Lieber & Štekauer, eds. 2009. 323–340.

Kayne, Richard. 1994. *The Antisymmetry of Syntax.* Cambridge, Mass. & London: MIT Press.

Keniston, Hayward. 1937. *The Syntax of Castilian Prose.* Chicago: University of Chicago Press.

Kiparsky, Paul. 1982a. *Explanation in Phonology.* Dordrecht: Foris.

Kiparsky, Paul. 1982b. "Lexical Morphology and Phonology". *Linguistics in the Morning Calm,* Vol. II ed. by In-Seok Yang, 3–91. Seoul: Hanshin.

Kiparsky, Paul. 2009. "Verbal Co-compounds and Subcompounds in Greek". *Proceedings of the 2007 Workshop on Greek Syntax and Semantics at MIT* ed. by Claire Halpert, Jeremy Hartman & David Hill, 187–195. Cambridge, Mass.: MIT Working Papers in Linguistics.

Klingebiel, Kathryn. 1986. "Les noms composés et la dérivation en français et en provençal: Hommage à Antoine Thomas". *Romania* 107.433–458.

Klingebiel, Kathryn. 1988. "New Compounds from the Old: An unexpected source of verb + noun compounds in Romance". *Proceedings of the 14th Annual Meeting of the Berkeley Linguistics Society – General Session and Parasession on Grammaticalization* ed. by Shelley Axmaker, Annie Jaisser & Helen Singmaster, 88–99. Berkeley: Berkeley Linguistics Society.

Klingebiel, Kathryn. 1989. *Noun + Verb Compounding in Western Romance.* Berkeley & Los Angeles: University of California Press.

Klingebiel, Kathryn. 1994. "Nominal Compounding in the Occitan Dialects: Influences from French (with an inventory of Occitan compound types)". *The Changing Voices of Europe: Social and political changes and their linguistic repercussions, past, present, and future* ed. by Mair Parry, Winifred Davies & Rosalind Temple, 141–153. Cardiff: University of Wales & Modern Humanities Research Association.

Kornfeld, Laura Malena. 2009. "IE, Romance: Spanish". Lieber & Štekauer, eds. 2009. 436–452.

Labov, William. 1965. "On the Mechanism of Linguistic Change". *Report of the Sixteenth Annual Round Table Meeting on Linguistics and Language Studies* ed. by Charles Kreidler, 91–114. Washington, D.C.: Georgetown University Press.

Labov, William. 1972. *Sociolinguistic Patterns*. Philadelphia: University of Pennsylvania Press.

Labov, William. 2001. *Principles of Linguistic Change: Social factors*. Malden, Mass.: Blackwell.

Laka, Itziar. 1994. *On the Syntax of Negation*. New York: Garland.

Lakoff, George. 1990. *Women, Fire, and Dangerous Things*. Chicago: University of Chicago Press.

Lakoff, George & Mark Johnson. 1980. *Metaphors We Live By*. Chicago: University of Chicago Press.

Lang, Mervin. 1990. *Spanish Word Formation: Productive derivational morphology in the modern lexis*. London & New York: Routledge.

Lapesa, Rafael. 1980. *Historia de la lengua española*. Madrid: Gredos.

Lara, Luis Fernando. 1996. *Diccionario del español usual en México*. Mexico, D.F.: Colegio de México.

Larson, Richard & Gabriel Segal. 1995. *Knowledge of Meaning: An introduction to semantic theory*. Cambridge, Mass.: MIT Press.

Larsson, Jenny Helena. 2002. "Nominal Compounds in the Baltic Languages". *Transactions of the Philological Society* 100.203–231.

Lasnik, Howard. 1972. *Analyses of Negation in English*. Ph.D. dissertation, Cambridge, Mass: MIT.

Lasnik, Howard. 1990. *Essays on Restrictiveness and Learnability*. Dordrecht: Kluwer.

Lasnik, Howard. 1999. *Minimalist Analysis*. Malden, Mass.: Blackwell.

Leffel, Katherine. 1988. *Free X-bar Theory and Barriers to Movement and Government*. Ph.D. dissertation, Gainesville, Fla.: University of Florida.

Lehmann, Winfred. 1972. "Contemporary Linguistics and Indo-European Studies". *Publications of the Modern Language Association* 87.976–993.

Levi, Judith. 1978. *The Syntax and Semantics of Complex Nominals*. New York: Academic Press.

Libben, Gary. 2005. "Why Study Compound Processing? An overview of the issues". *The Representation and Processing of Compound Words* ed. by Gary Libben & Gonia Jarema, 1–22. Oxford: Oxford University Press.

Lieber, Rochelle. 1992. "Compounding in English". *Rivista di Linguistica* 4.76–96.

Lieber, Rochelle. 2004. *Morphology and Lexical Semantics*. Cambridge: Cambridge University Press.

Lieber, Rochelle & Pavol Štekauer, eds. 2009. *The Oxford Handbook of Compounding*. Oxford: Oxford University Press.

Lightfoot, David. 1993. *How to Set Parameters: Arguments from language change*. Cambridge, Mass. & London: MIT Press.

Lloyd, Paul. 1968. *Verb-Complement Compounds in Spanish*. Tübingen: Max Niemeyer.

Loi Corvetto, Inés. 1988. "Sardisch: Interne Sprachgeschichte II. Lexik. Evoluzione del lessico". *Lexicon der Romanistischen Linguistik. Italienisch, Korsisch, Sardisch. Italiano, corso, sardo* ed. by Günter Holtus, Michael Metzeltin & Christian Schmitt, 854–867. Tübingen: Max Niemeyer.

Mackenzie, Jean Gilkison. 1984. *A Lexicon of the 14th-Century Aragonese Manuscripts of Juan Fernández de Heredia*. Madison: Hispanic Seminary of Medieval Studies.

Mallinson, Graham. 1986. *Rumanian*. Dover, N.H.: Croom Helm.

Marchand, Hans. 1966. *The Categories and Types of Present-day English Word-formation: A synchronic-diachronic approach*. Tuscaloosa, Ala.: University of Alabama Press.

Marouzeau, Jules. 1953. *L'ordre des mots en latin. Volume complémentaire*. Paris: Éditions "Les Belles Lettres".

Martinell Gifre, Emma. 1984. "De la complementación a la composición en el sintagma nominal". *Revista Española de Lingüística* 14.223–244.

Mascaró, Joan. 1986. *Morfología*. Barcelona: Biblioteca Universitària. Enciclopèdia Catalana.

Menéndez Pidal, Ramón, Rafael Lapesa, Manuel Seco & Constantino García. 2003. *Léxico hispánico primitivo (siglos VIII al XII)*. Madrid: Espasa Calpe.

Meyer-Lübke, Wilhelm. 1923 [1895]. *Grammaire des langues romanes*. Leipzig: Stechert.

Micronet. 1992. *ADMYTE: Archivo Digital de Manuscritos y Textos Españoles*. Madrid: Micronet.

Miller, D. Gary. 1993. *Complex Verb Formation* (= *Current Issues in Linguistic Theory*, 95). Amsterdam & Philadelphia: John Benjamins.

Moliner, María. 1998. *Diccionario de uso del español*. Madrid: Gredos.

Mondini, Sara, Gonia Jarema, Claudio Luzzatti, Cristina Burani & Carlo Semenza. 2002. "Why is 'Red Cross' Different from 'Yellow Cross'? A Neuropsychological Study of Noun-Adjective Agreement within Italian Compounds". *Brain and Language* 81.621–634.

Mondini, Sara, Claudio Luzzatti, Paola Saletta, Nadia Allamano & Carlo Semenza. 2005. "Mental Representation of Prepositional Compounds: Evidence from Italian agrammatic patients". *Brain and Language* 94.178–187.

Mondini, Sara, Claudio Luzzatti, Giusy Zonca, Caterina Pistarini & Carlo Semenza. 2004. "The Mental Representation of Verb-Noun Compounds in Italian: Evidence from a multiple single-case study in aphasia". *Brain and Language* 90.470–477.

Moyna, María Irene. 2004. "Can We Make Head or Tail of Spanish Endocentric Compounds?" *Linguistics* 42.617–37.

Müller, Bodo. 1987–. *Diccionario del español medieval*. Heidelberg: Carl Winter.

Munthe, Ake. 1889. "Observations sur les composés espagnols du type *aliabierto*". *Recueil de mémoires philologiques présenté à M. Gaston Paris par ses élèves suédois le 9 août à l'occasion de son cinquantième anniversaire*, 31–56. Stockholm: Imprimerie centrale.

Muromatsu, Keiko. 1995. "The Classifier as a Primitive: Individuation, referability, and argumenthood". *University of Maryland Working Papers in Linguistics* 3.144–180.

Muromatsu, Keiko. 1998. *On the Syntax of Classifiers*. Ph.D. dissertation, College Park, Md.: University of Maryland.

Murphy, Victoria & Elena Nicoladis. 2006. "When Answer-phone Makes a Difference in Children's Acquisition of English Compounds". *Journal of Child Language* 33.677–691.

Muysken, Pieter. 1982. "Parametrizing the Notion 'Head'". *Journal of Linguistic Research* 2.57–75.

Nebrija, Antonio de. 1973 [1495?]. *Vocabulario romance en latín. Transcripción crítica de la edición revisada por el autor (Sevilla, 1516)*. Ed. by Gerald J. MacDonald. Philadelphia: Temple University Press.

Nicholas, Nick & Brian Joseph. 2009. "Verbal Dvandvas in Modern Greek". *Proceedings of the 2007 Workshop on Greek Syntax and Semantics at MIT* ed. by Claire Halpert, Jeremy Hartman, & David Hill, 171–185. Cambridge, Mass.: MIT Working Papers in Linguistics.

Nicoladis, Elena. 2007. "Acquisition of Deverbal Compounds by French-speaking Preschoolers". *The Mental Lexicon* 2.79–102.

Nieto Jiménez, Lidio & Manuel Alvar Ezquerra. 2007. *Nuevo tesoro lexicográfico del español (s. XIV-1726)*. Madrid: Arco Libros.

Núñez Cedeño, Rafael. 1992. "Headship Assignment in Spanish Compounds". *Theoretical Analyses in Romance Linguistics* ed. by Christiane Laeufer & Terrell A. Morgan (= *Current Issues in Linguistic Theory*, 74), 131–149. Amsterdam & Philadelphia: John Benjamins.

Oirsouw, Robert van. 1987. *The Syntax of Coordination*. London: Croom Helm.

Olsen, Birgit Anette. 2002. "Thoughts on Indo-European Compounds Inspired by a Look at Armenian". *Transactions of the Philological Society* 100.233–257.

Olsen, Susan. 2001. "Copulative Compounds: A closer look at the interface between syntax and morphology". *Yearbook of Morphology 2000* ed. by Gert Booij & Jaap van Marle, 279–320. Dordrecht: Kluwer.

O'Neill, John. 1997. *A Dictionary of the Spanish Contained in the Works of Antonio de Nebrija*. Ph.D. dissertation, Madison: University of Wisconsin.

O'Neill, John. 1999. *Electronic Texts and Concordances of the Madison Corpus of Early Spanish Manuscripts and Printings*. Madison: Hispanic Seminary of Medieval Studies.

Oniga, Renato. 1992. "Compounding in Latin". *Rivista di Linguistica* 4.97–116.

Penny, Ralph. 1991. *A History of the Spanish Language*. Cambridge: Cambridge University Press.

Pesetzky, David. 1996. *Zero Syntax: Experiencers and cascades*. Cambridge, Mass.: MIT Press.

Pharies, David. 1986. *Structure and Analogy in the Playful Lexicon of Spanish*. Tübingen: Max Niemeyer.

Picone, Michael. 1996. *Anglicisms, Neologisms and Dynamic French*. Amsterdam & Philadelphia: John Benjamins.

Piñeros, Carlos Eduardo. 1998. *Prosodic Morphology in Spanish: Constraint interaction in word formation*. Ph.D. dissertation, Columbus, Ohio: Ohio State University.

Plag, Ingo, Gero Kunter, Sabine Lappe & Maria Braun. 2008. "The Role of Semantics, Argument Structure, and Lexicalization in Compound Stress Assignment in English". *Language* 84.760–794.

Pollock, Jean-Yves. 1989. "Verb Movement, Universal Grammar, and the Structure of IP". *Linguistic Inquiry* 20.365–424.

Pustejovsky, James. 1995. *The Generative Lexicon*. Cambridge, Mass.: MIT Press.

Rainer, Franz. 1993. *Spanische Wortbildungslehre*. Tübingen: Max Niemeyer.

Rainer, Franz. & Soledad Varela. 1992. "Compounding in Spanish". *Rivista di Linguistica* 4.117–142.

Ralli, Angela. 2009. "Modern Greek V V Dvandva Compounds: A linguistic innovation in the history of the Indo-European languages". *Word Structure* 2.48–68.

Real Academia Española. 1884. *Diccionario de la lengua castellana por la Real Academia Española*. Madrid: Imprenta de D. Gregorio Hernando.

Real Academia Española. 1960–. *Diccionario histórico de la lengua española*. Madrid: Real Academia Española.

Real Academia Española. 1979 [1726–1739] *Diccionario de autoridades*. Madrid: Gredos.

Real Academia Española. 1986. *Esbozo de una nueva gramática de la lengua española*. Madrid: Espasa Calpe.

Real Academia Española. 1992. *Diccionario de la lengua española*. Madrid: Espasa Calpe.

Real Academia Española. 2001–. *Nuevo Tesoro lexicográfico de la lengua española*. Online version available at http://buscon.rae.es/ntlle/SrvltGUILoginNtlle

Real Academia Española. [2006–2010]. *Banco de datos (CORDE) Corpus diacrónico del español*. Available at http://www.rae.es

Real Academia Española [2006-2010]. *Banco de datos (CREA) Corpus de referencia del español actual*. Available at http:///www.rae.es

Roeper, Thomas, & Muffy Siegel. 1978. "A Lexical Transformation for Verbal Compounds". *Linguistic Inquiry* 9.199–260.

Roeper, Thomas, William Snyder & Kazuko Hiramatsu. 2003. *Learnability in a Minimalist Framework: Root compounds, merger, and the syntax-morphology interface.* Amherst, Mass.: University of Massachusetts. Unpublished manuscript.

Ruhstaller, Stefan. 2004. "Sobre la génesis del diccionario académico. Las Ordenanzas de Sevilla como fuente de material léxico en el *Diccionario de Autoridades*". *Zeitschrift für Romanische Philologie* 120.106–127.

Sánchez Méndez, Juan. 2009. "La formación de las palabras por composición desde un punto de vista histórico". *Revista de Filología Española* 86.103–127.

Saint-Dizier, Patrick. 2006. *Syntax and Semantics of Prepositions.* Dordrecht: Springer.

Scalise, Sergio. 1992. "Compounding in Italian". *Rivista di Linguistica* 4.175–199.

Schwyzer, Eduard. 1953 [1938]. *Griechische Grammatik.* München: C. H. Beck.

Seco, Manuel, Olimpia Andés & Gabino Ramos. 1999. *Diccionario del español actual.* Madrid: Aguilar.

Senghas, Ann. 1995. "The Development of Nicaraguan Sign Language via the Language Acquisition Process". *BUCLD 19: Proceedings of the 19th Annual Boston University Conference on Language Development* ed. by Dawn MacLaughlin & Susan McEwen, 543–552. Somerville, Mass.: Cascadilla Press.

Senghas, Ann & Marie Coppola. 2001. "Children Creating Language: How Nicaraguan Sign Language acquired a spatial grammar". *Psychological Science* 12.323–328.

Spence, Nicol Christopher. 1980. "The Gender of French Compounds". *Zeitschrift für Romanische Philologie* 96.68–91.

Spencer, Andrew. 1991. *Morphological Theory. An introduction to word structure in generative grammar.* Oxford & Cambridge, Mass.: Blackwell.

Spitzer, Leo. 1951. "Sur quelques emplois métaphoriques de l'impératif. Part 2". *Romania* 73.16–63.

Stowell, Timothy. 1991. "Determiners in NP and DP". *Views on Phrase Structure* ed. by Katherine Leffel & Denis Bouchard, 37–56. Dordrecht: Kluwer.

Stump, Gregory. 1998. "Inflection". *The Handbook of Morphology* ed. by Andrew Spencer & Arnold Zwicky, 13–43. Oxford: Blackwell.

ten Hacken, Pius. 1994. *Defining Morphology: A principled approach to determining the boundaries of compounding, derivation, and inflection.* Hildesheim & Zürich: Georg Olms.

Toman, Jindřich. 1998. "Word Syntax". *The Handbook of Morphology* ed. by Andrew Spencer & Arnold Zwicky, 306–321. Oxford: Blackwell.

Tuggy, David. 2003. "*Abrelatas* and *Scarecrow* Nouns: Exocentric verb-noun compounds as illustrations of basic principles of cognitive grammar". *International Journal of English Studies* 3.25–61.

Uriagereka, Juan. 1988. *On Government.* Ph.D. dissertation, Storrs, Ct.: University of Connecticut.

Uriagereka, Juan. 2008. *Syntactic Anchors: On semantic structuring.* Cambridge: Cambridge University Press.

Val Álvaro, José Francisco. 1999. "La composición". *Gramática descriptiva de la lengua española* ed. by Ignacio Bosque & Violeta Demonte, 4757–4841. Madrid: Espasa.

Vendler, Zeno. 1967. *Linguistics in Philosophy.* Ithaca, NY: Cornell University Press.

Vennemann, Theo. 1974. "Topics, Subjects, and Word Order: From SXV to SVX via TVX". *Historical Linguistics: Proceedings of the First International Congress of Historical Linguistics, Edinburgh, September 1973* ed. by John Anderson & Charles Jones, vol. I, 339–376. Amsterdam: North-Holland.

Villalva, Alina. 1992. "Compounding in Portuguese". *Rivista di Linguistica* 4.201–219.

Vogel, Irene & Donna Jo Napoli. 1992. "The Verbal Component in Italian Compounds". *Proceedings of the 22nd Linguistic Symposium on Romance Languages* ed. by Jon Amastae, Grant Goodall, Mario Montalbetti & Marianne Phinney (= *Current Issues in Linguistic Theory*, 123), 367–381. Amsterdam & Philadelphia: John Benjamins.

Vries, Mark de. 2005. "Coordination and Syntactic Hierarchy". *Studia Linguistica* 59.83–105.

Wälchli, Bernhard. 2005. *Co-compounds and Natural Coordination*. Oxford & New York: Oxford University Press.

Whitney, William Dwight. 1941 [1879]. *Sanskrit Grammar: Including both the classical language, and the older dialects of Veda and Brahmana*. Cambridge, Mass.: Harvard University Press.

Williams, Edwin. 1981. "On the Notions 'Lexically Related' and 'Head of a Word'". *Linguistic Inquiry* 12.245–274.

Wright, Roger. 1999. "Periodization and How to Avoid It". *Essays in Hispanic Linguistics Dedicated to Paul M. Lloyd* ed. by Robert Blake, Diana Ranson & Roger Wright, 25–41. Newark, Dela.: Juan de la Cuesta.

Zacarías Ponce de León, Ramón F. 2009. "Posesión inalienable en los compuestos N + i + A del tipo *pelirrojo*". *Lingüística* 21.1–19.

Zagona, Karen. 1990. "*Mente* Adverbs, Compound Interpretation and the Projection Principle". *Probus* 2.1–30.

Zwanenburg, Wiecher. 1990a. "Compounding and Inflection". *Contemporary Morphology: Selected papers from the 3rd International Morphology Meeting held under auspices of the International Association of Morphology, in Krems, Austria, 4–7 July 1988* ed. by Wolfgang U. Dressler, Hans Christian Luschützky, Oskar Pfeiffer & John Rennison, 133–138. Berlin: Mouton de Gruyter.

Zwanenburg, Wiecher. 1990b. "Französisch: Wortbildungslehre. Formation des mots". *Lexikon der Romanistischen Linguistik. Französisch/Le français* ed. by Günter Holtus, Michael Metzelin & Christian Schmitt, 72–77. Tübingen: Max Niemeyer.

Zwanenburg, Wiecher. 1992. "Compounding in French". *Rivista di Linguistica* 4.221–240.

Zwicky, Arnold M. 1985. "Heads". *Journal of Linguistics* 21.1–29.

Compound dataset

This appendix includes the complete dataset of compounds found in the lexicographical sources. Compound classes are presented in the order in which they appear in the book, identified first by chapter, and then by the specific pattern they represent. Within each pattern, they are classified chronologically by century, and then alphabetically. Compounds were alphabetized as if they were spelled in one word and any word separation was ignored.

Organization of dataset

In the column entitled "Compound," lexemes appear in the spelling that best represents their compounded status; if a compound appears sometimes as one word and sometimes as two, the former spelling is preferred. In general, the contemporary spelling is chosen, with the exception of compounds only attested in historical texts, in which case the original orthography is retained. Spelling variants are included if they involve more than alternative orthographies for the same sound.

The column entitled "Earliest form," presents the first form attested, in its original spelling and accompanied by any inflection marks. By default, earliest forms are from the CORDE/CREA databases; if the first attestation comes from a lexicographical source, then an abbreviation appears between brackets next to the form. Only forms that can be interpreted as compounds are counted, so that if a sequence of two lexemes in CORDE/CREA is identical to a compound but does not have the appropriate meaning and/or formal features, it is discarded for the purposes of dating the earliest form.

The column entitled "Source" presents the complete list of sources where the compound was found, in chronological order of publication.

Finally, the columns entitled "First attestation" and "Last attestation" present the earliest and latest dates for which there is textual evidence of the compound. The first attestation is the earliest one regardless of source (lexicographical or textual), whereas to ascertain the last attestation, only the CORDE/CREA databases or those dictionaries that are exclusively based on actual data (e.g., Seco et al. 1999) are taken into consideration. Given the tendency of some dictionaries to include in their wordlists items no longer in use, those dictionaries are not considered unless they are the only ones where a compound is attested.

Chapter 4

[Adv + V]$_V$

Century	Compound	Earliest form	Sources	First att.	Last att.
1000–1100					
	bienhacer	bien fer (LHP)	LHP, A, AD, K&N, N	1085–1109	1989
	malhacer	mal fazer	A	1155	2000
1200					
	bendecir	bendezir	A, K&N, N, Au, DRAE, M	c. 1200	2004
	bienestar	bienestar	T, DRAE, M, S	1240–1250	2004
	bienvivir	bien vivir	DRAE, M	1293	1998
	malbaratar	malbaratallo	A, Au, DRAE, M, S	1251	1965
	maldecir	maldezir	A, K&N, N, C, Au, DRAE, M, S	c. 1200	2004
	malestar	malestar	N, DRAE, M, S	1228–1246	2004
	malfaçar	malfaçaron	T	c. 1250	c. 1250
	mallevar	malleuamos	T	1212	ad 1530
	malmeter	malmeter	A, K&N, Au, DRAE, M, S	1213	1992
	malparar	mal parar	A, K&N, Au, DRAE, M, S	c. 1280	1957
	malpensar	mal pensar	S	ad 1284	2004
	malquerer	mal querer	A, K&N, N, Au, DRAE, M, S	1293	1973
	maltraer	maltraer	A, K&N, Au, DRAE, M, S	c. 1236	1963
	menoscabar	menoscabar	T, K&N, C, Au, DRAE, M, S	c. 1236	2004
	menospreciar	menospretiar	A, K&N, N, C, AU, DRAE, M, S	c. 1250	2004
	menosvaler	menosvaler	Au	c. 1250	2002
1300					
	bienquerer	bien querer	K&N, N, DRAE, M, S	1327–1332	1974
	malandar	malandar	M, S	1330–1343	1984
	malcasar	mal casar	DRAE, M, S	1330–1343	1982
	malcomer	mal comer	DRAE, M, S	1379–1384	1956
	malentender	malentender	M, S	1378–1406	1970
	malpagar	malpagar	A, S	1330–1342	1967

Century	Compound	Earliest form	Sources	First att.	Last att.
	malrotar	marrotar	A, K&N, Au, DRAE, M	1386	1958
	maltratar	mal tratar	C, Au, DRAE, M, S	1300–1305	2004
	maltrobar	mal trobe	A	1385	1481–1497
1400					
	bienaventurar	bienaventurar	A, K&N, DRAE, M	1456	1456
	malherir	maherir	A, N, DRAE, M, S	1450–1491	1979
	malcriar	mal criar	M, S	1493	2004
	maldormir	mal dormir	A, S	1470–1492	2003
	malhablar	mal hablar	S	1424–1520	1980
	malinterpretar	mal interpretar	M, S	1440–1455	2001
	malparir	mal parir	Au, DRAE, M, S	ad 1492	1972
	malpasar	mal pasar	A	1427–1427	1999
	malsonar	mal sonar	DRAE, M, S	1498	1977
	malvestir	mal vestir	S	c. 1430	1968
	malvivir	mal vivir	M, S	1411–1412	2004
1500					
	bienparar	bien parar	A	1541	1541
	bienquistar(se)	bienquistar	DRAE, M, S	1597–1645	1987
	malcreer	mal creer	DRAE, M	1528	1998
	malemplear	mal emplear	M	1535–1552	1998
	malgastar	malgastar	Au, DRAE, M, S	1517	2004
	malmirar	mal mirar	S	1543	1975
	malograr(se)	malograrte	C, Au, DRAE, M, S	c. 1550–1606	2004
	malquistar(se)	malquistar	A, Au, DRAE, M, S	1597–1645	1974
	malsinar	malsinar	T, Au, DRAE	1528	1921
1600					
	malvender	malvender	DRAE, M, S	1600	2002
1700					
	malversar	malversar	DRAE, M, S	1768	2004
1800					
	justipreciar	justipreciar (TL)	M	1803	2004
1900					
	malacostumbrar	malacostumbrar (TL)	M, S	1984	1979

Century	Compound	Earliest form	Sources	First att.	Last att.
	malcrecer	malcrecer (S)	S	1999	1980
	maleducar	se maleducaban	M, S	1972	2004
	malhumorar	malhumorar	M, S	1999	1991
	malperder	malperder (S)	S	1999	1990

[Adv + A]$_A$

Century	Compound	Earliest form	Sources	First att.	Last att.
1000–1100					
	malhechor	malfechor	K&N, S	1097	2004
	malcalzado	malcalçados	A	c. 1140	1990
	malfecha	malfecha	A	c. 1196	1483
	malherido	mal ferido	A, Au	c. 1140	2004
	menoscabado	menoscabada	T, Au, M	c. 1196	2004
1200					
	bendito	bendichos	A, K&N, N, Au, M	c. 1200	2004
	bienamado	bien amado	A, S	1240–51	2003
	bienandante	bienandante	A, K&N, Au, M	1240–1272	1924–1957
	bienapreso	bien apreso	T	c. 1236	1471–76
	bienaventurado	bienaventurada	A, K&N, N, Au, M, S	c. 1215	2004
	biencasado	bien casado	M, S	c. 1250	2000
	biencriado	bien criado	A, C	c. 1275	2003
	bien facero	bien facero	T	1246–1252	1246–1252
	bienfecho	bienfecho	A, AD, M	c. 1240	ad 1600
	bien formado	bien formado	S	c. 1255	2004
	bienfortunado	bien fortunada	M	c. 1250	1940–1947
	bien gent	bien e gent	T	1236	1246–1252
	bienhablado	bien fablado	K&N, N, M, S	1254–61	2001
	bienhablante	bienfablantes	T, K&N	1254–1260	1605
	bienhadado	bien fadada	Au, M, S	c. 1215	1996
	bienhechor	bienfechor	S	1240–1272	2003
	bienjustiçiero	bienjustiçiero	T	c. 1252–1270	c. 1252–1270
	bienmandado	bien mandado	M, S	1240–1250	2002
	bienoliente	bien olientes	A, K&N, M, S	1246–1252	2004

Century	Compound	Earliest form	Sources	First att.	Last att.
	bien parado	bien parado	A	1246–1252	2002
	bien parecido	bien parecida	S	c. 1277	2004
	bienquerencioso	bien querenciosa	T, K&N	c. 1275	c. 1275
	bienqueriente	bienquerientes	T, K&N, M	c. 1236	1874
	bienquisto	bienquisto	A, K&N, N, M, S	1246–1252	2001
	biensonante	bien sonantes	M, S	c. 1255	2002
	bienvenido	bien venida	A, K&N, M, S	c. 1236	1973
	bienventurado	bienventurados	T	1228–1246	1600
	bienvisto	bien visto	A, T	1277	1997
	malaconsejado	mal aconsejado	M	1230	1921
	malacostum- brado	mal acostum- brado	Au, M	1250–1300	2004
	malandante	mal andante	A, K&N, M, S	c. 1200	1905
	malapreso	malapreso	A	1228–1246	1435
	malastrado	malastrado	A	1260	1260
	malastrugado	malastrugada	T	1236–46	1246–1253
	malavenido	mal abenidos	Au, M	1270–1284	2002
	malaventurado	malabenturado	A, K&N, Au, C, M, S	c. 1235	2000
	malcasado	mal casado	Au, M, S	c. 1240	2003
	malcreyente	mal creyente	T	c. 1270	1880–1881
	malcriado	mal criadas	A, Au, C, M, S	c. 1275	2004
	maldiciente	maldizientes	A, K&N, N, C, Au, M, S	c. 1240– 1270	2003
	maldigno	maldignos	A	c. 1236– 1246	1550
	maldito (maldicha)	maldicho	A, K&N, C, S	c. 1200	1975
	mal dolado	mal dolado	A	c. 1275	1596
	maldoliente	mal dolient	A	c. 1270	1651
	mal domado	mal domados	CS	1240–1250	c. 1910
	malentendido	mal entendida	M, S	1228–1246	2004
	malfamado	mal famado	K&N, S	1284	2003
	malfecho	malfecho	A, N, Au, M	1223	1952
	malhadado	malfadados	A, K&N, Au, M, S	1236–1246	2004
	malhetrero	mal fetrero	T, K&N	1254–1260	1254–1260

Century	Compound	Earliest form	Sources	First att.	Last att.
	mal infamado	mal enfamado	K&N	1256	2001
	malmandado	mal mandado	C, Au, M, S	c. 1250	1936
	malparado	mal parada	T, Au, M	1240–1250	2004
	malquerido	malquerudo	T, Au	c. 1280	2003
	malqueriente	malquerientes	A, K&N, N, Au, M	c. 1200	2002
	malquerio	malquerio	T, K&N	c. 1275	c. 1275
	malquisto	mal quista	A, N, C, Au, M, S	1240–1250	2003
	mal razonado	mal razonado	K&N	c. 1240–1250	1895
	maltraedor	maltraedor	K&N	c. 1270	1337–1348
	maltraído	mal traído	T, M	c. 1236	1965–1971
	maltratado	mal tratada	Au	1293	2004
	maltrecho	maltrecho	A, AD, M, S	c. 1223	2004
	menospreciado	menospreciada	T, CS, Au	c. 1250	2004
1300					
	bien inclinado	bien inclinada	Au	1379–1426	1945
	bien pensado	bien pensados	S	1378–1406	2004
	bien tratado	bien tratada	C	1348–1379	2002
	bienfaciente	bienfazientes	T, K&N	1330–1343	1922
	bienfamado	bien famado	A, K&N, M, S	1378–1406	1982
	bienmereciente	bien meresciente	A	1382	1872
	bienvista	bienbista	M	c. 1300	c. 1300
	malbaratado	mal baratada	Au	c. 1350	2004
	malcocinado	mal cozinado	C, M	1300–1305	2002
	malcontento	mal contentos	A, Au, C, M, S	1379–1391	2001
	maldormidor	mal dormidor	S	1334–1340	1987
	malganado	malganado	T	c. 1370	1642–1643
	malhablado	malfablado	K&N, M, S	1300–1305	2003
	malnacido	mal nazido	S	c. 1300	2004
	malpensado	mal pensada	M, S	1378–1406	2003
	malsabido (malsabidillo)	malsabida	A	1330–1343	1938
	malsano	malsano	AD, C, M, S	1380–1385	2004
	menospreciable	menospreçiable	M, S	1376–1396	1926
	menospreciador	menospreçiador	S	1376–1397	1994

Century	Compound	Earliest form	Sources	First att.	Last att.
	menospreciante	menospreçiantes	M	1385	1968
	siempreviva	siemprebiua	AD, N, C, Au, M, S	c. 1381–1418	1999
1400					
	bendiciente	bendizientes	Au, DRAE	c. 1400	1949–1967
	bien acondicionado	bien acondicionado	Au	c. 1430	2003
	bien tallado	bien tallada	Au	c. 1400–1440	2004
	bienaparente	bien aparente	A	1430–1440	1978
	bienestante	bien estante	S	ad 1435	1995
	biengranado	bien granados	Au, M, S	1420	1996
	bienhallado	bien fallada	M	c. 1414	1962
	bienhecho	bienhecho	N	c. 1430	1991
	mal considerado	mal considerado	M	c. 1453	2004
	malacondicionado	mal acondicionada	Au	c. 1480	2001
	malagradecido	malagradecido	M	1430	2004
	malcomido	mal comidos	Au, M, S	1471–1476	1989
	maldecido	maldecidos	Au, M	1477–96	2004
	maldispuesto	mal dispuesta	M	1411–1412	1974
	maledicente	malediziente	S	1490	2000
	malencarado	mal encarados	S	1454–1501	2002
	malinclinado	mal inclinado	C, Au	1452	1965
	malmaridada	mal maridada	M, S	1407–1463	2002
	malmirado	mal mirado	Au, M, S	1424–1520	1988
	malogrado	malogrado	Au, C, S	1497	2004
	maloliente	mal oliente	M, S	1411–1412	2004
	malparido	mal parida	Au, M, S	1495	2004
	malpegado	mal pegado	A	c. 1499–1502	2004
	malsufrido	mal sufridas	C, M	1481–1496	1980
	malviviente	malbivientes	M	1427–1428	2004
	plenisonante	plenisonante	A	1423	1427–1428
1500					
	bien agestado	bien agestados	Au	1544	2002
	bien parido	bien parida	S	c. 1541–1550	2001

Century	Compound	Earliest form	Sources	First att.	Last att.
	bienintencio-nado	bienintenciona-dos	C, M, S	1535–1622	1970
	biennacido	bien nacida	S	1532	2004
	malagestado	mal agestado	Au	1549–1603	1997
	malcarado	malcarado	M, S	1561	2003
	malconten-tadizo	mal conten-tadiços	M	1521–1543	1972
	malintencio-nado	malintencionada	C, M, S	1535–1575	2002
	malquistado	malquistado	Au	1549–1603	1987
	malsonante	mal sonantes	Au, M, S	1527–1561	2004
1600					
	mal parecido	mal parecido	S	1615	2001
	malhumorado	malhumorada	M, S	1646	2004
1700					
	bienhumorado	bien humorado	M, S	1725	1967
	malbaratador	malbaratador	S	c. 1750	1974–75
	maleducado	mal educada	M, S	1781	2004
	malversador	malversador	S	1791	2000
1800					
	malfachado	mal fachada	S	1844	1957
	malgenioso	malgenios	M, S	1896	2002
	malnutrido	mal nutridos	S	1881	2002
	menosprecia-tivo	menospreciativo	DRAE, M, S	1884	2001
1900					
	biempensante	bien pensantes	S	1923–1974	2002
	maldecible	maldecible	S	1909	1975
	maldurmiente	maldurmiente	S	1970	1970
	malgastador	malgastador	S	1928	2004
	malgeniado	malgeniados	M, S	1908–1930	2002
	siempretieso	siempretieso	M	1916	2002

[Adv + N]$_N$

Century	Compound	Earliest form	Sources	First att.	Last att.
1000–1100					
	bendición	benedictione	LHP, A, K&N, N, C, Au	867–1043	2004
	behetría	benefectria	LHP, T	1072	2002
	beneficio	beneficio	LHP, T	1041	2004
	mafechura	mafechura	P	1156	1276
	malhechor	malfechor	A, AD, ON, C, Au, DRAE, M	c. 1129	1973
	malquerencia	malquerencia	A, K&N, N, Au, DRAE, M, S	ad 1141–1235	2002
	menoscabo	menoscabo	A, K&N, N, C, Au, DRAE, M, S	c. 1150	1975
	menosprecio	menosprez	A, AD, N, C, Au, DRAE, M, S	c. 1196	1974
1200					
	bienandanza	bien andança	A, K&N, Au, DRAE, M, S	c. 1240–1272	1998
	bienaventuranza	bienauenturança	A, K&N, N, C, Au, DRAE, M, S	ad 1260	2003
	bienestança	bienestança	A, K&N	1240–1250	1491
	bienhechor	bienfechor	A, Au, N, DRAE, M	1240–1272	2003
	bien parança	bien parança	A, K&N	1270–1284	1270–1284
	bienquerencia	bienquerencia	T, A, K&N, N, Au, DRAE, M	1236	1997
	malandanza	malandanza	T, A, K&N, DRAE, M, S	c. 1236–1246	1997
	malavenimiento	malauenimiento	A	c. 1275	1471–1476
	maldecidor	maldezidores	K&N, A, ON, DRAE, M	1256–1263	1984
	maldecimiento	maldezimiento	T, K&N, ON, Au, DRAE	1270	1931
	maldición	maldicion	K&N, A, N, Au, DRAE, M	c. 1200	2004
	malestanza	malestança	A, K&N, DRAE, M	1236–1246	1570–1579
	malfetría	malfetría	LHP, K&N, T	1246–1252	1500
	malqueria	malqueria	T	c. 1280	c. 1280
	malsín	malsin	T, N, C, Au	1273	2003

Century	Compound	Earliest form	Sources	First att.	Last att.
	maltraedor	maltraedor	A, DRAE	c. 1270	1337–1348
	maltraimiento	maltraymientos	K&N, A	1270–1284	ad 1300
	menospre-ciamiento	menospre-tiamiento	T, DRAE, M	c. 1250	1570–1579
1300					
	maltratamiento	maltratamiento	Au, DRAE	1376 –1396	2003
	menospreciador	menospreçiador	ON, Au, DRAE, M	1376	1994
1400					
	bendecidor	bendezidores	DRAE, M	c. 1400	1948
	bienvenida	bienvenida	DRAE, M, S	c. 1430	2004
	malbarato	mal barato	M	ad 1430	1963
	malentrada	malentrada	DRAE, M	1476	ad 1480
1500					
	maledicencia	maledicencia	Au	1538–1589	2004
	malogro	malogro	Au, DRAE, M, S	1585–ad 1643	1999
	menoscabador	menoscabador	Au, DRAE, M	1554	1990
	menoscaba-miento	menoscaba-miento	T	ad 1500	1500
1600					
	malogramiento	malogramiento	M	1604	1941
1700					
	bienfechoría	bienfechoría	A, Au, M	1770	1992
	cercandanza	cercandanza	A, DRAE	1729	1992
	malversación	malversaciones	DRAE, M, S	c. 1750	2004
1800					
	malcriadeza	malcriadeza	M	1896	1935–1936
	malparanza	malparanza (TL)	DRAE, M	1803	1992
	malsonancia	malsonancia	S	1898	2001
1900					
	malba-ratamiento	malba-ratamiento	M, S	1928	1929
	malcriadez	malcriadez	M	1954	1954
	malrotador	malrotador	M	1918–1932	1918–1932

Chapter 5

[N + V]$_V$

Century	Compound	Earliest form	Sources	First att.	Last att.
1000–1100					
	cabtener	captenere	A, T, DRAE, M	c. 1020–1076	ad 1500
	mantener	manteneant	LHP, A, AD, K&N, C, DRAE, M, S	1095	2004
	manutener	manutenebimus	DRAE, M	1113	1690
1200					
	caboponer	caboposieron	T	c. 1252–1270	c. 1252–1270
	caboprender	caboprender	A	c. 1252–1270	1360
	fazferir, zaherir	fazerir	A	ad 1250	2002
	mamparar	manparar	A, K&N, DRAE	1240–1250	1981
	mancomunar	mancomunauan	M, S	1266	2001
	manlevar	manleuando	A, K&N, DRAE, M	1247	1495
	salpicar	salpicarle	C, M	c. 1275	2004
1400					
	manferir	manferir	DRAE	1438	c. 1594
1500					
	maniatar	maniatan	C, M, S	1527–1550	2004
	pelechar	pelechan	C, M, S	1513	1966
	perniquebrar	perniquebró	C, DRAE, M, S	ad 1536–1538	1965
	pintiparar	pintipara	DRAE	1597–1645	1821
	salpresar	salpresar	A, DRAE, M, S	1589	1976
1600					
	aliquebrar	aliquebrar	DRAE, S	1654	1981
	cabizbajar	cabizbajándose	Au	1605	1605
	mancornar	mancornasen	DRAE, M, S	1673	2000
	salpimentar	salpimentar	S	1611	2004
1700					
	calosfriarse	calosfriarse (TL)	M	1780	1992
	maniobrar	maniobrar	DRAE, M, S	1731	2004
	manuscribir	manuscriben	M	1787–1788	2002

Century	Compound	Earliest form	Sources	First att.	Last att.
1800					
	alicortar	alicortar	S	1851	1981
	capialzar	capialzar (TL)	DRAE, M	1884	1992
	mampostear	mampostear (TL)	DRAE, M	1803	1992
	mampresar	mampresar (TL)	DRAE, M	1803	1992
	rabiatar	rabiatar (TL)	M	1803	1938
1900					
	capitidisminuir	capitidisminuir	S	1966	2004
	cojitranquear	cojitranquear (S)	S	1968	1968
	fotocopiar	fotocopiar	M, S	1912	2002
	helitransportar	helitransportar (S)	S	1992	1992
	machihembrar	machihembrar	M	1941–ad 1961	1995
	manicurar	manicurarse	S	1972	1972
	mantornar	mantornar (TL)	M	1914	1992
	radiodifundir	radiodifundir	M, S	1970	1995
	radiotelevisar	radiotelevisar (S)	S	1970	1970

Integral $[N + A]_A$

Century	Compound	Earliest form	Sources	First att.	Last att.
1000–1100					
	sanguinemixto	sanguinemixto (LHP)	LHP	1056	1056
1200					
	barbapuniente (cf. barbipo-niente)	barvaponiente	A	1240–1250	1240–1250
	barbirrapado	barbirrapado	M	c. 1280	1540–1579
	bocabierto	bocabierto	A, K&N	1240–1249	1500
	bocarroto	bocarroto	A	1246–1252	1246–1252
	boquimuelle	boquimuelle	A, Au, DRAE, M	c. 1275	1872
	racorto (cf. rabicorto)	racortos	K&N	1250	1250
	rostrituerto	rostrituertas	C, Au, DRAE, M	1240–1250	1893
	testerido	tiestherido	T	1246 –1252	1246–1252

Century	Compound	Earliest form	Sources	First att.	Last att.
1300					
	barbicano	barvicano	Au, DRAE	1300–1325	1990
	cuellealuo	cuellealvo	T	1330–1343	1330–1340
	pelicano	pelicano	Au, DRAE, M, S	c. 1350	1992
1400					
	barbiponiente (cf. barbapuniente)	barbiponiente	A, K&N, C, Au, DRAE, M, S	1499–1502	1945
	cabezcaído	cabezcaídos	N	1495	1737
	cabizcaído	cabizcaído	C, Au, M, S	1445–1519	1965
	cabiztuerto	cabiztuerto	Au	1445–1519	1626
	cazcorvo	cazcorvos	ON, M	1495	1927
	maniatado	maniatados	Au	1491–1516	2004
	mentecato	mentecato	C, DRAE	1491–1516	2004
	nariz aguileño	nariz aguileño (N)	N	1495	1495
	nariz romo	nariz romo (N)	N	1495	1495
	orejascaído	orejascaído (N)	N	1495	1495
	patihendido	patihendido (N)	N, Au, DRAE, M, S	1495	1986
	patimacizo	patimaciço (N)	N	1495	1737
	patitieso	patiteso	T, C, Au, DRAE, M, S	1406–1436	2000
	peliagudo	peliaguda	C, Au, DRAE, M, S	c. 1450	2004
	rabiahorcado	rabihorcados	Au, DRAE, M	1498	1991
1500					
	arisprieto	arisprieto	Au, DRAE, M	1513	1513
	barbiespeso	barviespeso	DRAE, M	1575	1601
	barbihecho	barbihecho	Au, DRAE, M	1514	1910–1926
	barbilindo	barbilindos	Au, DRAE, M, S	1597–1645	1998
	barbinegro	barbinegro	Au, DRAE, M, S	1545–1565	1989
	barbitaheño	barbitaheño	DRAE, M, S	1528	1975
	barbiteñido	barbiteñido	Au, M	1596	1613
	bocinegro	bocinegro	M, S	1554	1988
	boquiabierto	boquiabierto	Au, DRAE, M, S	1533	2004
	boquiancho	boquiancho	Au, DRAE, M	1583	1624

Century	Compound	Earliest form	Sources	First att.	Last att.
	boquiblando	boquiblando	DRAE, M	1585–ad 1643	1951
	boquiconejuno	boquiconejunos	Au, DRAE, M	1572	1572
	boquiduro	boquiduro	DRAE, M	1533	1881
	boquifruncido	boquifruncida	Au, DRAE, M	1580–ad 1627	1636
	boquihendido	boquihendidos	DRAE, M	1572	1572
	boquirrojo	boquirroxo	Au	1580–ad 1627	c. 1615–1644
	boquirroto	boquirroto	Au, DRAE, M, S	1508	1985
	boquirrubio	boquirrubio	Au, DRAE, M, S	1580–1627	1989
	boquiseco	boquisecos	Au, DRAE, M	1555	c. 1623
	boquisumido	boquisumida	Au, DRAE, M, S	1599	1975
	boquitorcido	boquitorcidos	DRAE, M	1589	1896
	boquituerto	boquituerto	C, Au, DRAE, M, S	1549	1960
	cabizbajo	cabezbaxo	C, Au, DRAE, M, S	1514–ad 1542	1974
	cabizmordido	cabezmordidos	M	1517	1625
	cachigordo	cachigordilla	DRAE, M, S	1566	1982
	callialto	callialto	DRAE, M	1564	1564
	capialzado	capialçado	Au, M, S	1526	2000
	capialzo	capialço	M	1591	1591
	cariacuchillado	cariacuchillado	M	1573	1574
	cariaguileño	cariaguileña	C, Au, DRAE, M	1570–1596	1972
	carialegre	carialegre	M	1585–ad 1643	1995
	cariampollado	cariampollados	Au, M	1540	1646
	cariancho	cariancho	Au, DRAE, M, S	1596	2001
	cariblanco	cariblanco	M	1561	2004
	caridoliente	caridoliente	Au, DRAE, M	1597–1645	1597–1645
	carigordo	carigordo	Au, DRAE, M	1580–ad 1627	1985
	cariharto	cariharto	Au, DRAE, M	1580–ad 1627	1972
	carilargo	carilargo	C, Au, DRAE, M	1597–1645	1989
	carilucio	carilucias	Au, DRAE, M, S	1589	1967
	casquiacopado	casquiacopado	DRAE, M	1564	1564

Century	Compound	Earliest form	Sources	First att.	Last att.
	casquiderra-mado	casquiderra-mado	DRAE, M	1564	1899
	casquilucio	casquilucios	Au, DRAE, M, S	1580–1627	1989
	casquimuleño	casquimuleño	DRAE, M	1564	1899
	cejijunto	cejijunta	A, Au, DRAE, M, S	1528	2004
	cejunto	cejunto	N, M	1529–1531	1874
	crestibermejo	crestibermejos	A	1589	1905
	cuellierguido	cuellierguido	C, Au, DRAE, M, S	c. 1550–1580	1987
	cuellilargo	cuellilargas	DRAE, M	1589	1973
	faldicorto	faldicorto	DRAE, S	1588	2000
	lengüilargo	lengüilargo	M, S	1597–1645	1988
	lominhiesto	lomienhiestos	Au, DRAE, M, S	1549–1603	1986
	maniblanco	maniblanco	M	1564	1978
	manicorto	manicorto	DRAE, M, S	1589	1986
	manilargo	manilargo	DRAE, M	1596	1997
	manirroto	manirroto	C, Au, DRAE, M, S	152 –1543	2004
	manisalgado	manisalgado	A	1509	1509
	manivacío	manivacío	T, Au, DRAE, M	ad 1598	1975
	ojinegro	ojinegras	Au, DRAE, M, S	1597–1645	2001
	ojituerto	ogituerta	M, S	c. 1550	1981
	ojizaíno	ojizaino	Au, DRAE, M, S	1597–1645	1974
	ojizarco	ojizarco	Au, DRAE, S	1597–1645	2000
	pasicorto	pasicorto	DRAE, M	1568–1575	1960
	paticorto	paticorto	M, S	c. 1568–1575	2004
	patimuleño	patimuleños	M	1564	1572
	patitendido	patitendido	A	1529	ad 1852
	patituerto	patituerta	C, Au, DRAE, M, S	c. 1528	1990
	pechiblanco	pechiblanco	DRAE, M	c. 1587	1896
	peciluengo	peciluengos	DRAE, M	1513	1513
	pelinegro	pelinegro	Au, DRAE, M	ad 1585–1643	1980
	perniquebrado	perniquebrado	C, Au, M	1554	1984
	pernituerto	piernituertos	DRAE, M	1589	1598
	pintiparado	pintiparado	Au, DRAE, M, S	1535–1536	2002

Century	Compound	Earliest form	Sources	First att.	Last att.
	puntiagudo	puntiagudos	C, Au, DRAE, M, S	c. 1500	2004
	rabicano	rabicano	Au, DRAE, M, S	1561	1981
	rostritorcido	rostritorcidos	M	1589	1589
	zanquivano	çanquivano	Au, DRAE, M	1549	1892
1600					
	alicaído	alicaído	Au, DRAE, M, S	1605	2004
	aliquebrado	aliquebrada	DRAE, M, S	1654	1993
	anquiboyuno	anquiboyuna	DRAE, M	1652	1889
	arisnegro	arisnegro	Au, DRAE, M	1606	1606
	barbiblanco	barbiblanco	DRAE, M	1605	1605
	barbicastaño	barbicastaño	M	1605	1619
	barbilucio	barbilucio	Au, DRAE, M	1615	1882
	barbiluengo	barbiluengo	M	1645	1645
	barbirrojo	barbirrojo	M, S	1651	1968
	barbirrubio	barbirrubio	Au, DRAE, M	c. 1610	1890
	boquidulce	boquidulce	M	1628–1629	1628–1629
	boquihundido	boquihundida	Au, M	1624	1624
	boquinegro	boquinegras	Au, DRAE, M	1625	1625
	boquirrasgado	boquirrasgado	DRAE, M	1600	1944
	capipardo	capipardos	M	1615	1971
	cariacedo	cariaceda	Au, M	1651	1651
	cariacontecido	cariacontecido	Au, C, DRAE, M, S	1610	2004
	caricuerdo	caricuerda	C, Au	1605	1625–1630
	carilindo	carilinda	M	1615	2003
	carilleno	carilleno	DRAE, M	1615	1948
	carininfo	carininfos	Au, M, S	1615–1645	1992
	carirredondo	carirredondo	C, Au, DRAE, M, S	1610–1645	2000
	casquivano	casquivano	DRAE, M, S	1605	2004
	colilargo	colilargo	S	1654–1658	2001
	cuellidegollado	cuellidegollado	Au, DRAE, M	1605	1605
	culcosido	culcusidos	Au, DRAE, M	1626–1628	1626–1628
	ojialegre	ojialegres	Au, DRAE, M	1605	1932
	ojienjuto	ojienjuta	Au, DRAE	1605	1605
	ojimoreno	ojimorena	DRAE, M	c. 1613	1982

Century	Compound	Earliest form	Sources	First att.	Last att.
	orejisano	orejisano	M	1652	1652
	pasilargo	pasilargo	DRAE, M	1617	1819
	patiabierto	patiabierto	Au, DRAE, M, S	1646	2001
	patialbillo	patialbillo	Au, DRAE, M	1644	1644
	patizambo	patizambo	Au, DRAE, M, S	c. 1611	1990
	peliblando	peliblando	Au, DRAE, M	1624	1624
	pelicorto	pelicorta	Au, DRAE, M	1600	2002
	pelirrubio	pelirrubia	Au, DRAE, M, S	1625	1991
	pelitieso	pelitieso	Au, DRAE, M, S	1624	1987
	perniabierto	pierniabierto	Au, DRAE, M, S	1604	2001
	piernitendido	pernitendido	Au, DRAE, M	1629	1629
	rabicorto (cf. racorto)	rabicortos	C, Au, DRAE, M, S	1601	2004
	rabilargo	rabilargo	Au, DRAE, M, S	1630–1655	2000
1700					
	alicortado	alicortada	S	ad 1700	1991
	anquiseco	anquiseco (TL)	DRAE, M	1770	1992
	barbilampiño	barbilampiño	DRAE, M, S	1772	2004
	barbirrucio	barbirrucio (TL)	DRAE, M, S	1770	1969
	barbizaeño	barbizaeño	Au	1726	1726
	boquiangosto	boquiangosto (TL)	DRAE, M	1770	1992
	boquifresco	boquifresco (TL)	DRAE, M	1770	1896
	boquinatural	boquinatural (TL)	DRAE, M	1770	1992
	cabeciancho	cabeciancho (TL)	Au, DRAE, M	1729	1992
	cabecijunto	cabecijunto (TL)	Au	1729	1936
	cañilavado	cañilavado (TL)	Au, DRAE, M	1729	1889
	caribobo	caribobo (TL)	Au	1729	1936
	cariescrito	cariescrito (TL)	Au	1729	1729
	carinegro	carinegro	DRAE, M, S	1780	1976
	caripando	caripando (TL)	Au	1729	1729
	casquiblando	casquiblando (TL)	DRAE, M	1780	1992
	colicano	colicano (TL)	M	1780	1992

Century	Compound	Earliest form	Sources	First att.	Last att.
	corniabierto	corniabierto	DRAE, M, S	1737	1970
	dentivano	dentivano	Au, M	1780	1889
	espalditendido	espalditendido (TL)	Au, DRAE, S	1732	1986
	fazferido	fazfirido (TL)	A, Au	1732	1852
	pamposado	pamposado	DRAE	1737	1992
	papialbillo	papialbillo (TL)	Au, DRAE, M	1737	1992
	patiestebado	patiestebado (TL)	Au, DRAE, M	1737	1993
	pechicolorado	pechicolorado (TL)	Au, M	1737	1992
	pintarrojo	pintarroxo (TL)	Au, DRAE, M	1737	1992
	zanquilargo	zanquilargo	Au, DRAE, M, S	1758	1994
1800					
	aliabierto	aliabiertas	DRAE, M	1839	1935–1936
	aliblanca	aliblancas	M, S	1895	2002
	alicorto	alicorto	S	1888	2001
	alirrojo	alirrojo (TL)	M	1899	2001
	alitierno	alitierno (TL)	DRAE, M	1817	1962
	anquialmen-drado	anquialmen-drado (TL)	DRAE, M	1884	1992
	anquiderribado	anquiderribado (TL)	DRAE, M	1884	1992
	anquirredondo	anquirredondo (TL)	DRAE, M	1884	1992
	arisblanco	arisblanco (TL)	DRAE, M	1869	1992
	barbipungente	barbipungente (TL)	DRAE, M	1884	1992
	cabecicaído (cf. cabezcaído)	cabecicaído	CORDE	1880–1881	1880–1881
	cabeciduro	cabeciduro	M	1895	1981
	cachigordete	cachigordeta	C, Au, M	1852–1882	1950
	cañihueco	cañihueco (TL)	DRAE, M	1869	1992
	cañivano	cañivano (TL)	DRAE, M	1884	1962
	caridelantero	caridelanterilla	DRAE, M	1849	1849
	carifruncido	carifruncido	DRAE, M	1876	1876
	cariparejo	cariparejo	DRAE, M	1849	1849

Century	Compound	Earliest form	Sources	First att.	Last att.
	carirraído	carirraído (TL)	Au, DRAE, M	1884	1992
	cascalbo	cascalbo	M, S	1899	1956
	colinegro	colinegras	S	1895	1970
	cornialto	cornialto	S	1801	1970
	corniancho	corniancho	S	1803	1970
	corniapretado	corniapretao	DRAE, M	1878	1994
	cornicorto	cornicorto	S	1803	2001
	cornidelantero	cornidelantero	S	1803	1994
	cornigacho	cornigacha	DRAE, M, S	1878	2002
	corniveleto	corniveleto	DRAE, M, S	1874	2001
	cuellicorto	cuellicorto	DRAE, M, S	1834	2000
	culinegro	culinegro (TL)	M	1899	1992
	lomitendido	lomitendido	S	1803	1977
	manialbo	manialbo	M	1881	1881
	palmitieso	palmitieso (TL)	M	1803	1889
	patialbo	patialbo (TL)	DRAE, M	1884	1992
	paticojo	paticojos	Au, DRAE, M, S	c. 1872	1997
	patidifuso	patidifuso	M, S	1882	2002
	pechirrojo	pechirrojo (TL)	DRAE, M, S	1884	1981
	pechisacado	pechisacados	DRAE, M, S	1874	1987
	petirrojo	petirrojos	M, S	1884–1885	2004
	petiseco	petiseca	M	1874	1922
	piquituerto	piquituerto (TL)	M, S	1899	1989
	rabisalsero	rabisalsera	Au, DRAE, M, S	1877	1981
	raspinegro	raspinegro (TL)	DRAE, M, S	1803	1962
	sangripesado	sangripesado	M	1896	1935–1936
	troncocónico	tronco-cónica	M, S	1870	2002
	troncopi-ramidal	tronco-piramidal	S	1881	1997
	zanquituerto	zanquituertas	Au, DRAE, M	1890	1890
1900					
	alitranco	alitranco (TL)	M	1983	1992
	astifino	astifino	M, S	c. 1966	2002

Century	Compound	Earliest form	Sources	First att.	Last att.
	astigordo	astigordo (S)	S	1970	1994
	astinegro	astinegro (S)	S	1970	1994
	barbimoreno	barbimoreno (TL)	M	1925	1992
	barbirralo	barbirralo (TL)	M	1970	1992
	barbirrojete	barbirrojete (S)	S	1971	1971
	barbitonto	barbitonto (TL)	M	1936	1992
	cabecinegra	cabecinegra (S)	S	1988	2004
	callalta	callalta (TL)	A	1936	1936
	capiblanco	capiblanco (S)	S	1944	1989
	carialzado	carialzado (TL)	M	1925	1992
	cariavacado	cariavacado	S	1966	1976
	caribello	caribello (TL)	M	1925	1992
	carichato	carichato (TL)	M	1925	1992
	carifosco	carifosco (S)	S	1983	1983
	carilampiño	carilampiño	M	1927	1986
	caripelado	caripelada (TL)	M	1927	ad 1936
	carniseco	carniseco (TL)	M, S	1925	1992
	colicuadrado	colicuadrado (S)	S	1970	2000
	colipinta	colipinta (S)	S	1970	1970
	colirrojo	colirrojo	M, S	1952	1962
	colirrubio	colirrubio (S)	S	1960	2002
	coliteja	coliteja (TL)	M, S	1956	1992
	colitrenzado	colitrenzado (TL)	S	1972	1972
	collalba	collalba (TL)	M, S	1927	2000
	cornibrocho	cornibrocho (TL)	M	1970	1992
	cornigordo	cornigordo (TL)	M	1992	1992
	cornivuelto	cornivuelto	S	1987	1994
	cuellinegro	cuellinegro (S)	S	1973	2003
	cuellirrojo	cuellirrojo (S)	S	1973	1986
	culialto	culialto (S)	S	1967	1987
	culibajo	culibajo	S	1965	2001

Century	Compound	Earliest form	Sources	First att.	Last att.
	culiblanco	culiblanco	S	c. 1920	1956
	dientimellado	dientimellado (TL)	M	1925	1992
	dorsirrojo	dorsirrojo (S)	S	1970	2000
	faldinegro	faldinegro (TL)	M, S	1925	1973
	franjinegro	franjinegro (S)	S	1975	1975
	franjirrojo	franjirrojo (S)	S	1990	2003
	franjiverde	franjiverde (S)	S	1964	1964
	granigrueso	granigrueso (S)	S	1989	1989
	haldiblanco	haldiblanco (S)	S	1970	1970
	haldinegro	haldinegro (TL)	M	1956	1992
	labihendido	labihendido (TL)	M	1925	1992
	lengüicorto	lengüicortado	M	1948	1992
	manicuerno	manicuerno (S)	S	1986	1986
	manigordo	manigordo (TL)	M	1936	2002
	ojigarzo	ojigarzo	M, S	1962	1962
	ojijunto	ojijunta	M, S	1961	1995
	ojiprieto	ojiprieto (TL)	M	1936	1992
	papialbo	papialbo (S)	S	1970	1970
	papirrojo	papirrojo (S)	S	1970	1970
	patiblanco	patiblanco	DRAE, M	1924	2000
	paticalzado	paticalzado (TL)	M	1985	1989
	patinegro	patinegro	S	1989	1998
	pechiazul	pechiazul (S)	S	1976	2000
	peliblanco	peliblancas	DRAE, M	1900	2001
	pelilargo	pelilarga	Au, DRAE, M, S	1970	2000
	pelirrojo	pelirroja	M, S	1911	2004
	pernicorto	pernicorto	M, S	1940	1991
	piernilargo	piernilargo	S	1955–1974	1994
	piquigualdo	piquigualda	S	1996	1996
	piquirrojo	piquirroja	S	2000	2003

Century	Compound	Earliest form	Sources	First att.	Last att.
	puntiseco	puntiseco (S)	M, S	1978	1978
	sangriligero	sangriligero	M	1927	1935–1936
	teticiega	teticiega (TL)	M	1925	1975
	tozalbo	tozalbo (TL)	M	1925	1992
	vetisesgado	vetisesgado (TL)	M	1914	1992

Deverbal [N + A]$_A$

Century	Compound	Earliest form	Sources	First att.	Last att.
1000–1100					
	caputmasso	caputmasum	LHP	1044	1044
	mampuesto	manpuesta	A, K&N, C, Au, DRAE, M	1146	2002
1200					
	cabopreso	cabo preso	A	1208	c. 1252–1270
	cabtenido	captenido	A	c. 1236	c. 1396
	fementido	fementido	C, M	1246–1252	2002
	mantenido	mantenida	A, Au, M, S	c. 1215	2004
	salpreso	salpresos	T, K&N, C, Au, DRAE, M, S	1246–1252	1988
	viandante	viandantes	K&N, N, C, Au, DRAE, M, S	1247	2004
1300					
	senadoconsulto	senado consult	DRAE, M	1377–1399	2002
1400					
	mancomunado	mancomunado	S	1469	2004
	manumiso	manumissi	Au	1450	1993
	salpicado˙	salpicada	Au	1448	2004
1500					
	manvacío	manvacíos	A, M	1527–1561	1975
	mantenible	mantenible	S	1550	2001
	manuscrito	manuscritos	Au, DRAE, M	1539	2004
	salpimentado	salpimentados	Au	1570	2004
	salpresado	salpresada	C, Au	1549–1603	1847–1857

Century	Compound	Earliest form	Sources	First att.	Last att.
	terraplén, terrapleno	terrapleno	Au, DRAE, S	1527–1550	2003
1600					
	armipotente	armipotente	Au, DRAE, M	1615	1882
	tiplisonante	tiplisonante	Au, DRAE, M	1630–1655	1992
1700					
	calseco	calseco (TL)	DRAE, M	1780	1992
	fehaciente	fehaciente	S	1770	1974
	mampesado	mampesado (TL)	Au	1734	1791
	manumitido	manumitido	Au	1768	2000
	ondisonante	hondisonante	M	c. 1798–1809	c. 1798–1809
	pampringada	panpringada	Au, M	1767	1997
1800					
	armisonante	armisonante (TL)	DRAE, M	1884	1992
	causahabiente	causa habiente	M, S	1861	2002
	cuentadante	cuentadante (TL)	DRAE, M, S	1869	1992
	derechohabiente	derecho habientes	M, S	1881	2004
	galiparlista	galiparlistas	DRAE	1855	1933
	salcocho	salcocho	M, S	1840–ad 1862	2004
	vasomotor	vasomotores	M, S	1870–1901	2004
1900					
	acidorresistente	ácidorresistentes	M	1943	1943
	aguallevado	aguallevado (TL)	M	1925	1992
	castellanohablante	castellano-hablantes	M, S	1980	2002
	catalanohablante	catalanohablante (S)	M, S	1975	2000
	catalanoparlante	catalanoparlante (S)	S	1970	1996
	cultiparlante	cultiparlante (S)	S	1986	1988
	drogadicto	drogadictos	M, S	1969	2004

Century	Compound	Earliest form	Sources	First att.	Last att.
	drogodependiente	drogodependiente	M, S	1981	2004
	gallegohablante	gallegohablante (S)	S	1993	2001
	gallegoparlante	gallegoparlante (S)	S	1977	1993
	girovagante	girovagantes	S	1929–1933	1969
	insulinodependiente	insulinodependiente	S	1987	2004
	letraherido	letraheridos	S	1989	1996
	maniobrable	maniobrables	S	1975	2003
	radiodifusor	radiodifusoras	S	1924	2004
	radioguiado	radioguiado (S)	S	1984	1984
	radiomarítimo	radiomarítimo (TL)	S	1934	1988
	rusohablante	rusohablante (S)	S	1989	1997
	rusoparlante	rusoparlantes	S	1989	1995
	teleadicto	teleadictos	M	1987	2004
	tonitronante, tronitonante	tonitronante	S	1961	2002
	toxicodependiente	tóxico-dependientes	S	1980	1996
	vascohablante	vascohablante	S	1984	1997
	vascoparlante	vascoparlantes	S	1977	2000
	vasoconstrictor	vasoconstrictora	S	1919–1936	2004
	vasodepresor	vasodepresor	S	1964	2001
	vasodilatador	vasodilatadoras	S	1906	2004
	vasoespástico	vasoespásticos	S	1964	1999
	vibroprensado	vibroprensado (S)	S	1958	1958

Cardinal $[N + A]_A$

Century	Compound	Earliest form	Sources	First att.	Last att.
1200					
	ostrogodo	ostrogodos	K&N	c. 1270	1997

Century	Compound	Earliest form	Sources	First att.	Last att.
1800					
	centroameri-cano	centroameri-canos	M, S	1867	2004
	norteafricano	norteafricanas	M, S	1899	2004
	norteameri-cano	norteameri-canos	M, S	1824	2004
	sudafricano	sudafricana	M	1896	2004
	sudamericano	sudamericana	M	1811	2004
	surafricano	surafricanas	M, S	1899	2004
	suramericano	suramericanos	M, S	ad 1822	2004
	suroccidental	suroccidental	S	1899	2004
1900					
	centroasiático	centroasiático	S	1987	1998
	centroeuropeo	centro europeos	M, S	1922	2004
	extremooriental	extremo-oriental	S	1926	1995
	guineoecuato-rial	guineoecuato-rial (TL)	M	1984	1992
	norcoreano	norcoreanos	M	1951	2004
	norirlandés	norirlandés	M	1977	2005
	norteoccidental	norteoccidental	S	1985	2001
	norteoriental	norteoriental	S	1946–1952	1997
	surcoreano	surcoreanos	M, S	1951	2004
	suroriental	suroriental	S	1947	2002
	survietnamita	survietnamitas	S	1980	2000

Denominal [N + A]$_A$

Century	Compound	Earliest form	Sources	First att.	Last att.
1900					
	ferromagnético	ferromagnéticos	M, S	1910	2004
	fotomecánico	fotomecánico (TL)	M	1984	2004
	medioambiental	medio ambiental	S	1968	2004
	mercadotécnico	mercadotécnico (TL)	S	1989	2003
	radiactivo	radiactiva	M	1919	2004

Century	Compound	Earliest form	Sources	First att.	Last att.
	radioeléctrico	radioeléctrica	S	1929	2004
	radiotécnico	radiotécnicos	S	1929	2003
	radiotelefónico	radiotelefónicas	M, S	1924	2002
	radiotelegráfico	radiotelegráfica	S	1910	1997
	tensioactivo	tensioactivos	S	1981	1996

Other [N + A]$_A$

Century	Compound	Earliest form	Sources	First att.	Last att.
1300					
	rabigalgo	rabigalga	T	1330–1343	1886
1500					
	cachicuerno	cachicuernos	Au, DRAE, M, S	1511	1996
	obtusángulo	obtusiángulos	Au, DRAE, M, S	1567	1969–1974
1600					
	oblicángulo, oblicuángulo	oblicuángulo	Au, M	1690	1992
1800					
	atrirrostro	atrirrostro (TL)	DRAE	1884	1992
	conivalvo	conivalvo (TL)	DRAE, M	1869	1992
	curvinervio	curvinervio	S	1896	1956
	palminervio	palminervias	M, S	1896	1957–1974
	puntiforme	puntiformes	S	1893	2002
	colipava	colipavas	M, S	1895	1949–1953
1900					
	conirrostro	conirrostro	M, S	1925	1990
	dentirrostro	dentirrostro (TL)	M, S	1925	1954–1967
	fisirrostro	fisirrostro (TL)	S	1925	1981
	parisilábico	parisilábico (TL)	M	1927	1992
	rabisaco	rabisaco	M, S	1966	1981
	tenuirrostro	tenuirrostro	M, S	1925	1981

Deverbal [N + N]$_N$

Century	Compound	Earliest form	Source	First att.	Last att.
1000–1100					
	animadversión	animadversionis	Au, DRAE, M, S	1098	2004
	capleuador	caplebator	LHP, A	1142	1492
1200					
	cablieva	cablieua	A, DRAE, M	c. 1250	c. 1250
	captenencia	captenencia	T, A, DRAE	c. 1230	1264
	mamparamiento	manparamiento	A	1254–1260	1430
	mampostería, mampostoría	mamposteria	C, Au, DRAE, M	1262	2004
	mampostero	mampostero	A, Au, DRAE, M	c. 1234–1275	1993
	mampostor	manpostor	A, DRAE, M	1289	1322
	manumisor	manumissores	LHP, Au	c. 1250	1484
	manlevador	manleuador	T, A, K&N	c. 1250	1254–1260
	manlieva	manlieva	A, K&N, Au, DRAE, M	c. 1236	1967
	manparador	manparadores	T, K&N	1254–1261	1552
	manparamiento	manparamiento	K&N	1254–1260	1431
	mansesor	manssessores	CS	ad 1260	1511
	mantenedor	mantenedor	A, M, S	c. 1218–1250	2004
	mantenencia	mantenençia	A, K&N, DRAE, M, S	c. 1215	2002
	manteniente	manteniente	T, DRAE	1234–1275	1834
	mantenimiento	mantenimiento	T, C, Au, M, S	c. 1236	2004
	manumisión	manumissio	C, Au	c. 1250	2002
	misacantano	misacantano	LHP, A, K&N, Au, DRAE, M, S	c. 1215	2004
1300					
	casateniente	casa tenientes	M	1321	2001
	logarteniente, lugarteniente	lugartenient	A, Au, DRAE, M, S	1347	2004
	mamparo	manparo	C, DRAE	1305–1328	1988
	manlieve	manlieue	C, Au, DRAE, M	ad 1325	ad 1325
	manobra	manobra	DRAE, M, S	1379–1384	1872
	terrateniente	terratenientes	DRAE, S	1396	2004

Century	Compound	Earliest form	Source	First att.	Last att.
1400					
	lugartenencia	lugartenencia	DRAE, M, S	1414	1965
	manferidor	manferidores	DRAE	1438	1438
	manobrero	manobrero	M	1482	1510
	manutención	mantençión	C, Au, M	1424	2004
1500					
	manifactura	manufactura	Au	1595	2004
	maniobra	maniobra	Au, DRAE, M, S	1535–1622	2004
	manutenencia	manutenencia	DRAE, M	c. 1527–1561	1607
	toricantano	toricantanos	S	1597–1645	1960
1600					
	poderhabiente	poderhabiente	Au, DRAE, M, S	1677–1678	1983
1700					
	animadvertencia	animadvertencia (TL)	DRAE, M	1770	1992
	maniobrero	maniobreros	DRAE, M	c. 1750	2002
	manobre	manobre	A, M	1734	1986
1800					
	maniobrista	maniobrista	DRAE, M	1872	1996
	manirrotura	manirrotura (TL)	Au, DRAE, M	1884	1992
	poderdante	poderdante	DRAE, M, S	1808	2004
1900					
	betabloqueador	betabloque-adores	S	1991	2003
	betabloqueante	betabloqueantes	S	1988	2003
	broncodilatador	broncodilatado-res	M	1979	2004
	drogodepen-dencia	drogodepen-dencia	M, S	1981	2004

Chapter 6

Head-initial [N + N]$_N$

Century	Compound	Earliest form	Sources	First att.	Last att.
1000–1100					
	capiscol	capiscol	LHP, T, K&N, N, C, Au, DRAE	1150	1901
	iglesia catedral	iglesia catedral	K&N	1079	2003
	mayordomo	maiordomus	LHP	920	2004
1200					
	aguapié	agua pie	A, N, C, Au, DRAE, M, S	1263	1991
	aguja salmar	aguja salmar	K&N	c. 1250	1486–1499
	can rostro	can rostro	DRAE	c. 1234–1275	1242–1275
	cañafístola, cañafístula	canafistola	AD, N, C, Au, M, DRAE	1252	1998
	cañaherla, cañahierla, cañaherra	canna fierla	N, Au, DRAE, M	1250	1962
	capapiel	capa pielle	A, K&N	c. 1234–1275	1924–1957
	cuerno cabra	cuernocabra	AD	1250	1250
	feliglesie	feliglesias	LHP	1268	1268
	ferropea	ferropeas	LHP, T, Au	c.1218– 1250	1626
	maestrescuela	maestrescuela	A, K&N, N, C, Au, DRAE, M, S	1231	2003
	malvavisco	maluauisco	C	1250	2004
	mapamundi, mapa-mundo	mapamundi	DRAE, S	c. 1223	2004
	paloma torcaza	paloma torcaza	K&N	1250	1992
	parte fortuna	parte fortuna	K&N, T	1254–1260	c. 1619
	piedra jaspe	piedra jaspe	DRAE	c. 1270	2001
	piedrabezar	piedra bezahar	C, Au, DRAE	c. 1250	1962
	piedra cal	piedra cal	M	1266	ad 1802
	piedra esmeralda	piedra esmeralda	K&N	1270–1284	c. 1625
	piedra gija	piedras guijas	K&N, ON, C	c. 1250	1535
	piedra mármol	piedra marmol	K&N, DRAE, M	c. 1270	1994

Century	Compound	Earliest form	Sources	First att.	Last att.
	piedrazufre	piedrasufre	AD, K&N, N, C, Au, DRAE, M	1250	1993
	punto equinoccio	punto equinoctio	K&N	c. 1277	c. 1277
	redmanga	redmanga	A	1246–1252	1246–1252
	reyes magos	reyes magos	K&N	c. 1200	2004
	sal amoníaco	sal armoniaco	AD, K&N, DRAE, M, S	c. 1250	1950
	salgema	sal gema	T, AD, K&N, DRAE, M	c. 1250	2001
	tiracol	tiracol (TL)	T, Au, DRAE, M	1252	1886
	uva espina	uva espina	DRAE, M	ad 1264	2004
1300					
	avestruz	avestruz	N, C, Au	1375–ad 1425	2004
	azúcar cande, azúcar candi	açucar candio	Au, DRAE, M	1337–1348	1996
	carta puebla	carta-puebla	DRAE, M, S	1340	2000
	casa fuerte	casa fuerte	Au, DRAE, M	1300–1305	2003
	casia fístola	casia fistola	N, C, Au	1300	1509
	condestable	condestable	A, N, C, Au, DRAE	c. 1340–1350	2004
	espicanardo	espicanardi	LHP, Au, DRAE	1380–1418	1606–1611
	hierba brenca	yerua brenca	C	c. 1381–1418	1606
	juez árbitro	juezes árbitros	Au	1311	2003
	libro becerro	libro becerro	M	ad 1352	1948
	maestresala	maestresala	A, AD, N, C, Au, DRAE, M, S	1393	2001
	puerco javalí	puercos jaualies	C	1326	1992
	puercoespín	puercoespín	T, N, C, DRAE, M, S	1379–1425	2002
	sal vidrio	sal vidrio	AD	1350–1400	1569
	sobrecarta	sobre cartas	DRAE, M	1371	1904–1947
	sortiagua	sortiagua	T	1379–1425	1379–1425
	telaraña	telarañas	N, C, Au, DRAE, M	1379–ad 1425	2004

Century	Compound	Earliest form	Sources	First att.	Last att.
1400					
	agualluvia	agualluvia	Au, DRAE	c. 1457	2004
	aguamanos	aguamanos	A, AD, C, Au, DRAE, M, S	1423	1980
	aguamiel	agua miel	A, DRAE, M, S	1400–1500	2003
	aguanafa	agua nafa	DRAE, M	ad 1448	1987
	agua purga	agua purga	AD	ad 1429	c. 1605
	aguasal	aguasal	A, AD	1490	2002
	azúcar piedra	açucar piedra	Au, DRAE	1477–1491	1962
	cañaheja	cañahexa	N, Au, DRAE, M	ad 1435	1998
	carapico	capapico	M	ad 1452	ad 1452
	cartacuenta	carta cuenta	C, Au, DRAE	1464–1485	2001
	cepacaballo	cepacaballo	M	1499–1502	1972
	copo azúcar	copo açucar	AD	1429	1429
	énula campana	enula campana	ON, DRAE	c. 1400–1500	1962
	estrellamar	estrella mars	Au, M, S	ad 1452	1997
	filigrana	filigrana	C, Au, DRAE, M, S	1477–1491	2004
	garrapata	garrapata	N, C, Au, DRAE, M, S	1495	2004
	mangamazo	mangamaço	A	1406–1435	1406–1435
	musaraña	musaraneo	A, C, Au, DRAE, M, S	1490	2003
	paño lino	paño lino	AD	ad 1429	ad 1429
	pejerrey	pexerey	DRAE, M, S	1431–1449	2004
	piedra alumbre	piedra lumbre	Au, DRAE	1493	1994
	piedra diamante	piedra diamante	K&N	1422–1425	1921
	piedraimán	piedra imán	K&N, ON, C, Au, DRAE, M	1406–ad 1435	1997
	pimpollo	pinpollos	A, ON, C, Au, DRAE, M, S	c. 1400	2003
	pinsapo	pinsapo	N, M, S	1495	2003
	salnitrio, sal nitro	sal nitro	AD, K&N	1493	2001
	uva moscatel	uva moscatel	ON	1438	2004
	verde esmeralda	verde esmeralda	M	ad 1424–1520	2003

Century	Compound	Earliest form	Sources	First att.	Last att.
	yerba golondrina	yerba golondrina	AD	c. 1471	c. 1540– 1550
1500					
	aguanieve	aguaniebe	C, Au, DRAE, M, S	ad 1536–1585	2001
	aguaviento(s)	aguavientos	DRAE, M	1575–1580	1993
	árbol paraíso	arboles paraysos	Au	1513	1988
	arcoiris	arco iris	DRAE, M, S	1572	2004
	aspaviento	aspaviento	Au, M	c. 1535	2004
	avechucho	avechucho	C	1597–1645	1996
	becuadrado	becuadrado	DRAE, M	c. 1535–1575	1982
	bocacalle	bocacalle	DRAE, M, S	1571	2002
	bocamanga	bocamanga	Au, DRAE, M, S	1580–1589	2004
	bollomaimón	bollo maymón	C, Au, S	1514	1996
	calvatrueno	calvatrueno	C, Au, DRAE, M, S	1592	1972
	cañiheja (cf. cañaheja)	cañihejas	M	1582	1606
	cardo huso	cardo huso	N, Au, DRAE	1557–1567	1557–1567
	carnemomia	carne momia	C, Au	1527–1550	1940–ad 1974
	carromato	carromatos	DRAE	1592	2004
	casamata	casamata	C, DRAE	1536	2003
	cornicabra	cornicabra	C, Au, DRAE	1513	2001
	goma adragante, goma gargante	goma dragante	AD, M	ad 1500	ad 1975
	hormiga león	hormiga león	S	1589	1996
	madreselva	madreselva	N, C, Au, DRAE, M, S	ad 1500	2003
	maesecoral, masecoral, maestre coral	maestrecorales	DRAE, M	1582	1641
	marimanta	marimanta	DRAE, M, S	1597–1645	1991
	pájaro carpintero	pájaros carpinteros	S	1535–1557	2003
	pájaro niño	pájaros niños	DRAE, M, S	1580–1590	1957–1974
	palmacristi	palma christi	S	1598	1981
	papel marquilla	papel marquilla	M	1572–1574	1935–1936

Century	Compound	Earliest form	Sources	First att.	Last att.
	perigallo	perigallo	C, DRAE, M	c. 1549	2002
	pez espada	pexe espada	DRAE, M	c. 1595–1615	2002
	piedrapómez	piedra pomez	C, Au, DRAE, M, S	1525	2004
	polvoraduque	pólvora duque	DRAE, M	1529	1607
	puntapié	puntapié	C, Au, DRAE, M, S	1528	2004
	saucegatillo (cf. sauzgatillo)	saucegatillo	N, M	1589	1962
	sauzgatillo (cf. saucegatillo)	sazgatillo	Au, DRAE, M, S	1582	2004
	trampantojo	trampantojos	C, Au, M, S	1517	2003
	uva canilla	uva canilla	ON, DRAE	ad 1500	1962
	zangamanga	zangamangas	Au	1597–1645	1715
	zarzamora	çarçamora	N, C, Au, DRAE, M, S	ad 1500	2004
	zarzaparrilla	zarzaparrilla	C, Au, DRAE, M, S	1536–1541	2004
1600					
	ave lira	aves lira	M	1613–1640	1642–1648
	bocamina	boca mina	M, S	1640	2004
	bolsicalavera	bolsicalavera	Au	1622	1622
	buzcorona	buzcorona	M	1603	1625
	caballo coraza	caballos corazas	Au, DRAE	1607–1645	1960
	cachopinito	cachopinito	Au	1615	1615
	colapez	cola pez	A, DRAE	1606	1999
	diamante tabla	diamantes tablas	M	c. 1600	1871
	hojalata	hojalata	DRAE, M, S	1692	2003
	lápiz plomo	lápiz plomo	M	1675	1977
	marimacho	marimacho (C)	C	1611	2003
	marimarica	marimaricas	M	1622	1994
	mesa escritorio	mesas escritorios	M	1603	1993
	molamatriz	molamatriz (C)	C	1611	c. 1618
	palabrimujer	palabrimujer	Au, DRAE, M	1604–1621	1604–1621
	pejesapo	pexe sapos	DRAE, M, S	1607	1999

Century	Compound	Earliest form	Sources	First att.	Last att.
	pez mujer	peje mulier	Au, DRAE, M	1676	c. 1754
	pez sierra	pesca sierra	DRAE, M, S	1607	1988
	piedralipe(s)	piedra lipis	Au, DRAE, M	1640	1896
	pincarrasco, pincarrasca	pino carrasca	DRAE, M	ad 1605	2003
	sardina arenque	sardinas arenques	M	1605	1993
	serpiente pitón	serpiente pitón	M	1602	2004
	silla poltrona	silla poltrona	Au	1657	1991
	sobrino nieto	sobrinos nietos	S	1673	2002
	testaferro	testaferros	DRAE	1685	2004
	verdemar	verdemar	Au, M	ad 1612	1996
	yerba brasince	yerba brasinque	AD	ad 1600	ad 1600
	zapato botín	zapato botín	Au	1627	1886
	zascandil	zascandil	Au	1626	2004
	zurribanda	zurribanda	Au, DRAE	1605	1986
1700					
	aguacal	aguacal	M, S	1758	1827
	aguamar	agua mar	DRAE	c. 1754	1995
	aguarrás	aguarrás	Au, DRAE, M, S	1726	2004
	babazorro	babazorros	Au, DRAE, M	1758	1927
	baño maría	baño maria	M, S	1791	2004
	bocacaz	bocacaz	DRAE, M	1770	1910
	brocamantón	brocamantón (TL)	Au, M, S	1726	1992
	carta orden	carta-orden	DRAE	1737	1994
	carta pécora	carta pécora (TL)	C, Au, DRAE	1737	1992
	cólera morbo	colera morbo	M, S	1710	1997
	filoseda	filoseda	DRAE, M	1795	1980
	goma laca	goma laca	M, S	1780	1999
	hierba mate	yerba mate	M	1710	2002
	jaque mate	jaque mate	K&N, M	1799–1815	2004
	madreperla	madreperla	Au, DRAE, M, S	ad 1704	2002
	mangajarro	mangajarro (TL)	Au, DRAE	1734	1992

Century	Compound	Earliest form	Sources	First att.	Last att.
	obra maestra	obras maestras	S	1790	2004
	palamallo	palamallo (TL)	C, DRAE, M, S	1737	1992
	palo campeche	palo campeche	DRAE, M, S	1705	1994
	papel moneda	papel-moneda	M	1786–1834	2004
	patagorrillo	patagorrillo (TL)	Au	1737	1992
	pelicabra	pelicabra (TL)	Au	1737	1803
	pezpalo	pezpalo (TL)	M	1783	1950
	verdeceledón	verde celedonio	M	1767	c. 1825–1828
	verdemontaña	verdemontaña (TL)	Au, DRAE, M	1739	1992
	verdevejiga	verdevexiga	Au, DRAE, M	1739	1890
	zarzagavillo	zarzagavillo (TL)	Au	1739	1791
1800					
	agua cuaderna	agua cuaderna (TL)	DRAE	1884	1992
	aguají	aguají (TL)	M	1899	1990
	aguaturma	aguaturma (TL)	M	1817	2004
	ajoarriero	ajoarriero	M	1872	2004
	ajo cañete	ajo cañete (TL)	M	1817	1992
	ajo chalote	ajo chalote (TL)	M	1817	1990
	ajopuerro	ajopuerro (TL)	DRAE, M	1817	1997
	algodón pólvora	algodón-pólvora	M	1862	1951
	amarillo canario	amarilllo canario	S	1881	2004
	azúcar pilón	azúcar piloncillo	M	1807	1807
	azul cielo	azul cielo	M	1852	2004
	azul cobalto	azul cobalto	M	1856	2003
	barniz copal	barniz copal	M	1878	c. 1935
	becuadro	becuadro	DRAE, S	1880	1999
	bocabarra	bocabarra (TL)	M	1899	2004
	bocajarro (a ~)	a bocajarro	M, S	1891	2004
	bocallave	bocallave	M, S	1851–1855	1999

Century	Compound	Earliest form	Sources	First att.	Last att.
	bocateja	bocateja (TL)	M	1817	1992
	bocatijera	bocatijera (TL)	DRAE, M	1884	1992
	bocatoma	bocatoma	M	1845	2004
	bote salvavidas	bote salvavidas	M	c. 1870–1905	2004
	buque insignia	buque insignia	M, S	1894	2004
	cañacoro	cañacoro (TL)	DRAE, M	1884	1963
	cañamiel	cañamiel	C, DRAE, M, S	1847	1963
	cartón piedra	carton piedra	M, S	1872–1878	2004
	casa-cuartel	casa cuartel	S	1815–1819	2004
	casa cuna	casas-cunas	M, S	1869	2001
	célula huevo	célula huevo	M	c. 1890	1992
	coche-salón	coche-salón	S	1878	2001
	damajuana	damajuana	DRAE, S	1847	2004
	diamante rosa	diamante rosa	S	1802	2002
	don pereciendo	don pereciendo (TL)	DRAE	1832	1992
	globo sonda	globos sondas	M, S	c. 1870–1905	2004
	granja escuela	granjas-escuelas	S	1898	2004
	gris perla	gris perla	M	1856	2004
	gris pizarra	gris pizarra	M	1885	1995
	hierba pastel	hierba pastel (TL)	DRAE, M	1884	1933
	hierro palanquilla	hierro palan- quilla (TL)	DRAE	1803	1992
	hierro planchuela	hierro planchuela (TL)	DRAE	1803	1992
	hierro varilla	hierro varilla (TL)	DRAE	1803	1992
	higo chumbo	higo chumbo	M	1828–1870	2003
	hombre lobo	hombres lobos	M	1879	2004
	idea-fuerza	idea-fuerza	S	1897	2004
	laurel cerezo	laurel cerezo	S	1882	1962
	laurel rosa	laureles rosa	S	ad 1896	1991
	madreclavo	madreclavo (TL)	DRAE, M	1803	1992
	malvarrosa	malva-rosa	M	1852	1995

Century	Compound	Earliest form	Sources	First att.	Last att.
	mantaterilla	mantaterilla (TL)	DRAE, M	1803	1992
	máquina herramienta	máquinas herramientas	M	c. 1885	2002
	marimoña	marimoña	M	1877	1941–1961
	martillo pilón	martillo pilón	M	c. 1870–1905	2004
	mierdacruz	mierdacruz	S	1807	1986
	pájaro burro	pájaro burro (TL)	DRAE, M	1817	1992
	pájaro diablo	pájaro diablo (TL)	DRAE, M	1807	1992
	pájaro mosca	pájaro mosca	DRAE, M, S	1817	1991
	pájaro moscón	pájaro moscón	DRAE, M, S	1817	2000
	pájaro polilla	pájaro polilla (TL)	DRAE, M	1817	1992
	pájaro trapaza	pájaro trapaza (TL)	DRAE, M	1817	1992
	palahierro	palahierro (TL)	DRAE, M	1832	1946
	palo áloe	palo áloe (TL)	DRAE, M	1817	1992
	palo brasil	palo brasil	DRAE, M	1815–1819	1994
	palorrosa	palo-rosa	S	1852	2003
	papel pergamino	papel pergamino	M	1881	1997
	papel tela	papel tela	M	1891	2001
	pared horma	pared horma (TL)	DRAE	1884	1992
	pejepalo	pejepalo	DRAE, M	1843	1891–1898
	perro lobo	perro-lobo	M	1880–1881	1998
	pimiento morrón	pimientos morrones	M	1885–1887	2004
	pino alerce	pino alerce (TL)	DRAE	1817	1992
	pino balsain	pino balsain (TL)	DRAE	1832	1992
	plomo plata	plomo plata (TL)	DRAE	1837	1884
	quechemarín	quechemarín (TL)	DRAE	1837	1956

Century	Compound	Earliest form	Sources	First att.	Last att.
	sombrero hongo	sombreros hongos	DRAE	1876–1888	2002
	tabaco rapé	tabaco rapé	Au	1881	1963
	tío abuelo	tío abuelo	S	1867	2002
	tren correo	tren correo	DRAE, M	1860	1999
	tren ómnibus	tren ómnibus (TL)	M	1884	1992
	uñagata	uña gata (TL)	DRAE	1803	1962
	uva verga	uva verga (TL)	DRAE	1803	1992
	uvayema	uvayema (TL)	DRAE, M	1803	1992
	vara alcándara	vara alcándara (TL)	DRAE	1832	1992
	verde botella	verde-botella	M	1853	2002
	zarzarrosa	zarzarrosa	DRAE, M, S	1879	1987
1900					
	acuerdo marco	acuerdo marco	M	1977	2004
	aguatinta	agua tinta	M, S	1935	2003
	ajicuervo	ajicuervo (TL)	M	1925	1992
	ala delta	ala delta	M, S	1980	2001
	año luz	años-luz	M, S	1957–1974	2004
	autobomba	autobomba	S	1950	2004
	autocaravana	autocaravana (S)	S	1985	2003
	autochoque	autochoque	M, S	1961	1990
	avetoro	ave toro	DRAE, M	1909	1998
	avión nodriza	avión nodriza (M)	M	1998	2003
	azúcar glas	azúcar glas	M	1947	2004
	azúcar lustre	azúcar lustre	M	1927	1997
	balompié	balompié	M, S	1932	2004
	baloncesto	baloncesto	M, S	1926	2004
	balonmano	balonmano	M, S	1975	2004
	balón tiro	balón tiro	S	1996	1996
	balonvolea	balonvolea	M, S	1975	2002
	barco diligencia	barco diligencia (S)	S	1976	1976

Century	Compound	Earliest form	Sources	First att.	Last att.
	barco tanque	barco-tanque	M	1983	1983
	bono basura	bonos basura	S	1989	2002
	bonobús	bonobús	M, S	1984	2001
	bonohotel	bonohotel	M	1997	1997
	bonometro	bonometro	M, S	1986	1993
	bonotrén	bono-tren	M, S	1982	1984
	boticuero	boticuero (S)	S	1970	1970
	buque escuela	buque-escuela	M	1903	2004
	buque nodriza	buque nodriza	M	1912	2002
	buque submarino	buques submarinos	M	1904–1905	1926
	cabrarroca	cabrarroca	S	1976	1985
	camión cisterna	camiones cisterna	M	1939	2004
	camión tanque	camiones tanques	M	1985	2001
	caña borde	caña borde	M	1963	1963
	canario flauta	canarios flauta	S	c. 1923	1996
	canción protesta	canción-protesta	M, S	1976	2002
	caravinagre	cara vinagre	S	1964	1972
	cardo garrapata	cardo garrapata (S)	S	1977	1977
	carro dormitorio	carros-dormitorios	M	1980	2001
	carro tanque	carros-tanques	M	1996	1996
	cestapunta	cesta punta	M, S	1949	2000
	cierre relámpago	cierre relámpago	M	1962	1999
	ciudad dormitorio	ciudades dormitorios	M	1968	2004
	ciudad jardín	ciudad jardín	M, S	1929	2002
	ciudad satélite	ciudad satélite	M	1945–ad 1972	2004
	coche-cama	coche-cama	M, S	1922	2001
	coche escoba	coche-escoba	M	1994	1994
	coche patrulla	coche patrulla	M	1966	2004

Century	Compound	Earliest form	Sources	First att.	Last att.
	coche-restaurante	coche restaurante	M, S	1925	1997
	comida basura	comida basura	S	1987	2004
	contrato basura	contrato-basura	S	1994	2004
	cuello cisne	cuello cisne	M	1976	1998
	efecto dominó	efecto dominó	M	1983	2004
	equivalente-gramo	equivalente gramo	S	1987	1998
	espato flúor	espato fluor	M	1953	1995
	espinapez	espinapez (TL)	M	1925	1992
	faro piloto	faros pilotos	S	1955	1961
	fútbol-sala	fútbol sala	M, S	1980	2004
	gas ciudad	gas ciudad	M, S	1962	2002
	gas grisú	gas grisú	M	1929–1933	1950
	gas mostaza	gases mostaza	M, S	1937	2004
	gato garduño	gato garduño	S	1924–1927	1995
	gilipolla(s)	gilipollas	M	1961	2004
	gilipuertas	gilipuertas	M	1972	1984
	gomaespuma	gomaespuma	M, S	1971	2004
	gramopeso	gramo-peso (S)	S	1961	1988
	grillotopo	grillo topo	S	1926	1980
	grulla damisela	grulla damisela (S)	S	1987	1987
	herpes zóster	herpes zóster	S	1919–1936	2003
	hierba carmín	hierba carmín	M	1900	1994
	hierba centella	hierba centella	M	1962	1962
	hierba doncella	hierba doncella	M	1962	1982
	hierba estrella	hierba estrella	Au, DRAE, M	1962	1962
	hijoputa	hijoputa	S	1956	2004
	hogar cuna	hogar cuna (S)	S	1964	1964
	hombre-anuncio	hombres anuncios	S	1948	2004
	hombre-araña	hombre araña	S	1994	2004
	hombre-masa	hombre-masa	S	1962	2002
	hombre objeto	hombre objeto	S	1985	2002

Century	Compound	Earliest form	Sources	First att.	Last att.
	hombre-orquesta	hombre orquesta	S	1947–ad 1975	2004
	hombre rana	hombres rana	M	1964–1967	2003
	hombre-sánd-wich	hombre-sánd-wich (S)	S	1965	1995
	hora hache	hora hache	S	1956	1977
	hora punta	horas punta	M	1968	2004
	horno microondas	hornos microondas	M	1988	2004
	jara estepa	jara estepa	M	1998	1998
	juego-pelota	juego-pelota (S)	S	1964	1964
	kilogramo masa	kilogramo-masa	S	1946	1961
	kilogramo peso	kilogramo-peso (S)	S	1961	1985
	kilovatio hora	kilovatios-hora	S	1912	2004
	lagarto canarión	lagarto canarión (S)	S	1976	1976
	marizápalos	marizápalos	M, S	1927	2000
	mecánico dentista	mecánicos-dentistas	S	1961	1996
	mesa camilla	mesa camilla	M, S	1903	2004
	molécula gramo	molécula-gramo	S	1906	1998
	mono araña	monos arañas	M	1909	2002
	motocarro	motocarro	M	1962	1994
	mujer objeto	mujer-objeto	S	1968	2003
	niño burbuja	niños burbuja	M	1993	1997
	niño prodigio	niño prodigio	S	1925	2004
	noticia bomba	noticia bomba	M	1958	2002
	oso panda	oso panda (S)	S	1972	2003
	papamoscas cerrojillo	papamoscas cerrojillo (S)	S	1973	1989
	papel aluminio	papel aluminio	M	1976	2004
	papel biblia	papel biblia	M	1971	2002
	papel carbón	papel carbón	M	1929	2002
	papel cebolla	papel cebolla	M	1972	1996

Century	Compound	Earliest form	Sources	First att.	Last att.
	papel celofán	papel celofán	M	1953	2003
	papel charol	papel charol	M	1976	1976
	papel confort	papel confort	M	1987	1987
	papel cristal	papel cristal	M	c. 1935	1982
	papel madera	papel madera	M	1945–1964	2002
	papel oficio	papel oficio	M	1988	1997
	papel pinocho	papel pinocho (M)	M	1998	2001
	papel pluma	papel pluma	M	1966	1976
	par motor	par motor	S	1940–1956	2003
	pase pernocta	pase pernocta	M	1992	2000
	pato cuchara	pato cuchara (M)	M	1998	2003
	pedolobo	pedolobo (S)	S	1965	1965
	peje ángel	pez ángel	M	1927	1999
	peje araña	peje-araña	M	1918	1918
	peje diablo	pez-diablo	M	1962	1977
	pejegallo	pejegallo (TL)	M	1925	1989
	perro salchicha	perro salchicha	M	1972	1997
	pez ballesta	pez ballesta	M	1909	1909
	pez globo	pez globo	M	2002	2004
	pez luna	pez luna	M	1909	2003
	pez martillo	pez martillo	M	1909	2001
	picorrelincho	picorrelincho (S)	M, S	1981	1981
	pinotea	pinotea	M	1911	1997
	política-ficción	política ficción	S	1950–1968	2003
	punto cero	punto cero	S	1900	2003
	radio macuto	radio macuto	M	1985	2003
	reina margarita	reina margarita	S	1969	1999
	reloj pulsera	reloj pulsera	M	c. 1908–1930	2004
	rollo primavera	rollo primavera (S)	S	1993	1993
	sapoconcho	sapoconcho	S	1972	1973
	televisión basura	televisión basura	S	1994	2004

Century	Compound	Earliest form	Sources	First att.	Last att.
	tortuga carey	tortuga carey	M	1981	2001
	traje pantalón	traje- pantalón	S	1987	2002
	traje sastre	trajes-sastre	M, S	1931	2003
	tren botijo	tren botijo	M	1928	2001
	tren cremallera	tren-cremallera	M	2001	2004
	vacabuey	vacabuey (TL)	M	1927	1992
	vacaburra	vacaburra (TL)	M	1985	1999
	varaplata	varaplata (TL)	M	1936	1992
	villa miseria	villas miseria	M	1964	2004
	western-spaghetti	western-spaghetti (S)	S	1971	1975
	zorromoco	zorromoco (S)	S	1964	1964

Head-final [N + N]$_N$

Century	Compound	Earliest form	Sources	First att.	Last att.
1000–1100					
	aurifreso (cf. orofrés)	aurifreso	LHP	1050	1050
	campidoctor	campidoctoris	LHP	1090	1992
	aguaducho	aguaducho	LHP, K&N, N, C, Au	c. 1196	1997
	mancuadra	manquadra	A, CS, DRAE, M	c. 1129	1540–1553
	sanguisuela	sanguisuela	T, K&N, N	1148	2004
1200					
	argenfrés	argenfres	T, K&N	1270–1285	1270–1285
	argentpel	argenpel	A, DRAE	1252	1886
	cera folia	cerafolia	T	c. 1275	c. 1275
	lignáloe	ligno aloe	AD, K&N, C, Au, M	c. 1250	1994
	litiscontestación	litis contestatione	DRAE, M	1247	1900–1928
	litisexpensas	litis expensas	DRAE, M, S	1246	1983
	lobombre	lobombres	T, K&N	1275	1275
	orofrés (cf. aurifreso)	orofres	A, K&N, Au, DRAE, M	1268	1927
	orofresadura	oro fresadura	T	1293	1293

Century	Compound	Earliest form	Sources	First att.	Last att.
	oropimente	orpiment	A, AD, K&N, N, C, Au, DRAE, M, S	c. 1250	1994
	terremoto	terremotos	T, K&N, DRAE, S	1259	2004
	tierra mouimiento	tierra mouimiento	T	1260	1260
1300					
	cabrahígo	cabrafigo	A, N, C, Au, DRAE, M, S	1379–1384	1995
	cabrahiguera	cabrafiguera	M	1380–1385	1963
	casapuerta	casas puertas	Au, DRAE, M, S	1303	1995
	gallocresta	gallocresta	AD, ON, C, Au, DRAE, M, S	c. 1300	2000
	jurisperito	jurisperito	Au	1311	2002
	maristela	maristela	T	1379–1425	1539
	oropel	oropel	A, N, C, Au, M, S	1332	2004
1400					
	aguatocho, aguatocha	aguatocho	N, Au	c. 1445–1480	ad 1969
	aguja paladar	aguja paladar	AD, N, DRAE, M	1423	1611
	burgomaestre	burgomaestre	Au, DRAE, M, S	1497	2004
	caprifigo	caprifico	A	1495	1636
	carpobálsamo	carpobalsamo	Au	1490	1599
	casamuro	casamuro	A, DRAE, M	1427–1428	2002
	fideicomiso	fidecomiso	Au, DRAE	1491–1516	2004
	giróvago	giróvagos	M	ad 1450	1996
	jurisconsulto	jurisconsultos	Au	1422	2002
	mármol coluna	mármol coluna (N)	N	1495	1495
	pezuña	pesuña	AD, DRAE, M, S	c. 1450–1470	2004
	ranacuajo	renacuajos	K&N, N, C, Au, DRAE, M	1445–1519	2003
	rata parte	rata parte	DRAE	1470	1627
	sangre lluvia	sangre lluja	Au	ad 1429	1962
	solrayo	sorayo	AD	1423	1423
	varapalo	varapalo	Au, DRAE, M, S	1471–1476	2004

Century	Compound	Earliest form	Sources	First att.	Last att.
1500					
	cabalfuste	caualfuste	A, K&N, Au, M	1512	1512
	cabrahigal	cabrahigal	Au	1527–1550	1527–1550
	cachidiablo	cachidiablos	Au, DRAE	1597–1645	1992
	cachiporra	cachiporra	Au, DRAE, M	c. 1550–1606	2004
	ceracate	ceracates	M	1589	1589
	chilmole	chilmole	M	c. 1568–1575	1996
	gatuña	gatuña	DRAE, M	c. 1549	1962
	jurispericia	jurispericia	Au	1575–1588	1648
	jurisprudencia	jurisprudencia	Au	c. 1550	2004
	jurisprudente	jurisprudente	Au	1597	1941
	litisconsorte	litis consortes	DRAE, M	1588	1588
	litispendencia	litispendencia	Au, DRAE, M	1540–1553	1930
	madre patria	madre patria	M, S	1592–ad 1631	2004
	mancomunidad	mancomunidad	DRAE, M, S	1532	2004
	signo servicio	signo servicio	Au	1562	1562
1600					
	espinpuerco	espinpuerco (C)	C	1611	1611
	fideicomisario	fideicomisario	Au, DRAE	1687	2000
	gallipuente	gallipuente	Au, DRAE, M	ad 1605	1797
	legisperito	legisperitos	Au	1640–1653	2002
	mancuerda	mancuerda	DRAE, M, S	1607–1645	1998
	manivela	manivela	S	c. 1600	2004
	porcipelo	porcipelo	Au, M	1615	1932
1700					
	ajicola	ajicola (TL)	M	1726	1992
	cachipolla	cachipolla (TL)	DRAE	1780	1992
	ceriflor	ceriflor	M	1795	1795
	mamporro	mamporro (TL)	Au, M	1734	2003
	pavipollo	pavipollos	DRAE, M, S	1781–1784	2000
	tripitropa	tripitropa (TL)	Au	1739	1803

Century	Compound	Earliest form	Sources	First att.	Last att.
1800					
	ajipuerro	ajipuerro (TL)	M	1803	1992
	altímetro	altímetro (TL)	DRAE	1803	2004
	amperímetro	amperímetro	M	1870–1905	2003
	bocateja	bocateja (TL)	DRAE	1817	1992
	calorimotor	calorimotor (TL)	M	1869	1992
	empleomanía	empleomanía	DRAE, M	1820–1823	1997
	espiritrompa	espiritrompa	M, S	1893	1957–1974
	ferrocarril	ferro-carriles	S	1828–1870	2004
	ferrocianuro	ferrocianuro	M	1881	1998
	ferrovía	ferrovía	S	1886	2001
	fotocopia	fotocopia	M, S	c. 1875	2004
	fotograbado	fotograbado	M, S	1880–1881	2004
	fotolitografía	fotolitografía (TL)	M, S	1869	2004
	gomorresina	gomoresinas, gomo-resinas	DRAE, S	1807	1993
	gurripato	gurripato	S	1898	1987
	gutiámbar	gutiámbar (TL)	M	1803	1992
	maestrepasquín	maestrepasquín (TL)	M	1803	1992
	mancuerna	mancuerna (TL)	DRAE, M, S	1884	2001
	pico cangrejo	pico cangrejo	M	1842	1842
	platinocianuro	platinocianuro	S	1882	1997
	plusvalía	plus valía	S	1896–1964	2004
	radio vector	radio vector	S	1861–1865	2002
	sismómetro	sismómetro	S	1883	2000
	trapatiesta	trapatiesta	S	1894	1986
	varaseto	varaseto (TL)	Au, DRAE	1884	1910–1926
	viaducto	viaductos	DRAE, M, S	1848	2004
1900					
	aerosolterapia	aerosolterapia	S	1970	2003
	aminoácido	aminoácidos	S	1906	2004

Century	Compound	Earliest form	Sources	First att.	Last att.
	aminoalcohol	aminoalcohol (S)	S	1968	1968
	audiofrecuencia	audiofrecuencia	M	1950	1997
	audiometría	audiometría	M	1992	2004
	audiómetro	audiómetros	M	1913	1997
	autobanco	autobanco	S	1974	1997
	autobús	autobuses	M, S	1914	2004
	autocarril	autocarril	M	1922	1922
	autocine	autocinema	M, S	1976	2003
	autoescuela	autoescuela (S)	M, S	1970	2003
	autorradio	autorradio	M, S	1974	1996
	autotrén	autotrén	S	1981	1997
	autoventa	autoventa (S)	S	1977	1988
	autovía	autovías	M	1940–1956	2004
	avifauna	avifauna (S)	M, S	1969	2003
	boldoglucina	boldoglucina (S)	S	1989	1989
	bonoloto	bonoloto, bono-loto	M, S	1990	2001
	borosilicato	borosilicato (S)	S	1958	1973
	borotalco	borotalco (S)	S	1961	1961
	bronconeu-monía	bronconeu-monía	M	1921	2004
	buhobús	buhobús (S)	S	1974	1975
	burofax	burofax	S	1985	2004
	calori-amperímetro	caloriam-perímetro (TL)	M	1925	1992
	calorímetro	calorímetro	M	1910	1999
	capultamal	capultamal (TL)	M	1925	1992
	carril-bus	carril-bus	S	1980	2001
	cartómetro	cartómetro (TL)	M	1925	1992
	ceroplástica	ceroplástica (TL)	M	1925	1992
	ciclocross	ciclocross	M	1989	2004
	ciclomotor	ciclomotores	M	1980	2004

Century	Compound	Earliest form	Sources	First att.	Last att.
	cicloturismo	cicloturismo	S	1992	2003
	cicloturista	cicloturista	S	1986	2003
	ciencia-ficción	ciencia-ficción	M, S	1950–1968	2004
	cinecámara	cinecámara (S)	S	1970	1970
	cinecassette	cinecassette (S)	S	1970	1970
	cineclub	cineclub	M, S	1947–1975	2004
	cinefórum	cine-forum	M, S	1970	2002
	cocainomanía	cocainomanía (TL)	M, S	1983	1992
	cocobacilo	cocobacilo	M	1943	2001
	cóctel-bar	cóctel-bar (S)	S	1970	1970
	colapsoterapia	colapsoterapia (S)	S	1964	1964
	cosmonauta	cosmonautas	M, S	1962	2004
	cosmonáutica	cosmonáutica (TL)	M	1970	1992
	cosmonave	cosmonave (TL)	M, S	1983	1992
	cosmovisión	cosmovisión	M, S	1947	2004
	craneoestenosis	craneoestenosis (S)	S	1988	1988
	cuaderna vía	cuaderna vía	M	1905	2003
	cuboflash	cuboflash (S)	S	1966	1992
	demoniomanía	demoniomanía (TL)	M	1925	1992
	drogadicción	drogadicción	M, S	1976	2004
	drogomanía	drogomanía (S)	S	1971	1971
	espatadanza	espatadanza	S	1926	1985
	espectrofo-tometría	espectrofo-tometría	M, S	1956	2003
	espectrofo-tómetro	espectrofo-tómetro	M, S	1956	2004
	espectrómetro	espectrómetro	M	1968	2004
	esporogénesis	esporogénesis	S	1957–1974	1963
	etanolamina	fosfatidil-etano-lamina	S	1969	1999

Century	Compound	Earliest form	Sources	First att.	Last att.
	etilbenceno	etilbenceno (S)	S	1975	1981
	etilenglicol	etilenglicol	S	1992	1992
	fangoterapia	fangoterapia	S	1994	2003
	farmacomanía	farmacomanía	S	1993	1997
	farmacopsiquia-tría	farmacopsiquia-tría (S)	S	1982	1992
	farmacoterapia	farmacoterapia	S	1966	2003
	farmacovigi-lancia	farmacovigi-lancia	S	1992	2003
	faxmanía	faxmanía (S)	S	1990	1990
	ferrobús	ferrobús (S)	S	1972	2001
	ferromanganeso	ferromanganeso	S	1900–1928	1964
	ferroprusiato	ferroprusiatos	M	1951	1991
	ferrosilicio	ferrosilicio	S	1900–1928	1997
	fibrocartílago	fibrocartílago	S	1989	2001
	fibrocemento	fibrocemento	M, S	1951	2004
	flamenco-pop	falmenco-pop	S	1995	2002
	fluidoterapia	fluidoterapia	S	1980	2003
	fluorocarburo	fluocarburos	S	1996	1996
	fotocopiadora	fotocopiadora	M, S	1978	2004
	fotomatón	fotomatons	M, S	1968	2004
	fotomecánica	fotomecánica	M, S	1962	2004
	fotomontaje	fotomontajes	M, S	1948	2004
	fotomural	fotomural	S	1972	1998
	fotonovela	fotonovela	M, S	1970	2002
	fotoperiodismo	fotoperiodismo	S	1986	2003
	fotoperiodista	fotoperiodista	S	1994	2001
	fotorradiosco-pia	fotorradiosco-pia (S)	S	1964	1964
	fotorromance	fotorromance (S)	S	1971	1971
	frentepopu-lismo	frentepopu-lismo	S	1979	1994
	frontón-tenis	frontón-tenis (S)	S	1984	1999
	fuelóleo	fuelóleo	M, S	1981	1999

Century	Compound	Earliest form	Sources	First att.	Last att.
	gammaglobu-lina	gammaglobu-lina	M, S	1964	2000
	gasoducto	gasoductos	M, S	1973	2004
	gelatinobro-muro	gelatino bromuro	S	1912	2001
	girómetro	girómetro (TL)	M	1927	1992
	giropiloto	giropiloto (S)	S	1975	1975
	helipuerto	helipuerto	S	1960	2004
	hormono-terapia	hormono-terapia	S	1964	2003
	huecograbado	huecograbado	M, S	1930	1997
	hueco-offset	hueco-offset (S)	S	1979	1979
	lab-fermento	lab-fermento	S	1943	1975
	laborterapia	laborterapia	M, S	1974	1997
	laserterapia	laserterapia (S)	M, S	1984	2000
	librofórum	librofórum (S)	S	1958	1991
	lumpenprole-tariado	lumpenprole-tariado	S	1978	2002
	mancomu-nación	mancomu-nación (S)	S	1964	1986
	meningococo	meningococo	M, S	1943	2003
	mercadotecnia	mercadotecnia	M, S	1971	2004
	metalmecánica	metalmecánica	S	1974	2004
	mimodrama	mimodrama	M, S	1975	2001
	mineralocorti-coide	mineralocorti-coides	S	1964	1981
	morfinomanía	morfinomanía	M, S	1944–1949	1981
	motocarro	motocarro	M, S	1966	1994
	motofurgón	motofurgón (S)	S	1958	1958
	mundovisión	mundovisión (TL)	M, S	1984	1989
	musicotera-peuta	musicotera-peuta (S)	S	1975	2003
	musicoterapia	musicoterapia (S)	S	1970	2002
	narcodinero	narcodinero	S	1990	1997
	narcodólar	narcodólares	S	1989	2003

Century	Compound	Earliest form	Sources	First att.	Last att.
	narcoterrorismo	narcoterrorismo	S	1987	2004
	narcoterrorista	narcoterroristas	S	1990	2004
	oleoducto	oleoducto	M, S	1911–1925	2004
	oleomargarina	oleomargarina (S)	S	1957	1988
	oleoneumático	oleoneumático (S)	S	1970	1970
	oleorresina	oleorresina	M, S	1962	2003
	opiomanía	opiomanía	M	1944–1949	1980
	organogénesis	organogénesis	M, S	1976	2003
	organoterapia	organoterapia	M, S	1912	1988
	ovninauta	ovninauta (S)	S	1988	1988
	oxigenoterapia	oxigenoterapia	S	1964	2004
	ozonoterapia	ozonoterapia (S)	S	1990	2004
	papamóvil	papamóvil	M, S	1985	2002
	petrolquímica	petroquímica	M, S	1975	2004
	piano-bar	piano-bar	M, S	1980	2002
	piezoelectri-cidad	piezoelectri-cidad	M, S	1902	1994
	plusmarca	plusmarca	M, S	1944	2004
	plusmarquista	plusmarquistas	M, S	1946	2004
	plusvalor	plusvalor	S	ad 1975	2004
	propilenglicol	propilenglicol (S)	S	1969	2000
	puticlub	puticlubs	M, S	1978	2002
	radiactividad	radiactividad	M, S	1945	2004
	radioaficionado	radioaficionado	M, S	1948–1963	2004
	radiobaliza	radio baliza	M, S	1974	1999
	radiocanal	radiocanal (S)	S	1991	1991
	radiocomedia	radiocomedia	S	1971	1989
	radiocomuni-cación	radiocomuni-cación	M, S	1931	2004
	radiodiagnós-tico	radiodiagnós-tico	M, S	1964	2004
	radiodifusión	radiodifusión	M, S	1924	2004

Century	Compound	Earliest form	Sources	First att.	Last att.
	radiodifusor	radiodifusoras	M, S	1950	2004
	radioelectrici-dad	radioelectrici-dad	M, S	1929	1970
	radioemisora	radioemisores	M	1929	2004
	radioescucha	radioescucha	M, S	1929	2004
	radiofaro	radiofaro	M, S	1934	1998
	radiofoto	radiofoto	S	1978	1997
	radiofrecuencia	radiofrecuencia	M, S	1929	2004
	radiolocal-ización	radiolocal-ización	S	1988	2002
	radiomensaje	radiomensaje	M, S	1958	2003
	radionave-gación	radionave-gación	M, S	1995	2001
	radionovela	radionovela	M, S	1972	2004
	radioonda	radioonda (M)	M	1998	2003
	radiopatrulla	radio-patrulla	S	1969	2002
	radiorreceptor	radiorreceptor	M, S	1929	2004
	radiosonda	radiosonda	M, S	1977	2000
	radiosondeo	radiosondeo (S)	S	1990	1996
	radiotaxi	radiotaxi	M, S	1994	2004
	radiotelefonía	radiotelefonía	M, S	1924	2004
	radioteléfono	radioteléfono	M, S	1963	2003
	radiotelegrafía	radiotelegrafía	M, S	1912	2002
	radio-telegrafista	radio-telegrafistas	M, S	1946	2001
	radiotelégrafo	radiotelégrafo	M	1980	1995
	radiotelegrama	radiotelegramas	M, S	1924	1980
	radiotelescopio	radiotelescopios	M, S	1976	2004
	radioteletipo	radioteletipo (S)	S	1971	1975
	radioterapeuta	radioterapeuta	M, S	1964	2002
	radioterapia, radiumterapia	radioterapia	M, S	1919–1936	2004
	radiotrasmisor	radiotransmisor	M, S	1929	2004
	radiotrasmisión	radiotrasmisión	M	1985	1992
	radioyente	radioyentes	M, S	1952–1956	2003
	reflejoterapia	reflexoterapia	M, S	1989	2004

Century	Compound	Earliest form	Sources	First att.	Last att.
	roentgenotera-pia	roentgenotera-pia (S)	S	1970	1970
	roentgenterapia	roentgenterapia (S)	S	1964	1970
	servodirección	servodirección	M, S	1972	1994
	servofreno	servofreno	M, S	1940–1956	2003
	servomecanismo	servomecanis-mos	M, S	1958	1996
	servosistema	servosistema	M	1986	1999
	sexoadicto	sexoadictos (S)	S	1991	2001
	sexofobia	sexofobia	S	1968	1973
	sexomaníaco	sexomaníacos (S)	S	1971	1971
	sueroterapia	sueroterapia	M, S	1912	2000
	telebasura	telebasura	M	1992	2004
	telecomedia	telecomedia	M, S	1966	2004
	telediario	telediarios	M, S	1965	2004
	teledifusión	teledifusión	M	1965	1995
	telefilme	telefilmes	M, S	1964	2004
	telenovela	telenovela	M, S	1970	2004
	teleserie	teleserie	M	1978	2004
	telespectador	telespectadores	M, S	1962	2004
	televidente	televidente	M, S	1955	2004
	tensiómetro	tensiómetro	M, S	1988	2002
	tour-operador	tour operadores	M, S	1977	2004
	toxicomanía	toxicomanía	M, S	1906	2004
	trolebús	trolebuses	M, S	1940–1953	2002
	turbodiesel	turbodiesel	M, S	1994	2002
	vacunoterapia	vacunoterapia	M, S	1943	1979
	varilarguero	varilarguero	M, S	1945	2001
	vasoconstric-ción	vasoconstric-ción	M, S	1912	2004
	vasodilatación	vasodilatación	M, S	1912	2004
	vasoparálisis	vasoparálisis (S)	S	1988	1988

Century	Compound	Earliest form	Sources	First att.	Last att.
	ventiloterapia	ventiloterapia (S)	S	1970	1970
	vibroflotación	vibroflotación (S)	S	1970	1970
	vibromasaje	vibromasaje (S)	S	1971	1997
	vibromasajista	vibromasajista (S)	S	1974	1974
	vibroterapia	vibroterapia (S)	S	1972	1972
	videoaficio-nado	videoaficiona-dos	M	1985	2004
	videoarte	videoarte	S	1986	2004
	videocámara	video-cámaras (S)	M, S	1981	2004
	videocasete	videocassettes	M, S	1980	2003
	videocasetera	videocasetera	M	1987	2004
	videocinta	videocintas	M	1991	2002
	videoclip	videoclip	M, S	1986	2004
	videoclub	videoclubes, video club	M, S	1979	2003
	videoconfer-encia	videoconfer-encia	M, S	1983	2004
	videoconsola	videoconsola	M	1995	2004
	videodisco	video disco	M, S	1979	2002
	videofórum	videofórum (S)	S	1983	1983
	videofrecuencia	videofrecuencia (M)	M	1998	2002
	videojuego	videojuegos	M, S	1983	2004
	videolibro	videolibro (S)	M, S	1990	2002
	videopelícula	videopelículas	S	1983	1991
	videoportero	videoportero	M, S	2002	2004
	videorregistra-dor	videorregistra-dor (S)	S	1974	1974
	videoteléfono	videoteléfono	M, S	1987	2004
	videoterminal	videoterminales	S	1984	1995
	videotexto	videotexto	M	1986	2002
	vitaminoterapia	vitaminoterapia	M	1943	1989

[N + A]ₙ

Century	Compound	Earliest form	Sources	First att.	Last att.
1000–1100					
	carnestolendas	carnestollendas	A, Au, DRAE, S	1037	2004
	batalla campal	batallam campalem	K&N, C, DRAE, S	ad 1100	2004
	carta falsa	carta falsa	Au, DRAE, M	c. 1196	1997
1200					
	avutarda (cf. avetarda)	aotardas	A, AD, K&N, N, C, Au, DRAE, M, S	1250	2003
	agua bendita	agua beneita	T, K&N, N, Au, DRAE	1236	2004
	aguadulce	agua dulce	T, K&N, DRAE, M	c. 1250	2003
	aguamanil	aguamanil	K&N, N, Au, DRAE, M, S	c. 1200	2001
	agua(s) muerta(s)	aguas muertas	C, Au, DRAE, S	1293	2002
	agua rosada	agua rosada	T, AD, K&N	c. 1250	2000
	agua santa	aguas santas	T	c. 1240–1250	2003
	alga marina	alga marina	K&N, S	c. 1250	2004
	año nuevo	anno nueuo	M, S	1290–1300	2004
	arco turqués	arcos turquis	K&N	1293	1604–1618
	argent vivo	argent uiuo	LHP, AD, K&N, C, Au	c. 1250	1970
	arte mayor	artes mayores	S	1293	2003
	arte poética	arte poética	DRAE, M	ad 1250	1997
	arte(s) liberal(es)	artes liberales	DRAE, M, S	c. 1275	2004
	asafétida	asa fétida	AD, K&N, ON, Au, M, S	1250	1990
	bienes raíces	bienes raíces	DRAE	1251–1285	2004
	bolarménico	bolo arménico	AD, C, Au, M	c. 1250	1962
	caballero nobel	cavallero novel	K&N, DRAE	1240–1250	1924–1957
	cabra montés	cabra montés	ON, Au, DRAE, M, S	c. 1280	2001
	camino francés	camino frances	K&N	1248	1996
	campo abierto	campo abierto	C, Au	c. 1250–1260	2004
	cañavera	cañaveras	A, AD, K&N, Au, DRAE, M, S	c. 1230	1997
	carne viva	carne viva	K&N, Au, DRAE	c. 1275	2004

Century	Compound	Earliest form	Sources	First att.	Last att.
	carta desaforada	cartas desaforadas	DRAE, M	1255–1280	1883–1884
	carta plomada	carta plomada	DRAE	1248	c. 1625
	casa santa	casa santa	Au, DRAE	c. 1252–1270	1967
	cera blanca	çera blanca	AD, K&N, Au	c. 1280	1994
	cera virgen	çera virgen	M	c. 1275	2002
	cielo abierto	cielo abierto	S	ad 1260	2004
	coco bistinto	coco bistinto	T	c. 1275	1605
	cólera bermeja	colera bermeja	K&N	1250	ad 1500
	cosa juzgada	cosa judgada	Au	1247	2004
	cosa pública	cosa pública	S	c. 1250	2004
	cuervo marino	cueruo marino	N, Au, M	1250	2002
	disanto	disanto	T, ON, C, Au, DRAE, M	1240–1250	2003
	espíritu santo	espíritu santo	K&N, Au, DRAE, S	c. 1275	2004
	fe católica	fe catholica	AD, K&N, Au	1256–1263	2004
	fe pública	fe publica	Au, M, S	1293	2004
	goma arábiga	goma aráuiga	AD, Au, DRAE, M	1250	2004
	hueste antigua, estantigua	hueste antigua	K&N, Au	1270–1284	2001
	leopardo	leon pardo	T, K&N, N, DRAE, M, S	c. 1200	2003
	lobo cerval	lobo cerual	T, N, C, Au, DRAE, M, S	1250	1987
	mancomún (de ~)	mancomún	A, Au, DRAE, M, S	1201	1986
	manderecha	manderecha	A, C, DRAE, M, S	1296	1949–1952
	mandoble	mandobles	A, C, Au, DRAE, M, S	1285	2004
	melcocha	miel cocha	A, N, C, Au, DRAE, M, S	c. 1250	1997
	mundo mugeril	mundo mugeril	T, K&N	c. 1280	c. 1280
	murciego	murciego	A, K&N	1250	1942
	nuez moscada	nuez moscada	AD, K&N, N, Au, DRAE, M, S	1240–1250	2004
	óleo rosado	olio rosado	AD, K&N	c. 1250	ad 1600
	óleo violado	olio uiolado	K&N	1250	ad 1600
	paños menores	pannos menores	T, K&N, C, Au	1252–1270	2003

Century	Compound	Earliest form	Sources	First att.	Last att.
	piedra preciosa	piedra preciosa	K&N, N, C, Au, DRAE, M	c. 1236	2004
	piedra viva	piedra uiua	K&N, DRAE	ad 1260	2002
	puerco montés	puerco montes	K&N, N	c. 1250	1981
	rosa silvestre	rosa silvestre	N, C, ON, DRAE	c. 1275	2000
	salmuera	salmuera	T, N, C, Au, DRAE, M, S	c. 1250	2004
	sal pedrés	sal pedres	AD, K&N, DRAE, M	1250	1431
	tierra firme	tierra firme	N, Au, DRAE, M, S	c. 1223	2004
	tierra santa	tierra santa	Au	1270–1284	2002
	uva pasa	uuas passas	N, Au	c. 1280	2003
	vinagre	uinagre	LHP, Ad, N, C, DRAE, M, S	c. 1250	2004
1300					
	aberramía	abderramias	A, N, Au	1326	1508
	abocasta, avucasta	auecastas	A, AD, N, C, Au, DRAE, M	1337–1348	c. 1550
	aceite rosado	azeyte rosado	N	c. 1381–1418	1994
	agua manantial	agua manantial	DRAE	ad 1300	1985
	ansar brava	ansares brauas	AD	1326	c. 1618
	arte mecánica	artes mecanicas	DRAE	1379–1384	1995
	arte militar	arte militar	DRAE	1300–1305	2003
	azúcar rosado	açucar rosado	AD, Au, DRAE	c. 1381	1996
	bemol	bemol	T	ad 1379–1425	2003
	caballero andante	caualleros andantes	DRAE, M, S	c. 1313–1410	2003
	camino real	camino real	S	1303	2004
	camposanto	camposanto	A, DRAE, M, S	1326	2004
	cancerbero	can cerbero	C, M, S	1385	2004
	carta blanca	cartas blancas	C, Au, DRAE, M, S	1312	2004
	carta forera	cartas foreras	C, Au, DRAE, M	1329	1540–1553
	carta mensajera	carta mensajera	N, DRAE	1378–1406	1905
	casa llana	casa llana	DRAE, M	1339	1936–1964
	casa pública	casa pública	Au, DRAE, M	c. 1300	1986

Century	Compound	Earliest form	Sources	First att.	Last att.
	casa real	casa real	N, Au, DRAE, M	1325	2004
	casa solar	casa solar	DRAE, M	1313	1998
	casialígnea	casialignea	AD	1350	1515
	ciruela pasa	ciruelas passas	C, Au, M	c. 1381–1418	2004
	cólera negra	colera negra	N	1376–1396	1606
	cólera quemada	colera quemada	N	1381–1418	1624
	gloriavana	gloria vana	N	c. 1378–1406	2000
	lechetrezna	lechetrezna	C	c. 1300	1998
	manjar blanco	manjar blanco	M, S	1381–1418	2001
	mar alta (cf. altamar)	mar alta	DRAE	1340–1350	1940–1947
	oromate	oro mate	C, Au	1339	1982
	vara alta	varas altas	Au, DRAE, S	1376–1391	2002
	verdescuro	verde escuro	DRAE, M	1362	2004
1400					
	añocasto	agnocasto	K&N, Au, S	ad 1450	1962
	aguafuerte	agua fuerte	AD, Au, DRAE, M, S	ad 1429	2004
	agua mineral	agua mineral	DRAE	1493	2004
	aguardiente	aguardiente	A, AD, Au, DRAE, M, S	ad 1424–1520	2004
	aguazul, aguazur	aguazul	M	1476	1969
	aire corrupto	aire corrupto	Au	1410	1987
	amor propio	amor propio	Au, DRAE, S	1438	2004
	arca pública	arca publica	K&N	1499	2004
	arte menor	arte menor	S	1492	2003
	avefría	avefría	Au, DRAE, M, S	1406–1435	2001
	avetarda	auetarda	M	1490	1490
	barcalonga	barca luenga	M	c. 1492	c. 1492
	barcolongo, barcoluengo	barco luengo	Au, DRAE, M	1492–1493	1957
	becerro marino	becerro marino	Au	1490	1780
	caballero aventurero	caualleros aventureros	DRAE, M	ad 1454	1882
	cámara oscura	cámara oscura	M, S	1482–1492	2003

Century	Compound	Earliest form	Sources	First att.	Last att.
	campo libre	campo libre	S	ad 1490	2004
	campo raso	campo raso	N, C, M	1445–1480	1995
	caña dulce, cañaduz	cañas dulçes	C, Au, DRAE, M, S	1477–1481	1996
	canto llano	canto llano	C, Au, S	ad 1460	2002
	caparrosa	caparosa	N, C, Au, DRAE, M	1431	1994
	carta acordada	cartas acordadas	DRAE	1432	1973
	carta ejecutoria	carta ejecutoria	Au, S	1493	2001
	caudatrémula	cauda tremula	DRAE, M	1495	1983
	cuerpo celeste	cuerpo celeste	Au	c. 1445	2004
	eléboro blanco	eleboro blanco	C, DRAE, M, S	ad 1450	1998
	fabordón	fabordon	C, Au, DRAE	c. 1430–ad 1480	1897
	fenogriego	fenogrecho	AD, Au, DRAE, S	1400–1500	2004
	fruta seca	frutas secas	ON, Au, M	ad 1429	2004
	gato montés	gato montés	C, Au, DRAE, M	1422–1425	2001
	gato pardo	gato pardo	M	1463	2001
	gota caduca	gota caduca	M	ad 1429	1471
	gota coral	gota coral	Au, DRAE, M	1471–1476	1994
	gota fría	gota fria	M, S	1471	2000
	hierbabuena	yeruabuena	A, AD, N, C, Au, DRAE, M, S	ad 1429	2004
	higuera loca	higuera loca	N, C, Au, M, S	1494	1657
	historia natural	historia natural	K&N, ON, DRAE, M, S	1477–1496	2004
	i griega	i griega	ON, S	1492	1990
	lengua mala	lengua mala	T	1407–1463	1981
	lirio blanco	lirio blanco	N, DRAE, M	1411–1412	2004
	mal francés	mal francés	DRAE, S	1445–1519	2002
	mampesadilla	manpesadilla	M	1471	1923
	manizquierda	manizquierda	C	1427–1428	1673
	mar bonanza	mar bonança	RAE	1492–1493	1863–1873
	miel virgen	miel virgen	C, Au	1400–1500	1993
	murciégalo	murciegalo	C	1482	1954
	oro blanco	oro blanco	M, S	c. 1400	2004

Century	Compound	Earliest form	Sources	First att.	Last att.
	oro molido	oro molido	Au, S	1477–1491	2002
	pamporcino	pan porcino	Au, DRAE, M	1493	1985
	paños calientes	panos calientes	Au, DRAE, S	ad 1429	2004
	partes vergonzosas	partes vergonzosas	K&N, DRAE, S	1437	1992
	patria celestial	patria celestial	S	ad 1485	2000
	pleamar	plenamar	DRAE, M, S	1431–1449	2004
	puente levadizo	puente levadiza	Au, DRAE	1431–1449	2003
	puerta falsa	puerta falsa	C, Au	1411–1412	2003
	ropa blanca	ropa blanca	Au, DRAE, M	1480–1484	2004
	rosmarinun	rosmarino	LHP	1490	1996
	sangre fría	sangre fría	S	1470–1480	2004
	sedevacante	sede vacante	Au	1470	2003
	sentido común	sentido común	M, S	1427–1428	2004
	tabla rasa	tabla rasa	Au, S	1446–1447	2004
	tablachina	tablachina	Au, M	1492–1493	1886
	verdegay	verdegay	DRAE, Au, M, S	1406–ad 1435	1991
	vía pública	vía pública	S	1408	2004
	visto bueno	visto bueno	DRAE	1400–1500	2004
	vómito negro	vómito negro	S	1495	1999
1500					
	aguachirle	aguachirle	Au, DRAE, M, S	1597–1645	2001
	aguamarina	aguamarina	DRAE, M, S	1515	2004
	agua negra	agua negra	S	ad 1500	2004
	árbol mayor	árbol mayor	M	1528	1898
	arena(s) movediza(s)	arena movediza	M	c. 1598	2004
	azul turquí	azul turquí	M	c. 1597	2000
	caballo marino	caballos marinos	Au, DRAE	1535–1557	1991
	cabeza visible	cabeza visible	S	c. 1527–1561	2004
	cabo suelto	cabos sueltos	DRAE, M	1587	2004
	caja fuerte	caja fuerte	M, S	1575	2004
	cambio seco	cambio seco	Au	1541	1612

Century	Compound	Earliest form	Sources	First att.	Last att.
	campo franco	campo franco	C	1517	1952
	cañahueca	caña hueca	K&N, M, S	1513	2002
	carta misiva	cartas misivas	DRAE	1519	1984
	casa solariega	casas solariegas	DRAE, M	1575–1580	2003
	cielorraso	cielo raso	Au, M, S	c. 1560–ad 1578	2004
	cuenta corriente	cuenta corriente	S	1535–1557	2004
	esfera celeste	esphera celeste	Au, DRAE, S	1535	2004
	espiadoble	espía doble	C, Au	1554	2000
	estrella fija	estrella fija	K&N, ON	1524	2004
	fuegos artificiales	fuego artificial	Au, M, S	c. 1500	2004
	fuerza pública	fuerza pública	S	1590–1610	2004
	gallina ciega	gallina ciega	N, C, Au, DRAE, M, S	c. 1550	2003
	hambre canina	hambre canina	C, S	1521–1543	1994
	letra muerta	letras muertas	DRAE, M, S	1530	2004
	llave maestra	llave maestra	Au, DRAE, M, S	ad 1580–1627	2002
	lobo marino	lobos marinos	N, Au, DRAE, M, S	ad 1504	2004
	mansalva (a ~)	mansalva, a ~	Au, DRAE, M, S	1580	2004
	manvacía	manvacía	DRAE	1589	1966
	maremagno	maremagno	S	1535–1557	2001
	mataparda	mata parda	DRAE, M, S	1575–1580	1962
	mozalbillo	moçalbillo	Au	c. 1540–1577	1986
	olla podrida	olla podrida	C, Au, DRAE, M, S	1539	2002
	oso hormiguero	osos hormigueros	M, S	1535–1557	2002
	pájaro bobo	pájaros bobos	Au, DRAE, M, S	1537	2002
	pájaro carpintero	pájaros carpinteros	Au, DRAE, M	1535–1557	2003
	palosanto	palo santo	Au, DRAE, M, S	1527–1550	2003
	papel pintado	papel pintado	M	1522	2003
	pavo real	pavos reales	DRAE, M, S	1598	2004
	puerto franco	puerto franco	Au, S	1597	2003
	puerto seco	puertos secos	C, S	1523	2004
	tejavana	tejavana	M, S	1549	1972

Century	Compound	Earliest form	Sources	First att.	Last att.
	tracamundana	tracamundanas	Au, S	1597–1645	1970
	vara larga	vara larga	Au, DRAE	1513	2001
	vía láctea	vía láctea	Au, DRAE	1575	2003
	viarrecta	vía recta	Au	1530	1995
	viejo verde	viejo verde	Au, S	1597–1645	2004
1600					
	aguamala	aguas malas	DRAE, M, S	c. 1605–1609	2002
	agua milagrosa	agua milagrosa	S	1602	2002
	amor platónico	amor platónico	Au, S	1602–1613	2004
	azúcar moreno	açucar moreno	DRAE, M	1606–1611	2004
	azul celeste	azul celeste	M	1610 –1620	2004
	balarrasa	balas rasas	Au, DRAE, M, S	1605	1995
	banco raso	banco raso	Au	1608	1890
	barrio(s) bajo(s)	barrio bajo	M, S	1600	2004
	bóveda celeste	bóveda celeste	M, S	1680	2003
	caña brava	cañas bravas	M	1607	2004
	capilla ardiente	capilla ardiente	Au, DRAE, M, S	c. 1619	2004
	caradura	caradura	M, S	ad 1611	2004
	carta pastoral	cartas pastorales	DRAE, S	1645	2004
	diablo cojuelo	diablo cojuelo	Au, S	ad 1600	2004
	fruto seco	frutos secos	S	c. 1601–1621	2004
	fuego fatuo	fuegos fatuos	Au, DRAE, M, S	1690	2004
	hierbacana	yerua cana	Au, DRAE, M	1606	1962
	huevo hilado	hueuos hilados	Au, DRAE, S	1611	2004
	linterna mágica	linterna mágica	Au, S	ad 1666–1695	2002
	lugar común	lugar común	DRAE, S	c. 1619	2004
	macho cabrío	macho cabrío	DRAE, S	c. 1611	2004
	mano muerta	mano muerta	Au, DRAE, S	1648	2001
	mozalbete	mozalbetes	Au	1602	2004
	nochebuena	noche buena	C, DRAE, Au, M, S	1604	2001
	nochebueno	nochebueno	C, Au, DRAE, M	1612	1984
	piel roja	piel roja	M, S	1624	2004
	ropa interior	ropa interior	M	1657	2004

Century	Compound	Earliest form	Sources	First att.	Last att.
	zarzaperruna	çarça perruna	C, Au, DRAE, M	1606	1962
1700					
	aguabresa	aguabresa (TL)	Au	1726	1938
	aguacibera	aguacibera (TL)	DRAE, M	1770	1992
	agua regia	agua regia	DRAE, M, S	1729	2003
	aire comprimido	aire comprimido	M	1728	2003
	bala perdida	bala perdida	M, S	1781	2004
	bancarrota	bancarrota	Au, DRAE, M, S	1730	2004
	canto rodado	cantos rodados	DRAE, M	1795	2004
	carta credencial	carta credencial	S	1789	2004
	círculo vicioso	círculo vicioso	M, S	1729	2004
	clase media	clase media	S	1787	2004
	cordón umbilical	cordón umbilical	M, S	1780	2004
	cuadrilongo	cuadrilongo	Au	1758	1994
	cuerpo extraño	cuerpos extraños	M	1772	2004
	educación física	educación física	S	1786	2004
	goma elástica	goma elástica	DRAE, M	1790	2003
	gramática parda	gramática parda	S	1727–1728	2004
	guardiamarina	guardia marina	M, S	1748	2002
	huevomol	huebos moles	Au, DRAE, M, S	1787	1997
	marimorena	marimorena	Au, DRAE, M, S	1715	2003
	marisabidilla	marisabidilla	DRAE, M, S	1792	2000
	montepío	montepío	M, S	1769	2003
	paloblanco	palo blanco	S	ad 1745	2004
	palo borracho	palo borracho	M, S	1774	2002
	rasoliso	rasoliso	M, S	c. 1763	1974
	tejamanil	tejamanil	M	1743	1996
1800					
	aguaverde	aguaverde (TL)	DRAE, M	1817	1950
	agua oxigenada	agua oxigenada	M, S	1856	2004
	ajoblanco	ajo-blanco	DRAE, M, S	1891–1894	2003

Century	Compound	Earliest form	Sources	First att.	Last att.
	amor libre	amor libre	S	1876	2004
	arco voltaico	arco voltaico	S	c. 1870–1905	2004
	artes gráficas	artes gráficas	M, S	1880–1881	2004
	artes plásticas	artes plásticas	M	1869	2004
	azul marino	azul-marino	M	1802–1805	2004
	burriciego	burriciego	M, S	1874	2001
	cabeza dura	cabeza dura	M	1834	2004
	cadena perpetua	cadena perpetua	M, S	1828–1870	2004
	café-cantante	café cantante	M, S	1880–1881	2002
	caldo corto	caldo corto	S	1891–1894	2001
	cama redonda	cama redonda	M, S	1828–1870	2002
	chivo expiatorio	chivo expiatorio	M, S	1898	2004
	circuito cerrado	circuito cerrado	M, S	c. 1870–1905	2004
	clases pasivas	clases pasivas	S	1843–1844	2003
	columna vertebral	columna vertebral	M, S	1867	2004
	cuarto oscuro	cuarto oscuro	M, S	1882	2004
	cuerda floja	cuerda floja	M, S	1818	2004
	cuerda vocal	cuerdas vocales	M, S	1870–1901	2004
	cuero cabelludo	cuero cabelludo	DRAE, M, S	1870–1901	2004
	cuerpo calloso	cuerpo calloso	M, S	1870–1901	2003
	cuerpo ciliar	cuerpo ciliar	M, S	1870–1901	1992
	cuerpo lúteo	cuerpos lúteos	S	1870–1901	2004
	defensa personal	defensa personal	S	1862	2004
	fiebre amarilla	fiebre amarilla	DRAE, M, S	1801	2004
	fuerza bruta	fuerza bruta	M, S	1842	2004
	guardiacivil	guardias civiles	M, S	1849	2004
	juego malabar	juegos malabares	M, S	1861	2004
	lengualarga	lengua larga	M, S	1896	1993
	línea férrea	línea férrea	M, S	1854	2004
	masa coral	masa coral	S	1872–1878	2003
	montaña rusa	montaña rusa	M, S	1842	2004

Century	Compound	Earliest form	Sources	First att.	Last att.
	mosca muerta	mosca muerta	Au, DRAE, M, S	1896	1990
	papel picado	papel picado	M	1851–1855	2001
	papel secante	papel secante	M	1852–1882	2004
	pasodoble	pasos dobles	M, S	1845	2004
	pastaflora	pasta-flora	M, S	1832	1999
	pintarroja	pintarroxa	Au, DRAE, M, S	1803	1997
	pomarrosa	pomarosa	M, S	1858	1998
	punto muerto	puntos muertos	M, S	1881–1883	2002
	rabiacana	rabiacana	DRAE, M	1884	1962
	ropa vieja	ropa vieja	DRAE, M, S	1891–1894	2002
	selva virgen	selva virgen	S	1885	2003
	sombras chinescas	sombras chinescas	DRAE, M, S	ad 1800	2003
	tinta china	tinta china	M	1870	2004
	tiovivo	tiovivo	M, S	1884	2004
	tirada aparte	tirada aparte	M, S	1878	1973
	tosferina	tosferina	M, S	1872–1878	2004
	varita mágica	varita mágica	M, S	1869	2004
	vasos comuni-cantes	vasos comuni-cantes	M, S	1870–1901	2004
	vía férrea	vías férreas	DRAE, M, S	1854	2004
	vía libre	vía libre	M, S	1876	2004
	vía muerta	vía muerta	M, S	1883	2004
1900					
	agua pesada	agua pesada	M, S	1945	2002
	agua viva	aguaviva	T, K&N, N, C, Au, DRAE	1989	1997
	agujero negro	agujeros negros	M, S	1977	2004
	aire acondicionado	aire acondicionado	M, S	1949	2004
	arco parlamentario	arco parlamentario	S	1985	2004
	arco reflejo	arco reflejo	S	1913	1995
	arte marcial	arte marcial	M, S	1932	2004
	aula magna	aula magna	M, S	1959–1960	2004

Century	Compound	Earliest form	Sources	First att.	Last att.
	banda magnética	banda magnética	S	1967	2004
	banda sonora	banda sonora	M, S	1947–1975	2004
	baño turco	baño turco	M , S	1928	2004
	caída libre	caída libre	M	1910	2004
	caja registradora	caja registradora	M	1970	2003
	cajero automático	cajeros automáticos	M, S	1982	2004
	cama turca	camas turcas	M	1930	2001
	cámara lenta	cámara lenta	M, S	1941–1961	2004
	camisa negra	camisas negras	M, S	1924	1995
	campo abonado	campo abonado	M, S	1904–1905	2004
	cañamelar	cañamelar	M, S	1923	1997
	cañarroya	cañarroya	M	1962	1963
	carta abierta	carta abierta	M, S	1923	2004
	carta astral	carta astral	M, S	1982	2004
	carta magna	carta magna	M	1927	2004
	casa rodante	casas rodantes	M	1975	2004
	casco azul	cascos azules	M, S	1970	2004
	ciervo volante	ciervo volante	M, S	1909	2000
	constantes vitales	constantes vitales	M, S	1977	2004
	control remoto	control remoto	M	1943–1974	2004
	crema pastelera	crema pastelera	M	1972	2004
	cristal líquido	cristales líquidos	M, S	1927	2004
	cuento chino	cuentos chinos	M	1941	2004
	cultura física	cultura física	S	1910	2003
	disco compacto	disco compacto	M	1986	2004
	disco duro	disco duro	M	1990	2004
	disco rayado	disco rayado	M, S	1953	2003
	efectos especiales	efectos especiales	M, S	1955	2004
	escalera mecánica	escalera mecánica	M	1940	2004

Century	Compound	Earliest form	Sources	First att.	Last att.
	espacio verde	espacio verde	S	1942–1958	2004
	espina bífida	espina bífida	M, S	1943	2004
	fiebre aftosa	fiebre aftosa	M, S	1943	2004
	fila india	fila india	S	1920–1924	2004
	fotofija	foto fija	S	1971	2004
	guardería infantil	guarderías infantiles	M	1946	2004
	hielo seco	hielo seco	S	1964–1967	2004
	hierbaloca	hierba loca	S	1962	1987
	hierbasana	yerbasana	S	1957	1962
	hilo musical	hilo musical	M, S	1975	2004
	inteligencia artificial	inteligencia artificial	M, S	1967	2004
	jalea real	jalea real	M, S	1951	2003
	lista negra	lista negra	M, S	1932	2004
	lucha libre	lucha libre	M, S	1944	2004
	mano larga	mano larga	M, S	1949–1953	2001
	marimandona	marimandona	S	1911	1995
	matarrubia	matarrubia	M, S	1960	1962
	mesa redonda	mesa redonda	M, S	1921	2004
	mingamuerta	mingamuerta	S	1972	1972
	naturaleza muerta	naturaleza muerta	M, S	1916	2004
	nochevieja	noche vieja	M, S	1908	2004
	oveja negra	oveja negra	M, S	1926	2003
	papocolorado	papocolorado (S)	S	1981	1981
	pastor alemán	pastor alemán	M	1956	2004
	pejeverde	pejeverde (S)	S	1967	1967
	perrechico	perrechico (S)	S	1975	1975
	perro caliente	perros calientes	S	1977	2002
	pichafría	pichafrías	S	1979	1995
	picocruzado	picocruzado (S)	S	1971	1971
	picofino	pico fino	S	1976	1999
	picogordo	picogordos	S	1976	2001

Century	Compound	Earliest form	Sources	First att.	Last att.
	platillo volante	platillo volante	M, S	1953	2004
	portero automático	portero automático	M, S	1974	2003
	puente aéreo	puente aéreo	M, S	1962	2004
	rabopelado	rabopelados	M	1924–1928	1929
	ruleta rusa	ruleta rusa	M, S	1966	2004
	sangregorda	sangre gorda	M	c. 1916	1991
	teletonta	teletonta (S)	S	1980	1980
	tiro libre	tiros libres	M	1977	2004
	tocomocho	tocomocho	S	1977	2004
	traje espacial	traje espacial	M	1963	2003
	viuda negra	viuda negra	M, S	1969	2002

$[A + N]_N$

Century	Compound	Earliest form	Sources	First att.	Last att.
1000–1100					
	falso testimonio	falso testimonio	K&N, Au, DRAE, M, S	950–1000	2004
	buen varón	buen varón	K&N, ON, Au, DRAE	c. 1140	1996
	mala voluntad	mala voluntad	C, DRAE , M	c. 1196	2004
	malas artes	malam artem	M, S	1103	2004
	medianoche	media nocte	A, Au, K&N, C, DRAE, M, S	c. 1160	2004
1200					
	altamar	alta mar	K&N, C, Au, M, S	c. 1223	2003
	aureonumero	aureonumero	K&N, T, Au	c. 1280	1865
	buen estança	buen estança	T	1251	1491
	buenandancia	buena andançia	A, T, K&N, ON, DRAE, M	1251	1830
	buenaventura	buenaventura	A, K&N, Au, DRAE, M, S	1228–1246	2004
	caduco morbo	caduco morbo	K&N	c. 1270	c. 1270
	gentil mujer	gentiles mujeres	N	ad 1260	1933
	mala hierba	mala yerva	M	c. 1275	2004
	mala maña	mala maña	CS, S	c. 1230	2004
	malasangre	mala sangre	M, S	1275	2002

Century	Compound	Earliest form	Sources	First att.	Last att.
	malaventura	malaventura	A, K&N, Au, DRAE, M, S	c. 1215	1997
	mala voz	malauoz	DRAE	1226	1750
	malfado	mal fado	A	1230	1627
	malgranada	malgranada	A, M	1246–1252	ad 1300
	malpecado	mal pecado	T	c. 1236	1982
	medio cielo	medio cielo	Au, M	c. 1250	1996
	medio oriente	medio oriente	K&N	1277	2001
	medio tiempo	medio tiempo	Au	c. 1280	2000
	mediodía	medio dia	A, K&N, N, C, Au, DRAE, M, S	1223	2004
	prima noche	prima noche	Au, S	c. 1250	2002
	primeras letras	primeras letras	K&N, DRAE, S	c. 1275	2003
	ricadueña	rica dueña	DRAE, M	1240–1250	1941
	ricohombre	ricome	A, AD, K&N, Au, DRAE, M, S	c. 1234–1275	1954
	salva fe	salva fe	T	1242–1275	1519–1547
	santo oficio	santo oficio	Au, S	c. 1275	1996
	vanagloria	vanagloria	A, K&N, N, C, Au, DRAE, M, S	c. 1230	2003
1300					
	altamisa	alta misa	Au, M	1303–1309	1985
	amigable componedor	amigables componedores	M	1324	2004
	extremaunción	extrema unccion	K&N, C, DRAE, M, S	1385–1396	2004
	gentilhombre	gentiles hombres	N, C, Au, DRAE, M, S	1376–1391	2003
	malhumor	mal humor	M, S	c. 1381–1418	2004
	mal testigo	mal testigo	T	1330–1343	1837–1840
	maltrato	maltrato	C, Au, DRAE, M, S	c. 1381–1418	2004
	última voluntad	última voluntad	DRAE, S	1364	2004
1400					
	blanquibol, blanquibolo	blanquibol (N)	N, DRAE, M	1495	1495
	duramadre	duramadre	Au, DRAE, M, S	1494	2003
	falsa abeja	falsa abeja	N	1495	1495

Century	Compound	Earliest form	Sources	First att.	Last att.
	falsarrienda	falsas riendas	C, Au, DRAE, M, S	1441	1940–1947
	fiel ejecutor	fiel executor	C, DRAE, M	ad 1454	1997
	gordolobo	gordolobos	AD, N, C, Au, DRAE, M, S	1423	2002
	granguardia	gran guardia	Au, DRAE, M	1491–1516	1900
	mala lengua	malas lenguas	DRAE, M, S	1424–1520	2004
	malaventuranza	malaventurança	A, DRAE, M	1400–1426	1973
	malavez	malavez	DRAE, M	1423	1905
	malcoraje	mal coraje	DRAE, M	c. 1471	c. 1471
	malhojo	malhojo	Au, DRAE	1475	2002
	malparto	mal parto	ON, Au, DRAE, M, S	c. 1481–1502	2002
	media anata	media anata	M, S	1419–1426	2002
	media blanca	media blanca	N	1450–1491	1589
	medialuna	media luna	Au, DRAE, M, S	1411–1412	2004
	medios vientos	medio viento	Au	1498	1907
	piamadre	piamadre	DRAE, M, S	1494	2003
	pleamar	plenamar	M, S	1431–1449	2004
	primeros principios	primeros principios	S	ad 1456	2002
	quintaesencia	quintaesençia	DRAE, M, S	1424	2004
	salvaguardia	salvaguarda	DRAE, M, S	c. 1440–1460	2004
	salvo conducto	salvoconducto	N, C, Au, DRAE, M, S	1439	2004
	santa sede	santa sede	M, S	1492	1995
	terciopelo	terciopelo	N, C, Au, DRAE, M	c. 1445–1519	2004
1500					
	altimetría	altimetría	M	1590	2003
	altobordo	alto bordo	Au	c. 1550	2001
	altorrelieve	alto relieve	M, S	1545	2001
	bajamar	bajamar	Au, DRAE, M, S	c. 1527	2004
	bajorrelieve	bajo relieve	M, S	1563	2004
	balsopeto	falsopeto	C, DRAE, M	ad 1540	1758
	buenaboya	buenas boyas	DRAE, M	1574	1990
	buena moza	buena moza	DRAE	c. 1568–1575	2004
	buen mozo	buen moço	DRAE, M, S	1594	2004

Century	Compound	Earliest form	Sources	First att.	Last att.
	casicontrato	casi contrato	M	1505	1818
	chicozapote	chicozapotes	Au, DRAE, M, S	1527–1550	1997
	claraboya	claraboyas	C, Au, DRAE, M, S	c. 1550	2004
	falsabraga	falsa braga	Au, DRAE, M, S	1542	1946
	liquidámbar	liquidámbar	Au, DRAE, M, S	1525	2003
	malasombra	mala sombra	M, S	1508	2002
	malpaís	malpais	S	1531–1555	2001
	maltrapillo	maltrapillo	M	1599	1927
	medias calzas	medias calças	M	1521–1543	1976
	media cama	media cama	Au	c. 1550	1944
	mediacaña	media caña	CS, M, S	1526	2003
	medias palabras	media palabra	Au, S	ad 1540	2004
	mediapunta	media punta	M	1541	2004
	media vuelta	media vuelta	DRAE	c. 1560–ad 1578	2004
	mediofondo	medio fondo	M, S	1585	2004
	medio hermano	medio hermano	M, S	1528	2004
	medio punto	medio punto	M, S	c. 1591	2004
	medio relieve	medio relieve	M, S	1535–1557	1983
	patria potestad	patria potestad	M, S	1533	2004
	pitipié	pitipié	C	1568	1994
	pobre diablo	pobres diablos	DRAE, M, S	1594	2004
	pocachicha	poca chicha	S	ad 1598	1984
	postrer trance	postrero trance	S	1547	1978
	rectángulo	rectángulo	Au, DRAE, M, S	1567	2004
	ricahembra	rica hembra	K&N, C, DRAE, M, S	1526	1996
	ricahombría	ricahombría	Au, DRAE, M, S	1579	1579
	salvohonor	salvohonor	ON, DRAE, M	1530	1984
	todo relieve	todo relieve	M	1563	1941
1600					
	agrifolio	agrifolio	Au, DRAE, M	ad 1605	1962
	bajamano	bajamano	Au, DRAE	1603	1876–1880
	corta pala	corta pala	Au, DRAE	ad 1678	1768
	gran visir	gran visir	M, S	1650–1660	2004

Century	Compound	Earliest form	Sources	First att.	Last att.
	malahoja	malahoja	C	1611	1958
	malbaratillo	malbaratillo	DRAE, M	1613	1613
	malgasto	mal gasto	S	1654–1658	2001
	media lengua	media lengua	Au, M, S	1604	2002
	media naranja	media naranja	Au, DRAE, M, S	1604–1618	2004
	media tinta	media tinta	Au, DRAE, M, S	c. 1673	2004
	plenipotencia	plenipotencia	Au, DRAE, M	1648	1995
	plenipoten-ciario	plenipoten-ciario	Au, DRAE, M, S	1636	2004
	primera dama	primera dama	M, S	1641	2004
	sexto sentido	sexto sentido	M, S	1642–1648	2004
1700					
	altisonancia	altisonancia	S	1737–1789	2002
	bajo vientre	baxo vientre	M, S	c. 1793–1801	2004
	bellas artes	bellas artes	M	1778–1822	2004
	bellas letras	bellas letras	M	1726	2004
	bonvarón	bonvarón (TL)	Au	1726	1962
	doblescudo	doble escudo	M	1797	1994
	franco cuartel	franco cuartel	Au, M	1732	1853–1929
	grandilocuencia	grandilocuencia	M, S	1742	2003
	justiprecio	justiprecio	DRAE, M, S	1785	2003
	mala cabeza	malas cabezas	DRAE, M	1762	1996
	rubicán	rubican (TL)	DRAE, M, S	1737	1889
1800					
	agripalma	agripalma (TL)	DRAE, M	1817	1992
	altarreina	altarreina (TL)	DRAE, M	1884	1962
	altiplanicie	altiplanicie	M	1880–1882	2002
	bajos fondos	bajos fondos	M, S	1882	2004
	belladona	belladona	DRAE, M, S	1870–1901	2003
	chirlomirlo	chirlomirlo	M	1896	1896
	clarividencia	clarividencia	M, S	1875	2004
	clarividente	clarividente	M, S	ad 1884	2003
	cochigato	cochigato (TL)	DRAE, M	1869	1992
	cortocircuito	corto circuito	M, S	c. 1870–1905	2004

Century	Compound	Earliest form	Sources	First att.	Last att.
	cultiparlista	cultiparlistas	Au, DRAE, M	1899	1931
	falsarregla	falsarregla (TL)	M	1899	1992
	galiparla	galiparla	M	1882	1882
	justipreciación	justipreciación	M	1845–1874	1845–1874
	legítima defensa	legítima defensa	M, S	1835	2004
	librecambio	libre cambio	M, S	1859	2001
	librecambista	librecambistas	M, S	1863	2004
	librepensador	libre pensador	M, S	1861	2004
	librepen-samiento	libre pen-samiento	M, S	1880–1881	1995
	malacuenda	malacuenda (T)	DRAE, M	1803	1992
	malapata	mala pata	M	1897	2004
	mediagua	mediagua	M	1896	2004
	medio ambiente	medio ambiente	M	c. 1870–1905	2004
	mediopaño	mediopaño (TL)	DRAE, M	1803	1992
	poca lacha	poca lacha	M, S	1872	1978
	sextaferia	sextaferia (T)	DRAE	1884	1992
	vivisección	vivisecciones	M, S	1876	2004
1900					
	altavoz	altavoz	M, S	1924–1942	2004
	altiplano	altiplano	M, S	1908–1930	2004
	altipuerto	altipuerto (S)	S	1976	1976
	altocúmulo, altocúmulus	altocúmulo	S	1900	2000
	altoestrato	altoestratos	S	1900	2000
	altoparlante	altoparlante	M, S	1948	2004
	altosaxofonista	altosaxofonista (S)	S	1988	1994
	amargamiel	amargamiel	S	1962	1962
	angliparla	angliparla (TL)	M	1986	1992
	bella época	bella época	S	1994	2003
	bellasombra	bella sombra	M, S	1961	1962
	cortometraje	cortometraje	M, S	1947–ad 1975	2004

Century	Compound	Earliest form	Sources	First att.	Last att.
	cristianode-mocracia	cristianode-mocracia	S	1967	1977
	doblemano	doble mano	M	1980	1997
	duraluminio	duraluminio	M, S	1946	1999
	fisicoculturismo	fisicoculturismo	S	1990	2004
	físicoquímica	fisicoquímica	M	1919–1929	2004
	francobordo	franco bordo	M, S	1929	1946
	francotirador	franco tirador	M, S	1910	2004
	gran mal	gran mal	S	1980	1987
	hueco relieve	hueco-relieve	S	1946	1997
	inmunodefi-ciencia	inmunodefi-ciencia	M, S	1984	2004
	inmu-nodepresor	inmu-nodepresor	M, S	1982	2002
	inmuno-globulina	inmuno-globulina	M, S	1976	2004
	inmunosu-presión	inmunosu-presión	M, S	1988	2004
	inmunoterapia	inmunoterapia	M, S	1979	2004
	largometraje	largometraje	M, S	1947–ad 1975	2004
	malabsorción	malabsorción	S	1964	2004
	maladaptación	maladaptación (S)	S	1943	1993
	mala follada	mala follada (S)	S	1980	1980
	mala hostia	mala hostia	S	1984	2003
	malaleche	mala leche	M, S	1920	
	malaúva	mala uva	M, S	1951–1969	2004
	malformación	malformación	M, S	1943	2004
	malfunciona-miento	mal funciona-miento	S	1940–1956	2003
	malherbología	malherbología (S)	S	1983	2003
	malnutrición	malnutrición	M, S	1964	2004
	maloclusión	maloclusión (S)	S	1970	2003
	malposición	malposición	S	1943	2003
	mediafuente	mediafuente (S)	S	1974	1975

Century	Compound	Earliest form	Sources	First att.	Last att.
	media verónica	medias verónicas	S	1961	2002
	mediocampista	mediocampista	M, S	1979	2004
	mediofondista	mediofondistas	M, S	1983	2004
	mediometraje	mediometraje	M, S	1977	2003
	mediomundo	mediomundo	M, S	1925	1985
	mediopensionado	medio pensionado (S)	M, S	1962	1989
	minibar	minibares	M, S	1985	2003
	minibásket	mini-básket (S)	M, S	1966	1988
	minibús	minibus	S	1974	2004
	minicadena	minicadena (S)	M, S	1989	2004
	minicine	minicine	M, S	1980	2004
	minicrisis	minicrisis	S	1977	2004
	minicumbre	minicumbre	S	1986	2000
	minifalda	minifalda	M, S	1966	2004
	minigabinete	minigabinete (S)	S	1991	1997
	minigolf	minigolf (S)	M, S	1966	2004
	minimosca	minimosca	M, S	1978	2004
	miniordenador	miniordenadores	M, S	1974	1999
	miniserie	miniserie	S	1987	2004
	minisubmarino	minisubmarino	S	1986	2003
	minitalla	minitalla (S)	S	1970	1987
	minivacación	minivacación (S)	S	1977	2004
	minivestido	minivestido (S)	S	1970	1995
	nacionalcatolicismo	nacional-catolicismo	M, S	1977	2004
	nacionalsindicalismo	nacionalsindicalismo	M, S	1946	1997
	nacionalsocialismo	nacionalsocialismo	M, S	1946	2004
	nuevo rico	nuevos ricos	M, S	1923	2001
	pequeñoburgués	pequeño burgués	M, S	1902	2003

Century	Compound	Earliest form	Sources	First att.	Last att.
	purasangre	pura sangre	M, S	1910	2003
	quinta columna	quinta columna	M, S	1941	2003
	quintacolum-nista	quintacolum-nista	M, S	1924–1942	2003
	séptimo arte	séptimo arte	M, S	1923	2004
	similicadencia	similicadencia	M, S	1930	1950
	socialcapital-ismo	socialcapital-ismo (S)	S	1967	1967
	socialde-mocracia	social democracia	M, S	1927	2004
	socialdemó-crata	socialdemó-cratas	M, S	1929	2004
	socialrealismo	socialrealismo (S)	S	1974	2003
	sociobiología	sociobiología	M, S	1985	2002
	sociolingüística	sociolingüística	M, S	1972	2003

Chapter 7

[V + N]ₙ

$[V + N]_N$

Century	Compound	Earliest form	Sources	First att.	Last att.
1000–1100					
	cubrepán	cubre pan	DRAE, M, S	c. 1196	1984
	guardamezir, guadamecí	guadamecís	A, K&N, CS, Au, DRAE, M, S	c. 1140	1996
1200					
	baticor	baticor	A, DRAE, M	1240–1250	c. 1252–1257
	calagraña	calagrañas	DRAE	1240–1250	1549
	calzatrepas	calcatrepas	DRAE	c. 1250	1450–1500
	guardacós	guardacos	A	c. 1260	1267
	matalahúva	matafalua	DRAE, M, S	c. 1295	1972
	papagayo	papagayos	N, C, M, S	1240–1250	2004
	quebranta-hueso(s)	quebranta-huessos	A, AD, K&N, N, C, CS, Au, DRAE, M, S	c. 1275	2002
	rastrapaja	rastrapaja	A	1246–1252	1246–1252

Century	Compound	Earliest form	Sources	First att.	Last att.
	tornaboda	torna bodas	T, N, C, Au, DRAE, M, S	1270–1284	2002
1300					
	botafuego, botafogo	botafuego	AD, A, Au, DRAE, M	1386	1995
	guadarnés	guadarniz	C, Au, DRAE, M, S	1337–1348	1994
	mataamigos	mata-amigos	T	1330–1343	1330–1343
	matacán	matacanes	A, Au, DRAE, M, S	1330–1343	2000
	pasatiempo	passatiempo	C, Au, DRAE, M, S	1300–1305	2004
	picafigo	pica figo	AD, Au, DRAE, M, S	1386	1913
	rozapoco (a ~)	roçapoco, a ~	A	1330–1343	1330–1343
	tornapeón (a ~)	tornapeón, a ~	M	1350	1946
	tornasol, tornašole	tornasol	LHP, T, K&N, N, C, CS, Au, DRAE, M, S	1348	2002
	trotaconventos	trotaconventos	A, DRAE, M	1330–1343	2000
	vagamundo	vagamundos	C, Au, M, S	1391	2002
1400					
	abreojos	abre ojo	M	c. 1482–1500	c. 1614
	aguzanieve(s)	aguzanieve(s) (N)	A, N, C, Au, DRAE, M, S	1495	1986
	andarraya	andarraya	A, N, DRAE, M	c. 1438–1456	c. 1438–1456
	armatoste	armatoste	A, N, Au, DRAE, M, S	1477–1491	2002
	atajasolaces	atajasolaces	A, M	1499–1502	1982
	batifulla	batifulla	Au, DRAE, M	1475	1587
	batihoja	batihoja	A, N, C, Au, DRAE, M, S	1493–1564	1982
	cazadotes	caçadotes	M, S	ad 1456	2001
	chotacabras	chotacabras	A, N, Au, DRAE, M, S	1495	1995
	desuellacaras	desuellacaras	Au, DRAE, M	1499–1502	1991
	echacuervo(s)	echacuervos	A, N, Au, DRAE, M	1411–1412	2001
	escarbadientes	escarbadientes	N, Au, DRAE, M	1495	2004

Century	Compound	Earliest form	Sources	First att.	Last att.
	escarbaorejas	escarbaorejas	N, Au, DRAE, M	1495	1992
	espantalobos	espantalobos	A, Au, DRAE, M, S	c. 1499–1502	1998
	fregadientes	fregadientes (N)	N	1495	1495
	ganapán	ganapán	A, N, C, Au, DRAE, M, S	1411–1412	2002
	guadafiones	guadafion	N	1475	1604
	guadramaña	guadramaña	Au	1429–1440	c. 1626–1628
	guardabrazo	guardabraços	A, Au, DRAE, S	c. 1425	1962
	guardamelena	guardamelena	T	1406–1435	1406–1435
	guardapolvo	guardapolvo	A, C, Au, DRAE, M, S	1402	2002
	guardarropa	guardarropa	Au, DRAE, M, S	1497–1515	2004
	machamartillo (a ~)	machamartillo, a ~	A, C, Au, DRAE, M, S	1438	2002
	majahierro	majafierros	A, M	c. 1438–1456	c. 1438–1456
	matacabras	matacabras	M, S	1427–1428	2000
	papafigo	papafigo	A, N, C, Au, DRAE, M, S	1438	1994
	pasamano(s)	pasamano	C, Au, DRAE, M, S	1493–1564	2004
	pasamuros	pasamuros	M	1487–1488	2000
	pasavante	pasabantes	DRAE, M	1483–1500	1997
	pasavolante	passavolantes	Au, DRAE, M, S	c. 1445–1519	1995
	pelacejas	pelacejas	A	1499–1503	1499–1503
	picapleitos	picapleitos (ON)	ON, DRAE, M, S	1492	2004
	picavento	picavientos	N	1495	1737
	pisaúva(s)	pisaúvas	DRAE, M, S	1442	1442
	portacartas	portacartas	N, Au, DRAE, M, S	1477–1491	2004
	portaleña	portaleña	C, Au	1462	1462
	portapaz	portapaz	Au, DRAE, M, S	1477–1491	1970
	pujavante	puxavante	N, C, Au, DRAE, M	1406–ad 1435	1964–1967
	rascacaballos	rascacaballos	A	c. 1499–1502	1625

Century	Compound	Earliest form	Sources	First att.	Last att.
	regañadientes (a ~)	regañadientes, a ~	M, S	1435	2004
	rompenecios	rompenecios	A, M	c. 1499–1502	1622
	sacabuche(s)	sacabuches	A, N, C, Au, DRAE, S	1454–1469	2001
	sacadinero(s)	sacadinero	C, Au, DRAE, M, S	1487	1992
	sacaliña	sacaliña	A, N, C, Au, DRAE, M	1438	1975
	sacaviento	sacauiento	LHP, AD	ad 1429	ad 1429
	sacomano(s) (a ~)	sacomano, a ~	A, N, C, Au, DRAE	c. 1407–1463	1963
	saltaparedes	saltaparedes	Au, DRAE, M	c. 1499–1502	1990
	salvapaz	salua paz	ON	1422	1626
	sanaojos	sanaojos (N)	N	1495	1737
	sanapotras	sanapotras (N)	N	1495	1918
	tirabraguero	tirabragueros	N, C, Au, DRAE, M	1477	1809
	tiracuello	tiracuello	Au, DRAE, M	c. 1414	1625
	torcecuello	torcecuello	N, C, Au, DRAE, M, S	1492	2000
	tornaire	tornaire	T	1409	1970
	trocatinte	trocatinte	N, C, Au, DRAE, M	1485	c. 1835
	volapié, vuelapié (a ~)	volapié, a ~	Au, DRAE, M, S	1431–1449	2001
	zapateta	çapateta	Au, S	1467–1482	2004
1500					
	aferravelas	aferravelas	Au, M	1519–1547	1587
	alzacuello	alçacuello	Au, DRAE, M, S	1580–ad 1627	2004
	alzapié(s)	alzapié	Au, DRAE, M, S	c. 1553–ad 1584	1972
	alzaprima	alzaprima	ON, Au, DRAE, M	c. 1553–ad 1584	1992
	arrebatacapas (puerto de ~)	arrebatacapas	Au, M, S	1599	1997
	atarraya	atarrayas	Au, M	1575–1580	2004
	baticulo	bateculo	M	ad 1520	1946

Century	Compound	Earliest form	Sources	First att.	Last att.
	besamanos	besamanos	Au, DRAE, M, S	1521–1543	2001
	bogavante	bogavante	Au, DRAE, M	1539	2004
	botifuera	botifuera	S	1508	1964
	buscapié(s)	buscapiés	Au, DRAE, M, S	1585–ad 1643	1997
	buscarruidos	buscaruido	DRAE, M, S	1589	2001
	cagafuego, cagafogo	cagafogo	C	1595	1854
	cantarrana	cantarranas	M	1550	1935–1936
	catarribera	catarriberas	Au, DRAE, M, S	1596	1613–1626
	cataviento(s)	cataviento	Au, DRAE, M, S	1575	2003
	ciegayernos	ziegayernos	Au, DRAE	1580–1627	1622
	cierraojos (a ~)	cierra ojos, a ~	M	1540	1987
	cortabolsas	cortabolsas	C, Au, DRAE, M, S	1545–1565	1994
	derramasolaces	derramasolaces	M	1576	1627
	desentie-rramuertos	desentie-rramuertos	DRAE, M	1589	1589
	destripaterrones	destripaterrones	C, Au, DRAE, M, S	1589	2000
	engañabobos	engañabobos	Au, DRAE, M, S	1575	2002
	engañamundo(s)	engañamundo	M	1585–ad 1643	1606–1611
	engañapastor(es)	engañapastores	C, DRAE, M, S	c. 1535–1575	1958
	escurribanda	escurribanda	CS, Au, DRAE, M	1573	1992
	espantavillanos	espantavillanos	Au, DRAE, M, S	1588	1962
	estafermo	estafermo	C, DRAE	1590	2002
	girasol	girasol	C, Au, M, S	1535–1557	2004
	guardadamas	guarda damas	Au, DRAE, M, S	1561	2002
	guardainfante(s)	guardainfante	C, Au, DRAE, M, S	1580–ad 1627	2003
	guardajoyas	guardajoyas	Au, DRAE, M, S	c. 1550	1990
	guardamangier, guardamangel	guardamangier	Au, M	c. 1550	1954–1967
	guardamano(s)	guardamano	DRAE, M, S	1580–ad 1627	1994
	guardapuerta	guardapuerta	Au, DRAE, M	1542	1873–1876
	guardasol	guardasol	Au, DRAE, M	1597–1645	1886

Century	Compound	Earliest form	Sources	First att.	Last att.
	hincapié	hincapié	Au, M, S	1528	2004
	lavadientes	lavadiente	M	1517	1599
	lavamanos	lavamanos	Au, DRAE, M, S	1589	2004
	ligagamba(s)	ligagambas	C, Au, DRAE, M	1545–1565	1886
	ligamaza	ligamaza	M	1513	1993
	lloraduelos	lloraduelos	Au, DRAE, M, S	1525	1966
	majagranzas	majagranças	C, Au, DRAE, M, S	1517	1983
	matacaballo(s) (a ~)	mata caballo, a ~	Au, M, S	1525	2004
	matacallos	matacallo	M	c. 1595–1615	c. 1595–1615
	matahombres	matahombres	M, S	1545–1565	1987
	matalascallando	matalascallando	S	1597–1645	1927
	matamaridos	matamaridos	M	1594	1778
	matamoros	matamoros	M, S	1585	1996
	matamoscas	mata moscas	M, S	ad 1500	2001
	matasanos	matasanos	Au, DRAE, M, S	c. 1540–1579	2004
	matasiete	matasiete	Au, C, DRAE, M, S	1554	2001
	mercachifle	mercachifles	S	c. 1595–1615	2004
	mirabel	mirabel	Au	1582	1993
	mirasol	mirasoles	Au, DRAE, M, S	1598	2004
	mondadientes	mondadientes	N, Au, DRAE, M, S	1532	2002
	parapoco	parapoco	DRAE, M, S	c. 1541	1927
	pasacalle	pasacalles	Au, DRAE, M, S	1597–1645	2004
	pasagonzalo	pasagonzalo	M, S	1589	1986
	pasajuego	pasajuego	Au, DRAE, M	c. 1550	c. 1550
	pasamanillo	pasamanillos	C, Au	1584	1632
	pasaporte	pasaporte	C, Au, DRAE, M, S	c. 1550–1606	2004
	pelafustán	pelafustán	DRAE	1593	1999
	picapuerco	picapuerco	DRAE, M	1565	1620
	pierdetiempo	pierde tiempos	S	1552	1999
	pintamonas	pintamonas	Au, DRAE, M, S	1597–1645	1997

Century	Compound	Earliest form	Sources	First att.	Last att.
	pisaverde	pisaverde	C, Au, DRAE, M, S	1545	2003
	portamanteo	portamanteo	Au, DRAE, M, S	1582	1905
	portanuevas	portanuevas	DRAE, M	1589	1621
	posapié(s)	posapies	M, S	1582	1991
	quitapesares	quitapesares	Au, DRAE, M, S	1589	1992
	quitasol	quitasol	C, Au, DRAE, M, S	1535–1557	2002
	restañasangre	restañasangre	DRAE, M	1580–1590	1580–1590
	rodapelo	rodapelo	Au	1591	1871
	rodapié	rodapie	Au, DRAE, M, S	1598	2003
	rodeabrazo (a ~)	rodeabrazo, a ~	DRAE, M	1535–1557	1535–1557
	rompepoyos	rompepoyos	M	ad 1598	1646
	sabihondo, sabijondo	sabiondo	Au, DRAE, M, S	1509	2001
	sacabocado(s)	sacabocados	Au, DRAE, M, S	1592	2003
	sacamanchas	sacamanchas	DRAE, M	1595	1779
	sacamuelas	sacamuelas	C, Au, DRAE, M, S	c. 1525	2003
	sacapelotas	saca pelotas	C, Au, DRAE, M	1575	1575
	sacatrapos	sacatrapos	C, Au, DRAE, M, S	1587	1986
	saltabardales	salta bardales	Au, DRAE, M, S	1585	1990
	saltaembanco(s)	saltaembanco	Au, DRAE, M	1599	1641
	saltamonte(s)	saltamontes	DRAE, M, S	c. 1550	2004
	saltarregla	saltareglas	Au, DRAE, M	c. 1591	1613
	salvatierra	salvatierra	Au, DRAE	1553	1997
	suplefaltas	suplefaltas	Au, DRAE, M	1597–1645	1872
	tajamar	tajamar	Au, DRAE, M, S	1502–1515	2004
	tapaboca(s)	tapaboca	C, Au, DRAE, M, S	1587	2004
	tardanaos	tardanaos	DRAE, M	1583	1606–1611
	tentemozo	tentemoso	M	1580–ad 1627	1985
	tientaparedes (a ~)	tientaparedes, a ~	M, S	ad 1598	1982

Century	Compound	Earliest form	Sources	First att.	Last att.
	tornalecho	tornalecho	M	1528	1528
	tornaviaje	tornaviage	Au, DRAE, M, S	1519	2004
	trabacuenta	trabacuentas	Au, DRAE, M, S	ad 1566	1948
	tragahombres	tragahombres	DRAE, M, S	1589	2000
	tragamalla(s)	tragamalla	C, Au, DRAE, M	c. 1549	1635
	tragasantos	tragasantos	M	1528	1994
	tragavino	tragavino	M	1589	1589
	trancahílo	trancahilo	C, Au, DRAE, M	1526	1646
	trincapiñones	trincapiñones	C, Au, DRAE, M	1518–1522	1984
1600					
	andaboba	andaboba	Au, DRAE, M	1613	1613
	andarríos	andarríos	M, S	1603	1989
	atapierna(s)	atapiernas	C, Au, DRAE, M	c. 1619	1886
	atizacandiles	atizacandiles	M	1620	1981
	azotacalles	azotacalles	Au, DRAE, M	1601	1896
	batiporte(s)	batiporte	Au, M	1631	1631
	besapié	besapies	S	1615	1991
	buscavida(s)	buscavida	Au, DRAE, M, S	c. 1617	2002
	calamoco	calamocos	Au, DRAE, M	1605	1982
	capapuercas	capapuercas (C)	C	1611	1611
	cascarrabias	cascarrabias	DRAE, M, S	ad 1688	2004
	castrapuercas, castrapuercos	castrapuercas	Au, DRAE, M	1641	1935–1936
	cazalaolla	cazalaolla (C)	C	1611	1726
	cortapiés	cortapiés	Au, DRAE, M	1615	1615
	cumpleaños	cumpleaños	DRAE, M, S	1654–1658	2004
	deshonrabuenos	deshonrabuenos	DRAE, M, S	c. 1607	1965–1971
	echacantos	echacantos	Au, DRAE, M, S	1624	1882
	echaperros	echaperros	M	1620	1620
	enjaguadientes	enjuagadiente	C, Au, DRAE, M, S	c. 1605	1970
	excusabaraja(s)	escusabaraja	C, Au, DRAE, M, S	ad 1629	1956
	espantaniños	espantaniños	C	1611	1655

Century	Compound	Earliest form	Sources	First att.	Last att.
	guardamigo	guardaamigo	DRAE, M	1605	1608
	guardacartu-chos	guarda-cartu-chos	Au, DRAE, M	1626	1906
	guardalado	guardalado	Au	1618	1885
	guardapiés	guardapiés	Au, DRAE, M	1641	2000
	guardapostigo	guarda postigo	Au	1609	1876–1880
	guardasellos	guardasellos	S	c. 1619	1979
	guardaviñas	guardaviñas	S	c. 1610	1964
	hurtacordel (a ~)	hurta cordel, a ~	Au, DRAE	1614	1982
	lameplatos	lameplatos	Au, DRAE, M	1617	2002
	ligapierna	ligapierna	DRAE, M	1615	1615
	matabuey	matabuey	M	1606	1998
	matacandil(es)	matacandiles	Au, DRAE, M, S	1609	1987
	matapalo	matapalo	M	1607	2004
	mataperros	mataperros	DRAE, S	1635	1996
	metemuertos	metemuertos	Au, DRAE, M, S	1614	1727–1728
	metesillas	metesillas	DRAE, M	1677–1678	1982
	mondapozos	mondapozos	M	c. 1629	c. 1629
	montambanco	montambanco	M	1646	1646
	papahuevos	papahuevos	DRAE, M	1615	1957
	papamoscas	papamoscas	DRAE, M, S	1617	2001
	papasal	papasal	Au, DRAE, M	1613–1626	1879
	pasacaballo	pasacaballos	DRAE, M	c. 1619	c. 1619
	pasapán	pasapán	DRAE, M, S	1605	1928
	pegatoste	pegatoste	M	1646	1646
	pelagallos	pelagallos	DRAE, M	ad 1600	2000
	pelamesa	pelamesa	C, Au, DRAE, M	c. 1626–1628	1948
	pelarruecas	pelarruecas	DRAE, M	1615	1927
	perdonavidas	perdona vidas	Au, DRAE, M, S	1639	2004
	picaporte	picaportes	C, Au, DRAE, M, S	1619	2004
	picatoste	picatostes	C, Au, DRAE, M, S	1611	2004
	posaverga(s)	posaverga	Au, DRAE, M	1631	1631

Century	Compound	Earliest form	Sources	First att.	Last att.
	quemarropa (a ~)	quemarropa, a ~	Au, DRAE, M, S	1659–1664	2004
	quitapelillos	quitapelillo	Au, DRAE, M	1604	1786
	rajabroqueles	rajabroqueles	Au, DRAE, M	1646	1992
	revientacaballo	revienta caballos	M	1607–1645	1989
	sacanabo	sacanabo	Au, DRAE, M	1631	1631
	sacapotras	sacapotras	DRAE, M	1605	1918
	sacasillas	sacasillas	DRAE, M	1614	1614
	saltabanco(s)	saltabanco	Au, M	ad 1607	1992
	saltacharquillos	saltacharquillos (C)	C, Au, DRAE, M	1611	1992
	saltarrostro	salta rostro	M	1605	1605
	saltatrás	saltatrás	M, S	1648	1993
	saltimbanco	saltimbarchi	Au, DRAE	1604	2004
	salvamano (a ~)	salvamano	M	1615	1883–1884
	sanalotodo	sanalotodo	Au, DRAE, M, S	1611–1650	1983
	soplamocos	soplamocos	Au, DRAE, M, S	1683	2003
	soplavivo	soplavivo	Au, M	c. 1600	1605
	tapapié(s)	tapapiés	Au, DRAE, M	1660	1898
	tirapiedras	tirapiedras	M	1630	2001
	tornapunta	tornapunta	DRAE, M, S	1663	1991
	tragaavemarías	tragaavemarías	M	1613	1613
	tragaluz	tragaluz	C, Au, DRAE, M, S	1611	2004
	tragavirotes	tragavirotes	C, Au, DRAE, M	1611	1877
	truecaborricos	trueca borricos	Au	1635	1726
	truecaburras	trueca burras	C	1605	1605
	tumbaollas	tumbaollas	M	1644	1644
	zambapalo	zambapalo	DRAE, M	1601	1997
	zampalimosnas	zampalimosnas	Au, DRAE, S	1615–1645	1995
	zampapalo	zampapalo	Au, DRAE, M	1622	1622
1700					
	aforragaitas	aforra gaitas (TL)	Au	1726	1726

Century	Compound	Earliest form	Sources	First att.	Last att.
	alzapuertas	alzapuertas (TL)	DRAE, M	1770	1992
	barrefosos	barrefosos	M	c. 1773	c. 1773
	batiborrillo	batiburrillo	DRAE	1769	2004
	baticola	baticola	DRAE, M, S	c. 1775	1994
	becafigo	becafigo (TL)	Au, M	1726	1992
	botavante	botavante (TL)	DRAE, M, S	1770	1986
	cagafierro	cagafierro (TL)	DRAE, M	1780	c. 1885
	cagalaolla	cagalaolla (TL)	DRAE, M	1791	1992
	calacanto	calacanto (TL)	Au	1729	1726
	calacuerda	calacuerda	DRAE, M	1775	1927
	cardaestambre	cardaestambre	DRAE, M	1737	1737
	cascanueces	cascanuezes	M, S	c. 1774	2001
	catalejo	catalexos	DRAE, M	1730	2003
	cataraña	cataraña	Au	1729	1992
	catavino(s)	catavino	Au, DRAE, M, S	1729	2003
	chupaflor	chupaflor	M	1780	1991
	chupamirto	chupamirto	DRAE, M	1780	1994
	cortapicos	cortapicos y callares	Au, DRAE, M	1729	1935–1936
	cortaplumas	cortaplumas	DRAE, M, S	c. 1723	2002
	cuajaleche(s)	cuajaleche	M, S	1797	1998
	cubrecama(s)	cubrecamas	M, S	1797	2004
	cucamona(s)	cucamonas	M, DRAE	c. 1790–1823	2002
	cuentagarbanzos	cuenta garbanzos (TL)	Au	1734	1734
	descuernacabras	descuerna cabras (TL)	Au, DRAE, M	1732	1992
	descuernapadrastros	descuerna padrastros (TL)	Au, DRAE	1732	1989
	detienebuey	detienebuey (TL)	Au, DRAE, M	1732	1992
	escondecucas	escondecucas (TL)	DRAE, M, S	1791	1982
	espantanublados	espantanublados	Au, DRAE, M, S	1732	1965

Century	Compound	Earliest form	Sources	First att.	Last att.
	guardalmacén	guardaalmagacen	DRAE, S	c. 1790	1946
	guardacabo	guardacabo (TL)	Au, M	1734	1842
	guardacadenas	guardacadenas (TL)	Au	1734	1992
	guardacoima	guardacoimas (TL)	Au, DRAE	1734	1989
	guardacostas	guardacostas	DRAE, M, S	1721	2004
	guardafrentes	guardafrentes (TL)	Au	1734	1791
	guardafuego(s)	guardafuegos (TL)	Au, DRAE, M	1734	1972
	guardaízas	guardaizas (TL)	Au, DRAE	1734	1992
	guardalobo	guardalobos	S	1795	1992
	guardaman-cebo(s)	guardaman-cebos (TL)	Au, M	1734	1842
	guardarraya	guarda raya	M, S	1765	2002
	guardarruedas	guardarruedas	DRAE, M	1789	1892
	guardatimón(es)	guardatimones (TL)	DRAE, M	1734	1992
	guardavela	guardavela (TL)	Au, DRAE, M	1734	1992
	halacuerda(s)	halacuerdas (TL)	Au, DRAE, M	1734	1992
	hurgamandera	hurgamandera (TL)	Au, S	1734	1995
	hurtagua	hurtaagua (TL)	DRAE	1780	1992
	juzgamundos	juzgamundos (TL)	Au, M, S	1734	1992
	lanzafuego	lanzafuegos	DRAE, M	1784	1881
	limpiadientes	limpiadientes (TL)	Au, DRAE, M	1734	1972
	majarrana	majarrana (TL)	Au	1734	1869
	mamacallos	mamacallos	Au, DRAE, M, S	ad 1772	1983
	matacandelas (a ~)	matacandelas (TL)	Au, DRAE, M, S	1734	1984
	matafuego(s)	matafuegos (TL)	Au, DRAE, M	1734	2000
	matahambre(s)	matahambre	M, S	c. 1775	2001
	matarrata(s)	matarrata (TL)	Au, DRAE, M, S	1734	2001

Century	Compound	Earliest form	Sources	First att.	Last att.
	matasapo	matasapo	M	1790	1790
	mondaorejas	mondaorejas	Au, DRAE, M, S	1737	1737
	papanatas	papanatas (TL)	Au, DRAE, M, S	1737	2004
	paparrabias	paparrabias (TL)	Au, DRAE, M	1737	1863
	paracaídas	paracaidas	DRAE, M, S	1762	2004
	paraguas	paraguas	M, S	1782	2004
	parasol	parasol	Au, DRAE, M, S	1737	2004
	pasavoleo	passavoleo (TL)	Au, DRAE, M, S	1737	1992
	paspié	paspie (TL)	Au, M	1737	1872
	pelagatos	pelagatos	DRAE, M, S	1761	2003
	pesalicores	pesalicor	DRAE, M	1791	1882
	picaflor	picaflores	M, S	1748	2004
	picamaderos	picamaderos (TL)	Au, DRAE, M, S	1737	2001
	picamulo	picamulo (TL)	Au, DRAE, S	1737	1992
	portanveces	portanveces (TL)	Au, DRAE	1737	1992
	quebracho	quebrachos	M	ad 1745	2003
	quiebrahacha	quiebra hacha	M, S	1710	2004
	rajatabla (a ~)	rajatablas, a ~	Au, M, S	1790–1823	2004
	rapabarbas	rapabarbas	M, S	ad 1797	2000
	rascamoño	rascamoños	DRAE, M	1758	1758
	repicapunto (de ~)	repicapunto (TL)	Au	1737	1822
	rodaplancha	rodaplancha (TL)	Au, DRAE, M	1737	1992
	sacabala(s)	sacabala (TL)	Au, DRAE, M	1739	1992
	saltabarrancos	saltabarrancos (TL)	Au, DRAE, M	1780	1992
	saltacabras	saltacabras (TL)	Au	1739	1803
	tapafunda	tapafunda (TL)	Au, DRAE, M	1780	1939
	taparrabo(s)	taparabo	DRAE, M, S	1774–1776	2004
	tirabuzón	tirabuzón (TL)	Au, DRAE, M, S	1739	2004

Century	Compound	Earliest form	Sources	First att.	Last att.
	tirapié(s)	tirapié	Au, DRAE, M, S	1732	1965
	tocateja (a ~)	tocateja, a ~	Au, M, S	1739	2002
	topatolondro (a ~)	topatolondro, a ~ (TL)	Au	1739	1992
	tornachile	tornachiles	DRAE, M	1792	1989
	tornaguía	tornaguía	Au, DRAE, M	1739	1822
	tornavirón	tornaviron (TL)	Au, DRAE, M, S	1739	1989
	tragafees	tragafees (TL)	DRAE, M	1739	1992
	tragaldabas	tragaldabas	Au, DRAE, M, S	1727–1728	2002
	tragaleguas	tragaleguas (TL)	Au, M	1739	1992
	vengainjurias	vengainjurias (TL)	Au, DRAE	1739	1989
	zafarrancho	zafarrancho	DRAE, M, S	1764	2004
	zampabodigos	zampabodigos	DRAE, M	1739	1992
	zampatortas	zampatortas	Au, DRAE, M, S	1739	2000
1800					
	ablandabrevas	ablandabrevas (TL)	DRAE, M, S	1884	1997
	ablandahígos	ablandahígos (TL)	DRAE, M	1884	1884
	abrelatas	abre-latas	M, S	1891–1894	2004
	aguafiestas	aguafiestas (TL)	M, S	1899	2004
	ahogaviejas	ahogaviejas (TL)	DRAE, M	1817	1992
	ahorcaperros	ahorcaperro	M	1842	1987
	alargavista	alargavista	S	1896	1963
	alborotapueblos	alborotapueblos (TL)	DRAE	1803	1905
	alzapaño	alzapaño	DRAE, M, S	1884	1981
	apagapenol(es)	apagapenoles	DRAE, M	1842	1842
	apañacuencos	apañacuencos	M	1872	1872
	apuracabos	apuracabos (TL)	DRAE, M, S	1869	1982
	arrastraculo	arrastraculo (TL)	M	1899	1992
	arrastrapiés	arrastrapiés	S	1821	1963

Century	Compound	Earliest form	Sources	First att.	Last att.
	atropellaplatos	atropella-platos	M, S	1878	1983
	baticabeza	baticabezas	M	1893	1893
	besalamano	besalamano (TL)	M, S	1869	1945
	botafumeiro	botafumeiro	M, S	1892	2004
	botasilla	botasilla	M, S	1869	1995
	botavara	botavara	DRAE, M, S	1842	2001
	cagaaceite	cagaaceite	DRAE, M, S	1817	1955
	cagarrache	cagarrache	M	1895	1895
	cagarropa	cagarropa (TL)	DRAE, M	1884	1992
	calientaplatos	calienta-platos	M, S	1891–1894	1963
	cascaciruelas	cascaciruelas	DRAE, M, S	1811	1997
	cascapiñones	cascapiñones (TL)	DRAE, M	1803	1992
	cascatreguas	cascatreguas (TL)	DRAE, M	1803	1992
	catacaldos	cata caldos	DRAE, M, S	1873	1971
	catasalsas	catasalsas	M, S	1880	1880
	cenaoscuras	cena-à-oscuras (TL)	DRAE, M	1869	1992
	chafalmejas	chafalmejas (TL)	M	1899	1992
	chupalámparas	chupalámparas	M	1843–1844	1897
	cortafrío	cortafríos	DRAE, M, S	1881	1992
	cortafuego(s)	cortafuegos	DRAE, M, S	1878	2004
	cortapastas	cortapasta	S	1822	2004
	cubrecorsé	cubrecorsé	M, S	1890	2002
	cubrefuego	cubrefuego	S	1874	1961
	cubrejuntas	cubrejuntas	M	1881	1946
	cubrenuca	cubrenuca	M	1881	1991
	cubreobjeto(s)	cubreobjeto	M, S	1893	2001
	cuelgacapas	cuelgacapas	DRAE, M	1884	1982
	cuentagotas	cuentagotas	M, S	1885–1887	2004
	curalotodo	curalotodo	M, S	1849	2004
	echapellas	echapellas (TL)	DRAE, M	1822	1950
	escarramanchones (a ~)	escarramanchones (TL)	DRAE, M	1832	1992
	espantamoscas	espantamoscas	M, S	1877	2001

Century	Compound	Earliest form	Sources	First att.	Last att.
	espantapájaros	espantapájaros	M, S	1834	2004
	espetaperro (a ~)	espeta perros	M, S	1885–1887	1992
	friegaplatos, fregaplatos	friega-plato	M, S	1867	1995
	guardaagujas	guardaaguja (TL)	DRAE	1869	1990
	guardabarrera(s)	guardabarreras	M, S	1878	2002
	guardabosque(s)	guardabosque	DRAE, M, S	1830	2004
	guardabrisa(s)	guardabrisa (TL)	DRAE, M, S	1869	1979
	guardacabras	guardacabras (TL)	DRAE, M	1803	1992
	guardacalada	guardacalada (TL)	DRAE, M	1803	1992
	guardacantón	guardacantón	DRAE, M, S	1832	2000
	guardacuños	guardacuños (TL)	M	1803	1991
	guardaespaldas	guarda-espaldas	M, S	1841	2004
	guardafreno(s)	guardafrenos	DRAE, M, S	1877	2003
	guardaguas	guardaaguas (TL)	M	1869	1992
	guardagujas	guardaaguja (TL)	M, S	1869	2001
	guardahúmo	guardahumo (TL)	DRAE, M	1869	1992
	guardamalleta	guardamalletas	DRAE, M	1878	1965
	guardamateriales	guardamateriales	DRAE, M	1803	1992
	guardamonte(s)	guardamonte (TL)	M, S	1803	2000
	guardamuebles	guardamuebles	DRAE, M, S	1849	2001
	guardamujer	guardamujer (TL)	DRAE, M	1832	1992
	guardapapo	guardapapo (TL)	DRAE, M	1803	1886
	guardapelo(s)	guardapelo	S	1846	1999
	guardarrío(s)	guardarrío (TL)	DRAE, M, S	1884	1992
	guardavía	guardavía	M, S	1877	2003
	halacabullas	halacabullas (TL)	DRAE, M	1803	1914
	hurtadineros	hurtadineros (TL)	M	1803	1992
	lanzacabos	lanza cabo	M	1845–1874	2002
	lavacara(s)	lavacaras	DRAE, M	1817	1951

Century	Compound	Earliest form	Sources	First att.	Last att.
	limpiabarros	limpia-barros	M, S	1885–1887	1978
	limpiabotas	limpiabotas	DRAE, M, S	1843–1844	2003
	limpiachimeneas	limpia-chimeneas	DRAE, M, S	1884–1885	1884–1885
	limpiaplumas	limpiaplumas (TL)	DRAE	1884	1995
	limpiaúñas	limpiaúñas (TL)	DRAE, M, S	1884	1992
	marchapié	marchapié	M, S	1872	1987
	matagallegos	matagallegos (TL)	M, S	1899	1992
	matagallina(s)	matagallina (TL)	DRAE, M, S	1884	1998
	matagatos	matagatos	S	1883–1954	1989
	matahúmos	matahumos (TL)	DRAE, M	1803	1992
	matajudío	matajudío (TL)	DRAE, M	1803	1992
	matalobos	matalobos (TL)	DRAE, M, S	1817	1962
	mataojo(s)	mataojos	M	1890	1999
	mataperrada	mataperrada	M, S	1875	1966
	matapollo	matapollo (TL)	DRAE, M, S	1884	1962
	matapolvo(s)	matapolvo (TL)	DRAE, M, S	1884	1992
	matapulgas	matapulgas (TL)	M, S	1899	1992
	matasellos	matasellos (TL)	M, S	1899	2003
	mondaoídos	mondaoídos (TL)	DRAE, M, S	1869	1992
	pararrayo(s)	pararrayo	DRAE, M, S	c. 1806	2003
	parlaembalde	parlaembalde (TL)	DRAE, M	1832	1992
	parteluz	parteluz	M, S	1857	2003
	pasacólica	pasacólica (TL)	DRAE, M	1884	1992
	pasatoro (a ~)	pasatoro	DRAE, M	1832	1874
	pesabebés	pesa-bebés	M, S	1891	1982
	picagallina(s)	picagallina (TL)	DRAE, M, S	1803	1992
	picagrega	picagrega (TL)	M	1822	1992
	picaposte	picaposte (TL)	DRAE, M	1822	1992

Century	Compound	Earliest form	Sources	First att.	Last att.
	picarrelincho	picarrelincho (TL)	DRAE, M, S	1803	1992
	pinchaúvas	pinchaúvas (TL)	DRAE, M, S	1803	1992
	pisapapeles	pisapapeles	M, S	1884	2004
	pisasfalto	pisasfalto (TL)	DRAE, M, S	1822	1992
	portaalmizcle	portaalmizcle	DRAE, M	1843	1992
	portabandera	portabandera	DRAE	1803	1992
	portacaja	portacaja (TL)	M	1899	1992
	portacarabina	portacarabina (TL)	DRAE, M	1803	1992
	portaestandarte	portaestandarte	DRAE, M, S	1803	2001
	portafolio(s)	portafolio	M, S	1853	2004
	portafusil	portafusil (TL)	DRAE, M, S	1803	1994
	portagayola (a ~)	porta-gayola	S	1885–1887	2001
	portaguión	portaguión (TL)	DRAE, M	1803	1988
	portaherramientas	porta-herramienta	M	1885	1961
	portainjerto	portainjertos	S	1893	2003
	portalápiz	portalápiz	M, S	1847	1987
	portamantas	portamantas (TL)	S	1899	1982
	portamonedas	portamonedas	DRAE, M	1856	1999
	portaobjeto(s)	porta-objetos	M, S	1881	2003
	portapliegos	portapliegos	DRAE, M	1866	1982
	portaplumas	portaplumas	M, S	1896	1987
	portaviandas	portaviandas	DRAE, M, S	1872	1991
	prensaestopa(s)	prensa estopas	S	c. 1885	1999
	prensapuré(s)	prensa-purés	S	1891–1892	1990
	pringamoza	pringamoza	M, S	1867	2002
	quebrantaolas	quebrantaolas (TL)	M, S	1899	1992
	quebrantapiedras	quebrantapiedras	M	1874	1962
	quitaguas	quitaguas (TL)	DRAE, M	1817	1992
	quitamanchas	quitamanchas (TL)	DRAE, M, S	1869	2003
	quitamiedos	quitamiedos	M, S	1892	2002

Century	Compound	Earliest form	Sources	First att.	Last att.
	quitamotas	quitamotas (TL)	DRAE, M	1869	c. 1933
	quitapenas	quita penas	M, S	1853	1996
	rabiazorras	rabiazorras (TL)	DRAE, M	1803	1992
	rapapiés	rapapiés (TL)	DRAE, M, S	1803	1992
	rapapolvo(s)	rapapolvo	DRAE, M, S	1820–1823	2001
	rapavelas	rapa-velas	M	1873	1912
	revientacinchas (a ~)	revienta cinchas, a ~	DRAE	1882	1996
	revuelvepiedras	revuelvepiedras (TL)	M, S	1899	1992
	rompecabezas	rompe-cabezas	DRAE, M, S	ad 1822	2004
	rompecoches	rompecoches (TL)	DRAE, M, S	1803	1992
	rompesquinas	rompeesquinas	DRAE, M	1884	1991
	rompegalas	rompegalas (TL)	DRAE, M	1869	1992
	rompeolas	rompeolas	M, S	1894	2004
	rompesacos	rompesacos (TL)	DRAE, M	1884	1951
	rompezaragüelles	rompezaragüelles (TL)	M	1899	1992
	sacabotas	sacabotas	DRAE, M	1835	1835
	sacabrocas	sacabrocas (TL)	DRAE, M	1884	1992
	sacacorchos	sacacorchos (TL)	DRAE, M, S	1803	2003
	sacafilásticas	sacafilásticas (TL)	DRAE, M	1803	1992
	sacamantas	sacamantas (TL)	DRAE, M	1869	1966
	sacamuertos	sacamuertos (TL)	DRAE, M	1884	1982
	sacatapón	sacatapon (TL)	DRAE, M	1822	2000
	saltacaballo	saltacaballo (TL)	DRAE, M	1884	c. 1992
	saltaojos	saltaojos (TL)	DRAE, M, S	1884	1962
	saltatumbas	salta-tumbas	DRAE, M, S	c. 1835	1996
	salvavidas	salvavida	DRAE, M, S	1878	1986
	silvamar	silvamar (TL)	DRAE	1884	1962

Century	Compound	Earliest form	Sources	First att.	Last att.
	sueldacostilla	sueldacostilla (TL)	DRAE, M	1803	1992
	tajaplumas	tajaplumas (TL)	DRAE, M	1803	1992
	tapagujeros	tapaagujeros (TL)	DRAE, M	1884	1989
	tapabalazo	tapabalazo	DRAE, M	1803	2004
	tapaculo	tapaculo (TL)	DRAE, S	1803	1995
	tentempié	tentempié	DRAE, S, M	1849	2004
	tientaaguja	tientaaguja (TL)	DRAE, M	1884	1992
	tirabala(s)	tirabala (TL)	DRAE, S, M	1869	1990
	tirabeque	tirabeque	DRAE, S	1876	2001
	tirabotas	tirabotas (TL)	DRAE, M	1884	1992
	tirafondo(s)	tirafondo (TL)	DRAE, M, S	1869	2002
	tiralíneas	tiralíneas	DRAE, M, S	1847	2004
	tocasalva	tocasalva (TL)	DRAE, M	1884	1992
	tornatrás	tornatrás (TL)	M, S	1899	1992
	tornavoz	tornavos	DRAE, M, S	1844	2001
	trabalenguas	trabalenguas	M, S	1847	2002
	tragabolas	tragabolas	M	1888–1889	1986
	tragavenado	tragavenado (TL)	M	1899	1985
	trepajuncos	trepajuncos (TL)	M	1899	1992
	trepatroncos	trepatroncos (TL)	M	1899	1961
	trocatinta	trocatintas	DRAE, M	1811	1996
	tumbacuartillos	tumbacuartillos	DRAE, M, S	1884	1992
	vendehúmos	vendehumos (TL)	DRAE, M	1803	1986
	vuelapluma (a ~)	vuela pluma, a ~	M	1830	2001
	zampabollos	zampabollos (TL)	DRAE, M, S	1803	1987
	zapatiesta	zapatiesta	M, S	1897	1992
	zurrapelo	zurrapelo (TL)	DRAE, M	1884	1992
1900					
	abrebocas	abreboca	M, S	1951	2004
	abrebotellas	abrebotellas	M, S	1990	1999

Century	Compound	Earliest form	Sources	First att.	Last att.
	abrecartas	abrecartas	M, S	1904–1905	2001
	abrecoches	abrecoches	S	1948	1977
	abrepuño	abrepuño	M, S	1902	1962
	afilacuchillos	afilacuchillos	S	1940	1984
	afilalápices	afilalápices (TL)	M	1927	1992
	aguaitacamino	aguaitacamino (TL)	M	1927	1929
	ahogagatos	ahogagatos	S	1977	1977
	amargacenas	amargacenas (S)	S	1988	1988
	apagafuegos	apagafuegos	S	1984	2002
	apagavelas	apagavelas	M, S	1927	1999
	aparcacoches	aparcacoches	M, S	1994	2001
	apoyabrazos	apoyabrazos	S	1985	2003
	apoyacabezas	apoyacabezas	S	1988	2002
	ardeviejas	ardeviejas (TL)	M, S	1925	1970
	arrancaclavos	arrancaclavos (TL)	M	1927	1992
	arrancamoños	arrancamoños	M, S	1940	1940
	arrancapinos	arrancapinos	M	1950	1950
	ataguía	ataguía	M, S	1946	2000
	atajaprimo	atajaprimo (TL)	M	1927	1989
	atarantapayos	atarantapayos (TL)	M	1925	1992
	atascaburras	atascaburras	S	1984	2001
	atrapamariposas	atrapamariposas	S	1986	1986
	atrapamoscas	atrapamoscas	M, S	1927	1996
	atraviesamuros	atraviesamuros (M)	M	1998	1998
	avisacoches	avisacoches (TL)	M	1956	1992
	azotacristos	azotacristos (TL)	S	1933	1988
	azotalengua(s)	azotalenguas	M, S	1962	1962

Century	Compound	Earliest form	Sources	First att.	Last att.
	azotaperros	azotaperros (TL)	S	1925	1983
	batifondo	batifondo	M, S	1970	2002
	botalomo	botalomo (TL)	M	1927	1992
	buscabroncas	buscabroncas (M)	M	1998	1998
	buscaniguas	buscaniguas	M	1933–1946	1949–1953
	buscapersonas	buscapersonas	M, S	1995	2003
	buscapiques	buscapiques	M	c. 1908–1930	c. 1908–1930
	cagancho	cagancho	S	1959	1959
	caganidos	caganidos (TL)	M	1936	1992
	cagaprisas	cagaprisas (S)	S	1991	1991
	cagarrope	cagarrope (S)	S	1967	1967
	cagatinta(s)	cagatintas	M, S	1927	2000
	calabobos	calabobos	M, S	1963	2004
	calapié	calapié	S	1988	1999
	calientabraguetas	calientabraguetas (M)	M, S	1998	2001
	calientapiernas	calientapiernas (S)	S	1983	1983
	calientapiés	calientapiés	M, S	1903	1975
	calientapollas	calientapollas	M, S	1981	1994
	cambiadiscos	cambiadiscos (S)	S	1970	1970
	cambiavía	cambiavía (TL)	M	1925	1992
	cantaclaro	cantaclaro	M, S	1978	1984
	cantamañanas	cantamañanas	M, S	1972	2004
	cantamisa	cantamisa (S)	S	1970	1977
	cascahueso	cascahuesos (TL)	S	1936	1972
	cascamazo	cascamazo (S)	S	1967	1967
	cascarrojas	cascarrojas (TL)	M	1925	1992
	catabejas	catabejas (TL)	M	1956	1992
	catafaro(s)	catafaros	S	1940–1954	1960
	catalicores	catalicores (TL)	M	1925	1992

Century	Compound	Earliest form	Sources	First att.	Last att.
	cazacerebros	cazacerebros (S)	S	1986	1986
	cazafortunas	cazafortunas	M	1986	2003
	cazamariposas	cazamariposas	S	1976	2002
	cazaminas	cazaminas	M, S	1982	2002
	cazamoscas	cazamoscas	S	1929	2003
	cazasubmarinos	cazasubmarinos	S	1987	1997
	cazatalentos	cazatalentos	M, S	1988	2000
	cazatesoros	cazatesoros (S)	S	1989	2001
	cazatorpedero	cazatorpederos	M, S	1909	1995
	chafarrocas	chafarrocas (S)	S	1983	1992
	chapacuñas	chapacuña	S	1960	1972
	chupacirios	chupacirios	M, S	1900	2002
	chupamiel(es)	chupamiel	M, S	1916	c. 1966
	chupapiedras	chupapiedras (TL)	M	1970	1992
	chupapoto	chupapoto (M)	M	1998	1998
	chuparrosa	chuparrosas	M	1955–1980	1998
	chuparrueda(s)	chuparruedas (S)	S	1975	1990
	chupasangre	chupasangres	S	1966	2003
	chupatintas	chupatintas	M, S	1911	2003
	comecocos	comecocos	M, S	1987	1996
	comecuras	comecura	S	c. 1910	2001
	comediscos	comediscos (S)	S	1970	2001
	correcalle(s)	correcalle	M, S	1944	2002
	correcaminos	correcaminos	S	1955–1980	2003
	correlimos	correlimos	S	1986	2001
	corremundos	corremundos (S)	S	1958	1958
	correturnos	correturnos	S	1961	1995
	cortaalambres	cortaalambres	S	1905	1974
	cortaángulos	cortaángulos (S)	S	1970	1970
	cortacallos	cortacallos (TL)	M	1936	1992
	cortacésped	cortacésped	M, S	1986	2004

Century	Compound	Earliest form	Sources	First att.	Last att.
	cortacigarros	cortacigarros (TL)	M	1927	1992
	cortacircuito(s)	cortacircuitos	M, S	1931	1996
	cortacristales	cortacristales	S	1986	1986
	cortafiambres	cortafiambres (S)	S	1987	1987
	cortafierro	cortafierro	M	1986	1991
	cortagrama	cortagrama (M)	M	1998	1998
	cortalápices	cortalápices (TL)	M	1927	1992
	cortapajas	cortapajas	S	1921–1944	1964
	cortapapeles	cortapapel	M, S	1929	1995
	cortapatillas	cortapatillas (S)	S	1967	1967
	cortapichas	cortapichas (S)	S	1967	1967
	cortapuros	cortapuros (TL)	M, S	1927	1992
	cortarraíces	cortarraíces	S	1933	1964
	cortasetos	cortasetos (S)	S	1989	1993
	cortaúñas	cortaúñas	M, S	1992	2004
	cortavidrio(s)	cortavidrio (S)	S	1983	1983
	cortaviento	cortavientos	M	1964	2003
	crecepelo	crecepelos	M, S	1961	2003
	cubrebandejas	cubrebandejas	S	1982	1982
	cubrebotón	cubrebotón (S)	S	1989	1989
	cubrecabeza	cubre-cabezas	S	1911	1993
	cubrecadena	cubrecadena (TL)	M	1927	1992
	cubrecaras	cubrecaras (M)	M	1998	1998
	cubrechimenea	cubrechimenea (M)	M	1998	1998
	cubrecosturas	cubrecosturas (S)	S	1969	1989
	cubremantillas	cubremantillas (S)	S	1962	1962
	cubrepiés	cubrepiés	M	1905	1905
	cubrepuntos	cubrepuntos (S)	S	1976	1976

Century	Compound	Earliest form	Sources	First att.	Last att.
	cubrerradiador	cubrerradiador (S)	S	1970	2003
	cueceleches	cueceleches (S)	S	1963	1963
	cuentacacao	cuentacacao (TL)	M	1927	1992
	cuentachiles	cuentachiles (TL)	M	1992	1992
	cuentahílos	cuenta-hilos	M	1912	1993
	cuentakilómetros	cuentakilómetros	M, S	1940–1956	2004
	cuentapasos	cuentapasos	M, S	1927	1970
	cuentarrevoluciones	cuentarrevoluciones	M, S	1994	2002
	cuentavueltas	cuentavueltas	S	1927	2004
	cumplemeses	cuentameses (S)	S	1966	1966
	cumplesiglo(s)	cumplesiglo	S	1903	1977
	cundeamor	cundeamor	M	1903–1905	1954
	cundiamor	cundiamor	M	1935–1936	1971
	curamagüey	curamagüey (M)	M	1998	1998
	derivabrisas	derivabrisas (S)	S	1972	1990
	derramaplaceres	derramaplaceres (TL)	M	1925	1992
	despideaguas	despideaguas	M	1998	1998
	destripacuentos	destripacuentos (TL)	M	1925	1992
	dragaminas	dragaminas (TL)	M, S	1927	2002
	echavino	echavinos	S	1946	1985
	elevalunas	elevalunas	M, S	1984	2004
	emborrachacabras	emborrachacabras	M, S	1962	1998
	enrollacables	enrollacables (S)	S	1992	1993
	escalatorres	excalatorres	S	1948	1972
	escampavía	escampavías	M, S	1911	2000
	escuernacabras	escuernacabras	S	1962	2001

Century	Compound	Earliest form	Sources	First att.	Last att.
	escurreplatos	escurreplatos (TL)	M, S	1925	2002
	escurrevasos	escurrevasos (S)	S	1958	1958
	escurreverduras	escurreverduras (S)	S	1975	1977
	esgarramantas	esgarramantas (S)	S	1977	1988
	espantagustos	espantagustos (M)	M	1998	1998
	espantasuegras	espantasuegras	S	1977	1999
	espantazorras	espantazorras	S	1962	1962
	espulgabuey, espurgabuey	espulgabueyes	S	1935	1998
	exprimelimones	exprimelimones (S)	S	1958	1970
	exprimenaranjas	exprimenaran-jas (S)	S	1968	1968
	fijapelo	fijapelo (S)	M, S	1973	2001
	follapavas	follapavas (S)	S	1971	1971
	fregasuelos, friegasuelos	fregasuelos (S)	S	1965	1993
	giradiscos	giradiscos	M, S	1980	1995
	guardabanderas	guardabanderas	M	1903	1903
	guardabarros	guardabarros	M, S	c. 1908–1930	2004
	guardacalor	guardacalor (S)	S	1957	1957
	guardacoches	guardacoches	M, S	1961	2002
	guardafango(s)	guardafangos	M, S	1926–1928	2001
	guardafronteras	guardafronteras	S	1985	2002
	guardajurado	guarda jurado	S	1980	2004
	guardallama	guardallamas (TL)	M	1984	1989
	guardalodo(s)	guardalodos	M	1989	2000
	guardameta	guardameta	M, S	c. 1919–1923	2004
	guardapesca	guardapesca (TL)	M, S	1914	1958
	guardapuntas	guardapunta	M	1932	1948
	guardarrail	guardarrail	S	1977	2001
	guardasilla	guardasilla (TL)	M	1925	1992
	guardavalla	guardavallas	M	1967	2001

Century	Compound	Earliest form	Sources	First att.	Last att.
	guardavivos	guardavivos (S)	S	1983	1983
	guiaondas	guiaondas (S)	S	1970	1970
	huelebraguetas	huelebraguetas (S)	S	1977	1977
	inflagaitas	inflagaitas (S)	S	1962	1969
	juntapulpa	juntapulpa	S	1962	1977
	lameculos	lameculos	M, S	1951	2004
	lanzabombas	lanzabombas	S	1946	1975
	lanzacohetes	lanzacohetes	M, S	1978	2002
	lanzagranadas	lanzagranadas	M, S	1982	2004
	lanzallamas	lanzallamas	M, S	1926	2003
	lanzamisiles	lanzamisiles	M, S	1978	2004
	lanzaplatos	lanzaplatos (S)	M, S	1970	1970
	lanzatorpedos	lanzatorpedos	M, S	1904–1911	1987
	lavacoches	lava-coches	M, S	1926	2004
	lavacristales	lavacristales (S)	S	1970	1976
	lavafaros	lavafaros (S)	S	1989	1994
	lavafrutas	lavafrutas	M, S	1929–1933	2004
	lavaojos	lavaojos	M	1948	2003
	lavaparabrisas	lavaparabrisas	S	1985	2003
	lavaplatos	lavaplatos	S, M	1928	2004
	lavatrastos	lavatrastos	M	1952	1992
	lavavajillas	lavavajillas	M, S	1972	2004
	levantapesos	levantapesos (S)	S	1959	1959
	limpiacoches	limpiacoches	M	1987	1987
	limpiacristales	limpiacristales	S	1962	2003
	limpiafondos	limpiafondos (S)	S	1966	1966
	limpiahogar	limpiahogar (S)	S	1988	1988
	limpialuneta	limpialuneta (S)	S	1991	1991
	limpiametales	limpiametales	S	1972	1992
	limpiaparabrisas	limpiaparabri-sas	M, S	1940–1956	2004

Century	Compound	Earliest form	Sources	First att.	Last att.
	limpiapiés	limpiapiés	M	1998	1998
	limpiavajillas	limpiavajillas (S)	S	1993	1993
	limpiavías	limpiavías (S)	S	1951	1972
	lustrabotas	lustrabotas	M, S	1946	2004
	mamaúvas	mamaúvas (S)	S	1959	1959
	manchalienzos	manchalienzos (S)	S	1972	1972
	mangaperas	mangaperas (M)	M	1998	1998
	marcapasos	marcapasos	M, S	1977	2004
	mascabrevas	mascabrevas (S)	S	1972	1972
	mataburros	mataburro	S	1928	2004
	matacantos	matacantos (M)	M	1998	1998
	matacucarachas	matacucarachas	S	1972	2002
	matagallo(s)	matagallos	M, S	1925	1962
	matagigantes	matagigantes (S)	M, S	1970	1996
	matagusanos	matagusanos	S	1928	1985
	matahormigas	matahormigas (S)	S	1967	1990
	matalegumbres	matalegumbres (M)	M	1998	1998
	mataniños	mataniños	S	1977	1991
	mataparientes	mataparientes	S	1951	1979
	matapeces	matapeces	S	1962	1962
	matapiojos	matapiojos	M, S	1935–1936	1987
	matapolilla(s)	mata polillas	S	1964	1984
	mataquintos	mataquintos	S	1921	1977
	matasellado	matasellado (S)	S	1964	1979
	matasuegras	matasuegras	M, S	1929–1933	2001
	matasueños	matasueños (S)	S	1975	1975
	matatías	matatías (TL)	S	1927	1989
	meapilas	meapilas	M, S	1958	2001
	metepatas	metepatas	M, S	1972	2002

Century	Compound	Earliest form	Sources	First att.	Last att.
	meteprisas	meteprisas	S	1987	1987
	miracielos	miracielos	S	1962	1962
	montacamillas	montacamillas (S)	S	1958	1958
	montacargas	montacargas	M, S	1925	2004
	montacoches	montacoches (S)	S	1983	1983
	montaplatos	montaplatos	M, S	1988	2001
	papatoste	papatoste (TL)	M	1925	1992
	papavientos	papavientos	S	1933	1991
	parabrisas	parabrisas	M, S	1926	2004
	parachispas	parachispas (S)	M, S	1970	1992
	parachoques	para choque	M, S	c. 1908–1930	2004
	paragolpe(s)	paragolpes	M, S	1922	2004
	paragranizo	paragranizo	M	1925	1993
	pasabala(s)	pasabalas (M)	M	1998	1998
	pasabola(s)	pasabola	S	1942	1994
	pasabolo	pasabolo (S)	S	1964	1964
	pasabombas	pasabombas (M)	M	1998	1998
	pasacasete	pasacassettes	M	1991	1997
	pasacintas	pasacintas	S	1948	2004
	pasadiscos	pasadiscos	M	1993	1998
	pasamontañas	pasamontañas	M, S	1914	2000
	pasapalo	pasapalos	M	ad 1936	2002
	pasaperro	pasaperro (TL)	M	1914	2000
	pasapuré(s)	pasapuré	M, S	1940	2004
	pasarratos	pasarratos	S	1950	1978
	pegacarteles	pegacarteles (S)	S	1996	1996
	pegamoscas	pegamoscas (TL)	M	1936	1992
	pegapases	pegapases	S	1979	1997
	pesacartas	pesacartas (TL)	M, S	1927	1992
	pesaleches	pesaleches	M	1940	1940
	picabuey	picabueyes	S	1990	1999

Century	Compound	Earliest form	Sources	First att.	Last att.
	picacaballos	picacaballos	M	1998	1998
	picapinos	picapinos	S	1975	1996
	picapoll	picapoll (S)	S	1962	1962
	pidevías	pidevías (M)	M	1998	1998
	pinchadiscos	pinchadiscos	M, S	1971	2004
	pintalabios	pintalabios	M, S	1980	2004
	pintaúñas	pintaúñas	M, S	1970	2002
	planchamangas	planchamangas (S)	S	1961	1961
	podalirio	podalirio (S)	S	1959	1959
	portaeronaves	portaaeronaves	S	1978	2004
	portaviones	portaaviones	M, S	1946	2004
	portabebés	portabebés	S	1985	1997
	portabrocas	portabrocas	S	1938	1995
	portacarné	portacarnets	S	1975	1985
	portacincha(s)	portacincha (TL)	M	1970	1992
	portacohetes	portacohetes (S)	S	1964	1967
	portacontainer	portacontainer, porta-container (S)	S	1970	1982
	portadocumentos	porta documentos	M	1970	2002
	portaequipaje(s)	portaequipajes	M, S	1963	2004
	portafirmas	portafirmas	S	1979	1984
	portafotos	portafotos	S	1988	2004
	portahelicópteros	portahelicópteros	M, S	1978	2001
	portalámparas	portalámpara	M, S	1927	1996
	portalibros	portalibros (TL)	M, S	1925	1981
	portaligas	portaligas	S	1966	2003
	portalira	portaliras	S	1907	2002
	portallaves	portallaves (S)	M, S	1970	1999
	portamaletas	portamaletas	M, S	1966	1997
	portaminas	portaminas	M, S	1912	1997

Century	Compound	Earliest form	Sources	First att.	Last att.
	portamira	portamira (TL)	M	1914	1991
	portamisiles	portamisiles	S	1995	1997
	portapapeles	portapapeles	S	1918	2003
	portarretrato(s)	portarretratos	M, S	1953	2004
	portarrevistas	portarrevistas (M)	M	1998	1998
	portarrollo(s)	portarrollos	M, S	1999	2003
	portaseno	portasenos	M	1992	1996
	portaservilleta	portaservilleta (M)	M	1998	1998
	portavoz	portavoz	M, S	1900–1902	2004
	posavasos	posavasos	M, S	1979	2004
	prensatelas	prensatelas	M, S	1939	1992
	quitaesmalte(s)	quitaesmalte	M, S	1986	1995
	quitameriendas	quitameriendas	M, S	1902	1961
	quitanieves	quitanieves	M, S	1949	2004
	quitasolillo	quitasolillo (TL)	M	1925	1992
	quitasueño	quitasueños	M, S	c. 1908–1930	1988
	rascacielos	rascacielos	M, S	1916	2004
	rascatripas	rascatripas	M, S	1903	2001
	raspalengua	raspalengua	S	1962	1998
	recogeabuelos	recogeabuelos (TL)	M	1914	1992
	recogecable	recogecable (S)	S	1988	1988
	recogecenizas	recogecenizas (S)	S	1989	1989
	recogefirmas	recogefirmas (S)	S	1958	1958
	recogehojas	recogehojas (S)	S	1976	1976
	recogemigas	recogemigas (TL)	M, S	1956	1999
	recogepapeles	recogepapeles (S)	S	1973–1976	1973–1976
	recogepelotas	recogepelotas	M, S	1961	2004
	recogevotos	recogevotos (S)	S	1988	1988
	remediavagos	remediavagos	M, S	1908	1996

Century	Compound	Earliest form	Sources	First att.	Last att.
	reposabrazos	reposabrazos	M, S	1987	2004
	reposacabezas	reposacabezas	M, S	1981	2003
	reposapiés	reposapiés (TL)	M, S	1985	2004
	resbalabueyes	resbalabueyes (S)	S	1977	1977
	revientapisos	revientapisos	S	1989	2001
	rizapestañas	rizapestañas	S	1953	1993
	robaperas	robaperas	M, S	1953	1997
	rodachina	rodachina (TL)	M	1927	1992
	rompecaldera	rompecaldera (TL)	M	1927	1992
	rompecorazones	rompecorazones	M, S	1994	2001
	rompehielos	rompe-hielos	M, S	1929–1933	2003
	rompehuelgas	rompe-huelga	M, S	1938	1997
	rompenueces	rompenueces	M	1927	1992
	rompepiernas	rompepiernas	S	1992	2001
	rompetechos	rompetechos (M)	M	1998	1998
	rompevejigas	rompevejigas	S	1910	1961
	rondaflores	rondaflor	S	1916	1936–1950
	sabelotodo	sabelotodo (TL)	M, S	1925	2003
	sacaclavos	sacaclavos (TL)	M	1927	1997
	sacacuartos	sacacuartos (TL)	M, S	1925	1989
	sacafaltas	sacafalta	M	1990	1990
	sacaleches	sacaleches	M, S	1981	2004
	sacamantecas	sacamantecas (TL)	M, S	1925	1992
	sacamuestras	sacamuestras (S)	S	1964	1964
	sacaperras	sacaperras	M	1941–ad 1961	1991
	sacapuntas	sacapuntas	M, S	1954	2002
	sacasebo	sacasebo (TL)	M	1927	1992
	sacatinta	sacatinta (TL)	M	1925	1990

Century	Compound	Earliest form	Sources	First att.	Last att.
	sacavinos	sacavinos (S)	S	1962	1989
	saltacabrilla	saltacabrilla (M)	M	1998	2000
	saltagatos	saltagatos (TL)	M	1925	1992
	saltapajas	saltapajas (TL)	M	1925	1992
	saltaperico	saltaperico (TL)	M	1927	1976
	saltaprados	saltaprados	M, S	1926	1976
	saltigallo	saltigallo (TL)	M	1925	1992
	saltimboca	saltimboca	S	1983	2001
	salvabarros	salvabarros (TL)	M, S	1925	1977
	salvamanteles	salvamanteles (TL)	M, S	1936	2004
	salva-slip	salva-slip (M)	M	1998	1998
	secafirmas	seca firmas	M	1948	1992
	secamanos	secamanos (S)	S	1983	1983
	secapelo(s)	secapelos (TL)	S	1984	1992
	secaplatos	secaplatos (S)	M, S	1969	1969
	soplagaitas	soplagaitas	M, S	1924–1957	2000
	soplapitos	soplapitos	S	1940	1996
	soplapollas	soplapollas	M, S	1975	2000
	sujetalibros	sujetalibros (S)	S	1984	2003
	sujetapapeles	sujetapapeles (TL)	M, S	1936	2001
	supleausencias	supleausencias (M)	M	1998	1998
	tajalápiz	tajalápiz (M)	M	1998	1998
	tapabarro(s)	tapabarro	M	c. 1908–1930	1997
	tapacamino	tapacamino (TL)	M	1925	1987
	tapacantos	tapacantos (M)	M	1998	1998
	tapacosturas	tapacosturas (TL)	M, S	1985	1992
	tapacubos	tapacubos	M, S	1940–1953	2003
	tapajuntas	tapajuntas (TL)	M, S	1925	1992
	tapaluz	tapaluz (S)	S	1964	1964

Century	Compound	Earliest form	Sources	First att.	Last att.
	tapaojo	tapaojos	M, S	1929	1984
	tapaporos	tapaporos (S)	S	1972	1999
	tapapuntos	tapapuntos (S)	S	1969	1969
	tentabuey	tentabuey (TL)	M	1925	1992
	tentenelaire	tentenelaire (TL)	M	1925	1992
	tentetieso	tentetieso	M	1940	2004
	tirabrasas	tirabrasas (TL)	M, S	1925	1992
	tiracantos	tiracantos (TL)	M	1925	1992
	tirachinas	tirachinas	M, S	1956	2003
	tirachinos	tirachinos (TL)	M, S	1925	1992
	tiracuero	tiracuero	M, S	1925	1986
	tirafuera	tirafuera (TL)	M	1925	1992
	tiragomas	tiragomas	M, S	1921	1990
	tirahílos	tirahílos (S)	S	1958	1974
	tiralevitas	tiralevitas, tira-levitas	M, S	1951	2002
	tiratacos	tiratacos (TL)	M	1925	1992
	tiratiros	tiratiros (TL)	M	1925	1992
	tiratrillo	tiratrillo (TL)	M, S	1925	1992
	tocadiscos	tocadiscos	M, S	1948–1963	2004
	tocatorre	tocatorre (TL)	M	1914	1992
	tomacorriente	tomacorrientes	M	1960	2003
	tomavistas	tomavistas	M, S	1947	2002
	tornagallos	tornagallos (TL)	M	1925	1992
	tornarratas	tornarratas	S	1949	1999
	tragahúmos	tragahúmos (S)	S	1969	1969
	tragamillas	tragamillas (S)	S	1985	1985
	tragaperras	tragaperras (TL)	S, M	1927	2003
	tragasables	tragasables	M	1963	2003

Century	Compound	Earliest form	Sources	First att.	Last att.
	treparriscos	treparriscos (S)	M, S	1976	1992
	trincaesquinas	trincaesquinas (TL)	M	1925	1992
	trotacalles	trotacalles	M, S	1911	1996
	trotamundos	trotamundos	M, S	1936	2003
	tuercebotas	tuercebotas	S	1953	2001
	vierteaguas	vierteaguas (TL)	M, S	1925	1999
	vuelvepiedras	vuelvepiedras (S)	M, S	1976	1976
	zafacoca	zafacosa	M	1906	1997
	zampalopresto	zampalopresto (TL)	M	1936	1992
	zurracapote	zurracapote (S)	S	1987	1999

[Num + A]$_A$

Century	Compound	Earliest form	Sources	First att.	Last att.
1200					
	cuatripartito, quadripartito	quadripartito	T	1254–1260	2002
	quatropartido	quatropartido	T	c. 1277	c. 1277
	todopoderoso	todopoderoso	N, DRAE, M, S	1236–1246	2004
1300					
	cadañera	cadañeros	C	1397	1994
	dosañal	dos añales	N, DRAE, M	1350	1350
1400					
	cadañal	cadañal	ON, DRAE	1499	ad 1852
	cientañal	cientañal (ON)	A, ON, DRAE	1495	1495
	cinco mesino	cinco mesino (N)	N	1495	c. 1640
	cincoañal	cinco añal (N)	N, DRAE, M	1495	1495
	cincuentañal	cincuentañal (ON)	A, ON, DRAE	1495	1495
	cuatrañal	quatrañal	A, ON, DRAE, M	1495	1737
	cuatrisílabo	quatrisilabos	DRAE, M	1490	1490

Century	Compound	Earliest form	Sources	First att.	Last att.
	diez añal	diez añal (N)	N	1495	1495
	diez mesino	diez mesino (N)	N	1495	1495
	doceñal	doceñal (N)	N	1495	1495
	seisañal	seisañal (N)	N	1495	1737
	sietañal	sietañal (N)	N	1495	1495
	treintañal	treintañal	ON	1495	1987
	tremesino	tremesino	ON	1490	1962
	tresdoblado	tresdoblados	Au	1493	1943
	veintañal	veintañal	N	1495	1495
1500					
	centimano	centimano	Au	1589	1653
	tresmesino	tresmesino	DRAE	1513	1618
	cuatralbo	cuatralbo	Au, DRAE, M, S	1588	2003
1600					
	tresalbo	tresalbo	DRAE, S	1609	2001
1700					
	cuarentañal	quarentañal	A	1737	1737
	ochentañal	ochentañal	A, DRAE	1737	1737
	sieteñal	sieteñal (TL)	Au, DRAE, M	1739	1992
	tredentudo	tredentudo (TL)	Au, M	1739	1992
	tresañejo	tresañejo (TL)	Au, DRAE, M	1739	1992
	unipersonal	unipersonal	DRAE	c. 1795	2004
1800					
	dosalbo	dosalbo	M, DRAE	1881	1889
	todabuena	todabuena (TL)	DRAE, M, S	1884	1962
	todasana	todasana (TL)	DRAE, M, S	1822	1962
	tresañal	tresañal (TL)	A, N, DRAE, M	1803	1992
	unalbo	unalbo	M	1881	1991
	unilateral	unilaterales	DRAE	1862	2004

Century	Compound	Earliest form	Sources	First att.	Last att.
	unisexual	unisexuales	DRAE	1817	2001
	univalvo	univalvo (TL)	DRAE	1803	1975
1900					
	cuatricentenario	cuatricentenario	S	1969	2002
	quinceañero	quinceañeros	M	1927	2004
	variopinto	variopinta	M, S	1910	2004

[Num + N]$_N$

Century	Compound	Earliest form	Sources	First att.	Last att.
1000–1100					
	cuatrotanto	quatro tanto	C, Au, DRAE, M	1196	1938
1200					
	cuadrinieto	quadrinieto	A	c. 1250–1260	1490
	cuatrángulo	quadrangulo	C	c. 1250	1997
	cuatropea	quatropedias	ON, C	1250	1984
	milgrana	milgranas	A, AD, DRAE, M	c. 1200	1518
	milgrano	milgrano	A	c. 1236	1921
	todos santos	todos santos	T, Au	1252–1284	1941
	tres duplo	tres duplos	T	1254–1260	1313
	tresabuelo, trasabuelo	trasavuelo	A, M	c. 1250–1260	1928
	tresdoble	tres dobles	Au, DRAE, M	1251–1255	1646
	tresmallo, trasmacho	trasmancho	A	1251–1284	1999
	tresnieto, trasnieto	trasnietos	A, M	1246–1252	1589
1300					
	trestanto	trestanto	DRAE, M	1385	1645
1400					
	diez cuerdas	diez cuerdas	N	1490	1495
	milhoja(s)	milhoja (N)	A, N, DRAE, M, S	1495	2002
	todopoder	todo poder	N, S	1450	2000
	tridente	tridente	AD, Au, DRAE, M, S	1423	2004

Century	Compound	Earliest form	Sources	First att.	Last att.
1500					
	cientopiés, ciempiés	cientopies	A, Au, DRAE, M, S	1513	2003
	dos puntos	dos puntos	S	1552	1958
1600					
	poca vergüenza	poca vergüenza	S	1605	1999
	siete durmientes	sietedurmientes	Au	1610	1610
	sietecolores	siete colores	C, M, S	1601	2004
1700					
	cuarenta horas	cuarenta horas (TL)	Au	1739	1992
	cuatro orejas	quatro orejas (TL)	Au, DRAE	1737	1800
	poca ropa	poca ropa (TL)	Au	1737	1791
	tres sietes	tres sietes (TL)	DRAE	1793	1992
1800					
	milamores	milamores (TL)	DRAE, M, S	1884	1992
	sietecueros	sietecueros	M	1880–1882	1985
	tresbolillo (al ~)	tresbolillo, al ~	DRAE, M, S	1862	2002
1900					
	cinconegritos	cinconegritos (TL)	M	1925	1992
	cuatricolor	cuatricolor (S)	S	1975	1993
	cuatrimotor, cuadrimotor	cuatrimotor	M, S	1956	1994
	cuatrirreactor	cuatrirreactor (S)	S	1983	1983
	cuatrojos	cuatrojos	S	1967	1981
	dos piezas	dos piezas (S)	S	1971	2003
	mil leches	mil leches (S)	S	1995	2000
	milhombres	milhombre	M, S	1960	1992
	milpiés	milpiés	M, S	1909	1996
	milrayas	mil rayas	M, S	1940	1997
	muchamiel	muchamiel (S)	S	1948	1975

Century	Compound	Earliest form	Sources	First att.	Last att.
	sietemachos	sietemachos	S	1995	1996
	sietesangrías	siete sangrías	M	1962	1996
	todo uso	todo uso (S)	S	1970	1970
	todogrado	todogrado (S)	S	1988	1988
	todoterreno	todo terreno	M, S	1947	2004
	tres cuartos	tres-cuartos	M	1992	2002
	tres erre	tres erre (S)	S	1958	1961

[Num + prep + N]$_N$

Century	Compound	Early form	Sources	First att.	Last att.
1500					
	cincoenrama	cincoenrama	M, S	ad 1500	1962
	sieteenrama	sieteenrama	M	1540–1550	1962
1800					
	milenrama	milenrama (TL)	DRAE, M, S	1817	2004
1900					
	cientoengrana	cientoengrana	S	1962	1962
	cientoenrama	cientoenrama	S	1962	1962
	milengrana	milengrana	S	1962	1962

[Num + V]$_V$

Century	Compound	Early form	Sources	First att.	Last att.
1400					
	tresdoblar	tresdoblar	Au, DRAE, M	1499	1733
1500					
	cuatrodoblar	quatrodoblar	DRAE, M	ad 1500	1775
1700					
	sietelevar	sietelevar (TL)	Au, DRAE, M	1780	1992

Chapter 8

Concatenative $[N + N]_N$

Century	Compound	Earliest form	Sources	First att.	Last att.
1200					
	abecé	abecé	A, ON, Au, DRAE, M, S	1236	2002
	alfa y omega	alfa y omega	S	1225	2000
	cab & quinal	cabo quinal	T, K&N	1276	1283
	casatienda	casas tiendas	DRAE, M	1272	1997
	donaire	donaires	K&N, ON, C, Au, DRAE, M	1236–1246	2003
	uso y costumbre	uso e costumbre	K&N	c. 1275	1973
	usofruto, usofructo	usofructo	A, ON, DRAE, M	c. 1250	1619
	usufructo, usufruto	usufructuum	C, Au, DRAE, M, S	1220	2004
1300					
	arquibanco	arquibancos	A, ON, Au, C, M, S	1325	1950
	calicanto	cal é canto	C, Au, M, S	1345	2002
	cornamusa	cornamusas	C, Au, DRAE, M, S	1385	1998
	nordeste	nordeste	DRAE, Au, M, S	1399	2004
	pendón y caldera	pendon y caldera	Au	c. 1340	1962
	pleito homenaje	pleito homenaje	ON, Au, S	1304	1991
	sal y pimienta	sal et pimienta	M, S	1337–1348	2004
1400					
	artimaña	arte y maña	A, N, C, Au, DRAE, M, S	1499	2004
	befabemí	befabemj	Au, M	1460	1460
	calicata	calicata	DRAE, M	1490	2001
	calofrío, calosfrío	calofrío	A, Au, DRAE, M, S	1481–1496	2000
	capasayo	capassayo	T	1406–1435	1582
	capisayo	capissayo	A, C, Au, DRAE, M	ad 1440	1962
	clavecímbalo, clavezímbano	clavezínbalos	A, DRAE, M, S	1481–1496	1962

Century	Compound	Earliest form	Sources	First att.	Last att.
	clavicordio	clavicordios	Au, DRAE, M, S	1481–1496	2002
	compraventa	compraventa	DRAE, M, S	1423	2004
	daños y perjuicios	daños y perjuizios	M, S	1490	2004
	dares y tomares	dares e tomares	DRAE	1438	1994
	horca y pendón	horca y pendón	S	1491–1516	1984
	ida y venida	ida y venida	Au, DRAE, M, S	1482–1492	2000
	nornorueste	nornoroeste	DRAE	1493–1505	2002
	noroeste, norueste	noroestes	DRAE, M, S	1471–1476	2004
	oriflama	oriflama	DRAE, M, S	1471–1476	1996
	pares y nones	pares y nones	Au	ad 1498	1996
	pezcola	pezcola (N)	N	1495	ad 1969
	puertaventana	puertas ventanas	DRAE, M, S	ad 1492	1997
	sudueste	sudueste	Au, DRAE, M	1431–1449	1797
	uessudueste	uessudueste	DRAE, M	1480	1540–c. 1550
1500					
	aguanieve	aguaniebe	S	1536–1585	1998
	ajaspajas	ajaspajas	M	1589	1962
	ajonuez	ajo nuez	M	1589	1992
	arquimesa	arquimesa	Au, DRAE, M, S	1588	1945
	barahuste	barahuste	C	c. 1540–1579	1929
	botivoleo	botiboleo	Au, DRAE, M	1553	1627
	calaycata	cala é cata	C, M	1549	1983
	capigorrón	capigorrones	Au, DRAE, M, S	ad 1595	1990
	cerapez	cerapez	AD, C, Au, M, S	1526	1972
	cervicabra	cervicabras	Au, DRAE, M	1591	1994
	clavicémbalo, clavicímbalo	clavicimbano	C, Au, DRAE, M, S	1563	2001
	dimes y diretes	dimes y diretes	DRAE	1597–1645	2002

Century	Compound	Earliest form	Sources	First att.	Last att.
	estenordeste, estenoreste	este nordeste	M	1524	2000
	estesudeste, estesureste	este-sudeste	M	1527	2000
	gallipavo	gallipavo	Au, DRAE, M, S	1549–1575	2001
	idas y venidas	idas y venidas	M, S	c. 1527–1561	2004
	ir y venir	ir y venir	Au	1549	2004
	jaque y mate, jaque mate	jaque y mate	Au, DRAE, M, S	1580	2004
	lesnordeste	lesnordeste	DRAE	1519	1629
	mojigato	mojigato	C, Au, DRAE, M, S	1597–1645	2003
	nornordeste, nornoreste	nornordeste	Au, DRAE, M	1502	1982
	oesnoroeste, oesnorueste	oesnoroeste	Au, DRAE, M	1519–1547	1900
	oesudueste, oessudoeste, oessuroeste	oessudueste	Au, DRAE, M	1519–1547	1900
	paniquesillo	pan y quesillo	C, Au, DRAE, S	1535–1557	2001
	pinabete	pinabete	Au, S	1580–ad 1627	2003
	salpimienta	salpimienta	M, S	1529	1933
	santiamén	santiamén	Au, DRAE, M, S	1535	2004
	sapos y culebras	sapos y culebras	M, S	1595	1969
	sudeste, sudest	sudeste	Au, DRAE, M, S	c. 1527	2004
	sudoeste, sudouest	sudoeste	Au, DRAE, M, S	1519–1547	2004
	sureste	sureste	M, S	c. 1527	2004
	suroeste	sur-suroeste	M, S	1575	2004
	sursudeste, sursureste	nornoroeste-sursuroeste	M	c. 1527	2004
	sursudoeste, sursuroeste, susudouest	sursudoeste	M	c. 1527	1900
	tripicallos	tripicallo	M	1545–1565	1971
	uesnorueste	uesnorueste	DRAE, M	1540–c. 1550	1540–c. 1550

Century	Compound	Earliest form	Sources	First att.	Last att.
1600					
	ajopollo	ajopollo	S	1607	1990
	ajoqueso	ajo queso	DRAE, M	1656	1657
	carricoche	carricoche	C, Au, DRAE, M, S	1605	1972
	casa y cabeza	casa y cabeza	K&N	c. 1604	1646
	chochaperdiz	chochaperdiz	DRAE, M, S	1644	1996
	claviórgano	claviórgano	A, C, Au, DRAE, M	c. 1600	1996
	coliflor	coliflores	DRAE, M, S	1629	2004
	demonichucho	demonichucho	Au	1629c. 1626–1628	
	duelos y quebrantos	duelos y quebrantos	Au, DRAE, M, S	1605	2001
	gozar y gozar	gozar y gozar	Au	1640	1705
	nordoeste	nordoeste	Au	1690	1884
	punto y coma	punto y coma	M, S	c. 1604–1614	2004
	punto y raya	punto y raya	M	1603	1960
1700					
	ajillo y mojillo	ajillo y mojillo (TL)	Au	1726	1726
	ajolio	ajolio (TL)	Au, DRAE, M, S	1726	2000
	ares y mares	ares y mares	M	1768	1768
	cidracayote	cidracayote (TL)	DRAE, M	1780	1989
	doncellidueña	doncellidueña (TL)	Au	1732	1783
	moros y cristianos	moros y cristianos	DRAE, M, S	1790	2002
	plano-plano	plano-plano (TL)	Au	1737	ad 1969–1974
	plano-sólido	plano-sólido (TL)	Au	1737	ad 1969–1974
	salto y encaje	salto y encaxe (TL)	Au	1739	1982
	sudsudeste, sudsudest	sudsudest	Au, DRAE, M	1773	1773
	zapapico	zapapicos	DRAE, M, S	1782–1783	2003
1800					
	ajiaceite	ajiaceite (TL)	DRAE, M, S	1817	1962

Century	Compound	Earliest form	Sources	First att.	Last att.
	café-teatro	cafés-teatros	M, S	1880	2004
	casa cuartel	casa cuartel	M	1815–1819	2004
	casaquinta	casa-quinta	S	1877	2000
	cilindroeje	cilindro eje	M, S	1870–1901	1992
	cuadrado-cuadrado	cuadrado-cuadrado	Au	1861–1865	1969–1974
	cuadrado-cubo	cuadrado-cubo	Au	1861–1865	1969–1974
	equipo y armamento	equipo y armamento	M	1815	1962
	lauroceraso	lauroceraso	DRAE, M, S	1817	1962
	mezzosoprano	mezzosoprano	S	1852–1882	2004
	mirliflor	mirliflor	M, S	1880	1958
	pan y toros	pan y toros	S	1863	1990
	parada y fonda	parada y fonda	S	1872–1878	2002
	pasitrote	pasitrote (TL)	DRAE, M, S	1803	1995
	punto y aparte	punto aparte	M, S	1842	2004
	santo y seña	santo y seña	M, S	1826	2004
	sopicaldo	sopicaldo	M, S	1863	1995
	trompa y talega (a ~)	trompa y talega	S	1841	1950
	truquiflor	truquiflor	M, S	1838	1895
1900					
	acoso y derribo	acoso y derribo	M	1966	2004
	aguagoma	aguagoma	M	1998	1998
	ajoaceite	ajo aceite	M, S	1961	2001
	anarcosindicalismo	anarco-sindicalismo	M, S	1925	1994
	autocamión	autocamiones	M, S	1920	1933
	autotaxi	autotaxi	S	1978	2001
	beca salario	beca salario	S	1977	1994
	bragapañal	bragapañal (S)	S	1988	1995
	burro-taxi	burro-taxi	S	1971	1996
	cantautor	cantautores	M, S	1977	2004
	carricuba	carricubas	M	1930	1930

Century	Compound	Earliest form	Sources	First att.	Last att.
	cazabombar-dero	cazabombar-dero	M, S	1978	2004
	chichinabo	chichinabo	M, S	1989	2000
	cirroestrato	cirroestratos	S	1900	2000
	cirujano dentista	cirujano dentista	M	1981	2000
	clorogás	clorogás	S	1992	1992
	colinabo	colinabo	M	1933	2003
	concurso-oposición	concurso-oposición	S	1946	2001
	conferencia-coloquio	conferencia-coloquio	S	1980	2004
	corte y confección	corte y confección	M	1912	2004
	cumulonimbo	cúmulonimbo	S	1900	2000
	discobar	disco-bar	M, S	1989	2002
	disco-pub	discopub	M, S	1983	2001
	elepé	elepé	M, S	1977	2004
	escultopintor	escultopintor (S)	S	1988	1996
	escultopintura	escultopintura	S	1986	2003
	espacio-tiempo	espacio-tiempo	M	1950–1959	2004
	estratocúmulo	estratocúmulos	S	1900	2000
	faja-pantalón	faja-pantalón	S	1997	1997
	falda-pantalón	falda-pantalón	M, S	1950	2003
	faringoa-migdalitis	faringoa-migdalitis	S	1993	2002
	gachasmigas	gachas-migas	S	1996	2003
	gallipato	gallipato	M, S	1909	2003
	justicias y ladrones	justicias y ladrones	S	1923	1982
	marxismo-leninismo	marxismo-leninismo	M, S	1943–1974	2004
	mercurocromo	mercurocromo	M, S	1960	2002
	metrobús	metrobus	M	1996	2003
	moquillanto	moquillanto (S)	S	1962	1962
	mortinatalidad	mortinatalidad	M, S	1962	1994

Century	Compound	Earliest form	Sources	First att.	Last att.
	mueble-bar	mueble-bar-cama	M, S	1951	2003
	mueble-cama	muebles-cama	S	1951	1991
	nabicol	nabicol	M	1913	1933
	nimboestrato	nimboestrato (M)	M	1998	2000
	ozonopino	ozonopino	S	1940	1992
	pelviperitonitis	pelviperitonitis	S	1943	1999
	pinabeto	pinabeto	S	1963	2003
	poli-mili	poli-mili	S	1992	1993
	punto y seguido	punto y seguido	M, S	1926	1973
	radio despertador	radio despertador	M, S	1987	2002
	radiocasete	radio-casette	M, S	1981	2004
	radiograbador	radiograbador	M	1988	1998
	radiograbadora	radiograbadora	M	1996	1998
	radiogramófono	radiogramófono (TL)	S	1955	1955
	radiotelevisión	radiotelevisión	S	1945	2004
	rectocolitis	rectocolitis	S	1943	1987
	rombododecaedro	rombododecaedro	S	1902	1990
	rosacruz	rosacruz	M, S	1935–1936	2002
	sadomasoquismo	sadomasoquismo	M, S	1968	2004
	sofá-cama	sofá-cama	M, S	1912	2004
	solisombra	solisombra	S	1986	1989
	tablestaca	tablestacas	M, S	1946	1975
	tecno-pop	tecno-pop (TL)	S	1988	2003
	terciopana	terciopana (S)	S	1970	1970
	titanomagnetita	titanomagnetita (S)	S	1974	1974
	tractocamión	tractocamiones	S	1986	2004
	urogallo	urogallo	M, S	1963	2004
	vida y milagros	vida y milagros	S	1973	1973

Concatenative [A + A]$_A$

Century	Compound	First attested form	Source	First att.	Last att.
1000					
	sacrosanto	sacrosanto	C, Au, DRAE, M, S	1046	2004
1200					
	agradulce	agras dulçes	A	c. 1250	1629
	celtíbero	celtiberos	K&N, CS, DRAE, M, S	c. 1275	1974
	corriente y moliente	corrientes e molientes	Au, DRAE, M	1290	2001
	occidental meridional	occidental meridional	K&N	1277	1930
	occidental septentrional	occidental. septentrional	K&N	1277	c. 1527
	oriental meridional	oriental meridional	K&N	1276–1277	1277
	oriental septentrional	oriental septentrional	K&N	1276–1277	1803–1806
	sano y salvo	sano et saluo	K&N, M, S	1218–c. 1250	1974
	santo & sagrado	santo e sagrado	N	c. 1275	1940–1942
1300					
	altibajo(s)	altibaxo	A, Au, C, DRAE, M, S	1330–1343	2004
	celtiberio	celtiberios	A, DRAE, M	1385	1603
1400					
	agrodulce	agrodulce	C	1493	1962
1500					
	agridulce	agridulce	Au, DRAE, M, S	1576–1577	2004
	anchicorto	anchicorta	Au, DRAE, M, S	1549–1603	1981
	claro y oscuro	claro y oscuro	Au, DRAE	1580	1974–1975
	cultipicaño	cultipicaña	DRAE	1597–1645	1994
	dulceamargo	dulceamargo	S	1588	2003
	hecho y derecho	hecho y derecho	M, S	1569	1973
	tontivano	tontivano	M	1599–1622	1599–1622
	verdinegro	verdinegra	CS, Au, DRAE, M, S	c. 1500	2004

Century	Compound	First attested form	Source	First att.	Last att.
1600					
	bobibellaco	bobibellacos	Au	1605	1605
	celtibérico	celtibéricos	DRAE, M, S	1640	2002
	loquitonto	loquitonto	S	1680	1995
	rojiazul	rojiazul	S	c. 1606	2003
	tiesierguido	tiesierguido	C	1611	1892
1700					
	bobiculto	bobiculto (TL)	Au	1726	1877
	céfalo-faríngeo	cephalo-pharingeos (TL)	Au	1726	1726
	claroscuro	claroscuro	A, DRAE, M, S	1780	2004
	dulciamargo	dulciamargo	S	1795	1992
	épico-burlesco	épico-burlesco	S	1778–1822	1778–1822
	grecolatino	grecolatino	DRAE, M, S	1772	2004
	lunisolar	lunisolar	Au, S	1780	1981
	sordomudo	sordos mudos	M, S	1793	2000
	verdiblanco	verdiblanco	S	1768–1771	2004
	verdiseco	verdiseco	Au, DRAE, M, S	1734	1992
1800					
	alcalinotérreo	alcalinotérreos	M, S	1882	1998
	austrohúngaro	austro-húngara	M, S	1884	2004
	blanquiazul	blanquiazules	S	c. 1840	2004
	blanquinegro	blanquinegras	S	1870	2004
	celtohispano	celto-hispanas	M	1880–1881	2000
	cerebrospinal	cerebro-espinales	M, S	1870–1901	2003
	cochifrito	cochifrito	Au, DRAE, M, S	1828–1870	2001
	concavoconvexo	cóncavo-convexa	M, S	1870–1901	2000
	contante y sonante	contante y sonante	M, S	1820–1823	2004
	contencioso-administrativo	contencioso administrativo	M, S	1840	2004
	cortilargucho	cortilargucho	DRAE	1834	1834
	craneocerebral	cráneo-cerebral	S	1870–1901	1970

Century	Compound	First attested form	Source	First att.	Last att.
	craneo-encefálico	cráneo-encefálica	M, S	1870–1901	2004
	dorsolumbar	dorso-lumbar	S	1870–1901	2001
	dulcamara, dulzamara	dulcamaras	DRAE, M, S	1881	1997
	fibrocartilaginoso	fibrocartilaginoso	M	1881	1992
	gallegoportugués	gallego portuguesa	M, S	1878	1995
	genitourinario	génito-urinarios	M, S	1870–1901	2003
	grecorromano	greco-romano	DRAE, M, S	1804	2002
	hebraicoespañol	hebraico-español	S	1880–1881	1997
	hispanoamericano	hispanoamericanos	S	1845–1874	2004
	hispanoárabe	hispano-árabes	S	1890	2002
	hispanobelga	hispano-belga	S	ad 1863	2002
	hispanoeuropeas	hispano-europeo	S	1897	1970
	hispanogodo	hispano-goda	S	1855–1875	1997
	hispanohebreo	hispano-hebreas	S	1855–1875	1985
	hispanorromano	hispanorromano	S	1852	2004
	hispanovisigodo	hispano-visigodas	S	1855–1875	2001
	histórico-artístico	histórico-artístico	M	1857	2003
	iberoamericano	iberoamericana	M, S	1897	2004
	iberrorromano	ibero-romano	M	1880–1881	2000
	indochino	indochina	M, S	1899	2000
	indoeuropeo	indo-europea	M, S	1859	2003
	indogermánico	indogermánica	M, S	1868	1979
	isquiopubiano	isquio-pubianas	S	1870–1901	2003
	liberoleñoso	liberoleñosos	S	1893	1957–1974
	metacarpofalángico	metacarpo-falángicas	S	1870–1901	1997

Century	Compound	First attested form	Source	First att.	Last att.
	mineromedicinal	mineromedicinales	DRAE, M, S	1881	2004
	negriverde	negriverde	S	1828–1870	1957
	palmadocompuesto	palmado-compuestas	M, S	1896	1957–1974
	pavisoso	pavisosa	M, S	1885 –1887	2004
	rubicán	rubicano	M	1881	1889
	sacrolumbar	sacro-lumbar	Au	1870–1901	2000
	tibioperoneo	tibio-peronea	S	1870–1901	1992
	tontiloco	tontiloco	M, S	1880–1881	2004
	toracicoabdominal	torácico-abdominal	S	1870–1901	1995
	uraloaltaico	uralo-altaica	M, S	1880–1881	1995
	vascofrancés	vasco-francés	M, S	c. 1802	2000
	vasculonervioso	vásculo-nervioso	S	1870–1901	1997
1900					
	acetilsalicílico	acetilsalicílico	M, S	1962	2004
	afroamericano	afroamericana	M, S	1938	2004
	afrocubano	afrocubanos	M, S	1906	2004
	alfanumérico	alfanumérica	M, S	1971	2004
	amaradulce	amaradulce	S	1962	1962
	arabigoandaluz	arábigoandaluza	S	1923–1974	1996
	asturleonés	astur-leonés	M, S	1910–1945	2002
	audiovisual	audiovisual	M, S	1965	2004
	azulgrana	azulgrana	S	1934	2004
	baltoeslavo	baltoeslavo (S)	S	1995	1996
	blanquiamarillo	blanquiamarillo	S	1932	1993
	blanquirrojo	blanquirrojo	S	1934	2004
	blanquiverde	blanquiverdes	S	1916	2003
	blanquivioleta	blanquivioleta	S	1982	2002
	bucofacial	bucofacial (M)	M	1998	2004
	castellanoleonés	castellanoleonés	M, S	1902–1919	2004

Century	Compound	First attested form	Source	First att.	Last att.
	castellanoman-chego	castellano manchego	M, S	1938	2004
	celtohispánico	celtohispánico (TL)	M	1925	1992
	cerebrotónico	cerebrotónico	S	1969	1982
	cerebrovascular	cerebrovascu-lares	S	1964	2004
	checoslovaco	checoeslovaco	M, S	1923	2004
	chino-tibetano	chinotibetano	S	1987	2002
	craneofacial	craneofaciales	M, S	1986	2003
	cristianosocial	cristiano-social	S	1927	2003
	democratacris-tiano	demócratas cristianos	M, S	1924	2004
	dorsopalatal	dorsopalatal	S	1918–1932	1953
	dorsoventral	dorsoventral	M	1989	2001
	equinovaro	equino varo	S	1943	1991
	escul-topictórico	escul-topictórico (S)	S	1971	1996
	espaciotem-poral	espacio-tem-poral	S	1932–1944	2004
	espectrofoto-métrico	espectrofoto-métricas	S	1921–1944	1985
	espinocelular	espinocelular	S	1943	2002
	estratocris-talino	estratocristali-nas	S	1927	1957–1974
	galaicoportu-gués	galaicoportu-gueses	M, S	1902–1919	1994
	galorromano	galo-romana	M	1904–1916	2001
	gilitonto	gilitontos	S	1972	1975
	grecochipriota	grecochipriota	S	1977	2004
	hispano-británico	hispano-británicas	S	1977	2004
	hispano-flamenco	hispano-flamenco	S	1946	2003
	hispano-holandés	hispanoholan-desa	S	1951	2003

Century	Compound	First attested form	Source	First att.	Last att.
	hispano-israelí	hispano-israelíes	S	1977	1995
	hispanojudío	hispanojudía	S	1942–1945	1998
	hispano-marroquí	judeo-hispano-marroquí	S	1953	2004
	hispano-mejicano	hispano-mexicano	S	1900–1902	2004
	hispanonorteam-ericano	hispano-norteamericanos	S	1974	2003
	hispano-yanqui	hispano-yanqui	S	1966	1985
	iberoatlántico	iberoatlánticas	S	1980	1998
	iberocretense	iberocretense (S)	S	1966	1966
	iberomauri-tánico	iberomauri-tánico (S)	S	1962	1962
	iberorrománico	iberorrománico	S	1959	1998
	inciso-cortante	inciso-cortante (S)	S	1970	1980
	inciso-punzante	inciso-punzante	S	1933	1963
	indoamericano	indoamericano	M, S	1928	2004
	indoario	indo-aria	M	1995	2003
	indogermano	indogermanos	S	1946	1990
	indoiranio	indo-iranio	M, S	1932–1944	1995
	indomalayo	indomalaya	S	1926	1991
	indopakistano	indopakistaníes	S	1996	2001
	infectoconta-gioso	infectoconta-giosa	M, S	1951	2003
	italoamericano	italo-americano	S	1970	2003
	italo-argentino	italoargentino	S	1944–1949	2004
	italo-español	italo-españoles	M, S	1917–1933	1991
	italo-francés	italo-francés	S	1904–1916	1995
	italo-germana	italo-germanos	S	1937	2004
	labiodental	labiodentales	M, S	1904–1905	1997
	labiovelar	labiovelar	S	1918–1932	1918–1932
	lumbociático	lumbociática	S	1987	2002
	lumbosacro	lumbosacra	S	1943	2003

Century	Compound	First attested form	Source	First att.	Last att.
	maniacodepre-sivo	maniacodepresi-vos	S	1919–1936	2004
	marxista-leninista	marxista-leninista	S	1943–1974	2004
	materno-infantil	materno infantil	S	1974	2004
	maxilofacial	maxilofacial	M, S	1980	2004
	medicolegal	médico-legales	M	1979	2002
	musicovocal	músico-vocal	S	1995	2002
	navarroara-gonés	navarroara-gonesa	M, S	1924–1957	2001
	negriblanco	negriblancos	M, S	1938	1938
	osco-umbro	osco-umbrío	S	1942	1970
	paternofilial	paterno-filiales	S	1970	1973
	pavitonto	pavitonto	M, S	1974	1974
	pinnadocom-puesto	pinnadocom-puestas	S	1957–1974	1979
	pleuropulmo-nar	pleuropulmo-nares	S	1912	1991
	reticuloendote-lial	reticuloendote-lial	S	1964	2001
	rojiamarillo	rojiamarilla	S	1958	2004
	rojiblanco	rojiblancos	S	1934	2004
	rojinegro	rojinegras	S	1910	2004
	rojiverde	rojiverde	S	1986	2004
	serbobosnio	serbo-bosnias	M	1994	2004
	serbocroata	serbocroata	M, S	1985	2002
	siderometalúr-gico	siderometalúr-gico	M, S	1946	2002
	simpaticomimé-tico	simpaticomimé-ticas	S	1962	2004
	socialcristiano	social-cristiano	S	1925	2004
	socialrealista	social realista	S	1964–1967	2002
	sociocultural	sociocultural	M, S	1950–1968	2004
	socioeconómico	socioeconómi-cas	M, S	1946–1974	2004
	sociolingüístico	sociolingüística	M, S	1972	2003

Century	Compound	First attested form	Source	First att.	Last att.
	sociopolítico	sociopolítica	M, S	1950–1968	2004
	sumeroarcadio	sumeroarcadio	S	1961	1961
	tempoespacial	tempoespacial	S	1975	2002
	temporoparietal	temporo-parietal	S	1989	1989
	toracolumbar	toracolumbar	S	1943	1989
	tupí-guaraní	tupí-guaraní	M, S	1965	1999
	turcochipriota	turcochipriotas	S	1977	1996
	verdiamarillo	verdiamarilla	S	1907–1917	2001
	verdiazul	verdiazules	S	1905	2004
	verdibermejo	verdibermejo	S	1956	1956
	verdigris	verdigrises	S	1933	1978
	verdirrojo	verdirroja	S	1977	1997
	viscerotónico	viscerotónico	S	1969	1970
	viscoelástico	viscoelástico (S)	S	1974	1991
	viscoplástico	viscoplástico (S)	S	1974	1974

Concatenative [V + V]$_N$

Century	Compound	Earliest form	Sources	First att.	Last att.
1200					
	lexa prenda, liexaprén, dexa prenda	dexaprén	T, ON	ad 1275	1956
1400					
	cortapisa	cortapisa	T, N, C, Au, DRAE, M, S	ad 1435	2004
	girapliega	gira pliega	C, Au, DRAE, M	ad 1471	1982
	pasapasa (juego de ~)	passa passa	C, Au, DRAE, M	1481–1496	2002
	sanamunda	sanamunda	M		1493	1962
	vaivén	vaivenes	ON, C, Au, DRAE, M, S	1427–1428	2004

Century	Compound	Earliest form	Sources	First att.	Last att.
1500					
	cantimplora	cantimploras	C, Au, DRAE, M, S	1585	2004
	chiticalla	chiticalla	Au, DRAE, M, S	c. 1549	1993
	chiticallando	chiticallando	DRAE, M	c. 1540	1932
	ciaboga	ciaboga	Au, DRAE, M, S	1539	1996
	ciaescurre	cia escurre	Au	1574	1630–1633
	ganapierde	ganapierde	Au, DRAE, M, S	c. 1521–1543	1995
	quitaipón (de ~)	quita y pon	DRAE, M, S	1597–1645	2002
	saltaembarca	saltaembarca	Au, DRAE, M	1580–ad 1627	1960
	tiramira	tiramira	C, Au, DRAE, M	ad 1536–1585	1946
1600					
	tira y afloja	tirafloja (C)	C, Au, DRAE, M, S	1611	1972
1700					
	arrancasiega	arrangasiega (TL)	Au, DRAE, M	1726	1992
	bullebulle	bullebulle	Au, M, S	1773	1995
	cascamajar	cascamajar (TL)	DRAE	1780	1992
	chita callando	chita callando	M	1773	2003
1800					
	duermevela	duermevela	DRAE, M, S	1825	2002
	picapica	pica-pica	M, S	1872	2003
	quitapón	quitapon	DRAE, M, S	1872	1980
	tejemaneje	teje maneje	DRAE, M, S	ad 1800	2004
1900					
	callacuece	callacuece (TL)	M, S	1925	1974
	comecome	comecome	M, S	1932	2004
	dormivela	dormivela (S)	S	1964	1964
	metisaca	metisaca	M, S	1909	2003
	picaraña	picaraña (S)	S	1977	1977
	subibaja	subibaja	M, S	1905	2004

Subject index

Word index